Contents

Preface xi

Acknowledgements xii

1 Accounting and Business 1

1.1 Accounting as an Aid to Business 2
1.2 The Nature of Business 3
1.3 Forms of Business Ownership 3
1.4 Why Study Accounting? 3
1.5 The Accounting Office 4
1.6 Becoming an Accountant 6

2 Accounting for Your Money 10

2.1 Types of Personal Bank Account 11
2.2 The Bank's Record of the Customer's Money 11
2.3 Keeping Personal Bank Records 13
2.4 Bank Reconciliation 14
2.5 Electronic Information Processing 18

3 The Balance Sheet 31

3.1 Financial Position 32
3.2 The Fundamental Accounting Equation 33
3.3 Preparing a Balance Sheet 33
3.4 Accounts Receivable and Accounts Payable 35
3.5 The Balance Sheet for a Business 35
3.6 Claims against the Assets 37
3.7 Basic Recordkeeping Practices 38

4 Analyzing Changes in Financial Position 49

4.1 Recording Business Transactions 49
4.2 Summary of Steps in Analyzing a Transaction 56
4.3 Developing Good Work Habits 57

5 The Simple Ledger 65

5.1 Ledger Accounts 66
5.2 Debit and Credit 69
5.3 Account Balances 75
5.4 Double Entry System of Accounting 76
5.5 The Trial Balance 77

6 The Journal 91

6.1 The Two-Column General Journal 92
6.2 Business Practices and Journalizing 96
6.3 Source Documents 97

Five Journals system

7 Posting 111

7.1 The Balance Column Account 112
7.2 Formal Posting 114
7.3 Correcting Errors in the Books 118
7.4 Forwarding Procedures 119
7.5 The Accounting Cycle 120

8 The Income Statement 130

8.1 The Income Statement 131
8.2 The Income Statement Put to Use 134
8.3 The Fiscal Period 134
8.4 Expanding the Ledger 135
8.5 Chart of Accounts 139
8.6 Debit and Credit in the Expanded Ledger 140
8.7 Trial Balance Procedure Unchanged 141
8.8 Trial Balance out of Balance 142

9 The Simple Work Sheet and the Financial Statements 162

9.1 The Simple Work Sheet 163
9.2 The Balance Sheet — Account Form and Report Form 167
9.3 The Classified Balance Sheet 168
9.4 The Work Sheet and Financial Statements 168
9.5 Typewritten Financial Statements 175
9.6 The Accounting Cycle 176

10 Closing Entries 188

10.1 Objectives of Closing Entries 190
10.2 Making the Closing Entries 192
10.3 Post-Closing Trial Balance 197
10.4 The Accounting Cycle 198

11 Source Documents 210

11.1 Cash Sales Slip 211
11.2 Sales Invoice 212
11.3 Dual Purpose Sales Slip 213
11.4 Purchase Invoice 214
11.5 Cheque Copy 216
11.6 Cash Receipts List 217
11.7 Bank Advice 218
11.8 Summary of Source Documents and Related Accounting Entries 220

Summary Exercise
J. Allen Lawson, Lawyer 231

12 Subsidiary Ledger Accounting 235

12.1 Growth of a Ledger 236
12.2 Subsidiary Ledgers and Control Accounts 237
12.3 Accounts Receivable and Accounts Payable on the Balance Sheet 240
12.4 Flowcharting Techniques Used in this Text 240
12.5 Accounting for Accounts Receivable 244

12.6 Accounting for Accounts Payable 244
12.7 Non-routine Entries to Subsidiary Ledgers 246
12.8 Posting to the General Ledger 246
12.9 Balancing the Ledgers 246
12.10 Customer's Statement of Account 248

13 Accounting for a Merchandising Business 272

13.1 Merchandise Inventory 273
13.2 Periodic Inventory Method 276
13.3 Work Sheet of a Merchandising Business 280
13.4 Closing Entries for a Merchandising Business 282
13.5 Perpetual Inventory Method 284

14 The Synoptic Journal 307

14.1 Petty Cash Fund 308
14.2 Credit Invoices (Basic Procedure) 311
14.3 The Synoptic Journal 314
14.4 Two-Journal System 329

15 The Five-Journal System 350

15.1 Sales Tax 350
15.2 NSF Cheques 353
15.3 The Five-Journal System 353

Summary Exercise Travel Trailers 383

16 Cash Register Accounting 388

16.1 Returns and Allowances 389
16.2 Cash Refunds 392
16.3 Cash Discounts 394
16.4 Cash Registers 399

Supplementary Exercise
Green Thumb Garden Centre 440

17 Accounting Controls 463

17.1 Internal Control 463
17.2 Procedures for Control of Cash 466
17.3 Control of Cash Expenditures 470
17.4 The Voucher System 471

18 Payroll Accounting 505

18.1 Legal Obligations of Employer 506
18.2 Methods of Paying Employees 506
18.3 Payroll Deductions 509
18.4 Recording the Payroll 524
18.5 Payment to Employees 528
18.6 Payment of Payroll Liabilities 530
18.7 Basic Payroll Records 530

19 Adjusting Entries and Classified Statements 545

19.1 The Work Sheet 546
19.2 Adjustment for Supplies 547
19.3 Adjustment for Prepaid Expenses 550

19.4 Adjustment for Doubtful Accounts of Customers 554
19.5 Adjustment for Depreciation 558

20 Completing the Accounting Cycle 584

20.1 Adjusting for Accounts Payable 585
20.2 Adjusting for Accrued Wages 587
20.3 Review of Adjustment for Cost of Goods Sold (Periodic Inventory Method) 589
20.4 Adjusting and Closing the Books of a Proprietorship 592
20.5 Reversing Entries 596
20.6 The Accounting Cycle 598
20.7 Fully Classified Financial Statements 600

Summary Exercise Universal Lumber 623

21 Partnerships 635

21.1 Formation of a Partnership 636
21.2 Accounting for Simple Partnership Formations 629
21.3 Distribution of Net Income or Net Loss in a Partnership 647
21.4 Financial Statements of a Partnership 651
21.5 Adjusting and Closing Entries for a Partnership 656
21.6 Termination of Partnerships 660

22 Accounting for Corporations 681

22.1 Characteristics of Corporations 682
22.2 Advantages and Disadvantages of Corporations 684
22.3 Accounts of a Corporation 685

22.4 Dividends 687

22.5 Different Classes of Shares 689

22.6 Retained Earnings 694

22.7 Equity Section — Presentation of the Balance Sheet 697

22.8 Market Value of Company Shares 698

22.9 Share Records 700

22.10 Adjusting and Closing Entries for a Corporation 703

22.11 Income Tax for Corporations 703

23 Analyzing Financial Statements 729

23.1 Comparative Financial Statements 730

23.2 Common-size Financial Statements 734

23.3 Trend Analysis 736

23.4 Key Ratios and Relationships 737

24 Accounting and the Computer 771

24.1 Basic Concepts of Data Processing 772

24.2 Components of the Computer System 779

24.3 Computer Applications in Accounting 788

24.4 Developing a Computerized System 789

24.5 Computer Applications in Accounting at Save-More 793

24.6 Internal Control 814

24.7 Computer Use in Accounting 815

24.8 Computerized Accounting in the Future 816

Glossary G-1

Index I-1

Acknowledgements

Accounting 1: Third Edition could not have been completed without the many talented people who participated so willingly in the project. To these contributors, I am sincerely indebted.

The extensive teaching knowledge and experience of Bill Riggs, Commercial Director of Sutton District High School, is evident throughout the Teacher's Guide that accompanies this text. Bill was also responsible for writing the numerous career profiles that enliven the chapter endings.

Bill Quinn, a former student of mine, possesses an incredible capacity for accuracy and detail, and a genuine love for accounting. It was a pleasure indeed to supervise his preparation of the two solutions manuals.

Steven Talsky, of East York Collegiate, and Tim Crawford, Commercial Director of Barrie's Eastview Secondary School, provided the expertise needed to examine the role of the computer in accounting. The book would not have been complete without a chapter on this topic.

Al Pippard, of the National Cash Register Company of Canada, Ltd., provided the expert advice needed for the chapter on the cash register, and did so with a wonderful combination of patience and enthusiasm. Stan Iwachniuk, Head of Business at Tagwi High School in Avonmore, contributed some of his excellent exercises, much to the benefit of the text. Pat O'Neill, of the Toronto-Dominion Bank in Barrie, provided the up-to-date information necessary for the chapter on banking.

Many teachers and students assisted in the development of the text with valuable comments and suggestions based on their experience with the Second Edition. I would especially like to thank the many teachers who reviewed the manuscript and offered their constructive criticisms.

I would be remiss indeed if I failed to acknowledge the major role played by the staff of Prentice-Hall Canada, Inc. in the production of *Accounting 1*. Steve Lane guided the project from the beginning, taking part in its planning and development and maintaining its high quality throughout. Heather Scott McClune worked patiently and tirelessly to coordinate the editorial production process. Jan Cheesman and Rand Paterson handled the technical aspects of production with efficiency and intelligence.

Finally, a number of other people gave their time and talents to *Accounting 1*. Joyce Watts and Janet MacLean contributed their considerable editorial skills to the style and organization of the original manuscript. Christopher Blackburn provided the clear, comprehensive index that follows the text. Acorn Technical Illustrators furnished the many attractive, informative illustrations. And Bob Garbutt's handsome, lucid design enhances the text immeasurably. To all of them, my appreciation and gratitude.

G.E.S.

Preface

Accounting 1 is an introduction to accounting procedures, concepts, and applications designed for one-year or two-year courses offered in Canadian schools. The text is suitable for students who will enter the work force soon after these courses as well as for those who will take other accounting courses beyond this level.

Accounting 1 opens with two introductory chapters intended for the many first-year accounting students who have not taken previous business courses. Chapter 1: *Accounting and Business*, discusses a number of aspects of business and accounting. Students learn about the nature of business, types of businesses, the relationship between accounting and business, and accountancy as a career or profession. Chapter 2: *Accounting for Your Money*, gives students practice at clerical record-keeping, which is helpful in learning bookkeeping procedures and accounting theory. These topics lead quite naturally into the study of accounting that begins in Chapter 3.

Chapters 3 through 10 comprise the core of *Accounting 1*. Chapter 3 introduces accounting procedures by presenting the simple balance sheet for a service business. The next seven chapters then continue to develop accounting concepts in a simple and logical progression. In these chapters, students learn the theory of debit and credit, formal bookkeeping procedures, the fiscal period and income statement, the balance sheet, and the closing entries. By the end of Chapter 10, students will be familiar with the complete basic accounting cycle; they will know all the accounting steps except for the adjusting and reversing entries.

Chapters 3 through 10 should be studied in order because they represent clear and logical steps in the learning of accounting. New topics are introduced in simple stages throughout, building on concepts already established.

In Chapter 11, the topic of source documents is covered fully. A number of source documents are identified and explained in detail. Chapter 11 is then followed by a summary exercise to reinforce the students' knowledge of the basic accounting cycle. Chapter 12 offers students a clear explanation of subsidiary ledger accounting. This topic has particular relevance for students who leave school with only one credit in accounting; the beginning office worker is often asked to work with accounts receivable or accounts payable. Furthermore, this relatively difficult topic of subsidiary ledgers is more easily understood when learned within a simple system — in our case, one that includes only the two-column general journal.

Chapter 13 deals with accounting for a merchandising business. This chapter discusses the nature of the trading business, the accounting entries for sales and purchases, the taking of an inventory, the periodic and perpetual inventory systems, and the relationship between inventory and cost of goods sold. The end-of-period inventory adjustment is also covered in Chapter 13. This allows students to work with the full accounting cycle for a merchandising company at an early stage of study. Finally, Chapters 14 and 15 introduce the techniques of using specialized journals. A summary exercise follows Chapter 15 to allow students to reinforce and consolidate their learning. Thus, the first fifteen chapters cover the accounting cycle in a logical progression, one major concept at a time.

After Chapter 15, teachers have a good deal of freedom to choose topics and order of presentation. Chapters 16 through 18 could be studied at any time. However, the chapters dealing with cash register accounting, accounting controls, and payroll contain a good deal of important and necessary accounting information. They also represent important material for students who are about to enter the work force.

After students have completed Chapter 18, they will have a basic understanding of accounting theory and daily accounting procedures. They will then be ready to advance to the study of end-of-period accounting. The topic of adjusting entries is taught partly in Chapter 19 and partly in Chapter 20. These concepts are presented over two chapters in recognition of the fact that accounting adjustments have to do with the preparation of accurate financial statements. The author has found that students find it easier to keep this relationship in focus if only a few adjustments are dealt with at a time.

Once Chapters 19 and 20 are complete, the full accounting cycle has been covered, and basic accounting theory and practice has been presented. A very challenging project, Universal Lumber, follows Chapters 20 to reinforce all that has been learned to that point.

Accounting 1 then features four additional chapters to complete the student's knowledge of accounting. Chapter 21 on partnerships explains accounting for this type of business ownership. In Chapter 22, students learn about accounting for corporations, our most important form of business ownership. Chapter 23, on analyzing financial statements, presents the most common methods of preparing financial statements for ease of analysis, and explains the usual ratios and percentages that are involved. The information presented in these chapters should help students immeasurably in their understanding of the business world.

Finally, the last chapter in the text shows how the practice of accounting has undergone radical changes since the advent of electronic data processing. This chapter deals with specific accounting applications of the computer in today's business world.

A detailed discussion of all chapters can be found in the Teacher's Guide.

Flexibility

Accounting 1 has been written to suit the needs of teachers with varying teaching styles and ways of organizing courses, and of students with different abilities, goals, and interests.

The subject matter is presented in a logical and systematic order. However, the presentation is flexible enough to enable teachers to approach the material in other ways, to use alternative chapter orders, and to omit certain chapters altogether. Chapters 1 and 2 are optional; they have been included because we can no longer assume that students choosing first year accounting have taken any previous business courses. Chapters 3 through 15 cover the accounting cycle in a logical progression.

After Chapter 15, however, teachers have a good deal of freedom to choose topics and order of presentation. Chapters 16 to 18 and Chapter 24 could be studied at any time. Chapters 19 and 20 are prerequisite to Chapters 21 to 23, although each of these latter three is relatively independent of the other two.

A more complete description of how the text may be utilized can be found in the Teacher's Guide. It is my hope that *Accounting 1* will be a book that teachers can use without feeling restricted by a limited choice of topics.

Practice and Reinforcement

Accounting 1 features a wealth of practice exercises, review questions, and case studies to reinforce accounting theory.

- *Review Questions*: Comprehension questions at the end of each chapter check the student's understanding of the major concepts.
- *Exercises*: The exercises at the end of each chapter are arranged in groups according to the order of topics in the chapter. Within each group, these exercises are graduated according to three levels of difficulty; these range from simple exercises, to those of intermediate difficulty, to exercises requiring greater insight into accounting theory.
- *Cases*: Case studies at the end of each chapter focus the student's attention on realistic business problems that require action or decision. These cases are designed to provoke discussion concerning practical solutions to business problems and the role of values in making business decisions.
- *Summary Exercises*: Three long-term projects are provided at the end of Chapters 10, 15, and 20. These provide students with the opportunity to consolidate their learning of concepts that have been covered over a number of chapters.

Readability

The text offers thorough explanations in a simple, straightforward writing style. This clear presentation assists individualized instruction as it allows students to work on their own or to catch up on missed work.

The reading level has been carefully controlled with the needs of the target audience in mind. Particular attention has been paid to such factors as vocabulary and sentence length.

Study Aids

As a further aid to readability and to help students learn and study more effectively, the following study aids are featured in *Accounting 1*.

- *Easy-To-Follow Layout: Accounting 1* features a format designed to make the material readable.
  1. *Attractive Format*: The text uses an uncluttered, single-column page format to appeal to students and encourage them to use the book. Ample illustrations

and charts provide visual reinforcement of the text material and generous use is made of second colour.

2. *Topic Development*: Chapters are divided into major sections, each of which is clearly marked. Longer sections are further broken down into subheadings to enable students to better follow the development of a particular topic.
3. *Reinforcement of New Terms and Concepts*: New accounting terms are printed in boldface and defined in context when first encountered. These terms are then listed at the end of the chapter. In addition, a glossary and a comprehensive index are provided at the back of the text.

- *Abundant Questions and Exercises*
- *Chapter Preview*: Each chapter opens with a list of the sections in the chapter to give students an overview of topic development.
- *Key Objectives*: Student learning objectives follow the chapter preview to enable students to focus on the key goals of the chapter.

Personal and Practical Applications

The text emphasizes personal and practical applications of accounting whenever appropriate. Some of the problems and cases also involve accounting situations that would be familiar to most students.

Furthermore, most chapters feature the profile of someone involved in a job related to the material just covered in the chapter. These profiles describe people in common accounting positions, the steps they took to reach their position, and some of their job duties.

The Business Environment

Accounting 1 employs the following features in order to reflect the realities of the actual business world.

- *Source Documents*: Business source documents are included throughout the text to make the presentation more realistic and meaningful for the students. In Chapter 6, students are introduced to the concept that transactions originate from business documents. From Chapter 6 on, all transactions in the exercises are written in source document form. Then, in Chapter 11, the topic of source documents is covered more fully to give students a better understanding of how source documents relate to accounting entries.
- *Examples of Businesses*: The text makes frequent reference to various businesses to illustrate accounting concepts or to make the exercises more realistic. Whenever possible, the type of business chosen is one that would be familiar to students. In addition, the locations given for these businesses are from across Canada.
- *Flowcharts*: Simple and easy-to-follow flowcharts are used in the book for two purposes:

1. To show how symbols can be used to describe a system in a visual way.
2. To describe specific accounting systems and procedures in context.

Skill Development

Accounting 1 provides opportunities for students to:

- Interpret basic financial information.
- Develop decision-making skills.
- Make decisions and predictions based on accounting data.
- Develop communication skills in an accounting context.
- Apply problem-solving models to relevant accounting situations.
- Practise good work habits.
- Develop an awareness of the role of values in making business decisions.

Before beginning work on this revision, the author and publisher asked many teachers and students for suggestions as to how *Accounting 1* could be improved. In the light of their responses, we decided to produce two versions of the Third Edition. This complete version, with 24 chapters, contains enough material for two years of study. A brief edition is also available, designed for a one-year introductory course in accounting.

Both the brief and the complete versions of the Third Edition were prepared with the same fundamental goals as were the first two editions. At the urging of teachers and students, this text retains the approach, style, and organization of its predecessors. However, a comparison of this text with the earlier editions shows that the content of *Accounting 1* has been completely revised to meet the needs of accounting classes in the 1980s. The Third Edition has been expanded with six new chapters. All other chapters have been rewritten to improve readability, to incorporate more personal and practical applications, to reflect the real business world more accurately, and to update the content. Furthermore, important improvements have been made to the assignment material, workbooks, and layout. A new component has also been added to the program — a Teacher's Guide which includes helpful notes and aids.

New Chapters

There are six new chapters in the Third Edition.

- Chapter 1: *Accounting and Business* explores the nature and purpose of accounting, and explains how accounting relates to business.
- Chapter 2: *Accounting for Your Money* introduces some aspects of accounting through a familiar application — personal banking. This chapter draws students' attention to accounting procedures used in banking.
- Chapter 10: *Closing Entries* introduces this topic earlier than in previous editions. The concept is treated in a simple manner in this first half of the text, then covered in greater depth later (Ch. 20).

- Chapter 11: *Source Documents* describes the place of source documents in accounting. This chapter helps students better understand how source documents relate to accounting entries from Chapter 10. In addition, source documents are introduced earlier in the Third Edition, beginning in Chapter 6.
- Chapter 23: *Analyzing Financial Statements* is now expanded into a full chapter.
- Chapter 24: *Accounting and the Computer* recognizes the increased use of computers in accounting procedures.

Improved Content Presentation

Several internal revisions have also been made for this edition. Journalizing and posting are now presented in two separate chapters (Chapters 6 and 7), allowing students to concentrate on one major concept per chapter. Chapter 13: *Accounting for a Merchandising Business* expands the coverage of the trading business and the accounting for merchandise inventory to a full chapter.

Material on special transactions, cash, and banking activities, as well as on basic accounting systems and procedures, has been reorganized and rewritten for the new edition. Chapter 16: *Cash Register Accounting* deals with returns and allowances, cash refunds, cash discounts, and cash registers. Chapter 17: *Accounting Controls* treats internal procedures for control of cash, control of cash expenditures, and the voucher system.

The topic of adjusting entries has been rewritten to be easier for students to follow. Half of the adjustments are now presented in Chapter 19 and the remainder in Chapter 20. The traditional method of adjusting entries is used exclusively.

Improved Assignment Material

- *Review Questions*: The comprehension questions at the end of each chapter have been rewritten and more have been added.
- *Exercises*: Some new exercises have been included for each chapter. Exercises are now arranged in groups according to the order of topics presented in the chapter. Within each group, the exercises are graduated according to three levels of difficulty.
- *Cases*: Most of the case studies are new to this edition. Many of the new cases deal with the role of values in making business choices and decisions.
- *Summary Exercises*: Two of the exercises from the previous edition have now been expanded to become summary exercises: J. A. Lawson at the end of Chapter 11 and Travel Trailers at the end of Chapter 15.

Readability

The reading level of the Third Edition has been lowered to meet the needs of students of different ability levels. Particular attention has been paid to such factors as vocabulary and sentence length.

Study Aids

Many features in the Third Edition have been designed to help ensure effective learning.

- *New Format*: The revision develops student motivation and encourages use of the text by means of a new single-column page design. The number of illustrations and charts has been increased. Furthermore, the illustrations are now given figure numbers, thus enabling students to refer to them more easily. In addition, more use is made of second colour to enhance the content presentation.
- *Topic Development*: Especially in the early part of the book, chapters have been shortened in order to make the presentation more manageable for students. Moreover, chapters are now divided into major sections, each of which is clearly marked. Longer sections are further broken down under subheadings to enable students to better follow the development of a particular topic.
- *Reinforcement of New Terms and Concepts*: New accounting terms are printed in bold type and defined in context when first introduced. These terms are then listed at the end of the chapter. In addition, a glossary of these words is provided at the back of the text.
- *Chapter Preview*: Each chapter opens with a list of the sections of the chapter to give students an overview of topic development.
- *Chapter Objectives*: Student learning objectives follow the chapter preview. These are designed to enable students to focus on the key aims of the chapter.

Personal Applications, Careers, and Making Business Decisions

More personal and practical applications are presented throughout the text where appropriate. Furthermore, some exercises and case studies also involve personal applications of accounting.

Accounting-career profiles appear in most chapters. These describe people in common accounting positions, the steps they took to reach their positions, and some of their job duties.

Greater emphasis is placed on the analysis of accounting data to provide a source of information for business decisions. Some problems and cases address this topic, and Chapter 23 is spent exclusively on the presentation of financial statement analysis.

Updating

The basic content of the text has been updated in areas such as payroll and cash registers. Furthermore, the text recognizes the increased use of the computer in accounting.

Student Workbooks

As before, there are two companion workbooks, which supply all the business papers and accounting forms required to complete the exercises given in the student text. *Workbook A* covers Chapters 1–15 while *Workbook B* is used with Chapters 16–24.

Data is preprinted whenever it serves no educational purpose to have students copy data into the workbook. In addition, some special-purpose exercises are provided for specific objectives. For instance, students are given a journal and a ledger which is not in balance and then asked to locate the errors and to make the corrections.

A Teacher's Key for each workbook supplies worked-out solutions for all exercises, answers for all review questions, and comments on the case studies.

Teacher's Guide

To complete the package of teacher materials, a comprehensive *Teacher's Guide* has been prepared for the Third Edition. For each chapter, this guide offers:

- Teaching notes, including suggestions for the introduction of topics and ideas on how to extend particular concepts.
- Detailed student learning objectives.
- An indication of the degree of difficulty for each exercise in the student text and of the point in the chapter at which each exercise could be assigned.
- A bank of test items (including comprehension questions as well as exercises).

The *Teacher's Guide* also explains the program's basic philosophy and objectives. It discusses the text's flexibility and suggests ways to organize courses based on the book.

Two types of line master are also provided: illustrations of the major principles of accounting covered in the text, and masters for each form used in the workbooks.

It is impossible to overstate the value for today's students of a basic knowledge of accounting. For those who enter the business world, accounting skills can unlock the door to rewarding careers. But even for those who do not enter business, an understanding of basic accounting concepts can help in such areas as the management of personal finances or the unravelling of an increasingly complex world economic picture.

To help students to understand the value of accounting knowledge, I have tried to stress practical accounting applications whenever possible. And to help ensure that the students' introduction to the subject is rewarding, I have tried to capture their interest with a stimulating assortment of concepts, problems, and issues. Students embarking on the study of accounting are taking the first steps toward promising futures. It is my hope that for these students, and for their teachers, *Accounting 1* will provide an invaluable resource and guide.

G. E. S.

Prentice-Hall Canada Inc., Educational Book Division, and the author of *Accounting 1: Third Edition* are committed to the publication of instructional materials that are as bias-free as possible. This text was evaluated for bias prior to publication.

The author and publisher of this book also recognize the importance of appropriate reading levels and have therefore made every effort to ensure the highest possible degree of readability in the text. The content has been selected, organized, and written at a level suitable to the intended audience. Standard readability tests have been applied at several stages in the text's preparation to ensure an appropriate reading level.

Readability tests, however, can provide only a rough indication of a book's reading level. Research indicates that readability is affected by much more than word or sentence length; factors such as presentation, format, and design, none of which are considered in the usual readability tests, also greatly influence the ease with which the students read a book.

One other important factor affecting readability is the extent to which the text functions to motivate students. Thus, the following features were incorporated into this book to further increase reader comprehension. (Page references are given to provide examples of most features.)

Questions and Exercises

Accounting 1 features a wealth of practice exercises as well as questions to reinforce the theory.

1. *Review Questions*: Comprehension questions at the end of each chapter check student understanding of the major concepts. (p. 199, p. 664)
2. *Exercises*: The exercises at the end of each chapter are arranged in groups according to the order of topics in the chapter. Within each group they are graduated according to three levels of difficulty. (pp. 81–89, pp. 534–542)
3. *Cases*: Case studies at the end of each chapter focus students' attention on realistic business problems that require action or decision. (p. 108, p. 724)
4. *Summary Exercises*: Three long-term projects are provided (at the end of Chapters 10, 15, and 20). These exercises require students to consolidate their understanding of concepts covered over several chapters. (pp. 231–234, pp. 623–634)

Attractive Format

The book employs an attractive design to appeal to students and encourage the use of the text. It features an uncluttered, single-column format. In addition, generous use is made of headings and sub-headings, and of second colour.

Numerous Illustrations

Over 400 illustrations and charts provide visual reinforcement of the printed word.

Topic Development

Chapters are divided into clearly marked major sections. Lengthy sections are further broken down into sub-sections to help students follow the development of a particular topic more easily.

New Terms

Terms are printed in boldface type and defined in context when first introduced. These terms are then listed at the end of the chapter and defined in a glossary at the end of the text. (p. 121, p. 480)

Chapter Openings

Each chapter opens with a brief outline of content to enable students to see at a glance where the chapter is headed. These introductions consist of an overview of the sections that the chapter contains. (p. 130, p. 584)

Student Learning Objectives

A list of the key student learning objectives follows the introduction. These are designed to enable students to focus on the key ideas of the chapter. (p. 49, p. 545)

Chapter Conclusions

Each chapter ends with a list of the key terms followed by questions and exercises. (pp. 176–186, pp. 742–769)

End of Text

The book concludes with a glossary of terms and a comprehensive index to help students use and find important accounting terms and information.

Career Profiles

Most chapters feature a profile of a person involved in a job related to the material covered in the chapter. These profiles describe people in common accounting positions, the steps they took to reach their position, and some of their job duties. (p. 129, p. 679)

1

Accounting and Business

1-1 Accounting as an Aid to Business
1-2 The Nature of Business
1-3 Forms of Business Ownership
1-4 Why Study Accounting?
1-5 The Accounting Office
1-6 Becoming an Accountant

Objectives

When you have completed Chapter 1, you should:

1. Understand the objectives of business.
2. Know three ways in which accounting can be useful to business.
3. Know the three types of business, and the three forms of business ownership.
4. Know five ways in which a knowledge of accounting can benefit you.
5. Understand the type of work that is done in an accounting office and the background of some sample employees.
6. Know the different ways that you can learn accounting.
7. Know the three national accounting organizations and the requirements for admission to their programs.

Have you ever thought of starting your own business? What would be your goals? Your first goal would be to earn a good profit. In other words, after all your bills were paid, you would want to have enough money left over to make your work worthwhile.

In order to run a business you need to know how much profit the business is making. Accounting is the highly developed system that lets you keep track of your profits. Proper accounting methods provide a foundation for the financial success of a business.

1.1 Accounting as an Aid to Business

Accounting helps business people in these three important ways:

1. Accounting provides permanent records that are needed for the smooth running of any business. These records show, for instance, the amounts owed to the business by its customers, the amounts owed by the business to its suppliers, and the quantities of every item in stock. The records include copies, or written records, of all cheques issued by the business, documents as proof of all purchases, payroll records, and other relevant business forms.
2. Accounting provides necessary information about the business. The managers of the business and interested outsiders may need answers to questions like these: Is a satisfactory level of profit being earned? Is the selling price of the product high enough? Is there enough money on hand to pay the business's debts? Is the company successful in increasing its sales? Is there enough merchandise on hand? What does it cost to produce certain products? How much income tax will have to be paid? Can a bank loan be obtained to expand the business?
3. Accounting provides a number of controls to promote honesty and accuracy. As businesses grow, they often have to employ outside persons. The owners can no longer look after everything alone. They have to rely on the accounting system to keep their staff honest. A good accounting system establishes several safeguards. All cash must be deposited promptly in the bank. The person who handles cash should have no opportunity to falsify accounting records. All payments must be made by cheque and must be backed up by proper business papers. All items of stock should be counted periodically and compared with quantities worked out by the accounting department. Any stock shortages must be quickly identified and investigated.

Objectives of Accounting

Basically, accounting has two main goals.

1. Accounting must provide a record of all business transactions in a systematic manner to prevent theft, fraud, and error, and provide accurate data for interactions with outside individuals, companies, and governments.
2. Accounting must provide information and reports for owners and managers to assist them in making the best possible decisions for the company.

1.2 The Nature of Business

Businesses of all types are found in cities, towns, and villages throughout the country. Businesses are the economic framework upon which our society is built.

But what is a business? Generally, a business involves the sale of goods or services in order to earn a profit. Most businesses fall within one of the following three main categories.

1. *The service business.* This type of business sells a service to the public. A service business does not make or sell a product. To picture a service business, think of a bowling alley, a transport company, a rock group, or a medical clinic.
2. *The merchandising business.* This kind of business buys goods and resells them at a higher price for a profit. To picture a merchandising business, think of a hardware store, a marina, a department store, or a record store.
3. *The manufacturing business.* This kind of business buys raw materials, converts them into a new product, and sells these products to earn a profit. To picture a manufacturing business, think of a seamstress, a construction company, a paper mill, or a steel plant.

Although a farm is not a manufacturing company in the strict sense, it is closely related. It is known as a *producing business* because it produces products such as milk, beef, grain, and other foods.

1.3 Forms of Business Ownership

There are three main forms of business ownership. On a walk down any commercial street, you can see examples of each one. For example, you might notice a sign that reads 'J. Wouk, Carpenter'. This sign indicates that J. Wouk, alone, owns his business. A business in which one person works alone is known as a sole-proprietorship, and the owner is known as a sole-proprietor.

Or you might come across a sign that reads 'Fogle, Silver, Zimmerman, Accountants'. The three persons named on this sign are partners who own the business together and share in its profits. Their business is known as a partnership.

Again, you might find a sign that reads 'Red River Homes Limited'. This business is a 'limited company', also known as a 'corporation'. A corporation is a special form of business that is owned by a number of persons called shareholders. Almost all large businesses are corporations and some have several thousand shareholders.

1.4 Why Study Accounting?

Complexity of Business

The laws laid down by government concerning fair business practice, income taxes, and so on, have become so numerous and complex that only an expert can thoroughly understand them. A fully qualified accountant is expected to be expert in these laws. The increasing complexity of business transactions and the government regulations are major reasons why accounting has become the fastest growing of all the professions.

Accounting as a Job

Those of you who decide to enter the business world will find a job more easily if you have a background in accounting. A large percentage of jobs require accounting and recordkeeping skills. In simple terms, accountants are in demand.

As you improve your position in the business world, you will find your responsibilities growing. The higher positions in business require better qualifications. A thorough understanding of accounting will help you to improve your position in business. You will be a more valuable employee and you will be able to command a higher salary.

Owning Your Own Business

Many people want to own a business. Those who achieve their goal soon find themselves faced with accounting demands. They must keep track of their banking, the customers' accounts, the unpaid bills, the payroll, the sales tax, and so on. A knowledge of accounting gives the owner of a business a definite advantage.

Professional Accountancy

Some of you may choose a career as a professional accountant. By completing the requirements of one of the professional bodies of accountants, you can become a Chartered Accountant, a Certified General Accountant, or a Registered Industrial Accountant. Qualified professional accountants are eligible for senior management positions and have the right to practice as public accountants. Public accountants are those who offer their services to the general public for a fee in the same manner as doctors or lawyers. A professional accountant earns a good income and enjoys a respectable position in the community.

Accounting in Daily Life

If you choose not to work in the field of accounting, there are still benefits to be enjoyed from having a working knowledge of the subject. Persons with an accounting background are better able to understand the world around them, and can usually handle their own financial affairs very easily.

1.5 The Accounting Office

When you enter an accounting office, you can see a number of people, all very busy, operating business machines, speaking on telephones, holding conversations, and working with pen and paper. At first they all appear to be doing similar work, though they are not. Let's take a walk through the accounting office of Lombard-Brown, Ltd., a large merchandising firm, and see what some of the employees actually do.

The People

Samuel Kwong is the credit manager for Lombard-Brown. He decides whether to let a new customer buy on credit. He is responsible for all aspects of accounts receivable; that is, money owing from customers. Sam makes sure that customers' accounts are kept accurately and are collected promptly. If a customer's account becomes overdue, it is Sam who has to get tough. Because the business has a large number of credit customers, Sam is a busy man.

Sam has a secondary school diploma and has worked for the company for six years. Two years ago he enrolled in the CGA program and he expects to complete it in three years. He is gaining valuable experience in this office. But he realizes that he might have to change firms to improve his position.

Janet Liscombe is responsible for the daily banking. Among her duties, Janet opens, sorts, and distributes the mail. Any money received by the business must be listed for recordkeeping purposes. Then it is organized properly for depositing in the bank. Janet is responsible for delivering it to the bank each day.

Janet recently graduated from high school as a commercial specialist. Although her marks were good, she has no desire to go to college at this time. She wants to work for a year or two and then decide about her future. She is quite happy in her present job.

Frank Doucette is the paymaster. He and his staff prepare the company's weekly payroll. This is an important position. Lombard-Brown employs a large number of workers, and their cheques must be ready on time.

Frank has held several different accounting jobs since he left school fifteen years ago. He has gained a lot of knowledge and experience. Now he is in charge of the payroll department and enjoys this responsibility.

Susan Kusyk has an important position in the office. She is in charge of accounts payable, the paying of the company's bills. As bills are received from suppliers, they are sent to Susan's department. Here certain steps are taken to make sure that the bills are made out correctly and are proper charges against the business. Bills cannot be paid until Susan gives the final approval. Although she is not a qualified accountant, Susan is a college graduate and has taken several accounting courses. She expects to enrol in either the CGA or RIA programs in the near future. Without those initials after her name, Susan's career would be limited.

Dave Duncan is in charge of the accounting department. His official title is chief-accountant and office manager. As supervisor, Dave must bring all of the accounting systems and procedures into one smooth and efficient operation. Dave is a chartered accountant and is the only one in the office who knows and understands the entire system. If something goes wrong, Dave can be counted on to work it out. In addition to his many regular duties, Dave is part of the management team.

Someone always seems to need him. He spends a lot of time preparing data and reports for, and attending, executive meetings.

The Work

The accounting department of a business is expected to handle many jobs. These duties belong to one of the following three categories.

1. *Routine daily activities.* These are activities that occur in the same way nearly every day of the year. They include processing of bills, preparing of cheques, daily banking, recording of transactions, preparing business papers, and so on.
2. *Periodic accounting activities.* These are activities that occur at regular intervals. Pay cheques have to be made ready every week or two. Every month the bank accounts must be checked. Every year the annual financial reports must be prepared. Also, every year the income tax form must be prepared as required by government regulation.
3. *Miscellaneous activities.* Some accounting activities cannot be predicted. For example, if an accounting employee resigns, the position must be filled quickly. An advertisement must be prepared, interviews must be conducted, and so on. Or a bank manager may call, expressing concern over the size of a bank loan. A visit to the bank becomes necessary to discuss the matter. Or a salesperson may call about a new machine that she claims will reduce office costs. Time is taken to talk to her and to examine the machine.

As you can see, the accounting department of a business includes a wide variety of functions. In a small business, one or two people may do all the necessary accounting work. In a large business, several hundred people may be employed to carry out numerous accounting tasks.

1.6 Becoming an Accountant

A great many accounting positions exist in our society. Some are minor positions with small firms requiring basic accounting skills only. Others are high-level positions requiring exceptional competence and education. Between these two extremes, there lies a vast range of different accounting requirements. As a result, accountants often have widely different backgrounds and abilities. Some may have no formal training while others may have studied at a high level for several years.

Accountants obtain their formal training either in high-school, at college or university, or from a professional organization. All academic studies must be supplemented by job experience. You can't really call yourself a good accountant unless you have practical experience along with your formal training.

Most colleges and universities offer diplomas or degree courses in business. The study of Accounting is included as part of the curriculum in these courses.

Professional Accounting Organizations

To be a fully qualified accountant you must complete the course prescribed by one of three national professional accounting organizations. The names of these organizations and their national addresses are as follows:

Canadian Certified General
Accountants Association
535 Thurlow Street, Suite 800
Vancouver, B.C.
V6E 3L2

Professional Designation
CGA (Certified General Accountant)

The Society of Management
Accountants of Canada
M.P.O. Box 176
Hamilton, Ont.
L8N 3C3

Professional Designation
RIA (Registered Industrial Accountant)

Canadian Institute of Chartered
Accountants
250 Bloor Street, East
Toronto, Ont.
M4W 1G5

Professional Designation
CA (Chartered Accountant)

Each of the above professional bodies is a national association, but also functions at the provincial level. Members of these three organizations are highly regarded professional accountants.

The RIA and CGA programs are similar in a number of ways. To enrol in each of the courses you must have a grade 12 education or its equivalent. The programs are designed to be studied over a five-year period through the completion of a standard number of weekly lessons. However, the time can be shorter or longer, depending on the individual. People usually work full-time in accounting jobs while taking the course. Both associations have a practical experience requirement which must be completed before graduation. Both groups also offer lecture courses at universities and colleges across Canada. These courses offer an alternative method of covering the course. To fully qualify, a student must meet all the course requirements and then pass a final examination which is uniform across Canada.

The difference between the RIA and the CGA programs is one of emphasis. The RIA program concentrates on developing management accountants who are expected to work in industry at the management level. The CGA program allows for specialization in different areas, auditing for example, in the final year. CGA's work in all areas of accounting.

The Institute of Chartered Accountants is the oldest and largest body of professional accountants in Canada. Nearly 50 percent of Chartered Accountants, far more than any other body, are employed as public accountants. The Chartered Accountants are the only ones who require their members to have a university degree and to have practical experience in public accounting before graduation.

To become a chartered accountant a candidate must obtain a university degree, complete certain prescribed university courses, and complete a program of advanced professional study laid down by the institute. The candidate must also complete a term of service with a public accountant and pass a uniform final examination.

It usually takes five years after enrolment to become a Chartered Accountant. This time can be shortened or lengthened depending on the student. Although many CA's become public accountants, a large number of them hold senior executive positions in industry and government.

At one time, the accountancy profession was dominated by men. In recent years, however, women have been entering the profession in increasing numbers. It is a highly suitable career for women. This has been proven by the fact that in recent years three women have won the Institute's gold medal prizes for the highest marks across Canada.

Review Questions

1. Explain why profit is such an important factor in the lives of business people.
2. Accounting provides permanent records for a business. Explain, with examples.
3. Accounting provides information about a business. Explain, with examples.
4. Accounting provides controls within a business. Explain, with examples.
5. What is a business?
6. Name the three main types of business.
7. Describe a service business and give an example.
8. Describe a merchandising business and give an example.
9. Describe a manufacturing business and give an example.
10. A farm is considered to be more like a manufacturing than a merchandising business. Explain.
11. What is a sole-proprietorship?
12. What is a partnership?
13. What is a corporation?
14. Why is accounting the fastest growing profession?
15. Explain how a knowledge of accounting can help you in your career.
16. Explain how a knowledge of accounting can help those who own their own businesses.
17. Give five areas of activity within the accounting department.
18. Describe three different levels of competence within an accounting department.
19. There is a great deal of responsibility in some accounting jobs. Give two examples.
20. Describe the three categories of work in an accounting department. Give examples.

21. Name the three national professional accounting bodies.
22. Describe the steps necessary to become an RIA or a CGA.
23. Describe the steps necessary to become a CA.
24. In your opinion, why do chartered accountants go into public accounting more often than do the members of the other two accounting bodies?
25. In your opinion, how does one decide whether to become a CA, an RIA, or a CGA?
26. In your opinion, why is accounting a highly suitable career for women?
27. Explain why business courses in colleges or universities include accounting as one of the subjects in the curriculum.

2

Accounting for Your Money

2-1 Types of Personal Bank Account
2-2 The Bank's Record of the Customer's Money
2-3 Keeping Personal Bank Records
2-4 Bank Reconciliation
2-5 Electronic Information Processing

Objectives

When you have completed Chapter 2, you should:

1. Know five different types of personal bank account.
2. Know how to prepare a personal bank record.
3. Be able to reconcile a bank account.
4. Understand how a knowledge of banking is helpful when learning accounting.
5. Understand why banking activities are highly suited to electronic data processing.

Perhaps, like many students today, you have a part-time job. In that case, you have already discovered that when you earn money, you have to make choices about that money. How much will you spend? How much will you save? Where will you keep your savings?

Today's students are wise in the handling of money. They know what banks can do for them. Banks keep their money safely. Banks pay interest on their money. And that's not all. Banks also help students with their recordkeeping by offering personal bank accounts.

2.1 Types of Personal Bank Account

At one time, the only kind of personal bank account was the simple savings account. With a savings account, the bank pays you interest, or a percentage of your savings, for the use of your money. On savings accounts that are strictly for savings, the depositor earns interest at a healthy rate and may make withdrawals. Depositors are given a bank passbook as a record of their transactions. This is updated at any time on request.

The use of cheques to pay household and personal bills has now become a common practice. A **cheque** is a written order by a depositor to the bank authorizing the bank to pay out a certain sum of money to the person or organization named on the cheque. This method of making a payment is possible only through the banking system. It is only by means of the banking system that funds are transferred from one account to another.

For customers who write a lot of cheques, banks offer a special type of account called the 'Personal Chequing Account'. Customers with this type of account are allowed to write as many cheques as they wish. Once each month, the customers receive back all of their cheques cashed during the month, as well as a statement from the bank showing all of their transactions and the latest balance.

As you can see, bank accounts serve two basic functions: saving and chequing. You may have one or more accounts depending on your needs. The following accounts are available from banks today:

1. A **Personal Chequing Account** is for those who write a lot of personal cheques.
2. A **Premium Savings Account** is for those who want to earn interest on their savings at a fairly high rate, and for those whose account balance changes very little.
3. A **Daily Interest Savings Account** is for those who want to earn interest on their savings at a fairly high rate, and whose account balance changes frequently.
4. A **Chequing Savings Account** is for those who want to earn some interest but also want to write a few cheques on the account.
5. A **Daily Interest Chequing Account** is for those who want to earn interest on a fluctuating balance and also want to write a few cheques on the account.

2.2 The Bank's Record of the Customer's Money

A great deal of money is placed in banks by the general public. The banks have important obligations regarding these funds. They must keep them in a safe place. They must make them available when requested. And they must keep a record of them in an accurate, up-to-date, and proper manner.

The system by which banks keep track of their customers' accounts varies. Many branch banks have computer terminals, connected to a large central computer. The memory of the main computer stores all the data from all the customers of all the connected branches. Certain coded data is keyed at the branch terminal, and data stored in the central computer is made available at the branch. To bring a customer's passbook up to date, the book is placed in the printer, a few special keys are pressed, and the passbook is automatically updated. To find out the balance in a chequing account, a few keys are pressed and the customer's up-to-the-minute balance can be read on a small television screen.

Small remote branches may still use a handwritten and older machine-accounting system of maintaining customers' accounts. For each customer there is a **ledger sheet** such as the one illustrated in Figure 2.1.

This sheet is a simple business form, showing deposits, cheques and other deductions, and the running balance of the customer's account. When the customer

P.C.A. LEDGER No. 233454

Name John Wosney
Address 700 Main Street, Calgary, Alberta
Occupation Stonemason

Date	Cheques	Deposits	Balance
Feb. 12	Balance Forward		456.23
Feb. 14	40.02		416.21
Feb. 19		150.00	566.21
Feb. 24	25.00 56.00		485.21
Feb. 25		782.00	1 267.21
Mar. 3	313.15		954.06
Mar. 5	67.14		886.92
Mar. 7	10.45 19.50		856.97
Mar. 10	96.45		760.52
Mar. 14	412.00		348.52
Mar. 17	2.50 SC		346.02
Mar. 19	85.90		260.12

Figure 2.1 A ledger sheet for a personal chequing account.

asks that a passbook be brought up to date, the clerk copies the updating information into the passbook from the ledger sheet.

Chequing account customers do not have passbooks. For them, duplicate copies of the bank's ledger sheets are prepared. These **bank statements**, as they are known, are sent to the customers at regular intervals, along with the cheques that were cashed during the interval.

2.3 Keeping Personal Bank Records

If you write many cheques on your bank account, it makes good sense to keep a detailed record of your transactions and bank balance. There are three good reasons for this:

1. You will know your true bank balance at any time. Then you will not be guilty of writing cheques for amounts larger than your bank balance. Issuing cheques that 'bounce' is not good for your reputation and is a nuisance to your bank.

   It is unreliable to use the account balance shown by the bank. You may have written cheques that have not yet reached your bank for payment. In that case, the bank record will show a balance higher than you really have.
2. You can readily check back on any particular payment or analyze your payments for income taxes or some other purpose.
3. You will have a means of checking the accuracy of the bank's record. This is useful if there is any confusion between the bank's record and your own. You might forget a transaction, or the bank may make a wrong deduction against your account. Or someone could forge your signature on a cheque and get it cashed. Without a personal record, these problems could go unnoticed.

The simplest form of personal record is the three-column booklet shown in Figure 2.2. Banks usually hand out little 'registers' like this one free of charge.

CHEQUE NO.	DATE	CHEQUE ISSUED TO	AMOUNT OF CHEQUE	√	AMOUNT OF DEPOSIT	BALANCE FORWARD
						702 79
236	19– Sep. 26	Sterivision	7 92			694 27
237	27	Stevens	30 —			664 27
	30	Deposit Susan cheque			150 —	814 27
238	Oct. 1	Cullingford Motors	94 21			720 06
239	2	Bubbles	51 31			668 75
240	5	J. Crowe	102 60			566 15
241	5	Cash	100 —			466 15
242	11	Telephone	27 85			438 30
243	11	Banner	1 50			436 80

Figure 2.2 The three-column personal record book for a chequing account.

You can see that this is a simple record. It provides a running account of your balance with sufficient details so that you can use it in the ways mentioned above.

Always try to carry your register with your cheque book. Then whenever you write a cheque, or make a deposit, you can enter it in your personal record right away. If you happen to make a banking transaction at a time when you don't have your record with you, you will have to carry some kind of reminder with you until you make the entry later on.

2.4 Bank Reconciliation

As we have seen, the bank and the customer both keep a record of a chequing account. At regular intervals the bank sends the customer a bank statement. This statement is simply a copy of the bank's ledger sheets for the customer's account. When you compare your own record against the bank's, you will almost always find that the two records don't show the same balance. How do you know which balance is correct? Or, is either balance correct? These questions can only be answered by going through the process of checking the one record against the other. This process is known as **bank reconciliation**.

You may wonder why the two records show different balances. The most common causes are listed below.

1. You may have forgotten to record a transaction in your personal record.
2. You may have made a mistake in recording a transaction in your personal record.
3. You may have made an error in calculating the balance after recording a transaction.
4. The bank may have charged a cheque to your account in error.
5. Certain transactions recorded by you may be unknown to and not recorded by the bank.
6. Certain transactions recorded by the bank may be unknown to and not recorded by you.

The fact that both you and your bank keep a separate record of your banking activity can help in detecting errors and omissions, and in ensuring that the banking records are up to date and accurate. If both sets of records have all transactions recorded, and done properly, then both sets of records should have the same balance. If they don't have the same balance, there must be one or more causes for the discrepancy.

In order to be absolutely sure that your records are accurate, you must be able to account for the difference between your balance and the bank's. This requires the preparation of a bank reconciliation statement, usually done each time you receive your monthly bank statement.

Steps in Reconciling a Bank Account

1. As shown below, divide a sheet of paper in half down the middle, and write your

heading. Enter the latest balances shown by the bank statement and by your personal record.

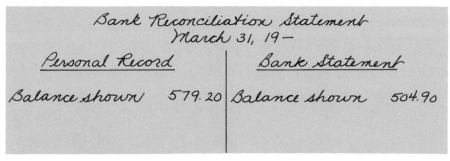

Bank Reconciliation Statement
March 31, 19—

Personal Record		*Bank Statement*	
Balance shown	*579.20*	*Balance shown*	*504.90*

2. Compare in detail the entries made on the bank statement with those made in your personal record. Be sure to use the 'cashed' cheques returned by the bank. Always mark the items with a coloured pen or pencil as you compare them. Only mark off items that match perfectly. The items that are not marked, then, are the ones that haven't been recorded equally in both sets of records. These are called the **discrepancy items**; they cause the two balances to disagree.

   Discrepancy items from one month are often cleared up in the bank statement for the next. Therefore, when performing step 2, it is necessary to check out each discrepancy item that appeared on the previous reconciliation. Most items will clear; that is, they will show up in the current period. Occasionally, however, an outstanding cheque will not clear. In other words, a cheque that is outstanding on the previous reconciliation will not appear in the bank statement of the current month, and, therefore, it is still outstanding. Any cheque in this category must be included with the outstanding cheques on the reconciliation.

   Let us assume that after comparing the two sets of records, the following items are not marked off:

   a. A deposit for $250, recorded in the personal record, did not show up on the bank statement. This happened because the deposit was made on the last day of the bank statement and the bank was late in processing it. This is known as a **late deposit**.

   b. Two cheques, No. 72 for $102.60 and No. 90 for $76.40, issued and recorded in the personal record, did not show up on the bank statement. The persons to whom these cheques were issued haven't cashed them yet. They are known as **outstanding cheques**.

   c. A bank service charge of $2.40, recorded on the bank statement, did not appear in the personal record. Usually, it is not until the depositor receives his bank statement that he finds out about a deduction for a service charge.

   d. One cheque, No. 80, issued for $75.40 and cashed by the bank for $75.40 was recorded incorrectly in the personal records as $74.50.

3. The unmarked items must be listed on the bank reconciliation. Remember that

the objective is to show how these items would affect the records if they had been recorded, and done correctly. Therefore, these items must be listed on the reconciliation statement on the side representing the record where they have not yet appeared.

Continuing our example, the following entries would be made on the reconciliation statement.

a. The late deposit of $250 is added to the balance shown by the bank.

Bank Reconciliation Statement
March 31, 19—

Personal Record		Bank Statement	
Balance shown	579.20	Balance	504.90
		Add: Late deposit	250.00
			754.90

b. The two outstanding cheques, $102.60 and $76.40, are deducted from the balance shown by the bank.

Bank Reconciliation Statement
March 31, 19—

Personal Record		Bank Statement		
Balance shown	579.20	Balance shown		504.90
		Add: Late deposit		250.00
				754.90
		Deduct: Outstanding cheques		
		#72	102.60	
		#90	76.40	179.00
				575.90

c. The bank service charge of $2.40 is deducted from the balance shown in the personal record.

Bank Reconciliation Statement
March 31, 19—

Personal Record		Bank Statement		
Balance shown	579.20	Balance shown		504.90
Deduct: Service charge	2.40	Add: Late deposit		250.00
	576.80			754.90
		Deduct: Outstanding cheques		
		#72	102.60	
		#90	76.40	179.00
				575.90

d. A deduction is made against the personal record for 90 cents. This will have the effect of correcting the deduction for cheque No. 80 from $74.50 to $75.40.

Bank Reconciliation Statement
March 31, 19–

Personal Record			Bank Statement		
Balance shown		579.20	Balance shown		504.90
Deduct: Service charge		2.40	Add: Late deposit		250.00
		576.80			754.90
Deduct: Adjustment on cheque #80			Deduct: Outstanding cheques		
Recorded as	$74.50		#72	102.60	
Should be	75.40		#90	76.40	179.00
Difference		.90			
					575.90
		575.90			

4. Ensure that the final balances on each side are equal. If they agree, the bank is reconciled, and the words 'true bank balance' may be written in. If they don't agree, you have not finished reconciling the bank account. Either you have not found all of the discrepancy items, or there is an adding error in the personal records. (An adding error is unlikely on the bank's part because their calculations are done by computer or accounting machine which have self-proving features.)

After listing all of the above items on the reconciliation statement and calculating the new balances, the finished reconcilation appears as follows:

Bank Reconciliation Statement
March 31, 19—

Personal Record			Bank Statement		
Balance shown		579.20	Balance shown		504.90
Deduct: Service charge		2.40	Add: Late deposit		250.00
		576.80			754.90
Deduct: Adjustment on cheque # 80.			Deduct: Outstanding Cheques		
Recorded as	$ 74.50		# 72	102.60	
Should be	75.40		# 90	76.40	179.00
Difference		.90	True Bank Balance		575.90
True Bank Balance		575.90			

5. Your reconciliation work is not finished after 4. You must remember to write into the personal record all items appearing on the 'personal' side of the reconciliation statement. Then the personal record will be up to date, be accurate, and reflect the true bank balance.

2.5 Electronic Information Processing

Banks have been quick to see the advantages of electronic recordkeeping. There is a great deal of data to be processed in a bank. Customers' accounts must be kept up to date, the interest on loans and deposits must be calculated and recorded, statements and reports for head office must be prepared, and so on. **Electronic data processing** allows all these functions to be carried out swiftly and efficiently.

Undoubtedly you have seen the strange-looking numbers coded on cheques. These numbers are a key part of the magnetic ink character coding system designed to speed up the processing of nearly two billion cheques written each year in Canada. These numbers are read by special sorting machines which greatly speed up the 'clearing' or transferring of cheques between banks. It is clear that as the volume of transactions to be processed increases, future banking will require the use of more and more electronic processing equipment and techniques.

Businesses today cannot get along without banking services. Money must be kept safely, cheques must be cleared, bank loans must be made, and foreign currencies must be converted. Everywhere, banking, business, and accounting work together.

Banking procedures and accounting procedures have much in common. The systematic recordkeeping techniques followed by banks belong to the world of accounting. The use of forms as proof of transactions is also a technique of business. And banks, like many businesses, are heavily influenced by new methods of electronic data processing.

You have just embarked on a study program in accounting. You will find that this first unit on banking will prove useful later on. It is impossible to be an effective accountant without having a thorough knowledge of banking procedures. And, by studying banking, you have already begun to acquire a feel for accounting in business.

Accounting Terms

cheque
personal chequing account
premium savings account
daily interest savings account
chequing savings account
daily interest chequing account
ledger sheet
bank statement
bank reconciliation
discrepancy item
late deposit
outstanding cheque
electronic data processing

Review Questions

1. Name the different types of personal bank account.
2. Briefly describe the factors that would affect the depositor's choice for each of the types of account.
3. The customer receives a copy of the bank's record of his account. Describe this record for a savings account and for a chequing account.

4. Give three reasons why a customer should keep his own banking record.
5. Why should a customer not feel that he can spend the balance in his account as shown by the bank?
6. Why should a depositor reconcile his chequing account?
7. After completing a reconciliation, what step is taken to ensure that the balance in the personal record is equal to the true bank balance?
8. Banks are leaders in the use of advanced data processing techniques. Give reasons for this.
9. By what name are the special numbers on a cheque known?
10. What is the purpose of these special numbers on cheques?

Exercises

1. Workbook Exercise: Complete a chart describing the features of bank accounts.

Maintaining a Personal Bank Record

2. Gerry O'Brien opened a personal chequing account on February 5, 19-- with a deposit of $500.

1. Record this deposit in Mr. O'Brien's personal record of his chequing account.

2. The transactions shown below were made by Mr. O'Brien between February 12 and April 4. Record these transactions in Mr. O'Brien's personal record, calculating the new balance after each entry.

February

12 Issued cheque No. 1 to Bell Telephone for $16.50.
15 Issued cheque No. 2 to Magic Insurance for $115.40.
28 Issued cheque No. 3 to General Realty for $250.

March

5 Deposited salary cheque in the amount of $850.
7 Issued cheque No. 4 to Admiral Department Store for $45.62.
7 Issued cheque No. 5 to Hi-Test Gasoline Co. in the amount of $35.71.
15 Issued cheque No. 6 to Growth Investment Company in the amount of $400.
20 Issued cheque No. 7 to United Way Fund in the amount of $50.
31 Issued cheque No. 8 to General Realty for $250.

April

4 Deposited salary cheque in the amount of $750.

3. Record the following transactions in the personal chequing account record of Frank Mazur.

	Balance brought forward, $374.20.
March	
6	Issued cheque No. 14 to Hydro for $54.75.
15	Issued cheque No. 15 to Brock Ratepayers for $20.
26	Issued cheque No. 16 to 'Cash' for personal use for $200.
31	Deposited salary cheque in the amount of $800.
April	
1	Issued cheque No. 17 to J. Belluz for rent in the amount of $300.
4	Issued cheque No. 18 to Bell Telephone for $15.
9	Issued cheque No. 19 to Sears for $29.50.
21	Issued cheque No. 20 to Jack Brown for $52.19.
30	Issued cheque No. 21 to the Receiver General (the federal government) for income tax in the amount of $78.40.
30	Deposited salary cheque in the amount of $800.
May	
1	Issued cheque No. 22 to J. Belluz for rent in the amount of $300.

Bank Reconciliations

4. The following data applies to the bank account of Carl Zimmer as of November 30, 19--:

Balance shown by Carl's personal record book		$657
Balance shown by the bank statement		$680
Late deposit, recorded by Carl on November 30 but not processed by the bank until December		$350
Outstanding cheques	No. 23	$ 75
	No. 27	$300
Bank service charge not recorded in the personal record		$ 2

1. **Prepare a bank reconciliation statement based on this data.**
2. **What entry or entries need to be made in the personal record to bring it to the true bank balance?**

5. The following are the personal chequing account record and bank statement for the account of D. Norman since he opened it on October 5.

1. **From these records, prepare a bank reconciliation statement as of December 31.**
2. **State the entries that need to be made in the personal record to bring it to the true bank balance.**

a. Bank statement for D. Norman.

THE NEIGHBOURHOOD BANK

IN ACCOUNT WITH

D. Norman
116 Grove Street

PERSONAL CHEQUING ACCOUNT

CHEQUES	DEPOSITS	DATE	BALANCE
Balance brought forward			
	1 000.00	Oct 5	1 000.00
15.20		Oct 21	984.80
S.C. .25		Oct 31	984.55
67.40		Nov 3	917.15
30.75		Nov 9	886.40
	900.00	Nov 10	1 786.40
320.00		Nov 12	1 466.40
120.00		Nov 15	1 346.40
200.00		Nov 25	1 146.40
S.C. 1.25		Nov 30	1 145.15
	900.00	Dec 1	2 045.15
36.75		Dec 2	2 008.40
300.00		Dec 9	1 708.40
320.00		Dec 14	1 388.40
20.75		Dec 28	1 367.65
19.00		Dec 31	1 281.25
S.C. 1.00		Dec 31	1 280.25

S.C. Service Charge

b. Personal record of D. Norman.

CHEQUE NO.	DATE	CHEQUE ISSUED TO	AMOUNT OF CHEQUE	✓	AMOUNT OF DEPOSIT	BALANCE FORWARD
	19-2 Oct 5	Deposit			1000 —	1000 —
1	10	Municipal Hydro	30 75	✓		969 25
2	20	Telephone	15 20	✓		954 05
3	31	Central Mortgage	320 —	✓		634 05
4	Nov 1	Triple C Finance	67 40	✓		566 65
5	9	Sparks Insurance	120 —	✓		446 65
	10	Salary			900 —	1346 65
6	15	Husky Oil	36 75	✓		1309 90
7	21	Qualified Accts Assoc.	200 —	✓		1109 90
8	31	Central Mortgage	320 —	✓		789 90
9	Dec 1	Triple C Finance	67 40			722 50
	3	Salary			900 —	1622 50
10	9	Withdrawal	300 —	✓		1322 50
11	15	Gino's Store	92 50			1230 —
12	26	Baker's Corner Store	20 75			1209 25
13	27	City Taxes	425 —			784 25
14	31	Central Mortgage	320 —			464 25
16	19-3 Jan 1	Triple C Finance	67 40			396 85
	2	Salary			925 —	1321 85

---

6. **The following are the personal chequing account record and the bank statement for the account of Paul Swartz for the month of June. Paul Swartz's bank reconciliation statement for May is also shown.**
   1. **From these records, reconcile the bank account of Paul Swartz as of June 30.**

67.40
92.50
20.75
425
320
67.40
993.05

2. State what entry or entries are necessary to bring the personal record to the true bank balance.

a. Paul Swartz's previous reconciliation.

Paul Swartz
Bank Reconciliation
May 31, 19–

Personal Record		Bank Statement	
Latest Balance	1 200.75	Latest Balance	1 450.75
		Deduct:	
		Outstanding cheques	
		#44 100 —	
		#45 150 —	250 —
True Balance	1 200.75	True Balance	1 200.75

b. Paul Swartz's personal record.

CHEQUE NO.	DATE	CHEQUE ISSUED TO	AMOUNT OF CHEQUE	√	AMOUNT OF DEPOSIT	BALANCE FORWARD 1 200 75
46	19– Jun 2	Rowlands Garage	237 50	✓		963 25
47	4	Joanne's Clothes	92 50	✓		870 75
48	9	Provincial Treasurer	9 —	✓		861 75
49	15	Rockway Gardens	7 73	✓		854 02
50	20	The Examiner	5 50	✓		848 52
51	20	Daily Times	6 30			842 22
	27	Salary			740 —	1 682 22
52	30	Marigold Apartments	275 —			1 407 22

c. Bank Statement sent to Paul Swartz.

GENERAL BANK

STATEMENT OF ACCOUNT WITH PAUL SWARTZ

CHEQUES	DEPOSITS	DATE	BALANCE
Balance forward		May 31	1 450.75
100.00		June 1	1 350.75
150.00		June 4	1 200.75
237.50		June 9	963.25
92.50 9.00		June 16	861.75
7.73		June 20	854.02
	740.00	June 27	1 594.02
5.50		June 30	1 588.52
S.C. 1.75		June 30	1 586.77

Challenge Question

7. The information given below includes the personal chequing account record and the bank statement for the account of Joy Lopez for the month of June. Joy Lopez's bank reconciliation sheet for May is also included.
   1. From these records, reconcile the bank account of Joy Lopez as of June 30.
   2. List the entries or corrections necessary in the personal record of Joy Lopez to bring the balance to the true figure.

a. Previous reconciliation.

Joy Lopez
Bank Reconciliation
May 31, 19—

Personal Record		Bank Statement		
Latest Balance	519 95	Latest Balance		424 40
Deduct: Bank Service Cheque	5 00	Add: Outstanding deposit		297 00
True Bank Balance	514 95			721 40
		Deduct: Outstanding cheques		
		#137	45 00	
		#138	37 50	
		#139	123 95	206 45
		True Bank Balance		514 95

b. Joy Lopez's personal record.

CHEQUE NO.	DATE	CHEQUE ISSUED TO	AMOUNT OF CHEQUE	√	AMOUNT OF DEPOSIT	BALANCE FORWARD
						681 40
138	19– May 29	Fred's Foods	37 50			643 90
139	31	Mountain Fuels	123 95			519 95
	Jun 1	Service charge	5 —			514 95
140	2	Telephone	26 75			488 75
141	5	Hydro	47 30			441 45
142	9	Property Tax	273 —			168 45
144	11	Bay Store	65 19			103 26
	12	Paycheck less $100			850 —	953 26
145	17	Ski club	33 —			920 26
146	19	Dr. McGail	30 —			890 26
147	22	Undercover	14 98			875 28
148	24	Eaton's	6 90			868 38
	26	Paycheck less $100			800 —	1668 38
149	29	Western Sails	410 —			1258 38
150	30	Frank Topa	335 —			923 38
151	31	Pete's Sports	46 20			877 18
152	31	Cash Withdrawal	150 —			727 18
	31	Insurance refund			135 —	862 18

c. Bank statement sent to Joy Lopez.

Municipal Bank

STATEMENT OF ACCOUNT FOR Joy Lopez

CHEQUES	DEPOSITS	DATE	BALANCE
Balance forward		May 31	424.40
	297.00	June 1	721.40
45.00		June 2	676.40
123.95		June 4	552.45
26.75		June 5	525.70
37.50		June 9	488.20
150.00		June 10	338.20
	850.00	June 12	1 188.20
273.00		June 15	915.20
47.30 65.19		June 16	802.71
30.00		June 23	772.71
14.98		June 24	757.73
	800.00	June 26	1 557.73
6.90		June 30	1 550.83
S.C. 2.20 150.00		June 30	1 398.63

Cases

Case 1 *Getting the Most Out of Your Bank Account*

Krista Lamer is an employee of a chartered bank. While having lunch one day with her friend, Judy Babych, the two ladies began to discuss finances, banking, interest rates, and so on. During the conversation, Krista learned that Judy had only one bank account, a chequing-savings account, and that the balance in this account was usually about $10 000. Judy thought that the chequing-savings account was ideal for her because she could write all the cheques that she wanted and still earn interest on the balance.

Krista knew that by a simple change in bank accounts Judy could earn more bank interest.

Questions

1. What would Krista advise Judy to do? Give reasons for your answer.

Case 2 *What Are Friends For?*

On Tuesday, February 5, Stephen and Stan Crockford, owners of a small business, met an old family friend, Mike Palmer. Several years earlier, before the Crockford brothers had inherited the business, Palmer had been their father's accountant. Now Palmer was in his late seventies. He no longer kept up with technological advances in accounting. However, he did remember some of the old tricks of the trade.

During the men's discussion over coffee, the talk eventually came around to the business. The Crockfords had a modest financing problem on their hands. In anticipation of receiving a $2 000 cheque from a customer that very morning, the brothers had issued a cheque for the same amount to a supplier who they knew would cash it that afternoon. Unfortunately, when the customer brought the cheque, the brothers didn't notice until too late that the cheque was postdated for Friday, February 8. They would not be able to deposit it until then.

The brothers also had a poor working relationship with their banker. This was due to a poor credit rating and a number of cheques that had bounced. Only yesterday the bank manager had refused to grant them a bank loan. He had also told them that he would not cash any of their cheques if there were not sufficient funds in their bank account.

Palmer believed that he could help the brothers out. First, he needed to know if either of them had an out-of-town bank account. Stan said that he had one in Bencrow where his cottage was located but that it only had a balance of a few dollars. Palmer said that the balance didn't matter.

Palmer suggested the following scheme. First, Stan was to write a cheque from his cottage account for $2 000 payable to the business and deposit it in the business bank right away. This would increase the bank account enough to cover the cheque that they were worried about. There would be no funds in the Bencrow account to cover Stan's cheque but this would not matter until Friday or perhaps even Monday. Palmer claimed that it took that long for a cheque to be cleared through to an out-of-town bank. Early Friday morning Stan would drive to Bencrow and deposit the post-dated cheque in his cottage account, providing the funds in that account to cover the cheque he had written on Tuesday.

As far as the Crockford brothers were concerned, the solution seemed too good to be true. They thanked their old friend and agreed to try it.

Questions

1. Do you think Palmer's scheme is legal?
2. Do you think Palmer's scheme is ethical?
3. Do you think the scheme will work?
4. Discuss.

Career

Rose McConnell / Bank Assistant Accountant

Rose McConnell went to high school in Bathurst, New Brunswick. After she graduated, Rose began work as a sales clerk for a local K-Mart Department Store. Her duties included stocking the shelves and pricing merchandise.

After two years, Rose left K-Mart to become a teller at the local branch of the Bank of Nova Scotia. She quickly learned how to cash cheques for customers, accept deposits, and balance her cash at the end of each day. She reported directly to the teller supervisor.

Rose's supervisor was very pleased with her efficiency and natural accounting ability. He recommended to the bank manager that she be quickly promoted. After just six months as a teller, Rose advanced to the accounting department as an accounting clerk. Her immediate supervisor was the assistant accountant.

The Bank of Nova Scotia then sent Rose on a management training program for one year. During this period, Rose gained experience in each phase of the accounting program. She learned, for example, how to process loans, keep ledgers, handle different types of bank account, calculate interest, and exchange foreign currencies.

After this training, Rose was promoted to assistant accountant and was transferred to another branch of the bank in Moncton, N.B. This is her present position. Rose responds to customers' enquiries concerning various services provided by the bank. She helps certain customers at the counter, such as those who want to certify a cheque or open a new bank account. Most importantly, Rose supervises the four tellers in the bank. She keeps track of and spot checks each teller's cash, trains new employees, and assigns each teller specific duties. Rose now reports directly to the bank accountant.

Rose likes the responsibility of her position and gets along well with the employees she supervises. She is grateful to the Bank of Nova Scotia for the faith it has shown in her future. She intends to reward that faith by someday becoming a bank accountant and then, perhaps, a bank manager. To help her fulfil her ambitions, she is presently taking evening classes twice a week in advanced accounting.

Career
Linda Osborne / Bank Accounting Clerk

Linda Osborne graduated from high school and immediately accepted a position as a secretary with the Bank of Nova Scotia in her home town, Calgary, Alberta. Her work involved typing correspondence, filing, and other general secretarial duties.

After two years, Linda was transferred to the loans department of the bank. Here she was involved in checking the credit ratings of people who wanted to borrow money. She did this by telephoning a central credit reference agency in order to obtain basic financial information about each person who applied for a loan. In addition, Linda typed out the forms for loan applications.

After working as a secretary for a few years, Linda decided she wanted to become more actively involved in banking. She became a bank teller. In this chapter you have read about various banking activities. From your own experiences, you probably have a good idea of some of the duties of a bank teller. In this position, Linda's major duties were to receive and pay out money, to verify deposits and examine cheques for endorsements, and to use the computer terminal to bring the customers' pass books up to date. Linda also sent all cheques to the bank's data centre for processing.

After three years as a teller, Linda was promoted to her present position of accounting clerk. One of her major duties is to prepare customers' bank statements and mail them, together with the cancelled cheques, to the customers. In addition, Linda certifies cheques, calculates the interest on savings accounts, and records the amount in the customers' accounts.

Recently, Linda has become responsible for talking to prospective customers about the various banking services available and assisting them in preparing application forms. She has also begun to process student loans. In her position, Linda reports directly to the accountant and the bank manager.

Linda very much enjoys her work at the bank. She finds the other employees friendly and co-operative. Because Linda has an aptitude for accounts, she hopes to become an operations officer (assistant accountant) and, then, to move to the position of senior operations officer (accountant).

3

The Balance Sheet

3-1 Financial Position
3-2 The Fundamental Accounting Equation
3-3 Preparing a Balance Sheet
3-4 Accounts Receivable and Accounts Payable
3-5 The Balance Sheet for a Business
3-6 Claims Against the Assets
3-7 Basic Recordkeeping Practices

Objectives

When you have completed chapter 3, you should:

1. Understand what is meant by the financial position of a business or a person.
2. Have started to build a vocabulary of accounting terms.
3. Be able to prepare a simple balance sheet in proper form for a business or an individual.
4. Understand the fundamental accounting equation.
5. Understand the meaning of 'claims against the assets'.
6. Know the four basic recordkeeping practices.

In the first two chapters, you learned that an accounting system reports and summarizes day-to-day financial information. One of the most important uses of this information is to show the **financial position** of an individual or a business.

3.1 Financial Position

The concept of financial position is simple and straightforward. If you wanted to determine someone's financial position, how would you go about it?

You would likely decide that the following three steps are necessary:

1. List and total the things owned that have dollar values; these are called **assets**.
2. List and total the person's debts; these are called **liabilities**.
3. Calculate the difference between the total assets and the total liabilities; this difference is called **capital** or **owner's equity**.

Example:

Let us follow the three steps given above to work out the financial position of Greg Bergman, a student, on July 15, 19--.

1. List and total the things of value owned by Greg. These assets might be as follows:

Cash	$ 30.75
Bank balance	75.00
Bicycle	136.00
Radio	47.00
Ski equipment	210.00
Total assets	$498.75

2. List and total Greg's debts. These liabilities might be as follows:

Owe to Philip	$10.00
Owe to Dad	15.00
Total liabilities	$25.00

3. Calculate the difference between total assets and total liabilities. The calculation is as follows:

Total assets	$498.75
Less total liabilities	25.00
Difference	$473.75

The difference of $473.75 is the amount that Greg Bergman is worth. This is known as equity or capital. A less commonly used term is **net worth**.

The above analysis shows the three steps taken to work out the financial position of an individual. The same three steps would be taken if you were trying to work out the financial position of a business.

3.2 The Fundamental Accounting Equation

The previous section showed that the total assets minus the total liabilities is equal to the capital or equity. This relationship is always true and can be written in the form of an accounting equation.

This **fundamental accounting equation** may be stated in two ways:

$$\text{Assets} - \text{Liabilities} = \text{Owner's Equity}$$

or

$$\text{Assets} = \text{Liabilities} + \text{Owner's Equity}$$

Now examine Greg Bergman's figures. From them you can see that the fundamental accounting equation is true.

$$\$498.75 - \$25.00 = \$473.75$$

or

$$\$498.75 = \$25.00 + \$473.75$$

This equation is an extremely important concept in the study of accounting. As you will soon see, all accounting theory is based on it.

3.3 Preparing a Balance Sheet

Accountants show the financial position of an individual or a business by means of a formal statement called a **balance sheet**. The steps involved in preparing the simple balance sheet of Greg Bergman from the data given above are shown in the following illustrations.

1. Write in the statement heading on columnar paper.

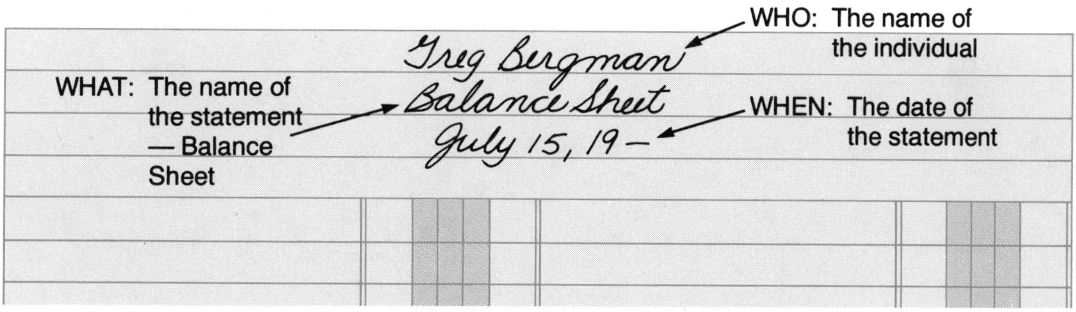

2. Write in the assets on the left side.

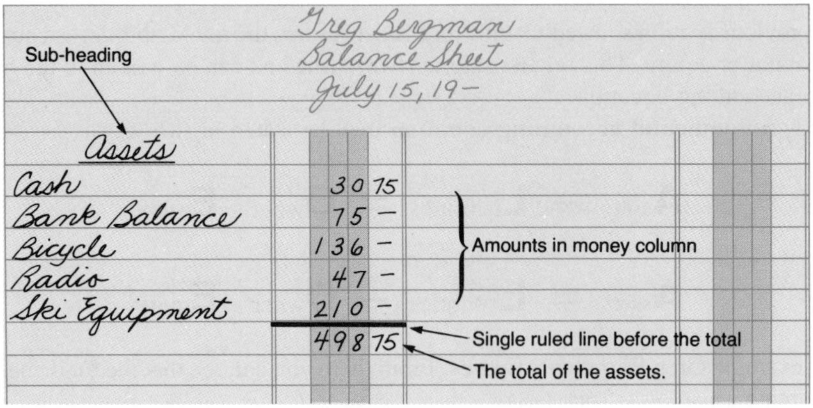
Greg Bergman
Balance Sheet
July 15, 19–
Sub-heading
Assets
Cash 30 75
Bank Balance 75 –
Bicycle 136 –
Radio 47 –
Ski Equipment 210 –
498 75
Amounts in money column
Single ruled line before the total
The total of the assets.

3. Write in the liabilities on the right side.

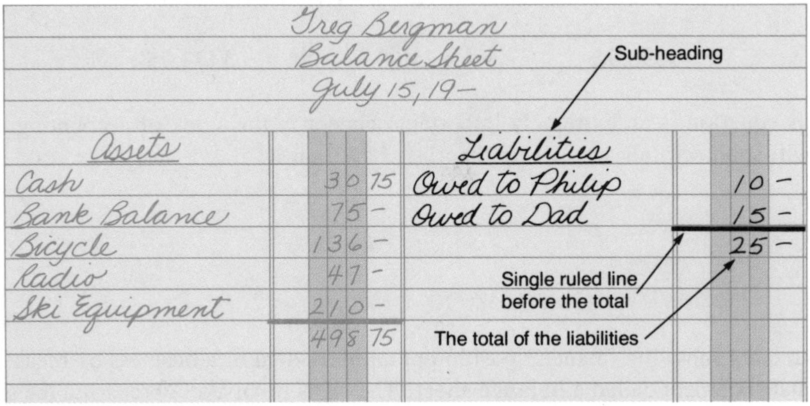
Greg Bergman
Balance Sheet
July 15, 19–
Sub-heading
Assets
Cash 30 75
Bank Balance 75 –
Bicycle 136 –
Radio 47 –
Ski Equipment 210 –
498 75
Liabilities
Owed to Philip 10 –
Owed to Dad 15 –
25 –
Single ruled line before the total
The total of the liabilities

4. Beneath the liabilities write in the owner's equity figure, the difference between the total assets and the total liabilities.

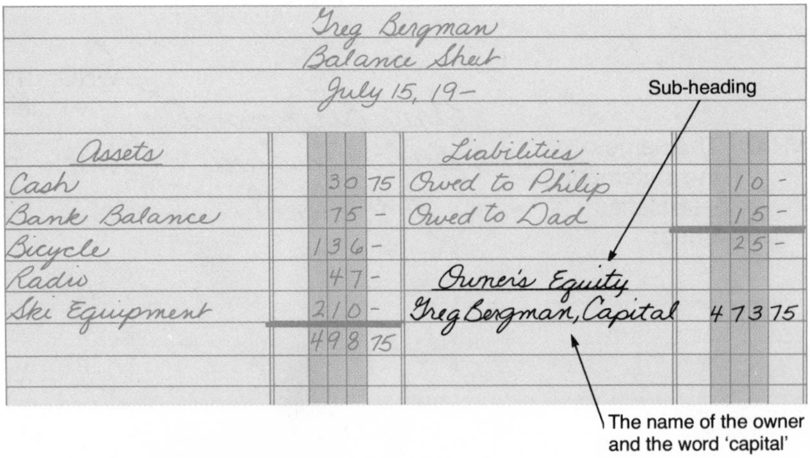
Greg Bergman
Balance Sheet
July 15, 19–
Sub-heading
Assets
Cash 30 75
Bank Balance 75 –
Bicycle 136 –
Radio 47 –
Ski Equipment 210 –
498 75
Liabilities
Owed to Philip 10 –
Owed to Dad 15 –
25 –
Owner's Equity
Greg Bergman, Capital 473 75
The name of the owner and the word 'capital'

5. Complete and rule off the balance sheet.

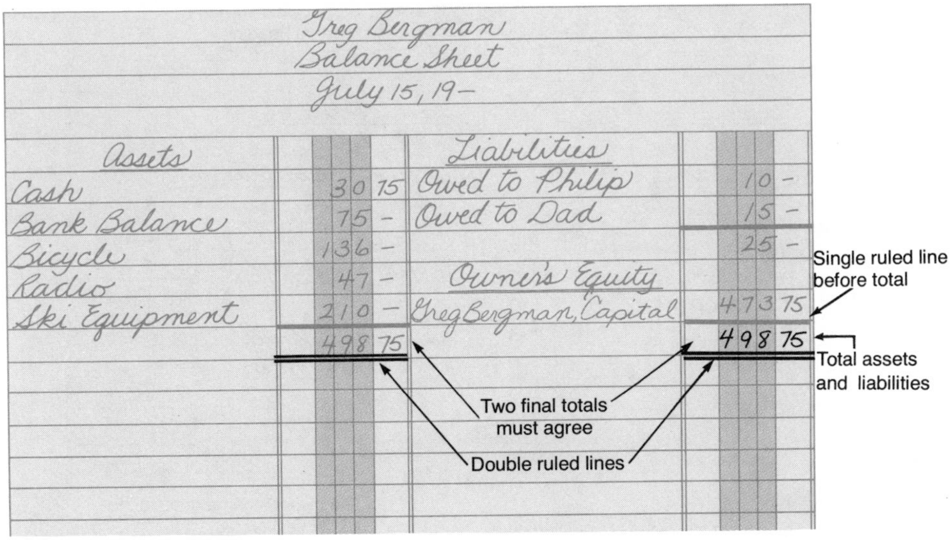
Greg Bergman
Balance Sheet
July 15, 19—
Assets
Cash 30 75
Bank Balance 75 —
Bicycle 136 —
Radio 47 —
Ski Equipment 210 —
498 75
Liabilities
Owed to Philip 10 —
Owed to Dad 15 —
25 —
Owner's Equity
Greg Bergman, Capital 473 75
498 75
Single ruled line before total
Total assets and liabilities
Two final totals must agree
Double ruled lines

3.4 Accounts Receivable and Accounts Payable

Customers often buy from a business with the understanding that they will pay later. These customers then owe money to that business. The business includes the money that is owed as one of its assets. This money is referred to as **accounts receivable** (accs recl). Each of the customers that owes money to a business is one of its **debtors**.

In turn, a business often purchases goods and services from its suppliers with the understanding that payment will be made later. The business includes these debts on the balance sheet in the liability section. These debts are referred to as **accounts payable** (accs payl). Each of the suppliers owed money by a business is one of the **creditors** of that business.

3.5 The Balance Sheet for a Business

You have already prepared a balance sheet for Greg Bergman, a student. The same five steps will be followed when preparing the balance sheet for a business. The balance sheet for a small business, A to Z Rent-Alls, is illustrated in Figure 3.1.

A to Z Rent-Alls
Balance Sheet
September 30, 19–

The business name goes in the statement heading.

Accounts Receivable – Debts owing from customers

Accounts Payable – Debts owed to suppliers

Assets		Liabilities	
Cash on hand	40 20	Bank Loan	10 000 –
Bank Balance	710 –	Accounts Payable	
Accounts Receivable		– Arrow Supply	1 950 40
– W. Boa	131 50	– Avco Finance	3 757 –
– T. Burns	350 –	Mortgage Payable	65 200 –
Rental Equipment	25 364 70		80 907 40
Delivery Trucks	12 965 –	Owner's Equity	
Land	38 000 –	Jerome Samas,	
Buildings	75 000 –	Capital	71 654 –
	152 561 40		152 561 40

Order of Assets
Assets are listed in the order of their liquidity, that is, how easily they can be turned into cash. Naturally, cash is listed first followed by bank balance, then accounts receivable, and so on.

The owner's name goes in the equity section.

Figure 3.1 The balance sheet of a small business, A to Z Rent-Alls.

Important Features of the Balance Sheet

1. A three-line heading is used. The heading tells three things: who, what, and when.
   The heading should list:
   a. the name of the business, organization, or individual;
   b. the name of the financial statement, in this case, Balance Sheet;
   c. the date on which the financial position was determined.
2. The assets are listed on the left side of the balance sheet and the liabilities and the capital are listed on the right side.
3. The assets are listed in the order of their **liquidity**, that is, in the order in which they can easily be changed into cash. Cash, being the most liquid, is listed first. Accounts receivable are listed next. Supplies and long-term assets such as land, buildings, and equipment are harder to change into cash quickly. Thus they are listed last.
4. The details of any item are fully disclosed on a balance sheet. For example, on the balance sheet of A to Z Rent-Alls, shown above, the used delivery truck is shown in the Assets section at its value of $12 965. The amount that is owed on

the truck, $3 757 to Avco Finance, is shown in the Liabilities section. This gives more information than showing the truck at a value of $9 208, the portion that has been paid for.

5. The two final totals, one for each side of the balance sheet, are recorded on the same line.

3.6 Claims Against the Assets

Consider this question. Who owns the assets of a business? If a business closed down, to whom would the assets belong?

The answers to these questions are straightforward. The assets would belong to those people who had provided the assets or the funds with which to acquire the assets.

A balance sheet shows who has a claim against the assets. Examine the balance sheet of Paramount Design, owned by Janet Korey, which is shown in Figure 3.2.

Paramount Design
Balance Sheet
December 31, 19—

Assets		Liabilities	
Cash	1 407 10	Bank Loan	4 000 —
Accounts Receivable		Accounts Payable	
R. Mason	350 —	Oakes Supply	150 —
H. Morgan	1 706 —	Modern Art Store	905 —
Supplies	1 250 —		5 055 —
Furniture	3 700 —	Owner's Equity	
Equipment	2 000 —	Janet Korey, Capital	15 108 10
Automobile	9 750 —		
	20 163 10		20 163 10

Figure 3.2 The balance sheet of Paramount Design.

As shown by the left side of the balance sheet, Janet's business assets are $20 163.10. The right side of the balance sheet shows that these assets, or the funds to obtain them, were provided by: the bank, $4 000; the other creditors, $150 and $905; and Janet herself, $15 108.10. Expressed in another way:

$$\underset{\$20\ 163.10}{\text{ASSETS}} = \underset{\underbrace{\$4\ 000 + \$150 + \$905}_{\text{creditors}} + \underbrace{\$15\ 108.10}_{\text{owner}}}{\text{CLAIMS AGAINST THE ASSETS}}$$

If for any reason a business is closed down, the claims of the creditors are settled first, and then the claim of the owner. This means that, if it is necessary to sell off any of the assets, the owner is responsible for any loss. The owner always gets what is left after the claims of the creditors have been satisfied.

Suppose that when Janet disposed of her assets and converted them into cash a loss of \$4 500 was suffered. The assets would be reduced from \$20 163.10 to \$15 663.10. However, the claims of the creditors would remain the same. Only the owner's claim or equity would have to be reduced — in this case to \$10 608.10.

The final balanced equation would be as follows.

$$\begin{array}{lcl} \text{ASSETS} & & \text{CLAIMS AGAINST THE ASSETS} \\ \$15\,633.10 & = & \underbrace{\$4\,000 + \$150 + \$905}_{\text{creditors}} + \underbrace{\$10\,608.10}_{\text{owner}} \end{array}$$

3.7 Basic Recordkeeping Practices

When to Abbreviate

Do not use abbreviations on financial statements such as balance sheets except when listing a business name which includes an abbreviation. For example, General Bakeries Limited is the name of the business; therefore the word Limited cannot be abbreviated. However, in the case of Canadian General Electric Co., the abbreviation for 'company' may be used as it is included in the name of the business.

Use of Columnar Paper

It is important for an accounting student to learn to use columnar paper. When columnar paper is used, notice how the figures are placed carefully in the columns. This is to help the accountant total the columns correctly. Observe also that dollar signs, periods, and commas are not used when recording amounts of money in the columns.

When using columnar paper, even dollar amounts may be shown by placing a dash in the cents column. Thus, in the following illustration, 12— is used instead of 12.00.

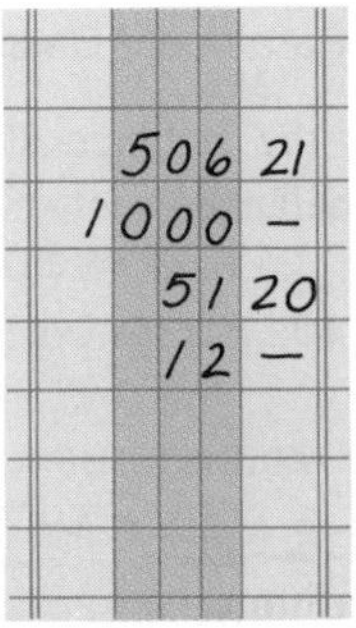

Use of Ruled Lines

If a column of figures is to be totalled (added or subtracted), a single line is drawn beneath the column and the total is placed beneath this single line as shown below:

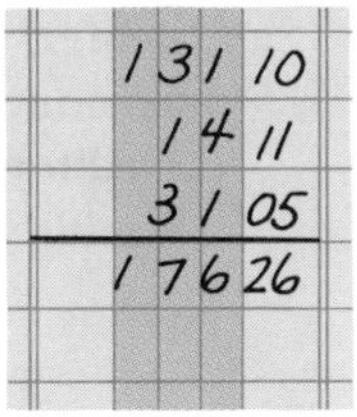

If a total happens to be a final total, such as the last amounts on the balance sheet, a double ruled line is drawn immediately beneath the total as shown below.

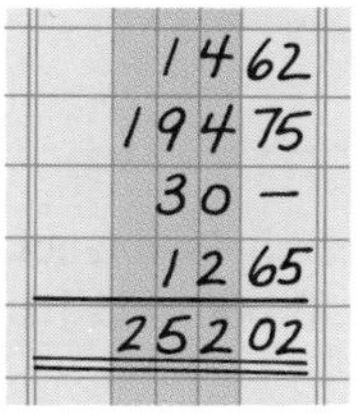

On most balance sheets, in order to place the two final totals on the same line, it is necessary to leave one or more blank lines between the figures in a column and the total. When this is done, place the single ruled line immediately above the total and not immediately beneath the figures in the column. Examine the following examples:

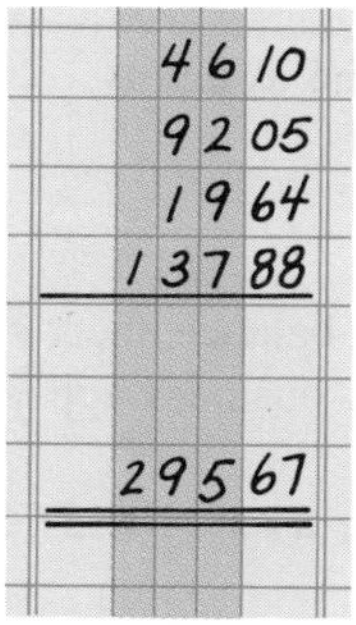

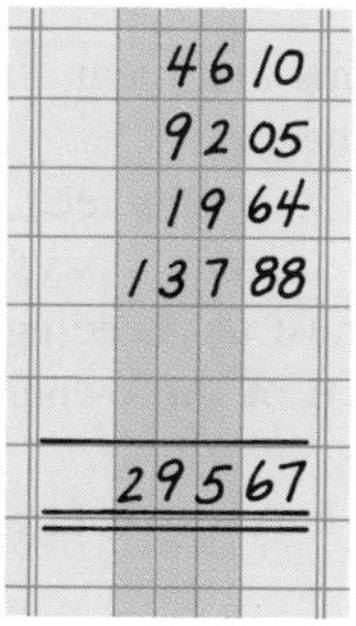

Neatness

It is most important that an accountant's work be neat and perfectly legible. This is necessary so that no one misinterprets the writing or the numbers. Although the work should never be untidy, at the same time it is not necessary that it be beautiful — only neat and legible.

From the very beginning you should make it a habit to strive for neatness and clarity in all of your exercises. Be sure to use your ruler to underline headings.

Accounting Terms

financial position
asset
liability
capital
owner's equity
net worth
fundamental accounting equation
balance sheet
accounts receivable
debtor
accounts payable
creditor
liquidity

Review Questions

1. Explain how you work out a person's financial position.
2. Karen Lipka has assets of $150 000 and liabilities of $65 000. What is her equity?
3. If a business has an equity of $125 000 and liabilities of $75 000, how much are its assets?
4. **a.** Define asset.
   b. Name five different assets a business may have.
5. **a.** Define liability.
   b. Name three different liabilities a business may have.
6. Define equity.
7. Name two other terms that mean the same as equity.
8. What is a balance sheet?
9. **a.** Explain the term 'accounts receivable'.
   b. Explain the term 'accounts payable'.
10. What three things must the heading of a balance sheet show?
11. When does the name of the owner of a business appear in the heading of a balance sheet?
12. On which side of a balance sheet are the assets listed? On which side are the liabilities listed?
13. How is an automobile that is not fully paid for shown on a balance sheet?
14. Who has a claim against the assets of a business?
15. When listing figures on columnar paper, what four items may be omitted?
16. **a.** What is a debtor?
    b. What is a creditor?
17. On which side of the balance sheet is a creditor listed?
18. What is meant by a single ruled line drawn beneath a column of figures?
19. Why is it important for an accountant's work to be neat?

20. Why does an accountant draw a double ruled line beneath a total?
21. When can short forms or abbreviations be used on financial statements?
22. Give two forms of the fundamental accounting equation.
23. Which is the most liquid asset?
24. Which is the more liquid asset, a government of Canada bond, or an account receivable? Explain your answer.

Exercises

Note: You will never be a successful accountant if, as you work through the exercises in this text, you merely memorize the solutions. Therefore, as you proceed through the text, always do your best to understand each topic completely.

Assets and Liabilities

1. List eight assets that a small business might own.

2. List three liabilities that a small business might owe.

3. Classify each of the following as an asset or a liability:

Office furniture	An amount owed by R. Jonas
An amount owed to H. Krueger	Supplies
Land	Mortgage payable
Supplies	Trucks
Bank Loan	A government bond
Buildings	An account receivable
An unpaid heating bill	An account payable

Fundamental Accounting Equation

4. If the total assets of a business are $37 486.49 and the total liabilities are $11 547.80, calculate the owner's equity.

5. On December 31, 1981, A. Lower's accounting equation was as follows:

Assets ($150 000) — Liabilities ($70 000) = Equity ($80 000)

If, during 1982, the assets increased by $70 000 and the liabilities decreased by $20 000, calculate the owner's equity at December 31, 1982.

6. If total assets increase by $10 000, and the equity increases by $5 000, what change has occurred in the liabilities?

7. If the liabilities increase by $15 000, and the equity decreases by $5 000, what change has occurred in the assets?

8. Paul Silva's assets and liabilities are listed below in alphabetical order.

Bank loan, $4 000; Building, $90 000; cash, $1 435; City Service (a debtor), $960; Emerson Electric Ltd. (a creditor), $1 200; Equipment, $13 750; Francis and Company (a debtor), $350; Frank's Service Station (a creditor), $375; Mortgage on building, $25 000; Supplies, $370.

1. **List the assets in one column and total them.**
2. **List the liabilities in another column and total them.**
3. **Calculate Paul Silva's equity.**

9. Claude Pineau, a factory worker in Hull, Quebec, asks you to help him find out how much he is worth. From a discussion with him you find out the following facts. List Claude Pineau's assets in one column, his liabilities in another, and calculate his net worth.

a. His bank balance is $754.
b. He owns a home valued at $82 500 which has a mortgage on it of $12 500.
c. He owns furniture and household equipment valued at $6 000.
d. He owns a summer property valued at $25 000 which he bought with money borrowed from the bank. Since the time of purchase he has paid back $1 000 of the loan.
e. He has unpaid bills amounting to $1 560.
f. He owes his father-in-law, M. Dupuis, the sum of $10 000 which he borrowed interest free several years ago at the time he bought his home.

The Balance Sheet

10. Kate Kramer is the owner and operator of The Kramer Company located in Revelstoke, B.C. On September 30, 19--, The Kramer Company had the following assets and liabilities. Prepare the September 30 balance sheet for The Kramer Company.

Assets	
Cash on hand	$ 106.70
Bank balance	530.00
J. Crothers (debtor)	1 100.00
R. Zack (debtor)	370.00
Supplies	200.00
Furniture and equipment	4 700.50
Delivery equipment	12 100.00
Liabilities	
Anglo Supply Co. (creditor)	740.46
C. P. Gregg (creditor)	3 000.00
Bank loan	5 000.00

11. From the following information as of June 30, 19--, prepare a balance sheet for Morgan & Associates, which is owned by Alice Morgan of Dryden, Ont.

Bank balance	$ 1 449.55
J. Radzio (debtor)	75.00
N. Ulrich (debtor)	100.00
Land	45 000.00
Buildings	142 000.00
Equipment	21 975.00
Trucks	14 925.00
Dominion Supply Company (creditor)	1 461.20
General Merchants Co. (creditor)	1 105.63
Beneficial Finance Co. (creditor)	3 163.00
Mortgage payable	63 251.00

12. The New Western Company in Brandon, Man., owned by Guy Albrecht, had the following assets and liabilities on March 31, 19--. Prepare a balance sheet for the company, as of that date.

Bank	$ 1 896.50
Tasty Beverages (debtor)	750.00
Food Haven (debtor)	400.00
Metro Mall (debtor)	1 235.00
Supplies	850.00
Furniture and Equipment	75 840.00
Land	50 000.00
Building	140 000.00
Trucks	35 000.00
Household Finance Company (creditor)	19 345.00
General Trading Company (creditor)	2 356.60
Lightning Electronics (creditor)	3 378.40
Bank Loan	10 000.00
Mortgage Payable	75 000.00

13. Michael Travis, the owner of Travis and Company located in Moncton, N.B., gave the following list of assets and liabilities to a public accountant and asked him to prepare a balance sheet as of March 31, 19––. Prepare the balance sheet as if you were the public accountant.

Amounts owed to Travis and Company:	
— G. Fordham	$ 1 042.16
— W. Gaines	743.86
— D. Samuelson	1 346.95
Amounts owed by Travis and Company to suppliers:	
— Raymond and Company	125.00
— Gem Finance Co.	1 236.45
— Empire Insurance Co.	150.00
— Beacon Company	1 567.25
— General Supply Co.	15 540.00
Office supplies	326.40
Building	135 000.00
Bank balance	4 946.03
Land	16 000.00
Office equipment	1 960.00
Shop equipment	535.00
Delivery equipment	4 240.00
Bank Loan	5 000.00
Mortgage payable	52 000.00

14. There are seven errors in the following balance sheet presentation. Find the errors and make a list of them.

BALANCE SHEET
MUSIC MAKERS
AUG. 31, 19––

Assets		*Liabilities*	
Accounts Receivable		Bank Loan	$ 3 500.00
W. Strothers	$ 128.40	Accounts Payable	
Waller Company	160.50	Circle of Sound	270.00
Supplies	74.50	A to Z Recordings	120.00
Sound Equipment	9 467.00		$ 3 500.00
Tapes and Records	2 674.00	*Mary Menari*	
Truck	7 500.00	Equity	17 269.40
Bank Balance	765.00		$20 769.40
	$20 769.40		

Claims Against the Assets

15. Joseph Litz is the owner of Bayliner Boat Charters, a business in Truro, N.S., that has six sailboats for hire. Mr. Litz has been able to make a comfortable living from renting out these boats during the sailing season.

The balance sheet of Bayliner Boat Charters is shown below.

BAYLINER BOAT CHARTERS
BALANCE SHEET
OCTOBER 31, 19--

Assets		*Liabilities*	
Bank	$ 900	Bank Loan	$ 18 000
Accounts Receivable	1 050	Accounts Payable	3 740
Supplies	1 250	Mortgage Payable	80 000
Equipment	4 390		$101 740
Boats	32 850	*Owner's Equity*	
Property	175 000	J. Litz, Capital	113 700
	$215 440		$215 440

Mr. Litz is past retirement age and is finding the business more than he can comfortably handle. He has attempted to sell it intact, but was unsuccessful. He has decided, therefore, to sell the assets for cash and pay off the claims of the creditors. In this way he can get his equity out of the business.

Mr. Litz hires a liquidator to help him. Through this man's services, the accounts receivable are collected in full. The supplies are sold for $500; the equipment is sold for $2 000; the boats are sold for $20 350; and the property is sold for $180 000. The liquidator charges $1 500 for his services.

Prepare a detailed calculation showing how much Mr. Litz will receive as a result of his claim against the assets.

Cases

Case 1 *A Balance Sheet Interpretation*

Shown below is the balance sheet of S. Magbool.

S MAGBOOL
BALANCE SHEET
JANUARY 31, 19--

Assets		*Liabilities*	
Cash	$ 6 000	Accounts Payable	$35 000
Accounts Receivable	14 000	Mortgage Payable	60 000
Land	40 000		$95 000
Buildings	95 000	*Owner's Equity*	
Equipment	25 000	S. Magbool, Capital	85 000
	$180 000		$180 000

Questions

1. Based on the limited information given, would you say that Mr. Magbool has any kind of a financial problem? Explain.

Case 2 *Can We Borrow?*

On December 31, 19--, you present your balance sheet, shown below, to the manager of the local bank, with the hope of obtaining a bank loan. During your conversation with the manager, certain facts are brought out.

a. About $8 000.00 owing from customers is considerably overdue.
b. A yearly mortgage payment of $4 000.00 is due next March 1.
c. All creditors' accounts are due within 30 days.
d. The average earnings of the business for the past five years have been very good.

BALANCE SHEET
DECEMBER 31, 19--

Assets		*Liabilities*	
Cash	$ 5 000.00	Accounts Payable	$17 000.00
Accounts Receivable	25 000.00	Mortgage Payable	35 000.00
Land	10 000.00		$52 000.00
Equipment	20 000.00		
Building	30 000.00	*Capital*	38 000.00
	$90 000.00		$90 000.00

Questions

1. Would the bank manager grant the loan?
2. What concerns might the manager have?

Career
Sandra Essex / Sole Proprietor

In high school, Sandra Essex of Vernon, B.C., took a number of business courses including accounting. After graduation, she was hired as a bookkeeper for a branch office of the Trane Service Agency, an international corporation. Sandra worked with cash receipts, customers' accounts, and suppliers' accounts.

After two years, Sandra decided to leave and start her own business. Following months of preparation, she opened Sandy's Fabric Shoppe in a rented store on Vernon's main street. So far, the business has been successful. Sandra sells a high quality selection of fabrics, wool, and needlepoint supplies. She enjoys the independence, variety, and contact with people that owning a store provides.

As the sole proprietor of a small business, Sandra does all her own accounting; her training and experience in this area have proven invaluable. Sandra's accounting duties include keeping track of accounts receivable and accounts payable, reconciling her monthly bank statement, and making sure that the correct amount of sales tax is sent to the provincial government. Sandra also must make sure that she has enough stock on hand to meet the demands of her customers.

Sandra has recently approached her local bank for a loan of $10 000. She wants to buy her stock in larger quantities to take advantage of supplier discounts and to increase her merchandise inventory. The loan manager, following standard procedure, has asked Sandra to produce a balance sheet for her business.

Sandra's balance sheet contains the following assets, liabilities, and owner's equity.

SANDY'S FABRIC SHOPPE
BALANCE SHEET
JUNE 30, 19--

Assets		*Liabilities*	
Cash on Hand	$ 50.00	Accounts Payable	
Bank Balance	3 000.00	Northcab Silk Co.	$ 800.00
Accounts Receivable		H. A. Kidd Co.	2 200.00
			$ 3 000.00
Bodley & Son	350.00		
Lukes	200.00	Owner's Equity	
Merchandise Inventory	7 000.00	Sandra Essex Capital	12 000.00
Supplies	400.00		
Furniture & Fixtures	3 000.00		
Office Equipment	1 000.00		
	$15 000.00		$15 000.00

Having prepared the balance sheet, Sandra now sees that all the assets do not belong to her. If the loan is granted, then the claims against the assets of Sandy's Fabric Shoppe will total $13 000. Nonetheless, Sandra is determined to proceed with the expansion of her business. She feels that the risk is justified by the prospect of increased success in the future.

4

Analyzing Changes in Financial Position

4-1 Recording Business Transactions
4-2 Summary of Steps in Analyzing a Transaction
4-3 Developing Good Work Habits

Objectives

When you have completed Chapter 4, you should:

1. Understand the factors that cause financial position to change.
2. Be able to give a definition of 'business transaction'.
3. Be able to work out the necessary changes that occur in any of the assets, liabilities, or the capital for any simple transaction.
4. Be able to explain why capital does or does not change for any transaction.
5. Be able to record a series of transactions on an equation analysis sheet.
6. Prepare a balance sheet from an equation analysis sheet.
7. State the five steps in analyzing a business transaction.

You have now been shown how to work out the financial position of a business (or individual) and how to present this information by means of a balance sheet. But financial position does not remain constant. In this chapter you will learn what causes the financial position to change, and how these changes affect the items on the balance sheet.

4.1 Recording Business Transactions

The financial position of an active business is always changing. A business day usually involves many business transactions. A **business transaction** may be defined as a financial event that changes the value of items on the balance sheet, and therefore changes the financial position of the business. Whenever any business transaction takes place, there is a change in the values of some of the assets, liabilities, or capital.

Your next step in the study of accounting is to learn how the various business transactions affect and change the financial position. To begin, consider the balance sheet of Metropolitan Movers in Burnaby, B.C. as shown by Figure 4.1.

METROPOLITAN MOVERS
BALANCE SHEET
DATE

Assets		*Liabilities*	
Cash	$11 500	Accounts payable	
Accounts Receivable		Central Supply	$ 750
K. Lincoln	500	Mercury Finance	18 370
B. Cava	1 300		$19 120
Equipment	7 500	*Owner's Equity*	
Trucks	24 500	J. Hofner, Capital	26 180
	$45 300		$45 300

Figure 4.1 The balance sheet of Metropolitan Movers.

The balance sheet of Metropolitan Movers shows the value of the assets, liabilities, and capital on a particular date. As business transactions occur, the values of assets, liabilities, and capital change. The balance sheet is not suitable for recording these changes. Therefore, let us arrange the items on the balance sheet in a different manner. Let us transfer the assets, liabilities, and capital from the balance sheet to an equation analysis sheet. This sheet is ideal for studying and recording changes in financial position.

	ASSETS					= LIABILITIES		+ OWNER'S EQUITY
	Cash	Accounts Receivable		Equipment	Trucks	Accounts Payable		J. Hofner Capital
		K. Lincoln	B. Cava			Central Supply	Mercury Finance	
Beginning balance	11 500	500	1 300	7 500	24 500	750	18 370	26 180
			45 300		=	19 120		+ 26 180

Figure 4.2 Equation analysis sheet for Metropolitan Movers.

The balance sheet items of Metropolitan Movers are entered on an equation analysis sheet as shown in Figure 4.2. Note that this arrangement is in the form of the fundamental accounting equation.

Updating the Equation Analysis Sheet

Let us now examine how transactions affect financial position.

Transaction 1 $500 cash is paid to Mercury Finance.

After this payment is made, the financial position shown in Figure 4.2 will no longer be right. Two changes are necessary: Cash must be reduced by $500; and the amount owed to Mercury Finance must also be reduced by $500. These changes are recorded on the equation analysis sheet shown in Figure 4.3.

	ASSETS					=	LIABILITIES		+	OWNER'S EQUITY
	Cash	Accounts Receivable		Equipment	Trucks		Accounts Payable			J. Hofner Capital
		K. Lincoln	B. Cava				Central Supply	Mercury Finance		
Beginning balances	11 500	500	1 300	7 500	24 500		750	18 370		26 180
Transaction 1	-500							-500		
New balances	11 000	500	1 300	7 500	24 500		750	17 870		26 180
			44 800			=	18 620			+26 180

Figure 4.3 Equation analysis sheet after transaction 1.

In analyzing transaction 1, observe that:

1. The amounts for Cash and for Mercury Finance are updated; Cash is decreased by $500, and Mercury Finance is decreased by $500.
2. The amounts for other items are unchanged but are correct.
3. After the changes are recorded and the new balances determined, the equation is still in balance.

Transaction 2 K. Lincoln, who owes Metropolitan Movers $500, pays $300 in part payment of his debt.

Can you figure out the changes to be made on the equation analysis sheet? Try to do this mentally before looking at Figure 4.4.

	ASSETS					= LIABILITIES		+ OWNER'S EQUITY
	Cash	Accounts Receivable		Equipment	Trucks	Accounts Payable		J. Hofner Capital
		K. Lincoln	B. Cava			Central Supply	Mercury Finance	
Beginning balances	11 500	500	1 300	7 500	24 500	750	18 370	26 180
Transaction 1	− 500						− 500	
New balances	11 000	500	1 300	7 500	24 500	750	17 870	26 180
Transaction 2	+ 300	−300						
New balances	11 300	200	1 300	7 500	24 500	750	17 870	26 180
			44 800			= 18 620		+26 180

Figure 4.4 Equation analysis sheet after transaction 2.

In analyzing transaction 2, observe that:

1. The figure for Cash is increased by $300, the amount received.
2. The figure for K. Lincoln is decreased by $300. He now owes $200.
3. After the changes are recorded, the equation is still in balance.

Transaction 3 Equipment costing $950 is purchased for cash.

Again, try to make the changes mentally before looking at the entries recorded in Figure 4.5.

	ASSETS					= LIABILITIES		+ OWNER'S EQUITY
	Cash	Accounts Receivable		Equipment	Trucks	Accounts Payable		J. Hofner Capital
		K. Lincoln	B. Cava			Central Supply	Mercury Finance	
Beginning balances	11 500	500	1 300	7 500	24 500	750	18 370	26 180
Transaction 1	− 500						− 500	
New balances	11 000	500	1 300	7 500	24 500	750	17 870	
Transaction 2	+ 300	−300						
New balances	11 300	200	1 300	7 500	24 500	750	17 870	26 180
Transaction 3	− 950			+ 950				
New balances	10 350	200	1 300	8 450	24 500	750	17 870	26 180
			44 800			= 18 620		+26 180

Figure 4.5 Equation analysis sheet after transaction 3.

In analyzing transaction 3 observe that:

1. Cash is decreased by $950, the amount paid out.
2. Equipment is increased by $950, the cost of the new equipment acquired.
3. After the changes are recorded, the equation is still in balance.

Transaction 4 A new pick-up truck is purchased at a cost of $15 000. Metropolitan Movers pays $10 000 cash and arranges a loan from Mercury Finance to cover the balance of the purchase price. (Note: This is considered to be a single transaction. Mercury Finance will pay $5 000 directly to the truck dealer.)

Again, try to work out the changes mentally before looking at the equation analysis sheet in Figure 4.6.

	ASSETS					= LIABILITIES		+ OWNER'S EQUITY
	Cash	Accounts Receivable K. Lincoln	Accounts Receivable B. Cava	Equipment	Trucks	Accounts Payable Central Supply	Accounts Payable Mercury Finance	G. Hofner Capital
Beginning balances	11 500	500	1 300	7 500	24 500	750	18 370	26 180
Transaction 1	− 500						− 500	
New balances	11 000	500	1 300	7 500	24 500	750	17 870	26 180
Transaction 2	+ 300	− 300						
New balances	11 300	200	1 300	7 500	24 500	750	17 870	26 180
Transaction 3	− 950			+ 950				
New balances	10 350	200	1 300	8 450	24 500	750	17 870	26 180
Transaction 4	−10 000				+15 000		+5 000	
New balances	350	200	1 300	8 450	39 500	750	22 870	26 180
			49 800			= 23 620		+26 180

Figure 4.6 Equation analysis sheet after transaction 4.

In analyzing transaction 4 observe that:

1. Cash is decreased by $10 000, the amount paid out.
2. Trucks is increased by $15 000, the cost of the new truck.
3. The liability to Mercury Finance is increased by $5 000, the additional amount borrowed.
4. After all of the changes are recorded, the equation is still in balance.

Transaction 5 Metropolitan Movers completes a storage service for B. Cava at a price of $500. A bill is sent to Cava indicating to him that he now owes the additional $500.

Work out the changes necessary on the equation analysis sheet. These are shown in Figure 4.7.

	ASSETS					= LIABILITIES		+ OWNER'S EQUITY
	Cash	Accounts Recievable		Equipment	Trucks	Accounts Payable		J. Hofner Capital
		K. Lincoln	B. Cava			Central Supply	Mercury Finance	
Beginning balances	11 500	500	1 300	7 500	24 500	750	18 370	26 180
Transaction 1	−500						−500	
New balances	11 000	500	1 300	7 500	24 500	750	17 870	26 180
Transaction 2	+300	−300						
New balances	11 300	200	1 300	7 500	24 500	750	17 870	26 180
Transaction 3	−950			+950				
New balances	10 350	200	1 300	8 450	24 500	750	17 870	26 180
Transaction 4	−10 000				+15 000		+5 000	
New balances	350	200	1 300	8 450	39 500	750	22 870	26 180
Transaction 5			+500					+500
New balances	350	200	1 800	8 450	39 500	750	22 870	26 680
			50 300			= 23 620		+26 680

Figure 4.7 Equation analysis sheet after transaction 5.

Transaction 5 is a little more difficult to understand than the previous four. But understanding is important in order to see the reasoning behind the entries on the equation analysis sheet. Transaction 5 may be explained as follows:

1. $500 is added to B. Cava's balance. He now owes $500 more.
2. No other asset or liability is affected.
3. J. Hofner's Capital is increased by $500.

There are two ways to explain this increase in capital. First, remember that Metropolitan Movers is in the business of providing a service to earn profit. When the service for Cava is completed, and Cava legally owes the $500, a profit has been earned. The owner of Metropolitan Movers is then better off by the amount of this profit, and to show this his capital is increased.

Secondly, the increase in capital can be shown by arithmetic. Remember that capital is the difference between the total assets and the total liabilities.

Prior to transaction 5:
Assets ($49 800) − Liabilities ($23 620) = Capital ($26 180)
After transaction 5:
Assets ($50 300) − Liabilities ($23 620) = Capital (26 680)

Clearly, there is an increase in capital of $500. This increase must be recorded on the equation analysis sheet.

Transaction 6 An old truck which had originally cost $6 000 and which is included in the Truck figure at that amount is found to be no longer adequate and is sold to Morrison Brothers for $2 000 cash.

Work out the changes necessary to bring the equation analysis sheet up to date. The updated sheet is shown in Figure 4.8.

	ASSETS					= LIABILITIES		+ OWNER'S EQUITY
	Cash	Accounts Receivable		Equipment	Trucks	Accounts Payable		G. Hofner Capital
		K. Lincoln	B. Cava			Central Supply	Mercury Finance	
Beginning balances	11 500	500	1 300	7 500	24 500	750	18 370	26 180
Transaction 1	− 500						−500	
New balances	11 000	500	1 300	7 500	24 500	750	17 870	26 180
Transaction 2	+ 300	−300						
New balances	11 300	200	1 300	7 500	24 500	750	17 870	26 180
Transaction 3	−950			+950				
New balances	10 350	200	1 300	8 450	24 500	750	17 870	26 180
Transaction 4	−10 000				+15 000		+5 000	
New balances	350	200	1 300	8 450	39 500	750	22 870	26 180
Transaction 5			+500					+ 500
New balances	350	200	1 800	8 450	39 500	750	22 870	26 680
Transaction 6	+2 000				−6 000			−4 000
New balances	2 350	200	1 800	8 450	33 500	750	22 870	22 680
			46 300			= 23 620		+22 680

Figure 4.8 Equation analysis sheet after transaction 6.

In analyzing transaction 6 observe that:

1. Cash is increased by $2 000, the amount received from the sale of the truck.

2. Trucks is decreased by $6 000. The truck that was sold was included in the Trucks figure at $6 000. Since it is no longer on hand, the Trucks figure must be reduced by $6 000 in order to be correct.
3. Capital is decreased by $4 000. After changing the necessary assets and liabilities, the difference between total assets and total liabilities is $22 680, which is $4 000 less than it was immediately before the transaction.
4. After all of the changes are recorded, the equation is still in balance.

Updating the Balance Sheet

The figures for an updated balance sheet for Metropolitan Movers are taken from the last line of the equation analysis sheet. Figure 4.9 shows the new balance sheet.

METROPOLITAN MOVERS
BALANCE SHEET
DATE

Assets		*Liabilities*	
Cash	$ 2 350	Accounts Payable	
Accounts Receivable		Central Supply	$ 750
K. Lincoln	200	Mercury Finance	22 870
B. Cava	1 800		$23 620
Equipment	8 450	*Owner's Equity*	
Trucks	33 500	J. Hofner, Capital	22 680
	$46 300		$46 300

Figure 4.9 The updated balance sheet of Metropolitan Movers.

4.2 Summary of Steps in Analyzing a Transaction

You have seen how each of six transactions caused the financial position to change. You are now ready to think of the concept of financial change in general.

The following suggestions will help you in analyzing transactions:

1. In thinking about the transactions try to be logical and to use good common sense.
2. For any transaction, carefully analyze the information given. Your objective is to make all the necessary changes in any of the assets, the liabilities, or both.
3. Recalculate the Assets total and the Liabilities total. Then calculate Assets minus Liabilities to see if Capital has changed.

   Eventually you will come to know intuitively if Capital has changed. Generally, if a business is better off as a result of a transaction, then Capital has increased. And, if the business is worse off, then Capital has decreased.

4. Make certain that at least two of the individual items (any of the assets, liabilities, or the capital) have changed. It is possible for several items to change, but never only one.
5. Make sure that the equation is still in balance.

4.3 Developing Good Work Habits

The first step in the accounting process is to analyze a transaction to determine the financial changes that result from it. It is necessary that you recognize the importance of performing this step correctly. Accounting must be accurate, and for this reason you must be very careful in carrying out all the steps in the accounting process.

You must also realize that the possible number of different transactions is very large. It is not practical to memorize all of the changes caused by all of the transactions. In fact it is almost impossible. In the first place, it is unlikely that you could remember them all. But secondly, and more important, if you tried to rely on memory alone you could never become a really good accountant. Good accountants use their memory of course, but they rely on common sense, practical knowledge, and clear thinking. They are able to handle any transaction, not just certain ones.

Accounting Terms

business transaction

Review Questions

1. Give the definition of a business transaction.
2. List the five steps in analyzing a transaction.
3. a. Name the form used in this text for analyzing transactions.
b. Explain how this form is related to the fundamental accounting equation.
4. Is it possible for the Equation Analysis Sheet to be out of balance? Explain.
5. State the conditions under which capital increases. Use an example to explain your answer.
6. State the conditions under which capital decreases. Use an example to explain your answer.
7. Do the following events represent business transactions? Give a reason for each of your answers.
a. Supplies are ordered for delivery next month.
b. A truck is purchased.

c. A prospective employee is interviewed.
d. The owner of the business withdraws cash from the business for his personal use.
e. A service is performed for a customer for a fee.

8. Dieter Krupp, owner of Krupp Enterprises, states that he is one of the creditors of his business. Can he be correct? Explain.
9. Sandra Beck is the owner of a local coin laundromat. She has an automatic washer in the basement which is no longer in use. The machine is still in good running condition, but its design is out-dated. The old machine could be sold for scrap for $30, but it would cost that much to move it away. Is this machine an asset? Explain.

Exercises

Transaction analysis

1. The opening financial position is shown here for Sheila's Interior Decorating, owned by Sheila Kostiuk. In your workbook, or on columnar paper, record in the correct columns the changes required for the transactions below. After each transaction, calculate the new totals and make sure that the equation balances.

	Cash	Accounts Receivable	Supplies	Office Furniture	Accounts Payable		S Kostiuk Capital
		D Murray			Ace Supply	Pine Motors	
Opening balances	1 000	50					1 050

Transaction 1. Stationery and supplies are purchased from Ace Supply, $75 on credit. They will be paid for within 30 days.

2. A new desk for the office costing $450 is purchased for cash.
3. D. Murray, a debtor, pays his debt in full.
4. A $100 service is performed for a customer who pays immediately in cash.
5. A used truck costing $6 500 is purchased from Pine Motors. A down-payment of $500 is made. It is agreed that the remainder of the purchase price will be paid within three months.
6. $75 is paid to Ace Supply, a creditor.
7. The owner, Sheila Kostiuk, withdraws $100 from the business for her own use.

2. The balance sheet of Triangle Real Estate, at the close of business on September 30, 19--, is as follows:

TRIANGLE REAL ESTATE
BALANCE SHEET
SEPTEMBER 30, 19--

Assets		*Liabilities*	
Cash	$ 216	Account Payable	
Accounts Receivable		Acme Supply	$ 562
P. Adams	375		
N. Swartz	200	*Owner's Equity*	
J. Hahn	150	J. Morse, Capital	3 521
Supplies	175		
Equipment	2 967		
	$4 083		$4 083

1. **Record the above balance sheet figures on the equation analysis sheet provided in your workbook.**
2. **Analyze the transactions of October 1, listed below, and record the necessary changes on the equation analysis sheet. After each transaction, ensure that the equation is still in balance.**
3. **After completing transaction 5, prepare a new balance sheet.**

Transactions of October 1

1. $100 cash is received from N. Swartz in part payment of the amount owed by him.
2. $200 cash is paid to Acme Supply in part payment of the debt owed to them.
3. Supplies costing $35 are purchased for cash from the Standish Company.
4. Triangle Real Estate sells a home for A.J. Buhler. For this service, Triangle Real Estate receives a commission of $2 700 cash.
5. A new desk is purchased from Ideal Furniture for $450 cash.

3. Alliance Appliance Service, in Renforth, Ont., owned by Wayne Dalli, has the following assets and liabilities at the close of business on October 20, 19--.

Assets		*Liabilities*	
Cash	$ 516	Bank Loan	$ 5 000
Accounts Receivable		Mortgage Payable	$22 700
N. Chang	100		
P. O'Neil	527		
Equipment	1 316		
Delivery Truck	15 750		
Building	80 000		

98209
27700
70509

1. Record the above items on an equation analysis sheet. Don't forget to calculate and include the capital figure.

2. Analyze the transactions of October 21, listed below, and record the necessary changes on the equation analysis sheet.

3. After completing transaction 5, calculate the new balance and ensure that the equation is still in balance. Then, prepare a new balance sheet.

Transactions of October 21

1. The owner, in need of money for his personal use, draws $500 cash out of the business.
2. P. O'Neil pays his debt of $527.
3. A repair service is performed for a customer. The customer pays the full amount of the bill in cash, $90.
4. A new electrical tester is purchased and paid for in cash, $210.
5. The regular monthly mortgage payment is made, $350 in cash.

---

4. Patricia Severs is a lawyer who owns her own law firm in Lethbridge, Alta. On the morning of May 6, 19--, the business has the following assets and liabilities:

Assets		*Liabilities*	
Cash	$ 761	Accounts Payable	
Accounts Receivable		Wilson's Co.	$ 56
V. Brabson	100	Beneficial Finance	4 320
T. Carlisle	50		
Office Supplies	442		
Office Equipment	2 330		
Automobile	7 500		

1. Set up the assets, the liabilities, and the capital on an equation analysis sheet.

2. Analyze the transactions of May 6, listed below, and record the necessary changes on the equation analysis sheet.

3. After completing transaction 5, calculate the new balances, and ensure that the equation is still in balance. Then, prepare a new balance sheet.

Transactions of May 6

1. $750 cash is paid for an air conditioner for the office.
2. Because the cash position of the business is very low, Pat Severs transfers $1 000 cash from her personal bank account into the business.
3. A cash payment of $35 is paid to Beneficial Finance.

4. Arthur Kushner, a client of Pat Severs, is given legal advice for which he is charged $200. Mr. Kushner pays immediately.
5. Pat Severs has a minor repair done to her automobile. She pays the bill of $35 immediately.

---

5. Merrymen Window Washing is a business owned and operated by Carl Savich in Timmins, Ont. On November 30, 19--, at the end of the day, the financial position of the business is as shown by the following balance sheet.

MERRYMEN WINDOW WASHING
BALANCE SHEET
NOVEMBER 30, 19--

Cash	$ 750	Accounts Payable	
Accounts Receivable		Simplex Finance	$1 560
D. Pederson	75	Cleanall Co.	124
T. Brock	120	Hipp Co.	475
Supplies	80		
Truck	5 050	*Owner's Equity*	
Equipment	2 947	C. Savich, Capital	6 863
	$9 022		$9 022

1. **Set up the balance sheet items on an equation analysis sheet. Leave a blank column for a new account payable.**
2. **Analyze the transactions of December 1, listed below, and record the necessary changes on the equation analysis sheet.**
3. **After completing transaction 5, calculate the new balances, ensure that the equation is still in balance, and prepare a new balance sheet.**

Transactions of December 1

1. The regular monthly instalment payment of $300 is paid to Simplex Finance.
2. $200 of supplies is purchased from Hipp Co. but not paid for.
3. $100 cash is received from T. Brock in part payment of his debt.
4. A new cash register is purchased from NCR Co. A cash down-payment of $300 is made. The balance of the purchase price of $825 is to be paid at a later date.
5. The old cash register, included in the Equipment figure at $350, is sold for $100 cash.

---

6. Workbook Exercise: Complete a chart showing the effect of transactions on total assets, total liabilities, and equity.

Using Your Knowledge

7. Shown below is an equation analysis sheet for the business of Brad Provost, a painter and decorator in Sydney, N.S.

Examine the entries made on this sheet. Then prepare a list of five transactions that would have caused the changes in the financial position indicated by the entries.

	ASSETS					LIABILITIES			OWNER'S EQUITY
	Cash	Accounts Receivable		Supplies	Equipment	Bank Loan	Accounts Payable		B. Provost Capital
		C. Sully	F. Vanweers				P.M. Co.	Norpaints	
	400	135	250	500	2 500	500	300		2 985
1.	+250		−250						
2.				+150				+150	
3.	+300								+300
4.		115							+115
5.	−300						−300		
	650	250	−0−	650	2 500	500	−0−	150	3 400

8. Shown below is an equation analysis sheet for the business of Brian Lee, an architect.

After studying this sheet, prepare a list of five transactions that would have caused the changes in financial position as shown.

	ASSETS					LIABILITIES		OWNER'S EQUITY
	Cash	Acc. Rec'l L. Swan	Supplies	Equipment	Auto	Bank Loan	Acc. Pay'l High Finance	B. Lee, Cap'l
	500		300	2 000	7 000	1 000	5 000	3 800
1.	+500	+1 300						+1 800
2.	+1500				−7 000		−5 000	−500
3.	−1000				+10 000	+9 000		
4.	−150							−150
5.			−50					−50
	1 350	1 300	250	2 000	10 000	10 000	−0−	4 900

9. At December 31, 19–1, Dowse Corporation had assets totaling $85 000. At December 31, 19–2, the assets totaled $115 000. During the same period, liabilities increased by $35 000. If the equity at the end of the first year amounted to $60 000, what was the amount of the owner's equity December 31 of the second year? Show how you arrive at your answer.

10. Describe four transactions that would cause the owner's equity to decrease.

11. Describe two transactions that would cause the owner's equity to increase.

Cases

Case 1 *Is it an Asset?*

Bill Katz is the owner of Katz Hardware Store in Weyburn, Sask. He has followed the practice of increasing the item Automobile for purchases of gasoline and oil for his car and for any minor repairs and tune-ups. During the current year the motor in his car was completely overhauled, which caused the item Automobile to be increased by $400.

Questions

1. As the accountant for Katz, do you agree with this procedure? Explain.

Case 2 *Can You Spend the Equity?*

Raj Singh is a young man who has just inherited a business from his father who was killed in an accident. Raj has little business experience but is anxious to learn and willing to work hard.

The business has not been operating very profitably lately because it badly needs to replace out-dated equipment. This will cost $35 000.

The latest balance sheet of the business shows the following:

Assets		*Liabilities*	
Cash	$ 3 000	Accounts Payable	$ 5 000
Accounts Receivable	17 000	Bank Loan	30 000
Land	30 000	Mortgage Payable	50 000
Building	50 000		$ 85 000
Equipment	20 000	*Owner's Equity*	35 000
	$120 000		$120 000

After examining the balance sheet, Raj believes that he sees the solution to the problem. He wants to use the equity to purchase the new equipment. The accountant hastens to point out to Raj that this is not possible. Raj demands an explanation.

Questions

1. What explanation will the accountant give?

5

The Simple Ledger

5-1 Ledger Accounts
5-2 Debit and Credit
5-3 Account Balances
5-4 Double Entry System of Accounting
5-5 The Trial Balance

Objectives

When you have completed Chapter 5, you should:

1. Know what an account is and what a ledger is.
2. Know the meaning of debit and credit.
3. Know the rules of debit and credit as they apply to assets, liabilities, and capital.
4. Be able to record transactions in T-accounts.
5. Be able to calculate the balance in a T-account.
6. Know what the balance in a T-account means.
7. Understand the concept of double-entry accounting.
8. Be able to take off a trial balance using both the handwritten and machine method.

The purpose of Chapter 4 was to show you the effect that transactions have on financial position. In Chapter 4, you practised analyzing several transactions and keeping a financial position up to date. The method used to deal with the transactions was a very simple one. However, that method is not satisfactory when working with a complete business operation. In an active business, many transactions occur each day. To record them all, accountants use a universal system which is based on the ideas you studied in the previous chapter. While the system is more complex, it is also more efficient and orderly. As you will learn, it is a very effective system.

5.1 Ledger Accounts

In this chapter, you will be concerned with maintaining an up-to-date financial position. For this purpose, accountants long ago developed the account and ledger. An **account** is a specially designed page on which changes are recorded in a special way. There is one account for each different item affecting the financial position. All of the accounts are called a **ledger**.

A ledger can be prepared in different forms (see Figure 5.1). The accounts may

a.

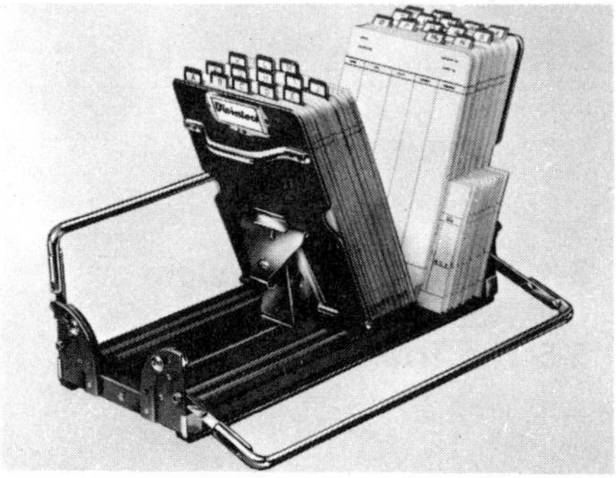

Card ledger (courtesy of Luckett Loose Leaf, Ltd.).

b.

Loose-leaf ledger (courtesy of Luckett Loose Leaf, Ltd.).

c.

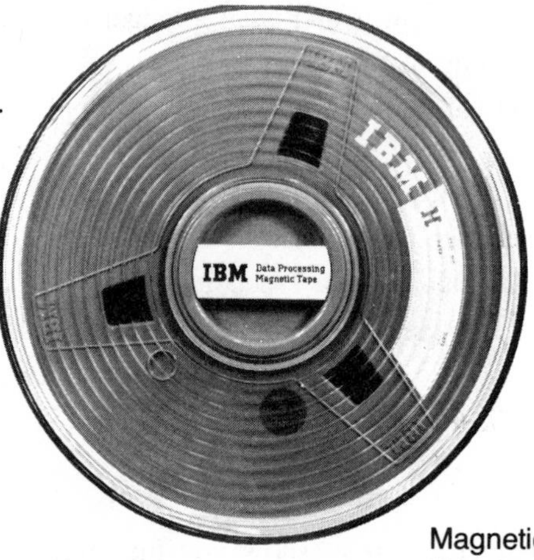

Magnetic tape (courtesy of IBM Canada Ltd.).

Figure 5.1 Three forms of the ledger.

be printed on cards, thus forming a card ledger. They may be printed on loose-leaf pages, thus forming a loose-leaf ledger. Or the accounts may be recorded on a magnetic tape or disc that can be read by a computer.

Let us begin our study of ledger accounts by referring to the records of Pacific Trucking owned by Byron Rissien of Prince Rupert, B.C. The balance sheet of this business is shown in Figure 5.2.

PACIFIC TRUCKING BALANCE SHEET — DATE —			
Assets		*Liabilities*	
Cash	$ 765	Bank Loan	$ 8 000
Accounts Receivable		Accounts Payable	
R. Van Loon	620	Packham Supply	946
W. Caruso	150	Dini Bros.	1 516
Supplies	465		$10 462
Trucks	35 075	*Owner's Equity*	
Equipment	14 674	B. Rissien, Capital	41 287
	$51 749		$51 749

Figure 5.2 The balance sheet of Pacific Trucking.

The data from the balance sheet is used to set up a separate account page for each item. Thus, Pacific Trucking will have ten ledger accounts, one for each item on its balance sheet. These accounts are:

Cash
Accounts Receivable—R. Van Loon
—W. Caruso
Supplies
Trucks
Equipment
Bank Loan
Accounts Payable — Packham Supply
— Dini Bros.
B. Rissien, Capital

Figure 5.3 shows the information from the balance sheet of Pacific Trucking presented as accounts in a ledger. These accounts are called T-accounts because, as you can see, each one looks like a T. The T-account is a simple kind of account, used to demonstrate the basics of accounting theory. Other kinds of account will be introduced in later chapters.

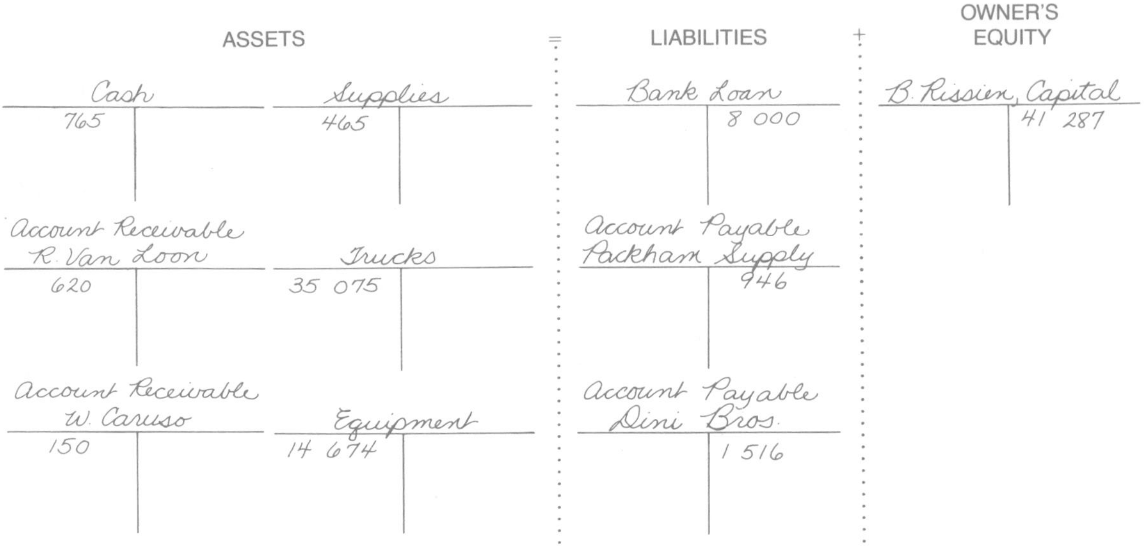

Figure 5.3 The simple ledger accounts of Pacific Trucking.

Important Features of Ledger Accounts

There are three important features of ledger accounts that must be carefully examined.

1. Each individual balance sheet item is given its own specially divided page with the name of the item at the top. Each of these pages is called an account. In Figure 5.3, there are ten accounts. You must learn to call them the Cash account, the R. Van Loon account, the Packham Supply account, the Bank Loan account, the B. Rissien, Capital account, and so on.
2. The dollar figure for each item, as taken from the Pacific Trucking balance sheet, is recorded in the account on the first line. It is especially important to record the dollar figure on the correct side of the account. For any item, the correct side is the side on which the item would appear on a simple balance sheet. Observe that for each of the asset accounts, the dollar amount is placed on the left side of the account page. For each of the liability accounts and the capital account, the dollar amount is placed on the right side of the account page.
3. The ledger and the balance sheet both show financial position, although in different ways. It follows therefore that, given a ledger, a balance sheet can be prepared from it, and, given a balance sheet, a ledger can be prepared from it.

5.2 Debit and Credit

In your work so far you have learned that the idea of 'left side' and 'right side' is important in accounting. This is especially true when dealing with accounts. The theory of accounting using ledger accounts is based entirely on the understanding that there are two distinct sides to every account page.

The two sides of an account page are given the names that have become accepted by accountants everywhere. **Debit** is the word associated with the left-hand side of an account. **Credit** is the word associated with the right-hand side of an account. Remember that the two new terms apply to every account page. This is shown by the following illustration using a T-account.

any account	
The debit side (short form Dr.)	The credit side (short form Cr.)

These two new words — debit and credit — are probably the two most important words in the accountant's vocabulary. You will have to use them a great deal.

Let us now begin to use these two new accounting terms. Looking back at the simple ledger in Figure 5.3 you will notice that the values of the assets were placed on the left side — the debit side — of their accounts. The values of the liabilities and of the capital were placed on the right side — the credit side — of their accounts. You may correctly conclude from this that assets are considered to be debit accounts and that liabilities and capital are considered to be credit accounts.

The Rules of Debit and Credit

Now that you have been introduced to the simple ledger and to the terms debit and credit, you are ready to learn how to record changes in the accounts. There is a simple set of rules for recording changes in accounts. These rules are summarized in the chart below.

THE RULES OF DEBIT AND CREDIT

Increase or Decrease	*Asset Accounts*	*Liability Accounts and Capital Account*
To record increases	Record the amount of the increase on the debit side of the account	Record the amount of the increase on the credit side of the account
To record decreases	Record the amount of the decrease on the credit side of the account	Record the amount of the decrease on the debit side of the account

Applying the Rules of Debit and Credit

To give you practice in using the new rules of debit and credit, a number of transactions are analyzed below. In applying these rules to the transactions, you should try to do the analyses before reading the explanations. And you must remember, too, the importance of the new theory. You must master the technique of analyzing transactions if you want to be a good accountant.

In analyzing the transactions that follow, refer to the ledger of Pacific Trucking, which appears in Figure 5.3.

Transaction 1 $200 of supplies is purchased from Packham Supply, to be paid for later.

Analysis

To correctly analyze a transaction it is helpful to use a 'transaction analysis sheet'. This sheet, shown below, provides a place to organize your thoughts about the transaction.

1. In column (1), write down the names of the accounts that are affected by the transaction. In this example:

(1) Account Names	(2) Account Classification: Asset, Liability, or Capital	(3) Increase (+) or Decrease (−)	(4) Debit or Credit	(5) Amount
Supplies				
Packham Supply				

2. In column (2), write down whether each of these accounts is an asset, a liability, or the capital. In this example:

(1) Account Names	(2) Account Classification: Asset, Liability, or Capital	(3) Increase (+) or Decrease (−)	(4) Debit or Credit	(5) Amount
Supplies	Asset			
Packham Supply	Liability			

3. In column (3), write down whether the accounts are to be increased or decreased. In this example:

(1) Account Names	(2) Account Classification: Asset, Liability, or Capital	(3) Increase (+) or Decrease (−)	(4) Debit or Credit	(5) Amount
Supplies	Asset	+		
Packham Supply	Liability	+		

4. In column (4), write down whether the accounts are to be debited or credited. Apply the rules given in the previous section. To increase an asset, you debit the account. To increase a liability, you credit the account. In this example:

(1) Account Names	(2) Account Classification: Asset, Liability, or Capital	(3) Increase (+) or Decrease (−)	(4) Debit or Credit	(5) Amount
Supplies	Asset	+	DR	
Packham Supply	Liability	+	CR	

5. In column (5), write in the amounts by which the accounts are increased or decreased. In this example:

(1) Account Names	(2) Account Classification: Asset, Liability, or Capital	(3) Increase (+) or Decrease (−)	(4) Debit or Credit	(5) Amount
Supplies	Asset	+	DR	200 —
Packham Supply	Liability	+	CR	200 —

After this step is completed, the accounting entry is worked out. An accountant would state it as follows: Debit Supplies and credit Packham Supply, $200. After the entry is recorded, the accounts appear as shown below:

Supplies	
465	
200	

Account Payable

Packham Supply	
	946
	200

Transaction 2 $500 is paid to Dini Bros. in part payment of the amount owed to them.

Analysis

This transaction is recorded on a transaction analysis sheet as follows.

(1) Account Names	(2) Account Classification: Asset, Liability, or Capital	(3) Increase (+) or Decrease (−)	(4) Debit or Credit	(5) Amount
Dini Bros.	Liability	−	DR	500 −
Cash	Asset	−	CR	500 −

An accountant would read this accounting entry as follows: Debit Dini Bros. and credit Cash, $500. After the entry is recorded, the accounts appear as shown below.

Cash	
765	500

Account Payable Dini Bros.	
500	1 516

Transaction 3 $200 cash is received from R. Van Loon in part payment of his debt.

Analysis

This transaction is recorded on the following transaction analysis sheet:

(1) Account Names	(2) Account Classification: Asset, Liability, or Capital	(3) Increase (+) or Decrease (−)	(4) Debit or Credit	(5) Amount
Cash	Asset	+	DR	200 —
R. Van Loon	Asset	−	CR	200 —

Read the entry as follows: Debit Cash and credit R. Van Loon, $200. After the entry is recorded, the accounts appear as shown below.

Cash	
765	500
200	

Account Receivable R. Van Loon	
620	200

Transaction 4 A delivery service is provided for a customer at a price of $100. The customer pays cash at the time the service is completed.

Analysis

This transaction is recorded on the transaction analysis sheet below.

(1) Account Names	(2) Account Classification: Asset, Liability, or Capital	(3) Increase (+) or Decrease (−)	(4) Debit or Credit	(5) Amount
Cash	Asset	+	DR	100 —
B. Rissien, Capital	Capital	+	CR	100 —

Read this entry as follows: Debit Cash and credit B. Rissien, Capital, $100. After the entry is recorded, the accounts will appear as shown below.

Cash	
765	500
200	

B. Rissien, Capital	
	41 287
	100

Transaction 5 A used truck costing $4 000 is purchased from Dini Bros. A cash down payment of $250 is made at the time of the purchase and the balance is to be paid at a later date.

Analysis

This transaction affects three accounts. The transaction analysis sheet entries for it are recorded on the following sheet.

(1) Account Names	(2) Account Classification: Asset, Liability, or Capital	(3) Increase (+) or Decrease (−)	(4) Debit or Credit	(5) Amount
Trucks	Asset	+	DR	4 000 –
Cash	Asset	−	CR	250 –
Dini Bros.	Liability	+	CR	3 750 –

Read this entry as follows: Debit Trucks, $4 000, credit Cash, $250, and credit Dini Bros., $3 750. After the entry is recorded, the accounts will appear as shown below.

Cash	
765	500
200	250
100	

Trucks	
35 075	
4 000	

Account Payable Dini Bros.	
500	1 516
	3 750

Transaction 6 A delivery is completed for R. Van Loon at a price of $150. Van Loon does not pay for the service at the time it is made but agrees to pay within sixty days.

Analysis

The transaction analysis sheet entries for this transaction are recorded below.

(1) Account Names	(2) Account Classification: Asset, Liability, or Capital	(3) Increase (+) or Decrease (−)	(4) Debit or Credit	(5) Amount
R. Van Loon	Asset	+	[redacted]R	150 –
B. Rissien, Capital	Capital	+	CR	150 –

Read this entry as follows: Debit R. Van Loon and credit B. Rissien, Capital, $150. After the entry is recorded, the accounts will appear as shown below.

Account Receivable

R. Van Loon	
620	200
150	

B. Rissien, Capital	
	41 287
	100
	150

Transaction 7 One of the lifting machines (part of Equipment) breaks down. $112 cash is spent on repairing the machine. (A common mistake made by beginners in respect to this type of transaction is to increase Equipment. To help you avoid this mistake, here is a clue: The owner is worse off financially because he has to repair the machine.)

Analysis

The following transaction analysis sheet records this transaction.

(1) Account Names	(2) Account Classification: Asset, Liability, or Capital	(3) Increase (+) or Decrease (−)	(4) Debit or Credit	(5) Amount
Cash	Asset	−	[redacted]R	112 –
B. Rissien, Capital	Capital	−	DR	112 –

Read this entry as follows: Debit B. Rissien, Capital and credit Cash, $112. After the entry is recorded, the accounts will appear as shown below.

Cash	
765	500
200	250
100	112

B. Rissien, Capital	
112	41 287
	100
	150

5.3 Account Balances

Calculating the Balance of an Account

In the ledger of Pacific Trucking there are ten accounts (see Figure 5.3). The following information is stored in each account:

1. The name of the account, which is written at the top.
2. The dollar value of the account.
3. Whether the value of the account is a debit or a credit.

To calculate the balance of a T-account, two steps are performed. These two steps are shown in Figure 5.4, using accounts from the ledger of Pacific Trucking.

1. Add separately the two sides of the account. Write down the totals beneath the last item on each side, using tiny pencil figures. These totals are called **pencil footings**, or **pin totals**.
2. Subtract the smaller total from the larger total and write the result beside the larger of the two totals. Circle the amount just written. This circled amount is the **account balance**, or the **balance of the account**.

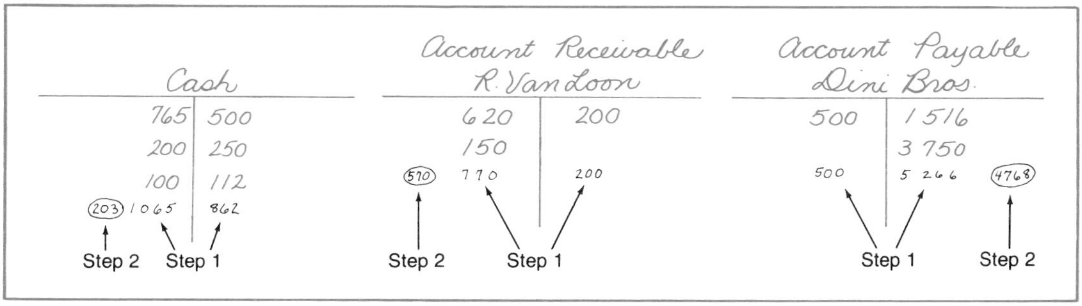

Figure 5.4 Calculating the balance of a T-account.

Interpreting the Balance of an Account

You must now learn to interpret the information stored in an account. It is not enough to simply determine the account balances. They must mean something to you. Look at the accounts in Figure 5.4 and see what you can learn from them.

The account balances should be clear to you. The Cash account has a balance of $203, DEBIT. The R. Van Loon account has a balance of $570, DEBIT. The Dini Bros. account has a balance of $4 766, CREDIT.

So far you are only familiar with three types of account: assets, liabilities, and the capital. Therefore, at this stage, all accounts must fall into one of those categories.

Remember that all accounts with debit balances are assets. Therefore, the Cash account, having a debit balance, is an asset. And, the R. Van Loon account, having a debit balance, is also an asset.

Also remember that accounts with credit balances are either liabilities or the capital. The Dini Bros. account has a credit balance and is not the capital account. Therefore, it is a liability.

5.4 Double Entry System of Accounting

Whenever a transaction occurs, changes in accounts must be made. All of the account changes together are referred to as the **accounting entry** for the transaction.

In this chapter, so far, there have been seven transactions. To record these seven transactions, seven accounting entries were necessary. These accounting entries are summarized in Figure 5.5.

Transaction	*Account Debited*	*Amount*	*Account Credited*	*Amount*
1.	Supplies	$ 200	Packham Supply	$ 200
2.	Dini Bros.	$ 500	Cash	$ 500
3.	Cash	$ 200	R. Van Loon	$ 200
4.	Cash	$ 100	B. Wilson, Capital	$ 100
5.	Trucks	$4 000	Cash	$ 250
			Dini Bros.	$3 750
6.	R. Van Loon	$ 150	B. Rissien, Capital	$ 150
7.	B. Rissien, Capital	$ 112	Cash	$ 112

Figure 5.5 The accounting entries for seven transactions.

If you have been observant, you will have noticed something about these seven transactions that is very special, something that is basic to the whole accounting process. Each of these seven transactions balances within itself; that is, the total of the debit amounts is equal to the total of the credit amounts. This is a condition that will hold true for every possible transaction. If, in your work, you ever arrive at an accounting entry that does not balance within itself, you can be certain that the entry is not correct. On the other hand, just because you have worked out a balanced entry is no guarantee that the entry is correct. It merely means that it is likely to be correct. If it doesn't balance, there is no such possibility.

It is probably easier for you now to understand why the system that you have been working with is known as the **double entry system of accounting**. In this system, every transaction is recorded both as a debit in one or more accounts and as a credit in one or more accounts so that the total of the debit entries equals the total of the credit entries. The double entry system of accounting is in general use throughout the business world.

5.5 The Trial Balance

A ledger is an alternate method of presenting the information on a balance sheet. Just as a balance sheet must balance, a ledger must also balance.

When setting up a ledger, as in Figure 5.3, the information for the accounts is usually obtained from a balance sheet. This way, the ledger begins in a balanced position with the total of the accounts with debit balances equal to the total of the accounts with credit balances. Then, the ledger is used to record the changes caused by business transactions. These changes are all in the form of balanced accounting entries.

As a result, after each full accounting entry, provided of course that it is done correctly, the ledger will still be balanced.

Periodically, it is necessary to check the accuracy of the ledger. This is done by means of a **trial balance**. A trial balance is a simple procedure used to find out if a ledger is in balance. To take a trial balance you must see if the total value of all the accounts with debit balances is equal to the total value of all the accounts with credit balances. If the two totals are the same the ledger is said to be **in balance**. If they are not the same the ledger is said to be **out of balance**. The whole process is called **taking off a trial balance** and is usually done at the end of each month.

The completed ledger of Pacific Trucking is shown in Figure 5.6. Let us see if it is in balance.

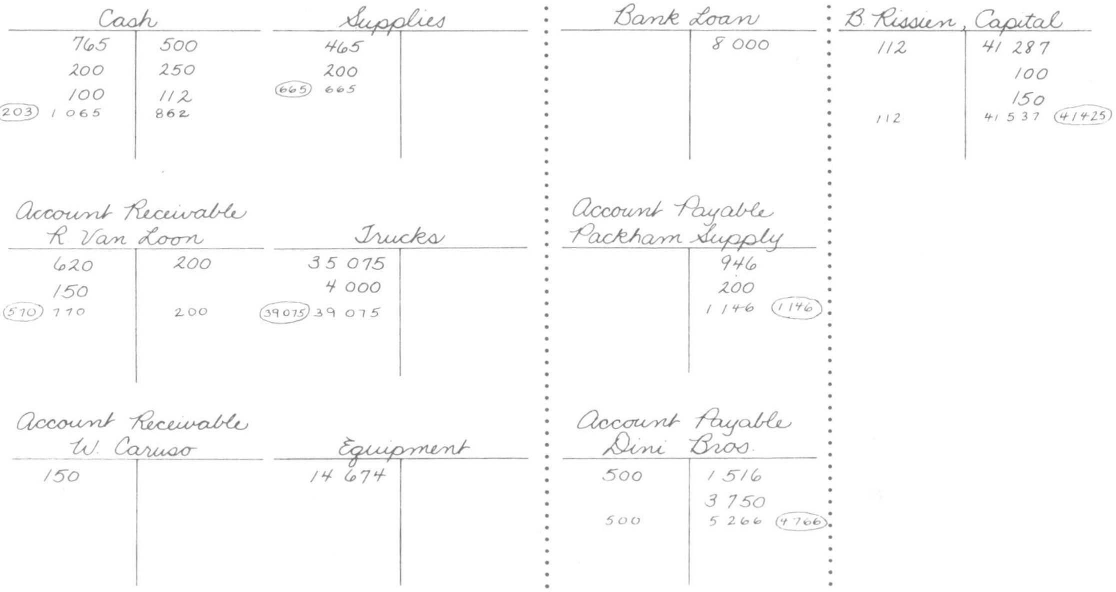

Figure 5.6 The completed ledger of Pacific Trucking.

To take off a trial balance, list all of the accounts and their balances, placing the debit balances in a debit column and the credit balances in a credit column. Then add up the two columns. Only if the two column totals agree is your work arithmetically correct. A heading is necessary on the trial balance showing the name of the individual or business, the title 'Trial Balance', and the date.

The completed trial balance for the above ledger is shown in Figure 5.7.

Heading: Who? What? When?

Pacific Trucking
Trial Balance
date

Accounts	Debits	Credits
Cash	203	
Accounts Receivable – R. Van Loon	570	
– W. Caruso	150	
Supplies	665	
Trucks	39075	
Equipment	14674	
Bank Loan		8000
Accounts Payable – Packham Supply		1146
– Dini Bros.		4766
B. Rissien, Capital		41425
	55337	55337

Accounts listed in ledger order.

Account balances listed in correct columns.

Column totals should agree.

Figure 5.7 The trial balance for the ledger of Pacific Trucking.

An Alternative Method of Taking Off a Trial Balance

An alternative method of taking off a trial balance is by using an adding-listing machine. This is an easier method and is therefore very commonly used.

The procedure is as follows:

1. Clear the machine by pressing the total button.
2. Enter the balances in the machine in ledger order, but enter the debit balances as +'s, and the credit balances as −'s.
3. Take off a total by depressing the total button. If your ledger work is correct, the sum of the debit balances, or +'s, will be equal to the sum of the credit balances, or −'s. Therefore, your total will be 0.00 if your work is correct.

The adding machine method of taking off a trial balance is illustrated in Figure 5.8. Be certain that you understand the principle involved. If you get zero for your total, your work is arithmetically correct. If you do not get zero for a total, your ledger is out of balance, and you must begin a search for the errors.

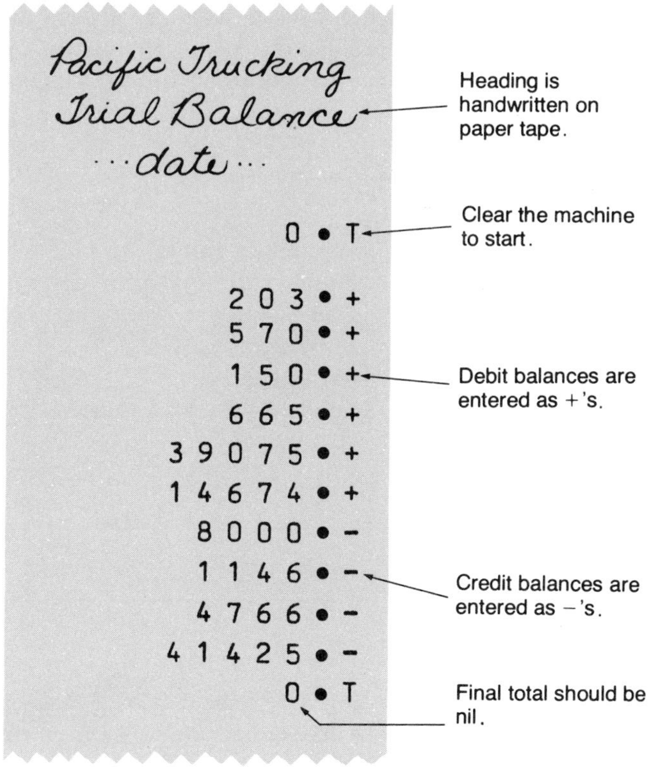

Figure 5.8 Trial balance done on an adding machine.

Importance of the Trial Balance

It is important to an accountant to have the ledger in balance. If the ledger is not in balance the work cannot be accurate. A ledger out of balance is a sign that one or more errors have been made in the accounts.

A good accountant cannot rest until all errors are found and corrected. Moreover, the accountant must test the ledger fairly frequently. It is standard practice to take off a trial balance at least every month.

A ledger that is in balance proves only that it is mechanically or mathematically correct. It may be in balance and still have inaccuracies in it. For instance, the accountant may have made incorrect entries even though they were balanced ones.

When a ledger is not in balance it has mechanical errors in it. The errors may have been caused by faulty addition, or entering an item on the wrong side, and so on. Sometimes, errors can be found easily; at other times, they are quite difficult to detect. The technique for finding errors when a trial balance is out of balance is fully discussed in Chapter 8.

Regardless of the method used, a trial balance should be kept on file for a short time, at least until a new one is prepared at the end of the following month. More commonly, it is kept on file until after the visit of the official auditors.

Accounting Terms

account	**accounting entry**
ledger	**double entry system of accounting**
debit	**trial balance**
credit	**in balance**
pencil footings	**out of balance**
pin totals	**taking off a trial balance**
account balance	

Review Questions

1. What is an account?
2. What is a ledger?
3. When setting up, or 'opening' a ledger from the data on a balance sheet, how many accounts will there be? How are the opening balances entered?
4. Each side of an account is given a special name. What are these names? What are their short forms?
5. Prepare a chart to summarize the rules of debit and credit. Use the form of the fundamental accounting equation.
6. Why are the rules of debit and credit identical for liabilities and owner's equity?
7. Explain the procedure for finding the balance of a T-account.
8. What are pin totals? What is another name for pin totals?
9. The K. Gaswa account has a debit balance of $400. Interpret this data.
10. The H. Henke account has a credit balance of $1 250. Interpret this data.
11. What type of account is an account with a debit balance?
12. What type of account is an account with a credit balance?
13. What is meant by 'accounting entry'?
14. Describe a special characteristic of every accounting entry.
15. Describe a special characteristic of the ledger.
16. List the steps necessary to take off a trial balance.
17. Explain the importance of a trial balance.
18. What is meant by a trial balance that does not balance?
19. How do you know if a trial balance does not balance?
20. Explain the meaning of 'double entry bookeeping'.

Exercises

Setting up the Ledger

1. The balance sheet for Stevens Woodworking is shown below.

STEVENS WOODWORKING
BALANCE SHEET
— DATE —

Assets		*Liabilities*	
Cash	$ 2 000	Bank Loan	$ 20 000
Accounts Receivable		Account Payable	
C. Prentice	1 150	Gem Lumber	2 500
A. Marks	375	Mortgage Payable	55 000
Land	30 000		$ 77 500
Building	75 000	*Owner's Equity*	
Equipment	17 800	T. Stevens Capital	63 325
Truck	14 500		
	$140 825		$140 825

Name the accounts that would appear in the ledger of Stevens Woodworking. Indicate the dollar value of each account, and tell whether it has a debit or credit value.

2. The balance sheet of Doctor Pauline Inaba is shown below.

DOCTOR PAULINE INABA
BALANCE SHEET
— DATE —

Assets		*Liabilities*	
Cash	$ 500	Accounts Payable	
Accounts Receivable		Medico Supply	$ 300
P. Auul	350	A. B. Associates	1 200
S. Wouke	1 250		$ 1 500
Supplies	900	*Owner's Equity*	
Furniture and Equipment	7 320	Pauline Inaba, Capital	18 860
Automobile	10 040		
	$20 360		$20 360

Set up the ledger of Dr. Inaba in the T-accounts provided in your workbook.

Debit and Credit Theory — The Transaction Analysis Sheet

3. Flora Monday is the owner-operator of a fitness clinic. The ledger used in her business contains the following accounts:

Cash
Accounts Receivable (several)
Supplies
Furniture
Equipment
Automobile
Accounts Payable (several)
Flora Monday, Capital

Listed below are transactions of Flora's business. Examine these transactions and record your analysis on the transaction analysis sheet provided in your workbook and shown below. To help you understand how the transaction analysis sheet works, the first transaction has been done for you. Be sure that each entry balances within itself.

Transactions

1. $300 cash is received from J. Parker, one of the accounts receivable.
2. $200 of supplies is purchased for cash.
3. Little Bros., one of the accounts payable, is paid $100.
4. The owner withdraws $250 for her personal use.
5. A piece of new equipment costing $500 is purchased from Champion Sports. $125 cash is paid at the time of purchase with the balance of $375 to be paid within 30 days.
6. A new customer signs up for a fitness course. The $300 fee is paid in cash.

Transaction Analysis Sheet

Transaction No.	Account Names	Account Classification: Asset, Liability, or Owner's Equity	Increase (+) or Decrease (−)	Debit or Credit	Amount
1.	Cash	Asset	+	DR	300 –
	Acct. Receivable J. Parker	Asset	—	CR	300 –

4. Crooks Garage is a small business operated by James Crooks. Shown below are ten selected transactions of Crooks Garage. Analyze these transactions on a transaction analysis sheet. When performing your analysis, choose from the following accounts.

Cash
Accounts Receivable (various)
Supplies
Equipment
Truck
Bank Loan
Accounts Payable (various)
J. Crooks, Capital

Transactions

1. A car is repaired for a customer who pays the $150 charge in cash.
2. $75 of supplies are purchased for cash.
3. $125 is paid to Rossi Co., an account payable.
4. $90 is received from G. Rawl, an account receivable.
5. A welding unit, included in the Equipment account at $210, is run over by a truck. It is so badly damaged that it has to be thrown away.
6. A new welding unit is purchased on credit from Bly Co. at a cost of $350.
7. For the repair of his car, F. Stefryk pays $100 cash and owes $250, the balance of the repair charge.
8. Arrangements are made with the bank to borrow $1 000. A promissory note for this amount is signed by Mr. Crooks for the bank after which the bank provides the business with $1 000 cash.
9. Albert McCann, a mechanic employed by Crooks Garage, is paid wages of $225.
10. A towing service is performed for a customer for $20 cash.

Calculating the Balance of T-Accounts

5. The accounts below appear in your workbook. Calculate their balances. Remember to make your pencil footings in tiny figures, and to circle the balance on the correct side of the account.

Cash	
250	190
1 210	48
360	512
29	750
1849	

Account Receivable H. Devrie	
25	175
150	
70	
35	
280	

Account Payable P. Helka	
30	75
45	40
	175
75	290
	215

R. Smart, Capital	
150	3 140
	2990

1. What does the debit balance in the H. Devrie account mean?
2. What does the credit balance in the P. Helka account mean?

Balancing the Ledger

6. From the following information, prepare a trial balance for the R. K. Bach Co. dated September 30, 19--. Use the formal handwritten method illustrated in the text.

Accounts and Balances

Cash, $7 000; W. Nishi (an account receivable), $300; Equipment, $1 400; Land, $45 000; Buildings, $90 000; Cheryk Company (an account payable), $1 700; Mortgage Payable, $80 000; R. K. Bach, Capital, $62 000.

7. Using an adding machine with a paper tape printout, prepare a trial balance from the accounts and balances of Ceco. Co. shown below. Remember to write in the three-part heading: Date the trial balance June 30, 19--.

Accounts and Balances

Cash, $1 200; J. Blanc (an account receivable), $700; M. Legris (an account receivable), $3 750; Supplies, $1 295; Equipment, $7 296; Automobiles, $22 970; Jondahl Co. (an account payable), $1 350; P. Swartz (an account payable), $4 250; Bank Loan, $10 000; Cecil Oke, Capital, $21 611.

8. Mr. J. Strom is the owner of a hardware store in Lethbridge, Alta. At the end of the year he attempted to prepare a trial balance of the accounts in the general ledger as shown below. The balances themselves are correct. But Mr. Strom has no knowledge of double entry bookkeeping and so he has made many errors in listing the balances. Find the errors and prepare a corrected trial balance.

J. STROM
TRIAL BALANCE
DECEMBER 31, 19--

	Debit	*Credit*
Cash	$ 3 000.00	
Land	24 680.00	
Accounts Receivable		$ 10 940.00
Supplies	690.00	
Office Equipment	7 150.00	
Automobile		15 200.00
Building	140 000.00	
Accounts Payable	5 160.00	
Bank Loan		22 000.00
J. Strom, Capital		96 000.00
Mortgage Payable		78 500.00
	$180 680.00	$222 640.00

9. Why don't the following accounting entries balance?

Cash	
4 000	9 000
10 000	250
3 000	75
375	
(7750) 17 075	9 325

Acc Rec'l - P. Jarvis	
3000	3 000

Supplies	
500	
75	
425	

Equipment	
2 000	
9 000	
11 000	

Truck	
5 000	

Bank Loan	
	10 000

Acc Pay'l - Supply House	
9 000	9000
250	500
250	
9 500	9 500

R. House, Capital	
	11 000
	300
	735
	12 035

Trial Balance

DR.	CR.
7 750	10 000
425	12 035
11 000	
5 000	
24 175	22 035

Transactions and the Ledger

10. Reliable Janitorial Service, owned and operated by Margot Finley, begins business with the following assets. There are no liabilities.

Assets	
Cash	$ 750.00
Supplies	156.00
Equipment	3 175.00
Truck	12 500.00

1. **Set up the beginning financial position in T-accounts. Don't forget the equity account.**
2. **In the T-accounts record the accounting entries for each of the transactions listed below. Some extra transaction analysis sheets are provided in the workbook for you to use if necessary.**
3. **After all of the transactions have been recorded, calculate and record the balances in the accounts.**
4. **Take off a trial balance to see if the ledger is in balance.**

Transactions

1. Purchased $150 of cleaning supplies from Special Chemicals Limited but did not pay for them.
2. Purchased a large vacuum cleaner from Proust Bros. and paid $800 cash.
3. Performed a cleaning service for S. Pearson at a price of $115. Mr. Pearson paid cash.
4. Performed a service for M. King at a price of $70. Mr. King agreed to pay in thirty days.
5. Paid $50 cash to Special Chemicals Limited.

---

11. A. Hoysted is a sign painter and truck letterer. His business has the following assets and liabilities:

Assets		*Liabilities*	
Cash	$ 216.00	Bank Loan	$ 500.00
Accounts Receivable		Accounts Payable	
G. Anderson	57.00	Consumers' Supply	375.20
N. Ostrowski	102.00	Nu-Style Furniture	951.65
Office Supplies	80.00	Traders Finance	3 980.00
Painting Supplies	1 120.00		
Office Furniture	4 090.00		
Automobile	8 000.00		

1. Set up A. Hoysted's financial position in T-accounts. Include the equity account.

2. For the transactions listed below record the accounting entries in T-accounts. If it is helpful for you, use a transaction analysis sheet.

Transactions

1. Received $75 cash from a customer for painting a sign.
2. Paid $100 to Consumers' Supply.
3. Received $102 cash from N. Ostrowski.
4. Sold an extra office desk (which is included in the Office Furniture figure at $150) to G. Brand at a price of $60. Mr. Brand paid $10 cash and owed the balance.
5. Borrowed an additional $500 from the bank.
6. Paid the regular monthly finance payment to Traders Finance, $125.
7. Paid the balance owing to Consumers' Supply.

3. Calculate the account balances and balance the ledger by taking off a trial balance.

12. Rainbow Real Estate is a business owned by Cathy Rogers. The assets and liabilities of the business are as follows:

Assets		*Liabilities*	
Cash	$ 1 056.25	Bank Loan	9 000.00
Accounts Receivable		Account Payable	
A. Niemi	516.00	Tuck Corporation	1 520.00
D. Murray	351.00		
Office Supplies	115.00		
Furniture and Equipment	1 916.00		
Properties Owned	18 042.00		
Automobile	17 965.00		

The financial position of Rainbow Real Estate is set up in T-accounts in the workbook. Use a transaction analysis sheet if necessary. Calculate and record the balances in the accounts and take off a trial balance.

Transactions

1. Received $516 cash from A. Niemi.
2. Sold a home for V. Morris. For this service Mr. Morris owes $2 150 to Rainbow Real Estate.
3. Paid $35 cash for office supplies.
4. Received $9 000 cash for sale of a property. (The property is included in the Properties Owned figure at $5 000.)
5. Paid $4 000 cash to the bank to reduce the amount of the bank loan.
6. Paid $100 cash to Tuck Corporation.
7. Paid $16 cash for a new headlight for the automobile.
8. Received $351 cash from D. Murray.
9. The owner withdrew $200 cash for her personal use.
10. Received $250 cash from V. Morris.
11. Paid the balance of the debt to Tuck Corporation in cash.
12. Purchased a new office desk at a cost of $195 from Pioneer Furniture but did not pay cash for it.
13. Sold a home for A. McIntosh. Mr. McIntosh paid Rainbow Real Estate $2 100 cash for the service.

Using Your Knowledge

13. The ledger of a small service business appears below.

ASSETS

Cash

Dr	Cr
1 500	300
450	250
	50

Supplies

Dr	Cr
400	

Account Receivable W. Brandt

Dr	Cr
700	450
190	

Equipment

Dr	Cr
3 000	
600	

LIABILITIES

Account Payable Perrier Co.

Dr	Cr
300	500

Account Payable S. Bloom Co.

Dr	Cr
	350

OWNER'S EQUITY

M. Barr, Capital

Dr	Cr
50	5 100
	190

Do the following exercises in your workbook or on columnar paper.

1. **Write down the opening financial position.**
2. **Give a brief description of five transactions that would have caused the entries recorded in the accounts. It is not important to list these in the correct order.**

14. The ledger of Dorothy Prouse, a lawyer, appears below.

ASSETS

Cash

Dr	Cr
500	412
78	250
300	5 000
5 000	75

Supplies

Dr	Cr
385	
75	

Account Receivable R. Burke

Dr	Cr
125	
985	

Equipment

Dr	Cr
2 956	

Account Receivable O. Patterson

Dr	Cr
78	78

Automobile

Dr	Cr
3 050	
8 000	

LIABILITIES

Bank Loan

Dr	Cr
	5 000

Account Payable Fincham Co.

Dr	Cr
412	412

Account Payable Master Finance

Dr	Cr
	3 000

OWNER'S EQUITY

D. Prouse, Capital

Dr	Cr
250	6 682
	300
	985

Do the following exercises in your workbook or on columnar paper.

1. **Write down the opening financial position.**
2. **Describe briefly eight transactions that would have caused the entries recorded in the accounts. The order of the transactions is not important.**

---

15. The trial balance prepared by your company at the end of the month did not balance. In reviewing the entries for the month, the accountant noticed that one of the transactions was recorded as a debit to Furniture & Fixtures, $500, and a debit to Cash, $500. Answer the following questions and explain your answer for each.

1. **Was the Cash account overstated, understated, or correctly stated on the trial balance? If overstated or understated, show by how much.**
2. **Was the total of the debit column of the trial balance overstated, understated, or correctly stated? If overstated or understated, show by how much.**
3. **Was the total of the credit column of the trial balance overstated, understated, or correctly stated? If overstated or understated, show by how much.**

---

16. The accountant for M. Finney, owner of a janitorial service business, prepared a trial balance at the end of December. When Mr. Finney examined the trial balance, he noticed that the S. Pearson Co. had a debit balance of $375. Mr. Finney remembered depositing a cheque received from Pearson for that amount. He wants to know why a debit balance still exists on the records. Give three different explanations of how this could happen.

---

17. State whether the following errors would cause a trial balance to be out of balance and by how much. Explain why or why not.

1. The entry to record the purchase of delivery equipment was omitted from the Delivery Equipment account, $150.
2. A new desk was purchased for cash. Cash was credited but the Office Supplies was debited instead of Office Equipment. The cost of the desk was $400.
3. Cash of $100 was received from a client for services performed. Cash was debited for $100 and Capital was credited for $10.
4. Cash of $500 was borrowed from the bank. Cash was credited for $500 and Bank Loan was debited $500.

Cases

Case 1 *A Fair Billing Procedure?*

The field of energy conservation has become an important one. Allan Timura has gained prominence in his community by specializing in this interesting field. The quality of his knowledge and ideas is unquestioned and there is a large demand for his services. He is a busy man.

Allan knows the value of his work and charges a high fee for his services. At the present time the rate for his services is $50 an hour. He charges all of his working days to his clients.

All of Allan's time, however, is not spent working directly for his clients. He frequently takes time to work on a few projects of his own, or to visit his stockbroker regarding his investments. This is time he charges to his clients.

When questioned about his billing practice, Allan defended it. He believed that, regardless of what he was actually doing, his mind was at work for his clients. He claimed that his own projects were used to experiment and test ideas that would ultimately benefit his clients. Also, he claimed, his projects relaxed him and prevented him from becoming tired or stale, keeping him sharp for his clients.

Questions

1. Is Allan's billing procedure a fair one? Are his arguments sound? Discuss.

Case 2 *Does a Balance Sheet Show the Worth of a Business?*

As you have seen, the accounting entry for any business transaction is recorded at the cost or price prevailing on the day of the transaction. For example, a building acquired in 19-1 for $40 000 would be set up in a Building account at that figure. In 19-2 and subsequent years the $40 000 figure would still remain in the accounts.

Questions

1. Is this good accounting practice?
2. Would you recommend changes?
3. Does a balance sheet show the worth of a business? Discuss fully.

6

The Journal

6-1 The Two-Column General Journal
6-2 Business Practices and Journalizing
6-3 Source Documents

Objectives

When you have completed Chapter 6, you should:

1. Know the purpose of a journal and its place in the accounting cycle.
2. Know how to correctly journalize accounting entries in the two-column general journal.
3. Know the four ways in which the words 'on account' are used.
4. Understand why businesses prefer to make purchases on credit.
5. Understand the advantages offered to businesses by banking services.
6. Understand that source documents form the basis for accounting entries and provide necessary evidence of business transactions.

You have now been introduced to some important basic accounting concepts. In particular, you have learned about the balance sheet, transaction analysis, and the ledger. But so far your learning has been based on theory. In this chapter, you will begin to make practical use of your new knowledge, just as you would in the real business world.

The ledger by itself does not fill all accounting needs. An accounting entry is split up when it is recorded in the ledger accounts. Information is transferred into two or more accounts. As transactions mount up, bits and pieces of many entries become scattered throughout the ledger. The details of any one transaction become difficult to find, yet sometimes this is necessary. Therefore another book, the **journal**, is also used in the accounting system.

The journal lists accounting entries as they occur. Each entry is recorded in the journal *before* being recorded in the ledger. The journal provides an important daily record, or history, of all accounting transactions.

An accounting entry in the journal is called a **journal entry**. The process of recording entries in the journal is called **journalizing**. Because the journal contains the first or original recording, the journal is known as a **book of original entry**. The basic process of recording transactions first in the journal and then in the ledger is shown by the following chart.

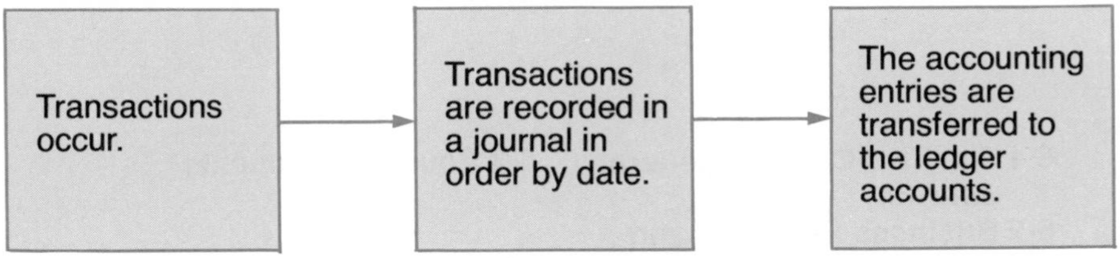

6.1 The Two-Column General Journal

There are several types of journal in use today. First we will study the simplest one — the **two-column general journal**. Figure 6.1 shows the overall appearance of the two-column general journal. From left to right, columns are provided for date, particulars, posting reference (P.R.), debit, and credit. The Posting Reference column, often called the Folio (Fo.) column, is used to cross-reference the journal and the ledger. (Cross-referencing is explained fully in Chapter 7.)

Recording The Date

On each page, the year is entered in small figures in the top half of the first line of the date column. The year is not repeated for each journal entry. The figure at the top of the page is meant to serve all the entries on the page. If it happens that the year changes in the middle of a page, then the new year is entered in small figures at the point on the page where it changes.

The month is entered in the first section of the date column on the first line of each page. There is no need to make an entry for the month again until the month changes. When the month changes, the new month is entered at the point of change.

The day is entered in the day section of the date column on the first line of each journal entry. Notice that the day is recorded on the first line of each journal entry no matter how many journal entries may occur on any given day.

GENERAL JOURNAL PAGE 16

DATE		PARTICULARS	P.R.	DEBIT	CREDIT
19– Nov.	9	Supplies	3	135 –	
		Bank	1		135 –
		Letterhead and envelopes;			
		cheque # 40			
	12	Equipment	4	900 –	
		Supplies	3	400 –	
		Accs Payl - Olivetti			1100 –
		Bank			200 –
		IBM typewriter; ribbons and			
		stationery; cheque # 41			
	28	Accs Payl - Woodwards	21	750 –	
		Bank	1		750 –
		Partial payment; cheque #42			
Dec.	3	Accs Recl - W. Hill	2	300 –	
		S. Cassar, Capital	31		300 –
		Service on account			
	17	Bank	1	5000 –	
		Bank Loan	22		5000 –
		Increase in bank loan			

Figure 6.1 A page from a two-column general journal.

Steps in Recording a Journal Entry

There are four steps in recording a general journal entry. These steps are outlined below.

1. Enter the day in the date column.

GENERAL JOURNAL PAGE 16

DATE		PARTICULARS	P.R.	DEBIT	CREDIT
	12				

2. Enter the names of the accounts to be debited at the left margin of the Particulars column. Enter the debit amounts in the 'debit' money column.

	12	Equipment		900 –	
		Supplies		400 –	

3. Indent the names of the accounts to be credited about one inch in the Particulars column. Enter the credit amounts in the 'credit' money column.

	12	Equipment		900 –	
		Supplies		400 –	
		Accs Payl - Olivetti			1100 –
		Bank			200 –

4. Write a brief explanation of the entry beginning at the left margin of the Particulars column on the line beneath the last credit item.

	12	Equipment		900 –	
		Supplies		400 –	
		Accs Payl - Olivetti			1100 –
		Bank			200 –
		I.B.M. typewriter; ribbons and			
		stationery; cheque #41.			

General Journal Facts

Observe the following facts about the two-column general journal.

Transactions are journalized in order by date.
The transactions are recorded as balanced accounting entries.
The accounting entries are separated by a blank line.
The journal pages are numbered consecutively.
Explanations are simple, brief, and meaningful.
Abbreviations are permitted in the journal.

Purpose of the General Journal

The most important purpose of the general journal is to provide a continous record of the transactions of a business in the order in which they occur. But, the journal is also useful in another way.

If you are the accountant you have to work out the accounting entry for each transaction and record it in the journal. It is at this time that you do your 'brain work'.

The journal is an important stage in your accounting process. While preparing the accounting entry for each transaction and recording it in the journal, you also have a chance to see your work before you in an organized manner. This helps you to ensure that the accounting entries are logical and sensible, and that they are balanced, as all accounting entries must be.

The journalizing process is more important than might first appear. A good job done at this stage reduces errors and prevents problems from occurring later.

The Opening Entry

A basic rule in accounting states that before any entry is recorded in the ledger it must first be recorded in the journal. This must be done for every accounting entry, even the first one that sets up the beginning financial position.

To begin or open a set of books, the beginning financial position must be established in the accounts. First, however, this position must be recorded as a journal entry in the journal. The journal entry that starts the books off, or 'opens' them, is known as the **opening entry**.

The opening entry for Shirley Cassar's photography business can be seen in Figure 6.2. This entry tells us that the assets at the start of the business include a bank balance of $1 400, supplies worth $425, equipment worth $3 715, and an automobile worth $9 550. The capital invested in the business is shown in the credit column as $15 090. There are no liabilities.

Oct	30	Bank		1400 –	
		Supplies		425 –	
		Equipment		3715 –	
		Automobile		9550 –	
		Shirley Cassar, Capital			15090 –
		Opening financial position			
		of Shirley Cassar			

Figure 6.2 The opening entry for a small business.

6.2 Business Practices and Journalizing

On Account

The term **on account** is used extensively in modern business. Therefore it is an essential part of business vocabulary.

The term is used in four specific ways.

1. When something is purchased on credit, that is, not paid for at the time the purchase is made, it is commonly referred to as a **purchase on account**.
2. When something is sold for credit, that is, no money is received for it at the time of the sale, it is commonly referred to as a **sale on account**.
3. When money is paid out to a creditor for the purpose of decreasing the balance owed to him, it is said to be **paid on account**.
4. When money is received from a debtor for the purpose of reducing the balance owed by him, it is said to be **received on account**.

Buying and Selling on Credit

It is an accepted feature of our modern economy that businesses with good reputations are able to buy the things that they need on short-term credit, usually from 10 days to one month. By being able to delay payment for a short period of time, the buyer gains the opportunity of thoroughly inspecting or testing the goods. If they are found to be unsatisfactory, the buyer can simply refuse to pay for the goods until they are made right.

Buying and selling on short-term credit is commonplace in the business world of today. Therefore, in the exercises in this text, expect to see this type of transaction occurring frequently.

Bank Account

Businessmen rely heavily on the banking system as the safest, cheapest, and most convenient way to make payments. It should be clear to you that the handling of large quantities of cash is unsafe. This is one important reason why people in business keep their money in a bank account.

Another and perhaps even more important reason is the convenience of being able to make payments by cheque. It is much easier to send a cheque to someone than it is to deliver cash in person. This is especially true if the buyer and the seller are dealing with each other over a long distance. Except in the case of retail stores in their dealings with the general public, it is usual for all except very small payments to be made by cheque.

In the books of account, therefore, you can expect to see an account called Bank rather than one called Cash. When money is paid out, it is the account Bank, not Cash, that is decreased. Similarly, when money is received, it is the account Bank, not Cash, that is increased.

The words 'bank' and 'cash' are often used interchangeably. When an item is said to be purchased for cash, it means that the item was paid for at the time it was purchased. But payment would most likely be by cheque, not cash. If the cash position of a business is reported as good, it really means that the business bank account has a healthy balance.

6.3 Source Documents

Accounting entries are not the product of someone's imagination. Accounting entries exist because business transactions take place.

Although transactions seldom occur inside the accounting office, the accounting department must examine and record them all. How does the accounting department find out about the business transactions that occur elsewhere?

Information about business transactions flows to the accounting department by means of business papers known as **source documents**. The accounting department is really at the centre of an information system. Data about business transactions flow to it from other departments. Accounting reports and statements flow to the other departments from the accounting office. An information system, with the accounting department at the centre, is shown in Figure 6.3.

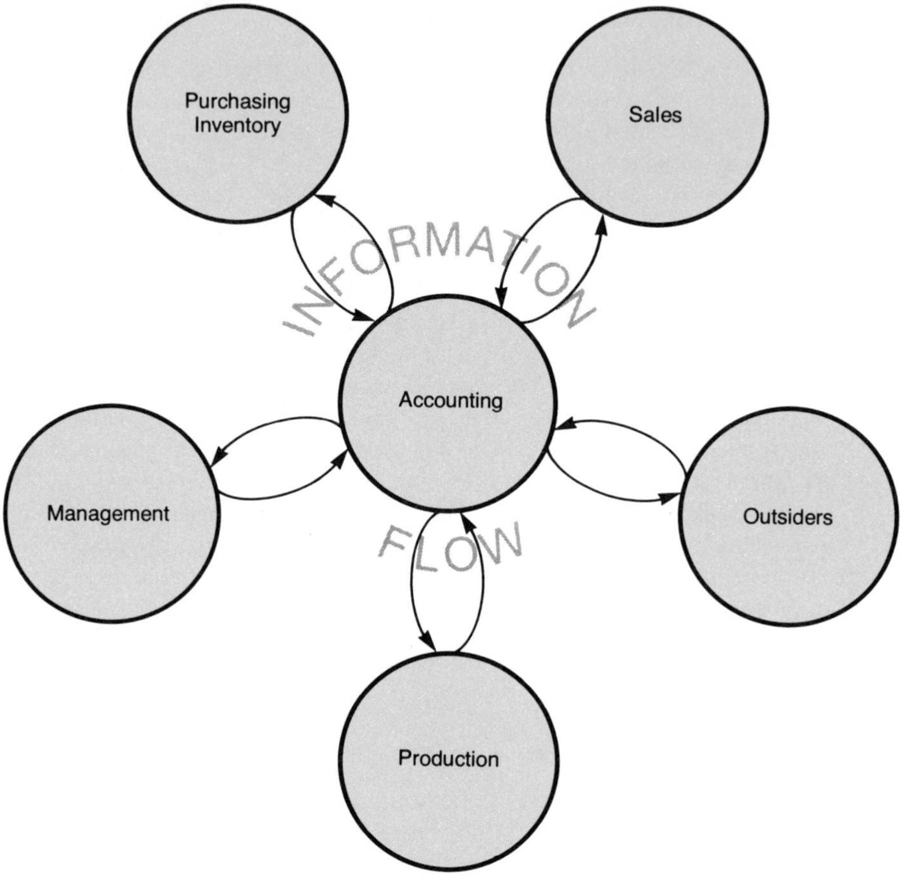

Figure 6.3 The central position of the Accounting Department in an information system.

Business papers provide the source documents for accounting entries. Source documents contain all the information necessary for the accounting entries. Source documents show the following:

1. The nature of the transaction.
2. The types of product or service involved.
3. The names of the customers or creditors.
4. The transaction date.
5. The amount of money involved.

Some examples of source documents, taken from the records of Pine Ridge Ski Club of Craighurst, Ontario, are shown in Figures 6.4, 6.5, 6.6, and 6.7.

ANNUAL FEES FORM

PINE RIDGE

Name Louis Tusek Phone Home 325-6410

Address 15 Cam Street Phone Bus. 325-4987

Street

Orillia

City

List all family members who will be skiing:

Name	Age Dec. 1	Annual fee
Louis	35	250.00
Teresa	32	200.00
Ginger	12	125.00
Dene	8	125.00
Roger	6	125.00
	TOTAL FEE	825.00

I (the undersigned) hereby agree to comply with and be governed by the By-Laws, Rules and Regulations of the Club now or hereafter in force or as amended from time to time and I agree to be responsible for any debts incurred by members of my family.

Dated this 15th day of November 19____

Signature Louis Tusek

I enclose my cheque for $ 825.00

PINE RIDGE SKI CLUB Box 94, Horseshoe Valley, Ont. (705) 835-2014

Figure 6.4 A fees form for a member of Pine Ridge Ski Club. This form, together with a cheque, shows the annual payment for this member's family. The cheque is made out to the ski club and is deposited in the bank.

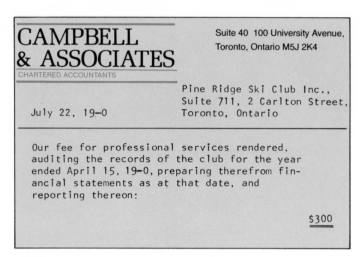

CAMPBELL
& ASSOCIATES
CHARTERED ACCOUNTANTS

Suite 40 100 University Avenue,
Toronto, Ontario M5J 2K4

July 22, 19-0

Pine Ridge Ski Club Inc.,
Suite 711, 2 Carlton Street,
Toronto, Ontario

Our fee for professional services rendered, auditing the records of the club for the year ended April 15, 19-0, preparing therefrom financial statements as at that date, and reporting thereon:

$300

Figure 6.5 A professional bill received by Pine Ridge Ski Club. This bill came from a firm of chartered accountants and shows the charge for auditing the club's records and preparing its financial statements.

Box 500, Orillia, Ontario L3V 6K7

THE DAVEY COMPANY

TROPHIES GIFTWARE ENGRAVERS

Sold to: Pine Ridge Ski Club

Date Dec 5, 19-0

PURCH. ORDER NO.	FED. SALES TAX	PROV. SALES TAX	DELIVERY DATE	TERMS	SHIP VIA	

35	Name tags		96.25
	Tax		6.74
			102.99

Figure 6.6 A purchase invoice received by Pine Ridge Ski Club. This document came from a small service business and shows the charge made for name tags worn by the members.

please return this portion with your payment

class of service	monthly amount	route number	account number
1G2-33		20270	75 7621 0639702

please quote this no. when making enquiries

OUR OFFICE IS NOW LOCATED AT 45 SARJEANT DRIVE, BARRIE

ONTARIO HYDRO
BOX 6700
BARRIE
ONTARIO, CANADA L4M 5N5

please insert so that address appears in window of return envelope

		$	¢
PAYMENT DUE BY	AUG 06 -1 *	156	32
AMOUNT PAYABLE AFTER DUE DATE		157	10

Ontario Hydro

please address enquiries to
BOX 6700
BARRIE L4M 5N5
705-728-5695 OR ZENITH 81120

billing date	class of service	monthly amount	account number
JUL 15 -1	1G2-33		75 7621 0639702

20270 0639702
PINE RIDGE SKI CLUB 7 7
R R 1 BOX 94 HORSESHOE V 2
BARRIE ONT 1
L4M 4Y8

present reading	reading date	meter number
1011	JUL 08	H007829
previous reading	**days since last reading**	**average kW.h used per day**
1011	35	0

reading difference		multiplier		energy used kW.h
0	X	150	=	0

	$	¢
PREVIOUS BALANCE	140	82
MINIMUM CHARGE	15	50
PAYMENT DUE BY AUG 06 -1	156	32
AMOUNT PAYABLE AFTER DUE DATE	157	10

form 968-3446.0 (front) rev 80-04 IBM 257-38C

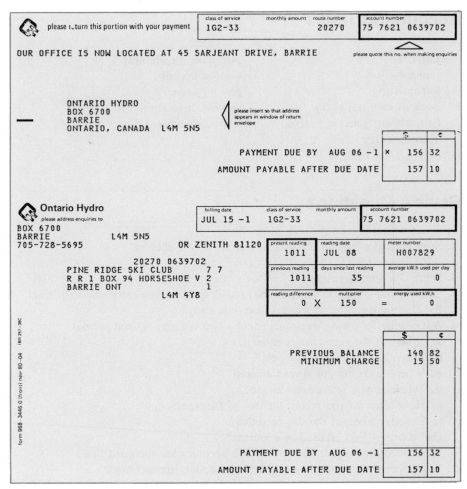

Figure 6.7 A utilities bill received by Pine Ridge Ski Club. This document came from the provincial hydro utility and shows the energy charge for a certain period of time.

Other examples of source documents include bills, invoices, cash sales slips, cash register slips, cheque copies, and memos.

Source documents serve two purposes. As we have seen, they are the source of information for accounting entries. Just as importantly, source documents provide permanent evidence of transactions. There is a set of rules, known as accounting standards, that are obeyed by all accountants. One of these rules states that factual evidence is necessary for all business transactions. Every business transaction must be backed up by business papers that provide good and proper evidence of the transaction. These business papers, which are kept on file, enable accountants to prove the accuracy and honesty of their work to owners, managers, auditors, governments, and other interested parties.

This section has given you a brief introduction to the concept of source documents. Later, in Chapter 11, the topic of source documents is discussed more fully.

Accounting Terms

journal	**purchase on account**
journal entry	**sale on account**
journalizing	**pay on account**
book of original entry	**receive on account**
two-column general journal	**source document**
opening entry	

Review Questions

1. State the basic rule of accounting learned in this chapter.
2. What is a journal?
3. What is a journal entry?
4. Give the name used to describe the process of recording entries in the journal.
5. Explain the meaning of 'book of original entry'.
6. Answer the following questions about a two-column general journal.
   a. Where is the year always entered?
   b. When do you rewrite the year?
   c. Where is the month always entered?
   d. When do you rewrite the month?
   e. How often do you record the day of the transaction?
   f. Exactly, where is the day recorded?
7. Can abbreviations be used in a journal?
8. When recording a journal entry, which accounts are recorded first?
9. When recording a journal entry, which accounts are indented?
10. Describe exactly how explanations are recorded in a journal.
11. Describe what is meant by the opening entry.
12. Besides a daily list of accounting entries, what else does the journal provide?
13. Give five examples of source documents.
14. Give two reasons for having source documents.
15. Give the accounting entry for a purchase invoice for $75 of supplies.

Exercises

Recording in a Two-column General Journal

1. **Rob Czank begins business with the following assets and liabilities:** Cash, $1 200; Office Equipment, $3 900; Land, $42 500; Building, $85 900; Account Payable to Diamond Equipment, $350; Mortgage on Building, $32 560;

After calculating the equity figure, record the opening entry for Rob Czank in a two-column general journal.

---

2. Using the accounts named below, journalize the transactions for February 1 to 5 on page 18 of the general journal of Mary Lamke, who operates a taped music service for dances in Thunder Bay, Ont.

Accounts: Bank
Account Receivable — T Burton
Account Receivable — Citizens' Hall
Sound Equipment
Tape Recordings
Automobile
Account Payable — Perry's Tapes and Records
Mary Lamke, Capital

Transactions

February

1 Purchased $220 of new tape recordings for cash.

1 Provided taped music for a dance at Citizens' Hall for $250, to be paid at a later date.

2 Received $75 from T. Burton on account.

3 Paid $85 cash for repairs to the sound equipment.

4 Paid $550 to Perry's Tapes and Records. This was the full amount owed to them.

5 Provided taped music for a dance at Municipal Arena and received $250 cash in full payment.

---

3. Syd Moyer is a house painter who is in business for himself in Charlottetown, P.E.I. In his ledger he uses the following accounts:

Bank
Accounts Receivable — several customers
Supplies and Materials
Equipment
Truck
Accounts Payable — several creditors
Bank Loan
S. Moyer, Capital

On page 70 of his general journal, journalize the transactions shown below for Syd Moyer.

Transactions

June

20 Received on account $125 from G. Ralph, an account receivable.

21 Purchased a supply of paint brushes for $87 cash.

21 Painted a porch for Mr. V. Laing at a price of $235. Mr. Laing promised promised to pay in 30 days.

22 Paid $350 on account to Performance Paints, an account payable.

23 Paid $58.50 cash to Jim's Garage to replace the old battery in the truck.

23 Paid the bank $500 to reduce the bank loan.

24 Completed a painting job for H. Chu and received the $275 charge immediately in cash.

---

4. In Forest Grove, N.B., Shauna Foulds owns and operates a car leasing business. She owns five cars which she financed through a large bank loan. Shauna Foulds' ledger contains the accounts shown below:

Bank
Accounts Receivable — several customers
Office Supplies
Office Furniture
Automobiles
Bank Loan
Accounts Payable — several creditors
Shauna Foulds, Capital

In a two-column general journal on page 19, record the following transactions for Shauna Foulds.

May

4 Finalized a car rental deal for $250 with G. Goldberg on account.

7 Paid Independent Car Servicing, $125 on account.

8 Received $215 on account from V. DelGrande.

12 Shauna Foulds withdrew $200 for her own personal use.

15 The telephone bill for $39.20 arrived in the mail. It was paid immediately.

20 Purchased a new car for $9 000 cash.

25 Finalized a car rental deal for J. Friest who paid the $315 charge in cash.

June

1 Paid cash for one month's rent, $300.

3 Paid Lecrois Brake Service $175 for repairs to a car.

Identifying Parts of a Two-Column General Journal

5. Workbook Exercise: Complete a chart identifying parts of the two-column general journal.

Identifying Errors in a Two-Column General Journal

6. The general journal shown below contains a number of errors. Study the given journal and prepare a list describing these errors.

GENERAL JOURNAL — PAGE

DATE		PARTICULARS	P.R.	DEBIT	CREDIT
Feb	3	Bank		200 -	
		Account Recivable - P. Simms			200 -
		Partial payment from customer.			
Feb	7	Bank			50 -
		Supplies		50 -	
		Pencils, pens, and papers			
		purchased from Reingolds.			
Feb	10	Bank		90 -	
		M. Farris, Capital		60 -	
		Equipment			250 -
		Sold equipment ($250) for $90 cash.			
Feb	22	Account Payable - General Finance		315 -	
Feb	22	Bank			315 -
		Account Receivable - N. Proulx		125 -	
		M. Farris, Capital			125 -
		Service performed for cash.			
Mar	3	Supplies			20 -
		Accounts Payable - Reingolds		20 -	
		Purchased folders on credit.			

Accounting Entries from Source Documents

7. The source documents described below are from transactions of Clare Lehto Window Cleaning, located in Fredericton, N.B. In a two-column general journal, record the accounting entries for these source documents using the following accounts.

Accounts: Cash
Accounts Receivable
Supplies
Accounts Payable
C. Lehto, Capital

Transactions

April

3 Received a cheque for $110 from P. Remus, a customer, in part payment of his debt to the business.

6 Issued cheque No. 713 for $300 to Walberg Bros., a supplier, in part payment of the debt owed to that company.

9 Received a purchase invoice from Merrick Products for $500 of cleaning supplies which were received in good order.

10 Issued cash sales slip No. 402 to R. Toogood, a customer, for cleaning services completed, $150.

15 Received a purchase invoice from Maritime Telephone for the telephone service for the month, $16.25.

20 Issued cheque No. 714 to C. Lehto for her personal use, $200.

8. Described below are source documents for Wayne Siebert, a professional photographer in Kelowna, B.C. Journalize the accounting entries for these transactions in a two-column general journal using the following accounts.

Accounts: Cash
Accounts Receivable
Supplies
Accounts Payable
W. Siebert, Capital

Transactions

November

9 Received a purchase invoice from Black Cameras for $700 of photo supplies.

15 Issued sales invoice No. 904 to Mr. and Mrs. B. Wooster for an album of their wedding pictures, $300.

19 Received a cheque from J. Manning paying his account of $250.

20 Issued cheque No. 121 for $425 to Black Cameras in part payment of the amount owed to them.

22 Received a memo from the owner stating that he had taken supplies worth $50 for his personal use.

27 Received a bill for $56 from Pacific Hydro for the monthly energy charge.

Using Your Knowledge

9. A number of journal entries are shown below without dates or explanations. These entries are for a beauty shop operated by Kelly Marshall in Kapuskasing, Ont.

Examine these entries and prepare a list of transactions that could have caused them.

Bank	25	
Kelly Marshall, Capital		25
Supplies	30	
Bank		30
Kelly Marshall, Capital	200	
Bank		200
Jan Vasko — Acc rec'l	20	
Kelly Marshall, Capital		20
Supplies	70	
Fain Bros. — Acc pay'l		70

10. The schedule below appears in your workbook. Complete the schedule by writing in '+', '−', or 'nil' for each transaction in the spaces provided

at the right. Each box should have an entry. The first transaction is done for you.

Transactions	*Total Assets*	*Accounts Receivable*	*Total Liabilities*	*Accounts Payable*	*Owner's Equity*
Purchased supplies on account	+	nil	+	+	nil
Received cash on account					
Reduced bank loan					
Paid telephone bill by cash					
Owner withdrew money for own use					
Paid M. Vincent on account					
Sold a service to a customer on account					
Purchased a car with a 20% down payment					
Sold a service to a customer for cash					
Purchased equipment on account					

Cases

Case 1 *Frustration for the Auditor*

Para Painting, of Montreal, Quebec, has applied to the bank for a loan. The bank manager has some doubts about this customer. The owner of Para Painting is Warren Dean, an aggressive young man with a reputation in the community for fast living. The records that Dean has submitted to the bank indicate that the business is quite profitable. However, Dean's recordkeeping techniques are unusual, and the bank manager is unsure about their accuracy. The bank manager asks Noel Des Roches, a public accountant, to audit the books.

Noel soon learns about Dean's methods. While at high school, Dean took an accounting course. Now he does his own bookkeeping. In order to save time, Dean does not use a journal but records all accounting entries directly in the accounts. In addition, he keeps a file of all business papers. He claims that he has never had a problem in backchecking on a transaction.

Noel finds it a slow process trying to figure out which debits correspond to which credits in the ledger. He always seems to need Dean to explain things to him and Dean is usually out on a job. On the third day, Noel finds that he cannot proceed further until Dean explains some puzzling entries. Unfortunately, Dean is not available, having left for a week's skiing in Europe.

Shown below are the unverified entries in the accounts. (These are not all of the accounts and entries of the business, but only the ones that Noel has not yet figured out.)

Bank	
5 000	5 000
	10 000

Acc Rec'l – P. Watt	
	5 000

Materials	
	5 000

Property	
10 000	

Automobile	
10 000	

Acc Pay'l – C.P. Paints	
5 000	

City Loan Co.	
	5 000

Questions

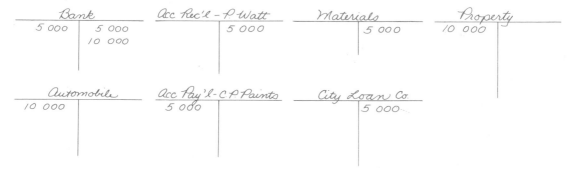

1. From an office clerk, Noel learns the following:

a. Dean bought either a car or an investment property from a customer. There was some talk of offsetting the customer's account balance against the cost price.

b. Dean has a habit of taking some of the files home with him. Since there are no files or banking records in the office pertaining to the car or the property, Noel assumes that Dean has taken them home. Because Dean lives alone, these records are unavailable.

Prepare three different lists of transactions that would explain the entries in the accounts.

2. Eventually, Noel realizes that he can't finish the audit until Dean returns from Europe, and reports this to the bank manager. The bank manager asks Noel to write up a report for Dean. Noel is to explain the difficulties he has encountered with Dean's records and how these difficulties are avoided by conventional accounting procedures.

Write this report as if you were Noel Des Roches.

Career

Jane Clarke / Bookkeeper for a Dentist

When Jane Clarke was a student in Peterborough, Ontario, she never imagined that one day she might work in the field of accounting. Jane took an arts and science course at high school; her school didn't offer business subjects.

After Jane graduated from high school, she spent several years working as a dental assistant. She enjoyed the variety that this position offered. Essentially, Jane's job was to ensure that the dental practice ran as smoothly and efficiently as possible. She saw that dental equipment and supplies were well maintained. She acted as receptionist, putting patients at ease in the waiting room. She kept the patients' files up to date, kept the dentist's appointment book, and sent out notices to remind patients of their appointments.

Jane also acted as the dentist's bookkeeper. She kept a cash receipts book and a two-column general journal. Jane sent out bills to the patients at the end of each month. As each cheque was received, she would match it with the appropriate bill, then endorse the cheque and list it for deposit. She made sure that every bill not paid in cash was listed as an account receivable. Jane also kept track of accounts payable; she checked invoices against the goods that were received and issued cheques periodically to creditors.

Jane performed various additional bookkeeping jobs for the dental practice. She purchased supplies and stamps for the practice and kept careful track of these in the journal. She made any necessary correcting entries in the two-column general journal. Each month, she also prepared the bank reconciliation statement.

After four years, Jane decided to leave work to marry and raise a family. This decision was not made easily. Jane found her work agreeably challenging and liked the man she worked for. She also liked the financial independence that accompanied a career. As we will see in Chapter 7, Jane Clarke eagerly returned to the work force as soon as her children were grown.

7

Posting

7-1 The Balance Column Account
7-2 Formal Posting
7-3 Correcting Errors in the Books
7-4 Forwarding Procedures
7-5 The Accounting Cycle

Objectives

When you have completed Chapter 7 you should:

1. Understand why both a journal and a ledger are used in the accounting process.
2. Be able to use a balance column account correctly and with ease.
3. Be able to first journalize and then post an account.
4. Know the six steps in the posting process.
5. Know how to make corrections in the journal and in the accounts, and how to make correcting journal entries.
6. Know how to forward the balance of an account to a new account page.
7. Know the first four steps in the accounting cycle.

You have now been introduced to the two important books in the accounting process. These two books, the journal and the ledger, are commonly referred to as **the books of account**, or simply **the books**. The journal provides a record of all transactions in the order they happen. The ledger provides detailed information on individual accounts.

7.1 The Balance Column Account

So far we have only considered the simple two-sided ledger account where debits and credits are recorded. But, in order to be really useful, a ledger account should supply more information. Therefore the usual ledger account does not look like the simple T-account. The form of account in common use today is the **balance column account**. The T-account and the balance column account are compared in Figure 7.1.

Numbering the Accounts

It is customary to number the accounts in the ledger in order to make them easier to identify. The method of numbering the accounts varies depending on the size and nature of the business and on the views of the accountant.

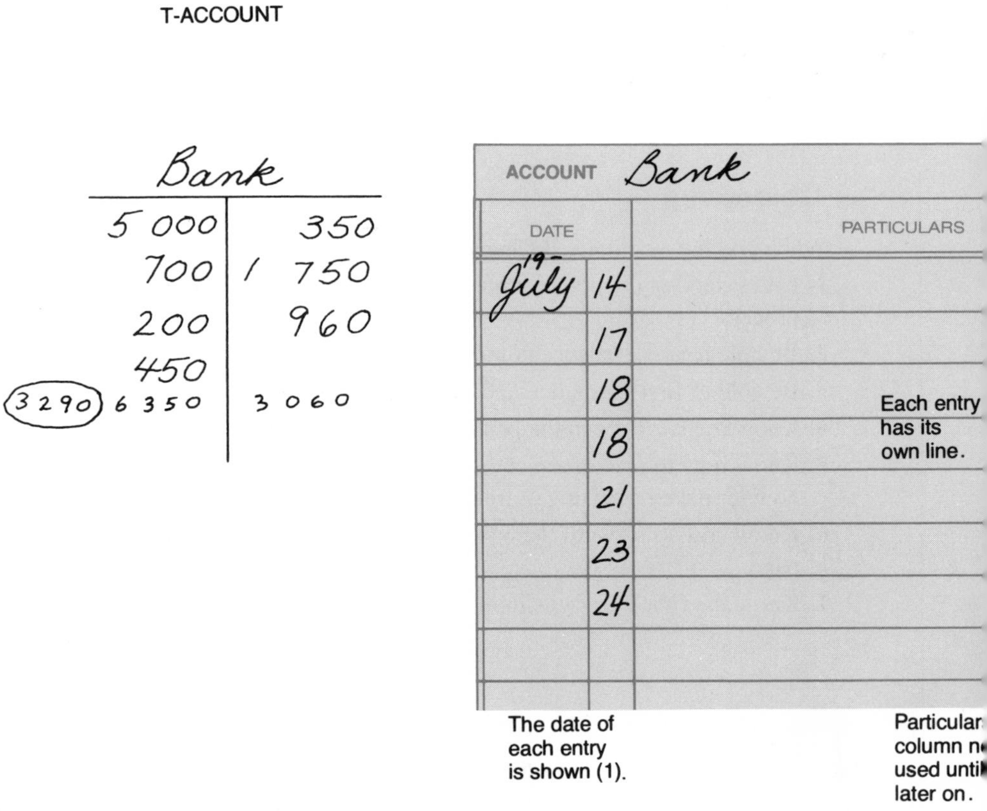

Figure 7.1 Comparison of entries made in a T-account *(left)* and in a standard balance column account *(right)*.

Notes:

1. The word 'entry' has different meanings in accounting. It may mean the full accounting entry with which you are already familiar. Or, as is intended in this instance, it may mean just one part of the full accounting entry.
2. An error commonly made by beginners is to use the Dr./Cr. column to show whether an entry was made in the debit column or the credit column. There is no need to show this because the kind of entry made can be seen at a glance.

   The purpose of the Dr./Cr. column is to show the kind of balance that the account has. In the Figure 7.1, it can be seen that the Bank account has a Debit balance of $3 290.

STANDARD ACCOUNT

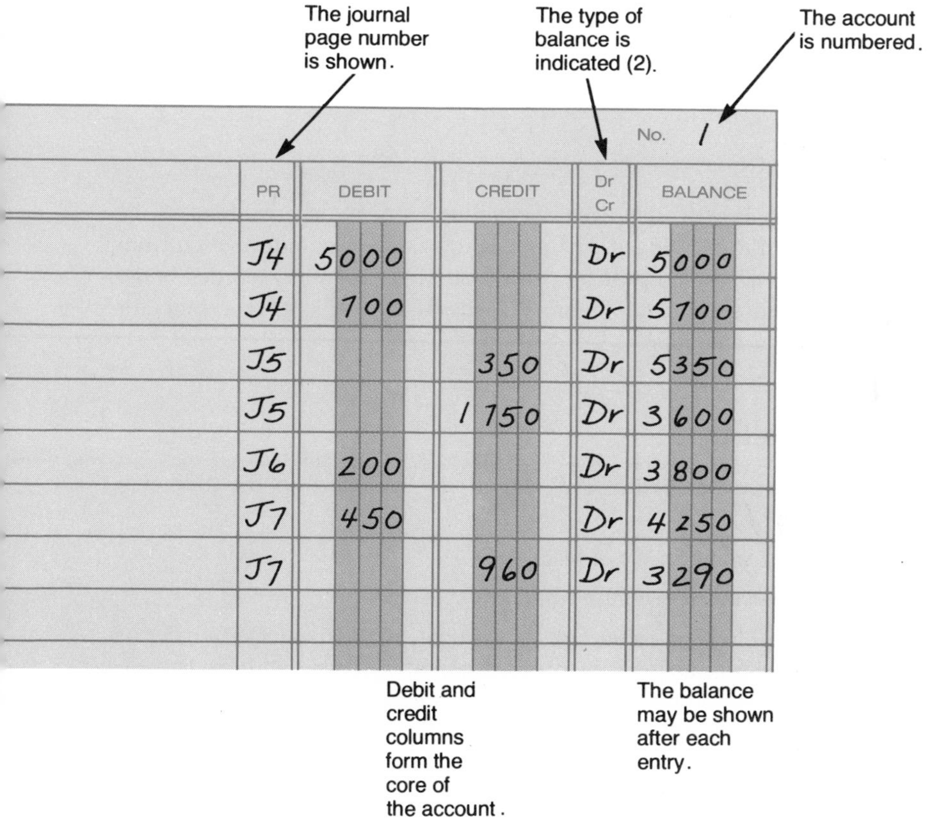
The journal page number is shown.
The type of balance is indicated (2).
The account is numbered.
No. 1
PR
DEBIT
CREDIT
Dr Cr
BALANCE
J4 5000 Dr 5000
J4 700 Dr 5700
J5 350 Dr 5350
J5 1750 Dr 3600
J6 200 Dr 3800
J7 450 Dr 4250
J7 960 Dr 3290
Debit and credit columns form the core of the account.
The balance may be shown after each entry.

In this text the numbering system follows the very simple scheme shown below:

Assets	No. 1 to No. 19
Liabilities	No. 20 to No. 29
Capital	No. 30

In larger businesses with automated accounting systems, coding of the accounts by means of a series of numbers is essential.

Opening an Account

An accounting entry often affects an item for which there is no account in the ledger. When this happens, it is necessary to prepare an account for the new item and insert it in the proper place in the ledger. This is called **opening an account**. To open an account you proceed as follows:

1. Obtain an unused page of account paper.
2. Write the name of the new item at the top of the page in the space provided. This is called the **account title**.
3. Write the number given to the new account in the space provided.
4. Insert the new account in its proper place in the ledger.

7.2 Formal Posting

In the last chapter you learned that each accounting entry is first recorded in the journal then transferred to the ledger. The process of transferring information from the journal to the ledger is called **posting**. Every individual amount recorded in the journal must be posted separately. Figure 7.2 shows the six-step procedure for posting these individual amounts.

Six Steps in Posting

For each individual amount entered in the journal, you must perform the following six steps in the ledger:

1. Turn to the proper account in the ledger.
2. Record the date. Use the next unused line in the account.
3. In the (PR) posting reference column of the account, record the page number of the journal where the transaction is recorded. Prefix this number with the letter J; for example, J14. You must use a journal code because, as you will see later, several journals are used at the same time and you must show which journal is being referred to.
4. Record the amount. Debit amounts are entered in the debit columns of the accounts. Credit amounts are entered in the credit columns of the accounts.
5. Calculate and enter the new balance of the account in the balance column and indicate whether it is a debit or a credit balance.

GENERAL JOURNAL

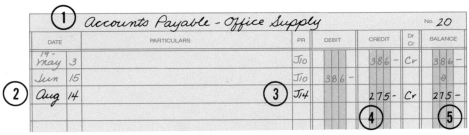

GENERAL JOURNAL — Page 14

DATE		PARTICULARS	PR	DEBIT	CREDIT
19– Aug	14	Office Furniture	6	425 –	
		Bank	1		150 –
		Acc. Payable - Office Supply	20		275 –

(6)

(The journal entry being posted)

LEDGER ACCOUNTS

(1) Bank — No. 1

DATE		PARTICULARS	PR	DEBIT	CREDIT	Dr Cr	BALANCE
19– Aug	3	Forwarded	–			Dr	704 15
	9		J13	502 –		Dr	1 206 15
(2)	14		(3) J14		150 –	Dr	1 056 15
					(4)		(5)

(1) Office Furniture — No. 6

DATE		PARTICULARS	PR	DEBIT	CREDIT	Dr Cr	BALANCE
19– Feb	2		J6	507 06		Dr	507 06
Apr	16		J9	370 –		Dr	877 06
(2) Aug	14		(3) J14	425 –		Dr	1 302 16
					(4)		(5)

(1) Accounts Payable - Office Supply — No. 20

DATE		PARTICULARS	PR	DEBIT	CREDIT	Dr Cr	BALANCE
19– May	3		J10		386 –	Cr	386 –
Jun	15		J10	386 –			0
(2) Aug	14		(3) J14		275 –	Cr	275 –
					(4)		(5)

(The ledger accounts affected)

Figure 7.2 Six steps in the formal posting of a journal entry.

6. Turn to the journal to perform the last step in posting. Record the number of the account to which the posting was made. Write this in the posting reference column in the journal and on the same line as the amount being posted.

Cross Referencing

Steps 3 and 6 of the posting sequence perform what is know as **cross-referencing**. Expressed in simple terms, the journal page number is recorded in the PR column of

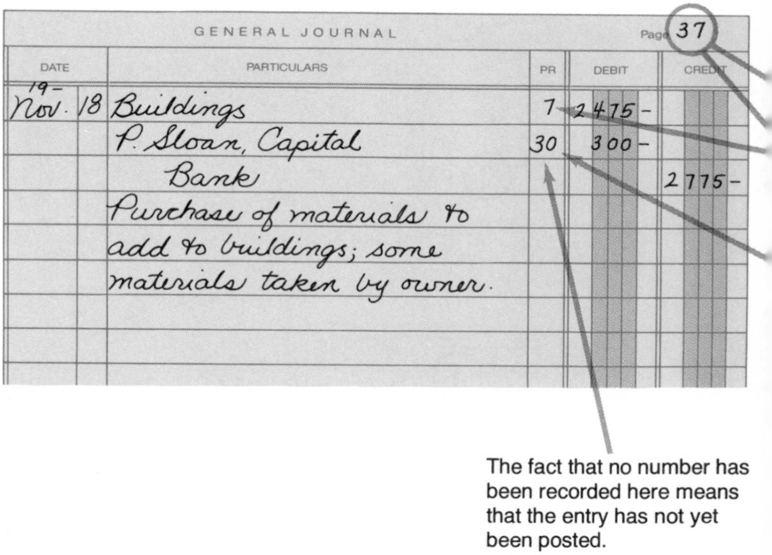

Figure 7.3 Cross-referencing.

the account. Then, the account number is recorded in the PR column of the journal. Cross-referencing is illustrated in Figure 7.3.

The recording of the account number in the journal is the final step in the posting of an individual item. The presence of the account number in the journal shows that the posting of an item is completed. The absence of the account number in the journal shows that the item has not been posted. If, for instance, a telephone call interrupts your posting of the journal, you can tell by a glance at the Posting Reference column where to begin again when you return.

LEDGER ACCOUNTS

Bank No. 1

DATE		PARTICULARS	PR	DEBIT	CREDIT	Dr Cr	BALANCE
19– Nov.	15	Forwarded	—			Dr	3 027 50
	17		J36	412 90		Dr	3 440 40

Buildings No. 7

DATE		PARTICULARS	PR	DEBIT	CREDIT	Dr Cr	BALANCE
19– Jan.	3		J30	18 432 –		Dr	18 432 –
Mar.	10		J32	2 170 –		Dr	20 602 –
Nov.	18		J37	2 475 –		Dr	23 077 –

P. Sloan, Capital No. 30

DATE		PARTICULARS	PR	DEBIT	CREDIT	Dr Cr	BALANCE
19– Nov.	10	Forwarded	—			Cr	20 250 –
	15		J34	250 –		Cr	20 000 –
	18		J37	300 –		Cr	19 700 –

7.3 Correcting Errors in the Books

Over the years professional accountants have made it a rule not to erase. Erasures in the books might arouse the suspicions of the auditors, the official examiners of the books and records. Therefore other methods have been devised for making corrections in the books.

For an error that is detected right away, the method of correction is very simple. This consists of stroking out the error neatly and writing above it the correct words or figures. Figure 7.4 illustrates this type of correction.

Clearly, a person with large handwriting will find it harder to make corrections. An accounting clerk should learn to write small so that errors can be corrected easily.

A single error may require several corrections. For example, if an incorrect journal entry is posted to the accounts, new account balances may be determined before the error is detected. To correct this error, then, it is necessary to change the amount in the journal, to change the posting in the account, and to recalculate and enter the correct account balance.

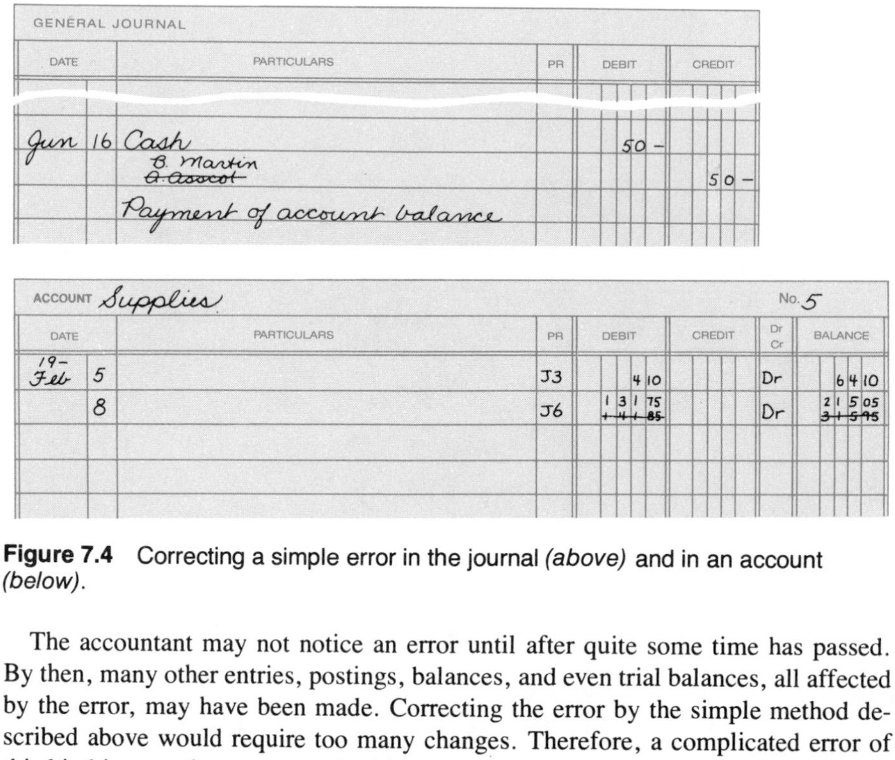

Figure 7.4 Correcting a simple error in the journal *(above)* and in an account *(below)*.

The accountant may not notice an error until after quite some time has passed. By then, many other entries, postings, balances, and even trial balances, all affected by the error, may have been made. Correcting the error by the simple method described above would require too many changes. Therefore, a complicated error of this kind is sometimes corrected with a **correcting journal entry**. By this method, the incorrect entry is left untouched and a new (correcting) entry is worked out and journalized. The correcting entry must allow the original transaction to have its proper effect in the accounts.

For example, suppose that a clerk incorrectly recorded a cash purchase of supplies as a credit purchase of supplies. The incorrect journal entry might be as follows:

Supplies	$105	
Account Payable — Weaver Brothers		$105

When posted to the accounts, the error has the following effect:

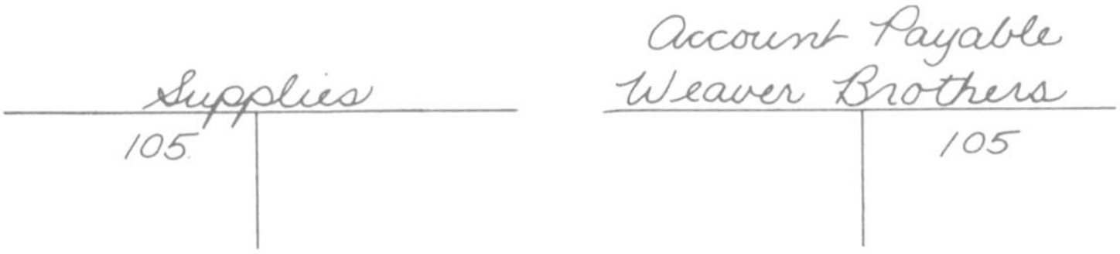

On discovering the error, the accountant will have to make the following correcting entry in the journal:

Account Payable — Weaver Brothers	$105	
Bank		$105

When this entry is posted to the accounts the effect is as follows:

The two entries together give the correct effect.

7.4 Forwarding Procedure

When an account page is full, the account must be continued on a new page. This new page begins with the information on the last line of the finished page. This process is called **forwarding** and involves the following steps.

1. Prepare a new account page by entering the account title and the account number. These are the same as on the finished account page.
2. On the last line of the finished account page, and in the Particulars column, write the words 'Carried Forward', or 'Forwarded'.
3. Obtain the necessary information from the last line of the completed page, and write the following on the first line of the new account page:
   a. The date of the last entry.
   b. In the Particulars column, the words 'Brought Forward', or 'Forwarded'.

c. In the P.R. column, a dash.

d. In the Balance Column, the last balance, including the balance indicator. Notice that nothing is written at this time in the Debit or Credit columns of the new page.

The completed account page and the new account page should look like the pages in Figure 7.5.

a.

ACCOUNT *T.J. Barker* No. 4

DATE		PARTICULARS	PR	DEBIT	CREDIT	Dr Cr	BALANCE
19– Feb	7		J1	150 62		Dr	150 62
	9		J3	374 50		Dr	525 12
	11		J5		150 62	Dr	374 50
	12		J5	216 51		Dr	591 01
	16		J8	75 62		Dr	666 63
	18		J9		374 50	Dr	292 13
	19		J9	583 62		Dr	875 75
	21	Forwarded	J10		292 13	Dr	583 62

b.

ACCOUNT *T.J. Barker* No. 4

DATE		PARTICULARS	PR	DEBIT	CREDIT	Dr Cr	BALANCE
19– Feb	21	Forwarded				Dr	583 62

Figure 7.5 The finished account page after being forwarded (a.) and the new account page with the balance brought forward (b.).

7.5 The Accounting Cycle

In order to meet the objectives of accounting, a definite set of procedures must be followed. This set of procedures is known as the **accounting cycle**. The steps in the accounting cycle are introduced gradually throughout the text, at the times considered most appropriate. The complete accounting cycle will eventually be covered.

You have already learned the first few steps in the accounting cycle. These steps are outlined in the flowchart in Figure 7.6.

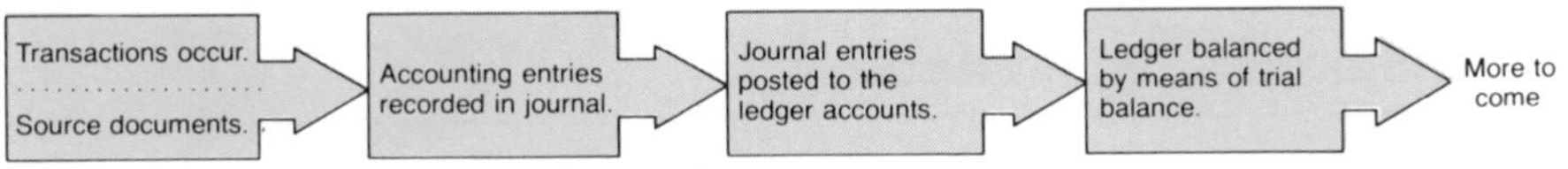

Figure 7.6 The first steps in the accounting cycle.

Accounting Terms

books of account
balance column account
opening an account
account title
posting
cross referencing
correcting journal entry
forwarding
accounting cycle

Review Questions

1. What are the books of account?
2. Where are accounting entries recorded first? Second?
3. How are the accounting entries arranged in the journal?
4. How are the accounting entries arranged in the ledger?
5. For what purpose is the T-account ideal?
6. How is the balance column account more useful than the T-account?
7. Describe the simple numbering system for accounts used in this text.
8. Explain the meaning of 'opening an account'.
9. Define 'posting'.
10. Give the six-step posting sequence.
11. How many of the above steps are performed in the account? How many are performed in the journal?
12. How can an accountant tell whether a journal entry has been posted?
13. Explain what is meant by cross referencing.
14. Why are erasures not permitted in accounting?
15. How would you correct a mistake made when entering an amount?
16. When would you use a correcting journal entry?
17. Briefly describe the forwarding procedure.
18. What steps in the accounting cycle have you studied so far?

Exercises

The Balance Column Account

1. The partially completed account shown below also appears in your workbook. Complete the balance column by calculating and entering the balance after each entry. Be sure to indicate each time whether the balance is debit or credit.

No. 21

DEBIT	CREDIT	Dr/Cr	BALANCE
1000 -			
	300 -		
	235 -		
100 -			
	600 -		
	215 -		
700 -			
120 -			
	302 -		
	417 -		
	914 -		
1500 -			

2. The following summary of data affecting the Bank account is taken from the journal of a local company. Using the standard account page in your workbook, properly record this data in the account.

Date		*Journal Page*	*Amount*	*Debit or Credit*
19 –				
May	7	1	$1 500.00	Dr
	8	2	890.00	Cr
	8	2	788.00	Dr
	9	3	375.50	Cr
	9	3	925.15	Cr
	9	4	634.00	Dr
	10	4	397.19	Cr
	10	4	246.02	Cr

Simple Posting

3. Workbook Exercise: Posting a single transaction.

4. Workbook Exercise: Posting several transactions.

Forwarding

5. Workbook Exercise: Forwarding an account balance.

Journalizing, Posting, and Balancing

6. Topflight Tool Rentals is a business owned and operated by W. Kuziki in Welland, Ont. The following trial balance shows the financial position of the business as of October 1, 19––.

TOPFLIGHT TOOL RENTALS
TRIAL BALANCE
OCTOBER 1, 19––

		Debits	*Credits*
1	Bank	$ 1 950.62	
2 - 1	Account Receivable — J. Hardie	110.00	
2 - 2	Account Receivable — S. Seward	25.00	
2 - 3	Account Receivable — M. Strauss	175.00	
3	Rental Tools	12 050.00	
4	Shop Equipment	5 047.00	
5	Delivery Truck	9 950.00	
20 - 1	Account Payable — Apoca Equipment		$ 4 750.00
20 - 2	Account Payable — Eastern Equipment		2 500.00
20 - 3	Account Payable — John's Garage		65.00
30	M. Kuziki, Capital		21 992.62
		$29 307.62	$29 307.62

The accounts of Topflight Tool Rental, with their balances, appear in the workbook. (Two workbook accounts are required for Bank.)

1. Journalize and post the transactions shown below. Use journal page 17.

Transactions

October

2 Received in the mail a cheque for $50 from J. Hardie on account.

3 Received an invoice from Apoca Equipment regarding the purchase on credit of rental tools worth $120.

3 Rented a tool to a customer for $15 cash. A cash sales slip was made out to the customer.

4 Rented a tool to a customer for $25 cash. A cash sales slip was made out to the customer.

5 A cheque for $500 was sent to Eastern Equipment in part payment of their account balance.

8 Received a cheque in the mail for $175 from M. Strauss in full payment of his account balance.

10 Issued a sales invoice to S. Seward who rented a large piece of equipment on account at a price of $400.

11 Sent a cheque for $750 to Apoca Equipment on account.

12 Received in the mail a cheque for $300 from S. Seward on account.

15 Issued a cheque to John's Garage in full payment of their account.

15 Received a memo from the owner stating that a tool valued in the accounts at $75 was broken beyond repair and was thrown out.

15 Received in the mail a cheque from S. Seward for the full amount of his account balance.

2. When finished posting, take off a trial balance to ensure that your work is accurate.

---

7. The Crown Repair Shop, owned by Wes Soo, is a business that has been in operation for several years in Moose Jaw, Sask. The trial balance of the business on March 31, 19-- is as follows.

CROWN REPAIR SHOP
TRIAL BALANCE
MARCH 31, 19--

		Debits	Credits
1	Bank	$273.60	
2 - 1	Account Receivable — J. Wernik	47.20	
2 - 2	Account Receivable — Amber Bros.	16.80	
3	Supplies	2 000.00	
4	Machinery	7 500.00	
5	Truck	8 068.00	
6	Office Furniture and Equipment	4 900.00	
20 - 1	Account Payable — Parker's Serv. St.		$27.60
20 - 2	Account Payable — Harold's Hardware		563.65
20 - 3	Account Payable — Regal Supply		729.56
30	W. Soo, Capital		21 484.79
		$24 805.60	$24 805.60

The accounts of Crown Repair Shop are set up in the workbook. (Two workbook accounts are required for Bank.)

1. Journalize and post the transactions below, beginning on page 32 of the journal.

Transactions

April

1 Received a cheque for $1 500 from the owner to increase the cash position of the business.

2 Received a cheque in the mail from J. Wernik in full payment of his account balance.

3 Issued a cheque to Parker's Service Station in full payment of the account balance.

4 Received in the mail a cheque for $25 from Amber Bros. on account.

4 Issued a cheque to Amber Bros. to pay them for the amount that they overpaid in the previous transaction.

5 Received an invoice from Regal Supply in regard to the purchase of $800 $100 of supplies on account.

8 Received an invoice from Peerless Machinery in regard to the purchase of new machinery for $246 on account.

9 Issued a cheque in the amount of $400 to Harold's Hardware on account.

9 Received a cheque for $35 along with a memo from the owner stating that a piece of office equipment had been sold. The equipment had originally cost $50 and was included in the Office Equipment and Furniture figure at that price. The equipment was sold for $35.

10 Issued a cheque to Regal Supply paying their account in full.

10 Purchased a filing cabinet for $170. As this was a cash sale a cheque for the full amount was issued to the supplier who provided a bill of sale for the cabinet.

11 Issued a cheque for $100 to Harold's Hardware on account.

15 Issued a cheque for $200 to the owner for his personal use.

15 Issued a cheque to Harold's Hardware for the full balance of the account.

2. Balance the ledger.

Opening Entry, Journalizing, Posting, and Balancing

8. The Northtown Gardening Service, owned by Carole Harlow, begins business on February 1, 19-- with the following financial position.

NORTHTOWN GARDENING SERVICE
BALANCE SHEET
FEBRUARY 1, 19--

Assets		*Liabilities*	
Bank	$ 2 650.20	Acc. Pay'l — Holland Bulbs	$ 1 150.00
Acc. Rec'l — F. Trottier	165.00	— Baxter Chemical	164.91
— C. Parlee	174.00		$ 1 314.91
— M. Rogers	316.00		
Supplies	2 116.50	*Owner's Equity*	
Equipment	4 967.20	Carole Harlow, Capital	9 073.99
	$10 388.90		$10 388.90

1. Journalize and post the opening entry. One workbook account is required for each account. Number the accounts in the usual way.

2. Journalize and post the transactions that appear below. You will start on journal page 1.

Transactions

February

1 Received a cheque on account from M. Rogers, $200.

2 Issued a cheque on account to Holland Bulbs, $700.

4 Issued a cheque to the owner for her personal use, $75.

5 Issued a bill of sale for $32 to G. Easter for a gardening service. Mr. Easter paid cash.

7 Issued a sales invoice to F. Trottier in the amount of $56 for a gardening service that was performed on account.

9 Received an invoice from Baxter Chemical in regard to the purchase of $300 of chemical fertilizer.

12 Issued a cheque to Baxter Chemical paying their account in full.

15 Received a cheque from M. Rogers in full payment of his account.

3. Take off a trial balance and check the accuracy of your work.

The Effect of Errors on the Trial Balance

9. Workbook Exercise: The effect of errors on the trial balance.

10. Workbook Exercise: Locating errors in a completed journal, a ledger, and a trial balance.

Using Your Knowledge

11. An accounting clerk has prepared his trial balance as of June 30, 19--, and determines that total debits equal total credits. He breathes a sigh of relief and informs his boss that his ledger is in balance and that therefore the accounts are correct. His boss, a chartered accountant, tells him that this is not necessarily the case. She asks him to prepare a list of all the possible errors that could occur and yet not cause the trial balance to be out of balance.

Prepare this list as if you were the accounting clerk.

12. An employee working on his first trial balance discovers that the Furniture and Equipment account has a credit balance of $5 000 and a customer's account has a credit balance of $200. Has the accountant made a mistake in his records or is this situation possible? Explain.

13. You have been employed by Wilson Building Supplies as an accounting clerk. Your main duty is to record journal entries daily and post to the general ledger. Your procedure in posting is to post the entries by account

order. For example, you first go through all your journal entries and post all Bank entries. You then proceed to the second account, and so on. Explain the advantage of this method.

14. Dean Perry posts from the journal to the ledger at the end of each week. Because he prepares a balance sheet once a year, he believes it is necessary to prepare a trial balance only once a year. What are the disadvantages of taking a trial balance only once a year?

Cases

Case 1 *Is Bank Accounting Different?*

Accounting is one of Susan Lott's favourite subjects at school. She often talks at the dinner table about what she has learned in class that day. Susan's brother Ed has no formal accounting training, but is a junior clerk at a bank and is involved in bank accounting. One evening, Ed questions Susan's explanation of debit and credit theory. Ed claims that a customer's bank account is increased by means of a credit and decreased by means of a debit, and he produces a bank statement to prove it. Susan admits that her brother is right, and next day Susan brings the issue up at her accounting class. As she suspected, her accounting teacher has a logical explanation.

Questions

1. Write out a brief explanation of this issue as if you were the teacher.

Case 2 *Does Automated Accounting Use Standard Theory?*

Andy, another relative of Susan Lott, works as a clerk in the data processing and computer centre of a large corporation in Montreal. He claims that accounting is no longer done as Susan is learning it. Susan has now spent several months studying Accounting. She is upset at Andy's suggestion that she is learning outmoded techniques.

Questions

1. Is there a different theory of accounting when it's computerized?
2. What kinds of businesses would still use handwritten records?
3. Even though accounting systems may use different journals and ledgers, do they use different theories of accounting?

Career
Jane Clarke / Office Manager

Jane Clarke did not find it easy to return to the work force after an absence of fifteen years. As we saw in Chapter 6, Jane had left work to raise a family. Fifteen years later, she found herself with little experience and few of the skills recognized in the modern business world.

Jane worked at a series of low-level clerical jobs. She found that in order to advance she would have to increase her knowledge of bookkeeping. After twenty years out of school, Jane enrolled in a night school program and received her first formal training in accounting. She did well in the courses and earned two accounting credits.

Soon after completing her program, Jane became a junior bookkeeper for Jacobi Television, a small chain of television and radio stores. Jane quickly impressed her employer with her maturity, responsibility and initiative. She was promoted to office manager for the company, a position she continues to hold.

As office manager, Jane supervises all office and clerical staff and acts as a liaison between employees and management. She advises the owner on financial matters and employee relations. She also performs a number of specific accounting functions.

Some of Jane's duties are related to accounts receivable. She keeps track of customers' accounts and sends monthly statements to customers. Jane also works with accounts payable. She makes sure that purchase invoices do not charge for goods that were never asked for or received. She approves purchase invoices for payment, and determines the accounts to be debited on these invoices, such as Supplies or Office Equipment.

As Jacobi Television's office manager, Jane has complete control over the general journal and the postings to the general ledger. She examines and records all business transactions in both the journal and the ledger. Each month she uses an adding machine to take off a trial balance of the ledger.

Finally, Jane handles a number of banking duties. She approves cheques for deposit, endorses cheques, and reconciles the bank statement each month.

Jane is delighted with her accounting career. She finds the variety stimulating and enjoys the responsibility. Jane feels that she has embarked on a second life, and looks forward with ever-increasing confidence to future success as an accountant.

8

The Income Statement

8-1 The Income Statement
8-2 The Income Statement Put to Use
8-3 The Fiscal Period
8-4 Expanding the Ledger
8-5 Chart of Accounts
8-6 Debit and Credit in the Expanded Ledger
8-7 Trial Balance Procedure Unchanged
8-8 Trial Balance Out of Balance

Objectives

When you have completed Chapter 8 you should:

1. Know the elements of net income.
2. Be able to prepare a basic income statement in good form.
3. Understand the difference between net income and net loss.
4. Understand the importance of the income statement to owners and managers.
5. Be able to make simple analyses and comparisons from income statement data.
6. Understand why net income has to be considered in relation to a period of time.
7. Understand that the data from the income statement is accumulated in special accounts in the equity section of the ledger.
8. Be able to define revenue, expense, and drawings.
9. Understand that the balance in the Capital account is normally the balance at the beginning of the accounting period.

10. Be able to journalize transactions that affect revenue, expense, and drawings.
11. Be able to prepare a chart of accounts.
12. Understand thoroughly the rules of debit and credit.
13. Know the normal types of balance for any account.
14. Know the five-step process for locating errors to be followed when the trial balance doesn't balance.
15. Know the four short-cut techniques for locating errors.

At this point in our work we will study the income statement and the expanded ledger. We will also examine the rules of debit and credit in their final form.

8.1 The Income Statement

The **income statement** is a very important financial statement. It provides the information that tells the owners and managers whether or not their business is making a profit. The income statement is a financial statement that summarizes the items of revenue and expense, and shows the net income or net loss of a business.

Net income results when revenues are greater than expenses. **Net loss** results when expenses are greater than revenues. Facts about the preparation and use of the income statement are given in Figures 8.1 and 8.2.

Source of Data for the Income Statement

The data for the income statement come from the ledger, but not the ledger exactly as you know it. The data are taken from a ledger that is enlarged in a special way to provide the necessary information. This new ledger has an expanded equity section.

Revenue and Expense Related to Equity

Look at the income statement of Cherub Air Service in Figure 8.1. You can see that net income is arrived at by deducting total expenses from total revenue. 'Expense' and 'revenue' are new words for processes that you are already familiar with. For example, when a payment was made, say to repair an automobile, an expense was incurred, and to record it you debited Equity and credited Bank. Or, when a service was performed for a customer for cash, revenue was earned, and to record it you debited Bank and credited Equity. Always remember that revenues and expenses cause increases and decreases in equity.

Cherub Air Service
Income Statement
Year Ended December 31, 19--

Revenue		
Charter Flights		$174 327.02
Flying Lessons		28 604.05
	Total Revenue	$202 931.07
Expenses		
Advertising		$ 500.00
Bank Interest and Charges		756.20
Building Maintenance		1 102.40
Depreciation - Aircraft		46 702.10
Depreciation - Equipment		3 071.64
Depreciation - Truck		2 042.19
Gasoline and Oil		35 962.12
Insurance		1 746.02
Light, Heat, and Water		2 017.00
Miscellaneous Expense		300.02
Rent		12 000.00
Repairs on Aircraft		15 072.16
Telephone		416.75
Wages		40 764.71
	Total Expense	$163 958.91
Net Income		$38 972.16

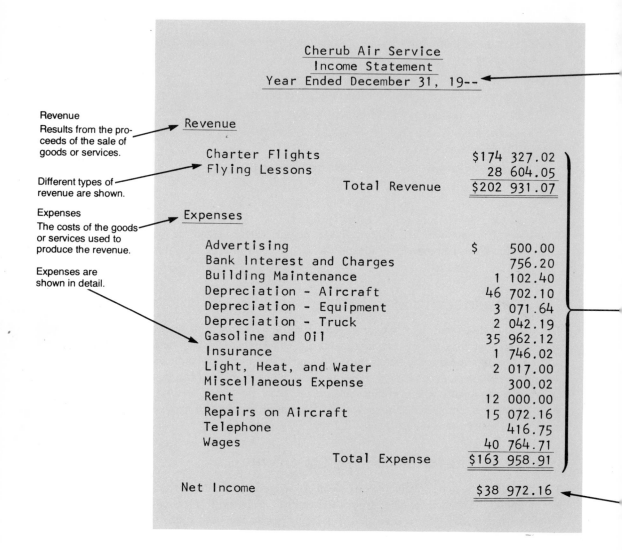

Revenue
Results from the proceeds of the sale of goods or services.

Different types of revenue are shown.

Expenses
The costs of the goods or services used to produce the revenue.

Expenses are shown in detail.

Figure 8.1 Income statement facts and preparation. This income statement is for a **service business**, one that sells a service but not goods.

The heading tells:
1. Name of business;
2. Name of statement;
3. Accounting period for which the figures have been accumulated.

This is the way to arrange the figures if only one column is used.

Net Income is also known as Net Profit or Net Earnings.

Net Income

	Total Revenue:	$202 931.07
minus	Total Expenses:	$163 958.91
equals	Net Income:	$ 38 972.16

Net income is not cash.

Net Loss results if the total revenue is less than the total expenses.

Master Trading Company
Income Statement
Year Ended June 30, 19--

Revenue		
Sales		$201 967
Cost of Goods Sold		117 381
Gross Profit		$ 84 586
Operating Expenses		
Advertising	$ 3 750	
Bank Charges	915	
Building Maintenance	1 219	
Depreciation of Building	5 037	
Depreciation of Equipment	1 432	
Depreciation of Automobiles	12 376	
Gasoline and Oil	11 064	
Insurance	1 942	
Licences	415	
Light, Heat, and Water	2 072	
Miscellaneous Expense	216	
Taxes	1 800	
Telephone	904	
Wages	26 372	
Total Operating Expenses		69 514
Net Income		$ 15 072

This is the way to arrange the figures if more than one column is used.

This net income figure is low. Management will be concerned with this low figure.

Figure 8.2 Income statement for a trading company. A **trading business** buys goods from wholesalers and manufacturers and sells them to the consumer.

8.2 The Income Statement Put To Use

Profitability

The income statement is an extremely useful tool. It tells the owners or managers whether their business is being run profitably. An analysis of the income statement also gives these people a great deal of useful information to guide them in their decision-making and help them form company policies.

A business will not survive for long if it does not produce a profit. **Gross profit** is the difference between the selling price of the goods sold by a trading business and the cost price of those goods. A business with a low gross profit figure may be setting its selling prices too low, paying too much for its goods, or not selling enough goods.

The owners and managers can use the income statement to compare the figures for the current year with those of the prior year (or years). This comparison helps them uncover unfavourable trends or problems that can be corrected. Management can make other mathematical comparisons to better guide the business in the future.

Income Tax

Every business is required by law to prepare an income statement once each year and to send it, along with an income tax return, to the government.

Income tax law states that the net income of a proprietorship is regarded as being earned by the owner on the last day of the annual fiscal period.

8.3 The Fiscal Period

Now that we are studying the income and expense accounts, it is time to introduce another new concept in accounting. Income and expenses must be measured in relation to a certain period of time.

The earnings figure of a business is meaningless unless it corresponds to a given length of time. If you were told that the net income of a business was $2 000, you would not be very well informed unless you also knew the length of time taken to earn this amount. If it took a period of one year, you would not be very favorably impressed. But if the $2 000 were earned in only one week, you would probably be very impressed indeed. The period of time over which earnings are measured is called the **fiscal period** or the **accounting period**, and sometimes the bookkeeping period.

In business today, the fiscal period is usually one year. This is hardly surprising. The year is a basic unit for the measurement of time. We pattern our lives around annual events, from birthdays to the filing of income taxes. However, the fiscal year does not have to be the same as the calendar year as long as it runs for 12 consecutive months. Half-yearly, quarterly, or monthly fiscal periods are quite common. Short fiscal periods allow owners and managers to keep more closely in touch with the progress of the business.

8.4 Expanding the Ledger

The ledgers that you have studied so far have only had a single account for capital. Any change in the equity of a business was recorded in this single account. Now you must become familiar with a system in which the ledger, instead of having a single account for capital, has a number of accounts in the equity section. The main purpose of the new accounts in the equity section of the ledger is to gather the information that is necessary for the preparation of the income statement. An illustration of an expanded ledger is shown in Figure 8.3.

After it is expanded, the equity section of the ledger must include the following accounts:

1. A capital account that is reserved for the beginning capital figure (plus any additional contributions from the owner).
2. One or more revenue accounts.
3. A number of expense accounts.
4. A drawings account.

Revenue

Revenue may be defined as increase in equity resulting from the proceeds of the sale of goods or services. For example, Eve Boa, a lawyer, draws up a legal agreement for a client and for her services is paid a fee of $75 cash. This transaction produces revenue.

This transaction has increased both Bank and Equity by the amount of $75. (If you need a review of the reasoning for changes in the equity, refer back to Chapter 4.) Previously, you would have debited Bank and credited E. Boa, Capital with the $75. But now, under the new and expanded system, you will debit Bank, as before, and credit an equity account which we shall call Fees Revenue. In general journal form, the entry is as follows:

Bank	$75.00	
Fees Revenue		$75.00

Remember that Fees Revenue represents an increase in equity. Since it has been shown earlier that an increase in equity requires a credit entry, it should come as no surprise to you that Fees Revenue will be accumulated in this account and it will have a credit balance.

Usually, a business has only one revenue account and it is given the appropriate name. A loan company, for example, which earns its revenue in the form of commissions, will very likely have a revenue account called Commissions Earned, or simply Commissions. Suitable names for the revenue accounts of other businesses might be Rental Revenue, Fees Earned, Royalties, and so on.

Assets

Bank #1	
439	

Acc Rec'l H. Gerousc #2-1	
1 420	

Acc Rec'l J. Magill #2-2	
57	

Acc Rec'l E. Parsons #2-3	
395	

Supplies #3	
316	

Office Equipment #4	
1 550	

Automobile #5	
6 800	

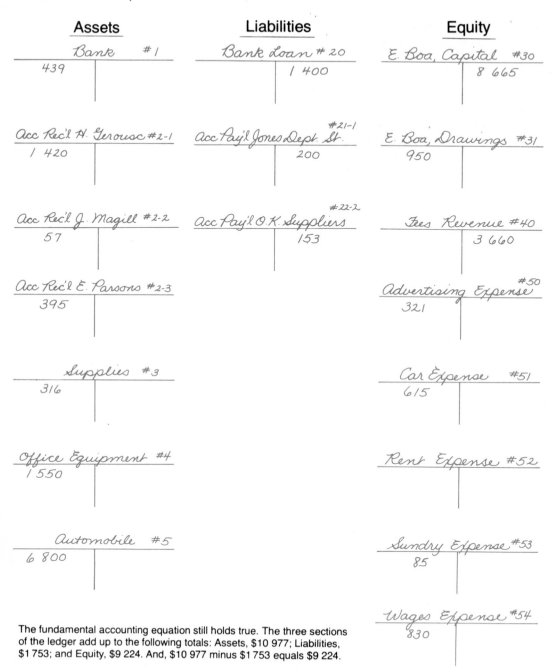

Liabilities

Bank Loan #20	
	1 400

Acc Pay'l Jones Dept. St. #21-1	
	200

Acc Pay'l O.K. Suppliers #22-2	
	153

Equity

E. Boa, Capital #30	
	8 665

E. Boa, Drawings #31	
950	

Fees Revenue #40	
	3 660

Advertising Expense #50	
321	

Car Expense #51	
615	

Rent Expense #52	

Sundry Expense #53	
85	

Wages Expense #54	
830	

The fundamental accounting equation still holds true. The three sections of the ledger add up to the following totals: Assets, $10 977; Liabilities, $1 753; and Equity, $9 224. And, $10 977 minus $1 753 equals $9 224.

Figure 8.3 Explanation of the expanded ledger of Eve Boa, a lawyer.

1. The Capital account shows the equity figure at the beginning of the fiscal period (plus any additional contributions from the owner, if any).

The new accounts in the equity section show changes in equity during the fiscal period.

2. A Revenue account shows an increase in equity resulting from the proceeds from the sale of goods or services. A revenue account is a credit account because it represents an increase in equity. There may be more than one revenue account.
3. An Expense account shows a decrease in equity resulting from the costs of materials or services used to produce the revenue. An expense account is a debit account because it represents a decrease in equity. There will be a number of expense accounts, arranged alphabetically.
4. The Drawings account shows a decrease in equity resulting from owner withdrawals. The Drawings account is a debit account because it represents a decrease in equity. Drawings has nothing to do with calculating net income or net loss.

Expense

An **expense** may be defined as a decrease in equity resulting from the costs of the materials or services used to produce the revenue. For example, Eve Boa must pay her secretary a regular weekly wage of $250 cash. She therefore incurs an expense of $250.

This transaction requires that both Bank and equity be decreased by $250. The decrease to Bank is handled in the usual way, as a credit to that account. But the decrease to equity is now to be debited to a new account called Wages Expense. In general journal form, the entry is as follows:

Wages Expense	$250	
Bank		$250

Keep in mind that Wages Expense represents a decrease in equity and as such requires a debit entry. It follows logically, therefore, that the Wages Expense account, or any expense account for that matter, will normally receive debit entries.

All Wages Expense will be accumulated in the one account. This account will have a debit balance.

There are many other transactions that involve expenses. For example, assume that Eve Boa receives the monthly furnace oil bill for $95 from Municipal Oil but does not pay the bill immediately. To record this transaction, it is necessary to decrease equity and to set up a liability to Municipal Oil. According to the rule just established, the accounting entry is as follows:

Heat Expense	$95	
Acc. Payl. — Municipal Oil		$95

In any business, there are usually several expense accounts, each one representing a reduction in equity of a specific type. The name of the account should suggest the nature of the expense. Other typical expense accounts are called by such names as Rent Expense, Delivery Expense, Insurance Expense, Bank Charges, Postage, and Property Taxes. Notice that the word 'expense' is not always included as part of the account title.

With experience you will come to know the usual names for these expense accounts.

Drawings

Drawings may be defined as a decrease in equity resulting from a personal withdrawal of the owner. The Drawings account may be thought of as the owner's personal withdrawal account. The decreases in equity entered in the Drawings account are *not* expenses of the business and are, therefore, considered to be the personal responsibility of the owner. Such decreases are debited or charged to the owner through the Drawings account.

The Drawings account is most commonly affected when the owner withdraws funds from the business for personal use. For example, assume that Eve Boa, the owner of the business, withdraws $125 cash to take care of personal expenses.

This transaction requires that both Bank and equity be decreased by $125. The decrease to Bank is handled in the usual way, as a credit to that account. But the decrease to equity, not being an expense, must be charged to the owner's Drawings account. The correct accounting entry to record the transactions is as follows:

E. Boa, Drawings	$125	
Bank		$125

All entries affecting Drawings follow the rules of debit and credit with which you are familiar. Drawings represent a decrease in equity, and decreases in equity require debit entries. Therefore, the Drawings account normally receives debit entries. All drawings must be gathered in this one account and will have a debit balance.

The Drawings account is also affected when the owner buys something for personal use but has the business pay for it. The owner may wish to take advantage of a special price that is offered to businesses but not to individuals. Or, this form of payment may be more convenient. In any event, when recording the transaction, the debit must be to Drawings and the credit must be either to Cash or to a creditor's account, depending on whether the item is paid for in cash.

For example, assume that Eve Boa purchases a new coffee-maker through the business. A bill for this coffee-maker in the amount of $85 arrives from Baystore. The $85 is not an expense of the business, but must be charged to Ms. Boa. The accounting entry to record this bill will be as follows:

E. Boa, Drawings	$85	
Accounts Payable — Baystore		$85
Coffee-maker for owner		

The Drawings account is also affected when the owner takes assets other than cash permanently out of the business for personal use. For example, the owner may take a spare office typewriter home for family use. If the typewriter is to be kept permanently at home, its value, as recorded in the books, must be charged to the owner's Drawings account. The correct accounting entry will be one that debits Drawings and credits Office Equipment.

For example, assume that Eve Boa purchased four paintings at $100 each for the office. The paintings are paid for and debited to Office Expense. Within a month, Eve decides that the wall has a crowded appearance and that one painting should be taken down. Eve decides to take one of the paintings home. Proper accounting requires that she be charged $100 for the painting. The accounting entry to record this is as follows:

E. Boa, Drawings	$100	
Office Expense		$100

Observe that the Office Expense account is reduced by $100.

8.5 Chart of Accounts

A **chart of accounts** is simply a list of the ledger accounts and their numbers all arranged in ledger order. Most businesses, except very small ones, have copies of their chart of accounts available for use of their own office staff, particularly new employees, and for auditors. The chart of accounts of E. Boa is shown in Figure 8.4. It is taken from the ledger in Figure 8.3.

The chart of accounts in Figure 8.4 uses the account numbers that have been adopted in this text for the expanded system. This numbering system is summarized below:

Assets	Nos. 1 to 19
Liabilities	Nos. 20 to 29
Capital	No. 30
Drawings	No. 31
Revenues	Nos. 40 to 49
Expenses	Nos. 50 on

E. BOA
CHART OF ACCOUNTS

Assets		*Equity*	
Bank	1	E. Boa, Capital	30
Accounts Receivable		E. Boa, Drawings	31
H. Geroux	2 - 1	Fees Revenue	40
J. Magill	2 - 2	Advertising Expense	50
E. Parsons	2 - 3	Car Expense	51
Supplies	3	Rent Expense	52
Office Equipment	4	Sundry Expense	53
Automobile	5	Wages Expense	54
Liabilities			
Bank Loan	20		
Accounts Payable			
Jones Dep't Store	21 - 1		
O. K. Suppliers	21 - 2		

Figure 8.4 E. Boa, chart of accounts.

8.6 Debit and Credit in the Expanded Ledger

When expanding the ledger, we also need to expand the chart of accounts to show the rules of debit and credit. The final summary is shown in Figure 8.5.

Debit and Credit Balances

An accountant needs to understand thoroughly the account balances in a ledger. At this stage it is not very difficult to tell whether an account is an asset or an expense, a liability or income. But it will not always be simple.

Remember these rules:

1. The accounts with debit balances are Assets, Expenses, and Drawings.
2. The accounts with credit balances are Liabilities, Capital, and Revenue.

a.

ACCOUNT	TO INCREASE	TO DECREASE
Assets	Debit	Credit
Liabilities	Credit	Debit
Equity Capital	Credit	Debit
Income	Credit	Debit
Expense	Debit	Credit
Drawings	Debit	Credit

b.

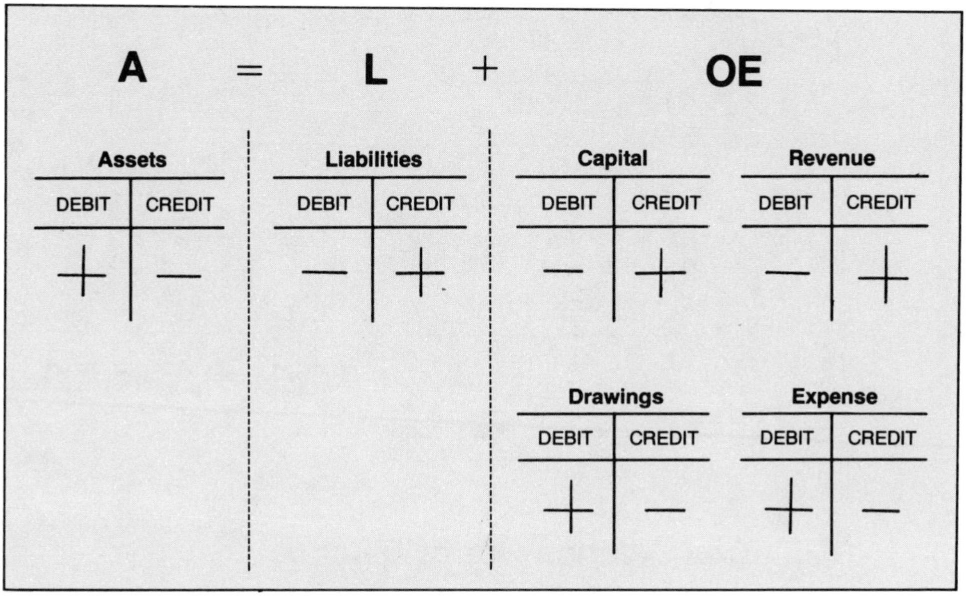

Figure 8.5 Summary of the rules of debit and credit (a.). A popular alternative method of showing these rules is by means of T-accounts (b.).

8.7 Trial Balance Procedure Unchanged

The new types of account do not change the trial balance procedure. You simply total the accounts with debit balances, total the accounts with credit balances, and see that the two totals agree. This is illustrated in Figure 8.6 with the trial balance of E. Boa's ledger (Figure 8.3).

E. Boa
Trial Balance
. . . date . . .

No.	Account	Debit	Credit
1	Bank	439 -	
	Accounts Recievable		
2-1	H. Giroux	1420 -	
2-2	J. Magill	57 -	
2-3	E. Parsons	395 -	
3	Supplies	316 -	
4	Office Equipment	1550 -	
5	Automobile	6800 -	
20	Bank Loan		1400 -
	Accounts Payable		
21-1	Jones Dep't Store		200 -
	O.K. Suppliers		153 -
30	E. Boa, Capital		8665 -
31	E. Boa, Drawings	950 -	
40	Fees Revenue		3660 -
50	Advertising Expense	321 -	
51	Car Expense	615 -	
52	Rent Expense	300 -	
53	Sundry Expense	85 -	
54	Wages Expense	830 -	
		14078 -	14078 -

Figure 8.6 Trial balance of E. Boa's ledger.

8.8 Trial Balance Out of Balance

Sometimes the trial balance does not balance. A trial balance out of balance indicates that one or more errors have been made in the journal, ledger, or trial balance. It is your responsibility as accountant to find and correct these errors.

Skill in finding errors is a real asset to an accountant. Ledgers are often out of balance. In more complex businesses, the trial balance is rarely found to be in balance after the first attempt. Even in your relatively simple classroom exercises, you will find that the trial balance frequently does not balance.

Some errors are very elusive and can be found only by a persistent and expertly conducted search. Without the skill to conduct this search properly, an accountant is unlikely to succeed in business. If you follow the steps below each time a trial balance does not balance, you can acquire skill in detecting errors. These steps are illustrated in Figure 8.7.

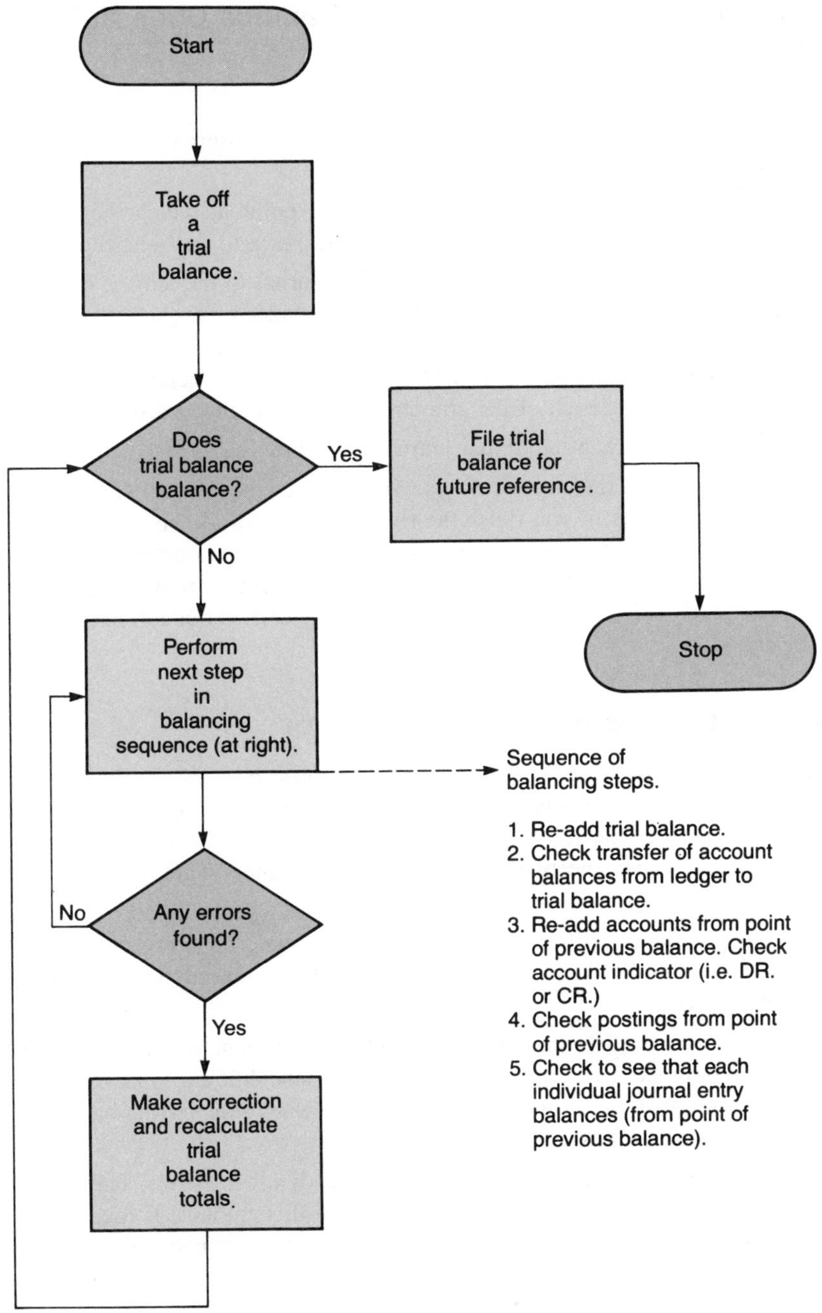

Figure 8.7 Flowchart of the procedure for balancing the general ledger.

Steps To Be Followed When Trial Balance Does Not Balance

1. Re-add the trial balance columns.
2. Check how accurately the account balances were transferred from the ledger to the trial balance.
3. Re-add the account balances beginning at the point at which the ledger was previously balanced. Ensure that the Dr. or Cr. prefix to the balance is correct.
4. Check the accuracy of the postings from the journal to the ledger, beginning at the point at which the ledger was previously balanced. In particular, watch for incorrect amounts, amounts not posted, amounts posted twice, and amounts posted in the wrong column. In performing step 4, it is generally necessary to make a mark beside each of the amounts as they are checked off.
5. Check to see that each individual journal entry is in balance.

On many occasions the error or errors will be detected before all steps are carried out. On the other hand, if you finish the five steps and still do not balance, it is not possible that the five steps were carried out properly. In this unhappy situation, it will be necessary for you to go through the sequence again, remembering to work with greater care. It is a certainty that if the steps are carried out correctly, the errors will be found.

Short Cuts in Detecting a Single Error

It takes a lot of time to go through the routine described above. So experienced accountants try to avoid this task whenever they can. If only one error has occurred, the error can often be located quickly by means of a few short tests. First, determine the difference between the two totals of the trial balance. Then apply any of the following tests:

1. If the trial balance difference is 1¢, 10¢, $1, etc., an error in addition has probably been made. Therefore, steps 1 and 3 of the correction routine should be performed first.
2. Examine both the ledger and the journal to find an amount that is equal to the trial balance difference. Each time that you find one, check it out to make sure that it is not an item that was omitted when posting or when transferring balances from the accounts to the trial balance.
3. If the trial balance difference is an even amount, divide it by two. Then search (a) the trial balance, and (b) the ledger accounts for this amount. If found, check to see if a debit amount has been placed in a credit column by mistake, or vice versa. An error of this type always produces a trial balance difference equal to twice the amount of the error.

   For example, consider the simplified trial balance shown below. It contains a single error. The $30 item listed as a credit should have been listed as a debit.

TRIAL BALANCE

110		
40		
	30	← Error
	55	
	200	
50		
25		
225	285	

Trial balance difference $60

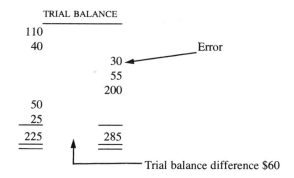

Notice that the difference between the totals is $60, twice the amount of the error. Whenever any amount is posted to the wrong side of the ledger, or transferred to the wrong side of the trial balance, a trial balance difference of twice the amount of the error will be produced.

4. Divide the trial balance difference by 9. If it divides evenly, a **transposition error** has likely occurred. A transposition error occurs when, for example, $35.60 is posted as $36.50, or when $1 200 is transferred as $120. Such errors always produce a trial balance difference that is exactly divisible by 9. When this happens, steps 2 and 4 of the checking sequence should be performed first.

Accounting Terms

income statement	**revenue**
net income	**expense**
net loss	**drawings**
gross profit	**chart of accounts**
fiscal period	**transposition error**
accounting period	

Review Questions

1. Give a general description of the income statement.
2. Define net income and net loss.
3. Explain the difference between a service business and a trading business.
4. What is the source of the data for the income statement?
5. Give the two basic reasons for preparing the income statement.

6. Describe the ways in which management uses the data on an income statement.
7. What is the fiscal period?
8. Besides the name of the statement, how is the heading of the income statement different from that of the balance sheet?
9. Name the four types of account that are found in the equity section of the ledger.
10. What do revenues, expenses, and drawings all have in common?
11. Explain the difference between revenues, expenses, and drawings.
12. Which accounts in the equity section of the ledger affect net income?
13. What does the balance in the capital account represent?
14. Give three examples of transactions that affect the drawings account.
15. What is a chart of accounts? Who uses a chart of accounts?
16. Describe the numbering system presently used in this text.
17. What types of balance are usually found in the following: an asset account; a liability account; the capital account; the drawings account; the revenue account; an expense account?
18. Draw a chart summarizing debit and credit theory in its final form.
19. List the five-step procedure to be followed when looking for errors in the books.
20. Why is skill in locating errors an advantage to the accountant?
21. Is it always necessary to carry out the five steps? Explain.
22. Briefly describe the four shortcuts in locating errors.
23. What is a transposition error?
24. If a credit item for $265 in the general journal is posted in error as a debit, by how much will the trial balance be out of balance? How might you detect such an error?
25. If the trial balance difference is $63, what type of error would you suspect?
26. If the trial balance difference is $10, what type of error would you suspect?

Exercises

Income Statement Preparation

1. From the following information for the month ended November 30, 19--, prepare an income statement for Atlas Associates. Use two money columns.

Fees Earned, $8 000; Salaries Expense, $600; Rent Expense, $750; General Expense, $185; Advertising Expense, $120; Car Expense, $158; Light and Heat Expense, $40.

2. From the following trial balance prepare an income statement for Booreman Enterprises after a six month period ended June 30, 19--. Use the single money column form.

BOOREMAN ENTERPRISES
TRIAL BALANCE
JUNE 30, 19--

1	Bank	$ 1 605	
2	Accounts Receivable	7 219	
3	Supplies	1 590	
4	Equipment	9 215	
5	Automobiles	16 498	
20	Bank Loan		$10 000
21	Accounts Payable		4 263
30	C. Booreman, Capital		11 538
31	C. Booreman, Drawings	15 000	
40	Revenue from Fees		65 702
50	Bank Charges	315	
51	Car Expenses	9 072	
52	Light, Heat, and Water	2 415	
53	Miscellaneous Expense	407	
54	Rent Expense	3 600	
55	Telephone	495	
56	Wages	24 072	
		$91 503	$91 503

3. Using the two-column form, prepare an income statement for Empire Trading Company for the month ended February 28, 19--.

EMPIRE TRADING COMPANY
TRIAL BALANCE
FEBRUARY 28, 19--

1	Bank	$ 505	
2	Accounts Receivable	9 219	
3	Merchandise	10 402	
4	Supplies	915	
5	Equipment	7 212	
6	Automotive Equipment	14 306	
20	Accounts Payable		$19 072
30	Frank Kappa, Capital		29 017
31	Frank Kappa, Drawings	1 340	
40	Sales		35 303
50	Cost of Goods Sold	27 062	
51	Car Expense	3 749	
52	Miscellaneous Expense	116	
53	Rent Expense	1 200	
54	Telephone Expense	76	
55	Utilities Expense	215	
56	Wages	7 075	
		$83 392	$83 392

Journalizing Transactions Involving Revenue, Expense, and Drawings

4. Eric Steele is in business for himself as a groundskeeper and gardener in Hamilton, Ont. He cuts grass, weeds gardens, and trims trees and shrubs for a number of customers on a regular basis.

The following accounts are in Eric Steele's ledger:

1	Bank	21-2	Account Payable — Pesticide Products
2-1	Account Receivable — G. Hung	21-3	Account Payable — Pro Hardware
2-2	Account Receivable — F. Sawchuk	30	E. Steele, Capital
2-3	Account Receivable — W. Scott	31	E. Steele, Drawings
3	Equipment	40	Revenue
4	Chemical Supplies	50	Advertising Expense
5	Truck	51	Miscellaneous Expense
20	Bank Loan	52	Telephone Expense
21-1	Account Payable — Banner News	53	Truck Expense

Journalize the following selected transactions for E. J. Steele.

Transactions

July

2 Received an invoice from Pesticide Products regarding the purchase of $97.90 worth of insecticide on account.

5 Received an invoice from Pro Hardware for $95 for the purchase of a new ladder on account.

6 Issued a cheque for $129 to W. Decorte for part-time wages.

10 Received $50 from a customer for services performed for cash. A cash sales slip was issued to the customer.

13 Issued a sales invoice to G. Hung for $100 for services rendered on account.

13 Received an invoice from the Banner News regarding a $15 advertisement placed in the newspaper on account.

16 Received a memo from E. J. Steele, the owner, stating that he had received $70 from a cash customer. The money was not put in the bank as usual but was kept by Mr. Steele and put into his pocket. Mr. Steele paid $15 of this money for gasoline for the truck and kept the rest for his personal use. A cash sales slip had been issued to the customer.

19 Received a notice from the bank stating that $56.20 had been taken by them from the business's bank account to pay for interest charges on the bank loan.

5. Journalize the following selected transactions of Alison Morphy, a self-employed photographer. Select from the accounts listed below.

1	Bank
2-1	Account Receivable — D. Khan
2-2	Account Receivable — W. Leroux
2-3	Account Receivable — R. Parke
3	Office Supplies
4	Photographic Supplies
5	Equipment
6	Automobile
20-1	Account Payable—Master Chemical Co.
20-2	Account Payable—Saddler Photo Service
30	A. Morphy, Capital
31	A. Morphy, Drawings
40	Revenue
50	Car Expense
51	Miscellaneous Expense
52	Rent Expense
53	Wages Expense

Transactions

June

5 Received $35 cash from M. Tyler who came to the studio for passport photos. A cash sales slip was issued.

9 Issued a cheque for $74 to Prince Motors for repairs to the car.

12 Issued a cheque for $300 to Milrig Investments for the rent for the month.

17 Issued an invoice for $250 to Ross Parke for wedding photos taken on account.

20 Received an invoice from Master Chemical Co. regarding the purchase of $164.50 of photographic supplies on account.

25 Issued a cheque for $24.75 for the monthly telephone bill, paid by cash.

25 Issued a cheque to the owner for $175 for her personal use.

27 Issued a cheque for $355 to West End Garage. The payment was as directed by the owner for the repairs to the owner's husband's car.

Short-Cut Techniques for Locating Errors

6. The four mini-exercises below will give you practice at using the short-cut techniques for locating errors when a trial balance doesn't balance. Each exercise has one error in it which you are to find. For each mini-exercise, go through the sequence of steps outlined below. Once you locate the error you need not continue with the subsequent steps.

Short-cut Steps to Locating an Error

a. Write down the trial balance difference.

b. Is it a round amount like $1, or $10, or $100? If no, go to step c. If yes, then re-add the trial balance and re-add the accounts in the ledger.

c. Search the journal, ledger, and trial balance for an entry equal to the trial balance difference. Check any such entries to ensure that a posting was not missed or posted twice, or an account balance was not missed or listed twice.

d. Does the trial balance difference figure divide evenly by 9? If no, go to step e. If yes, check for a transposition error in transferring account balances onto the trial balance or in posting from the journal to the ledger.

e. Is the trial balance difference an even amount? If yes, divide the amount by two and write down the result. Then, search the records for this amount. Check any entry for this amount to ensure that the entry was not posted to the wrong side of an account, or an account balance was not listed on the wrong side of the trial balance.

1. Why doesn't it balance?

JOURNAL

PARTICULARS	DR	CR
Bank	4500	
Equipment	3600	
Capital		8100
Supplies	73	
Accounts Payable		73
Expense	47	
Bank		47
Bank	195	
Revenue		195
Drawings	100	
Bank		100
Accounts Receivable	63	
Revenue		63
Supplies	38	
Bank		38

LEDGER

Bank	
4 500	47
195	100
	38
(4510) 4695	185

Accounts Receivable	
63	

Supplies	
73	
38	
111	

Equipment	
3600	

Accounts Payable	
	73

Capital	
	8100

Drawings	
100	

Revenue	
	159
	63
	222

Expense	
47	

TRIAL BALANCE

DR	CR
4510	73
63	8100
111	222
3 600	
100	
47	
8 431	8395

2. Why doesn't it balance?

JOURNAL

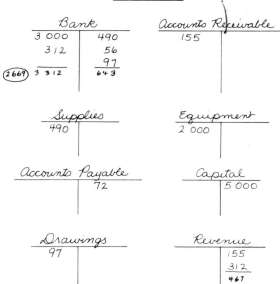

PARTICULARS	DR	CR
Bank	3 000	
Equipment	2 000	
Capital		5000
Supplies	490	
Bank		490
Accounts Receivable	155	
Revenue		155
Expense	56	
Bank		56
Expense	72	
Accounts Payable		72
Bank	312	
Revenue		312
Drawings	97	
Bank		97

LEDGER

Bank

Debit	Credit
3 000	490
312	56
	97
(2669) 3 312	643

Accounts Receivable

Debit	Credit
155	

Supplies

Debit	Credit
490	

Equipment

Debit	Credit
2 000	

Accounts Payable

Debit	Credit
	72

Capital

Debit	Credit
	5 000

Drawings

Debit	Credit
97	

Revenue

Debit	Credit
	155
	312
	467

Expense

Debit	Credit
56	

TRIAL BALANCE

DR	CR
2669	72
155	5000
490	467
2000	
97	
56	
5467	5539

3. Why doesn't it balance?

JOURNAL

PARTICULARS	DR	CR
Bank	2 500	
Equipment	7 000	
Capital		9 500
Accounts Receivable	371	
Revenue		371
Bank	269	
Revenue		269
Supplies	53	
Accounts Payable		53
Drawings	127	
Bank		127
Expense	86	
Bank		86
Expense	49	
Accounts Payable		49

LEDGER

Bank	
2 500	127
269	86
(2 556) 2 769	213

Accounts Receivable	
371	

Supplies	
53	

Equipment	
7000	

Accounts Payable	
	53
	49
	102

Capital	
	9 500

Drawings	
127	

Revenue	
	371
	269
	540

Expense	
86	
49	
135	

TRIAL BALANCE

DR	CR
2556	102
371	9500
53	540
7000	
127	
135	
10242	10142

4. Why doesn't it balance?

JOURNAL

PARTICULARS	DR	CR
Bank	4 000	
Equipment	3 000	
Capital		7 000
Supplies	216	
Accounts Payable		216
Accounts Receivable	321	
Revenue		321
Expense	73	
Bank		73
Expense	34	
Accounts Payable		34
Drawings	41	
Bank		41
Bank	150	
Accounts Receivable		150

LEDGER

Bank

4000	73
150	41
(4036) 4 150	114

Accounts Receivable

321	150
(171)	

Supplies

216	

Equipment

3000	

Accounts Payable

	216
	34
	250

Capital

	7000

Drawings

41	

Revenue

	321

Expense

73	
34	
107	

TRIAL BALANCE

DR	CR
4036	250
171	7000
216	41
3 000	321
107	
7530	7612

7. Workbook Exercise: Locate the errors in a given journal, ledger, and trial balance.

Journalizing, Posting, Balancing, and Income Statement

Note on the Handling of Supplies: It is common practice in accounting to allow certain accounts to become incorrect during the accounting period and to make them correct at the end of the accounting period. This is a technique used by accountants for convenience. The Supplies account is one account to which this shortcut technique is applied.

During the accounting period, make your accounting entries for supplies as follows:

1. Whenever supplies are purchased:
   Dr. Supplies
   Cr. Bank or the creditor } with the cost price of the supplies.
2. Whenever supplies are used in the business: Make no accounting entry.
   The effect of this step is to permit the Supplies account to become incorrect. The technique for updating this account at the end of the accounting period is explained in a later chapter.

8. The accounts required for this exercise are shown below. If you are not using the workbook for this text, allow 14 lines for Bank.

N. A. JAMES
CHART OF ACCOUNTS

1	Bank	30	N. A. James, Capital
2-1	Account Receivable — Jenkins and Co.	31	N. A. James, Drawings
3	Office Supplies	40	Fees Earned
4	Office Equipment	50	Advertising Expense
5	Automobile	51	Car Expense
20-1	Account Payable — Office Supply Company	52	Donations Expense
		53	Miscellaneous Expense
		54	Rent Expense

N. A. James, a public accountant, decided to begin a business of his own on October 1, 19--. At that time he invested in the business a bank balance of $2 497 and an automobile worth $5 000.

1. **Journalize and post the opening entry.**
2. **Journalize and post the following subsequent transactions for the month of October.**

Transactions

October

2 Purchased $165.55 of office supplies for cash. Issued a cheque in payment and received a bill of sale.

2 Issued a cheque for $375 in payment of the rent for October.

5 Issued a cheque for $25 for an advertisement in a local newspaper.

5 Received an invoice from Office Supply Company in regard to the purchase of a desk, a chair, and a filing cabinet at a total cost of $705 on account.

8 Mr. James was hired by a client, Jenkins and Co. At the conclusion of the work Mr. James charged Jenkins and Co. $370. A sales invoice was issued for this service on account.

9 Cash sales slips were made out for two transactions. B. Masters paid $55.00 in cash for a bookkeeping service. W. Shields paid $35.00 in cash for a tax return service. The total of $90 was deposited in the bank.

12 A cheque for $50 was sent as a donation to the Salvation Army.

12 Received a cheque for $100 from Jenkins and Co. on account.

13 Issued a cheque to the Office Supply Company in full payment of their account balance.

14 Paid Louis' Service Station $46.50 for gasoline and repair service on the business automobile. A cheque was issued and a bill from the service station was received.

16 Issued a cash sales slip to R. Andrews for a service performed and received $200 cash in full payment. The owner, N. A. James, did not deposit this money in the bank as usual but kept it for his own use.

19 Purchased $86.75 of office supplies from Woolworth's for cash. A cheque was issued and a bill received.

22 Issued a cheque for $18 for an advertisement in a local newspaper.

23 Issued a sales invoice for $600 to Jenkins and Co. for services performed on account.

26 Issued a cheque for $35 for postage stamps. (**Note:** Stamps are not considered to be supplies.)

27 Issued a cheque for $200 to the owner for his personal use.

3. Balance the ledger by means of a trial balance.

4. Prepare an income statement for the month of October.

---

9. The accounts required for this exercise are shown in the chart of accounts below. If you are not using the workbook for this exercise, allow 24 lines for Bank account.

GENERAL ENGINEERING
CHART OF ACCOUNTS

1	Bank	30	P. Schelling, Capital
2-1	Account Receivable W. J. Thomson	31	P. Schelling, Drawings
2-2	Account Receivable L. Pero	40	Service Revenue
3	Supplies	50	Bank Charges
4	Equipment	51	Loss on Sale of Equipment
5	Truck	52	Miscellaneous Expense
20	Bank Loan	53	Rent Expense
21-1	Account Payable Home Hardware	54	Telephone Expense
21-2	Account Payable Imperial Garage	55	Truck Expense
		56	Wages Expense

P. Schelling, a millwright, began a business called General Engineering. His beginning financial position was as follows.

GENERAL ENGINEERING
BALANCE SHEET
AUGUST 31, 19--

Assets		*Liabilities*	
Bank	$ 2 000.00	Bank Loan	$ 4 500.00
Supplies	450.00	*Owner's Equity*	
Equipment	1 732.50	P. Schelling, Capital	8 639.50
Truck	8 957.00		
	$13 139.50		$13 139.50

1. Journalize the opening entry and post it in the accounts.
2. Journalize and post the transactions for September shown below.

Transactions

September

1 Issued a cheque for $360 for the rent for the month of September.

3 Purchased supplies on account from Home Hardware; an invoice for $235 was received.

5 Issued sales invoices for $560 to W. J. Thomson and $500 to L. Pero for services performed on account.

9 Sold a piece of equipment for $150 cash. This piece of equipment had cost $200 and was included in the Equipment account at that figure. A cash sales slip was issued for the transaction. (**Note**: Although a sale has been made, this transaction does not affect the revenue account which is used only for the normal revenue of the business.)

10 Issued a cash sales slip for $180 to a customer for services performed for cash.

11 Issued a cheque for $200 to the owner for his personal use.

12 Issued a cheque for $135 to Home Hardware on account.

15 Received an invoice from Imperial Garage charging for gasoline and oil purchased on account; $142.

16 Purchased $65.45 of supplies for cash. A cheque was issued and a bill received.

18 Received a cheque from W. J. Thomson in full payment of his account balance.

18 Issued a cheque for $60 to the owner to repay him for out-of-pocket expenses: Postage, $15; Parking, $10; Gas and Oil, $35.

19 Received a memorandum from the bank stating that $52 had been deducted from the business bank account to pay for bank interest and bank charges.

19 Issued a cheque for $375 paying the wages of an employee.

19 Issued a cash sales slip for $600 to a customer for services rendered and cash received.

22 Received a memo from the owner stating that the bank had acted on his instructions to reduce the bank loan by $500.

24 Issued a cheque for $24 in payment of the telephone bill.

25 Received a cheque from L. Pero for $100 on account.

26 Issued a cash sales slip for $400 to a customer for services performed and cash received.

26 Issued a cheque for $150 to the owner for his personal use.

26 Issued a cheque to Home Hardware paying its account in full.

29 While on the job, the owner needed some additional supplies immediately and purchased them at a local store paying $19 cash from his personal funds. The owner wishes to credit the bill to his Drawings account.

30 Issued a cash sales slip for $750 to a customer for services performed and cash received.

30 Issued a cheque for $374 in payment of an employee's wages.

30 Received an invoice from Imperial Garage charging for gasoline and oil purchased on account; $112.

3. Balance the ledger by means of a trial balance.

4. Prepare an income statement for the month of September.

Using Your Knowledge

10. For each of the accounts listed, indicate whether it would normally have a debit or credit balance.

Supplies; Advertising Expense; A. Bryce, Drawings; G. Wright, a creditor; Rent Expense; Fees Earned; Bank Loan; W. Magill, a debtor; A. Bryce, Capital; Mortgage Payable.

11. Mrs. E. Foreman owns and operates a small florist shop in Gander, Nfld. She deposits all cash received in the bank and makes all payments by cheque. At the end of the last fiscal period, the Bank account showed a credit balance of $1 350 after all balances were found to be correct.

1. **Assuming no errors, how is it possible for the Bank, an asset account, to have a credit balance?**
2. **How should this item be shown on the balance sheet?**
3. **If, during the fiscal period, the revenues exceeded the expenses by $2 000 and the drawings amounted to $2 600, what is the net income figure for the period?**

12. The income statement of Bianco Company is shown below.

BIANCO COMPANY
INCOME STATEMENT
YEAR ENDED DECEMBER 31, 19--

Revenue		$47 416
Expenses		
Car Expense	$ 1 732	
Rent	3 500	
Utilities	1 075	
Wages	23 072	29 379
Net income		$18 037

Two errors were found in the books after the above statement was prepared:

a. A bill for $750 for automobile repairs had been incorrectly debited to automobiles.

b. $5 000 of owner's drawings had been incorrectly debited to Wages.

Prepare a corrected income statement.

13. The account balances in the ledger of Pamela Garside, a sculptress, are shown below in the T-accounts.

Account	Debit	Credit
Bank	1 745	
A.R.-P. Adler	50	
A.R.-A. Jackson	70	
Equipment	5 000	
Supplies	610	
Automobiles	7 900	
A.P.-Century Finance		5 500
A.P.-B.&B. Stone		110
P. Garside, Capital		10 150
P. Garside, Drawings	200	
Revenue		1 920
Car Expense	25	
Light, Heat, Water	280	
Rent	300	
Wages	1 500	

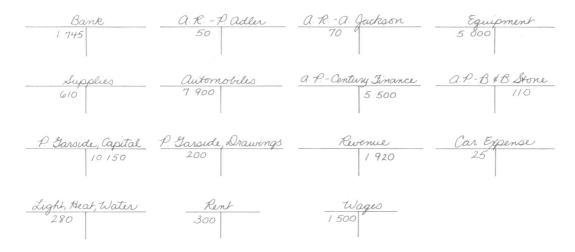

Pamela's auditor discovered the following errors when checking the records:

a. $150 of cash revenue was posted incorrectly to the Capital account.

b. $500 of the owner's drawings was posted incorrectly to the Wages account.

c. $400 of automobile expense was posted incorrectly to the Automobiles account.

d. $110 of equipment was incorrectly debited to Car Expense.

1. **Write out the accounting entries necessary to correct the above errors in the two-column general journal page in your workbook. Ignore dates and explanations.**
2. **The net income figure prior to the auditor's discoveries was determined to be $2 715. What will the corrected income figure be?**

Cases

Case 1 *Analyzing Income Statements*

Shown below, side by side for your easy comparison, are the income statements for two different companies in the furniture business.

INCOME STATEMENTS
YEAR ENDED DECEMBER 31, 19--

	Company A	*Company B*
Revenue		
Sales	$121 206	$415 072
Cost of Goods Sold	70 704	220 716
Gross Profit	$50 502	$194 356
Operating Expenses		
Advertising	—	$ 43 072
Bank Charges	$ 990	5 765
Building Maintenance	140	3 500
Delivery Expense	10 403	35 206
Insurance	509	1 532
Licenses	120	435
Light, Heat, and Water	1 850	5 775
Miscellaneous Expense	119	717
Rent	4 800	12 000
Telephone	275	716
Wages	10 402	40 307
Total Expenses	$29 608	$149 025
Net Income	$20 894	$45 331

Questions

1. Describe your mental picture of these two companies (large or small, high profile or low profile, etc.) giving specific reasons for your impression.
2. B's expenses are much larger than A's, and yet B is able to earn more than twice the net income of A. How is this possible?
3. The relationship between the cost price of the goods and the selling price of the goods is crucial in any business. Consider the following analysis for Company A:

Sales	$121 206 —	100%
Cost of Goods Sold	70 704 —	58%

Company A's goods cost 58% of their selling price.

a. Calculate this same percentage figure for Company B.

b. If the figure for Company B was 58 percent, the same as for Company A, how much lower would Company B's net income be?

Case 2 *A Poor System*

Suppose that you are hired as an accountant for a small gas station. When looking over the records, you find that the proprietor, who kept the records previously, has recorded all his cash payments into one account headed 'Expenses'.

Questions

1. Briefly outline what you would say to the proprietor in an effort to explain why this is not a good system.

Career

Cyndi Jones / Junior Accountant

Cyndi Jones enjoyed her accounting courses in high school and decided early on an accounting career. Shortly after graduating, she went to work as a payroll clerk with C. P. Clare, a firm that manufactures computer parts and printers. As payroll clerk, Cyndi calculated the hours worked by employees, calculated employee bonuses, and prepared various reports for the cost accountant.

Cyndi was quickly promoted to general accounting clerk. In this job, she controlled accounts receivable and accounts payable, prepared bank reconciliation statements, and kept track of the cash payments of the company.

Cyndi decided to obtain a professional degree in accounting. She enrolled in the Registered Industrial Accountants (RIA) program and began taking courses at night. While working full time, Cyndi has so far completed nine courses of the RIA program.

Cyndi presently works as a junior accountant for two of the companies controlled by Direct Transportation Systems, an American firm that transports freight. She reports directly to the accountant supervisor. Her duties include weekly journal entries and the preparation of the monthly income statement and balance sheet.

Each month, Cyndi must reconcile four different bank accounts. She must also maintain control of all the fixed assets of the business and prepare the monthly trial balance of the general ledger. In addition, Cyndi makes sure that the company's taxes are paid. Finally, she prepares Statistics Canada reports for the government, providing a list of major expenditures and other statistical information.

Cyndi's career in accounting is well underway. If she continues her hard work and study, she should rise quickly to a key accounting position.

9

The Simple Work Sheet and the Financial Statements

9-1 The Simple Work Sheet
9-2 The Balance Sheet — Account Form and Report Form
9-3 The Classified Balance Sheet
9-4 The Work Sheet and Financial Statements
9-5 Typewritten Financial Statements
9-6 The Accounting Cycle

Objectives

When you have completed Chapter 9 you should:

1. Be able to prepare a simple work sheet.
2. Understand the two basic purposes of the simple work sheet.
3. Be able to prepare simple classified financial statements from the work sheet.
4. Know the first six steps in the accounting cycle.

In the preceding chapters you learned how to record transactions in the books of account. Next we will see how accountants use this information to produce the two financial statements: the income statement and the balance sheet.

Financial reports are prepared from the information in the ledger at the end of every accounting period, and whenever else they are needed. The preparation of financial statements is advanced and complex work, as you will see later. Statements are usually prepared by an accountant rather than a clerk, because expert knowledge is needed.

9.1 The Simple Work Sheet

Accountants use a business form called a **work sheet** to help them organize and plan for financial statements. This sheet is ordinarily prepared in pencil so that any necessary changes can be made easily. The work is done on columnar bookkeeping paper.

The steps in the preparation of a work sheet are detailed below.

1. *Write the headings on columnar paper.* Examine the headings in Figure 9.1 very carefully. Observe, in particular, the precise way in which the accounting period is described. Notice that, for our simple exercises, six money columns are used.

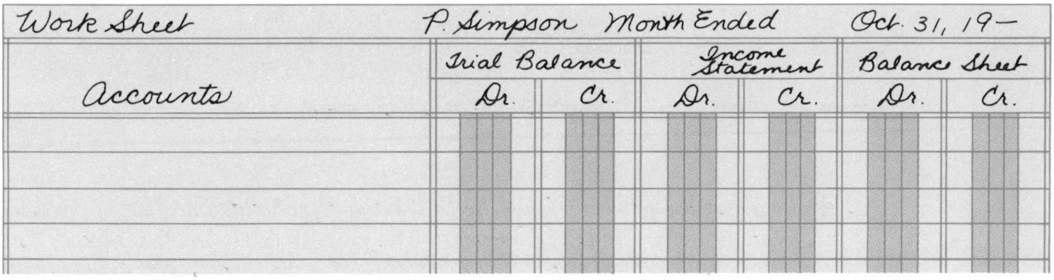

Figure 9.1 The headings of a work sheet.

2. *Record the trial balance in the manner shown in Figure 9.2.* It is a firm rule that the trial balance columns be balanced and correct before any further work is done on the work sheet.

Work Sheet	P. Simpson		Month Ended Oct. 31, 19–			
	Trial Balance		Income Statement		Balance Sheet	
Accounts	Dr.	Cr.	Dr.	Cr.	Dr.	Cr.
Bank	582 54					
Acc. Rec'l - J. Morrison	420 –					
Acc. Rec'l - N. Martin	755 –					
Supplies	645 –					
Office Equipment	2725 –					
Automobile	7400 –					
Acc. Pay'l - Ace Finance Co.		5216 –				
Acc. Pay'l - Grand's Stationers		474 –				
Acc. Pay'l - Industrial Suppliers		1007 40				
P. Simpson, Capital		4862 79				
P. Simpson, Drawings	1000 –					
Fees Revenue		3740 51				
Car Expenses	407 80					
Light and Heat	74 20					
Miscellaneous Expense	37 50					
Rent	275 –					
Telephone	42 16					
Wages	936 50					
	15300 70	15300 70				

Figure 9.2 Recording the trial balance on a work sheet.

3. *Extend each of the amounts from the trial balance columns into one of the four columns to the right, as in Figure 9.3.* The process is simple and logical. The Income Statement columns of the work sheet receive the income and the expenses — the items that make up the net income or the net loss. The Balance Sheet columns receive everything else — the assets, the liabilities, the capital, and the drawings. Remember that the drawings is definitely not an element of net income and therefore cannot be included in that section.

   Be careful to transfer the amount accurately and to record debit amounts into Debit columns and credit amounts into Credit columns. Be sure, too, that no single amount is transferred to two places and that no item is missed.

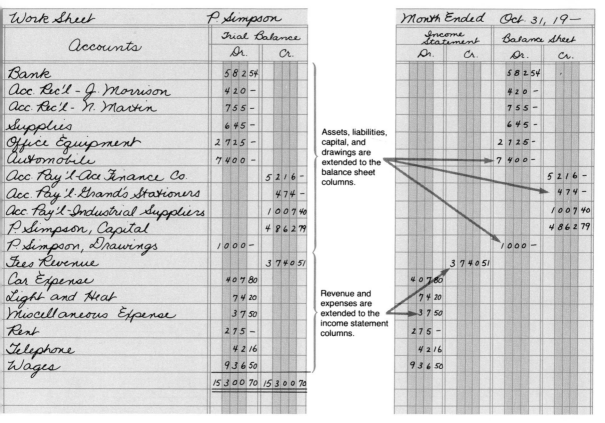

Work Sheet — P. Simpson — Month Ended Oct. 31, 19—

Accounts	Trial Balance Dr.	Trial Balance Cr.	Income Statement Dr.	Income Statement Cr.	Balance Sheet Dr.	Balance Sheet Cr.
Bank	582 54				582 54	
Acc. Rec'l - J. Morrison	420 -				420 -	
Acc. Rec'l - N. Martin	755 -				755 -	
Supplies	645 -				645 -	
Office Equipment	2 725 -				2 725 -	
Automobile	7 400 -				7 400 -	
Acc. Pay'l-Ace Finance Co.		5 216 -				5 216 -
Acc. Pay'l Grand's Stationers		474 -				474 -
Acc. Pay'l-Industrial Suppliers		1 007 40				1 007 40
P. Simpson, Capital		4 862 79				4 862 79
P. Simpson, Drawings	1 000 -				1 000 -	
Fees Revenue		3 740 51		3 740 51		
Car Expense	407 80		407 80			
Light and Heat	74 20		74 20			
Miscellaneous Expense	37 50		37 50			
Rent	275 -		275 -			
Telephone	42 16		42 16			
Wages	936 50		936 50			
	15 300 70	15 300 70				

Assets, liabilities, capital, and drawings are extended to the balance sheet columns.

Revenue and expenses are extended to the income statement columns.

Figure 9.3 Extending the amounts on a work sheet.

4. *Balance the work sheet as in Figure 9.4.* There are three objectives in balancing the work sheet. First, total the four right-hand money columns. Next, make sure that the difference between the two Income Statement columns is equal to the difference between the two Balance Sheet columns. This difference is known as the balancing figure. Finally, record the above information in a neat and orderly manner on the work sheet.

The work sheet must balance, so the balancing work must be done very carefully. If the two figures do not agree, then one or more errors have been made in preparing the work sheet. You may not proceed to the preparation of the financial statements until the errors have been found and corrected. It is mathematically impossible for the work sheet to be correct if it does not balance.

Work Sheet	P. Simpson Month Ended		Oct. 31, 19—			
	Trial Balance		Income Statement		Balance Sheet	
Accounts	Dr.	Cr.	Dr.	Cr.	Dr.	Cr.
Bank	582 54				582 54	
Acc. Rec'l - J. Morrison	420 –				420 –	
Acc. Rec'l - N. Martin	755 –				755 –	
Supplies	645 –				645 –	
Office Equipment	2725 –				2725 –	
Automobile	7400 –				7400 –	
Acc. Pay'l-Ace Finance Co.		5216 –				5216 –
Acc. Pay'l-Grand's Stationers		474 –				474 –
Acc. Pay'l-Industrial Suppliers		1007 40				1007 40
P. Simpson, Capital		4862 79				4862 79
P. Simpson, Drawings	1000 –				1000 –	
Fees Revenue		3740 51		3740 51		
Car Expense	407 80		407 80			
Light and Heat	74 20		74 20			
Miscellaneous Expense	37 50		37 50			
Rent	275 –		275 –			
Telephone	42 16		42 16			
Wages	936 50		936 50			
	15300 70	15300 70	1773 16	3740 51	13527 54	11560 19
Net Income			1967 35			1967 35
			3740 51	3740 51	13527 54	13527 54

These two figures must be equal.

Figure 9.4 Balancing the work sheet (net income situation).

Net Income or Net Loss

The balancing figure on the work sheet tells the amount of the net income or net loss for the accounting period. An intelligent look at the Income Section column totals will tell you which it is.

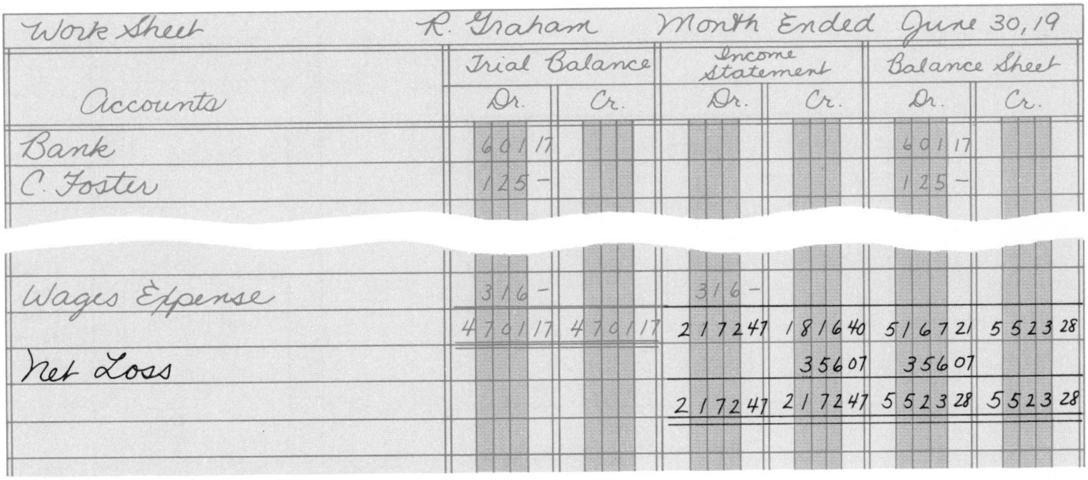

Work Sheet	R. Graham	Month Ended June 30, 19				
	Trial Balance		Income Statement		Balance Sheet	
Accounts	Dr.	Cr.	Dr.	Cr.	Dr.	Cr.
Bank	601 17				601 17	
C. Foster	125 –				125 –	
Wages Expense	316 –		316 –			
	4 701 17	4 701 17	2 172 47	1 816 40	5 167 21	5 523 28
Net Loss				356 07	356 07	
			2 172 47	2 172 47	5 523 28	5 523 28

Figure 9.5 Balancing the work sheet (net loss situation).

Net income has been earned when the credit column (revenue) is greater than the debit column (expense).

A net loss has been suffered when the debit column (expenses) is greater than the credit column (revenue).

Finalizing the work sheet for a loss situation is done slightly differently than for a profit situation. When there is a profit, as in Figure 9.4, the balancing figure (1 967.35) is placed in the two outside columns. When there is a loss as in Figure 9.5, the balancing figure (356.07) is placed in the two inside columns.

9.2 The Balance Sheet — Account Form and Report Form

The balance sheets in this chapter differ in general appearance from those discussed in Chapter 3. The earlier balance sheet had a horizontal or side-by-side arrangement known as the **account form of balance sheet.**

Here we will use a balance sheet with a vertical or one-above-the-other arrangement. This new style is known as the **report form of the balance sheet**. The two forms are contrasted in Figure 9.6. Because it can be presented on standard stationery, the report form of the balance sheet is the one in general use.

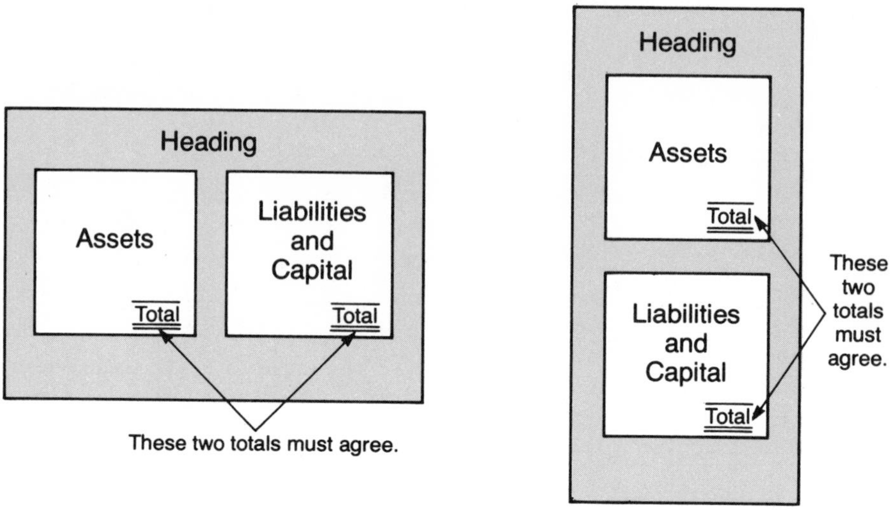

Figure 9.6 The balance sheet in the account form *(left)* and in the report form *(right)*.

9.3 The Classified Balance Sheet

A statement in which the data is grouped according to major categories is known as a **classified financial statement**. A sample classified balance sheet is shown in Figure 9.7. Observe the general appearance of this balance sheet. When reading the comments surrounding the statement be sure to relate them directly to the sample. Note in particular the meanings of the terms **current asset**, **fixed asset**, and **current liability**.

9.4 The Work Sheet and the Financial Statements

The financial statements act as the accountant's report to the owners or managers on the financial affairs of the business. Owners and business executives rarely need to look at the actual accounting records since they rely on the skill of the accountant to maintain them accurately. All that they want to see are the finished financial reports. It is up to the accountant to make sure that reports are perfectly accurate.

The completed work sheet contains, in an organized form, all of the information that is needed for the preparation of the financial statements. Develop the habit of taking this information only from the work sheet. Later, with more advanced work, it will not be available in any other place.

The partial worksheet for R. Wall in Figure 9.8 shows the information necessary for the balance sheet (Figure 9.9) and the income statement (Figure 9.10).

R. Wall
Balance Sheet
June 30, 19–

Assets			
Current Assets			
Bank		1507.10	
Accounts Receivable			
R. Carson	917.80		
W. Randolph	1309.62		
S. Tabone	1523.48	3750.90	
Supplies		560.–	5818.–
Fixed Assets			
Equipment		4925.60	
Automobile		9436.75	14362.35
			20180.35
Liabilities and Owner's Equity			
Current Liabilities			
Bank Loan		5000.–	
Accounts Payable			
Apex Ltd.	875.33		
J.C. Paul	1819.42	2694.75	7694.75
R. Wall, Capital			
Balance June 1		12276.53	
Net Income	1709.07		
Drawings	1500.–		
Increase in Capital		209.07	
Balance June 30			12485.60
			20180.35

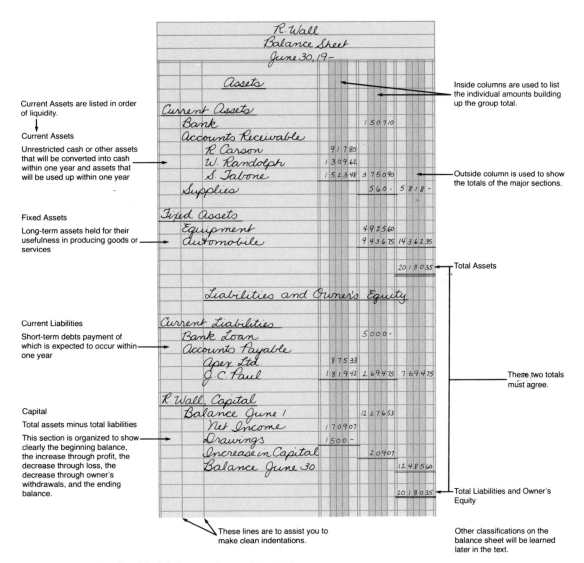

Current Assets are listed in order of liquidity.

Current Assets
Unrestricted cash or other assets that will be converted into cash within one year and assets that will be used up within one year

Fixed Assets
Long-term assets held for their usefulness in producing goods or services

Current Liabilities
Short-term debts payment of which is expected to occur within one year

Capital
Total assets minus total liabilities
This section is organized to show clearly the beginning balance, the increase through profit, the decrease through loss, the decrease through owner's withdrawals, and the ending balance.

Inside columns are used to list the individual amounts building up the group total.

Outside column is used to show the totals of the major sections.

Total Assets

These two totals must agree.

Total Liabilities and Owner's Equity

These lines are to assist you to make clean indentations.

Other classifications on the balance sheet will be learned later in the text.

Figure 9.7 The classified balance sheet of R. Wall.

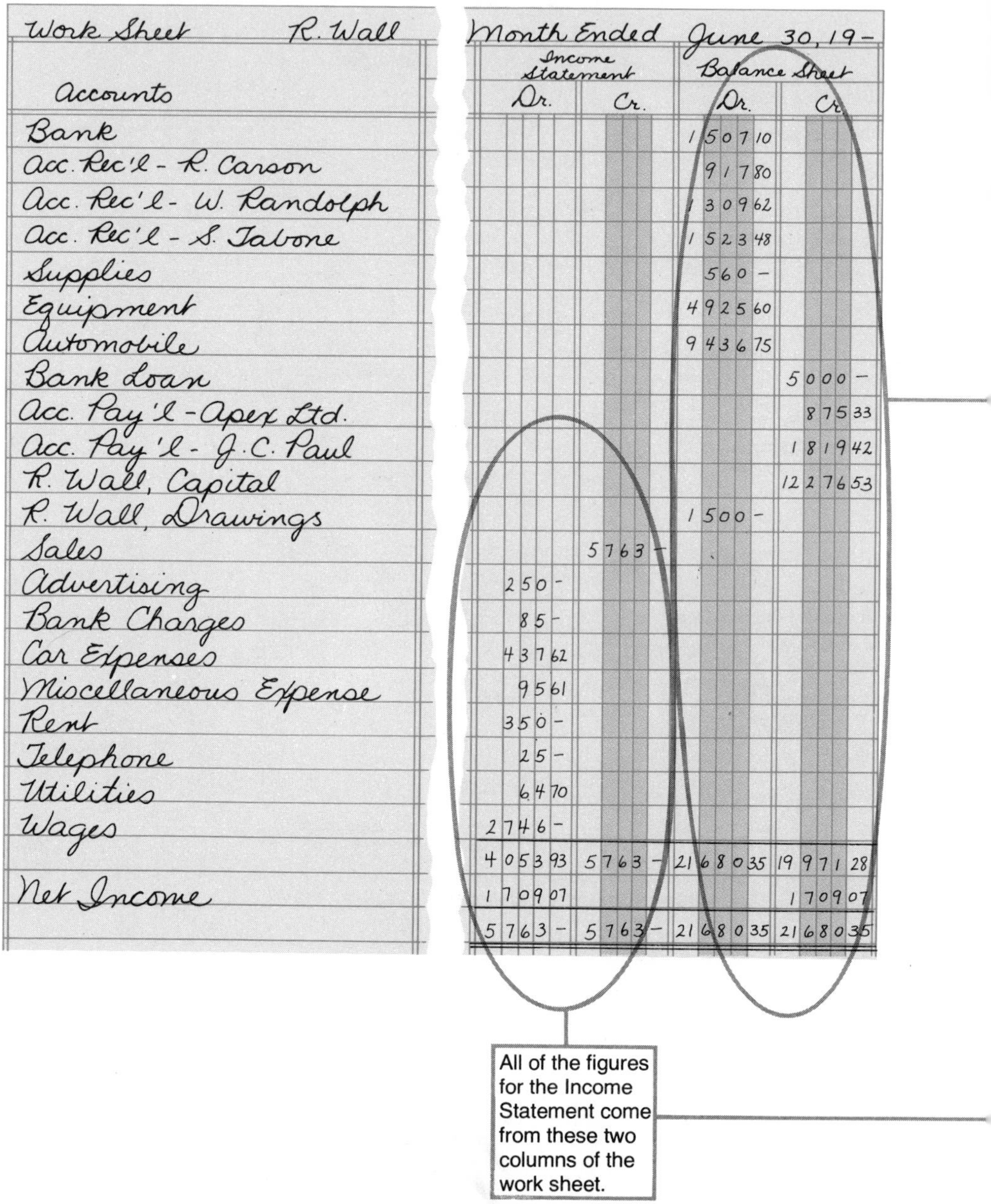

Work Sheet R. Wall — Month Ended June 30, 19–	Income Statement Dr.	Income Statement Cr.	Balance Sheet Dr.	Balance Sheet Cr.
Accounts				
Bank			1507 10	
Acc. Rec'l - R. Carson			917 80	
Acc. Rec'l - W. Randolph			1309 62	
Acc. Rec'l - S. Tabone			1523 48	
Supplies			560 –	
Equipment			4925 60	
Automobile			9436 75	
Bank Loan				5000 –
Acc. Pay'l - Apex Ltd.				875 33
Acc. Pay'l - J.C. Paul				1819 42
R. Wall, Capital				12276 53
R. Wall, Drawings			1500 –	
Sales		5763 –		
Advertising	250 –			
Bank Charges	85 –			
Car Expenses	437 62			
Miscellaneous Expense	95 61			
Rent	350 –			
Telephone	25 –			
Utilities	64 70			
Wages	2746 –			
	4053 93	5763 –	21680 35	19971 28
Net Income	1709 07			1709 07
	5763 –	5763 –	21680 35	21680 35

All of the figures for the Income Statement come from these two columns of the work sheet.

Figure 9.8 A partial work sheet for R. Wall giving the information for the financial statements in Figures 9.9 and 9.10.

All of the figures for the Balance Sheet come from these two columns of the work sheet.

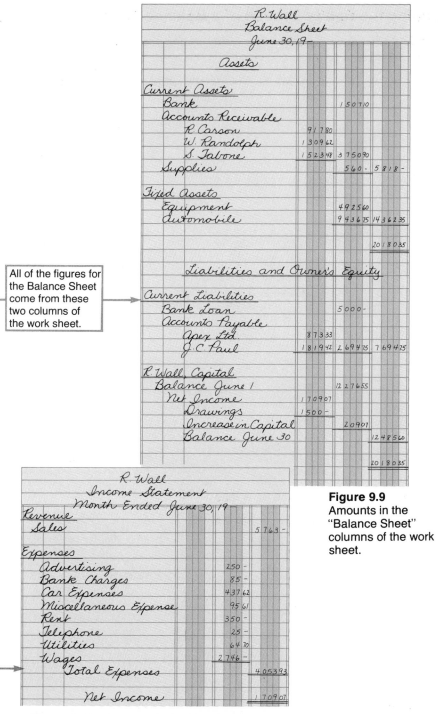

R. Wall
Balance Sheet
June 30, 19–

Assets			
Current Assets			
Bank		1 507.10	
Accounts Receivable			
R. Carson	917.80		
W. Randolph	1 309.62		
S. Tabone	1 523.48	3 750.90	
Supplies		560.–	5 818.–
Fixed Assets			
Equipment		4 925.60	
Automobile		9 436.75	14 362.35
			20 180.35
Liabilities and Owner's Equity			
Current Liabilities			
Bank Loan		5 000.–	
Accounts Payable			
Apex Ltd.	873.33		
J.C. Paul	1 819.42	2 694.75	7 694.75
R. Wall, Capital			
Balance June 1		12 276.55	
Net Income	1 709.07		
Drawings	1 500.–		
Increase in Capital		209.07	
Balance June 30			12 485.60
			20 180.35

Figure 9.9 Amounts in the "Balance Sheet" columns of the work sheet.

R. Wall
Income Statement
Month Ended June 30, 19–

Revenue		
Sales		5 763.–
Expenses		
Advertising	250.–	
Bank Charges	85.–	
Car Expenses	437.62	
Miscellaneous Expense	95.61	
Rent	350.–	
Telephone	25.–	
Utilities	64.70	
Wages	2 746.–	
Total Expenses		4 053.93
Net Income		1 709.07

Figure 9.10 Amounts in the "Income Statement" columns of the work sheet.

Building the Equity Section of a Balance Sheet

Figure 9.11 gives three examples of the equity section of a balance sheet, and shows how the information for them is derived from the work sheet.

Case 1. Net income greater than drawings.

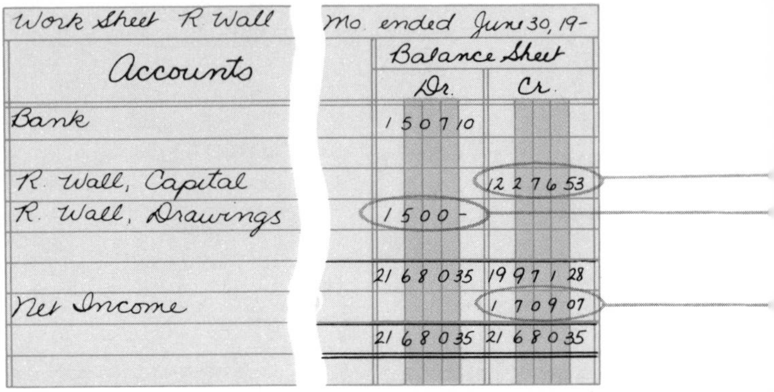

Case 2. Drawings greater than net income.

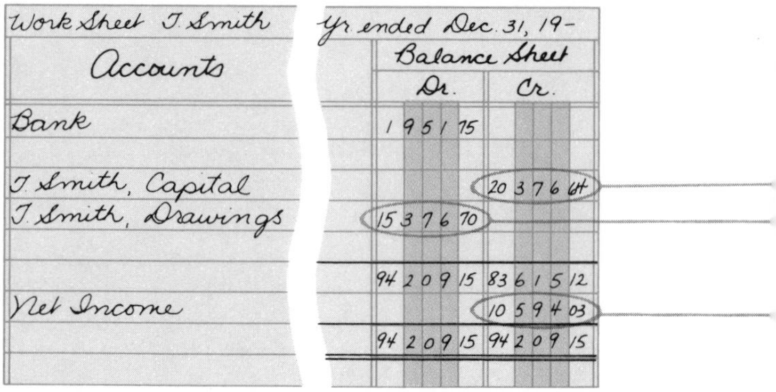

Case 3. A loss.

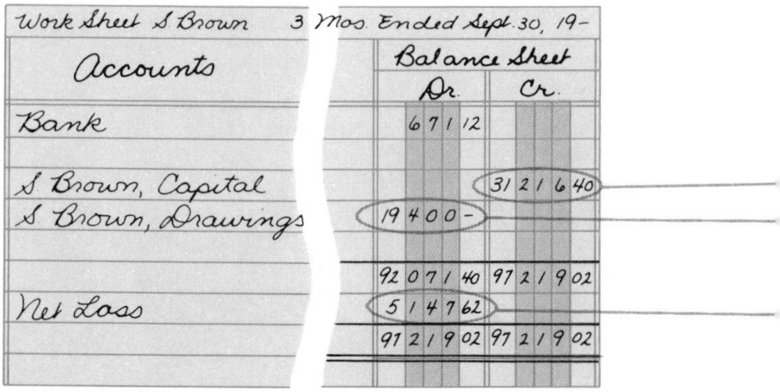

Figure 9.11 Equity items are transferred from the work sheet *(left)* to the balance sheets *(right)* for three different situations.

R. Wall, Capital			
Balance June 1		12 276 53	
Net Income	1 709 07		
Drawings	1 500 –		
Increase in Capital		209 07	
Balance June 30			12 485 60

T. Smith, Capital			
Balance January 1		20 376 64	
Net Income	10 594 03		
Drawings	15 376 70		
Decrease in Capital		4 782 67	
Balance December 31			15 593 97

S. Brown, Capital			
Balance, July 1		31 216 40	
Net Loss	5 147 62		
Drawings	19 400 –		
Decrease in Capital		24 547 62	
Balance December 31			6 668 78

Understanding the Equity Section of the Balance Sheet

The three equity sections from the previous page are examined again from a different viewpoint. In each case, the equity section starts with the capital figure at the beginning of the fiscal period, shows the changes in capital during the period, and finishes with the capital at the end of the period.

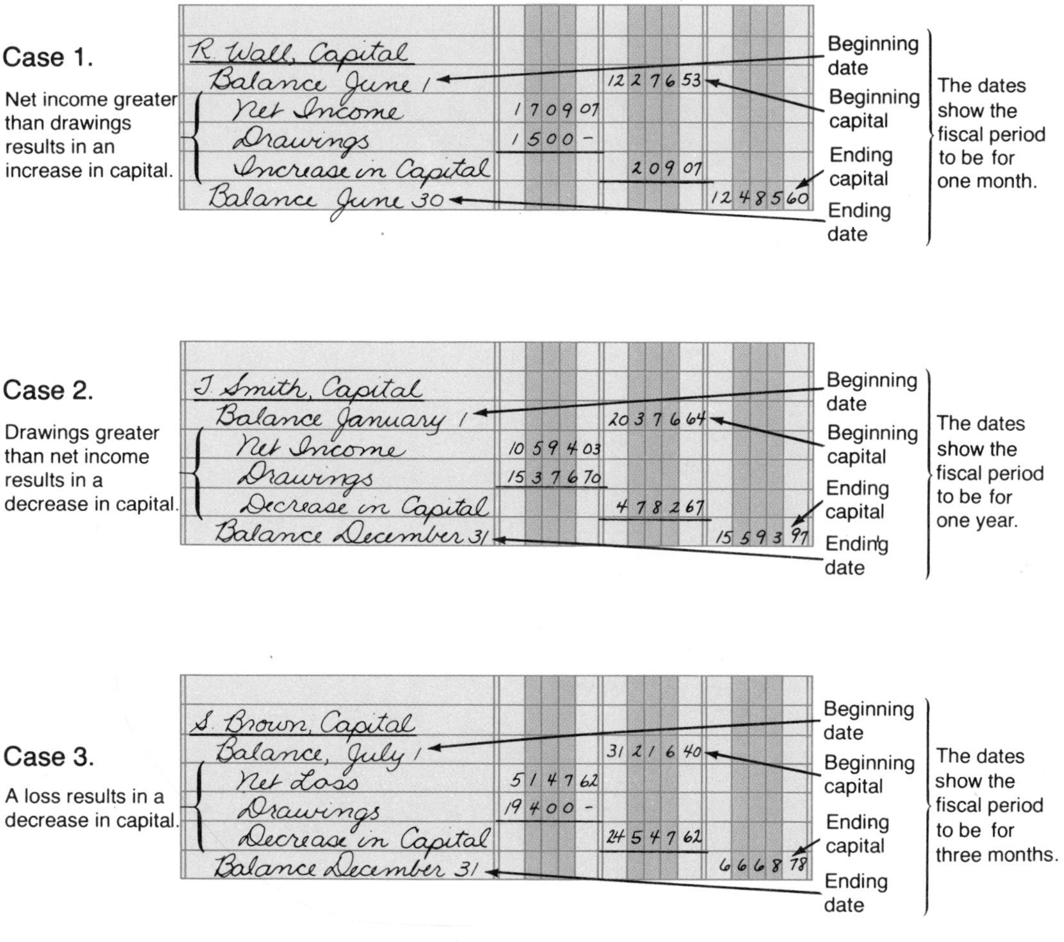

Figure 9.12 Three equity sections showing how equity changes in a fiscal period.

9.5 Typewritten Financial Statements

In the business world, financial reports are usually prepared in typewritten form by skilled typists who copy from the accountant's handwritten work. However, as a student you will find it easier to prepare your statements in handwritten form.

Examine the typewritten statement shown in Figure 9.13. Notice in particular the two ways in which it differs from the handwritten form.

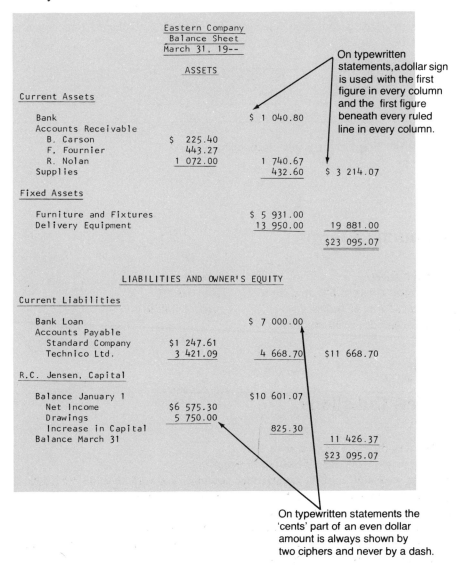

Eastern Company
Balance Sheet
March 31, 19--

ASSETS

Current Assets			
Bank		$ 1 040.80	
Accounts Receivable			
B. Carson	$ 225.40		
F. Fournier	443.27		
R. Nolan	1 072.00	1 740.67	
Supplies		432.60	$ 3 214.07
Fixed Assets			
Furniture and Fixtures		$ 5 931.00	
Delivery Equipment		13 950.00	19 881.00
			$23 095.07

LIABILITIES AND OWNER'S EQUITY

Current Liabilities			
Bank Loan		$ 7 000.00	
Accounts Payable			
Standard Company	$1 247.61		
Technico Ltd.	3 421.09	4 668.70	$11 668.70
R.C. Jensen, Capital			
Balance January 1		$10 601.07	
Net Income	$6 575.30		
Drawings	5 750.00		
Increase in Capital		825.30	
Balance March 31			11 426.37
			$23 095.07

On typewritten statements, a dollar sign is used with the first figure in every column and the first figure beneath every ruled line in every column.

On typewritten statements the 'cents' part of an even dollar amount is always shown by two ciphers and never by a dash.

Figure 9.13 An example of a typewritten balance sheet.

9.6 The Accounting Cycle

You have already learned that certain procedures are regularly followed during a fiscal period. The first three of these procedures are journalizing, posting, and balancing of the ledger. These are carried out by junior employees. The remaining procedures involve the preparation of the financial statements and advanced accounting entries. These are the direct responsibility of the accountant. All of the steps together constitute the accounting cycle.

The steps of the accounting cycle studied in the first nine chapters are shown in Figure 9.14.

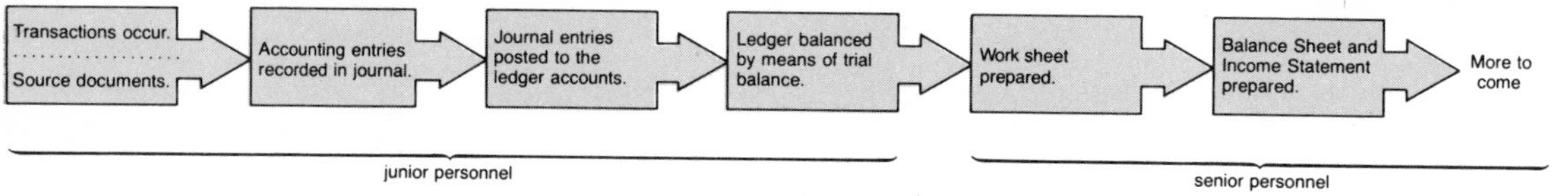

Figure 9.14 Steps in the partial accounting cycle.

Accounting Terms

work sheet
account form of balance sheet
report form of balance sheet
classified financial statement
current asset
fixed asset
current liability

Review Questions

1. What is the purpose of a work sheet?
2. Why is the work sheet prepared in pencil?
3. What does it mean if the trial balance columns of a work sheet do not balance?
4. Describe the third step in the preparation of a work sheet.
5. Describe how the work sheet is balanced.
6. If the work sheet does not balance, what must be done?
7. Describe the difference in the balancing of a work sheet for a 'profit' situation as compared to a 'loss' situation.
8. Explain the difference between the 'report' form and the 'account' form of the balance sheet.

9. What is meant by a classified financial statement?
10. When preparing financial statements, where does one obtain the necessary information? Be specific.
11. Why does an accountant take the trouble to prepare the financial statements very carefully?
12. Define current asset.
13. Define fixed asset.
14. Define current liability.
15. The balance sheet shows a brief history of the equity. Explain what is meant by this.
16. What is the most significant difference between the heading of the income statement and that of the balance sheet?
17. What steps in the accounting cycle have you learned so far in your study of accounting?

Exercises

Extending Accounts on a Work Sheet

1. **For each account listed below, indicate whether it would be extended to Income Statement Debit, Income Statement Credit, Balance Sheet Debit, or Balance Sheet Credit.** (A chart for this exercise is provided in the workbook).

Accounts Payable	Bank Loan
Miscellaneous Expense	Accounts Receivable
Revenue	Automobile
Advertising	Bank
Wages	G. Rojek, Drawings
Mortgage Payable	Sales
Light and Heat	Bank Charges
Equipment	Rent
G. Rojek, Capital	Supplies
Delivery Expense	Trucks

Simplified Work Sheets

2. **From the simplified data shown below, complete a work sheet for N. Foreman and Company for the month ended April 30, 19--.**

TRIAL BALANCE APRIL 30, 19--

Bank	5	
Acc Rec'l — R. Boddy	7	
Supplies	4	
Equipment	25	
Automobiles	15	
Bank Loan		12
Acc Pay'l — Greer Co.		2
N. Foreman, Capital		81
N. Foreman, Drawings	50	
Fees Revenue		70
Bank Charges	1	
Car Expenses	10	
Miscellaneous Exp.	2	
Light and Heat	8	
Rent	15	
Telephone	3	
Wages	20	
	165	165

3. From the simplified data shown below, complete a work sheet for Fox and Associates for the year ended December 31, 19--.

TRIAL BALANCE DECEMBER 31, 19--

Bank	3	
Acc. Rec'l — N. Toller	2	
Acc. Rec'l — P. Knapf	4	
Supplies	7	
Equipment	31	
Automobiles	16	
Bank Loan		15
Acc. Pay'l — Mercier Ltd.		21
A. Fox, Capital		57
A. Fox, Drawings	25	
Commissions Earned		91
Bank Charges	2	
Car Expenses	15	
Miscellaneous Expense	3	
Light and Heat	12	
Rent	27	
Telephone	5	
Wages	32	
	184	184

Locating Errors on a Work Sheet

4. The work sheet below contains a number of errors. Locate the errors, make the necessary corrections, and balance the work sheet. (A work sheet has been provided in the workbook.)

Work Sheet — The Arthur Company — Month Ended Oct. 31, 19–

Accounts	Trial Balance Dr.	Trial Balance Cr.	Income Statement Dr.	Income Statement Cr.	Balance Sheet Dr.	Balance Sheet Cr.
Bank	1 722 16				1 722 16	
Acc. Rec'l - J. Young	323 –				332 –	
Acc. Rec'l - M. Watson	72 –				72 –	
Acc. Rec'l - H. Chan	116 –				116 –	
Supplies	1 255 –				1 255 –	
Office Equipment	5 863 –				5 863 –	
Automobiles	13 200 –				1 320 –	
Acc. Pay'l - O.K. Supply		421 72				421 72
Acc. Pay'l - City Hydro		116 42				116 42
Acc. Pay'l - Slick Oil Co.		331 19				331 19
Bank Loan		10 000 –				10 000 –
P. Arthur, Capital		10 504 82				10 504 82
P. Arthur, Drawings	1 000 –			1 000 –		
Revenue		4 903 17		4 903 17		
Advertising	465 12		465 12			
Automobile Expense	270 –				270 –	
Bank Charges	56 40		56 40			
Miscellaneous Exp.	113 74		113 74			
Rent	400 –		400 –			
Salaries	1 280 –		1 280 –		1 280 –	
Telephone	25 60		25 60			
Utilities	115 30					
	26 277 32	26 277 32	2 340 86	5 903 17	12 230 16	21 074 15
Net Income			3 562 31			8 843 99
			5 903 17	5 903 17	12 230 16	29 918 14

Classifying Accounts

5. Classify the accounts given below into one of the categories named at the right.

Accounts	*Categories*
Accounts Receivable	Current Assets
Accounts Payable	Fixed Assets
Advertising	Current Liabilities
Bank	Owner's Equity
Bank Charges	Revenue
Bank Loan	Operating Expenses
Buildings	
Delivery Expense	
F. Rybak, Capital	
F. Rybak, Drawings	
General Expense	
Insurance Expense	
Commissions Earned	
Postage	
Rent	
Supplies	
Telephone	
Wages	

Equity Section Of A Balance Sheet

6. Complete the following schedule by filling in the blanks in the copy provided in your workbook.

Items	*Opening Capital*	*Net Income or Net Loss (−)*	*Drawings*	*Ending Capital*
a.	$ 30 000	$15 000	$10 000	$
b.	50 000	−2 000	7 000	
c.	70 000	32 000		75 500
d.		16 000	19 500	33 200
e.	56 000		30 000	40 000
f.	45 000		25 000	15 000
g.	22 000		10 000	28 000
h.		25 000	18 000	42 000
i.	120 000	42 000		112 000

7. Prepare the Equity section of the balance sheet from the data given for each case below.

Owner's name	T. Hunter	S. Robb	W. Head
Fiscal period	Year ended December 31, 19--	Three months ended March 31, 19--	Month ended May 31, 19--
Opening capital	$27 042.62	$19 641.25	$20 196.74
Net income	39 171.04	22 462.67	−3 750.20
Drawings	35 000.00	25 575.00	10 047.17

Preparing Work Sheets and Statements

8. Prepare the income statement and the classified balance sheet from the following completed work sheet.

Work Sheet — Sturdy Insurance Agency — Year Ended Dec. 31, 19

Accounts	Trial Balance Dr.	Trial Balance Cr.	Income Statement Dr.	Income Statement Cr.	Balance Sheet Dr.	Balance Sheet Cr.
Cash	2 704 30				2 704 30	
Acc. Rec'l - P. Norman	1 735 57				1 735 57	
Acc. Rec'l - V. Perczyk	3 760 -				3 760 -	
Supplies	1 767 -				1 767 -	
Office Equipment	5 437 50				5 437 50	
Automobiles	16 438 -				16 438 -	
Acc. Pay'l - Winston Motors		916 40				916 40
Acc. Pay'l - Gage News		1 504 31				1 504 31
D.K. Sands, Capital		24 353 92				24 353 92
D.K. Sands, Drawings	48 763 18				48 763 18	
Commissions Earned		92 403 50		92 403 50		
Advertising	6 130 75		6 130 75			
Car Expenses	3 640 20		3 640 20			
Miscellaneous Expense	216 91		216 91			
Rent	4 200 -		4 200 -			
Telephone	1 270 87		1 270 87			
Utilities	1 737 70		1 737 70			
Wages	21 376 15		21 376 15			
	119 178 13	119 178 13	38 572 58	92 403 50	80 605 55	26 774 63
Net Income			53 830 92			53 830 92
			92 403 50	92 403 50	80 605 55	80 605 55

9. The trial balance of P. C. Taylor, a lawyer, on June 30, 19--, after a fiscal period of six months, is as follows:

Bank	$ 516.20	
Acc. Rec'l — C. Carlisle	731.00	
Acc. Rec'l — G. Wu	1 650.00	
Office Supplies	2 789.80	
Automobile	10 800.00	
Office Equipment	4 550.00	
Professional Library	3 270.00	
Acc. Pay'l — Goodman's Stationery		$ 1 202.50
Acc. Pay'l — Farrow's Garage		525.40
P. C. Taylor, Capital		15 702.23
P. C. Taylor, Drawings	25 000.00	
Fees Earned		44 721.61
Car Expense	2 074.20	
Light and Heat	632.92	
Miscellaneous Expense	124.90	
Rent	3 000.00	
Salaries	6 645.51	
Telephone	367.21	
	$62 151.74	$62 151.74

Complete a six-column work sheet and prepare the financial statements.

10. The trial balance of Star Delivery Company on December 31, 19--, after a fiscal period of one year, is as follows:

Bank	$ 1 212.70	
Acc. Rec'l — R. Kowalchuk	170.00	
Acc. Rec'l — H. Kramer	351.00	
Acc. Rec'l — P. Schill	112.00	
Supplies	651.00	
Furniture and Equipment	13 900.00	
Trucks	27 050.00	
Bank Loan		$ 23 000.00
Acc. Pay'l — Civic Traders		1 746.00
L. Pugh, Capital		21 006.39
L. Pugh, Drawings	35 000.00	
Revenue		118 500.00
Gas and Oil Expense	21 874.00	
Insurance	2 171.40	
Miscellaneous Expense	225.00	
Rent	12 000.00	
Telephone	574.25	
Truck Repairs	3 146.90	
Utilities Expense	907.64	
Wages	44 906.50	
	$164 252.39	$164 252.39

Complete a six-column work sheet and prepare the financial statements.

Using Your Knowledge

11. Stacey Worrell, an accounting student, has discovered a slight variation in the procedure for balancing a work sheet. Her method is shown below.

Work Sheet — Morton Enterprises — Mo. Ended Dec. 31, 19–

Accounts	Tr. Bal. Dr.	Tr. Bal. Cr.	Inc. St. Dr.	Inc. St. Cr.	Bal. Sht. Dr.	Bal. Sht. Cr.
Bank	12 –				12 –	
Acc. Rec'l – G. Flavelle	8 –				8 –	
Supplies	15 –				15 –	
Equipment	40 –				40 –	
Truck	120 –				120 –	
Acc. Pay'l – Tops Hardware		17 –				17 –
V. Maswich, Capital		141 –				141 –
V. Maswich, Drawings	75 –				75 –	
Revenue		300 –		300 –		
General Expense	10 –		10 –			
Light and Heat	50 –		50 –			
Rent	90 –		90 –			
Telephone	8 –		8 –			
Wages	30 –		30 –			
	458 –	458 –	188 –	300 –		
Net Income			112 –			112 –
			300 –	300 –	270 –	270 –

1. Give your opinion of this method.
2. Explain why the balance sheet columns balance with the $112 net income figure included, but would not if the figure was excluded.

12. The balance in the Capital account of the O.K. Suppliers on January 1, 19––, was $26 000. The balance in this account was $27 500 at the end of the year. Net income for the year was $5 000. Explain why the balance in Capital was not $31 000.

13. The accounts used by Lakeview Taxi of Belleville, Ont., are listed below in alphabetical order.
1. Rearrange the accounts into their normal categories.
2. Design a numbering system for these accounts that is different from the one used in the text. In planning your system consider ways to allow easy inclusion of new accounts as the business expands.

Accounts

Advertising
Accounts Payable (various)
Accounts Receivable (various)
Automobiles
Bank
Bank Charges
Bank Loan
Building
Car Repairs
Car Supplies
Equipment
Gas and Oil Expense
Insurance Expense
Land
Legal Expense
Light and Heat
T. Malone, Capital
T. Malone, Drawings
Miscellaneous Expense
Office Supplies
Revenue
Telephone Expense
Wages Expense

Cases

Case 1 *Interpreting Balance Sheets*

Firewood Supply is a small business operated on a seasonal basis by Gerry Chowsky, a student in St. Boniface, Man. A comparative condensed balance sheet for the business for the 19–1 and 19–2 seasons is shown below.

FIREWOOD SUPPLY
BALANCE SHEET
DECEMBER 31, 19–2
(with comparative figures for 19–1)

	19–1	*19–2*
ASSETS		
Bank	$ 1 000	$ 2 000
Accounts Receivable	7 000	10 000
Equipment	12 000	22 000
Truck	10 000	10 000
	$30 000	$44 000
LIABILITIES AND EQUITY		
Bank Loan	$ 6 000	$ 6 000
Accounts Payable	7 000	11 000
Owner's Equity	17 000	27 000
	$30 000	$44 000

Questions

1. If the owner's drawings during 19–2 amounted to $5 000, calculate the net income for 19–2.

2. How could the accounts receivable have increased by $3 000?
3. Is the business in a good position to pay its debts?
4. What has happened to the net income (that is, the figure arrived at in question 1.)?

Case 2 *Financing Student Council Activities*

At the beginning of the school year, the Riverview High School student council has inherited a bank balance that was overdrawn by $935. The council has no assets.

The members of the council executive are extremely concerned and have asked you, the treasurer, to examine the records of the council to find out the reasons for the poor financial position. They have also asked you to make recommendations for providing good management in the coming year.

As a result of your investigation you find out that the previous council began its year with a positive bank balance of $200 and an inventory of five hundred fully paid-for T-shirts which had cost $1 each.

The bank book shows that the following transactions took place during the previous year.

	Cheques	Deposits	Balance
Beginning balance			200
Sale of student cards (940 × $2.50)		2 350	2 550
Cost of printing student cards	350		2 200
Grant to drama club	1 000		1 200
Proceeds from dance (Nightmare)		2 000	3 200
Profit on refreshments (Nightmare)		70	3 270
Charge for musicians (Nightmare)	1 500		1 770
Grant to choir	1 000		770
Proceeds from sale of 500 T-Shirts		375	1 145
Proceeds from variety show		140	1 285
Grant to athletic department	1 000		285
Proceeds from dance (Brainstorm)		300	585
Charge for musicians (Brainstorm)	1 600		−1 015
Profit on refreshments (Brainstorm)		80	−935

The previous student council had decided to have only top-notch entertainment at dances. Although this meant that the musical groups were expensive, a large profit was expected to be made on every dance. However, the 'Brainstorm' dance fizzled because of bad weather and poor scheduling.

The T-Shirts were sold at a bargain rate in order to promote school spirit. The three $1 000 grants were normal annual commitments made to the three school organizations.

Questions

1. Prepare a summary of receipts and expenditures for the year just completed so that it shows clearly how the bank balance dropped from $200 to negative $935.
2. Describe the factors which, in your opinion, contributed directly to the poor financial position.

3. Give recommendations for better managing the financial affairs of the student council in the future.
4. Suggest ways to remedy the negative bank balance.

Case 3 *Responsibility For Loss?*

Sue Zabjek, a history teacher, had 90 students who needed textbooks. The local bookstore had not provided good service in previous years. Therefore, to save money for her students and to avoid delay, Sue decided to buy the textbooks directly from the publisher. Sue clearly stated to her classes that she intended to sell the books at cost with no profit to her. The books arrived with an invoice for $1 350.

Sue's system for selling the books was very informal. As students crowded around her desk, Sue would take money from each one, give out a text, put the money in her drawer, and then repeat the process.

At the end of a week, Sue decided to take stock of her sales. She found that she had $1 050 in her desk. She also had 14 unsold books. By simple arithmetic, Sue calculated that she was missing either $90 or six books.

Before deciding on a course of action, Sue surveyed her classes to learn the status of the texts. Her survey showed that 76 students had their texts and 14 did not.

Questions

1. a. Did the publisher send the correct number of books?
   b. How could the shortage have been caused? Give three possibilities.
   c. Describe measures that Sue could have taken to prevent such an occurrence.

Sue did not believe that she should bear the $90 loss. Therefore, she decided to increase the charge per book by $1 for all 90 students. The increased price of the text was still lower than the bookstore price of $18.50. However, when she announced her decision to her students she met considerable resistance.

A few students refused to pay as a matter of principle, and others began to follow suit. They claimed that the teacher had agreed to sell the texts at cost price and should keep her word. These students did not believe they should be penalized for the teacher's failure to take adequate precautions.

Another student, whose father owned the bookstore, was furious at the price increase. From the beginning she had felt that Sue's plan brought unfair competition against her father. Now she could no longer restrain herself; she registered a formal complaint to the school principal against the teacher. The principal didn't like to get involved, but finally agreed to discuss the matter with the teacher.

Questions

2. a. Should a teacher be allowed to bypass local competition in the purchase of textbooks? Give reasons for your answer.
   b. Should Sue Zabjek have to suffer the $90 loss, or is her course of action a reasonable one? Give reasons to support your response.
   c. What should the principal say to Ms. Zabjek?

Career
Debbie Walesa / Accounting Supervisor

After Debbie Walesa graduated from high school in Chatham, Ontario, she travelled through Europe for a year. When she returned to Chatham, she went to work as a receptionist for McCoy Chrysler Dodge, a car dealership.

During the next three years, Debbie received on-the-job training in accounting. She also studied accounting by herself at home in the evenings. When this training was completed, Debbie became bookkeeper for the dealership. In this job, she took charge of accounts receivable and prepared the payroll for the company's employees.

Three years later, Debbie was promoted to her present position, supervisor of the accounting department. As supervisor, Debbie oversees all the company's accounting. She is responsible for all journal entries and is in charge of all postings to the general ledger. Every month, she prepares the general ledger trial balance and the work sheet. Debbie also prepares the company's financial statements, the income statement, and the balance sheet. Because the dealership is a trading business, she must also keep track of its inventory.

Debbie reports directly to the owner of the dealership and sends all financial reports to the head office of Chrysler Corporation in Canada. She pays all gasoline taxes, retail sales taxes, and payroll taxes. At the end of each year, she prepares the T4 slips for all 40 employees. She also contacts customers by telephone regarding overdue accounts, statement billing, and customer complaints.

Debbie's position offers challenge, variety, and responsibility. Her work encompasses all the steps in the accounting cycle that you have studied to date, including the journal, the ledger, the trial balance, the work sheet, and the financial statements.

10

Closing Entries

10-1 Objectives of Closing Entries
10-2 Making the Closing Entries
10-3 Post-Closing Trial Balance
10-4 The Accounting Cycle

Objectives

When you have completed Chapter 10 you should:

1. Understand the purpose of the closing entries.
2. Know the specific accounting objectives of the closing entries.
3. Be able to prepare the closing entries from data found on the work sheet.
4. Be able to prepare a post-closing trial balance.
5. Know the seven steps in the basic accounting cycle.

In Chapter 8 the equity section of the ledger was expanded by the addition of new accounts for revenues, expenses, and drawings. These new accounts are used to gather data for the preparation of the income statement and the equity section of the balance sheet. They are shown in the simplified ledger in Figure 10.1.

Remember that the income statement and the equity section of the balance sheet relate to a specific period of time known as the fiscal period. Most businesses choose a fiscal period of one year, the maximum period allowed by law. Some businesses, however, want financial statements more often, and choose shorter fiscal periods.

The balances in the accounts for revenues, expenses, and drawings all relate to a specific period of time. At the end of each fiscal period, these accounts have served their purpose. They have nothing to do with the next accounting period and are no

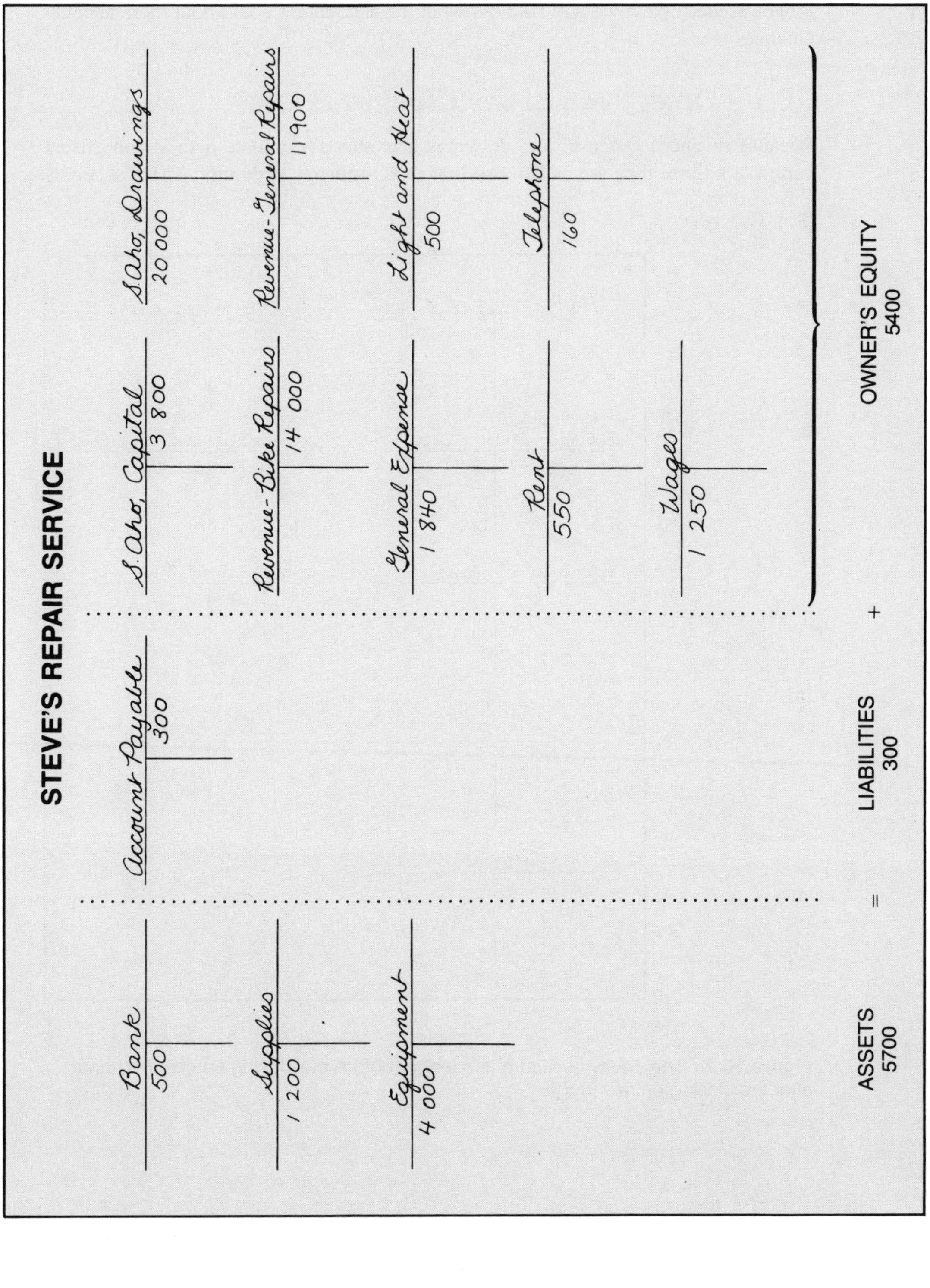

Figure 10.1 The expanded ledger of Steve's Repair Service.

longer needed. Now we will find out what the accountant does about these account balances.

10.1 Objectives of the Closing Entries

Because revenue, expense, and drawings accounts accumulate data for one fiscal period at a time, they are called **nominal** or **temporary accounts.** These accounts

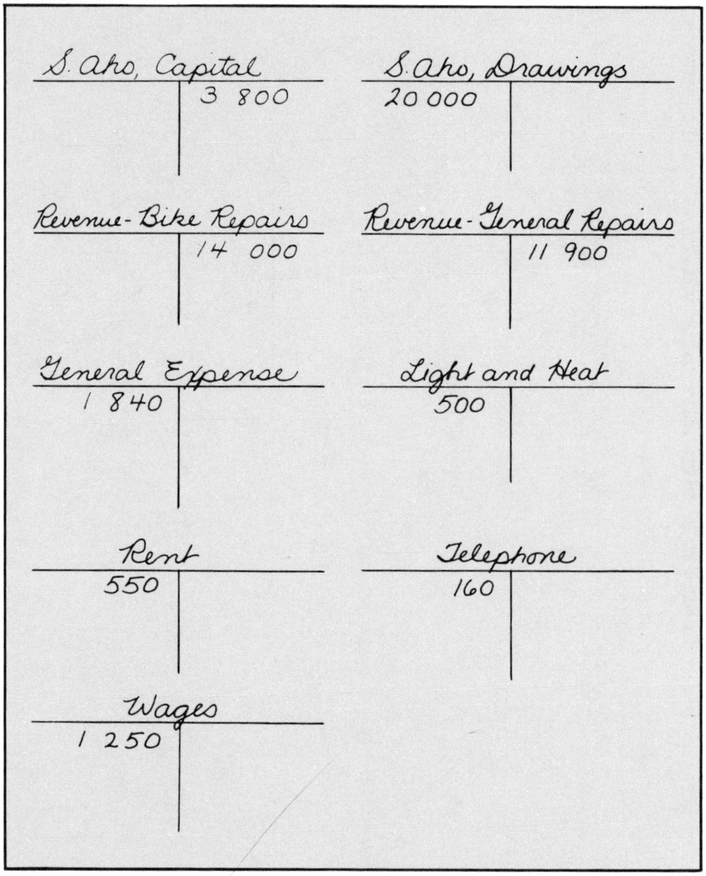

Figure 10.2 The equity section of the ledger before the closing entries *(left)* and after the closing entries *(right)*.

must be cleared of their old balances in order to prepare the equity section of the ledger for the next accounting period. They must begin the next period with nil balances. At the same time, the capital account must be updated to show the beginning balance for the new fiscal period.

The accounting entries that make these changes are known as the **closing entries**. The objectives of the closing entries can be seen in Figure 10.2. The equity section of the ledger is shown before and after the closing entries.

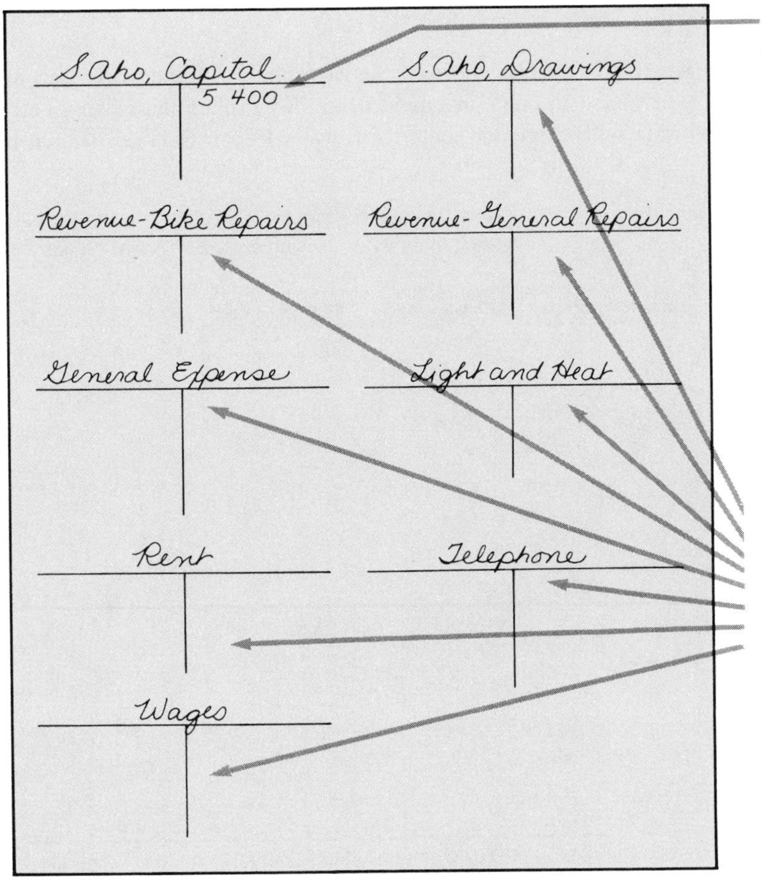
S. Aho, Capital
5 400
S. Aho, Drawings
Revenue-Bike Repairs
Revenue-General Repairs
General Expense
Light and Heat
Rent
Telephone
Wages
The Capital account has been updated. It represents the beginning balance for the new fiscal period (which is the same as the ending balance for the old fiscal period).
Revenue, expense, and drawings accounts all have nil balances. They have been closed out and are ready to accumulate the data for the next fiscal period.

The data contained in the nominal accounts does not disappear into thin air. To produce the nil balances, accounting entries are journalized and posted in the usual manner.

What are these closing entries? Perhaps you think you can simply transfer each nominal account balance individually to the capital account. This would have the desired result, but it is not the usual method. The customary method of making the closing entries is the four-step procedure outlined below.

10.2 Making the Closing Entries

The source of the data for the closing entries is the work sheet. On the work sheet all of the necessary figures exist in one convenient place. To explain the closing entry process, let us continue with the work sheet for Steve's Repair Service, shown in Figure 10.3.

The figures for closing entry #2 — The figures for closing entry #1 — The figure for closing entry #4

Work Sheet — Steve's Repair Service — Yr. Ended Dec. 31, 19-

Accounts	Trial Balance Dr.	Trial Balance Cr.	Income Statement Dr.	Income Statement Cr.	Balance Sheet Dr.	Balance Sheet Cr.
Bank	500 -				500 -	
Supplies	1 200 -				1 200 -	
Equipment	4 000 -				4 000 -	
Acc's Payable		300 -				300 -
S. Aho, Capital		3 800 -				3 800 -
S. Aho, Drawings	20 000 -				20 000 -	
Revenue-Bike Repairs		14 000 -		14 000 -		
Revenue-General Repairs		11 900 -		11 900 -		
General Expense	1 840 -		1 840 -			
Light and Heat	500 -		500 -			
Rent	550 -		550 -			
Telephone	160 -		160 -			
Wages	1 250 -		1 250 -			
	30 000 -	30 000 -	4 300 -	25 900 -	25 700 -	4 100 -
Net Income			21 600 -			21 600 -
			25 900 -	25 900 -	25 700 -	25 700 -

The figure for closing entry #3

Figure 10.3 Work sheet for Steve's Repair Service.

Closing Entry No. 1

The first closing entry transfers the balances in the revenue accounts to a new nominal account called Income Summary. The figures for this entry are found in the income statement credit column of the work sheet, as seen in Figure 10.3.

Since revenues have credit balances, debit entries are needed to close them out. This will help you work out the first closing entry for Steve's Repair Service.

19--			
Dec 31	Revenue — Bike Repairs	14 000	
	Revenue — General Repairs	11 900	
	Income Summary		25 900
	To close out the revenue accounts to Income Summary		

Closing Entry No. 2

The second closing entry transfers the balances in the expense accounts to the Income Summary account. The figures for this entry are found in the income statement debit column of the work sheet as illustrated in Figure 10.3.

Since expenses have debit balances, credit entries are needed to close them out. Remember this, as you work out the second closing entry for Steve's Repair Service.

19--			
Dec 31	Income Summary	4 300	
	General Expense		1 840
	Light and Heat		500
	Rent		550
	Telephone		160
	Wages		1 250
	To close out the expense accounts to Income Summary		

Examine Figure 10.4, which shows the ledger of Steve's Repair Service as it would be after posting the first two closing entries.

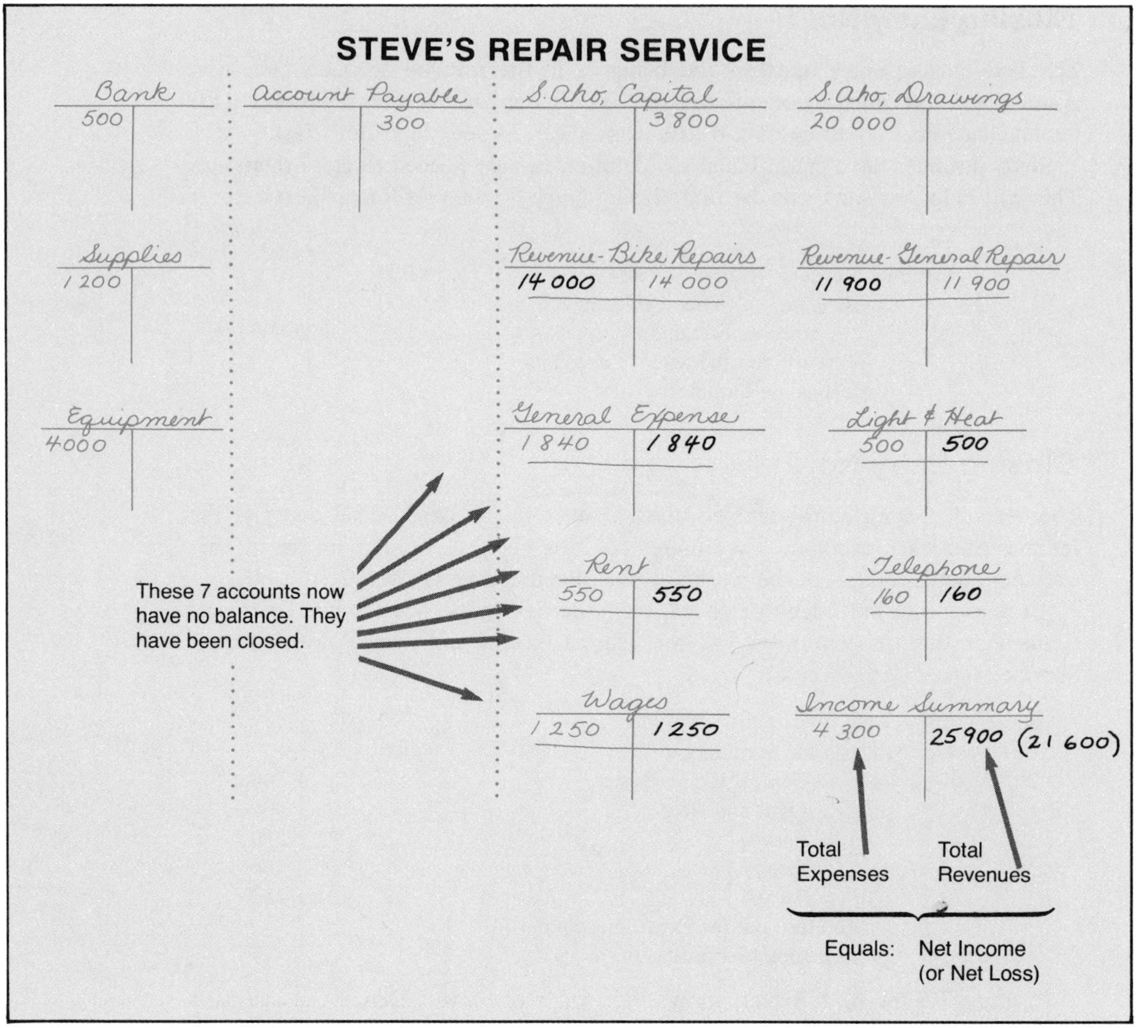

Figure 10.4 The ledger of Steve's Repair Service after the first two closing entries.

Closing Entry No. 3

The third closing entry transfers the balance in the Income Summary account to the Capital account. If the first two closing entries are correct, the balance in this account will be equal to the net income, or the net loss.

If a net income has been earned, the account will have a credit balance because the credits to it will exceed the debits. If a loss has been incurred, the opposite is true and the account will have a debit balance. The figure for this entry can be picked up from the work sheet.

Since the balance of the account in this case is a credit, a debit entry will be needed to close it out. Here is the third closing entry for Steve's Repair Service for you to work out.

19--			
Dec 31	Income Summary	21 600	
	S. Aho, Capital		21 600
	To close out Income Summary to Capital		

Closing Entry No. 4

The fourth closing entry transfers the balance of the Drawings account to the Capital account. Again, the figure for this entry is picked up from the work sheet.

Since the Drawings account always has a debit balance, a credit entry is needed to close it out. Here is the fourth closing entry for Steve's Repair Service for you to work out.

19--			
Dec 31	S. Aho, Capital	20 000	
	S. Aho, Drawings		20 000
	To close out Drawings to Capital		

The ledger for Steve's Repair Service with all four of the closing entries posted appears in Figure 10.5. Compare this to the ledger in Figure 10.1 and you will see that the objectives of the closing entries have been achieved.

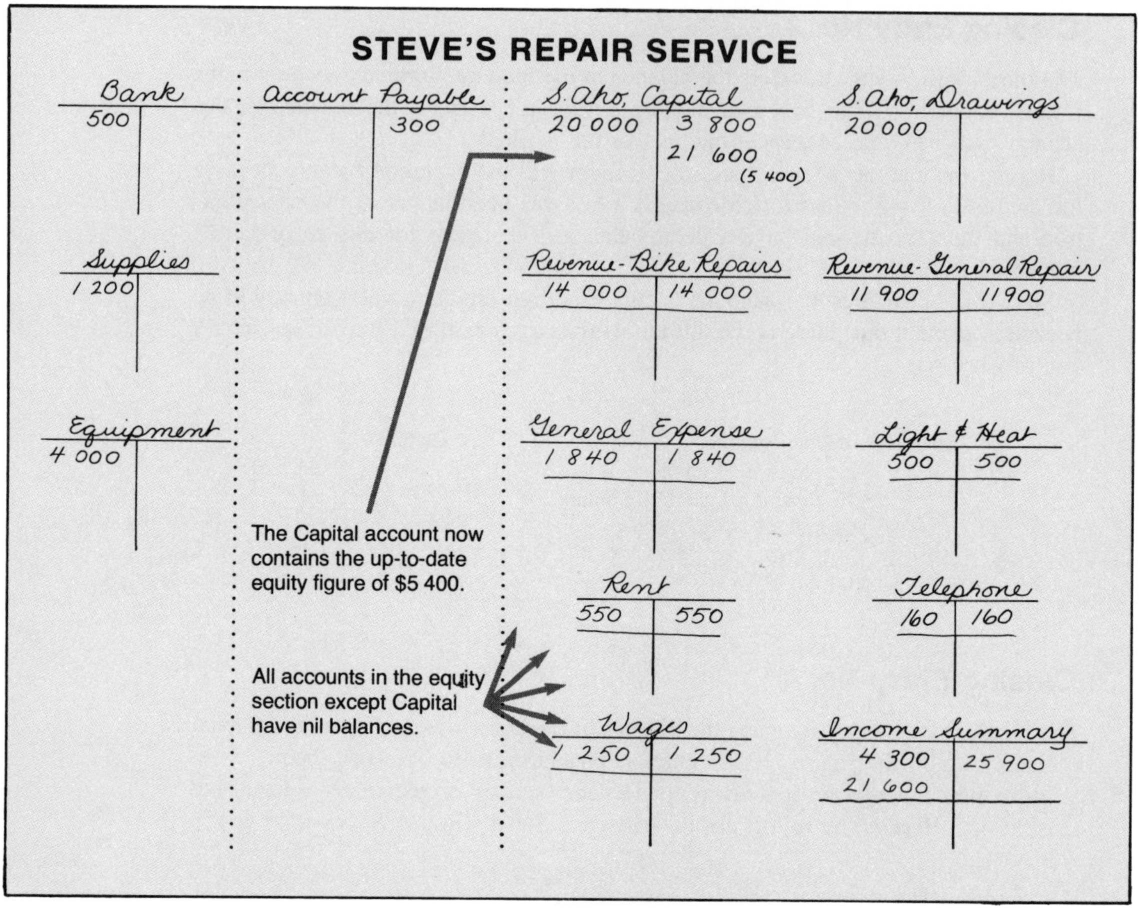

Figure 10.5 The ledger for Steve's Repair Service after all of the closing entries have been made.

Summary of the Closing Entries

The closing entry process consists of the following four entries:

1. An entry to close out the revenue accounts to the Income Summary account.
2. An entry to close out the expense accounts to the Income Summary account.
3. An entry to close out the Income Summary account to the Capital account.
4. An entry to close out the Drawings account to the Capital account.

After these four entries have been journalized and posted, the accounts in the equity section of the ledger will all have nil balances *except* the Capital account, which will contain the up-to-date equity figure.

10.3 Post-Closing Trial Balance

After you have journalized and posted the closing entries, you must check the accuracy of your work by taking off a trial balance. The trial balance that is taken after the closing entries are posted is known as the **post-closing trial balance**. This trial balance is shown in Figure 10.6 for the ledger of Steve's Repair Service.

STEVE'S REPAIR SERVICE
POST-CLOSING TRIAL BALANCE
DECEMBER 31, 9--

	DR.	*CR.*
Bank	500	
Supplies	1 200	
Equipment	4 000	
Account Payable		300
S. Aho, Capital		5 400
	5 700	5 700

Figure 10.6 The post-closing trial balance for the ledger of Steve's Repair Service.

10.4 The Accounting Cycle

The closing entries and the post-closing trial balance can now be added to the sequence of steps in the accounting cycle. The basic cycle is shown in Figure 10.7. This version of the accounting cycle is almost, but not quite, in its final form.

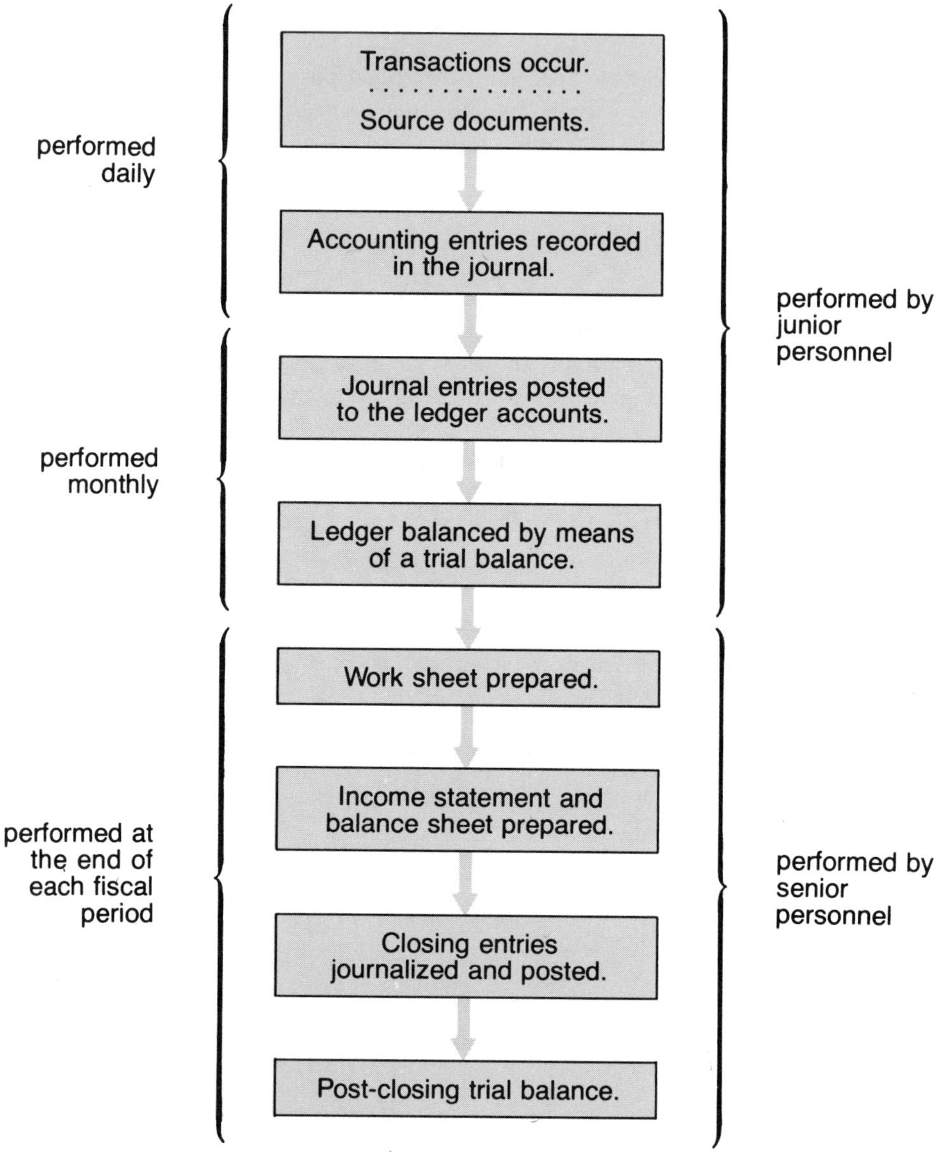

Figure 10.7 The basic accounting cycle.

Accounting Terms

nominal account
temporary account
closing entry
post-closing trial balance

Review Questions

1. What accounts are contained in the equity section of the ledger?
2. Explain the purpose of the accounts in the equity section of the ledger.
3. What is a fiscal period?
4. What is the most common length of fiscal period?
5. What other time spans may be used for a fiscal period?
6. Why would short fiscal periods be chosen?
7. What is a nominal account?
8. Give the two main objectives of the closing entries.
9. Where is the information for the closing entries located?
10. Describe the specific objective of the first closing entry.
11. Describe the specific objective of the second closing entry.
12. Describe the specific objective of the third closing entry.
13. Describe the specific objective of the fourth closing entry.
14. After all of the closing entries have been posted, what is the condition of the equity section of the ledger?
15. Describe how to take off a post-closing trial balance.
16. Explain the purpose of the post-closing trial balance.
17. In correct order state the eight steps in the accounting cycle as you have learned them.

Exercises

Identifying Nominal Accounts

1. A list of accounts appears below and in your workbook. Indicate which of these are nominal accounts.

Accounts

Accounts Payable
Accounts Receivable
Advertising
Automobiles
Bank
Bank Charges
Bank Loan
Building
Capital — Sylvia Magill
Car Expenses
Delivery Expense
Drawings — Sylvia Magill
Equipment
Insurance Expense
Land
Legal Expense
Mortgage Payable
Postage
Rent
Revenue from Commissions
Salaries
Sales
Supplies
Telephone
Wages

Simple Closing Entries Directly from T-Accounts

2. A simplified ledger appears below.

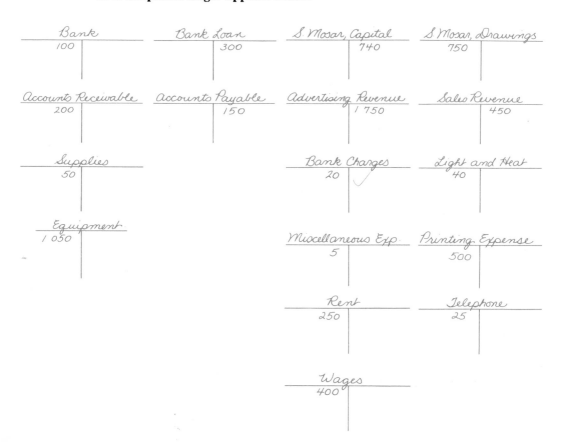

Account	Debit	Credit
Bank	100	
Bank Loan		300
S. Mosar, Capital		740
S. Mosar, Drawings	750	
Accounts Receivable	200	
Accounts Payable		150
Advertising Revenue		1 750
Sales Revenue		450
Supplies	50	
Bank Charges	20	
Light and Heat	40	
Equipment	1 050	
Miscellaneous Exp.	5	
Printing Expense	500	
Rent	250	
Telephone	25	
Wages	400	

1. Calculate the total assets, total liabilities, and the owner's equity. Prove the accuracy of your figures.
2. Journalize the closing entries with information taken directly from the ledger accounts.
3. Post the closing entries to the T-accounts in your workbook. If you are not using the workbook, set the above ledger up on work paper before making the postings.
4. Calculate the balance in the equity account and verify it by comparing it to the owner's equity figure calculated in question 1.

Relating Closing Entries To The Work Sheet

3. A partial work sheet appears below and in your workbook.

Work Sheet

Accounts	Income Statement Dr.	Income Statement Cr.	Balance Sheet Dr.	Balance Sheet Cr.
Bank			150 -	
Accounts Receivable			350 -	
Supplies			75 -	
Equipment			2 000 -	
Bank Loan				500 -
Accounts Payable				125 -
H. Braun, Capital				2 460 -
H. Braun, Drawings			400 -	
Sales Revenue		2 200 -		
Royalties Revenue		1 020 -		
Advertising	90 -			
Bank Charges	60 -			
General Expense	1 390 -			
Power Expense	140 -			
Rent	240 -			
Telephone	60 -			
Wages	1 350 -			
	3 330 -	3 220 -	2 975 -	3 085 -
Net Loss		110 -	110 -	
	3 330 -	3 330 -	3 085 -	3 085 -

closing entry #1

closing entry #2

closing entry #3

closing entry #4

1. Draw a line around the figure or group of figures for each of the closing entries. By means of a line, connect the encircled data to the appropriate number listed at the right.
2. Record the four closing entries in a two-column general journal.
3. Calculate the ending capital balance.

4. A partial work sheet appears below and in your workbook.

Work Sheet

Accounts	Income Statement Dr.	Income Statement Cr.	Balance Sheet Dr.	Balance Sheet Cr.
Bank			100 -	
Accounts Rec'l			400 -	
Supplies			75 -	
Bank Loan				200 -
E. Cyr, Capital				115 -
E. Cyr, Drawings			500 -	
Sales		2200 -		
General Expense	125 -			
Power Expense	215 -			
Rent	400 -			
Wages	700 -			
	1440 -	2200 -	1075 -	315 -
Net Income	760 -			760 -
	2200 -	2200 -	1075 -	1075 -

closing entry #1

closing entry #2

closing entry #3

closing entry #4

1. **Draw a line around the figure or group of figures for each of the closing entries. Use a line to connect the encircled data to the appropriate number listed at the right.**
2. **Record the four closing entries in a two-column general journal.**
3. **Calculate the ending capital balance.**

Simplified Ledger, Work Sheet, Closing Entries, Post-Closing Trial Balance

5. The trial balance of Kenny Company is shown below as of October 31, 19--, the end of a one-month fiscal period.

Bank	$ 740	
Accounts Receivable	13 685	
Supplies	940	
Land	20 000	
Building	50 000	
Furniture and Equipment	10 000	
Accounts Payable		$ 7 500
Mortgage Payable		35 500
L. Kenny, Capital		51 634
L. Kenny, Drawings	3 500	
Revenue		9 870
Advertising	575	
Delivery Expense	416	
Insurance Expense	80	
Miscellaneous Exp.	147	
Salaries	4 261	
Utilities	160	
	$104 504	$104 504

If you are using the workbook for this text, the above accounts and balances are set up for you in T-accounts. Also, the trial balance has been recorded on the work sheet.

If you are not using the workbook, set up the ledger in T-accounts, and complete the first stage of the work sheet.

1. **Complete the work sheet.**
2. **Journalize the closing entries.**
3. **Post the closing entries to the T-accounts.**
4. **Take off a post closing trial balance.**

Accounting Cycle

6. Workbook Exercise: Complete a chart related to the accounting cycle.

Closing Entry Process Done Formally

7. The trial balance of Dick Koehler, who operates a dance hall for the general public in Yorkton, Sask., is shown below. The trial balance is after a fiscal period of six months.

DICK KOEHLER
TRIAL BALANCE
JUNE 30, 19--

Bank	$ 375.20	
Supplies	215.45	
Sound Equipment	15 972.15	
Tapes and Records	4 706.70	
Truck	5 083.30	
Account Payable — Echo Records		$ 126.90
Account Payable — Electronic Shop		2 315.85
D. Koehler, Capital		33 080.95
D. Koehler, Drawings	18 000.00	
Revenue — Admissions		25 700.00
Revenue — Concessions		5 202.30
Advertising	1 040.80	
General Expense	1 790.55	
Musicians' Fees	12 740.85	
Rent	5 200.00	
Wages	1 301.00	
	$66 426.00	$66 426.00

The ledger represented by the trial balance above is included in your workbook. If you are not using this workbook, set this ledger up on columnar paper.

1. **Prepare the work sheet for the six-month period.**
2. **Prepare the balance sheet and the income statement.**
3. **Journalize the closing entries.**
4. **Post the closing entries to the accounts.**
5. **Take off a post-closing trial balance. Verify capital by comparing with the balance sheet.**

Using Your Knowledge

8. Given the following limited information, prepare the closing entries for O. Como.

O. COMO
BALANCE SHEET
NOVEMBER 30, 19--

Assets			
Bank			$100
Accounts Receivable			300
Supplies			70
			$470
Liabilities			
Accounts Payable			$150
Owner's Equity			
Balance November 1		$170	
Net Income	$650		
Drawings	500		
Increase in Equity		150	
Balance November 30			320
			$470

O. COMO
INCOME STATEMENT
MONTH ENDED NOVEMBER 30, 19--

Revenue	$1 800
Expenses	
General Expense	$ 50
Utilities	100
Wages	1 000
	$1 150
Net Income	$650

9. John, a student in accounting, comes to you, his teacher, with the following difficulty. After a great deal of time and effort, John has failed to balance the post-closing trial balance, and has become quite frustrated. 'Everything was going fine,' he states. 'My balance sheet balanced. My income statement agreed. I just can't figure it out.'

John's balance sheet, income statement, and post-closing trial balance are given below.

1. **How can you tell quickly which figure(s) on the post-closing trial balance are probably the incorrect ones.**
2. **Which figure(s) are wrong in this trial balance?**
3. **Explain what error or errors John has made.**

BALANCE SHEET

Assets			
Bank		$ 1 301	
Accounts Receivable		7 406	
Supplies		385	
Land		21 900	
Buildings		75 382	
Equipment		19 462	
			$125 836
Liabilities			
Bank Loan		$12 000	
Accounts Payable		5 726	
Mortgage Payable		52 672	$ 70 398
Owner's Equity			
Beginning balance		$71 314	
Net Loss	$ 876		
Drawings	15 000		
Decrease in equity		15 876	
Ending balance			55 438
			$125 836

INCOME STATEMENT

Revenue		$19 462
Expenses		
Advertising	$ 3 902	
Delivery	3 764	
Wages	12 000	
Utilities	672	20 338
Net Loss		$ 876

POST-CLOSING TRIAL BALANCE

Bank	$ 1 301	
Accounts Receivable	7 406	
Supplies	385	
Land	21 900	
Buildings	75 382	
Equipment	19 462	
Bank Loan		$ 12 000
Accounts Payable		5 726
Mortgage Payable		52 672
Owner's Equity		57 190
	$125 836	$127 588

Cases

Case 1 *Once a Liability, Always a Liability?*

Birch Contracting Company in Nanaimo, B.C., was obliged by law to provide vacation pay to every employee equal in amount to 2 percent of the gross pay of the employee. This liability for vacation pay became due and payable on June 1 of each year.

Most of the company's work was seasonal in nature and required a lot of manual labour. Therefore, Birch Contracting employed many migrant workers who stayed for only one season. These workers were often new Canadians who didn't know Canadian laws and regulations.

Birch Contracting provided for the necessary vacation pay and the accounting entries were properly recorded in the books. However, the company made no effort to contact former employees when the payment came due. Locating former employees was difficult, time-consuming, and often impossible. Therefore, the company chose to wait until the employees made the contact. Consequently, all former employees who did not contact the company were never paid their vacation pay.

Over a period of years, the liability for vacation pay as shown by the ledger grew to a sizable amount. The company accountant felt that something should be done about the liability, but the owner directed her to leave things as they were.

Questions

1. Is the company policy a reasonable one?
2. Should an unpaid liability be left on the books indefinitely?
3. What two advantages are gained by leaving the unpaid liability on the books indefinitely?
4. How would correct accounting practice deal with the above situation?

Case 2 *Keeping Branch Managers on the Alert*

The 11-UP Company produces a soft drink for sale to the general public. The owner and general manager, W. Bully, operates the head office plant in Toronto, Ont. In addition to the main plant, Bully has set up branch plants in three smaller centres to serve a large region in southern Ontario.

The success of 11-UP is based on its particular flavour. Bully developed the recipe for 11-UP some years ago and he is still the only one who knows the formula. The recipe is locked up in a vault in the office of a trust company.

Bully's branch system is very simple. Bully selects the site, builds the plant, and equips it according to a standard plan. He then hires local people to run the branch operation. At the branches, the product is made by combining a special syrup concentrate with sugar and water. The branches purchase the syrup concentrate from head office for a uniform price. The selling price of the soft drink is also uniform throughout the entire area.

Once a year Bully calls the branch managers to head office for a meeting at which the branch results for the year are discussed and analyzed. Bully calls this meeting his 'show down'. The branch managers don't particularly enjoy the proceedings.

Before the annual meeting, the branch offices are required to send their financial reports to head office. A grand summary of the results of all of the branches is then prepared for the meeting. The grand summary for the next annual meeting is shown in Table 10-1.

Table 10-1 Financial Summary of Branch Operations of the 11-UP Company

	LONDON BRANCH		HAMILTON BRANCH		WINDSOR BRANCH	
General Data						
Manager	A. Slaughter		M. Masconi		R. Bogart	
Population of area served	410 000		700 000		330 000	
Number of employees	9		12		8	
Number of trucks	5		8		4	
Profit and Loss Data	*in $000's*	*% of Sales*	*in $000's*	*% of Sales*	*in $000's*	*% of Sales*
Sales	760	100.0	1 108	100.0	620	100.0
Controllable Expenses						
Advertising	21	2.8	37	3.4	15	2.4
Sales Promotion	5	.7	6	.5	4	.6
Concentrate	185	24.4	269	24.3	176	28.4
Sugar	20	2.6	30	2.7	19	3.1
Maintenance						
—Equipment	2	.3	5	.4	2	.3
—Trucks	2	.3	9	.8	1	.2
—Plant	1	.1	1	.1	—	.0
Gasoline and Oil	265	34.8	320	28.9	160	25.8
Wages	91	12.0	127	11.5	95	15.3
Electricity	1	.1	1	.1	1	.2
Heating	1	.1	1	.1	1	.2
Bottle Breakage	1	.1	4	.3	—	.0
Non-Controllable Expenses						
Depreciation	80	10.5	87	7.8	85	13.7
Taxes	2	.3	2	.2	3	.5
Manager's Salary	35	4.6	40	3.6	35	5.6
Total Expenses	712	93.7	939	84.7	597	96.3
Net Profit	48	6.3	169	15.3	23	3.7

Mr. Bully is a thorough manager. He takes the trouble to analyze the financial summary thoroughly, looking for items that are deficient or excessive which may indicate a weakness in branch operations. Mr. Bully's objective is to eliminate weaknesses, such as theft, carelessness, and wastage, in order to maximize profits.

Questions

1. Analyze the statements as if you were Mr. Bully. Prepare a list of five items that seem to be unusual enough to warrant an explanation from the particular manager affected.
2. Provide reasons that would explain the unusual items on your list.

Career
Barbara Blaney / Senior Bookkeeper

Barbara Blaney graduated from high school and went to work as a bank teller. Two years later, she accepted a clerical position with Bell Canada. Soon thereafter, Barbara left the work force for 15 years to raise a family. During this period, she took some accounting courses in the evening.

Barbara returned to work as a part-time bookkeeper and treasurer for the Association for the Mentally Retarded. She handled all cash receipts and cash payments. Each month Barbara prepared a statement of receipts and payments that showed the Association's current bank balance. Barbara also prepared the monthly bank reconciliation statement.

For the past five years, Barbara has been a full-time senior bookkeeper in the business office of the Association for the Mentally Retarded. Her bookkeeping duties have increased immensely. She continues to journalize all cash receipts and payments, to prepare a monthly statement of receipts and payments, and to produce the monthly bank reconciliation statement. In addition, Barbara now prepares the monthly trial balance, the work sheet, the income statement, and the balance sheet. Each month, Barbara issues customers' statements to those companies that hire employees through the Association. She also oversees the preparation of the Association's biweekly payroll.

Each year, Barbara prepares all the closing entries and takes a post-closing trial balance. She closes out all revenue and expense accounts to an Income Summary account. Each year, Barbara also supervises the planning of annual budgets for many of the Association's programs.

Barbara is one of an increasing number of women who are rejoining the work force after their children are grown. She is pleased with the success she has achieved. Although most of her accounting knowledge has been gained through experience, she feels that the accounting courses she took at night school provided her with important background and a competitive edge in the marketplace.

11

Source Documents

11-1 Cash Sales Slip
11-2 Sales Invoice
11-3 Dual Purpose Sales Slip
11-4 Purchase Invoice
11-5 Cheque Copy
11-6 Cash Receipts List
11-7 Bank Advice
11-8 Summary of Source Documents and Related Accounting Entries

Objectives

When you have completed Chapter 11 you should:

1. Be able to recognize a number of source documents.
2. Be able to answer questions about specific source documents.
3. Know the purposes of source documents.
4. Understand that source documents are part of a system for controlling and recording business transactions.
5. Know the accounting entries for specific source documents.
6. Be able to tell the difference between a purchase invoice and a sales invoice.

The topic of source documents was briefly introduced in Chapter 6. Here we will examine this topic thoroughly using detailed illustrations and explanations.

Business transactions usually take place outside the accounting department. These transactions are usually not initiated by accounting personnel, but by the owner, by salesmen, by department heads, and others. How, then, does the accounting department find out about these transactions?

The accounting department learns of transactions from business papers called source documents. Source documents are sent to the accounting department by those who have been involved in business transactions. The accounting department then uses these source documents to make its journal entries. Almost every accounting entry is based on a source document. A source document is a business paper that records the nature of a transaction and provides all the information needed to account for it properly.

When there is no source document to back up an accounting entry, the entry must be supported in some other way. The following records may be substituted if there is no source document:

1. A memorandum from the owner.
2. Detailed calculations or a valid explanation by the accountant.
3. A previous source document, such as a long-term rental agreement, which covers a series of transactions.

Source documents do not only function to initiate accounting entries. They also prove that the entries are accurate. Owners, bankers, or government auditors may demand verification of the accounting records at any time. The source documents provide this verification and prove that the records are accurate. If there are errors, the source documents help to pinpoint them. Source documents also have other routine uses, as you will see in the following pages.

Several basic source documents will be explained and illustrated throughout this chapter. These are considered basic source documents because they pertain to the basic transactions that take place frequently in the business world. A company called Masthead Marine, owned by David Scott of Vancouver, B.C., will be used to illustrate these source documents. Masthead Marine is in the business of selling boats, marine equipment, and boat supplies and parts.

11.1 Cash Sales Slip

A **cash sales slip** is a business form that is prepared whenever goods or services are sold for cash. Usually there is an original and two copies. The features of a cash sales slip and the uses for the copies are shown in Figure 11.1.

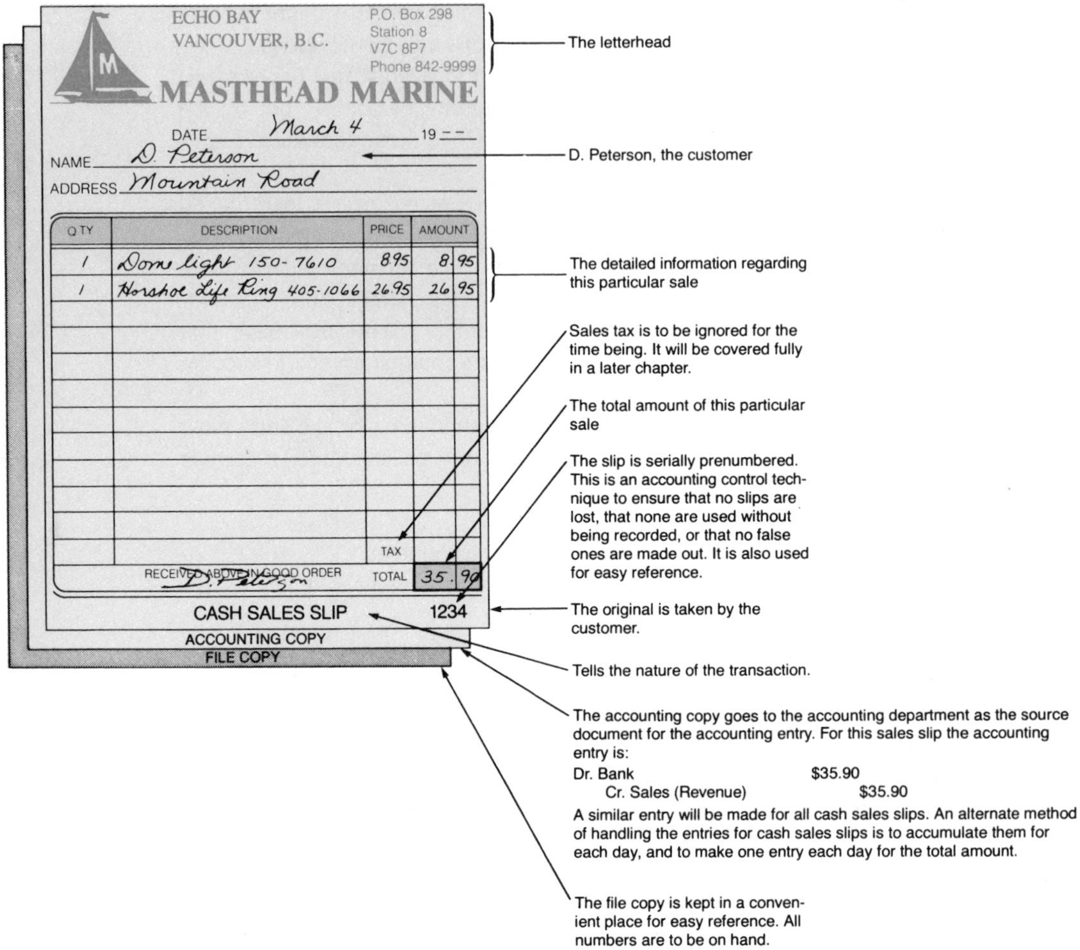
ECHO BAY
VANCOUVER, B.C.
P.O. Box 298
Station 8
V7C 8P7
Phone 842-9999
MASTHEAD MARINE
DATE March 4 19--
NAME D. Peterson
ADDRESS Mountain Road
QTY
DESCRIPTION
PRICE
AMOUNT
1 Dome light 150-7610 8.95 8.95
1 Horseshoe Life Ring 405-1066 26.95 26.95
TAX
TOTAL 35.90
RECEIVED ABOVE IN GOOD ORDER
D. Peterson
CASH SALES SLIP
1234
ACCOUNTING COPY
FILE COPY
The letterhead
D. Peterson, the customer
The detailed information regarding this particular sale
Sales tax is to be ignored for the time being. It will be covered fully in a later chapter.
The total amount of this particular sale
The slip is serially prenumbered. This is an accounting control technique to ensure that no slips are lost, that none are used without being recorded, or that no false ones are made out. It is also used for easy reference.
The original is taken by the customer.
Tells the nature of the transaction.
The accounting copy goes to the accounting department as the source document for the accounting entry. For this sales slip the accounting entry is:
Dr. Bank $35.90
Cr. Sales (Revenue) $35.90
A similar entry will be made for all cash sales slips. An alternate method of handling the entries for cash sales slips is to accumulate them for each day, and to make one entry each day for the total amount.
The file copy is kept in a convenient place for easy reference. All numbers are to be on hand.

Figure 11.1 Cash sales slip representing a sale of goods or services for cash.

11.2 Sales Invoice

A **sales invoice** is a business form that is prepared whenever goods or services are sold on account. Usually there is an original and several copies. The features of a sales invoice and the uses for the copies are shown in Figure 11.2.

In any sales transaction, the party that sells is known as the **vendor** and the party that buys is known as the **purchaser**. In this case, Masthead Marine is the vendor and S. and S. Boatworks is the purchaser.

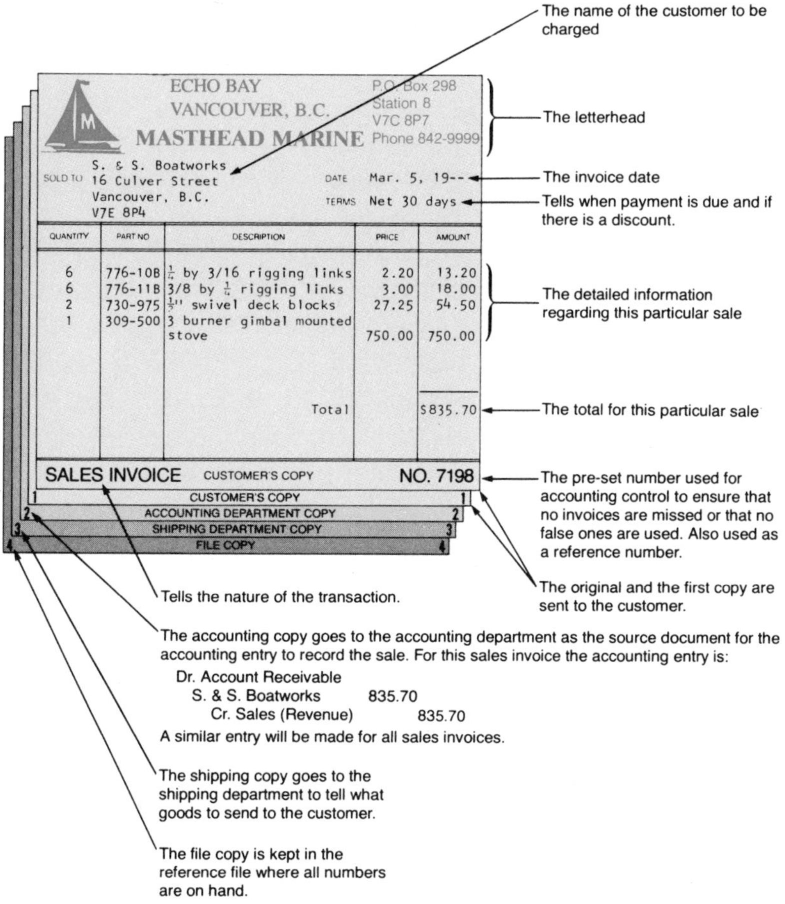

Figure 11.2 A sales invoice representing a sale of goods or services on account.

11.3 Dual Purpose Sales Slip

It is possible to handle all sales, whether charge or cash, on a single form. Two distinctly different business forms for sales are not necessary. All that is needed is a place on the form for the sales person to check off whether the sale is a 'cash' or a 'charge' sale. An example of a dual purchase sales slip is shown in Figure 11.3.

Small businesses, whose sales are mostly over the counter for cash, would choose this type of form. Because charge sales are a small part of their business, they don't require a formal system for handling them.

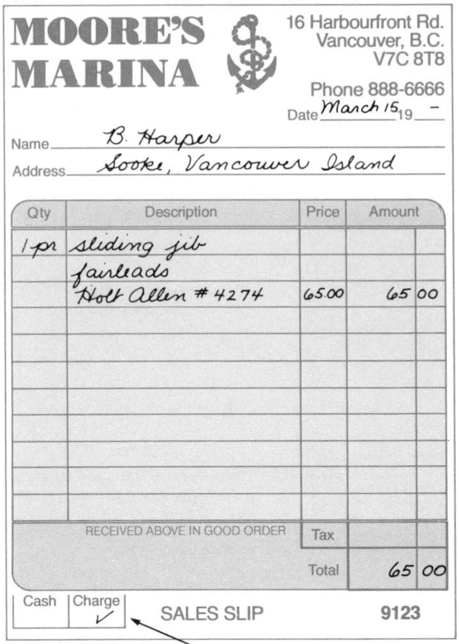
MOORE'S MARINA
16 Harbourfront Rd.
Vancouver, B.C.
V7C 8T8
Phone 888-6666
Date March 15 19 –
Name B. Harper
Address Sooke, Vancouver Island

Qty	Description	Price	Amount
1 pr	sliding jib fairleads Holt Allen # 4274	65.00	65 00
	RECEIVED ABOVE IN GOOD ORDER	Tax	
		Total	65 00

Cash | Charge ✓ | SALES SLIP | 9123

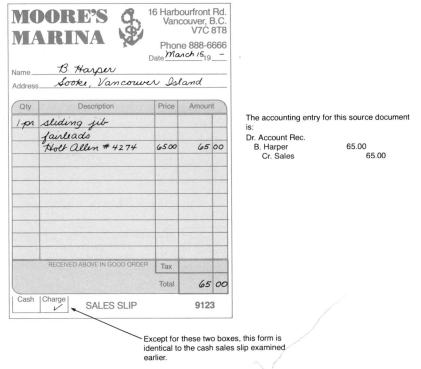

The accounting entry for this source document is:

Dr. Account Rec.		
B. Harper	65.00	
Cr. Sales		65.00

Except for these two boxes, this form is identical to the cash sales slip examined earlier.

Figure 11.3 Dual purpose sales slip.

11.4 Purchase Invoice

Masthead Marine is not always the vendor. Often it makes purchases on account from other companies. When Masthead Marine makes a charge sale to a customer it issues a sales invoice to that customer. Similarly, when Masthead Marine is the customer in a charge sale, it receives a sales invoice from the vendor. When the other company's invoice arrives at the office of Masthead Marine, it becomes known as a **purchase invoice**. A purchase invoice is a business form representing a purchase of goods or services on account.

Because Masthead Marine buys goods and services from a number of different companies, many different purchase invoices are on hand. Because these invoices are for the purchase of many different goods and services, no single accounting entry can be satisfactory in all cases. The account credited, an Account Payable, is common to all purchases on account, but the account debited varies according to what particular goods or services were purchased. The summary below illustrates this point.

The nature of the purchase invoice	*The account debited*	*The account credited*
1. For car repairs	Car Expense	Account Payable
2. For paint for building	Building Maintenance	Account Payable
3. For goods for resale	Merchandise Inventory	Account Payable
4. For advertising	Advertising Expense	Account Payable

It should be clear to you from this summary that the account debited depends on the nature of the goods or services purchased, and that the account credited is always an account payable.

Let us now look at two examples of purchase invoices. Figure 11.4 shows a purchase invoice for repairs to a lift truck. Figure 11.5 shows a purchase invoice for merchandise for resale.

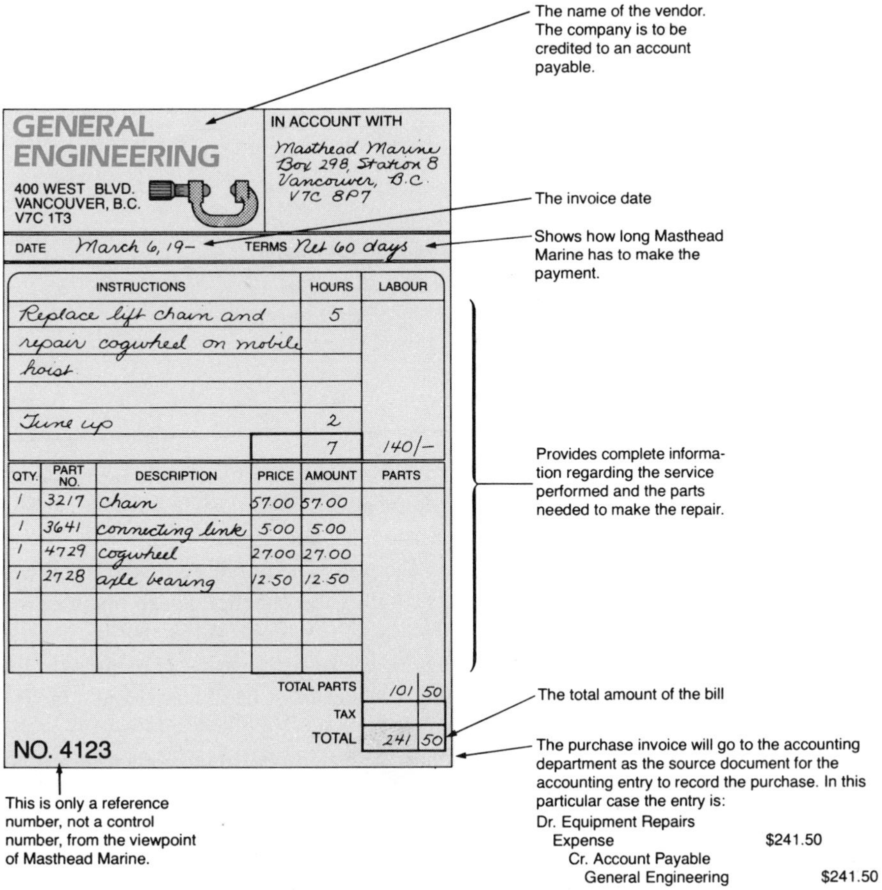
GENERAL ENGINEERING
400 WEST BLVD.
VANCOUVER, B.C.
V7C 1T3

IN ACCOUNT WITH
Masthead Marine
Box 298, Station 8
Vancouver, B.C.
V7C 8P7

DATE March 6, 19– TERMS Net 60 days

INSTRUCTIONS	HOURS	LABOUR
Replace lift chain and	5	
repair cogwheel on mobile		
hoist		
Tune up	2	
	7	140/–

QTY.	PART NO.	DESCRIPTION	PRICE	AMOUNT	PARTS
1	3217	chain	57.00	57.00	
1	3641	connecting link	5.00	5.00	
1	4729	cogwheel	27.00	27.00	
1	2728	axle bearing	12.50	12.50	

TOTAL PARTS 101 50
TAX
TOTAL 241 50

NO. 4123

Figure 11.4 A purchase invoice for repairs to a lift truck.

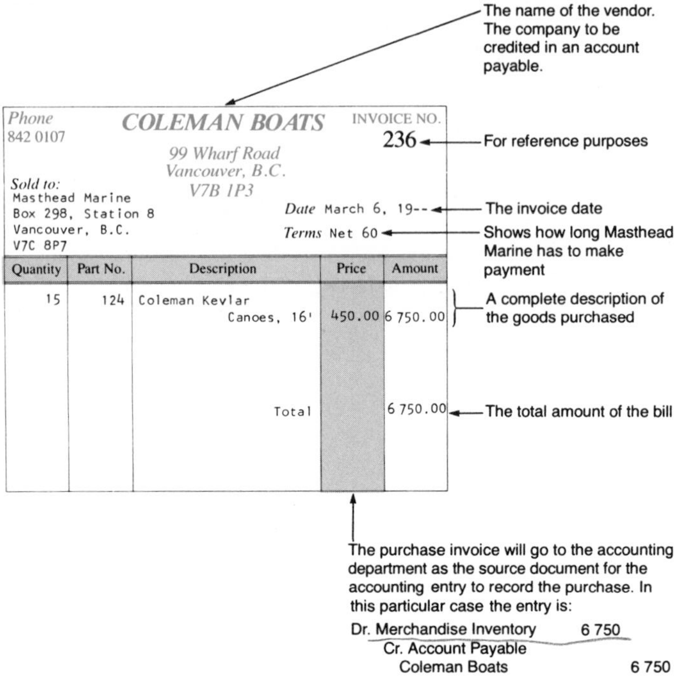

Figure 11.5 A purchase invoice for merchandise for resale.

11.5 Cheque Copy

A **cheque copy** is a business form that is used as a record of a payment made by cheque. Cheques may be issued for any of a number of things, such as cash purchases, wages, owner's withdrawals, payments on account, and so on.

Most cheques are issued for payments on account. The purchase invoices that are being paid are summarized on a tear-off portion of the cheque. These invoices are for purchases made in the past.

If the payment is for a cash purchase, that is, for something that is being paid for at the time it is being purchased, a supporting voucher must be obtained and attached to the cheque copy as proof of the purchase.

For some payments no supporting voucher is needed. For owner's withdrawals, the cashed cheque is proof that the owner received the money. For wages, the company's payroll records are the proof of proper payment.

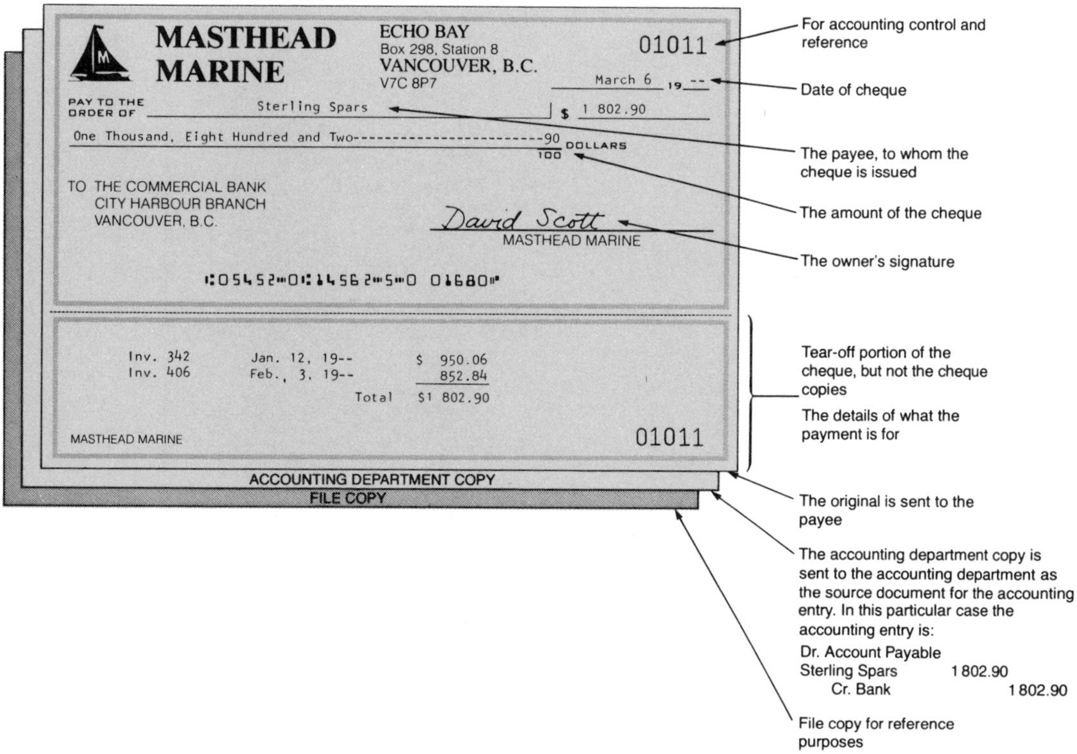

Figure 11.6 A cheque representing a payment made by the company. The accounting department copy of this cheque is the source document for the payment.

11.6 Cash Receipts List

Each day, in a business, some cheques are usually received from customers on account. The cheques themselves cannot be kept as the basis for accounting entries, as they must be taken to the bank for deposit. But before making the deposit an alphabetical listing of the cheques is prepared by a mail clerk or another employee.

The **cash receipts list** is a business paper representing the money coming in from customers on account. This listing shows all of the cheques received, the names of the senders, the cheque amounts, and an explanation of what each cheque is intended to pay. Some of the information for this listing is taken from the tear-off portion of the cheques received.

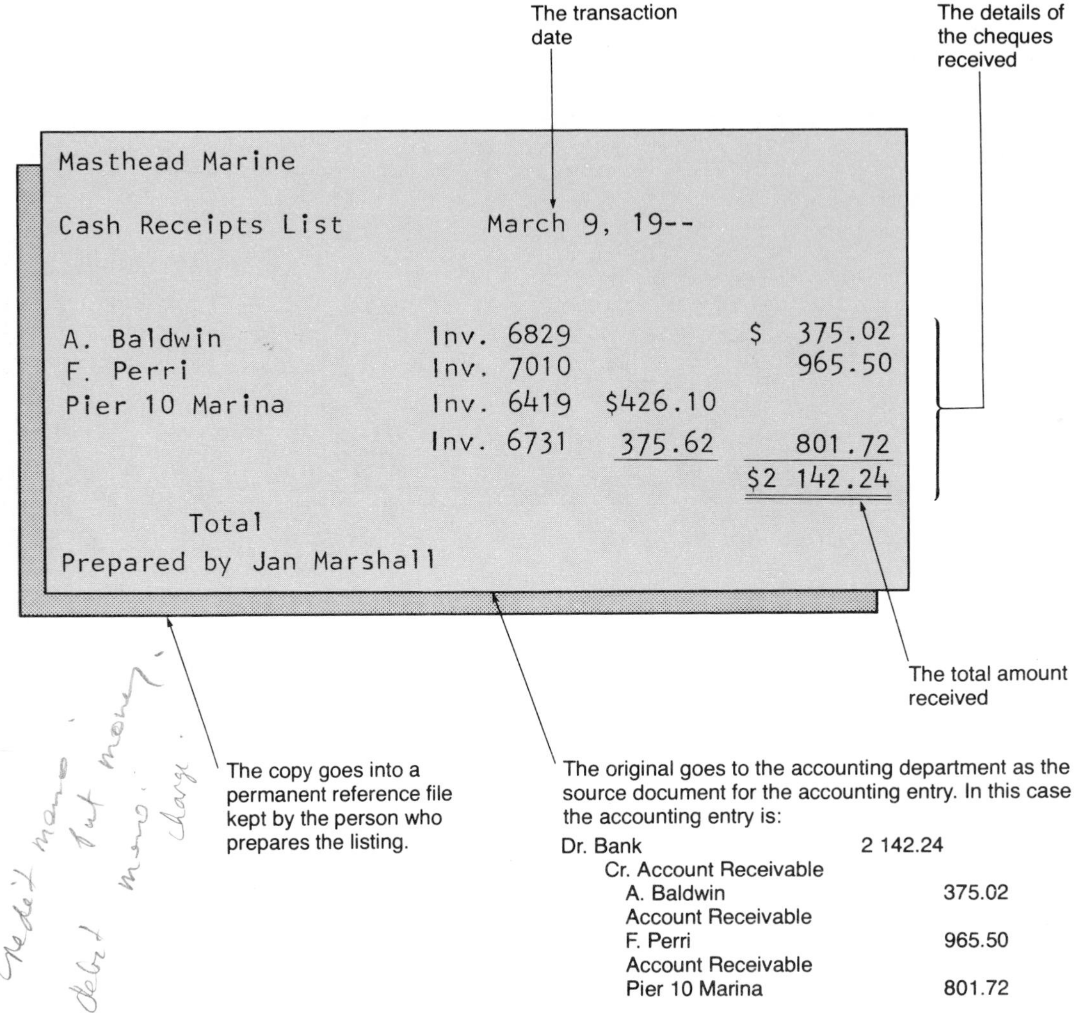
Masthead Marine

Cash Receipts List March 9, 19--

A. Baldwin	Inv. 6829		$ 375.02
F. Perri	Inv. 7010		965.50
Pier 10 Marina	Inv. 6419	$426.10	
	Inv. 6731	375.62	801.72
			$2 142.24
Total			

Prepared by Jan Marshall

The transaction date
The details of the cheques received
The total amount received
The copy goes into a permanent reference file kept by the person who prepares the listing.
The original goes to the accounting department as the source document for the accounting entry. In this case the accounting entry is:
Dr. Bank 2 142.24
Cr. Account Receivable
A. Baldwin 375.02
Account Receivable
F. Perri 965.50
Account Receivable
Pier 10 Marina 801.72

Figure 11.7 A cash receipts list.

11.7 Bank Advice

Whenever the bank initiates a change in the bank account of a business, it informs the business by means of a bank advice. A **bank advice** or **bank memo** is a business paper representing a bank account increase or decrease initiated by the bank.

In Figure 11.8 the Commercial Bank has sent a bank advice to Masthead Marine telling them that their account was charged interest on a bank loan on March 9, 19––.

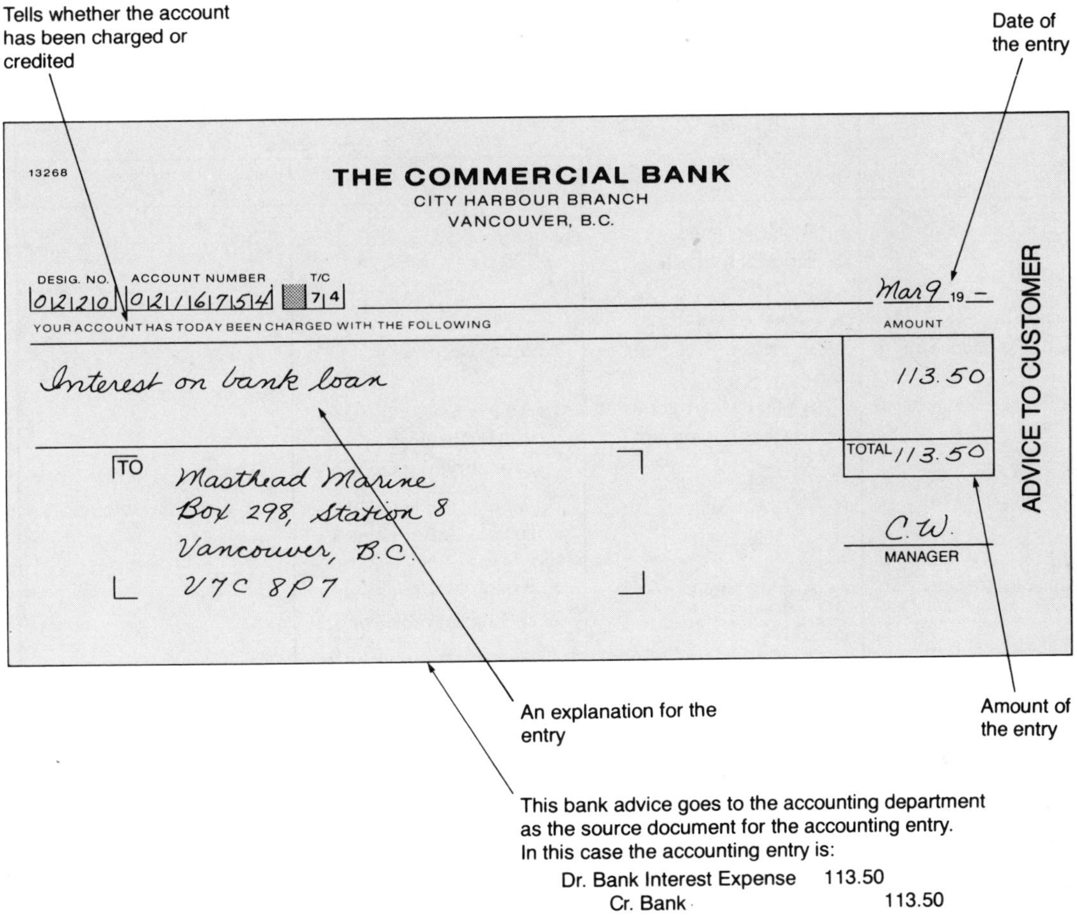

Tells whether the account has been charged or credited
Date of the entry
13268
THE COMMERCIAL BANK
CITY HARBOUR BRANCH
VANCOUVER, B.C.
DESIG. NO. 0 2 2 0
ACCOUNT NUMBER 0 2 1 / 6 7 5 4
T/C 7 4
Mar 9 19 –
YOUR ACCOUNT HAS TODAY BEEN CHARGED WITH THE FOLLOWING
AMOUNT
Interest on bank loan
113.50
TOTAL 113.50
TO Masthead Marine
Box 298, Station 8
Vancouver, B.C.
V7C 8P7
C.W.
MANAGER
ADVICE TO CUSTOMER
An explanation for the entry
Amount of the entry
This bank advice goes to the accounting department as the source document for the accounting entry. In this case the accounting entry is:
Dr. Bank Interest Expense 113.50
Cr. Bank 113.50

Figure 11.8 A bank advice.

11.8 Summary of Source Documents and Related Accounting Entries

Source Document	*Description of Transaction*	*Accounting Entry*	
		Account Debited	*Account Credited*
Cash Sales Slip	A sale of goods or services for cash	Bank	Sales
Sales Invoice Charge Sales Slip	A sale of goods or services on account	Account Receivable	Sales
Purchase Invoice	A purchase of goods or services on account	1. An asset account such as Merchandise Inventory, or 2. An expense account such as Advertising	Account Payable
Cheque Copy	Any payment	1. A liability such as an account payable, or 2. An asset account such as Automobiles, or 3. An expense account such as Car Expense, or 4. The Drawings account	Bank
Bank Debit Memo	A decrease in the bank account initiated by the bank	Bank Interest or Bank Charges	Bank
Cash Receipts List	The cheques received from customers on account	Bank	Accounts Receivable
Cash Register Tape	Will be covered in a later chapter		

Additional Supporting Documents and Vouchers

In addition to the source documents listed above you may encounter the following:

1. Cash register slips.
2. Receipts, such as those for donations or for postage.
3. Hydro bills, telephone bills.
4. Credit card or charge account statements.
5. Insurance endorsement certificates.

6. Written memos from owner.
7. Bank statements.
8. Bank credit memos.

Number of Copies of Source Documents

There is no fixed required number of copies of business documents. Each business develops a system of accounting suited to its own needs and preferences. Some owners and managers prefer a simple system, others a more elaborate one. The number of copies of any particular business document depends primarily on how elaborate the system is. Generally, the more elaborate the system, the greater the number of copies required to satisfy it.

Accounting Terms

cash sales slip
sales invoice
vendor
purchaser
purchase invoice
cheque copy
cash receipts list
bank advice
bank memo

Review Questions

1. Who initiates transactions in a business?
2. How does the accounting department learn of transactions?
3. What is a source document?
4. Explain why there is not always a source document for every accounting entry.
5. Describe the various uses of source documents.
6. Why are business forms prenumbered?
7. Explain why there are copies of source documents.
8. Explain the difference between a cash sales slip and a sales invoice.
9. Explain the difference between a sales invoice and a purchase invoice.
10. Explain what is meant by 'terms' on a sales invoice.
11. On a purchase invoice, why is there only a reference number and not a control number?
12. Why does a cheque have two parts to it?
13. Does a cheque copy have a tear-off part? Explain.
14. Describe the information that is put on the cheque and on the tear-off part.
15. Who is the payee of a cheque?
16. Why are there two business documents for a cash purchase?
17. When does a bank issue a debit or credit advice?
18. Explain the difference between a debit advice and a credit advice.

Exercises

Relating Source Documents, Transactions, and Accounting Entries

1. Identify the source document or documents that would support the following transactions:

a. Debt paid on account
b. Supplies purchased for cash
c. Service performed on account
d. Money withdrawn by owner
e. Bank loan reduced
f. Donation paid by cash
g. Receipt from customer on account
h. Supplies purchased on account
i. Sale made on account
j. Service performed for cash
k. Bank interest charged
l. Hydro bill paid by cash

2. Workbook Exercise: Complete a chart relating transactions to source documents.

3. Workbook Exercise: Complete a chart relating source documents to accounting entries.

4. Workbook Exercise: Complete a chart relating accounting entries to source documents to transactions.

Source Documents — Identifying and Explaining

5. Answer the following questions related to the source document below.

1. **What business document is it?**
2. **What is the purpose of the document?**
3. **Where does the information come from to prepare the list?**
4. **Why is a list prepared?**
5. **In the above listing what does 'on account' mean compared to 'Invoice 4502'.**
6. **Give the accounting entry that would be made as a result of the listing.**
7. **Who is G. Smalley?**

SAYERS AND ASSOCIATES
CASH RECEIPTS LIST MARCH 14, 19--

Degagne Machine Shop	on account	$ 500.00
Kivella Bake Shop	Inv. 4502	315.43
Molner Paints	Inv. 3909	214.60
Robitaille Taxi	on account	200.00
G. Smalley	Total	$1 230.03

---

6. Answer the following questions related to the source document below.

1. **What business document is it?**
2. **What is the purpose of the document?**
3. **Who is the issuer of the document?**
4. **Explain the purposes of the document number.**
5. **Give the accounting entry that would be made by the sender of the document.**

DAVIDSON TREE EXPERTS

Horseshoe Valley
Ontario, L4M 4Y8
Phone 321-8765

DATE *March 10* 19 *--*
NAME *F. Vailliant*
ADDRESS *Craighurst*

QUANTITY	DESCRIPTION	PRICE	AMOUNT	
6	*pruning of mature trees, removing dead wood*	*30*	*180*	*—*
2	*cut down and remove mature trees*	*75*	*150*	*—*
		TAX		
	RECEIVED ABOVE IN GOOD ORDER *F. Vailliant*	TOTAL	*330*	*—*

CASH SALES SLIP 2651

7. Answer the following questions related to the source document below.

1. **What business document is it?**
2. **Who is the sender of the document? Who is the receiver?**
3. **To which business is this document the equivalent of a sales invoice? To which business is it a purchase invoice?**
4. **Give the accounting entry that would be made by the sender of the document.**
5. **Give the accounting entry that would be made by the receiver of the document.**

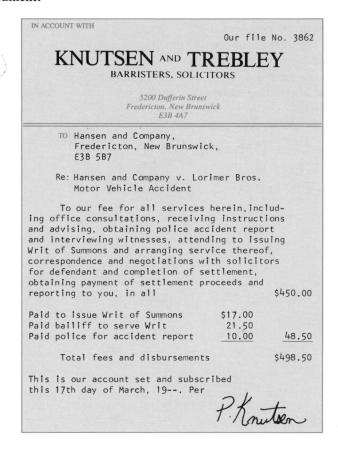

IN ACCOUNT WITH

Our file No. 3862

KNUTSEN AND TREBLEY
BARRISTERS, SOLICITORS

5200 Dufferin Street
Fredericton, New Brunswick
E3B 4A7

TO Hansen and Company,
Fredericton, New Brunswick,
E3B 5B7

Re: Hansen and Company v. Lorimer Bros.
Motor Vehicle Accident

To our fee for all services herein, including office consultations, receiving instructions and advising, obtaining police accident report and interviewing witnesses, attending to issuing Writ of Summons and arranging service thereof, correspondence and negotiations with solicitors for defendant and completion of settlement, obtaining payment of settlement proceeds and reporting to you, in all		$450.00
Paid to issue Writ of Summons	$17.00	
Paid bailiff to serve Writ	21.50	
Paid police for accident report	10.00	48.50
Total fees and disbursements		$498.50

This is our account set and subscribed this 17th day of March, 19--. Per

P. Knutsen

8. The document below arrives at your place of business by mail. Answer the following questions concerning it.

1. **What business document is it?**
2. **Who do you work for?**
3. **Why was this document sent to your company?**
4. **What does the broken line on the document represent?**
5. **Explain the information beneath the broken line.**
6. **Give the accounting entry that would be made in the books of your company to record the source document.**

CARBIDE TOOLS LIMITED
4000 Essex Drive
Vancouver, B.C.
V7R 8S8

No. 1101

May 10 19--

PAY TO THE ORDER OF Presto-Can Company $ 1 368.30

One Thousand, Three Hundred and Sixty-Eight----------------30/100 DOLLARS

THE COMMERCIAL BANK
CITY HARBOUR BRANCH
VANCOUVER, B.C.

Marianne Mayo
CARBIDE TOOLS LIMITED

⑈030800 3⑈041⑆ 004⑆ ⑈030800 3⑈

IN PAYMENT OF THE FOLLOWING

Invoice	Date	Amount
#6149	April 16	$ 217.02
#7002	April 30	400.12
#7109	May 7	751.16
	Total	$1 368.30

CARBIDE TOOLS LIMITED 1101

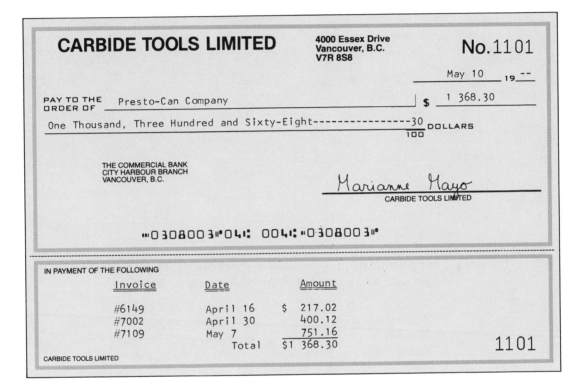

9. **Answer the following questions related to the source document below.**
   1. **What business document is it?**
   2. **In whose books of account is an accounting entry now necessary as a result of this source document?**
   3. **Give the accounting entry that would be made as a result of the source document.**

13268

THE COMMERCIAL BANK
LANSING AVENUE AND GROVE STREET
REGINA, SASKATCHEWAN

DESIG. NO.	ACCOUNT NUMBER	T/C	
0263	0947996	74	Mar. 6 19--

YOUR ACCOUNT HAS TODAY BEEN CREDITED WITH THE FOLLOWING

	AMOUNT
Interest on term deposit	362.04
	TOTAL 362.04

TO
Electroniks Company
Main Street
Flin Flon, Manitoba

A.S.
MANAGER

ADVICE TO CUSTOMER

Journalizing from Source Documents

10. Champion Rent-All, a business in Parry Sound, Ont., rents out tools and equipment. The accounts for the business are as follows:

1	Bank	40	Rental Revenue
2	Accounts Receivable	50	Bank Charges
3	Supplies	51	Delivery Expense
4	Rental Tools and Equipment	52	Light, Heat, and Water
5	Truck	53	Miscellaneous Expense
20	Bank Loan	54	Rent
21	Accounts Payable	55	Telephone
30	Frank N. Mazur, Capital	56	Wages
31	Frank N. Mazur, Drawings		

On page 76 of a two-column general journal, journalize the following selected transactions of Champion Rent-All.

Transactions

April

4 *Cash Sales Slip*
No. 409, to W. Franklin, $52.50

6 *Charge Sales Slip*
No. 410, to G. Fairbridge, $87.50

7 *Purchase Invoice*
From Vulcan Machinery, No. 3062 for one hydraulic jack, a rental tool, $315.

8 *Cheque Copy*
No. 1475, to Fair Supply Company, $215.90 on account.

11 *Cash Sales Slip*
No. 411, to R. Gullett, $47.50.

12 *Cash Receipt*
From P. Mathers, $92.75 on account.

14 *Cheque Copy*
No. 1476, to Municipal Hydro, for cash payment of hydro bill, $75.

15 *Cheque Copy*
No. 1477, to R. Klein, $300 for wages.

18 *Cash Sales Slip*
No. 412, to A. Heisse, $90.

20 *Cheque Copy*
No. 1478, to the owner, Frank Mazur, for his personal use, $350.

20 *Credit Card Statement*
From Husky Oil Company, $95 for gas and oil used in the delivery truck.

25 *Bank Debit Memo*
For bank service charge, $42.50.

30 *Cheque Copy*
No. 1479, to R. Klein, $300 for wages.

---

11. Janet Nuttall is in business as a commercial artist in Winnipeg, Man. The chart of accounts for her business is shown below.

CHART OF ACCOUNTS

1	Bank	30	Janet Nuttall, Capital
2	Accounts Receivable	31	Janet Nuttall, Drawings
3	Art Supplies	40	Fees Revenue
4	Equipment	50	Car Expenses
5	Automobile	51	Electricity Expense
		52	Miscellaneous Expense
20	Accounts Payable	53	Rent Expense
		54	Telephone Expense

On page 19 of a two-column general journal, journalize the following selected transactions of the business of Janet Nuttall.

Transactions

July

3 *Sales Invoice*
No. 192, to Mountain Distributors, $175.

4 *Sales Invoice*
No. 193, to Old Fort Trading Co., $300.

7 *Cheque Copy*
No. 316, to Central Garage for the cash payment for repairs to the business automobile, $115.

10 *Cheque Copy*
No. 317, to Twin City Hydro for the cash payment of the monthly hydro bill, $65.

12 *Purchase Invoice*
From C. & C. Equipment, No. 1401, for one large metal drawing table, $475.

12 *Cheque Copy*
No. 318, to Dejavu Art Supply for the cash payment for artist's supplies, $85.

15 *Cheque Copy*
No. 319, to the owner for her personal use, $350.

17 *Sales Invoice*
No. 194, to Display Design Company, $255.

19 *Cash Receipt*
From Victor Schilling, $150 on account.

20 *Cheque Copy*
No. 320, to C. & C. Equipment, $475 on account.

21 *Sales Invoice*
No. 195, to Scoville Sales, $235.

24 *Cheque Copy*
No. 321, to Fleming Properties, for the monthly rent, $375.

27 *Purchase Invoice*
From Lougherys Limited, No. 634, for drafting and artist's equipment, $215.

27 *Cheque Copy*
No. 322, to Twin City Telephone, for cash payment of the monthly telephone bill, $28.50.

28 *Credit Card Statement*
From Imperial Oil, for the gas and oil used in the automobile, $71.40.

30 *Cash Receipt*
From Old Fort Trading Co., $300 on account.

Cases

Case 1 *A Better Way to Account for Cheques Issued?*

Rather than continue her schooling, Maria Di Lorenzo decided to take a job in the accounting office of a small business. Maria had taken a basic accounting course in high school and was able to handle her new duties easily.

Maria was quick to learn and soon became very good at her job. She quickly thought that she could see where improvements could be made to make the system more efficient. In particular, Maria had a novel idea about the accounting for cheques.

According to the system already in effect a journal entry was written for each cheque issued. Maria suggested the following to replace this system.

a. Record the account number or numbers and the respective amounts to be debited on the tear-off portion of each cheque. (Remember that the tear-off portion of a cheque is detachable only on the original. All of the data on the cheque and on the tear-off portion are retained on the cheque copies.) As a result, the accounting entry for any cheque could be picked up from the cheque copy.

b. Make no journal entries for cheques as they are issued during any given month.

c. At the end of each month, record one grand accounting entry for all of the cheques issued during the month. The amounts on the cheque copies would be summarized with an adding machine and work paper; this would probably take about 2 or 3 hours to do.

e. Keep the copies of the cheques available for easy reference, should it be necessary to check back.

f. Keep the daily bank balance by adding the deposits for the day to the ending balance of the previous day and then deducting the total of the cheques issued during the day.

Questions

1. Is Maria's system workable?
2. What are the advantages and disadvantages of Maria's scheme? Discuss.
3. Think of a name for this system.

Case 2 *Profit Before Sentiment?*

John Pemberton had worked for T. W. Jones as chief accountant for six months. He was proud of the efficiency and enthusiasm shown by his staff.

One day, John was visibly upset after returning from a meeting with Mr. Jones. At the meeting, Mr. Jones had suggested that John dismiss the two senior employees in his department and bring in two young employees at the bottom of the salary scale. This would save the company several thousand dollars a year. "There is no room for sentiment in the business world," Mr. Jones had said.

John knew that his department would survive without the senior employees. There were intermediate level employees in the department who were waiting for an opportunity to move up to bigger responsibilities. There would be a slight inconvenience but not much more.

John considered the proposal for some time and could not feel comfortable with it. Both of the senior employees were older men, aged 55 and 60 respectively. John knew that it would not be easy for these men to find employment at the salary level they now enjoyed. Unfortunately, there was no union in the company to protect the rights of these men. John was also concerned about his own future. If he did not go along with the scheme, his employer would consider him 'soft' and his job might be endangered.

Questions

1. Is Mr. Jones's scheme a good one from a strictly business point of view?
2. Is Mr. Jones's scheme legal?
3. Does John have the right to consider his own future ahead of the future of others?
4. What do you think John should do?

Summary Exercise
J. Allen Lawson, Lawyer

You are to commence duties on November 1, 19--, at a salary of $365 per week, as accountant for J. Allen Lawson, a lawyer, who has been in business for some time. In your new position you will be required to perform all accounting tasks.

The chart of accounts for this exercise appears below.

J. ALLEN LAWSON
CHART OF ACCOUNTS

Assets		*Equity*	
Bank	1	J. Allen Lawson, Capital	30
Accounts Receivable		J. Allen Lawson, Drawings	31
Arnold's Paving	2-1	Fees Earned	40
Briggs Pharmacy	2-2		
Leyton and Leyton	2-3	Electricity Expense	50
Superior Stone	2-4	Insurance Expense	51
Warren Real Estate	2-5	Loss on Sale of Equipment	52
Office Supplies	3	Postage	53
Professional Library	4	Rent	54
Office Equipment	5	Salaries	55
Automobile	6	Telephone	56
		Travel Expense	57
Liabilities			
Accounts Payable			
C.H.C. Ltd.	20-1		
Grande Oil Co.	20-2		
Toronado Furniture	20-3		
Typewriters Limited	20-4		

On October 31, 19--, the trial balance of the business is as follows.

J. ALLEN LAWSON
TRIAL BALANCE
OCTOBER 31, 19--

	Dr.	*Cr.*
Bank	$ 2 062.54	
Accounts Receivable		
Arnold's Paving	75.00	
Brigg's Pharmacy	120.00	
Superior Stone	450.00	
Office Supplies	349.00	
Professional Library	330.75	
Office Equipment	501.60	
Automobile	6 475.00	
Accounts Payable		
C.H.C. Ltd.		$ 75.00
Grande Oil Co.		26.82
Toronado Furniture		125.00
J. Allen Lawson Capital		10 137.07
	$10 363.89	$10 363.89

1. The accounts and their balances for this exercise are set up in the workbook that accompanies this text. If you are not using the workbook, you must set up the ledger accounts as of October 31. Leave four accounts of 8 lines each for Bank. No opening entry is required for the exercise because it is a 'going concern', a business that is already functioning.

2. The business transactions for the month of November are listed below. These transactions are to be journalized starting on Journal page 62 and posted to the ledger. Assume that all money received is deposited daily in the bank.

Transactions

November

3 *Cash Receipt*
— From Superior Stone, $200 on account.

3 *Sales Invoice* – on account
— No. 76, to Warren Real Estate, $200 for services rendered.

5 *Cheque Copy*
— No. 71, $15 for the cash purchase of postage stamps.

6 *Cheque Copy*
— No. 72, to Grande Oil Co., in full payment of the account.

7 *Cheque Copies*
— No. 73, to J. A. Lawson, $150 for personal use.
— No. 74, for the accountant's weekly salary.
— No. 75, to the Provincial Law Association, $145 for the cash purchase of professional law books.

10 *Cheque Copy*
— No. 76, to Wilkins Bros., $75 for the cash purchase of office supplies.

10 *Sales Invoice*
— No. 77, to Leyton and Leyton, $375 for services rendered.

12 *Cash Receipt*
— From Briggs Pharmacy, $120 on account.

12 *Purchase Invoice*
— From Typewriters Limited regarding the purchase of a new typewriter. The price of the new typewriter is $315. As a down payment on the new machine, Typewriters Limited agreed to accept an old typewriter as a trade-in and gave an allowance of $75 for it. The old machine had originally cost $225 and was included in the Office Equipment account at that figure.
(**Note**: This is a challenge transaction. Work it out according to the rules that you have learned, and do not give up easily.)

13 *Cheque Copy*
— No. 77, to Local Garage, $137.25 as cash payment for repairs to the car.

13 *Cash Receipt*
— From G. Frankland, $50 for services rendered.

14 *Cheque Copies*
— No. 78, to J. A. Lawson, $90 for personal use.
— No. 79, for the accountant's weekly salary.

17 *Cheque Copy*
— No. 80, to C.H.C. Ltd., in full payment of the account.

18 *Cheque Copy*
— No. 81, to Toronado Furniture. A representative from Toronado Furniture phoned to request payment of their account which he claimed was $225. As a result of this phone call, it was found that an error of $100 was made by the previous accountant when recording the purchase of an office desk. After correcting the error, the account was paid in full.
(**Note**: This is a challenge transaction.)

19 *Sales Invoice*
— No. 78, to Arnold's Paving, $325 for services rendered.

20 *Cash Receipt*
— From P. Morgan, $40 for services rendered.

20 *Cheque Copy*
— No. 82, to Dean's Stationery, $55 for the cash purchase of office supplies.

21 *Cheque Copies*
— No. 83, to Mr. Lawson, $200 for his personal use.
— No. 84, for the accountant's weekly salary.
— No. 85, to Consumer's Insurance, $17.20 for the monthly insurance premium.

25 *Sales Invoices*
— No. 79, to Superior Stone, $1 400 for services rendered.
— No. 80, to Arnold's Paving, $250 for services rendered.

26 *Cheque Copy*
— No. 86, $15 for the cash purchase of postage stamps.

26 *Cash Receipts*
— From Superior Stone, for the full balance of their account.
— From Arnold's Paving, $400 on account.

27 *Sales Invoice*
— No. 81, to Warren Real Estate, $1 275 for services rendered.

27 *Cheque Copies*
— No. 87, to Civic Telephone, $36.50 for the cash payment of the phone bill.
— No. 88, to City Hydro, $48.27, for the cash payment of the electricity bill.

28 *Purchase Invoice*
— From Grande Oil Co., $78.60 for gasoline and oil used in company car during the month.

28 *Cheque Copies*
— No. 89, to E. French, $425 for the rent for the month.
— No. 90, to J. A. Lawson, $210 for his personal use.
— No. 91, for the accountant's weekly salary.

3. After completing the journalizing and posting for the above transactions, perform the following tasks.
a. Take off a trial balance.
b. Complete a work sheet.
c. Prepare an income statement for the month.
d. Prepare the balance sheet.
e. Journalize and post the closing entries.
f. Take off a post-closing trial balance.

12

Subsidiary Ledger Accounting

12-1 Growth of a Ledger
12-2 Subsidiary Ledgers and Control Accounts
12-3 Accounts Receivable and Accounts Payable on the Balance Sheet
12-4 Flowcharting Techniques Used in This Text
12-5 Accounting for Accounts Receivable
12-6 Accounting for Accounts Payable
12-7 Non-routine Entries to Subsidiary Ledgers
12-8 Posting to the General Ledger
12-9 Balancing the Ledgers
12-10 Customer's Statement of Account

Objectives

When you have completed Chapter 12, you should:

1. Be able to describe a subsidiary ledger.
2. Be able to describe a control(ling) account.
3. Understand the basic theory of accounting using subsidiary ledgers for accounts payable and accounts receivable, as well as a general ledger.
4. Know how to balance the books when a three-ledger system is used.
5. Know how accounts receivable and accounts payable are presented on the balance sheet.
6. Understand simple flowcharting techniques used to explain accounting tasks and procedures.
7. Understand a simplified accounting system for handling transactions that affect accounts receivable.
8. Know the accounting entries for the source documents that affect accounts receivable.

9. Know the accounting entries for the source documents that affect accounts payable.
10. Know how to handle non-routine transactions that affect subsidiary ledgers.
11. Be able to locate errors in a subsidiary ledger that is out of balance.
12. Understand that a customer's statement of account is a copy of the customer's account in the subsidiary ledger.

A growing business quickly reaches the point at which one person no longer can perform all the required accounting and office duties. The owner of an expanding business will generally try to hire additional staff for as little money as possible.

The least expensive employees are those whose skills, training, and experience are at an early stage of development.

To keep costs down, a system has evolved that permits most office duties to be handled by junior employees under the direction of a few senior persons. This system uses subsidiary ledgers and control accounts to divide duties in a business office.

12.1 Growth of a Ledger

As a business grows, its ledger grows too, but in a special way. The number of accounts for customers and creditors increases as the business expands. The other ledger accounts seldom increase in number; they increase in the size of their balances.

Figure 12.1 illustrates the growth of a ledger. Notice that the number of accounts for customers and creditors increases, while the number of other accounts remains unchanged.

Once a business gets beyond the small stage, its ledger may be dominated by the

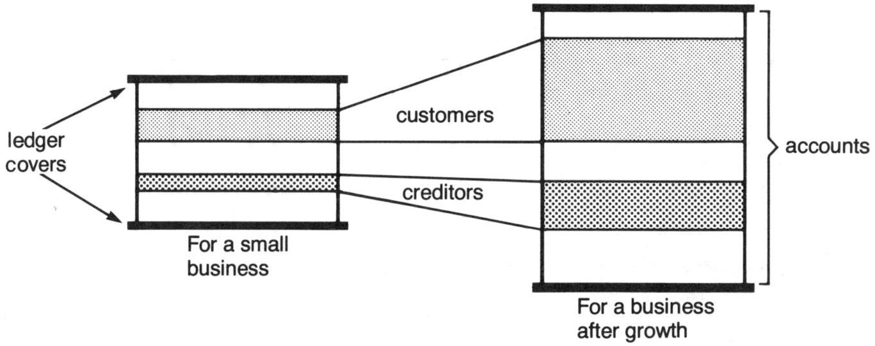

Figure 12.1 The growth of a ledger.

accounts of customers and creditors. In many large companies, Bell Canada for example, there are many thousands of customers' accounts.

12.2 Subsidiary Ledgers and Control Accounts

As stated earlier, in a mature business the office work is divided so that the bulk of it can be performed by less highly trained junior personnel under the guidance of a few senior persons. This is an economical way to run an office.

The recording of customers' and creditors' accounts is ideally suited to a division of duties. It makes good sense to separate these accounts from the rest of the ledger so that junior bookkeepers can look after them.

To begin the study of subsidiary ledgers, examine the T-account ledger in Figure 12.2. This ledger is typical except for the fact that the number of customers' and creditors' accounts is small.

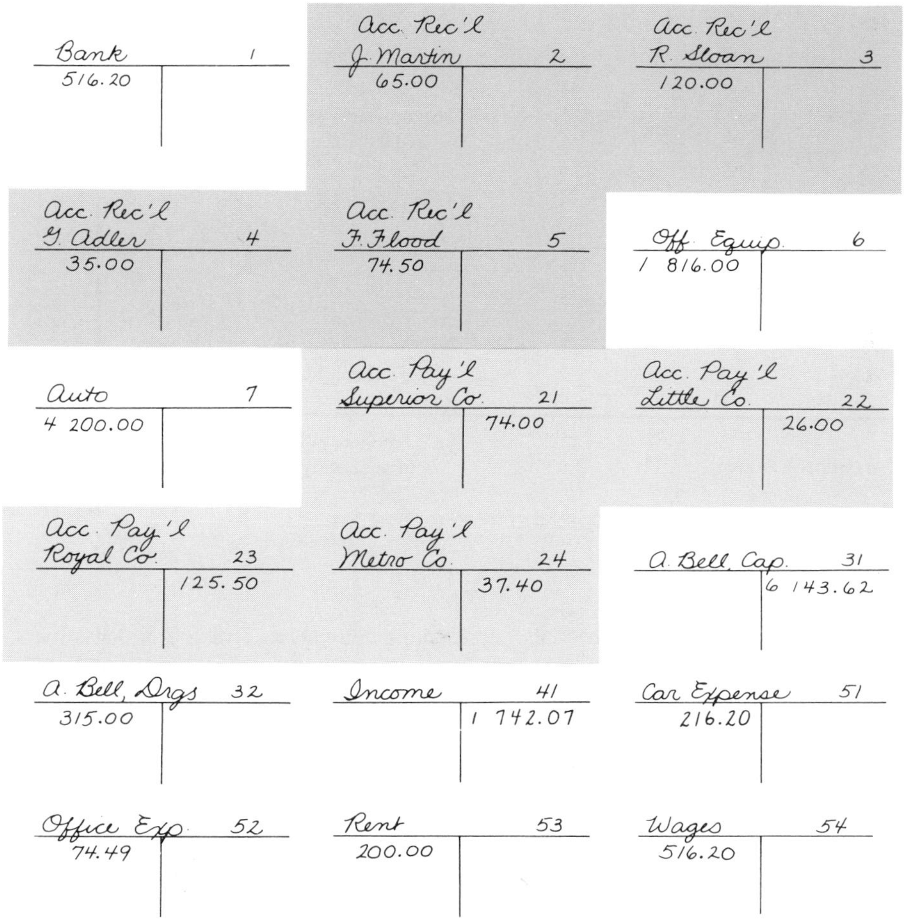

Figure 12.2 A simple ledger.

From this ledger extract all of the accounts of customers and creditors and set them aside in two separate groups.

In each new group, take out the account numbers, arrange the accounts in alphabetical order, and place the customers' and creditors' addresses on their account pages.

By definition, a group of accounts constitutes a ledger. Each of the two new groups of accounts conforms to this definition and is, therefore, itself a ledger. The two new ledgers, arranged alphabetically for greater convenience in handling, are shown in Figure 12.3.

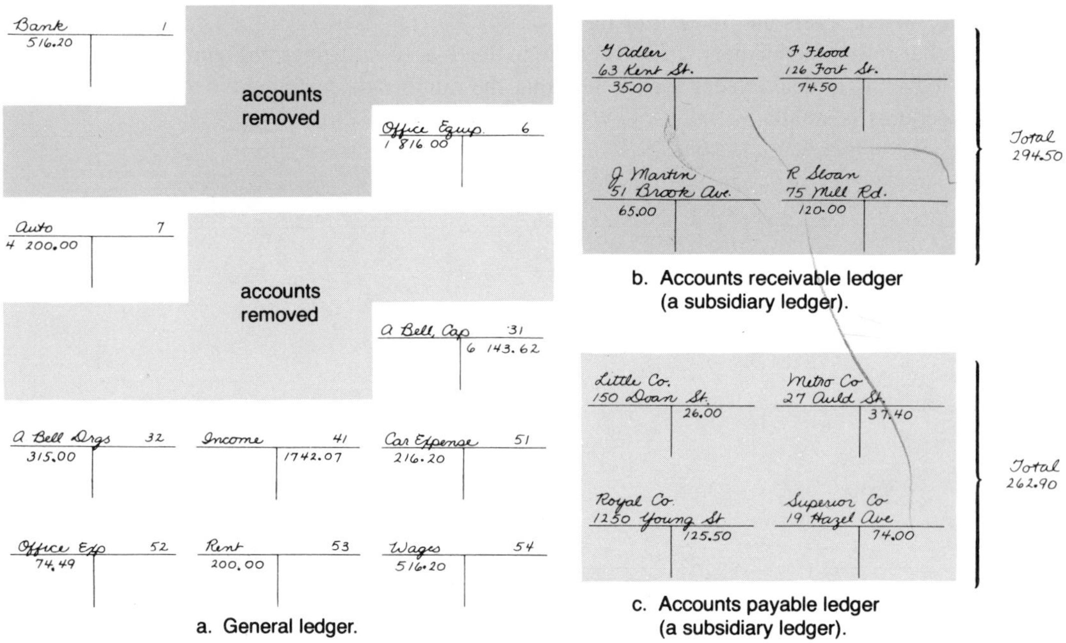

Figure 12.3 Partially developed three-ledger system.

The ledger of customers' accounts, representing amounts receivable from customers, is known as the **accounts receivable ledger** or sometimes as the customers' ledger. The accounts in it usually have debit balances. Occasionally, a credit balance may occur, as when a customer overpays his account. The ledger of creditors' accounts, representing amounts payable to creditors, is known as the **accounts payable ledger**. These accounts usually have credit balances.

Both of the new ledgers are called **subsidiary ledgers**. A subsidiary ledger is a separate ledger that contains a number of accounts of a similar type.

Now that there are three ledgers in the system it is necessary to identify each one individually in order to avoid any possible confusion. For this reason, the main ledger, the one you are accustomed to using, is given the name **general ledger**.

The changeover to the three-ledger system is not yet completed. Since certain accounts were removed from it, the general ledger in Figure 12.3 is no longer in balance, that is, it no longer balances within itself. For two reasons it cannot be left in this state. First, it is a basic principle of accounting that the ledger must always balance. Second, the general ledger, from which the financial statements are derived, must include the complete financial picture.

The next step, therefore, is to open two new accounts in the general journal to replace all of those accounts that were previously taken out and placed in separate ledgers. The two new accounts, given the names Accounts Receivable and Accounts Payable, are shown in Figure 12.4.

Notice that the Accounts Receivable account in the general ledger is given a balance of $294.50 Dr. which is equal to the total value of all the customers' accounts that it replaced. Similarly, the Accounts Payable account in the general ledger is given a balance of $262.90 Cr. which is equal to the total value of all the creditors' accounts that it replaced. The final appearance of the three-ledger system is shown in Figure 12.4.

Each of the two new accounts in the general ledger is called a **control account** or controlling account. A control account is a general ledger account the balance of which represents the sum of the balances in the accounts in a subsidiary ledger.

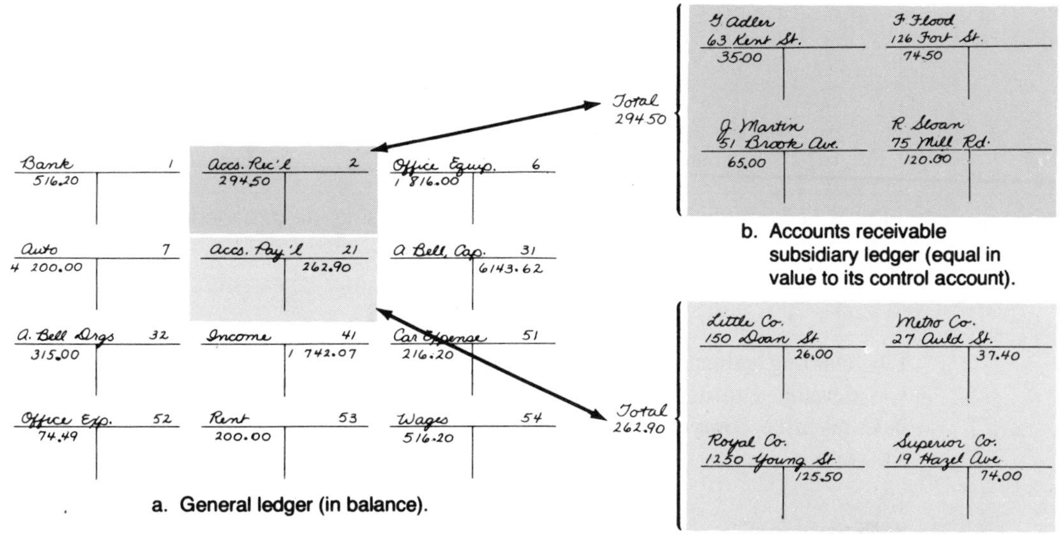

a. General ledger (in balance).

b. Accounts receivable subsidiary ledger (equal in value to its control account).

c. Accounts payable subsidiary ledger (equal in value to its control account).

Figure 12.4 The simple three-ledger system.

12.3 Accounts Receivable and Accounts Payable on the Balance Sheet

In the three-ledger system, the financial statements should not be prepared until the three ledgers are balanced. Only then can one be sure that the books of account are mechanically correct.

With this system, it is no longer necessary to list the individual customers and creditors on the balance sheet. In fact, these individual accounts will not even appear on the work sheet, the source of information for statement preparation. Now the balance sheet will show the total of Accounts Receivable and the total of Accounts Payable as illustrated by the partial balance sheet shown in Figure 12.5.

DR. P. R. HAYASHI
BALANCE SHEET
MARCH 31, 19–3

ASSETS		
Current Assets		
Bank	$1 650.21	
Accounts Receivable	7 086.14	
Supplies	1 276.00	$10 012.35
Fixed Assets		
Equipment	$3 040.00	
Automobile	5 075.00	8 115.00
		$18 127.35
LIABILITIES		
Current Liabilities		
Accounts Payable		$ 4 072.16

Figure 12.5 Partial balance sheet for a doctor using the three-ledger system.

12.4 Flowcharting Techniques

Flowcharting gained popularity with the use of computers. It is a technique that was developed to describe computer systems, and to aid in programming. If you have taken no computer-related programs, flowcharting will be a new experience for you.

What Is a Flowchart?

Until recently, an accounting system could only be described using many pages of handwritten notes. Such descriptions were generally hard to read and hard to understand. Fortunately, flowcharting has made such descriptions obsolete.

Flowcharting is a method of presenting a series of steps or operations in the form of a chart. A **flowchart** is a diagram or pictorial representation of a system or procedure. With flowcharts, accounting procedures can be easily visualized as a series of clearly defined, logical steps.

Understanding Flowcharting

Flowcharting is widely used for describing accounting procedures. In this text, simple flowcharts are used from time to time to describe small sections, or sub-systems, of the total accounting system.

Flowcharting Techniques Used in This Text

The flowcharts used in this text are based on the following simple principles. These are illustrated by the flowchart in Figure 12.6, describing the basic procedure for accounts receivable.

1. A flowchart may be marked off into sections, each one representing a particular department of the business. Figure 12.6 shows three departments: Sales, Mail Room, and Accounting.
2. Symbols are used to represent various business documents, books, ledgers, forms, and so on. Figure 12.6 uses symbols for the general journal and the general ledger.
3. A triangle is used to represent a permanent storage file. A letter appears within each triangle: N for numerical filing; A for alphabetical filing; and D for filing by date.
4. Symbols are used to show the functions of office workers, such as the Junior Accountant or Accounts Receivable Clerk.
5. Solid lines with arrows are used to indicate the physical movement or path of the documents through the various stages of processing to their final place of permanent storage (file). The chart is usually drawn so that the flow is from left to right and from top to bottom. In Figure 12.6, observe that the accounting copy of the sales invoice moves first to the accounts receivable clerk, next to the junior accountant, and finally to a numerical file.
6. Broken lines with arrows are used to indicate that information is taken from a document and is used to create another document, or to carry out an action. In Figure 12.6, observe that the accounts receivable clerk uses the invoice copies to make postings to the subsidiary ledger.
7. Circled numbers refer to notes that provide more detailed information where necessary.

Basic Accounts Receivable System

The flowchart below shows how the subsidiary ledger for accounts receivable is maintained, and the accounting controls that are part of the system. **Accounting controls** may be defined as the accounting procedures used to check the reliability of the information contained in accounting records.

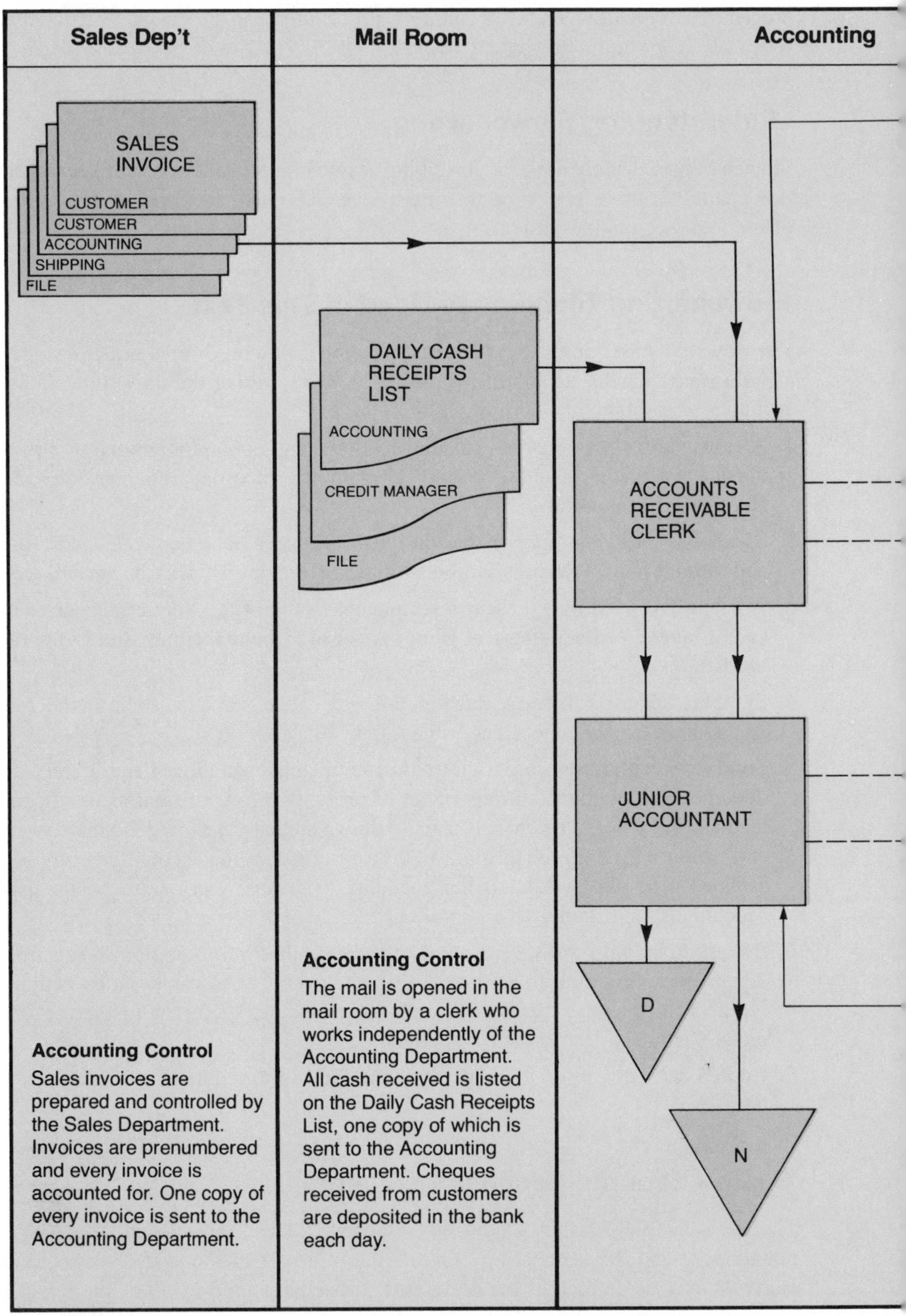
Sales Dep't
Mail Room
Accounting
SALES INVOICE
CUSTOMER
CUSTOMER
ACCOUNTING
SHIPPING
FILE
DAILY CASH RECEIPTS LIST
ACCOUNTING
CREDIT MANAGER
FILE
ACCOUNTS RECEIVABLE CLERK
JUNIOR ACCOUNTANT
D
N
Accounting Control
Sales invoices are prepared and controlled by the Sales Department. Invoices are prenumbered and every invoice is accounted for. One copy of every invoice is sent to the Accounting Department.
Accounting Control
The mail is opened in the mail room by a clerk who works independently of the Accounting Department. All cash received is listed on the Daily Cash Receipts List, one copy of which is sent to the Accounting Department. Cheques received from customers are deposited in the bank each day.

Figure 12.6 Flowchart of basic procedure for accounts receivable.

Dep't

Accounting Control

An accounting clerk maintains the subsidiary ledger independently. This person has no access to cash and no involvement with any other accounting records that affect accounts receivable.

The postings to the subsidiary ledger are made directly from the source documents that arrive from other departments. The clerk initials each document or item posted to indicate that the posting is completed.

The sales invoices represent debits (increases) to the customer's accounts.

The cash receipts represent credits (decreases) to the customer's accounts.

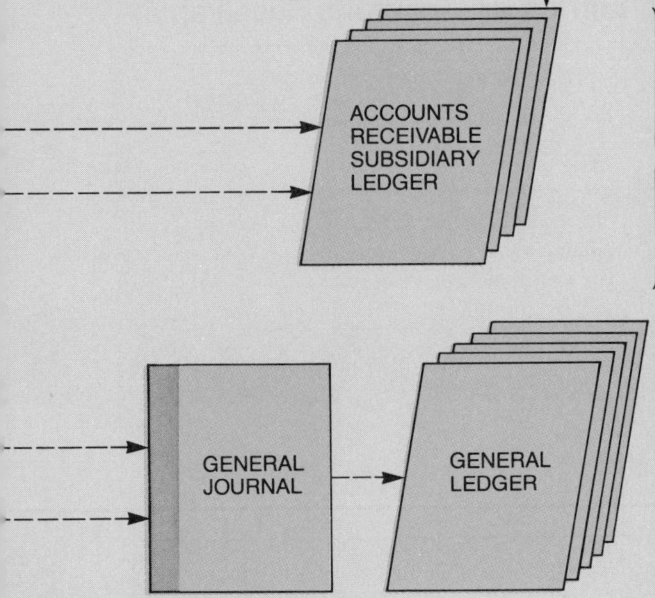

Schedule of Accs Rec'l

A. Adams	$ 50
B. Brown	100
C. Carter	30
S. Smith	25
T. Thomas	175
W. Wilson	35
	$415

General Ledger Trial Balance

Bank	$ 200	
Accs Rec'l	415	
Supplies	140	
Capital		$ 845
Drawings	400	
Revenue		1 200
Advertising	125	
Utilities	325	
Wages	450	
	$2 055	$2 055

Accounting Control

The junior accountant prepares journal entries from the source documents that arrive at his desk. This person does not initiate the source documents. Sales invoice copies and the daily list of cash receipts are not the only source documents.

Accounting Control

At the end of each month, the Schedule of Accounts Receivable, prepared by the accounts receivable clerk, must agree with the control account in the general ledger which is balanced independently by the junior accountant.

12.5 Accounting for Accounts Receivable

The flowchart in Figure 12.6 shows the following:

1. There are two source documents that affect customers' accounts.
2. An accounts receivable clerk independently maintains the subsidiary ledger for customers' accounts.
3. A junior accountant attends to the journalizing, posting, and balancing functions related to the general ledger.
4. A monthly summary of accounts receivable, prepared by the accounts receivable clerk, must agree with the balance in the Accounts Receivable control account, which is worked out by the junior accountant.

Summary of Accounting Entries for Accounts Receivable

Source Documents	*Subsidiary Ledger* Function of the Accounts Receivable Clerk	*General Journal and General Ledger* Function of the Junior Accountant
Sales invoice	To post to individual customers' accounts directly from the sales invoices. A debit entry is required to increase the customer's account. No cross-referencing is necessary. The invoice number is recorded in the particulars column of the customer's account.	For each sales invoice, record the following accounting entry in the general journal and post this entry to the ledger accounts. Dr. Accounts Receivable XXX Cr. Revenue XXX
Daily list of cash receipts	To post to individual customers' accounts directly from the list of cash receipts. A credit entry is required for each receipt to decrease the customer's account. No cross-referencing is necessary.	For each cash receipt, record the following accounting entry in the general journal and post this entry to the ledger accounts. Dr. Bank XXX Cr. Accounts Receivable XXX

12.6 Accounting for Accounts Payable

The system described above for accounts receivable is fairly simple. By comparison, the system for accounts payable can be quite complex. It involves the controlling of purchases, the proving of the receipt of goods, and the authorization of cheques for payment.

A common system for controlling accounts payable is fully explained in Chapter 16. For now, we will use a simplified system for accounts payable, similar to that for accounts receivable. Four features of this simplified system are as follows:

1. The two source documents that affect accounts payable are purchase invoices, and cheque copies (for payments on account, only).

   Note: Not all cheques issued affect accounts payable. For example, a cheque to the owner for personal use, or a cheque for a cash purchase of supplies, would not affect accounts payable. To have an effect on accounts payable a cheque must be in payment of an obligation for goods or services purchased previously on credit and recorded as a liability in the accounts payable ledger.
2. An accounts payable clerk independently maintains the subsidiary ledger for accounts payable.
3. A junior accountant attends to the journalizing, posting, and balancing functions related to the general ledger.
4. A monthly schedule of accounts payable, prepared by the accounts payable clerk, must agree with the balance in the Accounts Payable control account, which is worked out by the junior accountant.

Summary of Accounting Entries for Accounts Payable

Source Documents	*Subsidiary Ledger* Function of the Accounts Payable Clerk	*General Journal and General Ledger* Function of the Junior Accountant
Purchase invoice	To post to individual creditors' accounts directly from the purchase invoices. A credit entry is required to increase the creditor's account. No cross-referencing is necessary The purchase invoice number is recorded in the particulars column of the customer's account.	For each purchase invoice, record the following accounting entry in the general journal and post this entry to the ledger accounts. Dr. Asset, or Expense* XXX Cr. Accounts Payable XXX
Cheque copy	To post to individual creditors' accounts directly from cheque copies, if for payment on account. A debit entry is required to decrease the creditor's account. No cross-referencing is necessary.	For each cheque copy (payment on account only), record the following entry in the general journal and post this entry to the ledger accounts. Dr. Accounts Payable XXX Cr Bank XXX

*The account affected depends on what was purchased.

12.7 Non-routine Entries to Subsidiary Ledgers

You have seen that accounting systems are designed so that the information flows to the office clerks by means of business source documents or vouchers. However, there are some transactions for which there are no regular source documents and which do not fit into the regular accounting routine.

For example, suppose that Naomi Pavlo, the owner of a business, collects an overdue $200 account in full from her customer, B. Marr. Ms. Pavlo happens to be short of cash. Instead of turning in the cash to the business, she keeps it for her personal use.

First Ms. Pavlo would inform the accountant of the transaction. She has no wish to deceive anyone. The accountant would make the following accounting entry in the general journal.

N. Pavlo, Drawings	200	
Accounts Receivable		200
To record the receipt by N. Pavlo of the account of B. Marr in full. Funds were kept by N. Pavlo for her personal use.		

There is no regular source document for this type of transaction. Without the source document, the accounts receivable clerk will not learn in the usual way about the $200 credit to be made to Marr's account. The accountant understands this, and will make the entry in the subsidiary ledger himself. Or he will inform the clerk by means of a written memo. Because the subsidiary ledger must be kept up to date, the accountant must attend to this without delay.

12.8 Posting to the General Ledger

The general ledger is posted in the usual manner with one exception. It is no longer necessary to keep it always up-to-date. Only the customers' and creditors' accounts must be posted daily.

Now that the customers' and creditors' accounts are kept separately, it is general practice to refrain from posting to the general ledger until the end of the month. Then the posting is done in one concentrated effort. This is a far more efficient way of posting.

It is possible to keep track of the daily bank balance in various ways without having to post to the ledger.

12.9 Balancing the Ledgers

It is standard practice to balance all of the ledgers at the end of every month, after all postings have been completed.

The General Ledger

To balance the general ledger, there is no change in the procedure already described. The most common method is to use an adding machine to total all of the account balances. The accounts with debit balances are entered as additions and the accounts with credit balances are entered as deductions. If the ledger is in balance, the total of the tape will be zero.

The Subsidiary Ledgers

To balance a subsidiary ledger, obtain the total of all of the accounts in the ledger, and make sure that it agrees with the total in the general ledger control account. The balancing of a subsidiary ledger is usually the responsibility of the clerk in charge of the ledger. You must remember not to try to balance a subsidiary ledger until both the subsidiary ledger and the general ledger are posted up to date.

Examples of a subsidiary ledger trial balance are shown in Figures 12.7 and 12.8.

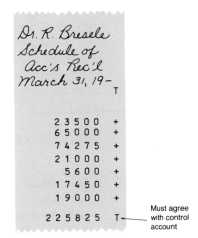

Dr. R. Brescle
Schedule of Accounts Recivable
March 31, 19–

G. Brophy	235 –
A. Delorenze	650 –
W. Hume	742 75
J. Murphy	210 –
P. Seswick	56 –
R. Tate	174 50
G. Wegenast	190 –
	2258 25

Must agree with control account.

Figure 12.7 A subsidiary ledger trial balance using the formal method.

Dr. R. Bresele
Schedule of
Acc's Rec'l
March 31, 19–

	T
2 3 5 0 0	+
6 5 0 0 0	+
7 4 2 7 5	+
2 1 0 0 0	+
5 6 0 0	+
1 7 4 5 0	+
1 9 0 0 0	+
2 2 5 8 2 5	T

Must agree with control account

Figure 12.8 A subsidiary ledger trial balance by the informal method which uses the adding machine listing.

Locating Errors When a Subsidiary Ledger Does Not Balance

The subsidiary ledger is not acceptable until it is balanced with the control account. To be balanced, the sum of all its accounts must agree with the balance of its control account. Only then can the balancing procedure be brought to a conclusion.

When a subsidiary ledger does not balance, a search for the errors must be made. In conducting the search, remember that whenever an amount is entered in any account in the subsidiary ledger, there must be an equivalent amount entered in the control account — and vice versa.

In your search for errors, there is no need to go back in the ledgers beyond the current month. The ledgers are balanced at the end of every month and there will be trial balance tapes on file as evidence. If errors exist in the accounts, you may be sure that they were made in the current month.

12.10 Customer's Statement of Account

You have seen that a business keeps detailed records of the accounts of its customers. To receive payments regularly, a business needs to notify customers about the status of their accounts. This is done by sending a statement of account to each customer at set intervals. A **statement of account** is a record of the customer's account for a period of time, usually a month. It gives the customer a list of the purchases made during the period and the unpaid balance at the end of the period. The statement of account is intended to serve as a gentle request for payment. The manner in which statements of account are prepared depends on how much automation there is in the accounting system.

Manual System

The following method is used in a manual system of accounting.

1. The customers' accounts are kept in a subsidiary ledger in the form that you have seen. Each customer is given an account page on which all transactions of the customer are recorded. The entries are continued on the account page until it is filled, at which time the account balance is forwarded to a new page and the process continued.
2. At the end of each month the transactions for each customer for the month, as well as the beginning and ending balances, are typed onto a statement of account form which is sent to the customer. This method is illustrated in Figure 12.9.

Customer Address H. Atkins
50 Placer Street
Thunder Bay, Ontario
P7E 3N6

Date		Reference	Debit	Credit	D/C	Balance
19- May	16	Forwarded			D	116 40
	20	Inv #3710	112 40		D	228 80
	29	Inv #3860	49 —		D	277 80
Jun	5			116 40	D	161 40
	26	Inv # 3992	176 90		D	338 30
Jul	9	Inv # 4019	84 50		D	422 80
	20			161 40	D	261 40
	31	Inv # 4198	90 —		D	351 40

COWELL'S LIMITED

9090 ARTHUR ST.
THUNDER BAY, ONT.
P7E 5M9

PHONE
999-6159

IN ACCOUNT WITH H. Atkins
50 Placer Street
Thunder Bay, Ontario
P7E 3N6

Date	Reference	Charges	Credits	Balance
Jun 30	Balance Forward			338.30
Jul 9	#4019	84.50		
20			161.40	
31	#4198	90.00		351.40

2% interest charged on overdue accounts

Figure 12.9 The ledger account and the statement of account for the month of June for H. Atkins.

Automated Accounting System

The manual system for producing customers' statements is too slow and time-consuming for a business with a large number of customers' accounts. A business with many credit customers requires a system that uses mechanical or electronic data processing equipment.

An automated accounting system uses the following method to keep the customers' ledger and produce the monthly statements of account.

1. In the customers' ledger, a new ledger sheet is set up each month for each customer's account. The ending balance of the old ledger sheet is forwarded to become the beginning balance on the new (current) sheet. The old sheet is then filled. As Figure 12.10 shows, each customer's account is made up of a number of monthly ledger sheets that follow one another in series.
2. The transactions for the current month are recorded on the current ledger sheet in the customary manner except that the entries are machine printed and calculated.

3. Since the ledger sheets are prepared in duplicate, the copy is used as the customer's statement of account. Under this system the customer receives an exact copy of his account. Banks use this method to produce bank statement copies for chequing accounts and business current accounts.

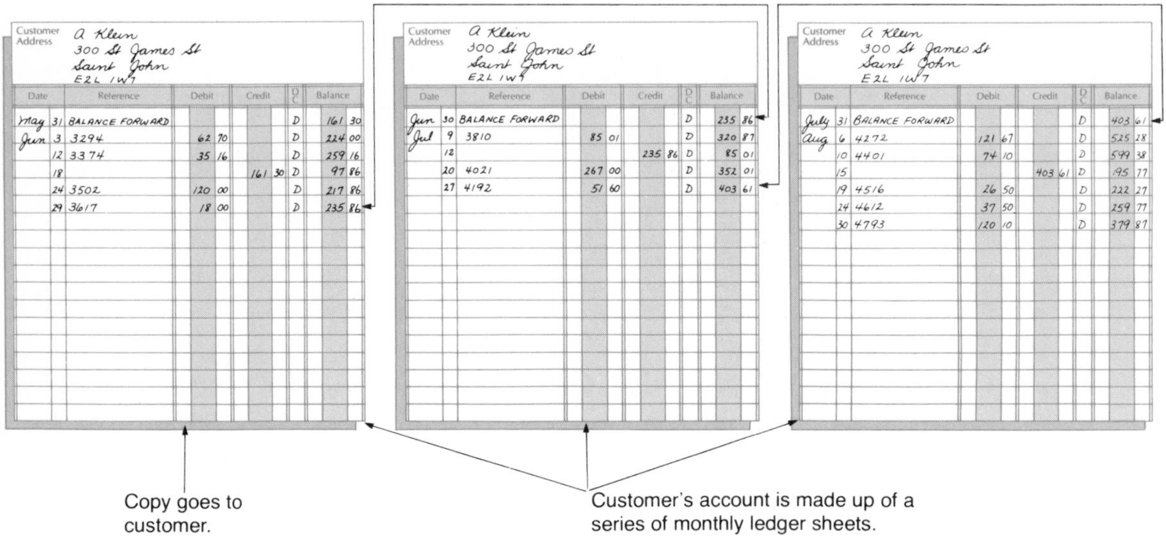
Copy goes to customer.
Customer's account is made up of a series of monthly ledger sheets.

Figure 12.10 A series of machine-printed statements for A. Klein.

Computer-Produced System

Computers are the most efficient way of handling business routines that are repetitive in nature, especially when the number of individual transactions is very large. Computers are ideal, therefore, for handling accounts receivable and monthly statements of account for a large business.

The computerized method is similar in principle to the machine accounting method. In both systems, new ledger sheets are set up for each customer each month. But with the computerized system the ledger sheets are not created on a daily basis. Instead, the computer is able to store all of the data for all of the customers for the entire month in its memory banks. At the end of the month, it produces all of the customers' accounts and monthly statements in a single operation that may take only a few hours.

More data can easily be shown on computer-produced statements than on the machine-produced or typed variety. Figure 12.11 shows a computer-produced monthly statement sent to a customer from a national department store.

A computerized system eliminates the need for carbon paper to produce the customer's copy of an account. The computer can easily be programmed to produce two originals at little additional time or expense.

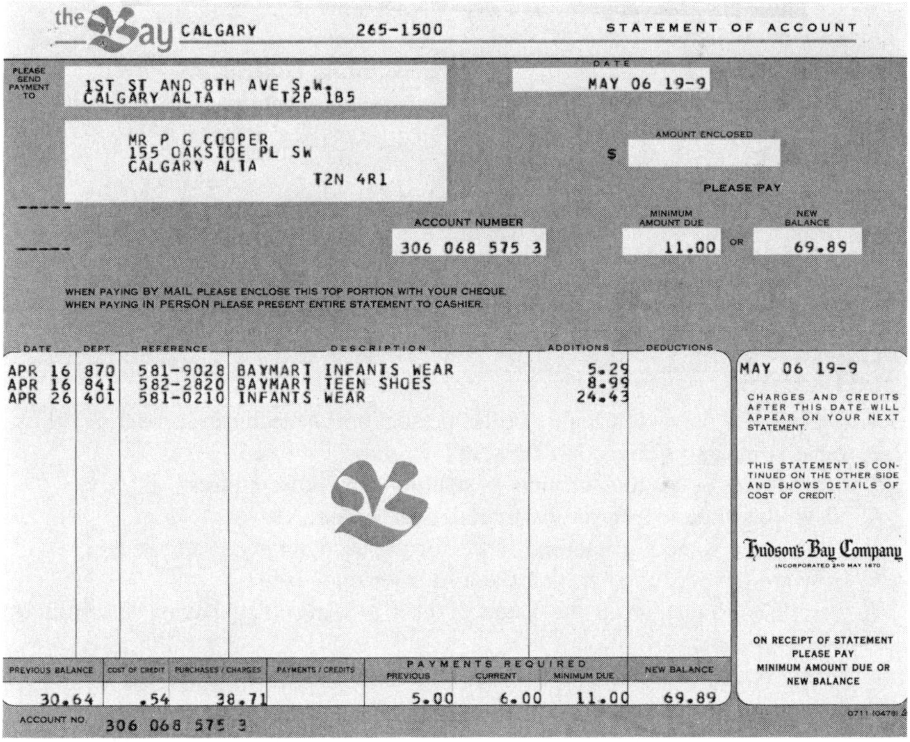

the Bay CALGARY 265-1500 STATEMENT OF ACCOUNT

PLEASE SEND PAYMENT TO: 1ST ST AND 8TH AVE S.W. CALGARY ALTA T2P 1B5

DATE: MAY 06 19-9

MR P G COOPER
155 OAKSIDE PL SW
CALGARY ALTA
T2N 4R1

AMOUNT ENCLOSED $

PLEASE PAY

ACCOUNT NUMBER: 306 068 575 3

MINIMUM AMOUNT DUE: 11.00 OR NEW BALANCE: 69.89

WHEN PAYING BY MAIL PLEASE ENCLOSE THIS TOP PORTION WITH YOUR CHEQUE.
WHEN PAYING IN PERSON PLEASE PRESENT ENTIRE STATEMENT TO CASHIER.

DATE	DEPT.	REFERENCE	DESCRIPTION	ADDITIONS	DEDUCTIONS
APR 16	870	581-9028	BAYMART INFANTS WEAR	5.29	
APR 16	841	582-2820	BAYMART TEEN SHOES	8.99	
APR 26	401	581-0210	INFANTS WEAR	24.43	

PREVIOUS BALANCE	COST OF CREDIT	PURCHASES / CHARGES	PAYMENTS / CREDITS	PAYMENTS REQUIRED PREVIOUS	CURRENT	MINIMUM DUE	NEW BALANCE
30.64	.54	38.71		5.00	6.00	11.00	69.89

ACCOUNT NO. 306 068 575 3

MAY 06 19-9

CHARGES AND CREDITS AFTER THIS DATE WILL APPEAR ON YOUR NEXT STATEMENT.

THIS STATEMENT IS CONTINUED ON THE OTHER SIDE AND SHOWS DETAILS OF COST OF CREDIT.

Hudson's Bay Company
INCORPORATED 2ND MAY 1670

ON RECEIPT OF STATEMENT PLEASE PAY MINIMUM AMOUNT DUE OR NEW BALANCE

Figure 12.11 Computer-produced statement of account of a national department store.

Statements of Account and the Customer

You have seen that a business produces a statement of account for each customer. Let us now examine this important document from the customer's point of view.

A statement of account should always be checked by the customer for errors. Although the degree of accuracy in business recordkeeping is remarkably high, errors and oversights do occur.

Keep a file of statements of account and of the bills of sale for your purchases. Along with adequate banking records, these enable you to check each statement of account as it arrives. You probably already keep the bills of sale for returning unsatisfactory purchases. Remember that all errors should be reported whether to your advantage or disadvantage.

Accounting Terms

accounts receivable ledger
accounts payable ledger
subsidiary ledger
general ledger
control account (controlling account)
flowchart
accounting control
customer's statement of account

Review Questions

1. Explain why only a few highly skilled persons are needed in an accounting office.
2. What is meant by division of labour?
3. In what ledger are the accounts of debtors kept? Of creditors?
4. Name the three ledgers in the three-ledger system.
5. What other name is sometimes used for the accounts receivable ledger?
6. How are the accounts in a subsidiary ledger organized?
7. Describe the change in the balance sheet as a result of having a subsidiary ledger system.
8. Give a brief description of a flowchart.
9. On a flowchart, what are symbols used for?
10. On a flowchart, what technique is used to indicate a flow of documents? Of information?
11. What two source documents affect accounts receivable?
12. What two source documents affect accounts payable?
13. Define a control account.
14. Define a subsidiary ledger.
15. When is the proper time to balance the three ledgers?
16. Describe the technique for balancing a subsidiary ledger.
17. When a subsidiary ledger does not agree with its control account, what must be done?
18. In searching for errors, how far back in the records must one investigate?
19. What is a statement of account?
20. Of what use is a statement of account to the sender?
21. Of what use is a statement of account to the receiver?
22. Describe the difference in organization between a subsidiary ledger that is automated and one that is not.

Exercises

Changing From A One-Ledger System To A Three-Ledger System

1. The trial balance of Proctor's Pet Store in Weyburn, Sask., is shown below.

PROCTOR'S PET STORE
TRIAL BALANCE
JUNE 30, 19--

Bank	$ 714	
Accounts Receivable		
P. Shewchuk	35	
J. Britt	75	
C. Powell	102	
D. Zecca	56	
W. Pritz	27	
Supplies	250	
Equipment	1 575	
Accounts Payable		
Cleaners' Supply House		$ 210
Wendell's Store		57
Arnwell Animal Hospital		135
Tracy Proctor, Capital		2 442
Tracy Proctor, Drawings	5 000	
Revenue		7 250
Light and Heat Expense	350	
Miscellaneous Expense	295	
Rent Expense	1 500	
Telephone Expense	115	
	$10 094	$10 094

1. **Calculate the value of the accounts receivable accounts.**
2. **Calculate the value of the accounts payable accounts.**
3. **T. Proctor changes over to a three-ledger system of accounting, with subsidiary ledgers and control accounts. Perform the following:**
   a. **Show the general ledger trial balance.**
   b. **Show the accounts receivable subsidiary ledger trial balance and agree it with the general ledger control account.**
   c. **Show the accounts payable subsidiary ledger trial balance and agree it with the general ledger control account.**

2. Hans Feebie decides to change his accounting system to a three-ledger system. On December 31, 19--, his trial balance is as shown below.

FEEBIE'S REPAIR SERVICE
TRIAL BALANCE
DECEMBER 31, 19--

Bank	$ 1 420	
Accounts Receivable		
N. Storey	112	
G. Wroe	75	
P. Baker	157	
C. Florio	35	
Supplies	1 057	
Delivery Truck	5 902	
Tools & Equipment	3 755	
Accounts Payable		
Watson Electric		$ 265
Jack's Machine Shop		315
Pete's Welding		75
City Gasolines		170
H. Feebie, Capital		11 207
H. Feebie, Drawings	7 500	
Revenue		10 055
Delivery Expense	257	
Light and Heat	195	
Miscellaneous Expense	105	
Rent	1 200	
Wages	317	
	$22 087	$22 087

1. Show the general ledger trial balance after the changeover.
2. Show the accounts receivable subsidiary ledger trial balance, balanced with its control account in the general ledger.
3. Show the accounts payable subsidiary ledger trial balance, balanced with its control account in the general ledger.

Preparing A Classified Balance Sheet

3. From the information below, prepare a classified balance sheet for Industrial Cleaners, as of May 31, 19--, the end of a one month fiscal period.

Bank	$ 3 150	
Accounts Receivable	7 420	
Supplies	950	
Equipment	4 260	
Automobiles	12 375	
Bank Loan		$ 5 000
Accounts Payable		7 210
P. Rye, Capital		13 920
P. Rye, Drawings	8 000	
Net Income		10 025
	$36 155	$36 155

Flowcharts

4. In your own words, provide a simple, point-form explanation of each of the following flowchart segments based on the system developed in this chapter.

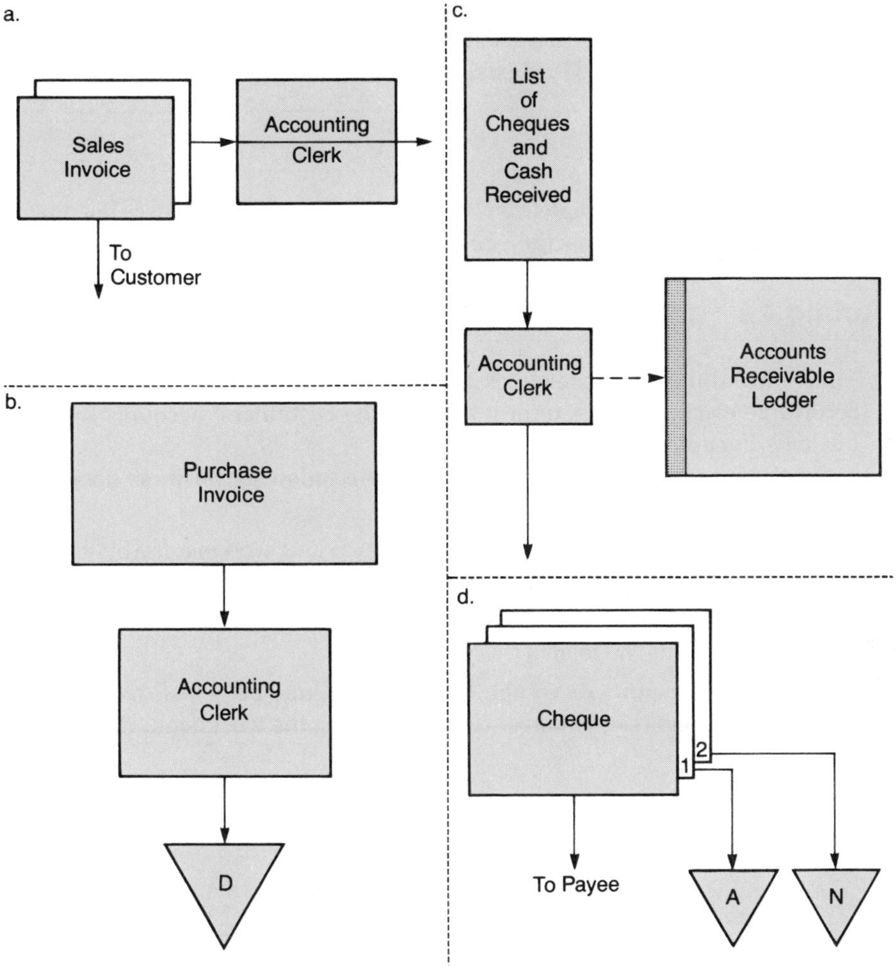

5. Study the flowchart in Figure 12.6 and answer the following questions.

1. **What system does it describe?**
2. **Name the departments involved in the flowchart.**
3. **Including the original, how many copies of the sales invoice are there?**
4. **Who receives the original and copy No. 1?**
5. **Where does the Sales Department send the accounting copy?**
6. **How does the accounts receivable clerk use the sales invoice copy?**
7. **How does the accounts receivable clerk show that a sales invoice copy has been handled?**

8. **Besides the sales invoice, what other source document is sent to the accounts receivable clerk?**
9. **What happens to these two source documents after the accounts receivable clerk is finished with them?**
10. **What are they used for at that point?**
11. **In what order are these source documents filed?**
12. **Describe the control that exists over cash receipts.**
13. **Describe the controls that exist over the subsidiary ledger and the clerk.**

Subsidiary Ledger Theory

6. **Workbook Exercise: Complete a chart showing the effect of source documents on subsidiary ledgers and the general ledger.**

Acting As The Subsidiary Ledger Clerk

7. **Your office duties with the Quick Distributing Co. include those of accounts receivable clerk. You are to post daily to the customers' accounts from the business documents that you receive.**

   On the morning of each working day, the following business documents arrive on your desk:

   a. Copies of all sales invoices issued on the previous working day by the Sales Department.

   b. A listing of the day's cash receipts, prepared first thing each morning by the clerk who opens the mail.

   1. **Set up the accounts receivable ledger as of June 30, 19--, from the following detailed trial balance. If you are using the workbook, the ledger is set up for you.**

QUICK DISTRIBUTING CO.
ACCOUNTS RECEIVABLE TRIAL BALANCE
JUNE 30, 19--

Adam Bros., 12 Mountain Avenue	Inv. No. 480	$ 67.20	
	507	94.20	$ 161.40
Rozo & Son, 620 Main Street	512		75.65
A. G. Farmer, 120A Blackwell Ave.	514		315.62
S. P. Handy, Ltd., 75 Porter Ave.	484	216.25	
	511	200.22	416.47
R. Mortimer, 60 Hawley Crescent	470	516.25	
	496	621.90	
	505	608.36	1 746.51
Renforth Sales, 192 Dale Place	510		137.62
Vista Limited, 2001 Central Ave.	515		50.00
			$2 903.27

2. Post to the customers' accounts from the following business papers.

July 2	*Invoices*	No. 516 Adams Bros.		$ 59.24
		No. 517 Renforth Sales		145.50
	Cash Receipts	A. G. Farmer	No. 514	315.62
		S. P. Handy, Ltd.	No. 484	216.25
3	*Invoice*	No. 518 Rozo & Son		75.85
	Cash Receipts	Nil		
4	*Invoices*	No. 519 A. G. Farmer		217.90
		No. 520 The Williams Company 417 Lake Street		150.00
	Cash Receipts	Adams Bros.	No. 480	67.20
		R. Mortimer	No. 470 & No. 496	1 138.15
5	*Invoices*	No. 521 Vista Limited		94.95
		No. 522 S. P. Handy, Ltd.		104.16
		No. 523 R. Mortimer		56.00
	Cash Receipt	Renforth Sales	No. 510	137.62
6	*Invoices*	No. 524 Adams Bros.		167.07
		No. 525 The Williams Company		75.00
	Cash Receipts	Rozo & Son	No. 512	75.65
		Vista Limited	No. 515	50.00

3. Take off a trial balance of the subsidiary ledger as of July 6 and balance the subsidiary ledger with the control account. The senior accountant has arrived at a control figure of $2 048.45.

---

8. On September 30, 19--, the detailed accounts payable trial balance of Magnetic Controls Company was as follows:

MAGNETIC CONTROLS COMPANY
ACCOUNTS PAYABLE TRIAL BALANCE
SEPTEMBER 30, 19--

Daiton Enterprises	106 Fleet Street, Barbary	516		$ 430.74
Gordon & Associates	7400 King Street, Oak City	B7407		216.92
Henderson Bros.	Box 65, Welton	16421	$ 507.00	
		16907	615.00	1 122.00
Kohler, R. M.	141 Nixon Avenue, Barbary	615		104.70
North State Packaging	1500 Middle Road, Lennox	901		74.87
Orenson & Sons	560 The Eastway, Dayson	1604	$1 046.26	
		1809	516.15	1 562.41
Riggs, J. B.	75 Baxter Road, Estwing	74621		502.00
Smithers, P. R.	106 Farr Street, Wibbling	74		57.05
Union Advertising	7900 Primeau Avenue, Marks County	16352	$ 436.21	
		17201	702.16	
		17306	518.90	1 657.27
				$5 727.96

1. **Set up the accounts payable ledger of Magnetic Controls Company. If you are using the workbook the ledger is already set up for you.**
2. **From the business documents listed below, perform the duties of the accounts payable clerk by posting to the accounts payable ledger.**

Transactions

October

1 *Purchase Invoices*
— Smithers, P. R., No. 104, $151.89.
— North State Packaging, No. 1046, $57.25.
Cheque Copies
— No. 65720, Union Advertising, on account, $800.
— No. 65721, Henderson Bros., Inv. 16421, $507.

2 *Purchase Invoices*
— Wrouse & Reid, 14 Kay Street, Saxton, No. 597G, $316.29.
— Union Advertising, No. 18002, $505.
— Orenson & Sons, No. 1856, $216.
Cheque Copies
— No. 65722, Daiton Enterprises, Inv. 516, $430.74.
— No. 65723, Orenson & Sons, on account, $500.

5 *Purchase Invoices*
— Gordon & Associates, No. B7502, $315.20.
— Kohler, R. M., No. 719, $174.90.
— Riggs, J. B., No. 74998, $472.47.
Cheque Copies
— No. 65734, North State Packaging, Inv. 901, $74.87.
— No. 65735, Union Advertising, balance of Inv. 17201, $338.37.

6 *Purchase Invoices*
— Daiton Enterprises, No. 702, $375.62.
— Henderson Bros., No. 17436, $1 746.21.
Cheque Copies
— No. 65739, Gordon & Associates, Inv. B7407, $216.92.

7 *Purchase Invoices*
— Henderson Bros., No. 17807, $65.25.
— Kohler, R. M., No. 792, $107.64.
— Wrouse & Reid, No. 602B, $392.61.
Cheque Copies
— No. 65744, Henderson Bros., Inv. 16907, $615.
— No. 65745, Orenson & Sons, balance of Inv. 1604, $546.26.
— No. 65746, Wrouse & Reid, Inv. 597G, $316.29.
— No. 65747, Smithers, P. R., Inv. 74, $57.05.

3. Take off an accounts payable ledger trial balance and see that it agrees with the balance of the control account. The correct control account figure is $6 221.79.

Acting as the Subsidiary Ledger Clerk and as the Junior Accountant in Simplified Situations

9. The simplified general ledger and accounts receivable ledger shown below are included in the workbook.

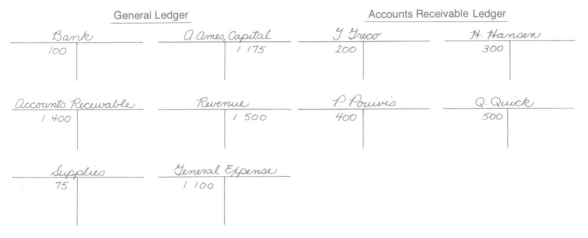

General Ledger

Account	Debit	Credit
Bank	100	
A. Ames, Capital		1 175
Accounts Receivable	1 400	
Revenue		1 500
Supplies	75	
General Expense	1 100	

Accounts Receivable Ledger

Account	Debit	Credit
G. Greco	200	
H. Hansen	300	
P. Pouwis	400	
Q. Quick	500	

1. Ensure that the accounts receivable ledger is in agreement with the control account.
2. Acting as the accounts receivable clerk post the source documents shown below directly to the subsidiary ledger. (Ignore dates.)
3. Acting as the junior accountant journalize the source documents shown below and post to the general ledger. (Ignore dates and cross-references.)

Source Documents

1. Sales Invoice — to G. Greco, $400
2. Cash Receipt — from P. Pouwis, $200
3. Sales Invoice — to Q. Quick, $100
4. Cash Receipt — from H. Hansen, $300
5. Cash Receipt — from Q. Quick, $500
6. Sales Invoice — to H. Hansen, $400

4. Acting as the junior accountant balance the general ledger.
5. Acting as the subsidiary ledger clerk agree the subsidiary ledger with the control account.

10. The simplified general ledger and accounts payable ledger, for the data shown below, appears in the workbook in formal accounts.

GENERAL LEDGER TRIAL BALANCE
MARCH 31, 19--

Bank	$1 500	
Equipment	5 400	
Accounts Payable		$2 200
S. York, Capital		2 900
Revenue		4 200
General Expense	2 400	
	$9 300	$9 300

ACCOUNTS PAYABLE TRIAL BALANCE
MARCH 31, 19--

Dow Company	$400
Frankle Corporation	500
Scampi Associates	600
Terrell Bros.	700
	$2 200

1. **Ensure that the accounts payable ledger is in agreement with the control account.**
2. **Acting as the accounts payable clerk, post the source documents shown below directly to the subsidiary ledger. Include dates and reference numbers.**
3. **Acting as the junior accountant, journalize the source documents shown below on page 75 of the journal and then post them to the general ledger. Include dates and cross-references but ignore journal explanations.**

Source Documents

1. Purchase Invoice; Dow Company; No. 492; April 1; for general expense; $200.
2. Cheque Copy; Frankle Corp.; No. 136; April 2; on account; $250.
3. Purchase Invoice; Scampi Assoc.; No. 604; April 2; for equipment; $200.
4. Purchase Invoice; Terrell Bros.; No. 316; April 3; for general expense; $150.
5. Cheque Copy; Terrell Bros.; No. 137; April 4; on account; $700.
6. Cheque Copy; Scampi Assoc.; No. 138; April 4; on account; $300.

4. **Acting as the junior accountant, balance the general ledger.**
5. **Acting as the subsidiary ledger clerk, agree the subsidiary ledger with the control account.**

Full Three-Ledger System

11. Rachel Bragg is a public accountant in Dartmouth, N. S. On March 31, 19--, her general ledger trial balance is as follows:

R. BRAGG
GENERAL LEDGER TRIAL BALANCE
MARCH 31, 19--

No. 1	Bank	$ 516.20	
2	Accounts Receivable	262.50	
3	Supplies	375.00	
4	Office Equipment	852.90	
5	Automobile	4 751.65	
20	Accounts Payable		$1 319.46
30	R. Bragg, Capital		3 181.23
31	R. Bragg, Drawings	400.00	
40	Fees Income		4 075.62
50	Car Expenses	196.50	
51	Light and Heat	62.75	
52	Miscellaneous Expense	47.51	
53	Rent	375.00	
54	Telephone	62.05	
55	Wages	674.25	
		$8 576.31	$8 576.31

1. Set up the general ledger accounts as of March 31, 19--. (Two workbook ledger accounts are required for Bank.) If you are using the workbook the ledger will be already set up for you.

2. Set up the accounts receivable ledger as of March 31, 19--. Observe that the total of the four accounts is equal to the balance of the control account in the general ledger. If you are using the workbook the ledger will already be set up for you.

The accounts receivable ledger on March 31, 19--, contains the following accounts:

Blue Cab Company	16 Fox Street	Inv. No. 74	$110.00
Champion Store	175 Main Street	75	37.50
Oasis Restaurant	325 Second Street	76	75.00
Village Restaurant	400 Main Street	77	40.00
			$262.50

3. Set up the accounts payable ledger as of March 31, 19--. Observe that the total of the four accounts is equal to the balance of the control account in the general ledger. If you are using the workbook the ledger will be already set up for you.

The accounts payable ledger on March 31, 19--, contains the following accounts:

M. Ball, Consultant	430 Red Road, Bigtown	$ 200.00
Queen Finance	151 King Street	1 047.21
Stirling Company	46 River Road	42.65
Tom's Garage	705 Victoria Street	29.60
		$1 319.46

4. Each day you are to perform the duties of both the accounts receivable clerk and the accounts payable clerk. From the list of business transactions shown below, you are to post daily to any customers' or creditors' accounts affected. Although it will be necessary for you to post directly from the list of transactions, try to imagine that you are posting directly from the source documents themselves. Also, remember that not all business transactions affect the accounts of customers and creditors.

Transactions

April

1 *Cheque Copy*
— No. 105, to P. Walters, $125, monthly rent.

3 *Sales Invoice*
— No. 78, to Blue Cab Company, $100.

5 *Cash Receipt*
— From Oasis Restaurant, $75, on account.

8 *Purchase Invoice*
— From Tom's Garage, $40.20, gasoline and oil.

9 *Cheque Copy*
— No. 106, to Queen Finance, $90, regular monthly payment.

12 *Sales Invoices*
— No. 79, to Champion Store, $175.
— No. 80, to Village Restaurant, $50.

15 *Cheque Copy*
— No. 107, to Municipal Telephone, $20.50, telephone for month.

15 *Cash Receipt*
— From Blue Cab Company, $110, on account.

19 *Sales Invoice*
— No. 81, to Oasis Restaurant, $75.

22 *Purchase Invoice*
— From Stirling Company, $35, for supplies.

24 *Cheque Copies*
— No. 108, to M. Ball, $200, on account.
— No. 109, to Stirling Company, $42.65, on account.

30 *Cheque Copies*
— No. 110, to Municipal Hydro, $15, electricity for month.
— No. 111, to R. Carter, $200, part-time wages for month.

5. **Each day you are to perform the duties of the junior accountant. Journalize each of the above transactions in the two-column general journal. Do not post to the general ledger accounts until the end of April.**

6. **As the junior accountant, you are to post the general journal to the general ledger at the end of the month. Then you are to take off a general ledger trial balance. It is your responsibility to see that the ledger balances.**

7. **As the accounts receivable clerk, you are to take off a trial balance of the accounts receivable ledger as of April 30, 19--. It is your responsibility to see that the accounts receivable ledger balances with the control account.**

8. **As the accounts payable clerk, you are to take off a trial balance of the accounts payable ledger as of April 30, 19--. See that this ledger balances with the control account.**

---

12. **Mr. E. W. Terry, an engineer, begins a small consulting business on a spare-time basis. He officially begins operations on July 1, 19--, with the following business assets:**

Bank Balance, $2 000; Office Furniture, $565; Automobile, $2 750; Equipment, $1 250.

He has no business liabilities.

1. **From the preceding information and the following chart of accounts, set up the general ledger of E. W. Terry as of July 1, 19--. Journalize and post the opening entry. Note:** Three workbook ledger accounts are required for Bank; two accounts required for Accounts Receivable; two accounts required for Accounts Payable.

E. W. TERRY
CHART OF ACCOUNTS

Account	*Number*	*Account*	*Number*
Bank	1	E. W. Terry, Capital	30
Accounts Receivable	2	E. W. Terry, Drawings	31
Office Supplies	3	Fees Earned	40
Office Furniture	4	Car Expense	50
Automobile	5	Rent Expense	51
Equipment	6	Miscellaneous Expense	52
Accounts Payable	20	Telephone Expense	53

2. **Record the following transactions of the business in the general journal. Open subsidiary ledger accounts as necessary and post to them on a daily basis. Postings to the general ledger accounts are left until the end of the month.**

Transactions

July

1 *Cheque Copy*
— No. 1, Chambers Bros., advance payment for monthly rent, $140.

2 *Purchase Invoice*
— Glen Printing, No. 651, for office supplies, $86.50.

4 *Sales Invoice*
— No. 1, J. R. Greenley, for services rendered, $150.

5 *Sales Invoices*
— No. 2, R. Grieve, for services rendered, $50.
— No. 3, P. Webb, for services rendered, $35.

7 *Purchase Invoice*
— Star Blueprinting, No. 370, for the printing of plans, $15.

8 *Purchase Invoice*
— Dynamic Engineering, No. B126, for consultation, $26.

9 *Purchase Invoice*
— McKay's Garage, No. B64, for gasoline and oil, $12.50.

10 *Sales Invoice*
— No. 4, M. Page, for services rendered, $50.
Purchase Invoice
— Star Blueprinting, No. 397, for printing of plans, $26.
Cheque Copies
— No. 2, Glen printing, re No. 651, $86.50.
— No. 3, Star Blueprinting, re No. 370, $15.
— No. 4, Dynamic Engineering, re No. B126, $26.
— No. 5, McKay's Garage, re No. B64, $12.50.

11 *Cash Receipt*
— J. R. Greenley, re No. 1, $150.

14 *Sales Invoice*
— No. 5, R. Grieve, for services rendered, $20.

15 *Sales Invoice*
— No. 6, J. R. Greenley, for services rendered, $40.
Purchase Invoice
— Automotive Electrical, No. 702, for repair to generator on car, $22.50.

16 *Sales Invoice*
— No. 7, P. Webb, for services rendered, $16.

17 *Purchase Invoice*
— Dynamic Engineering, No. B306, for consultation, $75.

18 *Cash Receipt*
— R. Grieve, re No. 2, $50.

22 *Sales Invoice*
— No. 8, M. Page, for services rendered, $18.

23 *Cash Receipt*
— M. Page, re No. 4, $50.

Purchase Invoice
McKay's Garage, No. B96, for gasoline and oil, $9.50.

24 *Cheque Copy*
— No. 6, E. W. Terry, for personal drawings, $100.

25 *Cash Receipt*
— J. R. Greenley, re No. 6, $40.

29 *Sales Invoice*
— No. 9, J. R. Greenley, for services rendered, $20.

30 *Cheque Copies*
— No. 7, Automotive Electrical, re No. 702, $22.50.
— No. 8, Star Blueprinting, re No. 397, $26.

31 *Cash Receipt*
— P. Webb, re No. 3, $35.
Cheque Copies
— No. 9, Township Hydro, for cash payment of hydro bill, $10.40.
— No. 10, Municipal Telephone, for cash payment of telephone bill, $16.50.
— No. 11, E. W. Terry, for personal drawings, $100.

3. Post and balance the ledger.

4. Take off subsidiary ledger trial balances and agree them with their respective control accounts.

Statements of Account

13. From the account of Richard Kott, shown below, prepare the statement of account for the month of April on the form provided in the workbook.

ACCOUNT R. Kott, 30 Beechwood Crescent, Baton Place, Manitoba No.

DATE		PARTICULARS	PR	DEBIT	CREDIT	Dr Cr	BALANCE
19- Feb.	28	Balance Forwarded	—			Dr	431 20
Mar.	12	# 3162		75 70		Dr	506 90
	18	on account			300 -	Dr	206 90
	26	# 3230		174 60		Dr	381 50
	31	# 3319		296 50		Dr	678 00
Apr.	5	on account			131 20	Dr	546 80
	12	# 3457		96 40		Dr	643 20
	19	# 3516		219 50		Dr	862 70
	24	on account			500 -	Dr	362 70
	28	# 3680		315 20		Dr	677 90
May	2	# 3775		61 30		Dr	739 20
	15	on account			46 80	Dr	692 40

14. Michele Penna received the statement of account shown below.

Lake Street
Thunder Bay
Ont. P9Z 1R3

Phone
326 1900

Lakeside Supply

In Account With
Michele Penna
1402 Archibald Street
Thunder Bay, P9Z 4Y6

Date	Reference	Charges	Credits	Balance
Mar 31	Balance Forward			372.16
Apr 9	#3126	115.70		
14	Payment Received		200.00	
17	#3296	131.50		
20	#3384	274.35		
23	#3410	164.53		
27	#3592	15.16		873.40

2% Interest on Overdue Accounts

Michele keeps complete records of her dealings with other businesses. An examination of her files reveals the following.

a. A check mark on Lakeside Supply's statement of account for March showed that the balance of $372.16 had been found to be correct.

b. Four bills of sale from Lakeside Supply showed that the purchases during the month were as follows:

April	9	No. 3126	$115.70
	14	No. 3296	131.50
	23	No. 3410	164.53
	27	No. 3592	15.16

c. The cheque register entries showed that two payments had been made to Lakeside Supply during the month as follows:

April	10	No. 376	$200.00
	30	No. 390	172.16

1. What discrepancies are there between Michele's records and the company's?
2. Give probable reasons for these discrepancies.
3. Suggest what Michele should do regarding these discrepancies.

Using Your Knowledge

15. Analyzing The Effect of Errors

At the end of June, the accountant for Marcus Company finds that the total in his accounts receivable subsidiary ledger does not agree with the balance in the control account. The subsidiary ledger total is $3 125 and the control figure is $13 500.

The accountant's investigation reveals five errors. Complete a schedule to show the effect of correcting each of the following errors. Be sure to arrive at the correct accounts receivable figure.

Errors

a. A sales invoice for $300, recorded correctly in the control account, was not posted to the subsidiary ledger.
b. A sales invoice for $325, recorded correctly in the control account, was posted twice in error to the customer's account in the subsidiary ledger.
c. A cash receipt for $100, recorded properly in the subsidiary ledger, was omitted from the control account.
d. A cash receipt for $75, recorded correctly in the control account, was posted to the wrong side of the customer's account in the subsidiary ledger.
e. An invoice for $500, posted correctly in the control account, was posted as $50 in the subsidiary ledger.

Challenge Question

16. Analyzing The Effect Of Errors

Five error situations and a response chart are given below. You are to analyze the error situations and complete the chart. In performing your analysis, keep the following in mind.

a. Subsidiary ledgers are posted directly from copies of source documents.
b. The general ledger is posted from journal entries in the general journal.
c. Unless you are informed otherwise, all accounting steps are deemed to have been done correctly.

Error Situations

1.	An entire general journal entry in respect to a \$200 sales invoice is not recorded.
2.	A cheque for \$100 received from a customer is credited to the wrong account in the accounts receivable ledger.
3.	A cheque for \$500 issued to a creditor is posted to the creditor's account as a \$50 debit.
4.	An invoice for \$125 is entered in the general journal as follows: Dr. Accounts Receivable \$135 Cr. Sales \$135
5.	A purchase invoice in the amount of \$75 is posted in the subsidiary ledger as a debit.

Response Chart (Appears in workbook also.)

	Case 1.	*Case* 2.	*Case* 3.	*Case* 4.	*Case* 5.
a. If the general ledger will be in balance and contain no errors, enter a checkmark.					
b. If the general ledger will be in balance but will contain one or more errors, enter a checkmark.					
c. If the general ledger will not be in balance, enter a checkmark.					
d. If you placed a checkmark in c. above, show the amount by which it will be out of balance.					
e. If the subsidiary ledger will be in agreement with the control account and contain no errors, enter a checkmark.					
f. If the subsidiary ledger will be in agreement with the control account but will contain one or more errors, enter a checkmark.					
g. If the subsidiary ledger will not be in agreement with the control account, enter a checkmark.					
h. If you placed a checkmark in g. above, show the amount of the difference between the control account and the subsidiary ledger.					
i. If you checked g. above, show which has the larger total, the control account or the subsidiary ledger, by entering a C or an S respectively.					

Cases

Case 1 *Overcoming a Lack of Control Over Accounts Receivable*

When James Egan went to work as the chief accountant for Durante Paving Company, he quickly noticed that the system of handling accounts receivable was quite different to any system that he had encountered before. The system was theoretically simple and worked as follows:

a. The production department issued sales invoices and sent them to the accounting department. The accounting department, after making the appropriate accounting entries, filed these invoices in an 'unpaid invoices' file, arranged alphabetically by customer.

b. As payments were received from customers, the appropriate invoices were withdrawn from the unpaid file, stamped PAID, and filed in a 'paid invoices' file.

c. The file of unpaid invoices represented the accounts receivable subsidiary ledger of the company.

Each month, the accounting department prepared a detailed list of the unpaid invoices for the owner. When the owner, Mr. Durante, looked over this list, he always found errors in it, such as an item on the list that he knew had been paid, or an item listed twice and showing slightly different amounts. Mr. Durante was annoyed by these errors, and often accused the accounting department of incompetence. Egan was also concerned because, since joining the company, he hadn't once been able to balance the subsidiary ledger with the general ledger control account.

Egan launched an investigation to find and overcome the weaknesses in the system. He found no fault with his own staff members who performed their duties correctly. But he did find a serious problem with the 'unpaid invoices' file. Other employees, particularly engineers and production foremen, were continually using the file, inserting and removing invoices without notifying the accounting department. These employees claimed that they needed the invoices for reference when discussing charges with customers, renegotiating a price, and so on. The engineering department did not keep its own file of invoices on special prenumbered forms. The invoices were typed up on ordinary letterhead paper.

Questions

1. The production engineers and foremen misused the 'unpaid invoices' file. Give examples of specific occurrences that would create errors in the accounts receivable.

2. Suggest changes to the system that would allow the accounting department to gain control over the accounts receivable.

3. After fixing the accounting system, Egan sees the owner, Mr. Durante, remove an invoice from the file without notifying the accounting department. How should Egan handle this problem?

Case 2 *Is the Policy Good or Bad?*

Jack Webster, the owner of a small business, decides that he should look after Number One, as he puts it.

Webster has a thorough system of recordkeeping for accounts receivable. He makes certain that every debt is collected on time, and his collection record is extremely good. However, Webster has an entirely different attitude toward accounts payable. 'Why,' he asks, 'should I keep records of how much I owe to others? Let them keep track of how much I owe them. And, if they don't do a thorough job of it, maybe I'll get away without paying for something.' He believes that other businesses should control their accounts receivable as he controls his.

As a result of this policy, Webster's procedure for handling incoming purchase invoices is very casual. After the purchase invoices are received and checked, they are placed in a pile on an office desk. The pile represents the accounts payable of the business, but no accounting entries are made to record them.

The purchase invoices stay in the pile on the desk until a request for payment is made. Then Webster removes the particular invoice in question and authorizes its payment. When the cheque in payment is issued, the purchase invoice is then accounted for as if it were a cash purchase of goods or services. The purchase invoice is filed with the cheque copy.

Questions

1. Is Webster a good businessman? Explain.
2. Is Webster's policy a reasonable one? Explain.
3. Would Webster's accounts be useful in providing information for management decisions?
4. When financial statements are prepared, how should the pile of unpaid bills be handled?

Career
Julie Devji / Accounts Receivable Clerk

Julie Devji took an introductory accounting course at her high school in India. After graduating, she emigrated to Montreal and took two courses in computer science at McGill University. Julie first worked in Canada as an office clerk for Stage 7 Knitting Company in Montreal. She recorded all the company's sales invoices in the sales journal and prepared daily and monthly summary sheets.

Julie next joined Cadbury's, a manufacturer of candy and other chocolate products, as junior accounts receivable clerk. She received payments from all the customers in eastern Canada and posted them to the accounts receivable ledger. She also credited the accounts of customers who returned merchandise to the company.

Julie was quickly promoted to her present position of senior accounts receivable clerk. She now oversees all customers' accounts for the province of Ontario. Julie receives all cheques from customers and prepares cheque remittance forms to enter these payments in the computer. She completes all weekly and monthly accounts receivable ledger balances for the computer.

Each month, Julie receives a computer printout of the accounts receivable trial balance and presents the total to the company controller for verification of the balance. She also issues monthly computer-produced customer statements and sends reminders to customers who are behind in their payments. If necessary, Julie contacts these customers by telephone and tactfully attempts to determine the reason for the arrears.

Julie's other duties include obtaining credit references for new customers and checking credit ratings. She also prepares data on accounts receivable for storage in the computer. She reports directly to the supervisor of accounts receivable and the credit control manager.

Julie is pleased with her progress at Cadbury's and intends to remain. In particular, she enjoys her work with the computer. She looks forward to meeting the challenges posed by the ever-increasing use of the computer in business accounting.

13

Accounting for a Merchandising Business

13-1 Merchandise Inventory
13-2 Periodic Inventory Method
13-3 Work Sheet for a Merchandising Business
13-4 Closing Entries for a Merchandising Business
13-5 Perpetual Inventory Method

Objectives

When you have completed Chapter 13, you should:

1. Understand what is meant by a merchandising business.
2. Understand what is meant by a merchandise inventory.
3. Know how merchandise inventory is presented on the balance sheet.
4. Understand what is meant by cost of goods sold.
5. Know how cost of goods sold is calculated.
6. Be able to prepare an income statement for a merchandising business.
7. Understand the difference between the periodic inventory method and the perpetual inventory method.
8. Know the accounting entries for transactions related to merchandise inventory.
9. Know the steps in taking a physical inventory.
10. Know how to handle merchandise inventory and cost of goods sold on a work sheet.
11. Be able to prepare the closing entries for a merchandising business.
12. Understand a basic inventory control and information system.

In the interest of simplicity, we have so far only studied businesses that sell services, rather than commodities. None of our examples or exercises have involved the buying or selling of goods. However, we are now ready to discuss accounting for the merchandising business. **Merchandise** means goods that may be bought or sold. Therefore, a merchandising business is one that sells goods rather than a service.

13.1 Merchandise Inventory

People who buy goods for the purpose of selling them at a profit are known as merchandisers. The goods that are handled by a merchandising business are commonly called **merchandise inventory**, merchandise, **stock-in-trade**, or just stock.

The merchandise inventory varies from one business to another depending on the nature of the business. For instance, the merchandise inventory of a lumber company consists of lumber and building materials. The merchandise inventory of a food retailer consists of the food commodities that are ordinarily seen on the store shelves. The merchandise inventory of an automobile dealer consists of new and used cars as well as replacement parts.

There are two common methods of accounting for merchandise inventory. Of the two, the **perpetual inventory method** is the more complex. Under this method a record of all items in stock is kept up to date.

The **periodic inventory method** offers a simpler way to account for merchandise inventory. With this method, the inventory figures are brought up to date only at the end of an accounting period. This is done by taking inventory, that is, by actually counting and valuing the items in detail. The periodic method is very common in businesses today.

Balance Sheet Presentation

Hardy's Hardware
Balance Sheet
June 30, 19--

ASSETS

Current Assets		
Bank	$ 1 205.60	
Accounts Receivable	12 961.70	
Merchandise Inventory	18 059.00	
Supplies	1 316.00	$33 542.30
Fixed Assets		
Store Equipment	$13 964.00	
Delivery Equipment	14 050.00	28 014.00
		$61 556.30

Merchandise Inventory is a large item.

Merchandise Inventory is a current asset.

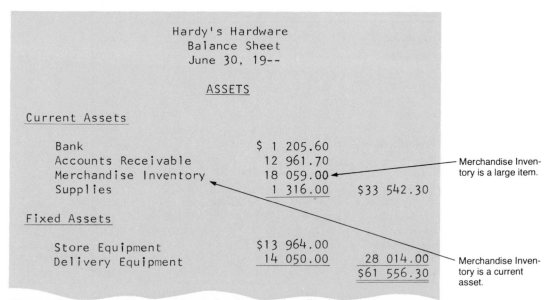

Figure 13.1 A partial balance sheet showing merchandise inventory.

Because a trading business sells goods directly to the customer, it must keep a large inventory on hand. This inventory has a monetary value to the business and must, therefore, be included as an asset on the balance sheet. The inventory is listed as a current asset because inventory items will usually be sold and converted into cash within a year. An illustration of merchandise inventory on the balance sheet is shown in Figure 13.1.

Relationship of Merchandise Inventory to the Net Income

The figure on the balance sheet is only one aspect of the accounting for merchandise inventory. The balance sheet figure represents only the cost of the merchandise on hand, that is, the cost of the merchandise that has not been sold. The cost of the merchandise that *has not been sold* is listed as a current asset on the balance sheet. The cost of the merchandise that *has been sold* is an income statement item.

The biggest overall expenditure of any trading business is the cost of its merchandise. An item that is sold for $100 may cost around $75, leaving a profit before other expenses of only $25. Clearly, the cost of the goods is a very significant expenditure. The purchase price of the stock that has been sold is known as the **cost of goods sold.**

The Inventory Pattern

In a successful business, merchandise is quickly sold and replaced. There is a definite pattern to the movement of merchandise inventory.

Table 13.1 Schedule of Inventory Movement Jan. - Dec., 19--.

Month of Sales and Purchases	*Units Purchased*	*Units Sold*	*Units on Hand*
Beginning inventory			1 700
January sales		500	1 200
February sales		400	800
March sales		700	100
purchases	1 500		1 600
April sales		800	800
May sales		300	500
purchases	2 100		2 600
June sales		900	1 700
July sales		500	1 200
August sales		350	850
purchases	1 000		1 850
September sales		650	1 200
October sales		200	1 000
November sales		400	600
purchases	900		1 500
December sales		100	1 400 ← Ending inventory
Totals	5 500	5 800	

1. There is a beginning inventory.
2. Merchandise is sold and moves out more or less continually during the accounting period.
3. Inventory is replenished by purchase of new stock from time to time.
4. An inventory remains at the end of the accounting period which roughly equals the beginning inventory.

Consider the schedule in Table 13.1 which shows the typical movement of inventory during a fiscal period.

Cost of Goods Sold Calculation

The data in Table 13.1 may be rearranged and summarized in the following form:

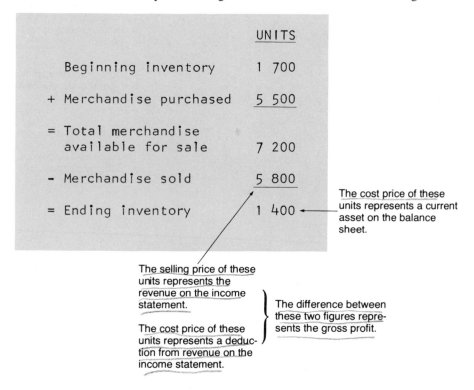

	UNITS
Beginning inventory	1 700
+ Merchandise purchased	5 500
= Total merchandise available for sale	7 200
- Merchandise sold	5 800
= Ending inventory	1 400

The cost price of these units represents a current asset on the balance sheet. (Ending inventory, 1 400)

The selling price of these units represents the revenue on the income statement. (Merchandise sold, 5 800)

The cost price of these units represents a deduction from revenue on the income statement.

The difference between these two figures represents the gross profit.

The inventory pattern summarized above may also be written in the form of an equation.

Beginning Inventory + Merchandise Purchased − Merchandise Sold = Ending Inventory

A simple mathematical rearrangement gives the equation for cost of goods sold as follows:

Beginning Inventory + Merchandise Purchased − Ending Inventory = Merchandise Sold

This simple equation is true whether it is expressed in units of merchandise or in dollars. The standard cost of goods sold calculation for financial statements is derived from this equation.

The majority of businesses use this method of calculating the cost of goods sold for the income statement. A formal example is shown in Figure 13.2.

Trident Trading Company

Income Statement

Year Ended December 31, 19--

Revenue		
Sales		$377 508
Cost of Goods Sold		
Merchandise Inventory, January 1	$ 72 074	
Purchases	230 853	
Freight-in	6 307	
Cost of Goods Available for Sale	$309 234	
Deduct Merchandise Inventory, December 31	83 562	
Cost of Goods Sold		225 672
Gross Profit		$151 836
Operating Expenses		
Advertising	$ 1 141	
Bank Charges	940	
Building Maintenance	375	
Car Expenses	2 994	
Delivery Expense	4 277	
Insurance	782	
Legal Expense	1 250	
Light, Heat, and Water	3 417	
Miscellaneous Expense	129	
Postage	318	
Rent	3 600	
Salaries	41 650	
Telephone	484	
Wages	47 563	
Total Operating Expenses		108 920
Net Income		$ 42 916

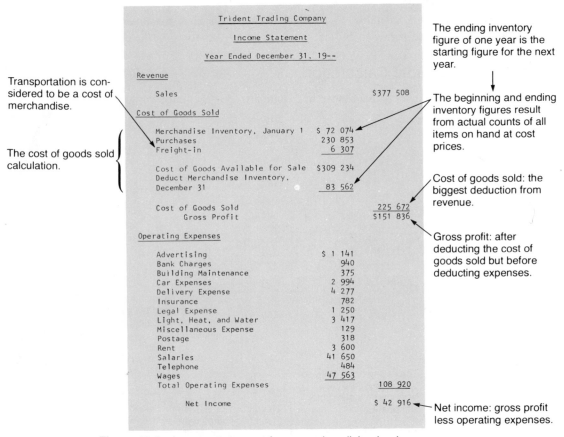

Transportation is considered to be a cost of merchandise.

The cost of goods sold calculation.

The ending inventory figure of one year is the starting figure for the next year.

The beginning and ending inventory figures result from actual counts of all items on hand at cost prices.

Cost of goods sold: the biggest deduction from revenue.

Gross profit: after deducting the cost of goods sold but before deducting expenses.

Net income: gross profit less operating expenses.

Figure 13.2 Income statement for a merchandising business.

13.2 Periodic Inventory Method

The preceding analysis was based on the periodic inventory method. Under the periodic inventory method, the merchandiser takes an actual count of the goods on hand at the end of the fiscal period and then values the goods to obtain the figure for the ending inventory. No attempt is made to account for the cost of goods sold as they are sold.

Consider a drug store that stocks a large number of different items of relatively low individual value. It is easy enough to record each sale at the selling price marked on each item. The cost price, however, is not marked on the item. The clerk cannot search out cost prices for every item so that an entry can be made at each sale to record the cost of goods sold. Instead, as we have seen, the cost of the goods sold is determined by calculation whenever financial statements are prepared.

The New Accounts for a Merchandising Business

The Merchandise Inventory Account

Under the periodic inventory method, the merchandise of a business is kept in two accounts. One of these, the Merchandise Inventory account, is used only to show the correct inventory figure at the end of an accounting period. At that time, after 'taking the inventory', the account is adjusted to reflect the correct inventory figure. This periodic adjustment is the only accounting entry made to the Merchandise Inventory account.

You will find a Merchandise Inventory account appearing in many of your exercises. Do not be confused by this account. Just remember that the balance in the account represents the adjusted inventory figure at the end of the preceding fiscal period. For your purposes at this time, consider the balance in the Merchandise Inventory account as representing the beginning inventory figure.

The Purchases Account

In order to handle the day-to-day transactions of a trading business, you must become familiar with the accounting entries for two important aspects of the business: merchandise buying and merchandise selling.

1. *Purchase of Merchandise.* During an accounting period, whenever merchandise intended for resale is purchased, the cost of the goods is debited to a new account called 'Purchases'. This name is short for 'Purchases of Merchandise for Resale'.

   If cash is paid for the merchandise, the accounting entry is:

Dr. Purchases	$XXX	
Cr. Bank		$XXX

   If the merchandise is bought on account, say from Victor Bros., the accounting entry is:

Dr. Purchases	$XXX	
Cr. Accounts Payable (Victor Bros.)		$XXX

   Not every item purchased is debited to the Purchases account. The **Purchases account** is used only for items of merchandise purchased with the intention of their being sold. For example, if a hardware store purchases a new delivery truck, the account to be debited is Delivery Truck. If the same hardware store purchases a shipment of hardware items to be put on sale, the account to be debited is Purchases. Similarly, if a tire dealer purchases some office supplies, the account to be debited is Office Supplies. But if the same tire dealer purchases a shipment of tires to be sold to the public, the account to be debited is Purchases.

2. *Sale of Merchandise.* Whenever merchandise is sold, the selling price of the goods is credited to a revenue account called 'Sales'.

   When goods are sold for cash the accounting entry is:

Dr. Bank	$XXX	
Cr. Sales		$XXX

   When goods are sold on account, say to J. Paus, the accounting entry is:

Dr. Accounts Receivable (J. Paus)	$XXX	
Cr. Sales		$XXX

   During the accounting period, nothing is done to record any decrease in Merchandise Inventory or to record the cost of goods sold. In this situation, it is easier to allow certain accounts to become incorrect during the accounting period and to correct them at the end of the period. But more about that later.

Freight-in

The **Freight-in account** is used to accumulate transportation charges pertaining to incoming merchandise. These charges are kept separate from the transportation charges on outgoing merchandise which are recorded in a Delivery Expense account. Freight-in is kept separately because it is one of the elements of the cost of merchandise, an information item very important to management.

The charges for freight-in or delivery expense may originate from invoices of trucking companies, railway companies, or shipping companies. If a business has its own delivery equipment, these charges will originate from bills related to the running of the equipment, such as garage bills, repair bills, and bills for gasoline and oil.

Physical Inventory

The periodic inventory method requires that a **physical inventory** be taken at the end of each fiscal period. This means that unsold goods are counted and valued to produce the ending inventory figure. This inventory figure is essential for two reasons. First, it is included as a current asset on the balance sheet, and second, it is an integral part of the cost of goods sold calculation on the income statement.

The procedure for taking inventory varies somewhat depending on the nature of the business. A common inventory-taking procedure for a merchandising business is outlined below. As you will see, it must be done in a very orderly manner.

To take inventory, a number of employees are needed who are familiar with the merchandise. Because inventory must be taken when the business is not in normal operation, the business may have to close down for a day or two.

Inventory Procedure

1. Prenumbered inventory tickets, such as the one shown in Figure 13.3 are given out to key employees.
2. Under the supervision of these key employees, the goods unsold are counted (or weighed). As each item is counted, an inventory ticket is prepared and the ticket attached to the merchandise.
3. The entire inventory is then checked over to make sure that no item has been missed or counted twice.
4. When the count seems satisfactory, the tickets are removed and sent to the accounting department for further processing.
5. The count tickets are checked to see that none are missing.
6. The details from the count tickets are listed on inventory summary sheets.
7. The unit cost price for each item on the sheets is obtained from the latest purchase invoices (or other records). This price is multiplied by the quantity of the item, and the resulting dollar value is entered on the summary sheets.
8. The individual dollar amounts are added to produce the inventory grand total.

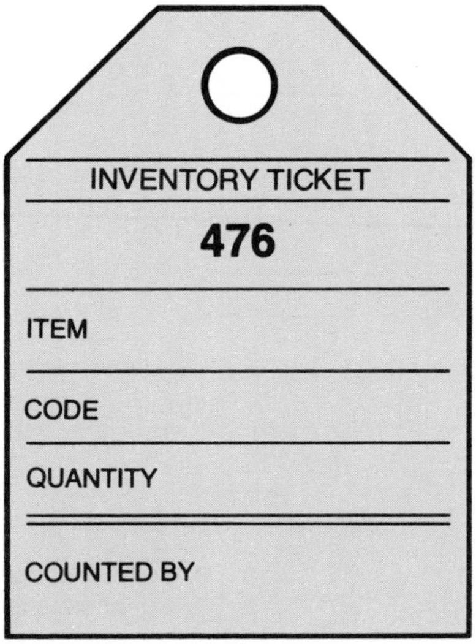

Figure 13.3 A prenumbered inventory ticket.

Limitations of the Periodic Method

You may have noticed that the periodic method of handling inventory has one serious weakness. Under this system it is impossible to produce a current inventory figure without taking a physical inventory. Why is the periodic system so extensively used despite this limitation? The answer is simple. The periodic system is much less expensive than an ongoing inventory control system. This is particularly true for businesses such as drug stores or hardware stores, with inventories that are made up of a large number of different items.

13.3 Work Sheet for a Merchandising Business

The ledger of a merchandising business contains three accounts that are new to you: Merchandise Inventory, Purchase, and Freight-in. These new accounts affect the financial statements. As you already know, the figures for the financial statements

How it is done

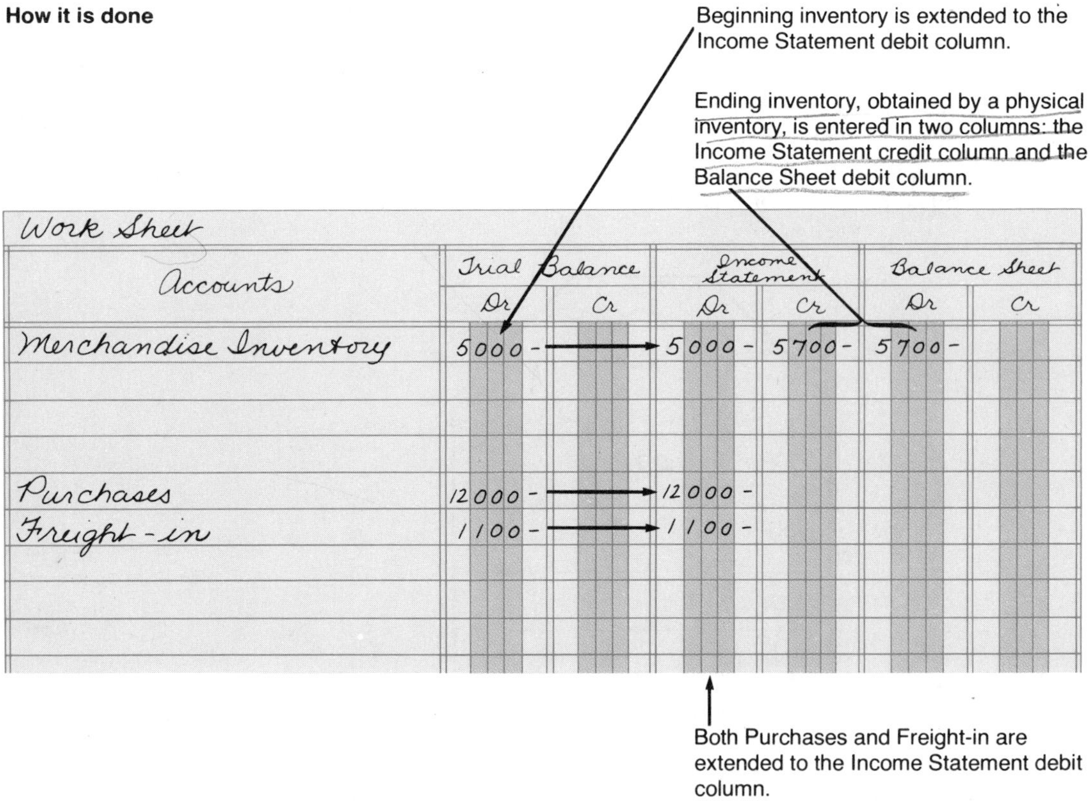
Beginning inventory is extended to the Income Statement debit column.
Ending inventory, obtained by a physical inventory, is entered in two columns: the Income Statement credit column and the Balance Sheet debit column.
Work Sheet
Accounts
Trial Balance
Dr
Cr
Income Statement
Dr
Cr
Balance Sheet
Dr
Cr
Merchandise Inventory
5000 -
5000 -
5700 -
5700 -
Purchases
12000 -
12000 -
Freight-in
1100 -
1100 -
Both Purchases and Freight-in are extended to the Income Statement debit column.

Figure 13.4a Partial worksheet showing the entries for the merchandise inventory, purchases, and freight-in accounts.

are obtained from a completed work sheet. Therefore, you must learn to handle these new accounts on the work sheet.

When working with the new accounts on the work sheet, remember two things. First, Merchandise Inventory, Purchases, and Freight-in are elements of the Cost of Goods Sold section of the income statement. Second, Merchandise Inventory is included as a current asset on the balance sheet. Also remember that the work sheet must be clear and easy to read.

To see how the new accounts are handled, examine the partial work sheet in Figure 13.4.

The three new accounts are highlighted on the completed work sheet for Trident Trading Company shown in Figure 13.5. You have already seen the income statement for this company in Figure 13.2.

Why it is done

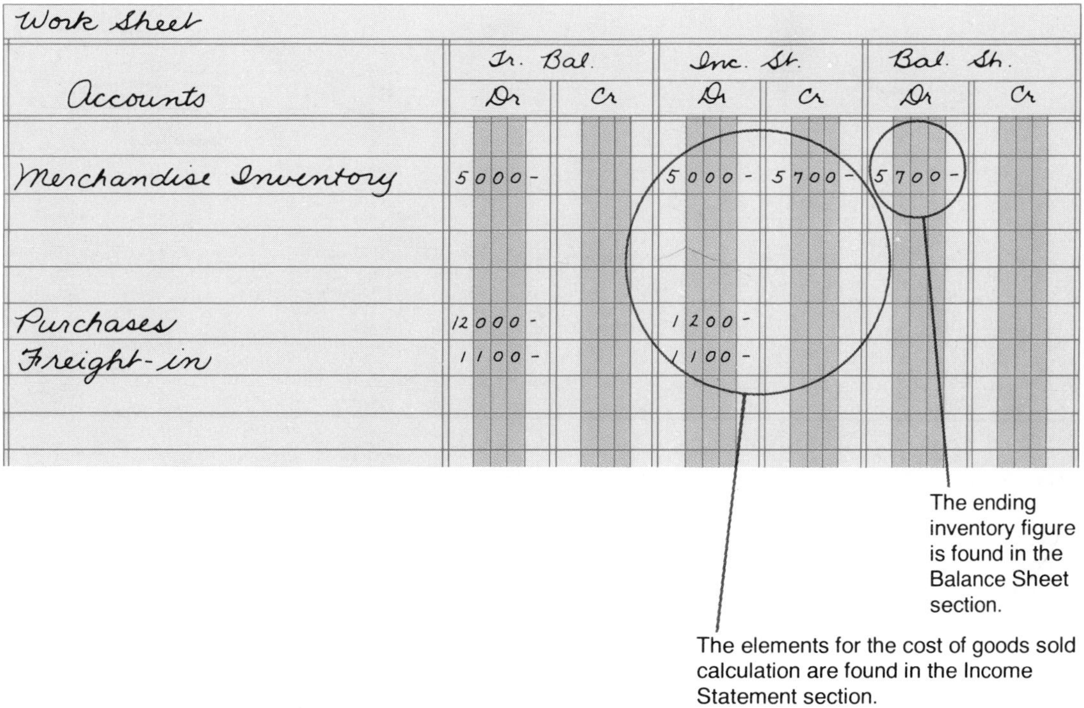

Figure 13.4b Partial work sheet showing how these figures affect the financial statements.

Work Sheet Trident Trading Company Year Ended Dec. 31, 19–						
Accounts	Trial Balance		Income Statement		Balance Sheet	
	Dr	Cr	Dr	Cr	Dr	Cr
Bank	2 463 -				2 463 -	
Accounts Receivable	27 374 -				27 374 -	
Merchandise Inventory	72 074 -		72 074 -	83 562 -	83 562 -	
Supplies	1 883 -				1 883 -	
Equipment	12 316 -				12 316 -	
Automobile	9 427 -				9 427 -	
Bank Loan		5 000 -				5 000 -
Accounts Payable		34 372 -				34 372 -
R. Kehoe, Capital		79 737 -				79 737 -
R. Kehoe, Drawings	25 000 -				25 000 -	
Sales		377 508 -		377 508 -		
Purchases	230 853 -		230 853 -			
Freight-in	6 307 -		6 307 -			
Advertising	1 141 -		1 141 -			
Bank Charges	940 -		940 -			
Building Maintenance	375 -		375 -			
Car Expenses	2 994 -		2 994 -			
Delivery Expense	4 277 -		4 277 -			
Insurance Expense	782 -		782 -			
Legal Expense	1 250 -		1 250 -			
Light, Heat, and Water	3 417 -		3 417 -			
Miscellaneous Expense	129 -		129 -			
Postage Expense	318 -		318 -			
Rent Expense	3 600 -		3 600 -			
Salaries Expense	41 650 -		41 650 -			
Telephone Expense	484 -		484 -			
Wages Expense	47 563 -		47 563 -			
	496 617 -	496 617 -	418 154 -	461 070 -	162 025 -	119 109 -
Net Income			42 916 -			42 916 -
			461 070	461 070 -	162 025 -	162 025 -

Figure 13.5 The work sheet for a trading company with the inventory-related accounts highlighted.

13.4 Closing Entries for a Merchandising Business

A very interesting result occurs when the closing entry process, described in Chapter 10, is applied to a merchandising business. The process very neatly cancels out the old inventory figure and sets up the new one. In other words, the closing entry automatically adjusts the inventory account at the end of the fiscal period.

To see how this is done, examine Figures 13.6 to 13.8.

Work Sheet

Accounts	Tr. Bal. Dr	Tr. Bal. Cr	Inc. St. Dr	Inc. St. Cr	Bal. Sh. Dr	Bal. Sh. Cr
Bank	500 -				500 -	
Merchandise Inventory	8 000 -		8 000 -	7 500 -	7 500 -	
B. Lee, Capital		7 000 -				7 000 -
B. Lee, Drawings	2 500 -				2 500 -	
Sales		21 000 -		21 000 -		
Purchases	12 000 -		12 000 -			
Expense	5 000 -		5 000 -			
	28 000 -	28 000 -	25 000 -	28 500 -	10 500 -	7 000 -
Net Income			3 500 -			3 500 -
			28 500 -	28 500 -	10 500 -	10 500 -

Figure 13.6 A completed work sheet showing the ledger accounts and balances. Note that the beginning inventory figure is $8 000 and the ending inventory figure is $7 500.

General Journal

	Accounts	Dr.	Cr.
1.	Mdse. Inventory	7 500 -	
	Sales	21 000 -	
	Income Summary		28 500 -
2.	Income Summary	25 000 -	
	Mdse. Inventory		8 000 -
	Purchases		12 000 -
	Expense		5 000 -
3.	Income Summary	3 500 -	
	B. Lee, Capital		3 500 -
4.	B. Lee, Capital	2 500 -	
	B. Lee, Drawings		2 500 -

Figure 13.7 The four closing entries, derived from the above work sheet. Remember that the first two closing entries are taken from information in the income statement section of the work sheet. Remember, also, to include all of the figures in the columns down to, and including, the sub-totals. That includes the inventory figures.

Bank	
500	

Mdse. Inventory	
8 000	8 000
7 500	

B. Lee, Capital	
2 500	7 000
	3 500

B. Lee, Drawings	
2 500	2 500

Sales	
21 000	21 000

Purchases	
12 000	12 000

Expense	
5000	5 000

Income Summary	
25 000	28 500
3 500	

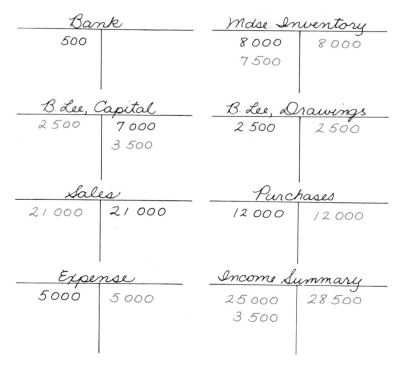

Figure 13.8 The general ledger. The account balances, before the closing entries, are entered in black, and the closing entries are posted in green.

As you can see, the closing entry process has had the following effects.

1. It has closed out all equity accounts except Capital.
2. It has updated the Capital account. The new balance is $8 000.
3. It has adjusted the Merchandise Inventory account. The new balance is $7 500.

This balance will remain in the account until the next time closing entries are recorded.

13.5 Perpetual Inventory Method

In certain kinds of business, a perpetual method of inventory control is favoured over the periodic inventory method. Under the perpetual inventory method a detailed inventory card file, known as a perpetual inventory file, keeps a running count of inventory and provides data for the inventory figures at any time. Figure 13.9 shows a card from a perpetual inventory file.

INVENTORY CONTROL CARD

Stock Number L591 Maximum 500 DOZ.

Description 200 Watt Light Bulbs Minimum 50 DOZ.

Location: Row 17 Bin 35

Date	Reference	Unit Cost	Quantity Received	Quantity Shipped	Balance on Hand
19– Nov. 5	Balance Forward				216
11	S.O. 436			100	116
14	S.O. 501			40	76
19	S.O. 530			35	41
21	S.O. 539			20	21
22	R.R. 1074	41¢	450		471
25	S.O. 561			75	396

Figure 13.9 A card from a perpetual inventory file.

The perpetual inventory file works as follows:

1. A perpetual inventory file is made up of a number of cards such as the one shown. One card is included for each item in the inventory.

   In the top portion of an inventory card (stock card), the following information is recorded:

   a. The stock identification number.
   b. A general description of the merchandise.
   c. The location of the merchandise in the warehouse.
   d. The maximum and minimum quantities to be kept in stock. The purpose of setting a maximum figure is to avoid having any more funds tied up in inventory than is necessary. The purpose of setting a minimum figure is to avoid running short of any item and therefore being unable to supply a customer.

2. The main body of the card is used to keep track of the quantity of the item in stock. Changes in the quantities result from goods being shipped out to customers or being received in from suppliers or returned by customers. Inventory clerks

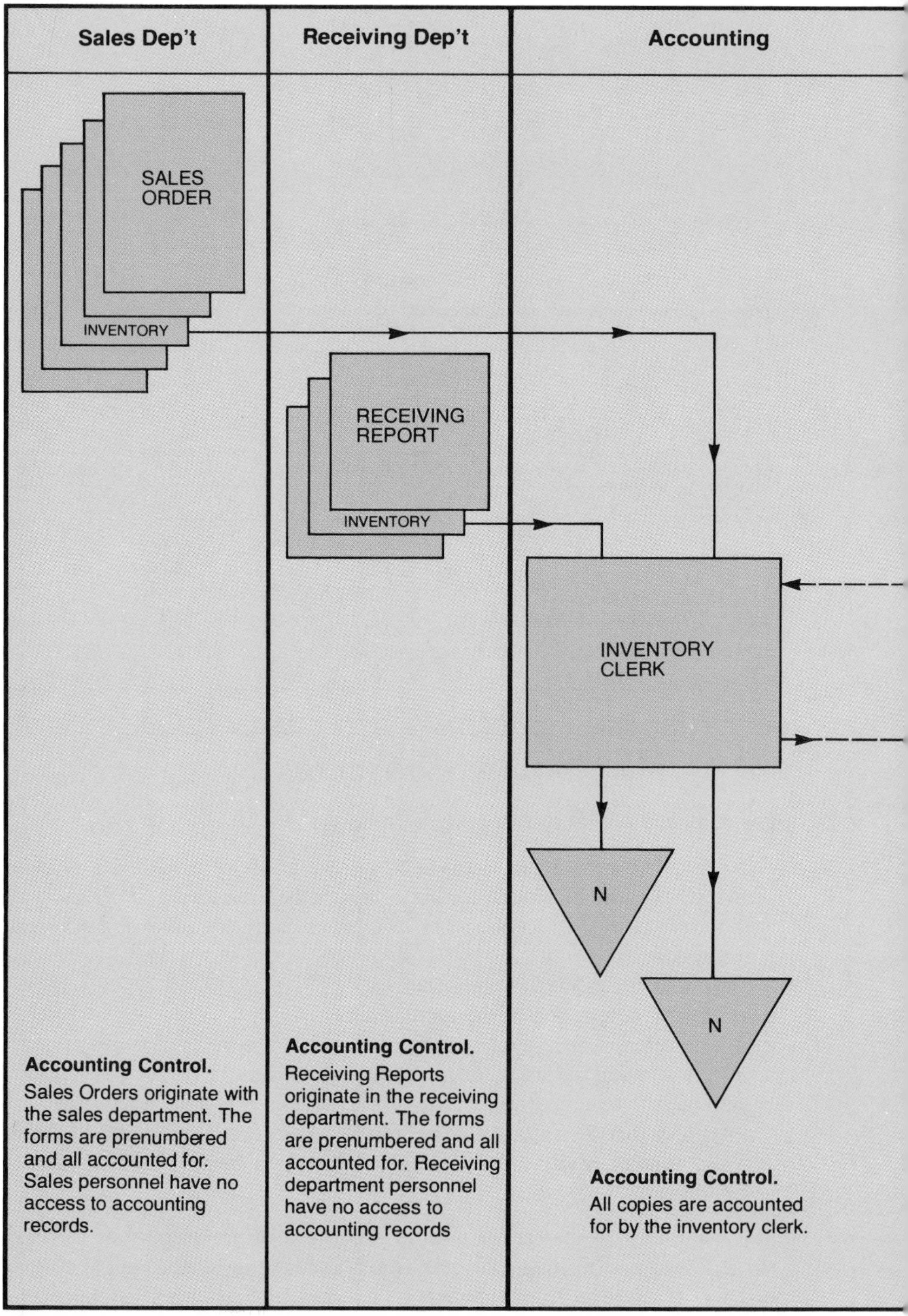

Figure 13.10 A flowchart of a simple perpetual inventory system.

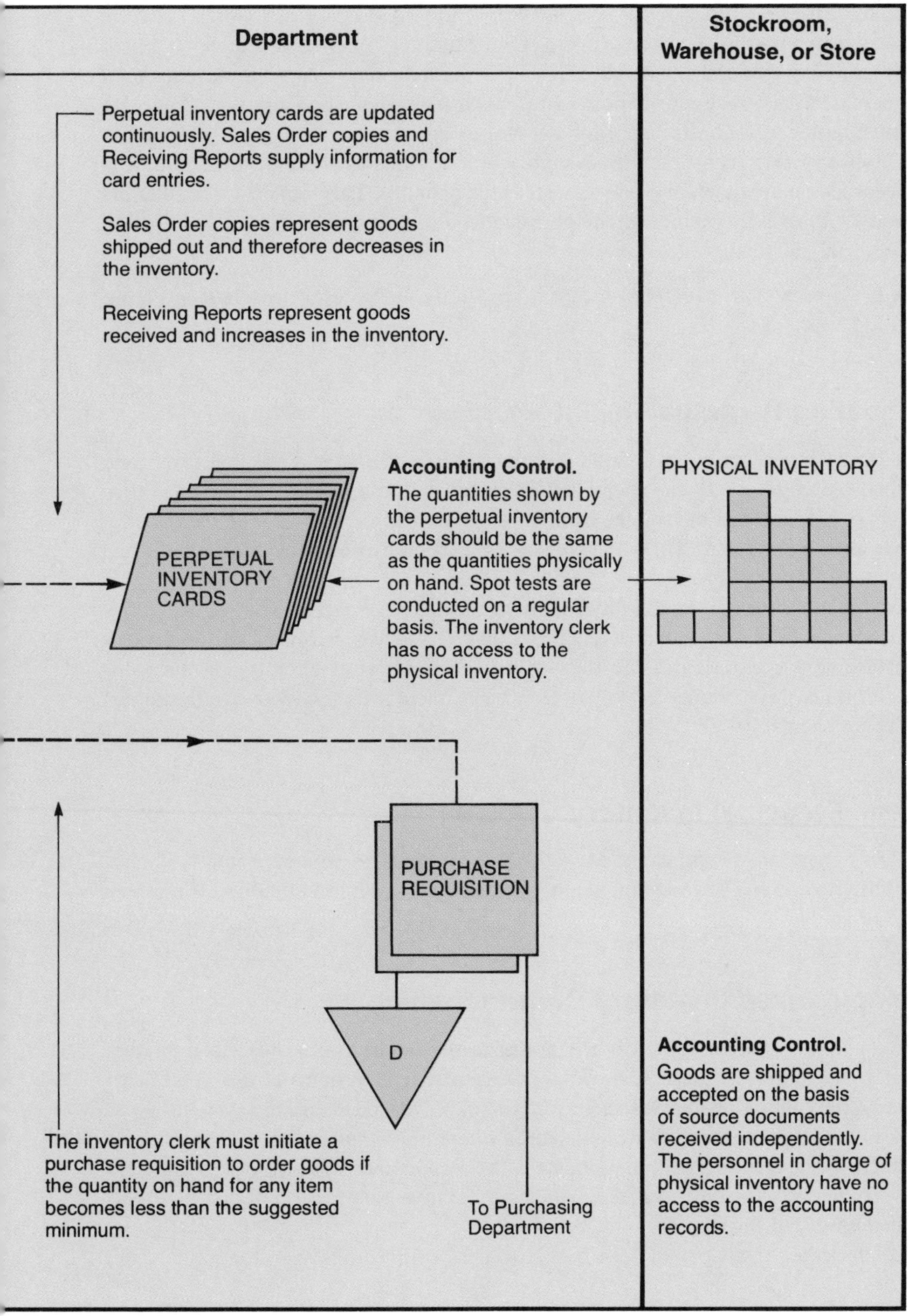
Department
Stockroom, Warehouse, or Store
Perpetual inventory cards are updated continuously. Sales Order copies and Receiving Reports supply information for card entries.
Sales Order copies represent goods shipped out and therefore decreases in the inventory.
Receiving Reports represent goods received and increases in the inventory.
PERPETUAL INVENTORY CARDS
Accounting Control.
The quantities shown by the perpetual inventory cards should be the same as the quantities physically on hand. Spot tests are conducted on a regular basis. The inventory clerk has no access to the physical inventory.
PHYSICAL INVENTORY
PURCHASE REQUISITION
D
The inventory clerk must initiate a purchase requisition to order goods if the quantity on hand for any item becomes less than the suggested minimum.
To Purchasing Department
Accounting Control.
Goods are shipped and accepted on the basis of source documents received independently. The personnel in charge of physical inventory have no access to the accounting records.

learn of these transactions by means of the shipping orders (sales orders) and the receiving reports that come to them. Each shipping order represents a shipment of goods out of the plant and must be recorded on the appropriate card as a decrease. Each receiving report represents a receipt of goods into the plant and must be recorded on the appropriate card as an increase.

Observe that each time a new supply of an item is purchased, the unit cost is recorded on the inventory card as well as the quantity. This unit cost is used at the end of the fiscal period when the merchandise inventory is evaluated for the financial statements.

A basic perpetual inventory system is shown by means of a flowchart in Figure 13.10.

Adjusting Perpetual Inventory

The file of inventory control cards is supposed to agree with the actual inventory, that is, the count of all the merchandise on hand in the stockroom. But, as time passes, it is found that the figures from the file do not always agree with the count of goods actually on hand. These differences are caused by unreported loss, theft, and damage of physical goods.

One or more times a year a physical inventory must be taken. That is, the goods on hand must be actually counted and listed. In this way, discrepancies are discovered. The inventory control cards are then adjusted by means of an entry on the cards which brings their figures for balance-on-hand into agreement with the figures on the count sheets.

Basic Perpetual Inventory System

The flowchart on the previous page shows a system for limited control of merchandise inventory. Advanced inventory systems are a subject suitable for a higher level of study.

Computerized Inventory Control System

Electronic information systems can perform all the functions described in this chapter and more. At present, however, these advanced systems cost a great deal. Usually, only major businesses can afford them. Advanced electronic systems are at work in the large modern department stores where individual cash registers serve as terminals connected to a central computer. The recent emergence of mini-computers will very likely bring the advantages of electronic inventory control within the reach of medium-sized businesses.

An electronic inventory system is able to perform the following functions.

1. It can produce daily inventory status reports, such as the one shown in Figure 13.11, which provide:
   a. The information needed by management to make decisions regarding purchasing or production.
   b. The information needed by management to test check the physical quantity of any inventory item, and, where losses occur, to take quick and effective action.
   c. The total value of the inventory, at cost prices, for use in preparing financial statements.

2. For each sale, an electronic system can search out the figure for goods sold. It can then record the following entries in the accounts:
   a. The debit to Cash or Accounts Receivable and the credit to Revenue with the selling price.
   b. The debit to Cost of Goods Sold and the credit to Inventory with the cost price.

   These two accounting entries allow management to determine the gross profit on each sale.

INVENTORY STATUS REPORT

STOCK NUMBER	DESCRIPTION	OLD BALANCE	QUANTITY RECEIVED	QUANTITY SHIPPED	NEW BALANCE	MAXIMUM	MINIMUM
EH-3703	BALL HAMMER 8 OZ	74	0	33	31	100	40
EH-3704	BALL HAMMER 16 OZ	52	50	26	76	100	25
EH-3705	BALL HAMMER 24 OZ	24	170	19	175	200	25
EH-3707	BALL HAMMER 32 OZ	36	150	170	16	200	25
EH-3709	BALL HAMMER 40 OZ	47	0	6	41	200	25
EG-4119	CLAW HAMMER 13 OZ	12	35	1	46	50	15
EG-4126	CLAW HAMMER 16 OZ	74	0	32	42	200	50
EG-4131	CLAW HAMMER 16 OZ (STANLEY)	156	0	53	103	300	100
EG-4132	CLAW HAMMER 16 OZ (NEOPHRENE HANDLE)	13	0	5	8	25	10
EG-4135	CLAW HAMMER 16 OZ (LEATHER HANDLE)	90	200	5	285	300	100
EG-4108	TACK HAMMER 8 OZ	54	95	3	146	150	50
EH-3725	BRICK HAMMER	12	60	2	70	75	25
BE-5263	RUBBER MALLET 14 OZ	32	0	12	20	100	25
BE-5266	RUBBER MALLET 28 OZ	27	70	13	84	100	25
EH-3753	SLEDGE HAMMER 6 LB	40	0	20	20	100	25
EH-3755	SLEDGE HAMMER 8 LB	11	90	3	98	100	25
EH-3757	SLEDGE HAMMER 10 LB	5	45	3	47	50	10
EG-3203	HAND DRILL 1/4 INCH	37	0	13	24	100	25
EG-3206	HAND DRILL 1/4 INCH HEAVY DUTY	46	0	15	31	100	25
EG-3224	AUTOMATIC PUSH DRILL (8 BITS)	56	0	27	29	100	25

Figure 13.11 A daily inventory status report produced by electronic inventory equipment.

A computerized inventory control system is suitable for businesses that fall into one of these two categories:

1. A business in which the inventory consists of a low number of goods of relatively high cost per unit, such as cars or major appliances.
2. A business in which a knowledge of the current status of the inventory is essential to management for decision-making purposes, in which financial statements are required frequently, and in which the volume of business is large enough to warrant having electronic data processing equipment.

For some merchandising businesses, such as Canadian Tire Corporation Limited, so many individual inventory items are carried that fast inventory reports are necessary to ensure that inventory shortages are kept to a minimum. For manufacturing businesses, a control over the supply of raw materials on hand is essential to ensure that a shortage of any one item does not cause a stoppage in production.

Accounting Terms

merchandise
merchandise inventory
stock-in-trade
perpetual inventory method
periodic inventory method
cost of goods sold
Purchases account
Freight-in account
physical inventory

Review Questions

1. Distinguish between a service business and a merchandise business.
2. What two names refer to the goods of a merchandising business?
3. Describe the merchandise inventory of a drug store and of a clothing store.
4. Where does merchandise inventory appear on the balance sheet?
5. What is meant by merchandise on hand?
6. State the equation for cost of goods sold.

7. Where does Freight-in appear on the income statement?
8. Distinguish between freight-in and delivery expense.
9. How does the ending inventory for the previous fiscal period relate to the current period?
10. What is the biggest deduction from revenue for a merchandising business?
11. What is gross profit?
12. What is the Purchase account used for?
13. Give the accounting entries for selling merchandise.
14. Give the accounting entries for purchasing merchandise.
15. What eight steps do you follow when taking physical inventory?
16. Describe how Merchandise Inventory is handled on the work sheet.
17. Describe how Purchases and Freight-in are handled on the work sheet.
18. Describe how the closing entries automatically adjust the inventory account.
19. What is the chief disadvantage of the periodic inventory method?
20. Why is the periodic method the most commonly used method of accounting for inventory?
21. For what types of business is the perpetual inventory method suitable?
22. Describe how a perpetual inventory file is maintained.
23. Give three advantages of the partial inventory control system.
24. What additional advantage does a computerized system have?

Exercises

Matching Inventory Items to Businesses

1. The chart shown below appears in the workbook. To the left of the chart, a number of common businesses are listed. To the right several products are listed and numbered.

1. In the columns headed 'Service' and 'Merchandising', classify the businesses as being either service, merchandising, or both by placing a checkmark in the appropriate box or boxes.

2. Match the products to the businesses that sell them by entering in the 'Goods Sold' column the numbers of the products that correspond to the businesses.
(**Note:** Some products apply to more than one business, and some businesses sell more than one product in the list.)

Business	*Service*	*Merchan-dising*	*Goods Sold*	*No.*	*Product*
Adjuster (insurance)				**1**	Automobiles
Accountant				**2**	Baseball gloves
Auto dealer				**3**	Bathroom tiles
Barber				**4**	Boat equipment
Boat dealer				**5**	Bricks
Brick and block factory				**6**	Building blocks
Builders' supply				**7**	Car and truck parts
Bus line				**8**	Carpets
Carpet store				**9**	Cheese
Furniture and appliance store				**10**	Film
Theatre				**11**	Hockey pucks
Sports store				**12**	Lumber
Florist				**13**	Meat
Grocery store				**14**	Milk
Hardware store				**15**	Plants
Hospital				**16**	Refrigerators
Insurance agency				**17**	Roses
Nursery (trees)				**18**	Rugs
Motel				**19**	Sailboats
Photography store				**20**	Shrubs
Radio station				**21**	Stoves (electric)
Real estate agency				**22**	Television sets
Trucking company				**23**	Trees
Television store				**24**	Tripods
				25	Trucks
				26	Wallboard

Gross Profit Analysis

2. The chart below appears in the workbook. Complete the chart by filling in the blank spaces. (Note: To calculate a percentage, convert it to a fraction and multiply by 100.)

	Selling price	*Cost price*	*Gross profit*	*Cost of goods sold as as a % of selling price*	*Gross profit as a % of selling price*
Easy	$250	$ 150	$100	60 %	40%
	$ 125	$ 85	$ 40	68 %	32 %
	$ 80	$ 56	$ 24	70 %	30 %
	$ 150	$ 75	$ 75	50 %	50 %
	$300	$195	$ 105	65 %	35 %
	$225	$ 162	$ 63	72 %	28 %
More difficult	$ 90	$ 54	$ 36	60 %	40%
	$500	$ 350	$ 150	70%	30 %
	$200	$ 130	$ 70	65%	35%
	$ 250	$120	$ 130	48 %	52%

3. Complete the right-hand column of the condensed Income Statement below. The Statement appears in the workbook.

	Dollars	*% of Sales*
Sales	$30 000	
Cost of Goods Sold	18 000	60%
Gross Profit	$12 000	
Operating Expenses	9 000	30%
Net Income	$ 3 000	10%

Cost of Goods Sold Equation

4. The chart shown below appears in the workbook.

1. Complete the chart by filling in the blank spaces.

	Year 1	*Year 2*	*Year 3*
Beginning inventory	100 units	300 units	50 units
Merchandise purchased	700 units	900 units	800 units
Goods available for sale	800 units	1200 units	850 units
Merchandise sold	500 units	1 000 units	800 units
Ending inventory	300 units	100 units	50 units

2. If the units cost $5 each throughout year 3, write up the Cost of Goods Sold section of the Income Statement.

Income Statement from Simple Data

5. Shown below are selected account balances taken from the ledger of Susan McTavish's Fashion Boutique. These balances are as of June 30, 19--, the end of a fiscal year.

Prepare the Income Statement from the following data. The ending inventory figure is $20 926.

	Dr.	*Cr.*
Merchandise Inventory	$18 316	
Sales		$77 585
Purchases	42 187	
Freight-in	1 572	
Advertising	1 675	
Bank Charges	219	
Car Expenses	1 318	
Miscellaneous Expense	516	
Rent	8 000	
Telephone	312	
Taxes	150	
Wages	15 726	

Accounting Entries for a Merchandising Business

6. Journalize the following transactions in a two-column general journal for Excel TV and Stereo:

Transactions

December

1 Received an invoice, No. 435, from Paramount Manufacturing for a shipment of television sets, $3 045.00

2 Received an invoice, No. B616, from Murray Transport Company for transportation charges on the above shipment of television sets, $435.

3 Received an invoice, No. 7042, from Swiss Stationers for a shipment of office forms and supplies to be used in the business, $236.

4 Issued Sales Invoice, No. 789, to W. Parker for stereo speakers and electronic parts, $417.

5 Issued Cash Sales Slip, No. 143, for the cash sale of merchandise from the store, $92.

6 Received an invoice, No. 902, from Haniko Electric for a shipment of electronic parts, $2 678.

7. From the following list of transactions for Plumbing Supply House, select those that have to do directly with purchase of merchandise inventory, sale of merchandise inventory, or cost of goods sold. Record the accounting entries for these selected transactions in a two-column general journal.

Transactions

Sales Invoice
— No. 6024, to P. Hamblin, for sale of plumbing supplies, $572.
Cheque Copy
— No. 174, to Jankowski Bros., $575.40 on account.
Purchase Invoice
— From Crane Fixtures, No. 767, for sink units, $3 742.50.
Cash Receipt
— From R. Parker, $200 on account.
Cash Sales Slip
— No. 371, to B. Mcleod, for plumbing supplies, $74.74.
Sales Invoice
— No. 6137, to R. Slaughter, for sale of plumbing supplies, $361.70.
Cheque Copy
— No. 362, for wages, $1 250.

Purchase Invoice
— From Maki Transport, No. 520, for transportation charges on incoming merchandise, $264.60.
Purchase Invoice
— From Asco Supply, No. 802, for shower units, $2 750.
Cheque Copy
— No. 402, to The Standard Company, for the cash purchase of plumbing supplies, $751.02.
Purchase Invoice
— From Bass Lake Garage, No. 327, for gas and oil used in the delivery truck, $324.70.
Cash Sales Slip
— No. 414, to W. Kell, for plumbing supplies, $125.37.
Cash Receipt
— From J. Farino, $315.70 on account.
Purchase Invoice
— From P. Koch, No. 614, for office supplies, $316.20.

End-of-period Accounting for a Merchandising Business

8. The simplified work sheet shown below appears in the workbook. Complete the work sheet. The ending inventory figure is $11 500.

Work Sheet

Accounts	Tr. Bal. Dr	Tr. Bal. Cr	Inc. St. Dr	Inc. St. Cr	Bal. Sh. Dr	Bal. Sh. Cr
Bank	500 -					
Accounts Receivable	7 000 -					
Merch. Inventory	10 900 -					
Equipment	12 000 -					
Accounts Payable		5 700 -				
R. Bok, Capital		30 200 -				
R. Bok, Drawings	18 000 -					
Sales		32 000 -				
Purchases	13 500 -					
Freight-in	1 700 -					
General Expense	300 -					
Wages	4 000 -					
	67 900 -	67 900 -				
Net Income			13 100 -			13 100 -

9. The trial balance for Small Engine Repair Shop at December 31, 19--, the end of an annual fiscal period, is given below.

1. Complete a work sheet.
2. Prepare an income statement.
3. Prepare a balance sheet.
4. Journalize the closing entries.

Small Engine Repair Shop
Trial Balance
December 31, 19—

Accounts	Tr. Bal. Dr.	Tr. Bal. Cr.
Bank	2 940.50	
Accounts Receivable	15 976.21	
Merchandise Inventory	39 076.–	
Supplies	1 275.–	
Store Equipment	18 357.70	
Delivery Equipment	11 902.50	
Accounts Payable		11 297.04
Bank Loan		12 500.–
H. Rohr, Capital		65 701.06
H. Rohr, Drawings	20 000.–	
Sales		108 376.02
Purchases	56 217.51	
Freight-in	1 178.36	
Bank Charges	1 364.70	
Delivery Expense	2 737.62	
General Expense	1 737.40	
Rent Expense	7 200.–	
Telephone Expense	743.50	
Wages Expense	17 167.12	
	197 874.12	197 874.12

10. The accounts and balances shown below appear in the workbook in a T-account ledger.

	Dr.	Cr.
Bank	100	
Accounts Receivable	1 400	
Merchandise Inventory	2 200	
Equipment	500	
Accounts Payable		700
Jennifer Roe, Capital		3 600
Jennifer Roe, Drawings	800	
Sales		6 000
Purchases	3 000	
Freight-in	300	
General Expense	900	
Wages	1 100	

1. If you are not using the workbook, set up the above accounts and balances in T-accounts.
2. Complete a work sheet (ending inventory, 2 000).
3. Prepare financial statements (month ended June 30, 19--).
4. Journalize the closing entries. Ignore dates and explanations.
5. Post the closing entries to the T-accounts.
6. Take off a post-closing trial balance.

Perpetual Inventory Cards

11. Two inventory cards from the perpetual inventory file of Outpost Marine are included in the workbook. These cards are shown below.

1. From the source documents listed below choose those that pertain to the two selected inventory items and record the increases or decreases on the cards as if you were the inventory clerk.

2. Assume that the quantities on hand are the latest ones purchased. Calculate the cost value for these two inventory items for inclusion in a summary for the grand inventory total.

Source Documents		*Stock No.*	*Quantity*	*Unit Price*
March	1 Shipping Order No. 921	730-0320	5	
	1 Shipping Order No. 922	713-3011	6	
	2 Receiving Report No. 630	736-0551	10	5.10
	3 Shipping Order No. 923	714-1018	35	
	3 Receiving Report No. 631	375-1000	20	10.50
	4 Receiving Report No. 632	931-4014	25	9.05
	5 Shipping Order No. 924	730-0320	15	
	8 Receiving Report No. 633	423-6757	5	25.60
	8 Shipping Order No. 925	713-3011	10	
	10 Receiving Report No. 634	703-1912	25	.50
	11 Receiving Report No. 635	602-4210	20	1.45
	11 Shipping Order No. 926	705-1912	15	
	12 Shipping Order No. 927	707-1129	100	

15 Receiving Report No. 636	713-3011	35	9.40
18 Receiving Report No. 637	920-0012	24	2.55
19 Shipping Order No. 928	730-0320	2	
20 Receiving Report No. 638	640-3121	30	40.25
23 Shipping Order No. 929	713-3011	15	
25 Receiving Report No. 639	730-0320	25	16.00
30 Shipping Order No. 930	730-0320	12	
31 Shipping Order No. 931	713-3011	20	
31 Receiving Report No. 640	715-6745	12	5.20

INVENTORY CONTROL CARD

STOCK NO. 730-0320

DESCRIPTION SCHAEFER CHEEK BLOCK MAXIMUM 30

LOCATION: ROW 16 BIN 3 MINIMUM 10

DATE	REFERENCE	UNIT COST	RECEIVED	SHIPPED	BALANCE
Feb. 20	Forward	15.50			28
26	S.O. 904			5	23

INVENTORY CONTROL CARD

STOCK NO. 713-3011

DESCRIPTION BARTON CAM CLEAT MAXIMUM 50

LOCATION: ROW 20 BIN 14 MINIMUM 20

DATE	REFERENCE	UNIT COST	RECEIVED	SHIPPED	BALANCE
Feb. 24	Forward	9.20			37
28	S.O. 910			10	20

Inventory Control Flowchart

12. Study the flowchart in Figure 13.10 and answer the following questions.

    1. Which source documents supply the data for the entries to the perpetual inventory cards?
    2. Where do these source documents originate?
    3. Describe the effect of each source document on the inventory record.
    4. Explain the role of the inventory clerk in the control of documents.
    5. In addition to updating the inventory cards the inventory clerk has another duty. Explain.
    6. What is the purpose of a purchase requisition?
    7. Explain how perpetual inventory cards act as an accounting control over physical inventory.
    8. The person who has custody of an asset should not have access to the accounting records for that asset. Explain how this principle applies to inventory control.
    9. Over a period of time, discrepancies develop between the physical inventory and the book inventory. What causes these differences?
    10. What steps should be taken when management learns of inventory discrepancies?

Using Your Knowledge

13. When the physical inventory was taken at the year-end, an entire department was overlooked. As a result, the inventory was understated by $10 000.

    Invent some hypothetical figures and use them to answer the following questions.

    1. How will the inventory understatement affect the gross profit?
    2. How will the inventory understatement affect the net income?
    3. How will the inventory understatement affect the net income of the following year?

4. Answer the preceding questions again this time for an *over*statement of $10 000.

---

14. Answer the questions related to the following source document.
    1. From the point of view of Masthead Marine, what is this source document?
    2. What accounting entry will be made in the books of Masthead Marine?
    3. From the point of view of Pier 11 Marina, what is this source document?
    4. What accounting entry will be made in the books of Pier 11 Marina?

Phone 842-9999

ECHO BAY
VANCOUVER, B.C.

P.O. Box 298
Station 8
V7C 8P7

MASTHEAD MARINE

SOLD TO Pier 11 Marina
4429 Marine Avenue
Powell River, B.C.
V8A 2L7

DATE June 15, 19--
TERMS 30 days

QUANTITY	PART NO.	DESCRIPTION	PRICE	AMOUNT
4	30-3002	Clew Outhaul Blocks	$11.40	$45.60
20	13-4101	Transom Drain Sockets	2.50	50.00
		Total		$95.60

SALES INVOICE — CUSTOMER'S COPY — NO. 9642

15. The following statement shows the results of operation for two successive years.

THE WALTON COMPANY
INCOME STATEMENT
YEARS ENDED DECEMBER 31, 19–8 AND 19–9

	19–8	19–9
Sales	$100 000	$120 000
Cost of Goods Sold		
Opening Inventory	$ 20 000	$ 25 000
Purchases		
	$	$ 63 000
Less Closing Inventory	25 000	
Cost of Goods Sold	$	$
Gross Income	$ 65 000	$
Expenses	$	$ 37 000
Net Income	$ 33 000	$ 42 000

1. **Fill in the blanks to complete the above statement.**
2. **Suppose that on December 31, 19–8, the merchandise inventory was miscounted. Instead of $25 000 as shown, it was counted as $21 000.**
   a. **What effect would this understatement have on the net income figure for 19–8?**
   b. **What effect would it have on the net income figure for 19–9?**
3. **What effect, if any, would the above noted error have on the balance sheet for 19–8?**

Cases

Case 1 *Irregularity Disclosed by Income Statement*

Mark Trewin is the owner of Spyhill Ski Shop. His accountant has just handed him the financial statements for the year. The income statement is shown below in condensed form.

SPYHILL SKI SHOP
INCOME STATEMENT
YEAR ENDED JUNE 30, 19--

Revenue			
Sales		$110 000	100%
Cost of Goods Sold			
Opening Inventory	$ 36 500		
Purchases	67 000		
	$103 500		
Deduct Closing Inventory	36 000	67 500	61%
Gross Profit		$42 500	39%
Operating Expenses		29 000	27%
Net Income		$13 500	12%

Mark is upset by this statement, and suggests to his accountant that an error has been made. His accountant assures him that everything was checked and double checked because of the low net income figure. No error was found.

Mark is particularly troubled by the gross profit figure. The operating expenses appear to be normal. Mark explains that all of his merchandise is marked up 100 percent and that there have been no special sales needed to move the goods. In other words, Mark feels that the gross profit should be at its normal figure of approximately 50 percent.

Because he has to be away a great deal, Mark relies heavily on his store manager. In past years Greg Zaba was the manager and no problems were encountered. A year ago, Greg left for a better position. This year the store was managed by Jon Yeo. Jon came from out of town and not much is known about him.

Questions

1. Assuming that the sales figure is correct, what should the figure for cost of goods sold have been?
2. What is the most likely reason for the high figure for cost of goods sold?
3. Try to show the cost of goods sold section as it would appear if there had been no irregularity.
4. Suggest how the owner can correct any irregularities.

Case 2 *A Scheme to Save Income Tax?*

Vince Lyons owns a large and profitable sporting goods business in Regina, Sask. He has recently had a run of bad luck on the stock market, which has left him very short of funds. Unfortunately, he is badly in need of money to pay his income tax which is almost due.

Vince desperately needs a way to reduce the amount of income tax that he will have to pay. After much searching, he comes up with a scheme that he thinks may work. He describes this scheme to his wife, Louisa, to get her reaction.

Vince explains to Louisa that his income tax is based primarily on the net income of the business. He shows her condensed figures for the current year and the projected figures for next year. These are shown below.

	This year's actual figures	Next year's projected figures
Sales	250 000	300 000
Cost of Goods Sold		
Beginning inventory	50 000	60 000
Purchases	147 500	170 000
Goods available for sale	197 500	230 000
Deduct ending inventory	60 000	65 000
	137 500	165 000
Gross Profit	112 500	135 000
Expenses	65 000	75 000
Net Income	47 500	60 000

Vince proposes to understate this year's ending inventory by $20 000, causing the net income tax to be understated by the same amount. This way, Vince expects to reduce his tax bill by $7 000.

Vince does not consider this action to be dishonest. He explains to Louisa that an understatement this year will cause an overstatement the next year. He shows her the figures as they would appear containing the suggested inventory change. As Vince points out, the net income for the two years is still $107 500 whatever way it's calculated. Although he will pay less tax this year, he will make it up by paying more next year. Rather than cheating, he is simply postponing tax payment for a while. According to Vince, he will have no problem paying his taxes next year.

	This year's actual figures (modified)	Next year's projected figures (modified)
Sales	250 000	300 000
Cost of Goods Sold		
Beginning inventory	50 000	40 000
Purchases	147 500	170 000
Goods available for sale	197 500	210 000
Deduct ending inventory	40 000	65 000
	157 500	145 000
Gross Profit	92 500	155 000
Expense	65 000	75 000
Net Income	27 500	80 000

Questions

1. Is Vince correct when he claims that the net income for two years remains the same no matter how it is arrived at?
2. Will Vince be breaking the law?
3. Does the scheme offer a hidden benefit to Vince apart from the $7 000 tax deferral?
4. What dangers do you see in this scheme?

Career

Slavka Fotak / Intermediate Accountant

Slavka Fotak was born in Yugoslavia. After graduating from high school, she came to Canada and studied accounting at a community college for one year. She enjoyed her accounting courses a great deal, and applied for work in this field.

Slavka's first position was in the accounts payable department of Domtar Inc., a company that manufactures paper products. Here, she learned how to handle accounts payable.

Slavka left Domtar to become an accounts payable clerk with Mennen Company, a manufacturer of men's toiletries. While employed with Mennen, Slavka used a computer for the first time. She kept the accounts payable ledger using data supplied by computer printout.

Slavka next worked as a bookkeeper with Galaxy 2000, a lighting firm. She maintained the ledgers for accounts receivable and accounts payable. She also kept the general ledger to the taking of the trial balance and prepared the company's payroll.

At present, Slavka is employed as an intermediate accountant with SSIH (Canada) Ltd., the agent in Canada for Omega watches. She verifies all invoices received for payment, records the amounts in the accounts payable journal, and posts the amounts to the ledger. Slavka also prepares the monthly bank reconciliation statements and the general journal entries for the company. She prepares the company payroll, and the salesmen's commission and expense reports; these are presented to the president of the company for his authorization. Slavka also maintains the accounts receivable ledger and supervises the accounts payable clerks in her department.

Each year, Slavka oversees a physical inventory of the company's merchandise. She uses the inventory figures to prepare schedules of cost of goods sold; these are sent to the controller for inclusion on the income statement. In addition, Slavka prepares all the closing journal entries and sets up the new inventories for the coming fiscal period. She then prepares the important Management Report which is sent to the head office in Switzerland. In her position, Slavka reports to the controller of the company.

Slavka is pleased that she chose accounting as her career. She finds her work challenging and absorbing and enjoys the people she works with. She feels that the accounting field offers substantial opportunities for future advancement and looks forward to a promising career.

14

The Synoptic Journal

14-1 Petty Cash Fund
14-2 Credit Invoices (Basic Procedure)
14-3 The Synoptic Journal
14-4 Two-Journal System

Objectives

When you have completed Chapter 14, you should:

1. Know the purpose of a petty cash fund.
2. Understand how the petty cash fund is operated.
3. Know the accounting entries to establish a petty cash fund, and to replenish a petty cash fund.
4. Be able to describe a credit note.
5. Know the purpose of a credit note.
6. Know the accounting entries for credit notes, both for the seller and for the buyer.
7. Be able to journalize transactions in a synoptic journal.
8. Understand the concept of a columnar journal.
9. Be able to balance and post a synoptic journal.
10. Understand the two-journal system using a synoptic journal and a general journal.
11. Be able to journalize using general journal vouchers.

Three new accounting concepts are introduced in this chapter. First you will study how to account for petty cash. Then you will be shown how to handle returns and allowances when merchandise sold is unsatisfactory. Finally, you will learn how to use a new style of journal with several columns.

14.1 Petty Cash Fund

The most common method of making payment for expenditures is by cheque. However, it is not always convenient to issue a cheque, and payment in 'cash' is sometimes expected. Consider the following transactions:

1. The janitor requires some electrical fuses. During his lunch period he purchases with his own money a quantity of fuses from the local hardware store. He then submits the cash register slip for $3.75 to the accounting department so that he may be repaid.
2. Two salaried employees are asked to work overtime in order to complete a special job. As a favour, they are each given $8 for supper money.
3. A parcel is delivered by an express company for which express charges of $12.50 must be paid immediately.

The most efficient way to pay for small expenditures of this type is with cash. For this reason a small quantity of cash, usually no more than $200, is kept in the office. It is called the **petty cash fund**.

Establishing a Petty Cash Fund

To establish a petty cash fund, a sum of money is withdrawn from the bank account and put in the care of some person in the office. More precisely, a cheque is issued (made out to Petty Cash usually) and given to the person chosen to be in charge of petty cash; this person cashes the cheque and brings the money (in the form of small bills and coins) back to the office. The petty cash fund is usually kept in a metal cash box (with lock). Outside office hours, the box is usually kept in the company safe or vault. Naturally, the keeper of the petty cash is instructed as to the type of expenditure that may be made out of petty cash funds.

The accounting entry to establish a petty cash fund is shown by the following:

Transaction It is decided to establish a petty cash fund of $50. A cheque in the amount of $50 is made out to Petty Cash and is given to the person chosen to keep the petty cash.

The journal entry to establish the petty cash fund is as follows:

Petty Cash	50.00	
Bank		50.00

The effect in the accounts is as follows:

PETTY CASH	
50.00	

BANK	
	50.00

After the cheque is cashed, the petty cash box will contain $50 in cash.

Operating the Petty Cash Fund

The keeper of the petty cash fund is authorized to make small payments out of the fund from time to time. But for every amount paid out of the fund, a bill for the expenditure (submitted by the person who received the money) must be put in. If a bill is not available, the recipient of the money must fill out a **petty cash voucher** such as the one shown in Figure 14.1.

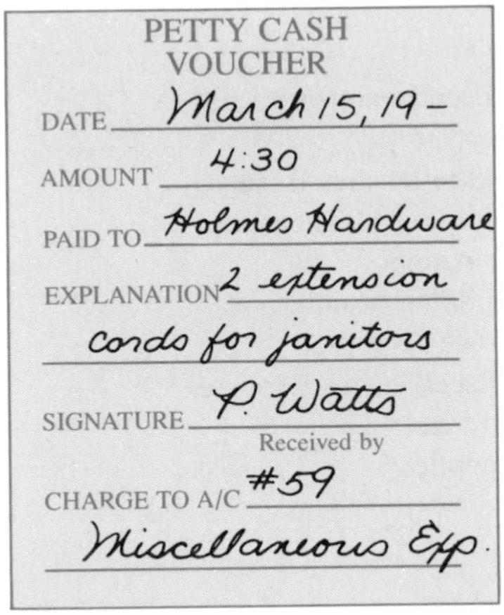
PETTY CASH VOUCHER
DATE March 15, 19–
AMOUNT 4:30
PAID TO Holmes Hardware
EXPLANATION 2 extension cords for janitors
SIGNATURE P. Watts
Received by
CHARGE TO A/C #59 Miscellaneous Exp.

Figure 14.1 A petty cash voucher.

The bill or petty cash voucher is then placed in the box. A supply of unused petty cash vouchers (also known as petty cash slips) is kept with the petty cash fund.

At any time, the total of the bills, vouchers, and cash in the petty cash box should be equal to the petty cash fund. The keeper of the fund is responsible for seeing that this is so.

The accounting for this aspect of petty cash is easy because no entry is made. It is one of those accounting situations where it is easier to allow the records to become temporarily incorrect. This method of handling petty cash is known as the **imprest method**.

Replenishing the Petty Cash Fund

As time passes, of course, the cash in the petty cash box will decrease as the bills and vouchers are paid. A point will be reached where there may not be enough cash in the fund to pay the next bill or voucher. To prevent this, a lower limit is usually placed on the fund. When the lower limit for the petty cash fund is reached, the fund is renewed. The procedure is known as **replenishing petty cash**.

To show the accounting for replenishing petty cash, let us continue with our earlier example of a petty cash fund of $50. After some time, the contents of the petty cash box are:

Cash	$ 4.15
Bills and Vouchers	45.85
Total	$50.00

The breakdown of the bills and vouchers by account charged is as follows:

Vouchers		
1.	Miscellaneous Expense	$ 2.59
2.	Postage	4.00
3.	Miscellaneous Expense	3.75
4.	Building Maintenance	1.56
5.	Donations	5.00
6.	Building Maintenance	4.75
7.	Truck Expense	5.15
8.	Miscellaneous Expense	4.30
9.	Postage	5.70
10.	Supplies	9.05
	Total	$45.85

The lower limit of the petty cash fund is set at $5. Because the petty cash box contains less cash than the lower limit of $5, the fund must be replenished. First the keeper of the fund prepares a summary of the charges from the bills and vouchers in the box. There is no definite form in which the summary must be prepared. The summary might be drawn up like the one in Figure 14.2. The bills and vouchers from which the summary is prepared are attached to this summary.

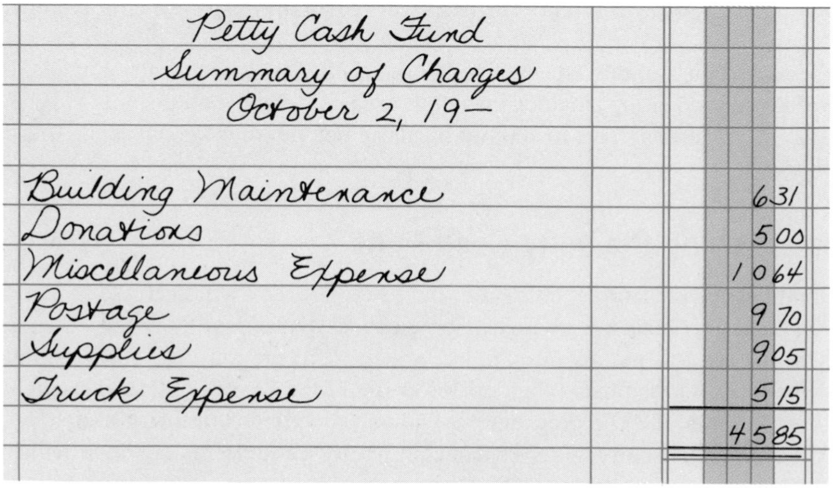

Petty Cash Fund
Summary of Charges
October 2, 19—

Building Maintenance	6 31
Donations	5 00
Miscellaneous Expense	10 64
Postage	9 70
Supplies	9 05
Truck Expense	5 15
	45 85

Figure 14.2 A summary of charges from a petty cash fund.

Next the petty cashier obtains a cheque with which to replenish the cash that has been spent from the fund. This is done by (1) submitting the summary, together with the bills and vouchers, to the department that issues cheques, and (2) obtaining a cheque, made out to petty cash, for an amount equal to the total shown on the summary (in this example, $45.85). The summary and the supporting papers are accepted as the source document for the cheque.

The cheque is then cashed and the money placed in the petty cash box along with the $4.15 already there. The fund is now restored to its original amount of $50 cash. It is now ready to begin another cycle.

The Accounting Entry to Replenish Petty Cash

The copy of the replenishing cheque, the petty cash summary, and the attached vouchers all act together as the source document for the accounting entry to replenish the petty cash fund. The accounting entry for the summary in Figure 14.2 is as follows:

Building Maintenance	$ 6.31		Debits taken from summary
Donations	5.00		
Miscellaneous Expense	10.64		
Postage	9.70		
Supplies	9.05		
Truck Expense	5.15		
Bank		$45.85 ←	Credit taken from cheque account

As we have seen, two types of accounting entry are necessary when the imprest method of petty cash is used.

1. The first entry establishes the fund. A similar entry is used to increase the fund.
2. The replenishing entry records the credit to Bank and distributes the charges to the various accounts.

14.2 Credit Invoices (Basic Procedure)

When a sale is made on account, the seller issues a sales invoice and makes the following accounting entry:

Dr. Accounts Receivable	XXX	
Cr. Sales		XXX

No further action is necessary for most sales transactions except to ensure that the customer pays the account. Occasionally, however, a correction or a cancellation of a sales invoice is necessary.

Examine the sales invoice shown in Figure 14.3.

Phone
842-9999

ECHO BAY
VANCOUVER, B.C.

P.O. Box 298
Station 8
V7C 8P7

MASTHEAD MARINE

SOLD TO Penticton Marina
4000 Skaha Lake Road
Penticton, B.C.
V2A 6G9

DATE April 14, 19--
TERMS 60 days

QUANTITY	PART NO.	DESCRIPTION	PRICE	AMOUNT
2	15-2500	Gusher '25' pump	$315.00	$630.00
8 Pacs.	48-1020	Skyblazer Red Signal Flares	18.00	148.00
		Total		$778.00

SALES INVOICE   CUSTOMER'S COPY   NO. 8321

Figure 14.3 The customer's copy of a sales invoice.

In the books of the vendor (Masthead Marine), the following accounting entry is made for this 'sales' invoice:

Dr. Accounts Receivable	778.00	
Cr. Sales		778.00

In the books of the buyer (Penticton Marina), the following accounting entry is made for the above 'purchase' invoice:

Dr. Purchases	778.00	
Cr. Accounts Payable		778.00

Correction or Cancellation of a Sales Invoice

Let us assume that several weeks after purchasing the items in our sample sales invoice (Figure 14.3), Penticton Marina learns from its customers that the Skyblazer flares are defective. After checking and verifying this claim, Penticton Marina notifies Masthead Marine that the flares are being returned for 'credit'. In other words, Penticton Marina expects that its account on the books of Masthead Marina will be decreased by means of a credit entry.

The standard procedure for dealing with this situation is for the vendor (Masthead Marine) to issue a 'minus' invoice known as a **credit invoice** or credit memorandum (memo). The credit invoice in this case would look like the one in Figure 14.4.

Phone 842-9999

ECHO BAY
VANCOUVER, B.C.

P.O. Box 298
Station 8
V7C 8P7

MASTHEAD MARINE

SOLD TO Penticton Marina
4000 Skaha Lake Road
Penticton, B.C.
V2A 6G9

DATE April 14, 19-
TERMS 60 days

QUANTITY	PART NO.	DESCRIPTION	PRICE	AMOUNT
8 Pacs	48-1020	Skyblazer Red Signal Flares (defective merchandise)	18.50	148.00
		Total		$148.00

CREDIT

CREDIT INVOICE CUSTOMER'S COPY NO. 841

The path of a credit invoice is the same as that of a regular sales invoice.

The word 'credit' is prominently displayed.

The invoice is printed in red or on pink paper.

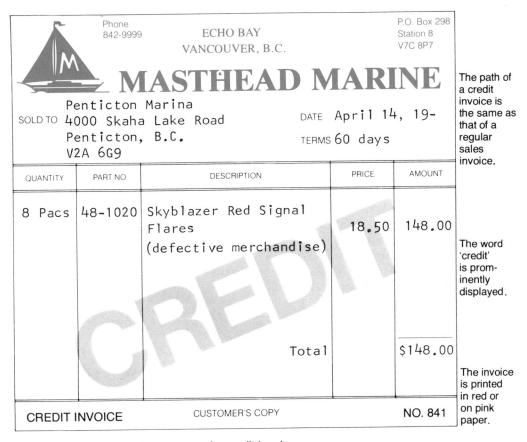

Figure 14.4 The customer's copy of a credit invoice.

The effect of a credit invoice is to reverse a charge on a regular sales invoice. Let us see how the credit invoice for Penticton Marina would be treated. Keep in mind that a credit invoice is the *opposite* to a regular sales invoice.

In the books of the vendor (Masthead Marine), the accounting entry for this credit invoice is as follows:

Dr. Sales	148.00	
Cr. Accounts Receivable		148.00

In the books of the buyer (Penticton Marina), the accounting entry for this credit invoice is as follows:

Dr. Accounts Payable	148.00	
Cr. Purchases		148.00

After the credit invoice has been processed by Masthead Marine, the balance in the account of Penticton Marina is $630, as it should be.

The Purpose of a Credit Invoice

Credit invoices are used to adjust or correct a customer's account for any of the following reasons:

1. If the goods prove to be defective and are returned. In this case the sales invoice will be cancelled.
2. If the goods prove to be less than satisfactory. In this case, the customer will be given an allowance (a reduction) in the price as shown on the sales invoice.
3. If an error is made on the sales invoice. In this case, the error will be corrected.

14.3 The Synoptic Journal

By now you should have a fairly good idea of the accounting process. You are ready to study a device that makes the whole system more efficient.

In the business world, the two-column journal is kept mainly for unusual transactions. Routine transactions are generally recorded in a many-columned type of journal, such as the **synoptic journal**. The synoptic journal is a journal with a number of columns to accumulate accounting entries by accounts.

Journalizing in the Synoptic Journal

An illustration of one style of synoptic journal appears in Figure 14.5. Observe the special money columns for Bank Dr., Bank Cr., Accounts Receivable Dr., Accounts Receivable Cr., Accounts Payable Dr., Accounts Payable Cr., Sales or Income Cr., Purchases Dr., and the blank column to be designated by the accountant.

SYNOPTIC JOURNAL MONTH OF 19 Page

DATE	PARTICULARS	CHQ NO.	BANK		ACCOUNTS REC'L		ACCOUNTS PAY'L			SALES	PURCH'S		OTHER ACCOUNTS			
			DR.	CR.	DR.	CR.	DR.	CR.	NO.	CR.	DR.		ACCOUNT	PR	DR.	CR.

Figure 14.5 The Synoptic Journal.

The idea of the synoptic journal is to put similar items in special columns during the journalizing process. Later, when posting to the general ledger, it is the totals of the special columns that are posted rather than the individual items contained within the columns. For each of the special columns, one posting is enough.

For example, if twenty individual amounts have been entered in the Bank Debit column of the synoptic journal, then it is the total of these twenty amounts, rather than each separate amount, that will be posted. The accountant saves a good deal of time and effort by posting the totals instead of the individual items.

In theory, one could have a special column for every general ledger account. But in practice it is common to have special columns only for the items that occur frequently, and a general section for the remaining items. Otherwise, the journal page would be too wide.

Journalizing in the synoptic journal is easy. Obtain a sheet of 'synoptic' paper and try the following sample entries.

Transaction 1 May 4: Sold $56 of merchandise for cash on sales ticket No. 57.

According to a recently learned rule, the accounting entry for this transaction is Dr. Bank, $56; Cr. Sales, $56. In the synoptic journal this entry is recorded as follows:

SYNOPTIC JOURNAL MONTH OF May 19 — Page 42

DATE	PARTICULARS	CHQ NO.	BANK		ACCOUNTS REC'L		ACCOUNTS PAY'L			SALES	PURCH'S		OTHER ACCOUNTS			
			DR.	CR.	DR.	CR.	DR.	CR.	NO.	CR.	DR.		ACCOUNT	PR.	DR.	CR.
19– May 4	Cash Sale		56 –						57	56 –						

Transaction 2 May 5: Sold $112 of merchandise to Paul Boxer on account. Invoice No. 165 was issued.

The accounting entry for this transaction is Dr. Accounts Receivable (Paul Boxer), $112; Cr. Sales, $112. This entry follows the previous entry in the synoptic journal in the manner shown below. For simple routine entries such as this, no explanations need to be written in.

You will recall that the postings to the customers' and creditors' accounts are made directly from the source documents.

SYNOPTIC JOURNAL MONTH OF May 19 — Page 42

DATE	PARTICULARS	CHQ NO.	BANK		ACCOUNTS REC'L		ACCOUNTS PAY'L			SALES	PURCH'S		OTHER ACCOUNTS			
			DR.	CR.	DR.	CR.	DR.	CR.	NO.	CR.	DR.		ACCOUNT	PR.	DR.	CR.
19– May 4	Cash Sale		56 –						57	56 –						
5	Paul Boxer				112 –				165	112 –						

Transaction 3 May 6: Purchased $316 of merchandise on account from Empire Wholesale; received their invoice.

The accounting entry for this transaction, which you have recently learned, is Dr. Purchases, $316; Cr. Accounts Payable (Empire Wholesale), $316. This entry is recorded in the synoptic journal as follows:

SYNOPTIC JOURNAL MONTH OF May 19— Page 42

DATE	PARTICULARS	CHQ NO.	BANK		ACCOUNTS REC'L		ACCOUNTS PAY'L			SALES	PURCH'S		OTHER ACCOUNTS			
			DR.	CR.	DR.	CR.	DR.	CR.	NO.	CR.	DR.		ACCOUNT	PR.	DR.	CR.
19– May 4	Cash Sale		56 –						57	56 –						
5	Paul Bozer				112 –				165	112 –						
6	Empire Wholesale							316 –			316 –					

Transaction 4 May 7: $37.20 of supplies is purchased and paid for with cheque No. 74 issued to Deluxe Stationers.

The accounting entry for this transaction is Dr. Supplies, $37.20; Cr. Bank, $37.20. It is recorded in the synoptic journal in the manner shown below.

Notice that the accountant has used the blank column for Supplies. This tells us that, for this business, Supplies is an item that often occurs.

SYNOPTIC JOURNAL MONTH OF May 19— Page 42

DATE	PARTICULARS	CHQ NO.	BANK		ACCOUNTS REC'L		ACCOUNTS PAY'L			SALES	PURCH'S	Supplies	OTHER ACCOUNTS			
			DR.	CR.	DR.	CR.	DR.	CR.	NO.	CR.	DR.	Dr.	ACCOUNT	PR.	DR.	CR.
19– May 4	Cash Sale		56 –						57	56 –						
5	Paul Bozer				112 –				165	112 –						
6	Empire Wholesale							316 –			316 –					
7	Deluxe Stationers	74		37 20								37 20				

Transaction 5 May 7: Issued cheque No. 75 in the amount of $400 to Arrow Realty in payment of the monthly rent.

This accounting entry — Dr. Rent Expense, $400; Cr. Bank, $400 — is recorded in the synoptic journal as shown below.

Notice that there is no special column for Rent Expense. The payment of the rent is a transaction that occurs only once a month and for that reason it is recorded in the section headed 'Other Accounts'. Observe in this case that the amount is placed in the Debit column.

SYNOPTIC JOURNAL MONTH OF May 19— Page 42

DATE	PARTICULARS	CHQ NO.	BANK		ACCOUNTS REC'L		ACCOUNTS PAY'L			SALES	PURCH'S	Supplies	OTHER ACCOUNTS			
			DR.	CR.	DR.	CR.	DR.	CR.	NO.	CR.	DR.	Dr.	ACCOUNT	PR.	DR.	CR.
19– May 4	Cash Sale		56 –						57	56 –						
5	Paul Bozer				112 –				165	112 –						
6	Empire Wholesale							316 –			316 –					
7	Deluxe Stationers	74		37 20								37 20				
7	Arrow Realty	75		400 –									Rent Expense		400 –	

Additional Transactions

A number of additional transactions of a routine nature are listed below. Try to journalize them on your own before comparing your work with the synoptic journal entries in Figure 14.6.

May 10 Issued cheque No. 76 in the amount of $73.50 to A. Baldwin — a payment on account.
May 10 Issued cheque No. 77 in the amount of $46.20 to G. English & Co. — a payment on account
May 11 Received a cheque for $96 from R. Smith on account.
May 11 Received a cheque for $375 from F. Jones on account.
May 13 Issued cheque No. 78 in the amount of $312 to M. Field in payment of his wages.
May 13 Issued cheque No. 79 in the amount of $285 to R. French in payment of his wages.
May 14 Issued sales invoice No. 166 for $250 to M. Birch.
May 14 Issued sales invoice No. 167 for $170 to Y. Ash.
May 17 Received an invoice from Continental Railway in the amount of $87.50 for freight charges on incoming merchandise.
May 18 Received an invoice from Budget Oil in the amount of $64.72. This invoice was for gasoline and oil used in the delivery truck.
May 19 Issued cheque No. 80 for $300 to G. Ripley, the proprietor, for his personal use.
May 20 Issued cheque No. 81 for $300 to Ideal Supply in payment of merchandise which was purchased for cash.
May 21 Received an invoice from Circle Supplies in the amount of $46; this invoice was in respect to the purchase of supplies on account.
May 21 Received an invoice from Deluxe Stationers in the amount of $420; this invoice was in respect to the purchase of a new office desk at a cost of $350 and some supplies at a cost of $70.
May 24 The owner of the business, G. Ripley, made an agreement with Crescent Bank to borrow $1 000. As a result of this agreement Crescent Bank deposited $1 000 in the business bank account and sent the business a notice to this effect.
May 26 Issued cheque No. 82 in the amount of $200 to Empire Wholesale on account.
May 26 Received an invoice from Prairie Manufacturing in respect to the purchase of merchandise on account; $160.
May 26 Received a cheque for $100 from R. Stoddard on account.
May 27 Issued cheque No. 83 for $312 to M. Field in payment of his wages.
May 27 Issued cheque No. 84 for $285 to R. French in payment of his wages.
May 31 Issued sales invoice No. 168 for $96 to Purity Company.

SYNOPTIC JOURNAL

DATE		PARTICULARS	CHQ. NO.	BANK DR.	BANK CR.	ACCOUNTS REC'L DR.	ACCOUNTS REC'L CR.	ACCOU DR.
19– May	4	Cash Sale		56 —				
	5	Paul Boxer				112 —		
	6	Empire Wholesale						
	7	Deluxe Stationers	74		37 20			
	7	Arrow Realty	75		400 —			
	10	A. Baldwin	76		73 50			73 5
	10	G. English & Co.	77		46 20			46 2
	11	R. Smith		96 —			96 —	
	11	F. Jones		375 —			375 —	
	13	M. Field	78		312 —			
	13	R. French	79		285 —			
	14	M. Birch				250 —		
	14	Y. Ash				170 —		
	17	Continental Railway						
	18	Budget Oil						
	19	G. Ripley	80		300 —			
	20	Ideal Supply	81		300 —			
	21	Circle Supplies						
	21	Deluxe Stationers						
	24	Crescent Bank		1 000 —				
	26	Empire Wholesale	82		200 —			200 -
	26	Prairie Mfg.						
	26	R. Stoddard		100 —			100 —	
	27	M. Field	83		312 —			
	27	R. French	84		285 —			
	31	Purity Company				96 —		
				1 627 —	2 550 90	628 —	571 —	319 7
				1 627 —	2 550 90	628 —	571 —	319 7

Figure 14.6 Synoptic journal with entries for transactions for the month.

MONTH OF *May* 19— Page *42*

...S PAY'L CR.	NO.	SALES CR.	PURCH'S DR.	*Supplies Dr*	OTHER ACCOUNTS ACCOUNT	PR.	DR.	CR.
	57	56 –						
	165	112 –						
316 –			316 –					
				37 20				
					Rent Expense		400 –	
					Wages Expense		312 –	
					Wages Expense		285 –	
	166	250 –						
	167	170 –						
87 50					Freight-in		87 50	
64 72					Delivery Exp.		64 72	
					Ripley Drugs		300 –	
			300 –					
46 –				46 –				
420 –				70 –	Office Equip.		350 –	
					Bank Loan			1 000 –
160 –			160 –					
					Wages Exp.		312 –	
					Wages Exp.		285 –	
	168	96 –						
094 22		684 –	726 –	153 20			2 396 22	1 000 –

Balancing the Columnar Journal

At the bottom of every page, and at the end of every month, a procedure called cross balancing is performed on the synoptic journal, or on any columnar journal. This procedure is often referred to as balancing the journal.

Cross balancing is checking the total of all the debits in the journal against the total of all the credits to make sure that these two grand totals agree. The steps in cross balancing a journal are described below. As you study these steps, refer to the illustration of the synoptic journal in Figure 14.6.

1. Immediately beneath the last entry on the page, and in ink, draw a single ruled line across all money columns of the journal.
2. Separately, total (foot) each money column and write in the total in small pencil figures just beneath the single ruled line. You will recall that these small pencil figures are known as 'pencil footings' or 'pin totals.'
3. Using an adding machine or a pencil and paper, separately add all of the pin totals of the debit columns and all of the pin totals of the credit columns. Include

A SYNOPTIC PAGE JUST COMPLETED

THE NEW PAGE BEING STARTED

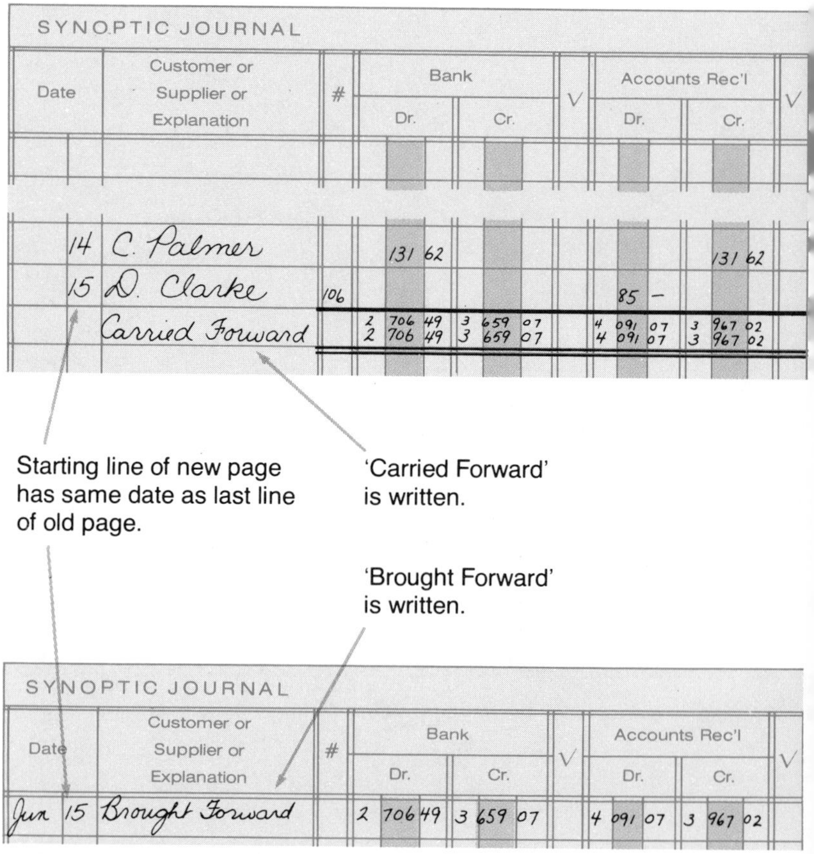

Figure 14.7 Forwarding in the synoptic journal.

all columns of the journal. These two additions should produce the same grand total. If the two sums are the same, the journal is 'in balance'. If the two sums are not the same, the journal is 'out of balance' or 'not in balance'. A journal out of balance indicates that one or more errors have been made in its preparation. You may not proceed to the posting of the journal until the errors have been located and corrected.

4. If step 3 indicates that the journal is in balance, write in the column totals in ink immediately beneath the pin totals.
5. In ink, draw a double ruled line beneath the column totals.

Forwarding the Columnar Journal

Whenever a new journal page is started, and it is not the beginning of a month, it is customary to start the new page with the totals from the previous page. The totals at the end of one page are 'forwarded' to the beginning of the next. This procedure is shown in Figure 14.7.

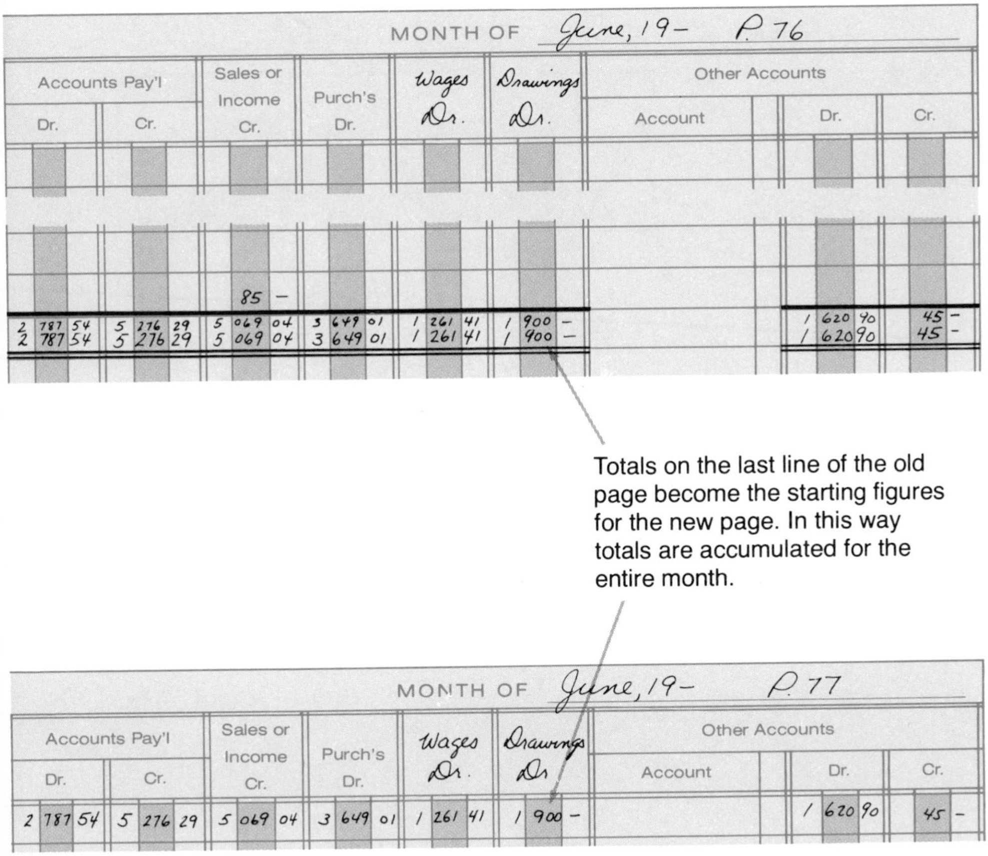
MONTH OF June, 19– P. 76
Accounts Pay'l
Dr.
Cr.
Sales or Income Cr.
Purch's Dr.
Wages Dr.
Drawings Dr.
Other Accounts
Account
Dr.
Cr.
85 –
2 787 54
5 276 29
5 069 04
3 649 01
1 261 41
1 900 –
1 620 90
45 –
Totals on the last line of the old page become the starting figures for the new page. In this way totals are accumulated for the entire month.
MONTH OF June, 19– P. 77
Accounts Pay'l
Dr.
Cr.
Sales or Income Cr.
Purch's Dr.
Wages Dr.
Drawings Dr.
Other Accounts
Account
Dr.
Cr.
2 787 54
5 276 29
5 069 04
3 649 01
1 261 41
1 900 –
1 620 90
45 –

SYNOPTIC JOURNAL MONTH OF June, 19 – Page 30

DATE		PARTICULARS	BANK DR.	BANK CR.	ACCS REC'L DR.	ACCS REC'L CR.	ACCS PAY'L DR.	ACCS PAY'L CR.	SALES CR.	PCH'S DR.		OTHER ACCOUNTS: ACCOUNT	PR.	DR.	CR.
Jun.	3	G. Peltier			10				10						
	7	R. Buie	65						65						
	8	S. Katz		50								Rent Exp.		50	
	10	T. Jones		7			7								
	12	W. Bye						15		15					
	14	S. Black	9			9									
	16	T. Thompson			12				12						
	18	V. Jackson		14			14								
	20	A. Adams						30		30					
	21	B. Yon	4			4									
	23	M. Carter	6						6						
	25	D. Davidson			11				11						
	30	S. Sloan		8								Car Exp.		8	
			84	79	33	13	21	45	104	45				58	

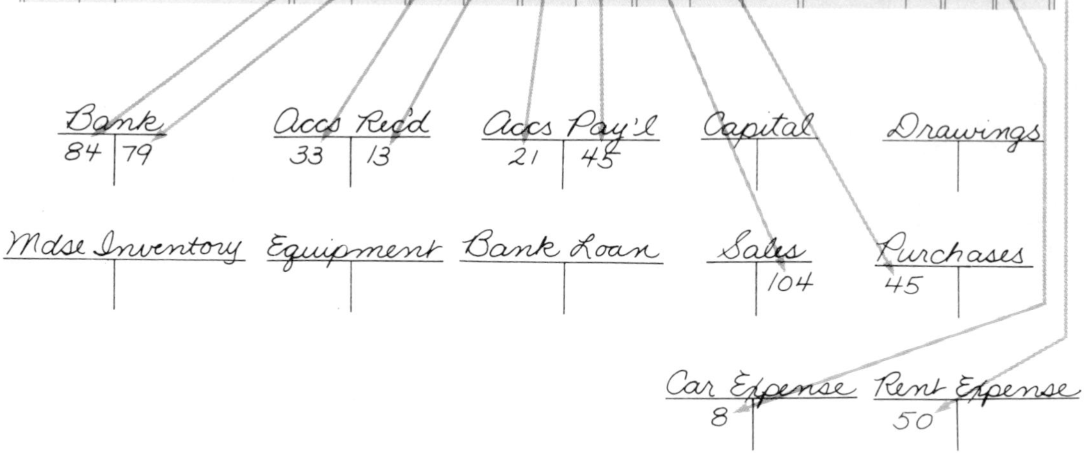

Figure 14.8 Posting the synoptic journal.

Posting the Synoptic Journal

Before we discuss how to post the synoptic journal, let us recall some facts about 'posting' in general. First, posting to the general ledger is done once a month. Therefore the synoptic journal, which is posted to the general ledger, is posted only once a month. Second, posting to the subsidiary ledgers is done daily, independently, and directly from copies of source documents.

Posting the synoptic journal requires a different procedure because it is a multi-columned journal. The basic procedure is illustrated in Figure 14.8 by means of a simplified example. Study this example and in particular observe that:

1. For each of the *Special Columns*, the column totals are posted rather than the individual amounts within the columns. By posting only the totals, a great deal of time is saved.
2. The *Other Accounts section* lists items that are generally unrelated. Therefore, the individual amounts contained within the columns are posted separately. Posting the Other Accounts section is very similar to posting from a two-column general journal.

Formal Technique for Posting the Synoptic Journal

Figure 14.9 shows an example of formal posting from the synoptic journal. Observe the following details:

1. The entries in the accounts are dated with the last day of the month.
2. *Sn* and the journal page number are used when cross referencing in the accounts.
3. When cross referencing in the journal, the following rules apply:
   a. The account number is entered in brackets immediately beneath the column total being posted.
   b. For items in the Other Accounts section, the account number is entered in the Posting Reference column beside the amount being posted.
4. The account balances are not calculated until all of the postings are completed. Then they are obtained with the help of an adding machine.

After being posted entirely, the synoptic journal, with posting reference numbers entered, appears as shown in Figure 14.10.

SYNOPTIC JOURNAL

DATE		PARTICULARS	CHQ. NO.	BANK DR.	BANK CR.	ACCOUNTS REC'L DR.	ACCOUNTS REC'L CR.
19– May	4	Cash Sale		56 —			
	5	Paul Boxer				112 —	
	6	Empire Wholesale					
	7	Deluxe Stationers	74		37 20		
	7	Arrow Realty	75		400 —		
	31	Purity Company				96 —	
				1 627 —	2 550 90	628 —	571 —
				1 627 —	2 550 90	628 —	571 —
				(1)	(1)		

Account Bank No. 1

Date		Particulars	P.R.	Debit	Credit	DR. CR.	Balance
19– Mar.	31	Balance brought forward	—			DR	1 351 4
Apr.	30		Sn 41	1 630 20			
	30		Sn 41		1 264 19	DR	1 717 4
May	31		Sn 42	1 627 —			
	31		Sn 42		2 550 90		

Figure 14.9 Formal posting from the synoptic journal. The illustration shows only three postings involving two ledger accounts.

MONTH OF May 19 — Page 42

ACCOUNTS PAY'L DR.	ACCOUNTS PAY'L CR.	NO.	SALES CR.	PURCH'S DR.	Supplies Dr	OTHER ACCOUNTS: ACCOUNT	PR.	DR.	CR.
		57	56 —						
		165	112 —						
	316 —			316 —					
					37 20				
						Rent Expense	58	400 —	
		168	96 —						
319 70	1 094 22		684 —	726 —	153 20			2 396 22	1 000 —
319 70	1 094 22		684 —	726 —	153 20			2 396 22	1 000 —

Account Rent Expense No. 58

Date		Particulars	P.R.	Debit	Credit	DR. CR.	Balance
19— Apr.	30	Balance brought forward	—			DR	800 —
May	31		Jn42	400 —			

SYNOPTIC JOURNAL

DATE		PARTICULARS	CHQ. NO.	BANK DR.	BANK CR.	ACCOUNTS REC'L DR.	ACCOUNTS REC'L CR.
19– May	4	Cash Sale		56 –			
	5	Paul Boyer				112 –	
	6	Empire Wholesale					
	7	Deluxe Stationers	74		37 20		
	7	Arrow Realty	75		400 –		
	10	A. Baldwin	76		73 50		
	10	G. English & Co.	77		46 20		
	11	R. Smith		96 –			96 –
	11	F. Jones		375 –			375 –
	13	M. Field	78		312 –		
	13	R. French	79		285 –		
	14	M. Birch				250 –	
	14	Y. Ash				170 –	
	17	Continental Railway					
	18	Budget Oil					
	19	G. Ripley	80		300 –		
	20	Ideal Supply	81		300 –		
	21	Circle Supplies					
	21	Deluxe Stationers					
	24	Crescent Bank		1 000 –			
	26	Empire Wholesale	82		200 –		
	26	Prairie Mfg.					
	26	R. Stoddard		100 –			100 –
	27	M. Field	83		312 –		
	27	R. French	84		285 –		
	31	Purity Company				96 –	
				1 627 –	2 550 90	628 –	571 –
				1 627 –	2 550 90	628 –	571 –
				(1)	(1)	(2)	(2)

Figure 14.10 Synoptic journal showing posting references.

MONTH OF *May* 19— Page *42*

ACCOUNTS PAY'L DR.	ACCOUNTS PAY'L CR.	NO.	SALES CR.	PURCH'S DR.	*Supplies Dr*	OTHER ACCOUNTS ACCOUNT	PR.	DR.	CR.
		57	56 —						
		165	112 —						
	316 —			316 —					
					37 20				
						Rent Expense	56	400 —	
73 50									
46 20									
						Wages Expense	58	312 —	
						Wages Expense	58	285 —	
		166	250 —						
		167	170 —						
	87 50					Freight-in	55	87 50	
	64 72					Delivery Exp.	53	64 72	
						Ripley Drugs	32	300 —	
				300 —					
	46 —				46 —				
	420 —				70 —	Office Equip	9	350 —	
						Bank Loan	22		1 000 —
200 —									
	160 —			160 —					
						Wages Exp.	58	312 —	
						Wages Exp.	58	285 —	
		168	96 —						
319 70	1 094 22		684 —	726 —	153 20				
319 70	1 094 22		684 —	726 —	153 20			2 396 22	1 000 —
(21)	(21)		(41)	(51)	(4)				

SYNOPTIC JOURNAL

DATE		PARTICULARS	CHQ. NO.	BANK DR.	BANK CR.	ACCOUNTS REC'L DR.	ACCOUNTS REC'L CR.	ACCOUNTS PAY'L DR.	ACCOUNTS PAY'L CR.
Aug	3	J. R. Borgo	42		150 –	(Painting buildings)			
	4	M. Hicks	43		57 –				
			(Refund of amount overcharged)						
	5	Midwest Oil	44		280 –				
			(Heating oil; part for owner's cottage)						

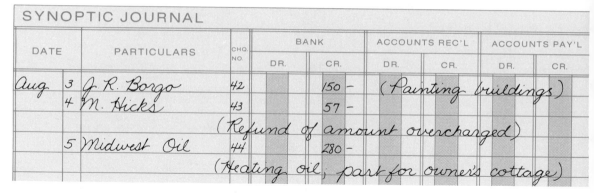

Figure 14.11 Recording non-routine transactions in the synoptic journal.

Variations in Journalizing in the Synoptic Journal

1. From time to time you may want to record a transaction of a non-routine nature in the synoptic journal. This is permitted as long as the accounting entry is explained (usually in parentheses) whenever it is not self-explanatory. When writing explanations, you are allowed to write through the money columns. (See all three transactions illustrated in Figure 14.11.)
2. Debit entries may be written in Credit columns or credit entries in Debit columns, but they must be circled or written in red. This special treatment of an entry indicates that its effect in the column is the opposite to that specified in the column heading. When the column is totaled, the circled item must be subtracted in order that the column total, when posted, will have the proper effect on the account. (See the second transaction illustrated in Figure 14.11.) This is an important technique.
3. Although most accounting entries require only one line in the synoptic journal, there are times when two or more lines may be required. This situation arises when at least two of the accounts affected by a transaction need to be recorded in the Other Accounts section of the journal, or when an explanation is written on a separate line. (See the second and third transactions illustrated in Figure 14.11.)

MONTH OF *August* 19 — Page *96*

SALES CR.	PURCH'S DR.		OTHER ACCOUNTS: ACCOUNT	PR.	DR.	CR.
			Bldg. Mtce.		*150 -*	
(57 -)						
			Heat Exp.		*200 -*	
			J. Roe Drugs		*80 -*	

14.4 Two-Journal System

Frequently, the synoptic journal and the two-column general journal are both used in a business. The synoptic journal is used to record the type of transaction for which it is most suitable, namely, routine transactions. Its preparation usually presents no difficulty for a junior employee. On the other hand, the two-column general journal is used by a senior accounting person to record entries of a non-routine and usually more complex nature. The basic structure of a two-journal system is illustrated in Figure 14.12 by means of a flowchart.

In a two-journal system, each journal is prepared apart from the other. At the end of every month, each of the journals is posted separately to the general ledger. If the general ledger is found to be out of balance after the postings have been completed, it is necessary to examine both journals when looking for errors.

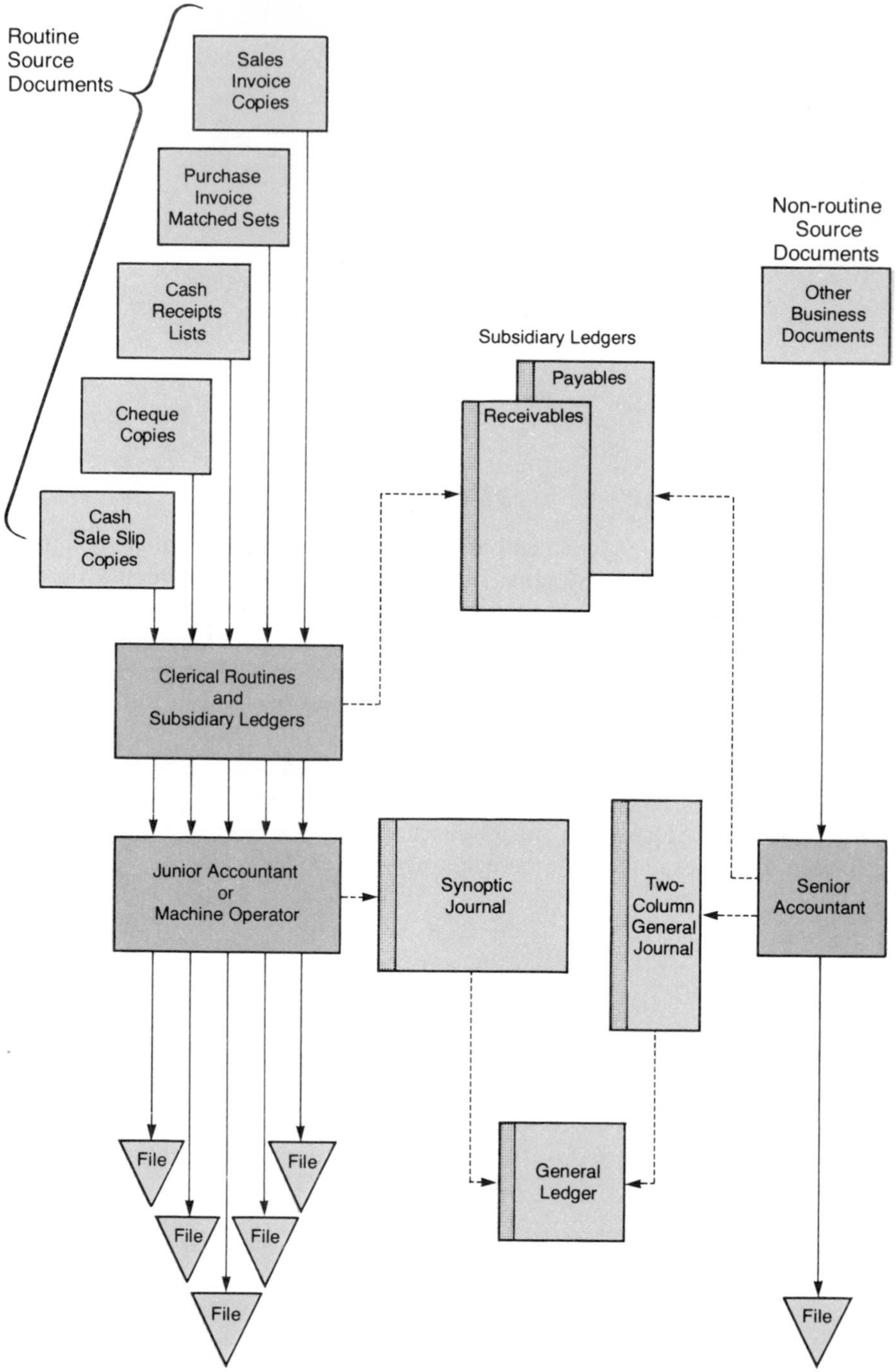

Figure 14.12 A flowchart of a basic two-journal system.

General Journal Vouchers

A popular alternative to the general journal in the form of a book is a file of **general journal vouchers**. An example of a completed general journal voucher is shown in Figure 14.13.

Unused journal vouchers are kept in the form of a pad at the desk of the person who is responsible for their preparation. As general journal entries come up, they are written on the vouchers. Each entry is written on a new voucher. The vouchers are numbered in order as they are written and are filed in numerical order on a type of ring binder.

At the end of each month, the general journal vouchers for the month are posted to the general ledger. A minor difference in procedure is the use of the journal voucher number in cross referencing the journal entry in the account.

GENERAL JOURNAL VOUCHER

DATE: June 14 19— VOUCHER NO. 146

Account	✓	Subsidiary Ledger	PR	General Ledger Debit	General Ledger Credit
Sales			41	230 95	
Accounts Receivable			2		230 95
Farrow Brothers	✓	84 75			
N. Robertson	✓	90 00			
S. Laing	✓	56 20			
		230 95			

EXPLANATION:

To cancel three Sales Invoices issued in error: #615; #616; #617.

Figure 14.13 A completed general journal voucher.

Accounting Terms

petty cash fund
petty cash voucher
imprest method
replenishing petty cash
credit invoice
synoptic journal
cross balancing
general journal voucher

Review Questions

1. What is the purpose of a petty cash fund?
2. Describe briefly how the petty cash imprest system works.
3. Under what circumstances is a petty cash voucher made out?
4. When is a petty cash fund replenished?
5. What eventually happens to the petty cash vouchers?
6. How does a credit invoice come by its name?
7. Who issues a credit invoice?
8. What circumstances give rise to credit invoices?
9. What special feature does the synoptic journal have as compared to the two-column general journal?
10. For what type of entry is the synoptic journal best suited?
11. Give two advantages of the synoptic journal.
12. How are the special columns allocated?
13. What is the limiting factor in regard to the number of special columns?
14. Describe the cross balancing procedure.
15. How often is the synoptic journal cross balanced?
16. Describe the forwarding procedure in the synoptic journal.
17. Describe the essential difference between posting the synoptic journal and posting the two-column general journal.
18. In the synoptic journal, what is the purpose of the two general columns?
19. Why can't you usually post the totals of the two general columns of a synoptic journal?
20. What date is used when posting from the synoptic journal?
21. Explain the cross referencing procedure as it relates to a synoptic journal.
22. Explain the meaning behind the circling of an amount in one of the special columns.
23. Briefly describe the two-journal system.
24. Describe the difference between a two-column general journal and a journal voucher file.

Exercises

Petty Cash

1. On January 15th, Markel Brothers issues a cheque in the amount of $200 to establish a petty cash fund. Give the accounting entry in general journal form to establish the petty cash fund.

2. On February 20th, Seneca Sales Company issues a cheque to increase the petty cash fund from $100 to $150. Give the accounting entry in general journal form to increase the petty cash fund.

3. On March 16, 19--, after a bill of $12.16 is paid, the contents of a petty cash fund with a lower limit of $5 are as follows:

Cash	$1.68	Building Expense	10.50
Bills and Vouchers		Miscellaneous Expense	2.05
Miscellaneous Expense	6.04	Postage	9.00
Miscellaneous Expense	1.25	Miscellaneous Expense	4.15
Sales Promotion	3.17	Building Expense	12.16

   1. Prepare the summary of charges necessary to replenish the fund.
   2. In general journal form, write out the accounting entry necessary to replenish the fund.

4. On June 10, 19--, a $25 petty cash fund with a lower limit of $2 is in the following condition:

Cash	$ .54	Office Expense	2.14
Bills and Vouchers		P. Martin, Drawings	10.00
Office Expense	5.02	Office Expense	1.20
Office Supplies	.75	Office Expense	2.00
Advertising	2.00	Office Supplies	1.35

   1. Prepare the summary of charges necessary to replenish the fund.
   2. In general journal form, write out the required accounting entry to replenish the fund.

5. You are the keeper of the petty cash fund for Graphic Art Supplies. Since the fund is very low, you are in the process of preparing the petty cash summary to be used to obtain the replenishing cheque.

   Below left is a listing of the vouchers in the petty cash box, giving a general description of the nature of the payment for each. Below right is the chart of accounts for Graphic Art Supplies.

Prepare the petty cash summary for the purpose of obtaining the replenishing cheque.

PETTY CASH VOUCHERS

1. Owner's parking receipt	$ 9.00
2. Paint for building	13.50
3. New broom for janitor	12.75
4. Typewriter ribbons	8.35
5. Supper money for employee	7.50
6. Postage stamps	15.00
7. New window pane	20.00
8. Telegram charge	10.50
9. Donation to boy scouts	10.00
10. Payment to student for cleaning up the grounds	10.50
11. Mileage to employee for using personal car for business	17.50
12. Coffee and doughnuts brought in for a business meeting	24.35
13. Dog licence for watch dog	10.00
14. Parking receipt of owner	7.00
15. Supper money for employee	7.50
16. Postage for parcel delivery	15.00

CHART OF ACCOUNTS

1	Bank
2	Accounts Receivable
3	Merchandise Inventory
4	Supplies
5	Equipment
6	Automobile
20	Bank loan
21	Accounts Payable
30	Judi Mavar, Capital
31	Judi Mavar, Drawings
40	Sales
50	Purchases
51	Freight-in
52	Advertising
53	Bank Charges
54	Building Maintenance
55	Car Expense
56	Delivery Expense
57	Donations Expense
58	Light and Heat Expense
59	Miscellaneous Expense
60	Telephone Expense
61	Wages Expense

6. Indicate whether each of the following statements is true or false. This exercise appears in the workbook.

1. The Petty Cash account in the general ledger must never change.
2. A petty cash voucher must be prepared for every payment out of the fund.
3. The petty cash fund is used for the purpose of cutting down on the number of cheques issued.
4. The accounting entry to replenish the petty cash fund is made by the keeper of the fund.
5. The petty cash box is locked and put away in a safe place outside business hours.
6. The keeper of the petty cash fund must never borrow from it.
7. The petty cash summary is organized by general ledger accounts.
8. A payment out of petty cash can only be charged to an expense account or an asset account.
9. The keeper of the fund is expected to make up any shortage in the petty cash fund.

10. To check the petty cash fund, the auditor would total all of the cash and all of the vouchers in the box and check this total against the Petty Cash account balance.

Credit Invoices

7. Answer the following questions related to the credit invoice below.

1. **Who issued the credit invoice?**
2. **Who received the credit invoice?**
3. **Who is the seller of the goods described?**
4. **Why was this credit invoice issued?**
5. **What will Northern Electric Supply do to its account for Magnus Hardware?**

NORTHERN ELECTRIC SUPPLY

CREDIT INVOICE
NO. 3941

4020 Henderson Highway, Winnipeg, Manitoba, R2E 0C9

SOLD TO Magnus Hardware
4 Main Street
Winnipeg, Manitoba
R3C 1A1

DATE Jan. 15, 19--

TERMS 60 days

QUANTITY	PART NO.	DESCRIPTION	PRICE	AMOUNT
4 doz	52-1220	Galvanized switchboxes	$7.20	$28.80
6	52-8480	Stab-Lox circuit breakers	3.99	23.94
		Total		$52.74

CREDIT

CUSTOMER'S COPY

8. Examine the two source documents below and answer the questions that follow.

EQUIPMENT RENTAL INVOICE

BOX 100, HALIFAX, N.S., B3L 2Z4 PHONE 233 6767

ACADIA
EQUIPMENT AND SUPPLY

CONTRACT NO.	DATE SHIPPED	SHIPPED VIA	INVOICE NUMBER
402	Sept. 10	Acadia	D4023
BILLING NO.	**DATE RETURNED**	**RETURNED VIA**	**INVOICE DATE**
36	Sept. 13	Acadia	Sept.14, 19--

RENTED TO
Cornwallis Construction
20 Cornwallis Street
Halifax, Nova Scotia
B3K 1A1

TERMS
Net 30 days

SHIPPED TO
Same

OVERDUE ACCOUNTS
2% per month

STOCK NO.	DESCRIPTION	NO. DAYS, WEEKS, MOS.	RATE	AMOUNT
146	Forklift truck	3 days	$100.00	$300.00

1. a. Which company is the sender of the document?

b. Which company is the receiver of the document?

c. From the point of view of Acadia Equipment Supply, what source document is it?

d. From the point of view of Cornwallis Construction, what source document is it?

e. If the invoice is to be charged to Equipment Rental Expense, what accounting entries should be made in the books of Acadia Equipment and Supply and in the books of Cornwallis Construction?

CREDIT INVOICE

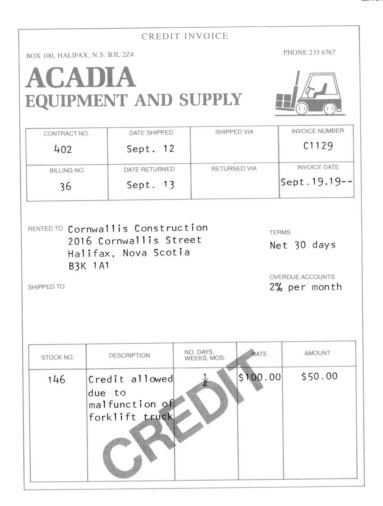

BOX 100, HALIFAX, N.S. B3L 2Z4

PHONE 233 6767

ACADIA
EQUIPMENT AND SUPPLY

CONTRACT NO.	DATE SHIPPED	SHIPPED VIA	INVOICE NUMBER
402	Sept. 12		C1129
BILLING NO.	**DATE RETURNED**	**RETURNED VIA**	**INVOICE DATE**
36	Sept. 13		Sept.19,19--

RENTED TO Cornwallis Construction
2016 Cornwallis Street
Halifax, Nova Scotia
B3K 1A1

TERMS
Net 30 days

OVERDUE ACCOUNTS
2% per month

SHIPPED TO

STOCK NO.	DESCRIPTION	NO. DAYS, WEEKS, MOS.	RATE	AMOUNT
146	Credit allowed due to malfunction of forklift truck	$\frac{1}{2}$	$100.00	$50.00

CREDIT

2. a. Which company is the sender of the document?
   b. Which company is the receiver of the document?
   c. Which company is the vendor?
   d. Which company is the purchaser?
   e. Which company is thought of as the supplier?
   f. There are three ways to tell that the above document is a credit invoice. What are they?
   g. In the Description column, the words 'Credit allowed' are used. What is meant by this?
   h. On what day will payment be due?
   i. Give the accounting entries to be made in the books of Acadia Equipment and Supply and Cornwallis Construction.

Synoptic Journal — Cross Balancing

9. At the end of July 19--, the totals in a synoptic journal are as follows:

SYNOPTIC JOURNAL

Date		Customer or Supplier or Explanation	#	Bank		√	Accounts Rec'l		√	Accounts
				Dr.	Cr.		Dr.	Cr.		Dr.
				2 694 62	3 016 21		3 096 17	2 546 21		1 596 12

Cross balance the synoptic journal.

10. At the end of June 19--, the pin totals in a synoptic journal are as follows:

SYNOPTIC JOURNAL

Date		Customer or Supplier or Explanation	#	Bank		√	Accounts Rec'l		√	Accounts
				Dr.	Cr.		Dr.	Cr.		Dr.
				6 092 10	5 961 02		10 060 22	6 142 10		4 092 17

Cross balance the synoptic journal.

Synoptic Journal — Simple Journalizing

11. 1. Record the following transactions in a synoptic journal.

Transactions

March

4 Issued cheque No. 56 for $300 to Martin and Martin on account.
9 Issued sales invoice No. 72 to O. P. Ploeg, $150.
10 Received invoice No. 692 from Andrews Brothers for a shipment of merchandise, $450.
11 Received $500 on account from P. S. Rak.
11 Issued cheque No. 57 for $65 to Municipal Telephone for the cash payment of the monthly telephone bill.

2. Rule and balance the synoptic journal.

MONTH OF *July, 19—*

Pay'l Cr.	Sales or Income Cr.	Purch's Dr.	*Supplies Dr.*	*Wages Dr.*	Other Accounts: Account	PR	Dr.	Cr.
1 842 94	3 309 42	1 706 40	156 97	746 02			729 74	11 26

MONTH OF *June, 19*

Pay'l Cr.	Sales or Income Cr.	Purch's Dr.	*Supplies Dr.*	*Wages Dr.*	Other Accounts: Account	PR	Dr.	Cr.
9 402 19	10 104 11	7 574 80	356 51	3 023 65			409 97	

---

12. 1. In the synoptic journal, page 19, of Donway Distributing Co., record the transactions listed below for August 19--. Use the spare column for 'Wages'. The chart of accounts for the business is as follows:

No. 1	Bank	No. 40	Sales
2	Accounts Receivable	50	Purchases
3	Merchandise Inventory	51	Freight-in
4	Supplies	52	Advertising
5	Building	53	Building Maintenance
6	Furniture and Equipment	54	Car Expense
20	Accounts Payable	55	Heat and Electricity
21	Bank Loan	56	Miscellaneous Expense
22	Mortgage Payable	57	Postage
30	A. Orlando, Capital	58	Telephone Expense
31	A. Orlando, Drawings	59	Wages

2. After journalizing the following transactions, cross balance and rule the journal.

Transactions

August

2 *Cheque Copy*
— No. 702, to D. Macdonald, $310, cash payment for painting the building occupied by the business.

3 *Sales Invoice*
— No. 210, to N. Rae, $84, for sale of goods.
Cash Receipt
— From B. Page, $100, on account.

5 *Cheque Copy*
— No. 703, to E. Pickard, $290, for wages.
Cash Sales Slip
— No. 91, to M. Franci, for cash sale of merchandise, $85.

8 *Cheque Copy*
— No. 704, to Receiver General for Canada, $80, for postage stamps. (**Note**: Cheques to the Government of Canada are made out to the Receiver General for Canada.)
Sales Invoice
— No. 211, to Atlas Stores, $502, for sale of goods.

9 *Purchase Invoice*
— From Diamond Wholesalers, $325, for purchase of merchandise.

10 *Purchase Invoice*
— From Continental Railway, $165, for freight charges on incoming merchandise.

11 *Cash Sales Slip*
— No. 92, to J. Vincent, for cash sale of merchandise, $56.50.

12 *Cheque Copies*
— No. 705, to Vance Brothers, $300, on account.
— No. 706, to E. Pickard, $290, for wages.

15 *Cheque Copies*
— No. 707, to Century 21, $40, for newspaper advertising.
— No. 708, to A. Orlando, $300, for proprietor's personal use.

18 *Cash Sales Slip*
— No. 93, to A. Anderson, for cash sale of merchandise, $27.40.

19 *Cheque Copies*
— No. 709, to Merry Manufacturing, $500, on account.
— No. 710, to E. Pickard, $290, for wages.
Cash Receipt
— From G. Price, $140.25, on account.

22 *Cheque Copy*
— No. 711, to Price-Vincent Ltd., $350, for mortgage instalment.
Sales Invoice
— No. 212, to T. Schmidt, $170, for sale of goods.

23 *Purchase Invoice*
— From Deluxe Oil Company, $75, for gasoline used in the proprietor's automobile — $50 for business purposes, $25 for personal use.

24 *Bank Debit Slip*
— From General Bank, $22, for bank service charges.

25 *Cheque Copy*
— No. 712, to A. Orlando, $500, for proprietor's personal use.

26 *Cash Sales Slip*
— No. 94, to K. Beka, for sale of merchandise, $65.
Cheque Copy
— No. 713, to E. Pickard, $290, for wages.

29 *Purchase Invoice*
— From Federated Supply, $1 240, for the purchase of merchandise.

30 *Cheque Copy*
— No. 714, to Public Utilities Commission, $85, electricity charges for light and heat.

31 *Sales Invoice*
— No. 213, to R. Snell, $190, for sale of goods.
Cash Receipt
— From U. Stewart, $106, on account.

---

13. From Exercise 12 above, summarize the postings that would be made to the general ledger. List the information in three columns: Account, Debit Amount, Credit Amount. Show that the postings are 'balanced' by totaling the two money columns.

---

14. On page 75 of the synoptic journal of Low Trading Company, journalize the transactions below. The spare column in the synoptic journal is used for Drawings. The following accounts are required for this exercise:

Bank	Purchases
Accounts Receivable	Freight-in
Merchandise Inventory	Advertising
Supplies	Bank Charges
Equipment	Delivery Expense
Bank Loan	General Expense
Accounts Payable	Rent Expense
Debra Low, Capital	Telephone Expense
Debra Low, Drawings	Utilities Expense
Sales	Wages Expense

Transactions

Date	Source Document	No.	Name	Explanation	Amount
May 2	Sales Invoice	165	P. Boshkoff	Sale of goods	$ 200
4	Purchase Invoice	375	Hoito Company	Merchandise for sale	340
4	Cash Receipt		H. Doerr	On account	150
6	Cheque Copy	315	Bell Telephone	Cash payment of telephone bill	35
6	Cheque Copy	316	Northland Supply	Cash payment for merchandise	130
6	Bank Credit Memo		Reliable Bank	Increase in loan	1 000
9	Cheque Copy	317	D. Low	Owner's personal use	175
9	Credit Note received	146	Hoito Company	Credit for goods returned	120
12	Sales Invoice	166	P. Olsen	Sale of goods	135
13	Purchase Invoice	902	Lucier Bros.	Merchandise for sale	90
16	Cheque Copy	318	Loumarr Corp.	On account	160
18	Cash Receipt		J. Lockwood	On account	215
23	Cheque Copy	319	B. Smid	Cash payment of wages	240
26	Cheque Copy	320	D. Low	Owner's personal use	175
27	Credit Note issued	14	P. Tremblay	Defective merchandise returned	60
30	Sales Invoice	167	D. Rybak	Sale of goods	180
31	Purchase Invoice	1742	General Machinery	New equipment	950
31	Purchase Invoice	37465	National Railway	Transportation on incoming goods	165

Posting the Synoptic Journal

15. Workbook Exercise: Posting synoptic journal totals to a simple ledger.

16. Workbook Exercise: Posting the synoptic journal to a simple ledger.

Forwarding in the Synoptic Journal

17. Workbook Exercise: Forwarding in the synoptic journal.

General Journal Vouchers

18. Workbook Exercise: Journalizing using a general journal voucher.

Journalizing, Posting, Balancing (3 Ledgers)

19. F. Dunn is the sole proprieter of Crest Hardware in Iona, N. S. He operates the store with the assistance of his wife and some occasional part-time help. Mrs. Dunn works in the store and is also responsible for all direct aspects of accounting. The financial statements are prepared annually from her records by a professional accountant.

The books of account are very simple and consist of a general ledger, an accounts receivable ledger, an accounts payable ledger, and a synoptic journal. The last page used in the synoptic journal is page 72 and it shows that the spare column is used for General Expense.

Most of the sales of the business are cash sales or C.O.D. sales. The cash receipts are deposited in the bank on a daily basis. All payments are made by cheque.

The number of accounts in both subsidiary ledgers is very small. Mr. Dunn grants credit to only a few customers and buys his stock from only a few suppliers. Because of the small number of debtors and creditors the subsidiary ledger routine is very simple. All transactions are recorded in the synoptic journal and the postings to the subsidiary ledgers are made directly from the source documents.

The three ledgers of Crest Hardware are set up in the workbook from the following trial balances.

CREST HARDWARE
GENERAL LEDGER TRIAL BALANCE
JANUARY 31, 19--

1 Petty Cash	$ 100.00	
2 Bank	1 400.00	
3 Accounts Receivable	365.25	
4 Merchandise Inventory	8 090.20	
5 Supplies	395.00	
6 Store Equipment	4 906.21	
7 Delivery Equipment	3 500.00	
21 Accounts Payable		$ 1 404.00
22 Federal Finance Co.		5 261.00
31 F. Dunn, Capital		11 739.12
32 F. Dunn, Drawings	860.00	
41 Sales		5 507.40
51 Delivery Expense	417.06	
52 Freight-in	269.50	
53 General Expense	164.10	
54 Purchases	3 064.20	
55 Rent Expense	300.00	
56 Wages Expense	80.00	
	$23 911.52	$23 911.52

CREST HARDWARE
ACCOUNTS RECEIVABLE TRIAL BALANCE
JANUARY 31, 19--

R. Dunlop (Invoice 1407)	$112.76
G. Langford (Invoice 1431)	157.06
R. Potts (Invoice 1436)	95.43
	$365.25

CREST HARDWARE
ACCOUNTS PAYABLE TRIAL BALANCE
JANUARY 31, 19--

City Hardware Supply (Their Invoice No. 17421)	$ 746.21
Special Steel Products (Their Invoice No. 147A)	657.79
	$1 404.00

1. Record the journal entries in the synoptic journal from the transactions listed below. Post to the subsidiary ledgers on a daily basis.

Transactions

February

2 *Cash Sales Slip* No. 206
— $86.01.
Sales Invoice
— No. 1475, to R. Dunlop, $26.40, for sale of goods.
Purchase Invoice
— No. 18021, from City Hardware Supply, $264.25, for purchase of merchandise.

3 *Cash Sales Slip* No. 207
— $102.51
Cash Receipt
— From R. Dunlop, $112.76 on account.

5 *Cash Sales Slip* No. 208
— $56.42

6 *Cash Sales Slip* No. 209
— $109.75.
Cheque Copy
— No. 316, to R. Niosi, $28, wages for part-time help.

7 *Cash Sales Slip* No. 210
— $245.90.
Purchase Invoice
— No. 18340, from City Hardware Supply, $316.25, for purchase of merchandise.

Cheque Copies
— No. 317, Special Steel Products, $500, on account.
— No. 318, City Hardware Supply, $746.21, for No. 17421.
— No. 319, F. Dunn, $250, drawings.

9 *Cash Sales Slip* No. 211
— $240.09

10 *Cash Sales Slip* No. 212
— $347.15.
Sales Invoice
— No. 1476, to G. Langford, $59, sale of merchandise.

12 *Cash Sales Slip* No. 213
— $75.87.
Purchase Invoice
— No. 192A, Special Steel Products, $375.00 for purchase of merchandise.
Cheque Copy
— No. 320, to J. Sacco, $25, wages for part-time help.

13 *Cash Sales Slip* No. 214
— $152.06.
Cheque Copy
— No. 321, to Special Steel Products, $157.79, balance of 147A.

14 *Cash Sales Slip* No. 215
— $310.02.
Sales Invoice
— No. 1477, to R. Potts, $243.67, sale of goods.
Purchase Invoice
— No. 1244, from Clix Oil Company, $63.75, for gasoline and oil used in the delivery truck.
Cheque Copy
— No. 322, F. Dunn, $150, drawings.

16 *Cash Sales Slip* No. 216
— $136.82.
Cash Receipt
— From G. Langford, $157.06, in payment of invoice No. 1431.

17 *Cash Sales Slip* No. 217
— $440.
Purchase Invoice
— No. 344, Joe Jay Transport, $76.45, charges for transportation on incoming merchandise.

19 *Cash Sales Slip* No. 218
— $129.65.
Cheque Copy
— No. 323, to Oak Investments, $300, for the rent for the month.

20 *Cash Sales Slip* No. 219
— $142.92.

21 *Cash Sales Slip* No. 220
— $264.08.
Cheque Copy
— No. 324, to F. Dunn, $250, drawings.

23 *Cash Sales Slip* No. 221
— $89.87.
Sales Invoice
— No. 1478, to R. Dunlop, $64.20, sale of goods.
Cheque Copies
— No. 325, to D. Phin, $29, part-time wages.
— No. 326, to Public Utilities Commission, $25.08, cash payment of electricity and water bills.
— No. 327, to City Telephone Company, $19.05, cash payment of telephone bill.

24 *Cash Sales Slip* No. 222
— $248.00.
Cash Receipt
— From R. Dunlop, $26.40, invoice No. 1475.

26 *Cash Sales Slip* No. 223
— $55.11.
Cheque Copy
— No. 328, to City Hardware Supply, $264.25, for invoice No. 18021.

27 *Cash Sales Slip* No. 224
— $74.23.

28 *Cash Sales Slip* No. 225
— $343.24
Cheque Copies
— No. 329, to F. Dunn, $250, drawings.
— No. 330, to Petty Cash, to replenish the petty cash fund for the following expenditures:

Delivery Expense	42.60
General Expense	51.20

Purchase Invoice
— No. 18472, from City Hardware Supply, $47.49, for store supplies.

2. Balance the synoptic journal.
3. Post the synoptic journal to the general ledger.
4. Balance the general ledger.
5. Balance the subsidiary ledgers.

Using Your Knowledge

20. Two columns of a synoptic journal are totalled incorrectly, but the errors offset each other. The total of the Sales column is $2 000 more than it should be, and the total of the Accounts Receivable credit column is $2 000 less than it should be. What will be the effect on the accounts? On the ledger? On income? On total assets? How might the errors be detected?

Cases

Case 1 *Crook or Saint?*

R. C. Bews was obsessed with building his business. He had started out by using an inheritance to establish a small paving company. Since then, R. C. had fashioned Bews Construction Limited into one of the major road construction companies in Ontario.

R. C. was a man of mixed temperament. He was often pleasant and kind, but he could be ruthless in business. R. C. could fire an employee without a twinge of conscience. His workers quickly learned not to waste a penny.

If performance is judged by profit alone, R. C. was a good businessman. Between 19–1 and 19–9, Bews Construction Limited's net income was never lower than $500 000 (before income tax). In two of those years, it was over $1 000 000.

Bews Construction was located in Toronto, Ontario. Metropolitan Toronto is a major city; its population then was over two million. The surrounding area, consisting of a number of counties, had an equivalent population. Four million people drive a lot of cars, and require a great many well-maintained roads and highways. Road and highway construction and maintenance is a function of government. Therefore, the bulk of Bews Construction Limited's business was with city, county, and provincial government departments.

R. C. always tried to foster good relationships with each government employee that he dealt with, whether a major executive or simply a project inspector on the site. R. C. wined and dined these employees, and also made sure that he was in a position to grant them favours. He always made it a point to have extra tickets for the big hockey or baseball game. If a theatre attraction was sold out, R. C. could always find an extra pair of tickets for a grateful executive. He kept a long Christmas list of civic employees. The least important recipients were given bottles of liquor, while the most important received colour television sets. Rarely was a gift refused. During the hot summer months, a very comfortable lakefront cottage, complete with boat and car, was kept fully stocked and available for important officials.

R. C. claimed to be an honest man who expected nothing in return for his generosity. The gifts merely expressed his appreciation for the past friendship and cooperation of the recipient. The gifts also allowed him to share his prosperity with those people who had innocently contributed to the growth and development of his company.

Questions

1. Was R. C. a good businessman?
2. What is your opinion of his policy of giving favours?
3. Is this policy consistent with his attitude toward his own employees?
4. Do you believe R. C.'s claim that there are no strings attached to his gifts? Discuss.
5. Suggest some advantages that R. C. might gain from his policy.
6. Are there any unfair income tax advantages to the company? To the recipients of the gifts?
7. If you had to express R. C.'s policy in one word, what would it be?

Career

Carol Smalley / Accounts Payable Processor

Carol Smalley enjoyed the accounting courses she took as part of a business and commerce program in high school. After she graduated, she applied for positions in this field. She first worked for State Farm Insurance as a cashier.

Carol's next job was as a payroll clerk for International Business Machines. After several months, she was promoted to the position of accounts payable clerk. During this period, Carol organized the invoices to be paid and made sure that discounts for early payment were taken where possible. She also matched invoices to packing slips and purchase orders so that they could be approved for payment by the general manager. She left this job to get married and have children.

After a four-year absence from the work force, Carol joined Prentice-Hall Canada Inc., a publishing company. She began by working in the customer service department and then moved to the accounts receivable department as a collection clerk.

At present, Carol works as an accounts payable processor. In this capacity, Carol checks all invoices for correction and eventual payment, with approval of the sales manager. She assigns an account code for each supplier so that invoices can be charged to the correct account. Carol also prepares computer data forms, which list the supplier's name, the date, the amount of the cheque, and how payment should be made. She matches cheques to the data forms and sends the cheques to suppliers.

Carol maintains the accounts payable ledger. She also controls the petty cash fund; she replenishes it when needed and submits all vouchers for approval by the vice president in charge of finance.

Although Carol's specific duties were learned on the job, she feels that her high school accounting courses laid a firm foundation for her career. They taught her early the importance of organization, accuracy, and thoroughness, and introduced her to key accounting concepts and procedures. Carol finds her work stimulating and rewarding. In particular, she enjoys her computer-related activities and anticipates working more closely with the computer in future.

15

The Five-Journal System

15-1 Sales Tax
15-2 NSF Cheques
15-3 The Five-Journal System

Objectives

When you have completed Chapter 15, you should:

1. Understand the purpose of sales tax.
2. Know the accounting entries for sales tax both for when sales tax is added to the price of goods on an invoice, and for when sales tax is remitted to the government.
3. Know what is meant by an NSF cheque
4. Know the accounting entry for an NSF cheque.
5. Understand what is meant by the five-journal system of accounting.
6. Know how to journalize using the five-journal system.
7. Be able to balance and post the journals when a five-journal system is used.

Three new accounting concepts are introduced in Chapter 15. You will learn how to account for sales tax and for NSF cheques. As well, you will study the five-journal system in which the journal entries are recorded in five separate journals.

15.1 Sales Tax

Sales tax is a popular method used by governments to raise revenue. Basically it is a percentage tax based on the price of goods. The seller must add on this tax at the time of sale and collect it from the customer. The seller then remits this tax to the government. The rate of sales tax varies from province to province, ranging normally from 4 percent to 8 percent.

Provincial sales tax, commonly called retail sales tax, is charged to the final customer only. A sale from a wholesaler to a retailer is not subject to sales tax.

Accounting for Sales Tax

The purchaser of goods does no accounting for sales tax. Purchased goods are recorded at the final cost shown on the sales slip or sales invoice, including tax.

It is the seller of goods who must do the accounting for sales tax. The seller is required to do the following:

1. Calculate the tax and add it to the selling price of the goods.
2. Accumulate the sales tax charged to customers in a Sales Tax Payable liability account.
3. Collect the tax from the customers.
4. Remit the accumulated tax periodically to the government. In many cases the seller will have to pay the tax to the government before it has been collected from the customers.

Sales Tax on a Cash Sale

The simplest transaction involving sales tax is the cash sale. The seller of the goods calculates the amount of tax or finds it from a tax table, adds the tax to the price of the goods, and collects the total amount from the customer.

With a cash sale, the seller collects the tax at the time of the sale. Because the tax portion must eventually be paid to the government, it represents a liability of the seller.

'Sales Tax Payable' is a liability account set up specially to accumulate sales tax. In an accounting system using a columnar journal, there will be a special column for Sales Tax Payable because it is a frequently occurring item.

Consider the following transaction. Taxable merchandise worth $40 is sold to R. Brown for cash. The rate of sales tax is 5 percent. The following accounting entry records the transaction:

Dr. Bank	42.00	
Cr. Sales		40.00
Cr. Sales Tax Payable		2.00

Sales Tax on a Charge Sale

Goods sold on account also involve sales tax. Consider the sales invoice in Figure 15.1 on which a 5 percent sales tax is charged. Note that with a charge sale the seller does not collect the tax at the time of the sale, but must wait until the customer pays his account, which in this case is supposed to be within 30 days, as stated by the terms of the invoice.

The following accounting entry records this sales invoice:

Dr. Accounts Receivable		
(Marathon Recreation)	337.84	
Cr. Sales		321.75
Cr. Sales Tax Payable		16.09

SPORTS EQUIPMENT LIMITED

2900 Desjardins Avenue
Montreal, Quebec, H1V 2H8

Phone
782-8360

SOLD TO: Marathon Recreation,
Marathon, Ontario
POT 2E0

DATE Nov. 16, 19--
P.O. NO. 4321
TERMS Net 30 days

SHIPPED BY	VIA	F.O.B.
C.P. Express	Rail	Montreal

QUANTITY	DESCRIPTION	UNIT PRICE	AMOUNT
3 pr	O.H.A. hockey nets	$36.00	$108.00
1 only	P.B.M. Playball	9.75	9.75
3 doz	Regulation hockey sticks	68.00	204.00
			$321.75
		SALES TAX 5%	16.09
		SHIPPING CHARGES	
		TOTAL	$337.84

ITEMS NOT EXTENDED OR SHIPPED WILL BE FORWARDED AS SOON AS POSSIBLE. NO GOODS RETURNABLE WITHOUT OUR WRITTEN PERMISSION. ALL CLAIMS FOR DAMAGES OR DEFICIENCY MUST BE MADE WITHIN FIVE DAYS FROM RECEIPT OF GOODS.

SALES INVOICE NO. 8373

Figure 15.1 Sales invoice on which a sales tax has been charged.

Remitting Sales Tax

Periodically, the seller must remit the accumulated sales tax to the government. This is usually done once a month. For example, the federal government of Canada requires that the sales tax collected during one month be sent to the government (to the Receiver General for Canada) by the fifteenth day of the following month. Taxes collected in January are due by the fifteenth of February, taxes collected in February are due by the fifteenth of March, and so on. Government auditors make periodic visits to businesses to ensure correctness of collections and remittances.

The accounting entry for remittance of sales tax to the government is:

Dr. Sales Tax Payable	XX.XX	
Cr. Bank		XX.XX

15.2 NSF Cheques

Many people prefer to pay for goods and services by cheque, either when they make their purchases or later when they receive their bills. As a result, this kind of payment has become commonplace.

A cheque, however, does involve some risk to the person who accepts it. As a rule, the recipient of a cheque cannot be sure that the issuer of the cheque has money in the bank to cover it. The recipient must bank the cheque and wait until the issuer's bank clears it, that is, decides whether or not it is good.

A cheque received into your business will probably pass through these stages:

1. Because most cheques are good, assume that any cheques you receive will be cleared. Therefore, you first record the receipt of the cheque in the cash receipts journal as a debit to 'Bank' and a credit to some other account. Then you deposit the cheque in your bank account. If the cheque turns out to be good, you will probably hear no more of it.
2. Your bank also acts on the assumption that all cheques are good, and increases the balance of your account by the amount of the cheque. The bank then forwards the cheque through the clearing house to the bank of the person who issued the cheque.
3. The issuer's bank attempts to deduct the amount of the cheque from the issuer's account. If the balance of the account is large enough to cover the cheque, the deduction is made. However, if the balance of the account is not large enough to cover the cheque, no deduction is made. Instead, the bank stamps the cheque 'Not Sufficient Funds' (NSF) and sends it back to your bank. The cheque has now been 'dishonoured'; in common speech, it has 'bounced'. An **NSF cheque**, then, is one that has been refused by the bank on which it is drawn due to lack of funds in the issuer's account.
4. The dishonoured cheque is then returned to your bank. Since your bank account was previously increased by the amount of the worthless cheque, your bank now makes an offsetting deduction in the account. It does this promptly and then sends the dishonoured cheque together with a memo explaining the debit in your account.
5. After receiving the 'bad news' from the bank, you must do two things:
   a. Immediately try to contact the person who wrote the bad cheque, and attempt to obtain proper payment. This may not be easy.
   b. In the cash payments journal, reverse the accounting entry that was previously made at the time of receiving the cheque. The required entry will be a credit to Bank and a debit to some other account.

15.3 The Five-Journal System

Because only one person at a time can work on it, the synoptic journal described in Chapter 14 is suitable for only a very small business or organization. Most businesses soon reach a point where more than one person has to be involved in the

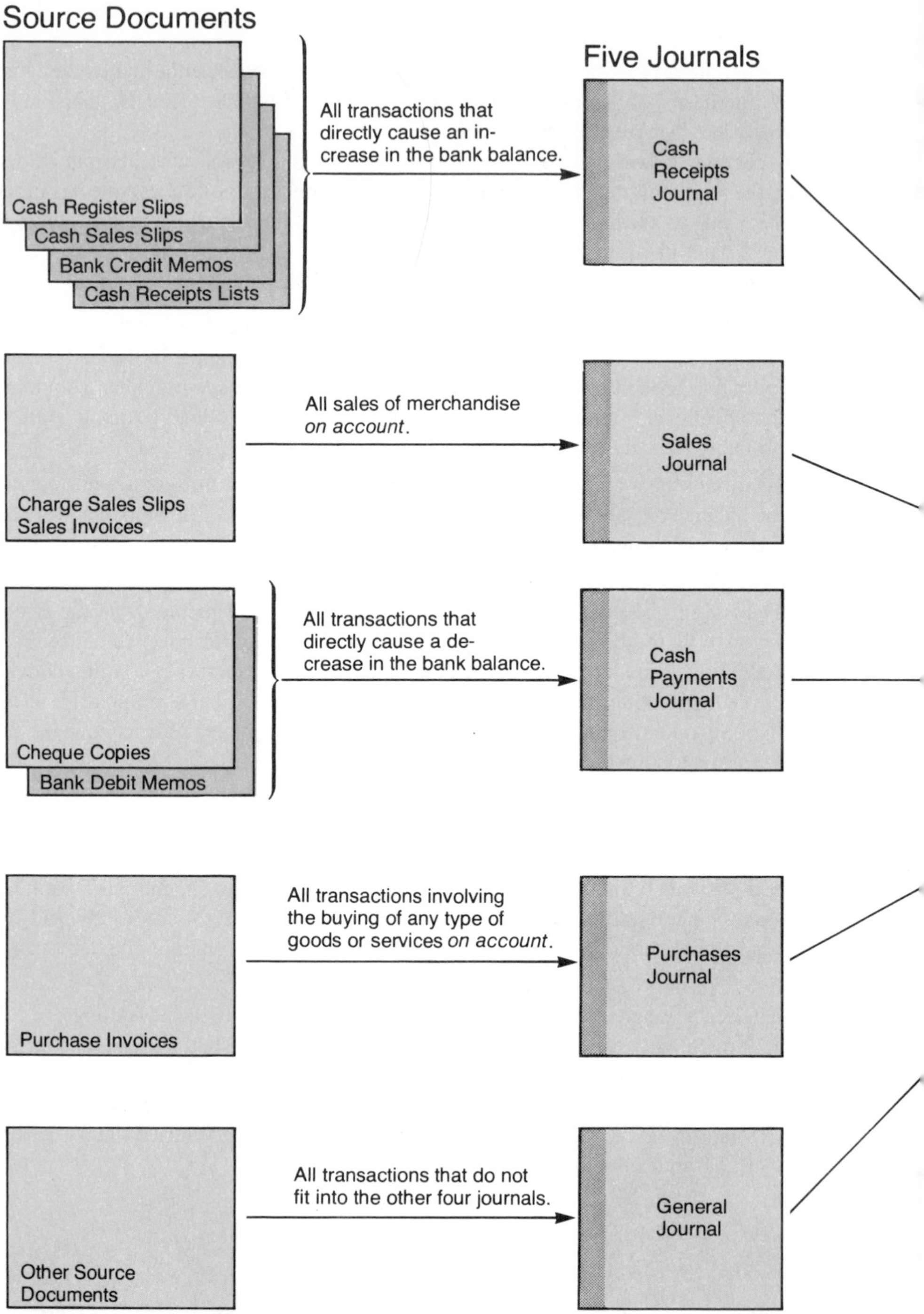
Source Documents
Five Journals
Cash Register Slips
Cash Sales Slips
Bank Credit Memos
Cash Receipts Lists
All transactions that directly cause an increase in the bank balance.
Cash Receipts Journal
Charge Sales Slips
Sales Invoices
All sales of merchandise on account.
Sales Journal
Cheque Copies
Bank Debit Memos
All transactions that directly cause a decrease in the bank balance.
Cash Payments Journal
Purchase Invoices
All transactions involving the buying of any type of goods or services on account.
Purchases Journal
Other Source Documents
All transactions that do not fit into the other four journals.
General Journal

Figure 15.2 Basic structure of the five-journal system.

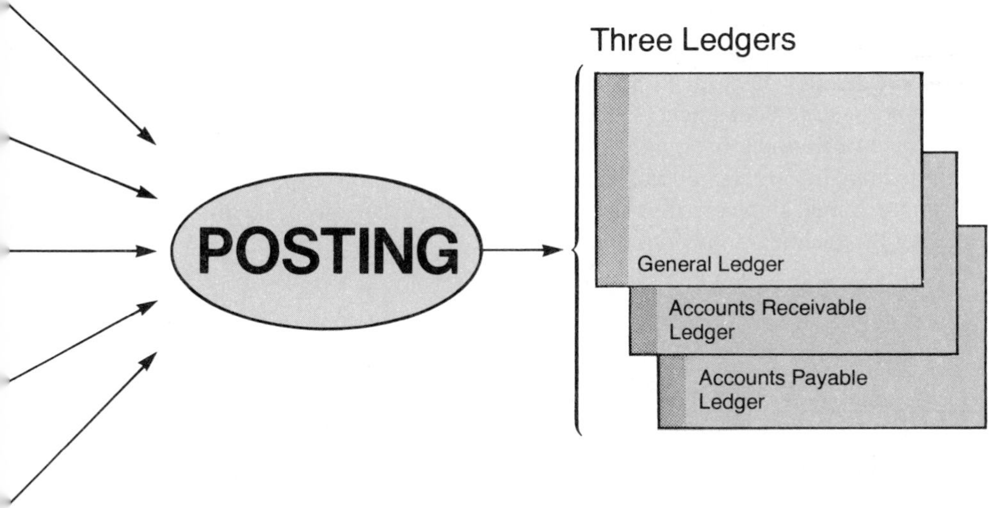
POSTING
Three Ledgers
General Ledger
Accounts Receivable
Ledger
Accounts Payable
Ledger

journalizing process. To make this possible, systems using more than one journal have been developed. One such system is the five-journal system.

Under the **five-journal system**, five journals are kept in process at the same time, each one separate from the others. A system of several journals has two main advantages. First, it allows several people to be journalizing at the same time. Second, it makes the accounting system more efficient by allowing greater specialization of duties among the staff. The degree of specialization needed depends on the type of business, the number of transactions, and other factors.

The basic structure of the five-journal system is illustrated in Figure 15.2. As you can see, the accounting entries are channelled from the various source documents into the five separate journals. Each journal is restricted to a particular type of transaction. Each of the special journals is posted individually to the three ledgers.

As Figure 15.2 shows, a number of specialists (or department heads) may come into existence in an accounting system. Large offices may require a specialist for each journal. Smaller offices often find that one person can specialize in the operation of two journals. For instance, there is a natural relationship between 'Sales' and 'Cash Receipts', and another natural relationship between 'Purchases' and 'Cash Payments'. Each of these pairs can make very effective units of work within the accounting department.

Learning to operate the five-journal system is not going to be difficult for you. You will find that the general journal has not changed. And each of the new journals is a columnar journal similar to the synoptic journal. The only significant difference is that all of the routine transactions do not go into one journal; they are directed to one of four special journals, as shown in the illustration.

Cash Receipts Journal

The **cash receipts journal** contains the accounting entries for all transactions that directly cause an increase in the bank balance. Every accounting entry in the cash receipts journal involves a debit to 'Bank'. The two most common transactions in the cash receipts journal are cash sales and receipts on account from customers.

A partially completed page from a typical cash receipts journal is shown in Figure 15.3. It was prepared from the source documents listed below.

February

4 *Cash Sales Slip*
— No. 64, to R. Smith, $147.50 plus sales tax of $7.38; down payment, $100; balance $54.88.

4 *Cash Sales Slip*
— No. 65 to P. Wylie, $26.37 plus sales tax of $1.32.

4 *Cash Receipts*
— D. Denison, $65.20, on account.
— W. Scott, $146.25, on account.

5 *Cash Sales Slip*
— No. 66, to O. Miles, $27.90 plus sales tax of $1.40.

5 *Cash Receipts*
— J. Kelly, $52.10, on account.
— S. Bruno, $19.02, on account.

5 *Bank Credit Advice*
— From Centennial Bank, $34.20, for interest earned.

Special Features

1. Special columns are used for frequently occurring items. The 'Other Accounts Cr.' section is used for infrequently occurring items.
2. Extra columns are used as necessary.
3. Because it is a columnar journal, the cash receipts journal follows the rules for columnar journals. The column labelled 'Amount of Deposit' (explained below) does not form part of the balanced journal.
4. The 'Amount of Deposit' column is not a compulsory column. The cash receipts journal can be prepared without it. For a variety of reasons, the financial records of the business do not always agree with those of the bank. Therefore, the 'Amount of Deposit' column has been included as a convenient way to tie in cash receipts with the bank record. This column does not form a part of the balanced accounting entries and must not be included when balancing or when posting the journal. The total of the 'Amount of Deposit' column will equal the total of the 'Bank' column.
5. Cash sales go in the cash receipts journal. Sales on account go in the sales journal. If a sale is partly for cash and partly on account, it goes into the cash receipts journal, as shown in the first entry of Figure 15.3.
6. At the end of each month, the cash receipts journal is balanced, ruled, and posted in the manner described in Chapter 14 for the synoptic journal.

Cash Receipts Journal — Month of February, 19–

Date		Particulars		Other Accounts Cr.			Sales Tax Payable Cr.	Sales Cr.	Accts. Rec'l.		Bank Dr.	Amount of Deposit
				Account	P.R.	Amount			Cr.	Dr.		
19– Feb.	4	R. Smith	64				7 38	147 50		54 88	100 –	
	4	P. Wylie	65				1 32	26 37			27 69	
	4	D. Denison							65 29		65 29	
	4	W. Scott							146 25		146 25	339 23
	5	O. Miles	66				1 40	27 90			29 30	
	5	J. Kelly							52 10		52 10	
	5	S. Bruno							19 02		19 02	100 42
	5	Bank Cr. Memo		Interest Rev.		34 20					34 20	34 20

Figure 15.3 A partially completed page of a cash receipts journal.

Sales Journal

The **sales journal** contains the accounting entries for all sales of merchandise on account. The sale on account is the only type of transaction that is recorded in this journal. The source document for an entry to this journal is either a sales invoice (most commonly) or a charge sales slip.

Figure 15.4 shows a partially completed page of a sales journal. As you can see, the journal uses ordinary columnar paper. In the sample, the sales tax rate is 5 percent.

Special Features

1. Only special columns are used in the sales journal. No provision is made for a general section.
2. Because it is a columnar journal, the rules for columnar journals apply to the sales journal. All of the money columns must be included when balancing the journal.
3. At the end of each month, the sales journal is balanced, ruled, and posted in the same manner as described previously for the synoptic journal.

Sales Journal — Month of February, 19–

Date		Particulars	Sales Tax Payable Cr.	Sales Cr.	Inv. #	Acc's Rec'l Dr.
19– Feb.	3	G. Barber	7 05	141 –	161	148 05
	3	F. Lees	3 50	70 –	162	73 50
	4	H. Meek	1 88	37 50	163	39 38
	4	S. King	71	14 19	164	14 90
	4	W. Horwath	1 25	25 –	165	26 25
	5	P. Keyer	2 95	59 –	166	61 95
	5	D. Ward	6 –	120 –	167	126 –
	6	G. Barber	(1 25)	(25 –)	168	(26 25)

Invoice No. 168 is a credit invoice.

Figure 15.4 A partially completed page of a sales journal.

Cash Payments Journal (Cash Disbursements Journal)

The **cash payments journal** contains the accounting entries for all transactions that directly cause a decrease in the bank balance. Every accounting entry in the cash payments journal involves a credit to 'Bank'. The most common type of transaction recorded in the cash payments journal involves the issuing of a cheque as a payment on account or for a cash purchase of goods or services.

Figure 15.5 shows a partially completed page of a cash payments journal. Again, the journal can use ordinary columnar paper. The journal was prepared from the source documents shown below.

February

3 *Cheque Copies*
— No. 72, G. Collins Co., $56, on account.
— No. 73, Taylor Bros., $175, on account.

4 *Bank Debit Advice*
— $34.10, for bank service charges.
Cheque Copies
— No. 74, F. Downes, $150, for wages.
— No. 75, K. Frost, $170, for wages.

5 *Cheque Copies*
— No. 76, R. G. Hall, $120, for proprietor's personal use.
— No. 77, Janson Trade Centre, $326.50, for cash purchase of merchandise.
— No. 78, Lumley's Limited, $226.50, for cash purchase of supplies.
— No. 79, Superior Engineering, $500, as a down payment on new equipment costing $1 740.

Special Features

1. The cash payments journal is also commonly known as the cash disbursements journal.
2. Special columns are used for frequently occurring items. The general section is used for infrequently occurring items.
3. The cash payments journal follows the rules for columnar journals. Therefore, all of the money columns must be included when balancing the journal.
4. Cash purchases go in the cash payments journal. Purchases on account go in the purchases journal. A purchase that is partly for cash and partly on account is entered in the cash payments journal, as seen in the last entry of Figure 15.5.
5. At the end of each month, the cash payments journal is balanced, ruled, and posted in the same manner as previously described for the synoptic journal.

Cash Payments Journal — **Month of February, 19–**

Date		Particulars	Other Accounts Dr. Account	P.R.	Other Accounts Dr. Amount	Wages Dr.	Supplies Dr.	Pch's Dr.	Acc's Pay'l Dr.	Acc's Pay'l Cr.	Chq #	Bank Cr.
19– Feb.	3	G. Collins Co.							56 –		72	56 –
	3	Taylor Bros.							175 –		73	175 –
	4	Bank Dr. Memo	Bank Chges		34 10							34 10
	4	F. Downes				150 –					74	150 –
	4	K. Frost				170 –					75	170 –
	5	R. G. Hall	Drawings		120 –						76	120 –
	5	Trade Centre						326 50			77	326 50
	5	Lumley's Ltd					226 50				78	226 50
	6	Superior Engineering	Equipment		1 740 –					1 240 –	79	500 –

Figure 15.5 A partially completed page of a cash payments journal.

Purchases Journal

The **purchases journal** contains the accounting entries for all transactions involving the buying of goods or services on account. Every accounting entry in the purchases journal involves a credit to Accounts Payable. The source documents for these entries are the matched sets of purchase invoices.

A partially completed page of a purchases journal is shown in Figure 15.6. This journal makes use of ordinary columnar paper. The journal was prepared from the source documents below.

February

3 *Purchase Invoices*
- Ref. No. 602, Williams' Equipment, $156, for repairs to equipment.
- Ref. No. 603, P. R. Trotter, $85.80, for supplies.

4 *Purchase Invoices*
- Ref. No. 604, Pascoe's, $56.40, miscellaneous expense.
- Ref. No. 605, Reliable Trading, $171, for merchandise.

5 *Purchase Invoices*
- Ref. No. 606, Mason & Mason, $37.90, for supplies.
- Ref. No. 607, ABC Supply, $470, for merchandise.
- Ref. No. 608, N. S. E. W. Railway, $116, for transportation charges on incoming goods.
- Ref. No. 609, Hector Oil Co., $119.60, for gas and oil for delivery truck.

Purchases Journal — Month of February, 19–

Date		Particulars	Other Accounts Dr.				Delivery Exp. Dr.	Misc. Exp. Dr.	Supplies Dr.	Pch's Dr.	Ref #	Acc's Pay'le Cr.
			Account	P.R.	Amount							
19– Feb.	3	Williams Equip.	Equip. Repairs		156 –						602	156 –
	3	P.R. Trotter							85 80		603	85 80
	4	Pascoe's						56 40			604	56 40
	4	Reliable Trading								171 –	605	171 –
	5	Mason & Mason							37 90		606	37 90
	5	ABC Supply								470 –	607	470 –
	5	N.S.E.W. Railway	Freight-in		116 –						608	116 –
	5	Hector Oil Co.					119 60				609	119 60

Figure 15.6 A partially completed page of a purchases journal.

Special Features

1. Special columns are used for frequently occurring items. The 'Other Accounts Dr' section is used for infrequently occurring items.

2. The purchases journal follows the rules for columnar journals. All of the money columns must be included when balancing the purchases journal.
3. Purchase invoice reference numbers are not used in all accounting systems. An accountant setting up a purchasing system has a choice of filing the purchase documents in either numeric or alphabetical order. In the latter case, no reference numbers are necessary. Where numeric order is used, however, a reference number must be placed on each of the purchase document sets. It is usually easier and faster to locate purchase invoices that are filed in numeric order.
4. At the end of each month, the purchases journal is balanced, ruled, and posted in the same manner as described previously for the synoptic journal.

Cross Balancing the Special Journals

Before the four special journals are posted at the end of each month, they must first be ruled and balanced. The procedure for cross balancing a columnar journal has been explained in Chapter 14. Basically, you must add the debit column totals, add the credit column totals, and see that the two additions are the same. If they are, the journal is ruled off ready to be posted.

Posting in the Five-Journal System

You have known for some time how to post the general journal and have recently learned how to post a columnar journal. This is practically all that you need to know in order to post in the five-journal system. Each journal is posted separately but the order in which they are posted does not matter. Only after all five of the journals have been posted should any attempt be made to balance the ledgers.

This development of a new system of journals does not affect the manner of posting to the subsidiary ledgers. They are still posted directly from the source documents.

Cross-referencing

Cross-referencing is an important part of posting. In the journals, show that each amount has been posted by writing in the number of the ledger account. In the accounts, beside each debit and credit entry, identify the journal and page number from which the entry came.

In Chapter 7's discussion of 'posting references in the accounts', you were told to record the journal page number from which the entry is taken and to prefix it with a code letter, for example, J14. You were told that the journal code is necessary because several journals may be used simultaneously. The code is a means of identifying the specific journal with which the page number is associated.

Now, perhaps, you can appreciate more fully the advantages of coding the posting references in the accounts. Each of the four new journals has its own code.

The codes are as follows:

Journal	*Code*
Cash Receipts Journal	CR
Cash Payments Journal	CP
Sales Journal	S
Purchases Journal	P
General Journal	J

The sample account in Figure 15.7 shows how the new coded posting references might appear.

ACCOUNT *Accounts Receivable* No. 2

DATE		PARTICULARS	PR	DEBIT	CREDIT	Dr Cr	BALANCE
19– Mar.	31	Balance Forwarded	–			Dr	6 474 07
	31		S67	13 047 25			
	31		Cr74		12 096 40		
	31		J19		42 42	Dr	7 382 50

Figure 15.7 Journal codes as they might appear in the ledger.

Accounting Terms

sales tax
NSF cheque
five-journal system
cash receipts journal
sales journal
cash payments journal
purchases journal

Review Questions

1. What is the purpose of sales tax?
2. Describe how sales tax is calculated.
3. When do the provincial governments levy sales tax?

4. Who must collect and account for sales tax?
5. How often is sales tax remitted to the government?
6. Why does sales tax usually occupy a special column in one or more of the journals?
7. What is an NSF cheque?
8. How does one learn about an NSF cheque?
9. Why is the bank entitled to deduct the amount of an NSF cheque from your account without first informing you?
10. Name the five journals in a five-journal system.
11. Give the two main advantages of a five-journal system.
12. State the rules for channelling transactions into the various journals.
13. In what journal is a sale recorded that is only partly paid for?
14. In what order are the five journals posted?
15. Give the new codes used when cross referencing in a five-journal system.

Exercises

Sales Tax

1. 1. Calculate the sales tax for each of the following if the rate of tax is 5 percent.

2. Calculate the total amount to be paid by the customer for each of the following.

3. Give the accounting entry for each transaction in the books of the vendor.

Transactions

a. A cash sale of goods at a price of $75.
b. A cash sale of goods at a price of $120.
c. A charge sale of goods at a price of $58.60.
d. A charge sale of goods at a price of $98.00.
e. A sale of goods at a price of $130 with a down payment of $50.

2. The invoice below was issued to Island Marina by Masthead Marine.

1. Give the accounting entry to be made in the books of the vendor.

2. Give the accounting entry to be made in the books of the purchaser.

MASTHEAD MARINE

ECHO BAY
VANCOUVER, B.C.

P.O. Box 298
Station 8
V7C 8P7
Phone
842-9999

SOLD TO Island Marina
4000 Island Highway
Campbell River, B.C.
V9W 2J4

DATE July 3, 19--
TERMS Net 30 days

QUANTITY	PART NO.	DESCRIPTION	PRICE	AMOUNT
6	77-1139	Saturn off-shore compasses	$ 95.00	$ 570.00
2	03-3295	LG2 dual log indicator	299.00	598.00
				$1 168.00
		5% sales tax		58.40
				$1 226.40

SALES INVOICE NO. 3267

3. Jack Pritchard paid $330.96, including 5 percent sales tax, for some furniture.

   1. Calculate the price of the goods before the sales tax is added.
   2. Calculate the sales tax on the goods.
   3. Prove your work.

4. Examine the account below and answer the questions that follow.

ACCOUNT *Sales Tax Payable* No. 22

DATE		PARTICULARS	PR	DEBIT	CREDIT	Dr Cr	BALANCE
19– Feb.	1	Forwarded	–			Cr	476.30
	15		CP80	476.30			
	28		SJ61		242.95		
	28		CR57	559.15	316.20	Cr	559.15
Mar.	15		CP82				
	31		SJ64		251.86		
	31		CR59		302.19	Cr	554.05

1. **How much sales tax was accumulated in January?**
2. **How much sales tax was accumulated in February?**
3. **What does the account balance represent?**
4. **How much sales tax was accumulated in March?**
5. **When will the sales tax accumulated in March be paid?**
6. **Give the accounting entry that will be made for the transaction of April 15.**

NSF Cheques

5. Pugh & Co. made a cash sale to H. Vernon for $55 plus $2.75 sales tax for a total of $57.75. Vernon gave his cheque in payment. A few days after depositing the cheque in the bank, Pugh & Co. was notified by its bank that Vernon's cheque was NSF.

1. **What entries would Pugh & Co. record at the time of making the sale?**
2. **What entries would record the fact that the cheque is NSF?**

6. Pugh & Co. sold goods on account to H. Vetiri. The goods were priced at $107, the sales tax was $5.35, and the total was $112.35. The next month, Pugh & Co. received a cheque from Vetiri for $112.35 and deposited it in the bank. A few days later, the company was informed that the cheque had bounced. Discussion with Mr. Vitiri disclosed that he was temporarily short of funds and would pay the bill in the near future.

1. **What entries would be made by Pugh & Co. at the time of the sale?**
2. **What entries would be made by Pugh & Co. upon receipt of Vetiri's cheque?**
3. **What entries would record the fact that the cheque is NSF?**

Using the Journals One at a Time

7. 1. **Record the following transactions in the cash receipts journal provided in the workbook. Calculate sales tax at 5 percent. Assume bank deposits are made at the end of each day.**

Transactions

December

1 The owner, P. Messer, increased his capital balance by depositing his personal cheque for $1 000 in the business account.
3 Merchandise was sold to H. Joseph for $150 cash. Sales ticket No. 103.
4 Received a cheque for $211 from S. Nolan on account.

4 Merchandise was sold to V. Kelly for $75 cash. Sales ticket No. 104.
5 Received a cheque for $165 from A. Cullen on account.
6 Merchandise was sold to R. Peckford for $200 on sales ticket No. 105. Peckford paid $100 cash and owed the balance.

2. Rule and balance the journal at this point.

---

8. 1. Record the following sales invoices in the sales journal provided in the workbook.

October

1 Sales invoice No. 70; goods $80; sales tax $4; total $84, to M. Sloboda.
2 Sales invoice No. 71; goods $140; sales tax $7; total $147, to R. McFee.
2 Sales invoice No. 72; goods $217; sales tax $10.85; total $227.84, to M. Greshuk.
3 Sales invoice No. 73; goods $596; sales tax $29.80; total $625.80, to E. Caban.
3 Sales invoice No. 74; goods $32.05; sales tax $1.60; total $33.65, to R. Van Horne.

2. Rule and balance the sales journal at this point.

---

9. 1. Record the following transactions in the cash payments journal provided in the workbook.

Transactions

April

1 Issued cheque No. 40 to R. Morris for the cash purchase of supplies, $76.02.
2 Issued cheque No. 41 to Cox Supply Co. for the cash purchase of merchandise, $361.40.
3 Issued cheque No. 42 to Municipal Hydro in payment of the hydro for the previous month, $56.20.
4 Issued cheque No. 43 to Franklin Wholesale on account, $300.
4 Issued cheque No. 44 to C. Foster, the owner, for his personal use, $200.
5 Received a debit memorandum from the City Bank to the effect that a $12.50 service charge had been made against the business's bank account.
5 Issued cheque No. 45 to S. Main for weekly wages, $155.
6 Issued cheque No. 46 for $100 to Cox Supply as a down payment on a purchase of merchandise costing $375.

2. Rule and balance the journal at this point.

---

10. 1. Record the following transactions in the purchases journal provided in the workbook. Ignore reference numbers.

Transactions

February

2 Received purchase invoice from Double Square Manufacturing for the purchase of merchandise, $710.38.
3 Received purchase invoice from North District Supply for the purchase of supplies, $67.20.
3 Received purchase invoice from Provincial Transfer Co. for freight charges on incoming merchandise, $147.50.
4 Received purchase invoice from Clarke's Service Station for gasoline and oil used in the delivery truck, $57.75.
5 Received purchase invoice from Circle Products for the purchase of merchandise, $525.
5 Received purchase invoice from Grant Auto Sales for the purchase of a new delivery truck, $5 259.45.

2. Rule and balance the journal at this point.

Selecting Which Journal to Use

11. State in which of the five journals each transaction below would be recorded.

Transactions

1. A cheque is issued to a supplier on account.
2. A purchase invoice is received from a supplier of merchandise.
3. A cheque is received on account from a customer.
4. A cash sale is made to a customer.
5. A sale on account is made to a customer.
6. A cheque is issued to the owner for his personal use.
7. A cheque is issued to pay the wages for the period.
8. A sales invoice is issued.
9. A correcting entry is made to transfer a debit amount from the Supplies account to the Miscellaneous Expense account.
10. A cheque is issued to pay for a cash purchase of merchandise.
11. A bank debit advice for a service charge is received.
12. A cheque is issued to a supplier on account.
13. A cheque is issued to pay for the monthly rent.
14. A bank debit advice is received with respect to an NSF cheque.
15. A bank credit advice is received with respect to interest earned.
16. A new typewriter is purchased and a down payment is required. A cheque is issued.
17. The owner collects a debt from a customer but keeps the money for his personal use.
18. The owner spends a sum of money out of his own pocket for business purposes and is reimbursed by means of a cheque.

Journalizing in the Five Journals

12. Journalize the transactions shown below in the five journals of Domino Wholesale Company. The chart of accounts for Domino Wholesale Company is as follows:

Petty Cash
Bank
Accounts Receivable
Merchandise Inventory
Supplies
Equipment
Accounts Payable
Sales Tax Payable
Anna Popov, Capital
Anna Popov, Drawings
Sales
Purchases
Freight-in
Bank Charges
Delivery Expense
General Expense
Light, Heat, and Water
Postage Expense
Rent Expense
Telephone Expense
Wages Expense

Transactions (**Note:** 5 percent sales tax to be added to all sales)

Date	*Source Document*	*No.*	*Name*	*Explanation*	*Amount*
May 1	Cheque copy	75	Morris and Hannah	Rent for May	$425.00
2	Purchase invoice		Grinnelco	Merchandise	378.00
2	Cash receipt		R. Jones	On account	436.80
4	Cash sales slip	97	A. Racicot	Merchandise sold	70.00
4	Information memo			An error was discovered in the general ledger. An amount of $30 which had been debited to General Expense should have been debited to Supplies.	30.00
5	Cheque copy	76	P. Fobert	Wages	275.00
8	Sales invoice	317	C. Perry	Goods sold	215.00
9	Cash receipt		S. Storey	On account	95.00
9	Purchase invoice		Wonder Mfg.	Supplies	110.25
9	Cheque copy	77	A. Popov	Personal use	300.00
10	Purchase invoice		Pressed Fittings	Merchandise	435.75
10	Sales invoice	318	Mercer Company	Goods sold	190.00
11	Cash receipt		R. Russell	On account	200.00
12	Purchase invoice		Newday Supplies	Supplies	210.00

Date	*Source Document*	*No.*	*Name*	*Explanation*	*Amount*
May 12	Cheque copy	78	General Supply	On account	125.50
15	Purchase invoice		Baldwin's	Supplies	78.75
15	Sales invoice	319	T. Ward	Goods sold	216.00
16	Credit invoice issued	320	C. Perry	Merchandise returned $70 plus $3.50 tax	$ 73.50
16	Cash receipt		R. Grant	On account	150.00
17	Cash sales slip	98	P. Fuhrman	Goods sold	65.00
17	Sales invoice	321	B. Adler	Goods sold	195.00
18	Cheque copy	79	Provincial Treasurer	Sales tax for prior month	497.07
19	Purchase invoice		Continental Railway	Freight-in	96.40
19	Sales invoice	322	G. Nolan	Goods sold	110.00
19	Information memo			An error was detected in the accounts receivable ledger. An amount of $62 which should have been credited to J. Walker's account was credited in error to M. Walker's account.	62.00
22	Cheque copy	80	Bell Telephone	Telephone	52.70
22	Cheque copy	81	Baldwin's	Cash purchase of supplies	26.25
23	Sales invoice	323	W. Phillips	Goods sold	280.00
23	Cash sales slip	99	P. Leonard	Goods sold $190 Down payment $50	190.00 50.00
23	Cash sales slip	100	H. Fogh	Goods sold	370.00
24	Credit invoice rec'd		Grinnelco	For goods returned $55 plus tax	57.75
25	Bank debit memo		Western Bank	Bank service charge	34.70
25	Cheque copy	82	A. Popov	Personal use	300.00
26	Cheque copy	83	O. K. Welding	On account	150.00
29	Cheque copy	84	Petty Cash	Replenishing cheque for petty cash expenditures: Gen Exp 26.40 Del Exp 8.60 Postage 10.00	45.00
29	Bank debit memo		Western Bank	NSF cheque of R. Russell	200.00
30	Cheque copy	85	S. Tybo	Wages	300.00
31	Purchase invoice		Jim's Garage	Gas and oil used in the delivery vehicle, $124.80; in the owner's car, $62.50	187.30

Posting Individual Journals

13. Workbook Exercise: Formal posting of a sales journal to selected accounts.

Journalizing, Posting, and Balancing with Five Journals and Three Ledgers

14. The general ledger of Bristol Appliances Company as of December 31, 19-- is set up in the workbook. On December 31, 19--, the combined chart of accounts and general ledger trial balance of Bristol Appliances Company was as follows:

1 Bank	$3 163.12	
2 Accounts Receivable	2 471.49	
3 Supplies	312.50	
4 Merchandise Inventory	7 416.40	
5 Store Equipment	800.00	
6 Delivery Truck	2 200.00	
20 Accounts Payable	1636351	$1 941.60
21 Bank Loan		8 000.00
22 Sales Tax Payable		360.00
30 S.C. Scales, Capital		6 061.91
31 S.C. Scales, Drawings		16363.51
40 Sales		
50 Purchases		
51 Delivery Expense		
52 Miscellaneous Expense		
53 Rent		
54 Salaries		

The subsidiary ledgers of Bristol Appliances Company as of December 31, 19-- are set up in the workbook. On December 31, 19--, the subsidiary trial balances appeared as follows:

ACCOUNTS RECEIVABLE TRIAL BALANCE
DECEMBER 31, 19--

C. Booth, 129 James Street	Inv. No. 325	$ 316.10
M. Howard, 881 Wilson Avenue	296	95.00
J. Hudson, 14 Brook Drive	306	912.75
O. Langley, 65 Finch Avenue	315	163.87
T. Miles, 110 Church Street	326	50.00
S. Thorpe, 375 Beckett Drive	217	135.00
D. Wilkins, 70 Dixon Avenue	331	500.00
	346	298.77
		$2 471.49

ACCOUNTS PAYABLE TRIAL BALANCE
DECEMBER 31, 19--

Stirling Company, 20 River Street	Ref. B245	$ 560.20
Triangle Electric, Roxborough	4701	316.47
Universal Vacuums, 20 Dexter Street	6508	1 000.00
Western Electric, 1000 Fleet Street	246R	64.93
		$1 941.60

The subsidiary ledgers of Bristol Appliances Company are posted daily, directly from the source documents.

1. **In the journals of Bristol Appliances Company, record the transactions shown below. Bristol Appliances uses a five-journal system. The five journals shown below are set up in the workbook. Use the following page numbers:**

Cash Receipts Journal	*Page* 61
Cash Payments Journal	*Page* 117
Purchases Journal	*Page* 74
Sales Journal	*Page* 82
General Journal	*Page* 29

A 5 percent sales tax is to be applied on all sales of merchandise.

Transactions

January

2 *Cash Sales Slip*
— No. 401, to T. Arthur, $125 plus sales tax.
Cash Receipt
— From C. Booth, $116.10, on account.
Cheque Copy
— No. 376, to J. C. Brown, $87.42, for the cash purchase of supplies.

3 *Purchase Invoice*
— No. 1212, from Smith's Service Station, 3 Cary Street, $63.50, for gasoline and oil used in the delivery truck.
Cash Sales Slip
— No. 402, to R. Malone, $475 plus sales tax.

4 *Sales Invoice*
— No. 347, to M. Howard, $310 plus sales tax.

5 *Cheque Copies*
— No. 377, to Universal Vacuums, $500, on account.
— No. 378, to 'Cash', $885, for the salaries for the week.

8 *Cash Receipt*
— From T. Miles, $50, in full payment of account.

Correcting Entry
— An error was discovered in an entry made in December. An amount of $16.10 was debited incorrectly to Delivery Expense; it should have been debited to Miscellaneous Expense.

9 *Cash Sales Slip*
— No. 403, to H. McPhee, $800 plus sales tax.

10 *Purchase Invoice*
— No. 306R, from Western Electric, $661.50, for the purchase of merchandise.

10 *Cheque Copy*
— No. 379, to Stirling Company, $708.75, for the cash purchase of merchandise.

11 *Sales Invoices*
— No. 348, to O. Langley, $137.50 plus sales tax.
— No. 349, to T. Miles, $200 plus sales tax.
— No. 350, to S. Thorpe, $475.12 plus sales tax.

12 *Cash Receipt*
— From Clover Stores, $105; because of a recent change in the system, certain supplies on hand were not usable and were sold for cash at their cost of $105.

Cheque Copy
— No. 380, to 'Cash', $710, for the salaries for the week.

15 *Cheque Copies*
— No. 381, to S. C. Scales, $300, for his personal use.
— No. 382, to the Provincial Government, $360, for sales tax for the previous month.

Cash Receipts
— From C. Booth, $100, on account.
— From J. Hudson, $512.75, on account.
— From S. Thorpe, $135, invoice No. 217.
— From D. Wilkins, $798.77, invoices No. 331 and 346.

Cash Sales Slips
— No. 404, to F. Lang, $480 plus sales tax.
— No. 405, to K. Klein, $750 plus sales tax.

16 *Purchase Invoice*
— No. 406, from Ritz Furniture, Melody Road, $157.50, for the purchase of merchandise.

17 *Purchase Invoice*
— No. 708, from Super Stationers, $76.40, for supplies.

18 *Cheque Copies*
— No. 383, to Triangle Electric, $316.47, paying invoice No. 4701.
— No. 384, to Stirling Company, $560.20, paying invoice No. B245.

— No. 385, to Western Electric, $64.93, paying invoice No. 246R.
— No. 386, to Smith's Service Station, $63.50, paying invoice No. 1212.

19 *Cheque Copy*
— No. 387, to 'Cash', $890, in payment of the weekly salaries.

22 *Sales Invoices*
— No. 351, to D. Wilkins, $300 plus sales tax.
— No. 352, to C. Booth, $281.63 plus sales tax.
— No. 353, to S. Thorpe, $31.12 plus sales tax.

23 *Purchase Invoice*
— No. 4912, from Triangle Electric, $68.25, for purchase of merchandise.

24 *Purchase Invoice*
— No. 842, from Super Stationers, $31.50, for supplies.

25 *Cheque Copy*
— No. 388, to local telephone company, $46.50, for monthly telephone bill.

26 *Cheque Copies*
— No. 389, to Boston Television Co., $112.60, for the cash purchase of merchandise.
— No. 390, to Admirable Company, $82.95, for the cash purchase of merchandise.
— No. 391, to 'Cash', $875, for the weekly salaries.
— No. 392, to Grayson Brothers, $450, for the rent for the month.

30 *Purchase Invoice*
— No. 864, from Super Stationers, $105, for supplies.

31 *Purchase Invoices*
— No. B319, from Stirling Company, $315, for merchandise.
— No. 6722, from Universal Vacuums, $261.81, for merchandise.
— No. 512, from Ritz Furniture, $86.40, for merchandise.

Cash Sales Slip
— No. 406, to M. Morse, $906.00 plus sales tax.

Sales Invoices
— No. 354, to J. Hudson, $1 200 plus sales tax.
— No. 355, to M. Howard, $12.08 plus sales tax.
— No. 356, to S. Thorpe, $19.65 plus sales tax.

Cheque Copy
— No. 393, to local hydro, $46.40, for hydro for the month.

2. Balance the special journals and post the five journals to the general ledger.

3. Balance the general ledger as of January 31.

4. Balance the subsidiary ledgers as of January 31.

15. C. D. Mould is the proprietor of Husky Hardware. He uses five journals and three ledgers in his accounting system. He posts the subsidiary ledgers daily, directly from the source documents. In his locality there is a 5 percent sales tax on all sales.

The three ledgers of Husky Hardware as of June 30, 19--, are set up in the workbook.

The general ledger trial balance of Husky Hardware as of June 30, 19--, is as follows:

HUSKY HARDWARE
GENERAL LEDGER TRIAL BALANCE
JUNE 30, 19--

1 Bank	$ 2 614.20	
2 Accounts Receivable	412.50	
3 Merchandise Inventory	4 095.12	
4 Supplies	300.00	
5 Store Equipment	2 675.00	
6 Delivery Equipment	3 500.00	
20 Accounts Payable		$ 5 063.94
21 Sales Tax Payable		108.52
30 C.D. Mould, Capital		7 864.36
31 C.D. Mould, Drawings	5 876.34	
40 Sales		19 800.00
50 Purchases	9 500.00	
51 Miscellaneous Expense	216.41	
52 Rent	1 800.00	
53 Wages	1 847.25	
	$32 836.82	$32 836.82

The subsidiary ledger trial balances are as follows:

HUSKY HARDWARE
ACCOUNTS RECEIVABLE TRIAL BALANCE
JUNE 30, 19--

J. Barkley, 260 Western Avenue	No. 490	$92.46	
	496	15.02	
	503	60.10	$167.58
T. Fairley, 300 Center Road	501		56.42
S. Harvey, 466 Keeley Street	502		76.50
R. Taylor, 588 Truway Drive	498		112.00
			$412.50

HUSKY HARDWARE
ACCOUNTS PAYABLE TRIAL BALANCE
JUNE 30, 19--

Household Utensils Company 487 Faith Avenue	Inv. No. 52	$1 067.50
J. & A. Hardware Supply 600 Young Street	596	505.25
Learner Bros. 5012 Direct Avenue	141	3 067.20
Specialty Manufacturing Co. Barbary	163	423.99
		$5 063.94

1. Journalize the transactions listed below in the five journals of Husky Hardware. These are provided in the workbook.

Cash Receipts Journal	*Page* 42
Cash Payments Journal	*Page* 93
Sales Journal	*Page* 56
Purchases Journal	*Page* 85
General Journal	*Page* 16

Transactions

July

2 *Cheque Copy*
— No. 187, to D. C. Harper, $300 for the rent for July.
Purchase Invoice
— From Household Utensils Company, No. 87, $184.50, for the purchase of merchandise.

3 *Sales Invoices*
— No. 504, to S. Harvey, $50 plus sales tax.
— No. 505, to R. Taylor, $26 plus sales tax.
— No. 506, to T. Fairley, $42 plus sales tax.
— No. 507, to J. Barkley, $64 plus sales tax.

4 *Cash Receipt*
— From the owner C. D. Mould, $1 000, for the purpose of increasing his investment in the business.

5 *Purchase Invoice*
— From Learner Brothers, No. 206, $35.60, for supplies.
Cheque Copy
— No. 188, to Supply House, $147, for the cash purchase of merchandise.

Cash Register Slips
— $863.26. The cash sales for the week amounted to $822.15 plus sales tax of $41.11.

8 *Cash Receipt*
— From T. Fairley, $56.42, paying invoice No. 501.

9 *Sales Invoices*
— No. 508, to L. Peck, 12 Semore St., $41 plus sales tax.
— No. 509, to S. Harvey, $18 plus sales tax.
— No. 510, to T. Fairley, $25 plus sales tax.

10 *Purchase Invoice*
— From J. & A. Hardware Supply, $315, for a shipment of hammers, saws, and other tools.

12 *Cash Register Slips*
— $982.80. The cash sales for the week amounted to $936 plus sales tax of $46.80.

Bank Debit Memo
— From Sovereign Bank, $10.20, bank account decreased because of bank service charge.

Cheque Copy
— No. 189, to Modern Manufacturing Company, $273, for the cash purchase of merchandise.

13 *Cash Receipts*
— From S. Harvey, $129, paying invoices No. 502 and No. 504.
— From J. Barkley, $107.48, paying invoices No. 490 and No. 496.

15 *Cheque Copies*
— No. 190, to Learner Brothers, $1 500, on account.
— No. 191, to Household Utensils Company, $500, on account.
— No. 192, to B. Wiley, $400, wages for the first half of the month.
— No. 193, to W. Brown, $425, wages for the first half of the month.
— No. 194, to C. D. Mould, $500, personal withdrawal by proprietor.
— No. 195, to the Provincial Government, $108.52, sales tax for the previous month.

17 *Sales Invoices*
— No. 511, to V. Parker, 466 Janes Road, $75 plus sales tax.
— No. 512, to L. Peck, $45 plus sales tax.
— No. 513, to S. Harvey, $19 plus sales tax.

Cash Receipt
— From R. Taylor, $112, paying invoice No. 498.

18 *Non-routine Transaction*
— The proprietor submits bills amounting to $24.08 for miscellaneous expenses which he has paid out of his own pocket. He asks that his Drawings account be credited.

19 *Cash Register Slips*
— $898.80. The cash sales for the week amounted to $856 plus $42.80 sales tax.
Cash Receipts
— From S. Harvey, $38.85, paying his account in full.
— From T. Fairley, $44.10, paying invoice No. 506.
— From L. Peck, $43.05, paying invoice No. 508.
22 *Purchase Invoice*
— From Maple Feed Company, Maple, No. 996, $603.75 for the purchase of merchandise.
23 *Purchase Invoice*
— From Household Utensils Company, No. 156, $412.65, for the purchase of merchandise.
26 *Cash Register Slips*
— $1 118.25. The cash sales for the week amounted to $1 065 plus sales tax of $53.25.
Cheque Copy
— No. 196, to Learner Brothers, $262.50, for the cash purchase of merchandise.
29 *Cheque Copies*
— No. 197, to Household Utensils Company, $567.50, paying the balance of invoice No. 52.
— No. 198, to J. & A. Hardware Supply, $505.25, paying invoice No. 596
— No. 199, to Specialty Manufacturing Company, $423.99, paying No. 163.
31 *Cheque Copies*
— No. 200, to B. Wiley, $400, wages for the last half of the month.
— No. 201, to W. Brown, $425, wages for the last half of the month.
— No. 202, to C.D. Mould, $500, for his personal use.

2. Balance and post the journals to the general ledger.

3. Balance the general ledger.

4. Balance the subsidiary ledgers.

Using Your Knowledge

16. Before posting to the general ledger, the equality of the Debit and Credit column totals in the journals should be proved. Suppose that this was not done, and that the total of a column in the cash receipts journal was incorrectly added by $100.

1. How would this error first be discovered?

2. What steps would normally be followed to find the cause of the error?

17. **M. Lunney Co. has two bank accounts, one with a balance on deposit of $100 000 and one, for payroll, which is overdrawn by $5 000. The bank charges interest on the $5 000. Is this fair? Explain.**

18. N. Howard conducts a small retail business. At the time of a sale she collects the tax from the customer but makes no attempt to distinguish on her books between the amount of the sale and the amount of the sales tax. In her entries involving cash sales she debits Cash and credits Sales for the total amount.
    1. **If Howard's total sales for the month amount to $52 500, how much sales tax would she remit to the provincial treasurer if the rate of tax is 5 percent? Assume that all sales are taxable.**
    2. **What entry would be made to record the sales tax?**

19. Bob Jarvis, the accountant for Wright Brothers, sets up an accounting system to eliminate the accounts receivable and accounts payable ledgers. All invoices owing to creditors and all invoices due from customers are kept in separate file folders until paid. When invoices are paid, they are removed from the customers' and creditors' files and placed in a file for paid invoices. At the end of the month the unpaid files are totalled and these totals agreed with the balances in the control accounts in the general ledger.

    What advantages and disadvantages are there to such a system?

20. Shoe store owner D. Mugami made approximately 300 credit sales and 100 credit purchases each month. Mr. Mugami recorded all these sales and purchases in a general journal. A friend asked him why he did not use a sales journal and a purchases journal. Mr. Mugami replied that he did not understand their use. He believed that they simply divided the work among several people. Since he did his own accounting, he had no need for these special journals.

    Is division of labour the only reason for using special journals? Explain.

21. The Ross Paper Box Company was a well-established business which sold a limited line of higher priced but profitable merchandise to an exclusive clientele. The books of account consisted of a two-column general journal and a general ledger. The accountant, J. Thomas, who did things his own way, had been with the company for 25 years and provided accurate and timely statements every month.

    Last year the firm hired a recent graduate in accounting and marketing as the general manager. He was very aggressive and wanted to see the business increase its sales. Within six months he introduced new lines of merchandise which added numerous customers. The volume of transactions increased from 200 to 3 000 per month. It became necessary for Thomas to take the books home and work on them at night. At the end of December, with the accounting statements for October 31 still not completed, Thomas resigned.

1. **What do you think caused Thomas to quit after 25 years with the company?**
2. **If you had been the accountant during the period of increased sales, what changes would you have made in the accounting system?**

22. **A review of the accounting records of Nixon Co. disclosed the following errors. Show how these errors should be corrected, giving journal entries where applicable.**
    1. Cash received from H. Latimer for $285.00 was entered correctly in the cash receipts journal, but posted to the accounts receivable ledger as $258.00.
    2. An invoice for 45 cartons at $1.75 each shipped to Best Drug Store was extended and entered in the sales journal as $87.75.
    3. Cash of $65.00 was entered correctly in the cash receipts journal as received from M. Smith, but was posted in the accounts receivable ledger to the account of M. Smythe.
    4. The footings of the 'Purchases' column in the cash payments journal were overstated by $100.
    5. A cheque for $150 payable to G. Graham for legal fees was entered incorrectly in the cash payments journal as $160. The journal has not yet been posted.

Cases

Case 1 *Does the Business Come First?*

J. C. Macdonald loved cars. He was lucky enough to own a Studebaker dealership, Macdonald Studebaker, during the years when that car enjoyed great popularity. During these peak years, Macdonald Studebaker became a large and very prosperous concern.

J. C. used some of his profits from Macdonald Studebaker to purchase a small speciality machine shop called Speciality Fittings. This company manufactured stainless steel fittings designed to meet the sanitation needs of the dairy and brewery industries.

Although J. C. owned Speciality Fittings outright, he left its management to hired executives. J. C. limited his own involvement to a weekly visit of one or two hours. This way, he could devote most of his time to his first love, the car business.

After a few years the Studebaker became less popular. Macdonald Studebaker made fewer sales and lower profits. Eventually, the business faced bankruptcy. After a series of substantial losses, Macdonald Studebaker had heavy debts and a severe shortage of cash. Meanwhile, the fortunes of Speciality Fittings were on an upswing. Good management and a good product combined to push Speciality Fittings ahead year after year.

J. C. began to draw funds out of Speciality Fittings and to put them into the ailing Macdonald Studebaker. At first this presented no problem to Speciality Fittings. However, as J. C.'s demands for cash persisted, Speciality Fittings also began to experience financial problems.

The accountant for Speciality Fittings, Ken Bond, was seriously upset by J. C.'s actions. Ken believed that J. C. was 'pouring good Speciality money down the Studebaker sewer'. To curtail J. C.'s withdrawals, Ken began to juggle the accounting records so that Speciality Fittings would seem to have less money than it really had. Ken didn't steal the money. He kept it safely tucked away in a secret bank account, out of the reach of J. C. Macdonald.

Eventually, the company's auditors discovered Ken's activities. They had no alternative but to report their findings to J. C. Three hours after learning about the deception, J. C. Macdonald fired Ken Bond.

Questions

1. As a businessman, what was J. C. Macdonald's problem?

2. Did Ken Bond have a moral right to protect the company for which he worked?

3. Was there an alternative approach that Ken Bond could have taken?

4. Should Ken have been fired?

5. Was there an alternative approach that J. C. Macdonald could have taken?

Career
Richard Savard
General Accountant

After finishing high school, Richard Savard completed a business program at a college in Halifax, Nova Scotia. This program included a number of accounting courses.

After graduation, Richard went to work for Moore Business Forms as a junior cost clerk. In this job, he determined the cost of goods sold and made recommendations on the selling price of the product. He was quickly promoted to intermediate cost clerk. After two years, Richard joined Lyon's Furniture Company as a senior cost clerk. During this period, he was asked to design an entire system for determining the company's costs.

Richard next joined Emerson Electric, a large manufacturer of electric motors, as a junior accountant. He enjoyed this work so much that he decided to try for a professional accounting degree. He enrolled in the Registered Industrial Accountant's (RIA) program and completed his courses at night while working full-time in the day.

At Emerson Electric, Richard established the standard cost of goods sold, coded all purchases to the appropriate account numbers, and calculated the cost of production. He was then promoted to cost accountant and office manager. In this capacity, Richard controlled the sales journal, the cash receipts journal, and the accounts receivable ledger. He also made sure that customers' accounts were collected. During this period, he reported directly to the general manager and indirectly to the controller at Head Office.

Richard was next promoted to plant accountant for one of the company's branch offices. In this position, he supervised the cost accountant and nine

clerks. He also prepared daily production and labour reports as well as monthly forecasts of sales and costs.

Richard currently works as general accountant, in charge of all accounting procedures and practices for his branch of Emerson Electric. He prepares all reports on earnings, profits, cash balances, and other financial concerns. He also develops general accounting practices to ensure accurate reporting.

Richard directs ten employees in the cost, payroll, and general accounting departments. He maintains control over all special journals and subsidiary ledgers. He approves all general journal entries and prepares the trial balance of the general ledger for use in his reports and financial statements. He also maintains a chart of accounts of the general ledger for all divisions.

As general accountant, Richard reviews and approves the weekly factory payroll, the biweekly salaried payroll, and the daily accounts payable cheques. In addition, he confirms the reconciliations of all bank accounts, makes sure that the correct sales tax is remitted to the government, and prepares the journal entries to record all NSF cheques.

One of Richard's responsibilities is to examine ways that the computer can be used by his department to make accounting procedures more efficient. He believes that the introduction of the computer will dramatically alter the nature of his job.

As general accountant, Richard will have to co-ordinate the changeover from manual to computerized accounting methods and redesign his department to take fullest advantage of the computer. He looks forward to meeting these challenges and considers this an exciting time to be an accountant.

Summary Exercise
Travel Trailers

Travel Trailers is a business owned and operated by Charles Fowler. The business earns its income for the selling and servicing of mobile homes and trailers. All sales and service transactions are subject to 5 percent sales tax.

Because of a special arrangement with an independent finance company, Travel Trailers is able to treat every trailer sale as a cash transaction. This is possible because the finance company pays Travel Trailers in full for any trailer sold. The finance company accepts the responsibility for collecting from the customer on an instalment basis including interest charges.

1. From the following combined chart of accounts and general ledger trial balance, set up the general ledger of Travel Trailers as of May 31, 19--. If you are using the workbook, the general ledger is set up for you.

TRAVEL TRAILERS
GENERAL LEDGER TRIAL BALANCE
MAY 31, 19--

Petty Cash	$ 50.00	
Bank	1 751.75	
Accounts Receivable	1 166.97	
Supplies	151.00	
Merchandise Inventory	25 423.32	
Equipment	8 472.94	
Delivery Truck	3 000.00	
Accounts Payable		$ 4 987.50
Bank Loan		20 000.00
Sales Tax Payable		817.40
C. Fowler, Capital		23 979.97
C. Fowler, Drawings	4 374.00	
Sales		49 423.51
Purchases	32 581.75	
Freight-in	174.72	
Bank Interest Expense	516.50	
Light and Heat Expense	4 350.40	
Miscellaneous Expense	94.72	
Rent Expense	1 000.00	
Telephone Expense	376.20	
Wages Expense	15 724.11	
	$99 208.38	$99 208.38

2. From the information shown below, set up the accounts receivable ledger of

Travel Trailers as of May 31, 19--. If you are using the workbook, the ledger is set up for you.

Customer	*Address*	*Invoice No.*	*Amount*
B. Fraser	15 Gay Street	634	$ 330.75
W. Hoyle	49 First Street	635	77.70
A. Newman	250 Fort Road	629	225.75
Schell Brothers	96 Garrison Avenue	633	204.75
N. Thompson	20 Wilson AVenue	630	315.00
L. Walker	4 Dennis Avenue	631	13.02
		Total	$1 166.97

3. From the following information, set up the accounts payable ledger of Travel Trailers as of May 31, 19--. If you are using the workbook, the ledger is set up for you.

Supplier	*Address*	*Invoice No.*	*Amount*
Double-G Industries	Manortown	420	$1 575.00
Maynard Cartage	49 Larry Lane		nil
Modern Mobile Homes	West City	2213	2 100.00
National Hardware	64 Venture Street	2309	787.50
Parker Manufacturing	10 Bergen Street		nil
Windsor Manufacturing	Windsor	404	525.00
			$4 987.50

4. Travel Trailers uses five journals in its accounting system as shown below.

Sales Journal *Page 19*

Date	Name							SalesTax Payable CR	Sales CR	Inv. No.	Acc's Rec'l DR

Purchases Journal *Page 74*

Date	Name	Other Accounts DR					Freight-in DR	Supplies DR	Pchs's DR		Accs Pay'l CR
		Account	PR	Amount							

Cash Receipts Journal *Page 37*

Date	Name	Other Accounts Cr				SalesTax Payable CR	Sales CR	Accs Rec'l CR	Bank DR		
		Account	PR	Amount							

Cash Payments Journal *Page 84*

Date	Name	Other Accounts DR			Wages DR	Drawing DR	Supplies DR	Pchs's DR	Accs Pay'l DR	Ch. #	Bank CR
		Account	PR	Amount							

General Journal *Page 5*

Date	Particulars	PR	Debit	Credit

Journalize the following transactions for June. Post to the subsidiary ledgers daily directly from source document data.

Transactions

June

1 *Sales Invoice*
— No. 636, to A. Newman, $190 plus 5 percent sales tax, for repairs to trailer.
Cheque Copy
— No. 755, issued to General Real Estate, $450 for the monthly rent.

2 *Sales Invoice*
— No. 637, to L. Walker, $300 plus 5 percent sales tax, for sale of trailer parts.
Cheque Copy
— No. 756, issued to Double-G Industries, $300, on account.

3 *Purchase Invoices*
— From Parker Manufacturing, No. 40, $136.50, for supplies.
— From Double-G Industries, No. 472, $551.20, for trailer parts.

4 *Cash Receipts*
— Received from W. Hoyle, $77.70, in payment of account.
— Received from Federated Finance Company, $9 135 cash, for sale of trailer, selling price $8 700, sales tax $435.
Bank Debit Advice
— From Central Bank, $120, for interest charged on bank loan.

5 *Cheque Copies*
— No. 757, issued to C. Fowler, $400, owner's personal use.
— No. 758, made out to Cash, $775 for the wages for the week.
Sales Invoice
— No. 638, to N. Thompson, $370 plus sales tax, for trailer repairs and parts.

8 *Cheque Copy*
— No. 759, to J. C. Pat Supply, $76.62, for cash purchase of supplies, $43.50, and miscellaneous expense, $33.12.
Non-routine Item
— Correction required. $12.50 item was charged incorrectly to Freight-in; it should be charged to Miscellaneous Expense.

9 *Cash Receipt*
— From A. Newman, $225.75, on account.
Purchase Invoices
— From Windsor Manufacturing, No. 452, $420, for trailer parts.
— Maynard's Cartage, No. 64; $67.50, for transportation on incoming merchandise.

10 *Bank Debit Advice*
— From Central Bank, $5 000, to reduce the bank loan.
Sales Invoice
— No. 639, to B. Fraser, $450 plus 5 percent sales tax for trailer parts.

Cash Receipt
— Received from Federated Finance Company, $15 225 cash, for sale of trailer, selling price $14 500, sales tax $725.
Credit Note Issued
— No. 27, to A. Newman, $131.25, goods returned, $125, tax, $6.25.
Cheque Copies
— No. 760, to Modern Mobile Homes, $1 000, on account.
— No. 761, to Double-G Industries, $500, on account.
Purchase Invoice
— From Windsor Manufacturing, No. 481, $4 803.75, for new trailer.

11 *Sales Invoice*
— No. 640, to Schell Brothers, $575 plus 5 percent sales tax, for trailer parts and service.
Cheque Copy
— No. 762, to C. Fowler, $400, owner's personal use.

12 *Cash Receipts*
— From Schell Brothers, $204.75, on account.
— From B. Fraser, $330.75, on account.
— From N. Thompson, $315, on account.
Cheque Copy
— No. 763, made out to Cash, $901, weekly wages.

15 *Cash Receipt*
— From Federated Finance Company, $8 505, cash for sale of trailer, selling price $8 100, sales tax $405.
Cheque Copies
— No. 764, to Provincial Government, $817.40, sales tax collected in May.
— No. 765, to Double-G Industries, $775, paying balance of invoice 420.
Purchase Invoice
— From Maynard's Cartage, No. 82, $142, for transportation on incoming merchandise.

16 *Purchase Invoices*
— From National Hardware, No. 2412, $92.50, for trailer parts.
— From Double-G Industries, No. 515, $7 680, for one new trailer.
— From Windsor Manufacturing Co., No. 499, $283.50, for trailer parts.

17 *Sales Invoice*
— No. 641, to W. Hoyle, $110 plus sales tax, for trailer service.
Cheque Copy
— No. 766, to Emerald Store, $40.50, for miscellaneous items.

18 *Cheque Copies*
— No. 767, to C. Fowler, $200, owner's personal use.
— No. 768, to National Hardware, $787.50, on account.
— No. 769, to Modern Mobile Homes, $1 100, on account.
Credit Note Received
— From Double-G Industries, No. 302, $1 050, price adjustment on invoice No. 515.

19 *Purchase Invoice*
— From National Hardware, No. 2480, $409.50, for trailer parts.
Cheque Copy
— No. 770, made out to Cash, $1 060 for the wages for the week.

22 *Sales Invoice*
— No. 642, to L. Walker, $290 plus sales tax of 5 percent, for trailer parts and service.
Purchase Invoice
— From Parker Manufacturing, No. 90, $58.80 for trailer parts.
Non-routine Transaction
— The owner collected $13.02 from L. Walker (for invoice No. 631) but he kept the money for his own use. (Debit his Drawings account.)

24 *Cash Receipt*
— Received from Federated Finance Company, $3 097.50 cash, for sale of trailer, selling price $2 950, sales tax $147.50.

25 *Cheque Copy*
— No. 771, to C. Fowler, $350, personal drawings.
Bank Debit Advice
— From Central Bank, $5 000, to reduce the bank loan.

26 *Sales Invoice*
— No. 643, to A. Newman, $236 plus sales tax, for trailer repairs.
Cheque Copies
— No. 772, to Windsor Manufacturing, $945.00, on account.
— No. 773, made out to Cash, $998, for the wages for the week.
— No. 774, made out to Petty Cash, $45.36, for petty cash expenditures: Miscellaneous Expense, $35.20; Freight-in, $10.16.
— No. 775, to City Hydro, $46.20, for the hydro for the month.
— No. 776, to Bell Telephone, $37.25, for the telephone bill for the month.

29 *Cash receipts*
— From B. Fraser, $472.50, on account.
— From Schell Brothers, $603.75, on account.
Purchase Invoices
— From Modern Mobile Homes, No. 2409, $3 050, for new trailer unit.
— From National Hardware, No. 2561, $93, for supplies.

30 *Sales Invoice*
— No. 644, to W. Hoyle, $230 plus sales tax, for trailer servicing.

5. **Balance the special journals.**
6. **Post the five journals to the general ledger.**
7. **Balance the general ledger as of June 30.**
8. **Balance the subsidiary ledgers as of June 30.**
9. **Prepare a six-column work sheet.** (The closing inventory is $27 062.)
10. **Prepare an income statement for a six-month fiscal period and a balance sheet.**
11. **Journalize and post the closing entries.**
12. **Take off a post-closing trial balance.**

16

Cash Register Accounting

16-1 Returns and Allowances
16-2 Cash Refunds
16-3 Cash Discounts
16-4 Cash Registers

Objectives

When you have completed Chapter 16, you should:

1. Understand the purpose of Returns and Allowances accounts for both purchases and sales.
2. Know the accounting entries for both sales returns and allowances and purchases returns and allowances.
3. Know how sales returns and allowances and purchases returns and allowances are presented on an income statement.
4. Understand the reason for giving cash refunds.
5. Know the accounting entries for cash refunds.
6. Know the most common terms of sale.
7. Understand the purpose of offering a cash discount.
8. Know the accounting entries for discounts earned and discounts allowed.
9. Know how discounts earned and discounts allowed are presented on the income statement.

10. Know the operating features of an intermediate level cash register.
11. Know how basic retail transactions are handled using the cash register.
12. Understand the nature of and uses for the detailed cash register audit tape.
13. Know the end-of-day procedure required of a cash register operator.
14. Know the accounting entries for the cash register daily summaries.
15. Understand the concept of cash short or over.

16.1 Returns and Allowances

Chapter 14 included a section on credit invoices. As we saw, credit invoices are issued to make an adjustment or a correction in a customer's account. Credit invoices are necessary when (1) goods are returned as unsatisfactory, (2) an allowance is made on goods, or (3) an error on a sales invoice is corrected.

In Chapter 14, the accounting entries for returns and allowances were the same as those for the original sales. The original entries were simply reversed. This is a common accounting practice.

However, some businesses, such as large department stores, require additional information in respect to returns, allowances, or refunds. They want to know what proportion of the merchandise sold is returned to them. They learn this information by keeping a separate account for sales returns and allowances.

Sales Returns and Allowances Account

Consider the following transactions:

Transaction 1 Simplex Company sells $50 of goods to A. Moss. An invoice is issued for the sale on November 12, 19--. Sales tax is at 5 percent.

The journal entry for the transaction in the Sales Journal of Simplex Company is as follows:

Accounts Receivable (A. Moss)	52.50	
Sales		50.00
Sales Tax Payable		2.50

The effect in the accounts is as follows:

Accs Recl (A. Moss)		Sales Tax Payable		Sales	
52.50			2.50		50.00

Transaction 2 Because a portion of the goods sold to A. Moss is defective and returned, Simplex Company issues a credit invoice for $18 plus tax on November 18, 19--.

Simplex Company, which uses a **Sales Returns and Allowances account,** records the following entry in the Sales Journal for this transaction:

Sales Returns and Allowances	18.00	
Sales Tax Payable	.90	
Accounts Receivable (A. Moss)		18.90

The cumulative effect in the accounts is as follows:

Accs Recl (A. Moss)		Sales Tax Payable		Sales Returns & Allowances		Sales	
52.50			2.50				50.00
	18.90	.90		18.00			

The account for Sales Returns and Allowances, together with the Sales Account, show the true sales figure, called **net sales**. In this case, the net sales figure is $32.

Observe that, because Simplex Company accumulates returns and allowances separately, there may be a special column provided for a Sales Returns and Allowances account in the sales journal. The Sales Returns and Allowances column is a debit column because entries to the Sales Returns and Allowances account are normally debits.

Purchases Returns and Allowances Account

There are certain businesses that consider it necessary to know the total amount of returns and allowances for merchandise purchased. They want to know what proportion of the merchandise purchased by them is returned to their suppliers. They obtain this information by using a separate account in which to accumulate purchases returns and allowances.

The **Purchases Returns and Allowances account** includes only items of merchandise inventory. It does not include items such as supplies or expense items such as truck parts. These latter items are handled by means of a direct credit to the account involved.

Consider the following transactions:

Transaction 1 On June 12, 19--, Baytown Drug Market receives a shipment of drugs and the sales invoice for them from Drug Wholesale Company. The total of the invoice is $147.

The following journal entry for the transaction appears in the purchases journal of Baytown Drug Market:

Purchases	147.00	
Accounts Payable		
(Drug Wholesale Company)		147.00

The effect in the accounts is as follows:

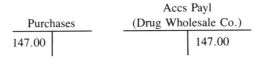

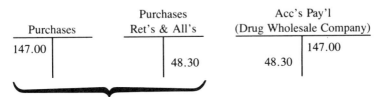

Purchases		Accs Payl (Drug Wholesale Co.)	
147.00			147.00

Transaction 2 On June 14, Baytown Drug Market notices that a number of the packages received from Drug Wholesale Company are damaged. The damaged goods are returned for credit and a credit note for $48.30 is received on June 16. Baytown Drug Market uses a Purchases Returns and Allowances account.

The following journal entry for the transaction appears in the purchases journal:

Accounts Payable (Drug Whols)	48.30	
Purchases Returns and Allowances		48.30

The cumulative effect in the accounts is as follows:

Purchases		Purchases Ret's & All's		Acc's Pay'l (Drug Wholesale Company)	
147.00					147.00
			48.30	48.30	

The account for Purchases Returns and Allowances together with the account for Purchases shows the true purchases figure, called **net purchases**. In this case, the net purchases figure is $98.70.

Returns and Allowances on the Income Statement

Both Sales Returns and Allowances and Purchases Returns and Allowances appear on the income statement. They are treated as deductions from Sales and Purchases, respectively. Their inclusion on the statement requires a slightly different presentation as shown on the partial income statement in Figure 16.1.

Mallon Company Income Statement Year Ended December 31, 19–			
Revenue			
Sales		92,657.20	
Less Sales Ret's and Allow's		3,763.50	
Net Sales		88,893.70	
Cost of Goods Sold			
Mdse. Invent. Jan. 1		31,652.30	
Purchases	46,307.12		
Less Purch. Ret's and Allow's	4,964.16		
Net Purchases		41,342.96	
Freight-in		2,617.17	
Cost of Goods Avail. for Sale		75,612.43	
Deduct Mdse. Invent. Dec. 31		27,406.90	
Cost of Goods Sold			48,215.53
Gross Profit			40,678.17

Figure 16.1 Returns and allowances on the income statement.

16.2 Cash Refunds

The cash sale is a very common business transaction. But dissatisfaction can occur with cash sales as well as with sales on account. When customers pay cash for goods and later find them unsatisfactory, they usually demand and get their money back — in other words, they obtain a **cash refund**. The accounting for cash refunds takes place as follows:

Transaction 1: On May 16, 19––, Star Supply makes a cash purchase of a new battery from Cut-Rate Auto Parts. The cost of the battery is $25 plus sales tax of 5 percent. A cheque is issued by Star Supply to pay for the goods. A cash sales slip is made out by Cut-Rate Auto Parts.

BOOKS OF BUYER (Star Supply)
Journal entry (in cash payments journal) is as follows:

Truck Expense	26.25	
Bank		26.25

The effect in the account is as follows:

TRUCK EXPENSE	
26.25	

BANK	
	26.25

BOOKS OF SELLER (Cut-Rate Auto)
Journal entry (in cash receipts journal) is as follows:

Bank	26.25	
Sales		25.00
Sales Tax Payable		1.25

The effect in the accounts is as follows:

BANK	
26.25	

SALES	
	25.00

SALES TAX PAYABLE	
	1.25

Transaction 2 On May 18, 19—, at the time the battery is being installed, the mechanic finds that it is cracked. It is, therefore, returned to Cut-Rate Auto Parts and a refund cheque for the full amount is obtained. The refund cheque is included in the day's cash receipts of Star Supply. A cash sales slip with 'Refund' prominently marked on it is issued by Cut-Rate Auto Supplies.

BOOKS OF BUYER (Star Supply)
Journal entry is as follows:

Bank	26.25	
Truck Expense		26.25

The cumulative effect in the accounts is as follows:

TRUCK EXPENSE	
26.25	26.25

BANK	
	26.25
26.25	

BOOKS OF SELLER (Cut-Rate Auto)
Journal entry is as follows:

Sales	25.00	
Sales Tax Payable	1.25	
Bank		26.25

The cumulative effect in the accounts is as follows:

BANK	
26.25	
	26.25

SALES	
	25.00
25.00	

SALES TAX PAYABLE	
	1.25
1.25	

As an alternative, some businesses debit the Sales Returns and Allowances account.

'No Cash Refunds' Policy

Rather than give a refund to a cash customer, many businesses prefer to issue a credit note. The issuing of a credit note sets up an account for the customer in which there is a credit balance. The customer is thus encouraged to make purchases from the business which are to be paid for out of the credit balance. This practice discourages the customer from spending the refund at another place of business.

16.3 Cash Discounts

Perhaps you are already acquainted with cash discounts. They are usually offered on the bills for utilities in the home, that is, the water, hydro, gas, or oil bills.

A **cash discount** is a reduction that may be taken off the amount of a bill if payment is made on or before the discount date stated on the bill. The purpose of a cash discount is to encourage the customer to pay promptly. Many businesses, as well as municipalities, offer cash discounts to their customers.

Terms of Sale

Every seller of goods or services makes certain arrangements with customers as to when the goods or services are to be paid for and whether a cash discount is to be offered. These arrangements are commonly known as the **terms of sale**.

Any terms of sale may be agreed upon by seller and buyer. Most often, however, the terms are standard ones such as those listed below.

Standard Terms of Sale

1. **C.O.D.** Cash on Delivery. The goods must be paid for at the time they are delivered.
2. **On Account** or **Charge**. The full amount of the invoice is due at the time the invoice is received but a brief time, usually 25 days, is given to make payment.
3. **30 Days** or **Net 30**. The full amount of the invoice is due 30 days after the date of the invoice.

   60 Days or **Net 60**. The full amount of the invoice is due 60 days after the date of the invoice.
4. **2/10,n/30**. This is read as '2 percent, 10; net, 30'. If the bill is paid within 10 days from the invoice date, a cash discount of 2 percent may be taken. Otherwise, the full amount of the invoice is due 30 days after the invoice date.

   Any variation of the above is possible. Another example is **1/15,n/60**. If the bill is paid within 15 days from the invoice date, a cash discount of 1 percent may be taken. Otherwise, the full amount of the invoice is due 60 days after the invoice date.

The terms of sale often depend on the customer's reputation for reliability in paying. A reliable customer of long standing will probably be granted very favourable terms. A new customer, about whom little is known, will probably be required to pay cash on delivery, at least for a short time.

The terms of every sale are recorded on the sales invoice (see Figure 16.2). Therefore, every time a sale is made and an invoice sent out, the customer is reminded of the arrangements for making payment.

Once the terms of sale for a particular customer have been decided on, they will likely remain unchanged for some time. Therefore, the customer's usual terms are often recorded on his account card for easy reference. This provides very helpful information to the credit manager, who is responsible for collecting the debts.

Accounting for Cash Discounts

Accounting for a cash discount begins at the time a credit sale is made to a customer and an invoice offering a cash discount is issued. Examine the invoice shown in Figure 16.2.

ECHO BAY
VANCOUVER, B.C.

P.O. Box 298
Station 8
V7C 8P7
Phone
842-9999

MASTHEAD MARINE

SOLD TO Nanaimo Marina
5000 Departure Bay Road
Nanaimo, B.C.
V9T 4B9

DATE June 4, 19--
TERMS 2/10,n/30

QUANTITY	PART NO	DESCRIPTION	PRICE	AMOUNT
12	HA 346	Tubular Jam Cleat $\frac{1}{2}$ in	$ 3.85	$ 46.20
6	HA 433	Mast Gate Muscle Box	35.95	215.70
12	HA 4872	Shroud Adjuster	12.50	150.00
		Total		$411.90

SALES INVOICE CUSTOMER'S COPY NO. 10094

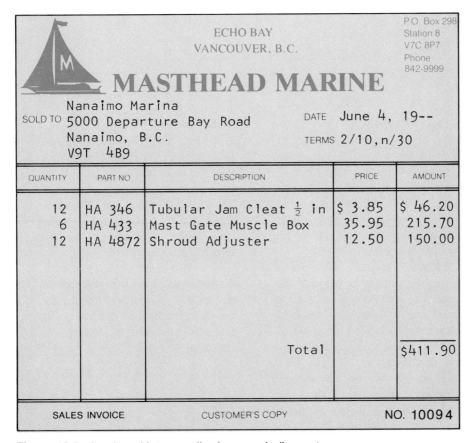

Figure 16.2 Invoice with terms allowing a cash discount.

IN THE BOOKS OF NANAIMO MARINA
(The Buyer)

The invoice, when received by Nanaimo Marina, is regarded as a purchase invoice. The following accounting entry is recorded from it in the purchase journal.

Purchases	411.90	
Accounts Payable (Masthead Marine)		411.90

In the T-accounts, the effect is as follows:

Purchases		Accounts Payable (Masthead Marine)	
411.90			411.90

IN THE BOOKS OF MASTHEAD MARINE
(The Seller)

From the data on the sales invoice copy, Masthead Marine makes the following accounting entry in the sales journal.

Accounts Receivable (Nanaimo Marina)	411.90	
Sales		411.90

In the T-accounts, the effect is as follows:

Accounts Receivable (Nanaimo Marina)		Sales	
411.90			411.90

IN THE OFFICE OF THE BUYER

Someone in the accounting department of the buyer must have the responsibility for checking each purchase invoice to see if a discount is offered. Where discounts are offered, special treatment is necessary to ensure that payment is made within the discount period.

Assume, in this case, that a cheque to pay the invoice is prepared immediately. However, the cheque is dated June 14 (ten days after the invoice date), and is held in the office for release one day before the date on the cheque. The cheque is made out for $403.66. This amount is arrived at by deducting the 2 percent discount ($8.24) from the amount of the invoice ($411.90). The tear-off portion of the cheque shows that the cheque is in payment of invoice No. 10094, and that a discount of $8.24 has been deducted.

IN THE OFFICE OF THE SELLER

Upon receiving Nanaimo's cheque in the office, Masthead Marine lists the cheque on the Daily List of Cash Receipts form, the source document for the transaction. This listing is forwarded first to the accounts receivable clerk for posting to the customers' accounts in the subsidiary ledger. This clerk verifies any cash discounts that have been taken, and ensures that full details of the transaction are recorded on the listing. In this particular case, the listing will appear as follows:

Customer:	Nanaimo Marina
Amount Rec'd:	$403.66
Cash Discount:	8.24
Gross Amount:	411.90

Notice that, for cash receipts where there is a cash discount, the gross amount ($411.90 in this case) is credited to the customer's account.

IN THE BOOKS OF NANAIMO MARINA
(The Buyer)

From the cheque copy, the following accounting entry is made in the cash payments journal.

Accounts Payable		
(Masthead Marine)	411.90	
Discounts Earned		8.24
Bank		403.66

This entry has the following effects in the accounts:

1. Bank is decreased by the amount of the cheque issued ($403.66).
2. The debt to Masthead Marine is eliminated in full for invoice No. 10094.
3. The earning of a discount of $8.24 is recorded.

In the T-accounts, the cumulative effect of the two transactions is as follows:

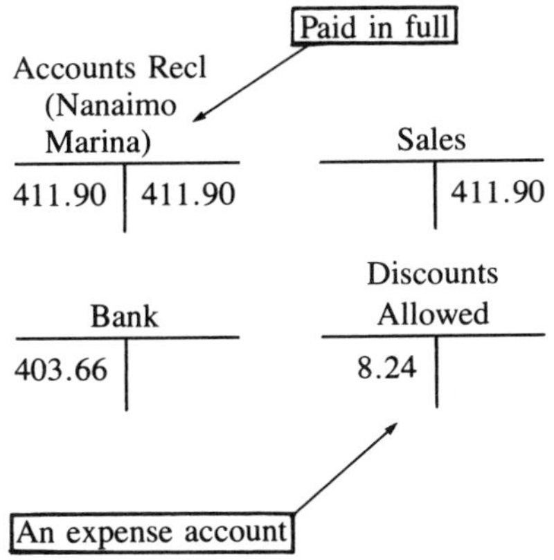

IN THE BOOKS OF MASTHEAD MARINE
(The Seller)

From the Daily List of Cash Receipts, the following accounting entry is made in the cash receipts journal.

Bank	403.66	
Discount Allowed	8.24	
Accounts Receivable		
(Nanaimo Marina)		411.90

This entry has the following effects in the accounts:

1. Bank is increased by the amount of the cheque received ($403.66).
2. The debt of Nanaimo Marina is eliminated in full for invoice No. 10094.
3. The giving of a discount of $8.24 is recorded.

In the T-accounts, the cumulative effect of the two transactions is as follows:

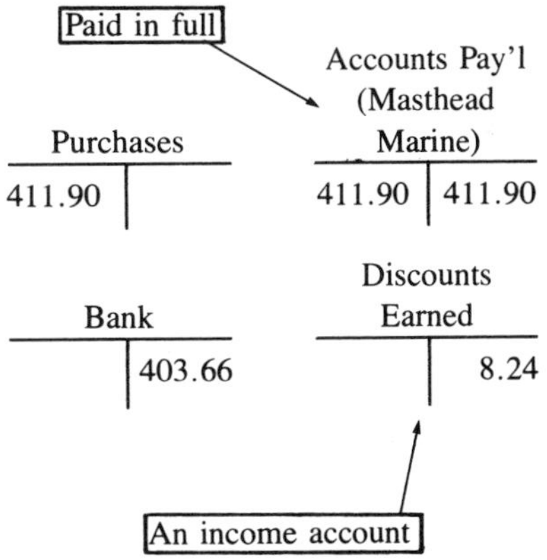

Additional Cash Discount Facts

1. Occasionally, a customer takes a late discount. In other words, the customer takes the discount after the discount period has expired.

   Business people try to be reasonable when faced with this situation. There may have been postal tie-ups or other legitimate delays. No business wants a reputation for being cheap. At the same time, however, a business does not want customers to take advantage of it.

If a business decides to disallow a late discount, the usual practice is to cash the customer's deficient cheque and write a polite letter requesting that the customer make up the deficiency in the payment.

2. The Discounts Earned account is often referred to as the Discount off Purchases account. The Discounts Allowed account is often referred to as the Discount off Sales account.
3. Every business will try to take advantage of cash discounts offered by its suppliers. Therefore, entries to the Discounts Earned account can be expected to occur frequently. These entries will normally require a special column in the cash payments journal of every business.

Only businesses that offer cash discounts to customers need a Discounts

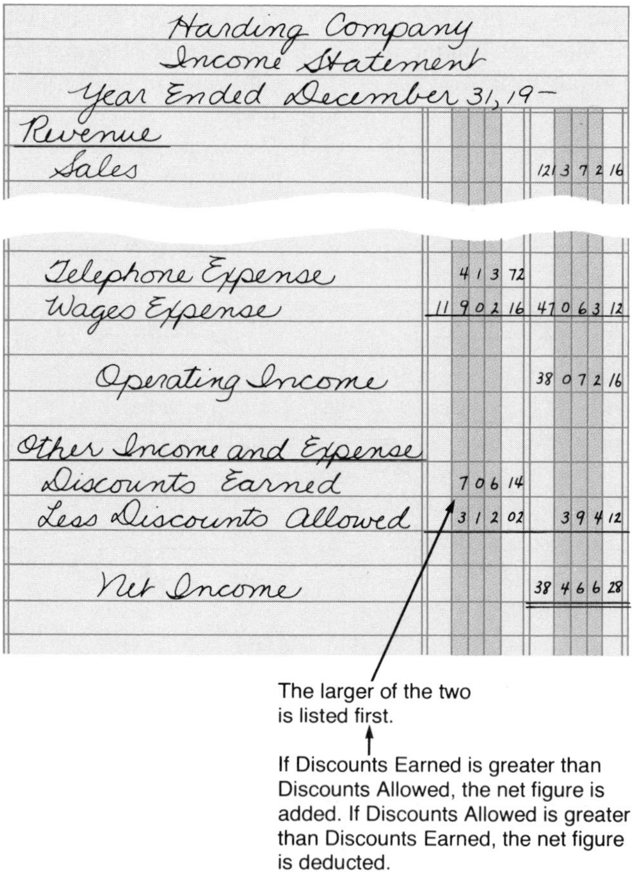

Harding Company
Income Statement
Year Ended December 31, 19–

Revenue		
Sales		121 372 16
…		
Telephone Expense	413 72	
Wages Expense	11 902 16	47 063 12
Operating Income		38 072 16
Other Income and Expense		
Discounts Earned	706 14	
Less Discounts Allowed	312 02	394 12
Net Income		38 466 28

The larger of the two is listed first.
If Discounts Earned is greater than Discounts Allowed, the net figure is added. If Discounts Allowed is greater than Discounts Earned, the net figure is deducted.

Figure 16.3 Presenting cash discounts on the income statement.

Allowed account. These businesses will need a special column for Discounts Allowed in the cash receipts journal.

4. Occasionally an invoice is received on which there is a cash discount, and some time before the discount date a portion of the goods is returned or an allowance obtained. In this case, the discount may be taken only on the net cost of the goods. The net cost is found by deducting the amount of the credit note from the amount of the sales invoice.

   When this happens, the purchaser should make certain of the discount date by discussing it with the vendor. Because of the circumstances, the discount date will probably be moved ahead, perhaps to the date of the credit note.

Cash Discounts on the Income Statement

Figure 16.3 shows a common method of presenting cash discounts on the income statement. Observe that the net discounts are either added to, or deducted from, the Operating Income figure. (Operating Income shows the net income remaining after the operating expenses are deducted.)

16.4 Cash Registers

Over the past few years, giant advances in electronics and micro-circuitry have revolutionized the business-data-processing industry. The new cash registers are just one example of machines that now possess capabilities undreamt of twenty years ago. In many businesses today, the cash register provides management with up-to-the-minute information essential for success in a highly competitive business world.

The most advanced cash registers serve as terminals, in direct two-way communication with a computer. They perform important services for the convenience of the customer and provide a cost benefit for the owner. Cash registers today can tell instantly if an item is in stock. They can update the inventory after each transaction. They can check out a customer's credit standing and update the customer's account. These advanced cash registers are fast becoming indispensable. Businesses that fail to use them may find themselves at a severe competitive disadvantage.

Stand-alone electronic cash registers are unconnected to a central information system. Even these have capabilities not known only a few years ago. Today, the operator doesn't have to make any mental or manual calculations. Price, sales tax, discount, and change computations are all done automatically. Electronic cash registers offer greater speed and accuracy, and more usable information, for the benefit of both customer and retailer.

A typical stand-alone electronic cash register is illustrated in Figure 16.4.

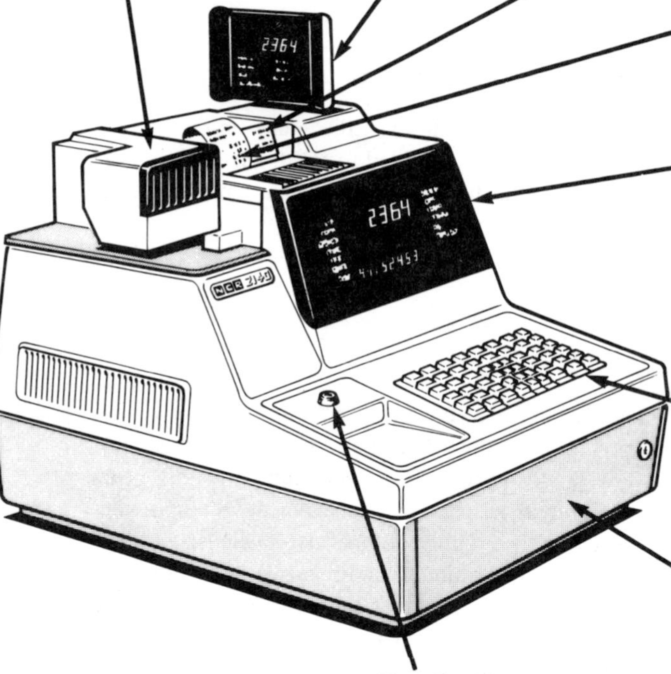
Document Printer
A device that prints the details of any transaction on the bill of sale or other document. Money received, money paid out, gift certificates, and so on are validated when the transaction details are printed on them by the company's own cash register. Also, the device can be set up to refuse to record a transaction unless a document is inserted in the opening of the slip printer.
Swivel Display Window
A window in which the details of the transactions are displayed for the customer. The customer acts as an auditor of the transaction, making sure that the operator records amounts correctly.
Detailed Audit Tape
A continuous paper-tape record of every entry in the order of occurrence. The machine assigns a reference number for each transaction which is printed on all related documents. This makes it easier to check back on any particular transaction.
Customer's Take-Home Receipt
A detailed machine-printed paper record of the transaction for the customer.
Operator's Display and Prompting Window
A display window that (1) provides a readout of the transaction details so that the operator may visually check them and (2) tells the operator what function has to be performed next on the machine.
Keyboard
The keys used by the operator to enter the transaction details, and to cause the data to be permanently recorded.
Cash Drawer
A sectioned drawer that provides a safe and convenient place for the cash.
Four-Position Control Lock
A locking device that controls different machine functions. The daily totals cannot be accessed except with a special key which is under the control of a supervisory person.
NCR 2140
ELECTRONIC CASH REGISTER

Figure 16.4 A typical stand-alone electronic cash register. Courtesy National Cash Register of Canada Limited.

Some Additional Cash Register Features

Basic Features

1. *Security.* The audit strip provides a continuous record of all transactions. This strip is locked inside the machine and is accessible only to supervisory personnel in possession of a special control key and identification number. The operator is prevented from tampering with the internal tape.
2. *Control.* A number of registers and activity counters provide totals in several categories, such as total cash sales, total charge sales, and total payments received on account. The operator is made to account for cash and supporting documents that agree with the machine-produced totals.
3. *Summaries.* Within two minutes of store closing, a number of detailed summaries can be made available to supervisors to assist them in their management function. These include summaries of sales by each clerk, sales by product, sales by department, and a complete breakdown of the day's cash register activity.

Advanced Features

1. *Coin Dispenser.* A device added to the machine will automatically present customers with the coin portion of their change.
2. *Updating Records.* Certain files, such as those for inventory and accounts receivable, can be stored in electronic memory and be updated after every transaction. Also, a card file for each account receivable can be kept close to the cash register and updated by the slip printer as each transaction is processed.
3. *Optical Character Recognition.* Data can be encoded on a label or a card using specially shaped numbers or bars. Data in this form can be scanned by a device and processed as if it had been entered on the keyboard. This feature is known as **optical character recognition**.

   Data are entered in this way more accurately and quickly because the operator does not have to read it or key it in. Prices can be recalled automatically from electronic memory. The entire process of reading, calculating, and transmitting data can be instantly completed.

Using the Cash Register

The cash register is a versatile piece of equipment. It can help process different types of transaction. It is most commonly used for the cash sale, but it can also be used for charge sales, amounts received from customers, refunds, issuing of credit notes, and paying of expenses.

This book is not going to teach you the detailed operation of a cash register. That information can be obtained from a manufacturer or can be learned on the job. In this section, you will, however, learn the basic techniques for processing transactions in a business that uses a cash register. You must learn how to account for cash register summaries.

The following transactions take place in a clothing store for women. A sales person assists the customer until the bill of sale is completed. The customer is then sent to the cash register where another salesperson finalizes the transaction.

Change Fund (Float)

The **change fund** is a small quantity of money, usually about forty or fifty dollars, in small bills and coins, which is used to make change for customers. At the beginning of each business day, this change fund, or float, is placed in the cash drawer of the cash register. At the close of business, some small bills and coins are taken from the cash register drawer to make the change fund for the next day. This money is stored in a safe place overnight.

Cash Sale

The cash sale is the simplest and most common type of transaction. For a cash sale, the following sequence of operations takes place:

1. The clerk depresses an identifying number on the keyboard.
2. The transaction type (cash, in this case) is entered through the keyboard.
3. A description of the merchandise is entered through the keyboard.
4. The price is entered through the keyboard.
5. The 'total' key is pressed. The machine then calculates the tax, adds the tax to the price of the merchandise, and displays the total in the display window.
6. The method of payment (cash, cheque, Visa, etc.) and the amount of money tendered is entered through the keyboard. The amount of the customer's change is calculated and displayed, the sales receipt is presented, and the cash drawer opens.
7. The money from the customer is put in the cash drawer and change is given.
8. The cash drawer is closed. The machine will not accept another transaction until the drawer is closed.

Charge Sale

The charge sale has to be recorded both through the cash register and on a sales slip similar to the one in Figure 16.5. The sales slip is made out in duplicate. The original is the source document for the debit entry to the customer's account and the copy is for the customer.

The following procedure for a charge sale may vary slightly from store to store:

1. A duplicate sales slip is prepared by the sales clerk.
2. The cashier's code number is entered into the keyboard.
3. The duplicate sales slip is placed in the document printer device.
4. The 'charge' function key is pressed to tell the machine the type of transaction.
5. The details of the transaction are entered through the keyboard.
6. The 'total' key is pressed to complete the transaction.
7. The customer is given the copy of the duplicate sales slip.
8. The original of the duplicate sales slip is placed in the cash drawer to be used later when posting to the customer's account. Note that no money is received as part of this particular transaction.

Receipt on Account

The procedure for recording a receipt on account is approximately as follows:

1. A duplicate sales slip, such as the one in Figure 16.6, is prepared by the sales clerk.
2. The cashier's code number is entered into the keyboard.
3. The duplicate sales slip is placed in the document printer device.
4. The 'received on account' function key is pressed to tell the machine the type of transaction.
5. The details of the transaction are entered through the keyboard.
6. The 'total' key is pressed to complete the transaction.
7. The money received from the customer is placed in the cash drawer.
8. The copy of the duplicate sales slip is given to the customer.
9. The original of the duplicate is placed in the cash drawer, to be used later in posting to the customer's account.

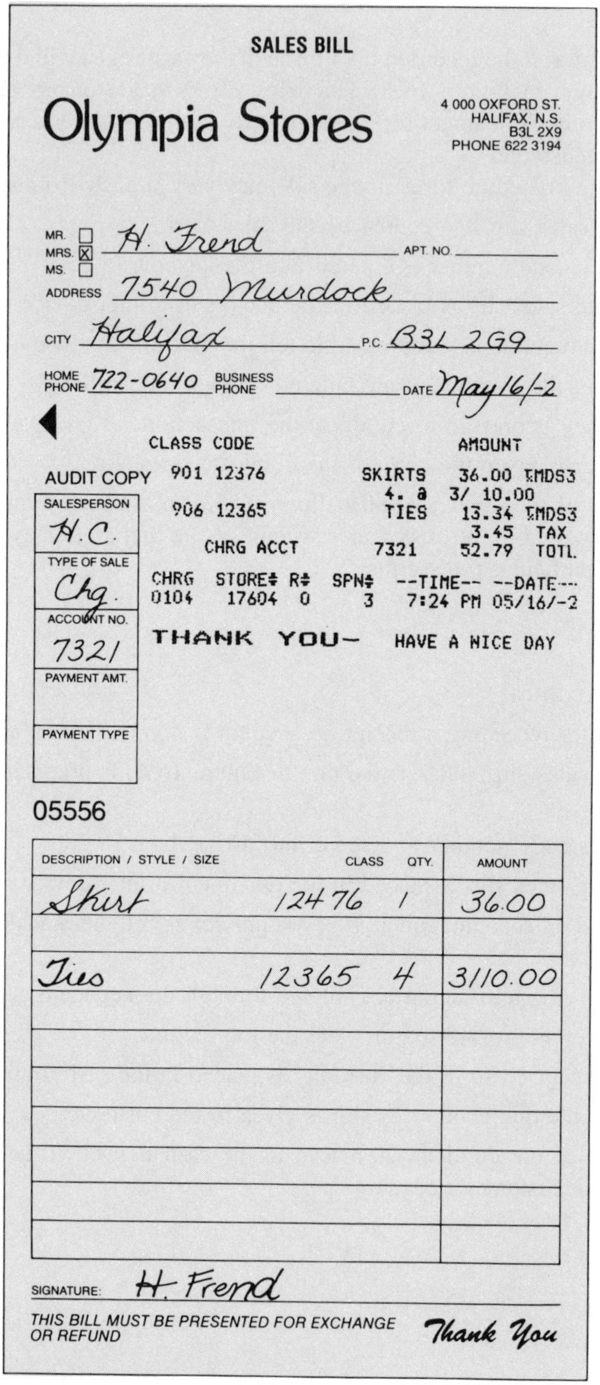
SALES BILL

Olympia Stores

4 000 OXFORD ST.
HALIFAX, N.S.
B3L 2X9
PHONE 622 3194

MR. ☐ MRS. ☒ MS. ☐ H. Frend APT. NO.

ADDRESS 7540 Murdock

CITY Halifax P.C. B3L 2G9

HOME PHONE 722-0640 BUSINESS PHONE DATE May 16/-2

CLASS CODE AMOUNT

AUDIT COPY 901 12376 SKIRTS 36.00 TMDS3
4. @ 3/ 10.00
906 12365 TIES 13.34 TMDS3
3.45 TAX
CHRG ACCT 7321 52.79 TOTL

CHRG STORE# R# SPN# --TIME-- --DATE--
0104 17604 0 3 7:24 PM 05/16/-2

THANK YOU— HAVE A NICE DAY

SALESPERSON H.C.
TYPE OF SALE Chg.
ACCOUNT NO. 7321
PAYMENT AMT.
PAYMENT TYPE

05556

DESCRIPTION / STYLE / SIZE	CLASS	QTY.	AMOUNT
Skirt	12476	1	36.00
Ties	12365	4	3/10.00

SIGNATURE: H. Frend

THIS BILL MUST BE PRESENTED FOR EXCHANGE OR REFUND

Thank You

Figure 16.5 A sales slip showing a charge sale.

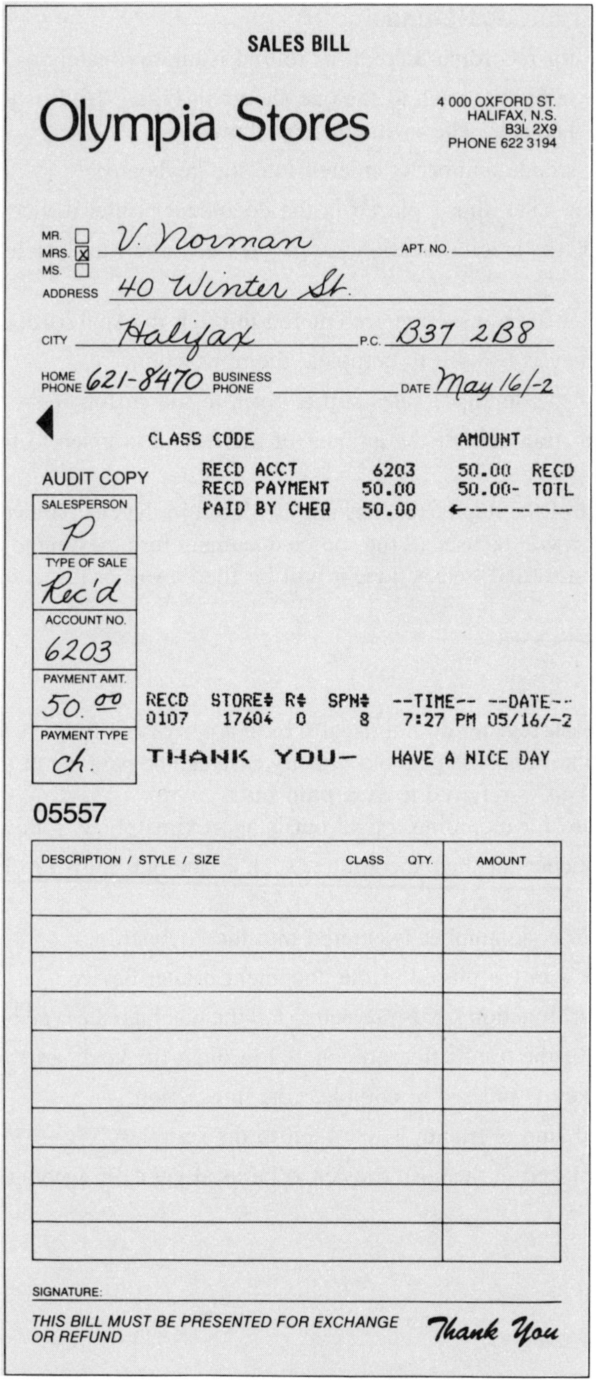

SALES BILL

Olympia Stores

4 000 OXFORD ST.
HALIFAX, N.S.
B3L 2X9
PHONE 622 3194

MR. ☐ MRS. ☒ MS. ☐ V. Norman APT. NO.

ADDRESS 40 Winter St.

CITY Halifax P.C. B37 2B8

HOME PHONE 621-8470 BUSINESS PHONE DATE May 16/-2

CLASS CODE AMOUNT

AUDIT COPY

RECD ACCT 6203 50.00 RECD
RECD PAYMENT 50.00 50.00- TOTL
PAID BY CHEQ 50.00 ←------

SALESPERSON P

TYPE OF SALE Rec'd

ACCOUNT NO. 6203

PAYMENT AMT. 50.00

RECD STORE# R# SPN# --TIME-- --DATE--
0107 17604 0 8 7:27 PM 05/16/-2

PAYMENT TYPE ch.

THANK YOU— HAVE A NICE DAY

05557

DESCRIPTION / STYLE / SIZE	CLASS	QTY.	AMOUNT

SIGNATURE:

THIS BILL MUST BE PRESENTED FOR EXCHANGE OR REFUND

Thank You

Figure 16.6 A sales slip used to record a receipt on account.

Return for Credit or Refund

The procedure for recording a credit or refund is approximately as follows:

1. A duplicate sales slip, such as the one shown in Figure 16.7, is prepared by the sales clerk. The sales slip is stamped as shown.
2. The cashier's code number is entered into the keyboard.
3. The duplicate sales slip is placed in the document printer device.
4. The 'refund' or 'credit' function key is pressed to tell the machine the type of transaction.
5. The details of the transaction are entered through the keyboard.
6. The 'total' key is pressed to complete the transaction.
7. The copy of the duplicate sales slip is given to the customer.
8. In a 'refund' transaction, the amount of the refund is given to the customer in cash.
9. The original of the duplicate sales slip is placed in the cash drawer. In a 'credit' transaction, it will be used as the source document for a posting to the customer's account. In a refund transaction, it will be filed away or discarded.

Paid Out

Stores with a cash register do not usually have a petty cash fund. A small expenditure that would normally be paid out of petty cash can be paid out of the funds in the cash register. This is referred to as **a paid out**.

The procedure for recording a paid out is approximately as follows:

1. A bill or voucher for the expenditure, such as the one shown in Figure 16.8, is obtained.
2. The cashier's code number is entered into the keyboard.
3. The supplier's bill is placed in the document printer device.
4. The 'paid out' function key is pressed to tell the machine the type of transaction.
5. The details of the transaction are entered through the keyboard.
6. The 'total' key is pressed to complete the transaction.
7. The required sum of money is paid out to the supplier.
8. The bill is placed in the cash drawer to be used later for accounting purposes.

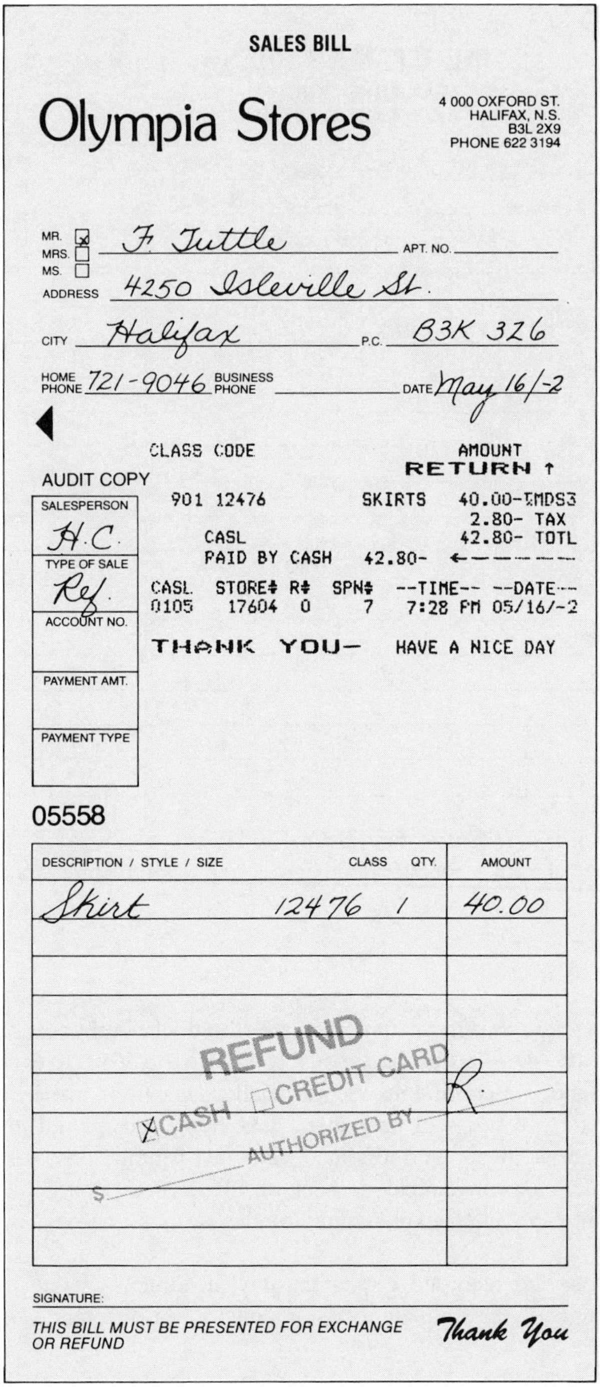

SALES BILL

Olympia Stores

4 000 OXFORD ST.
HALIFAX, N.S.
B3L 2X9
PHONE 622 3194

MR. ☒ MRS. ☐ MS. ☐ F. Tuttle APT. NO.

ADDRESS 4250 Isleville St.

CITY Halifax P.C. B3K 3Z6

HOME PHONE 721-9046 BUSINESS PHONE DATE May 16/-2

AUDIT COPY

SALESPERSON H.C.

TYPE OF SALE Ref.

ACCOUNT NO.

PAYMENT AMT.

PAYMENT TYPE

CLASS CODE AMOUNT
RETURN ↑
901 12476 SKIRTS 40.00-TMDS3
2.80- TAX
CASL 42.80- TOTL
PAID BY CASH 42.80- ←
CASL STORE# R# SPN# --TIME-- --DATE--
0105 17604 0 7 7:28 PM 05/16/-2
THANK YOU— HAVE A NICE DAY

05558

DESCRIPTION / STYLE / SIZE	CLASS	QTY.	AMOUNT
Skirt	12476	1	40.00

REFUND
☒ CASH ☐ CREDIT CARD
AUTHORIZED BY R.
$

SIGNATURE:

THIS BILL MUST BE PRESENTED FOR EXCHANGE OR REFUND

Thank You

Figure 16.7 A sales slip used to record a return for refund.

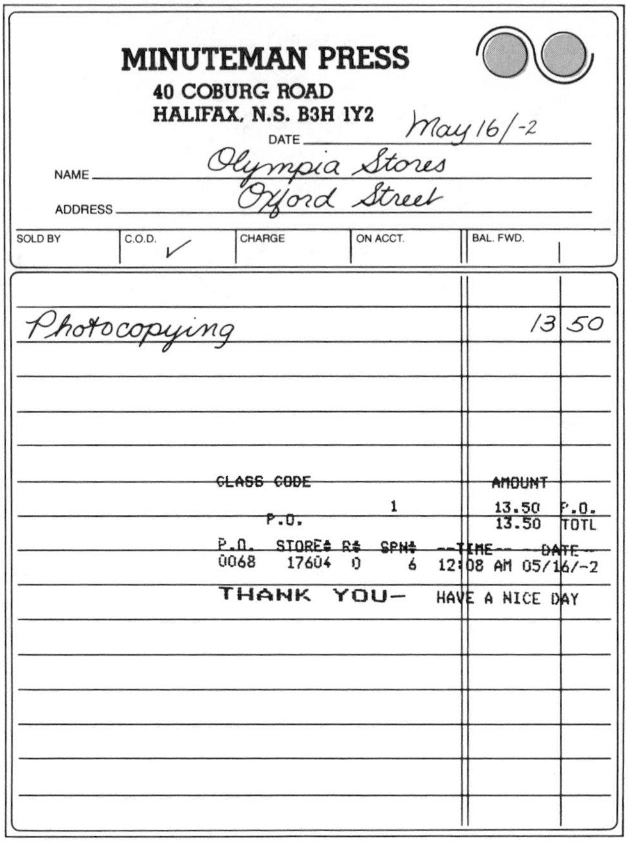

MINUTEMAN PRESS
40 COBURG ROAD
HALIFAX, N.S. B3H 1Y2

DATE May 16/-2

NAME Olympia Stores

ADDRESS Oxford Street

SOLD BY	C.O.D.	CHARGE	ON ACCT.	BAL. FWD.
	✓			

Photocopying	13	50

CLASS CODE AMOUNT
1 13.50 P.O.
P.O. 13.50 TOTL
P.O. STORE# R# SPN# --TIME-- --DATE--
0068 17604 0 6 12:08 AM 05/16/-2
THANK YOU— HAVE A NICE DAY

Figure 16.8 A bill from a supplier used to record a cash payment for a service.

Detailed Audit Tape

As transactions occur during the day, they are stored within the machine on a paper tape known as the **detailed audit tape**, the 'audit strip', or the 'audit trail'. The detailed audit tape is a continuous record of all transactions made during the day, and is equivalent to a series of customers' take-home receipts all joined together. Each transaction is given an individual reference number by the machine, in consecutive order, for convenience in back-checking on any particular transaction. A detailed audit tape, with explanations of the various codings, is illustrated in Figure 16.9.

As transactions are recorded during the day, a number of registers within the machine electronically accumulate totals in a number of different categories. These

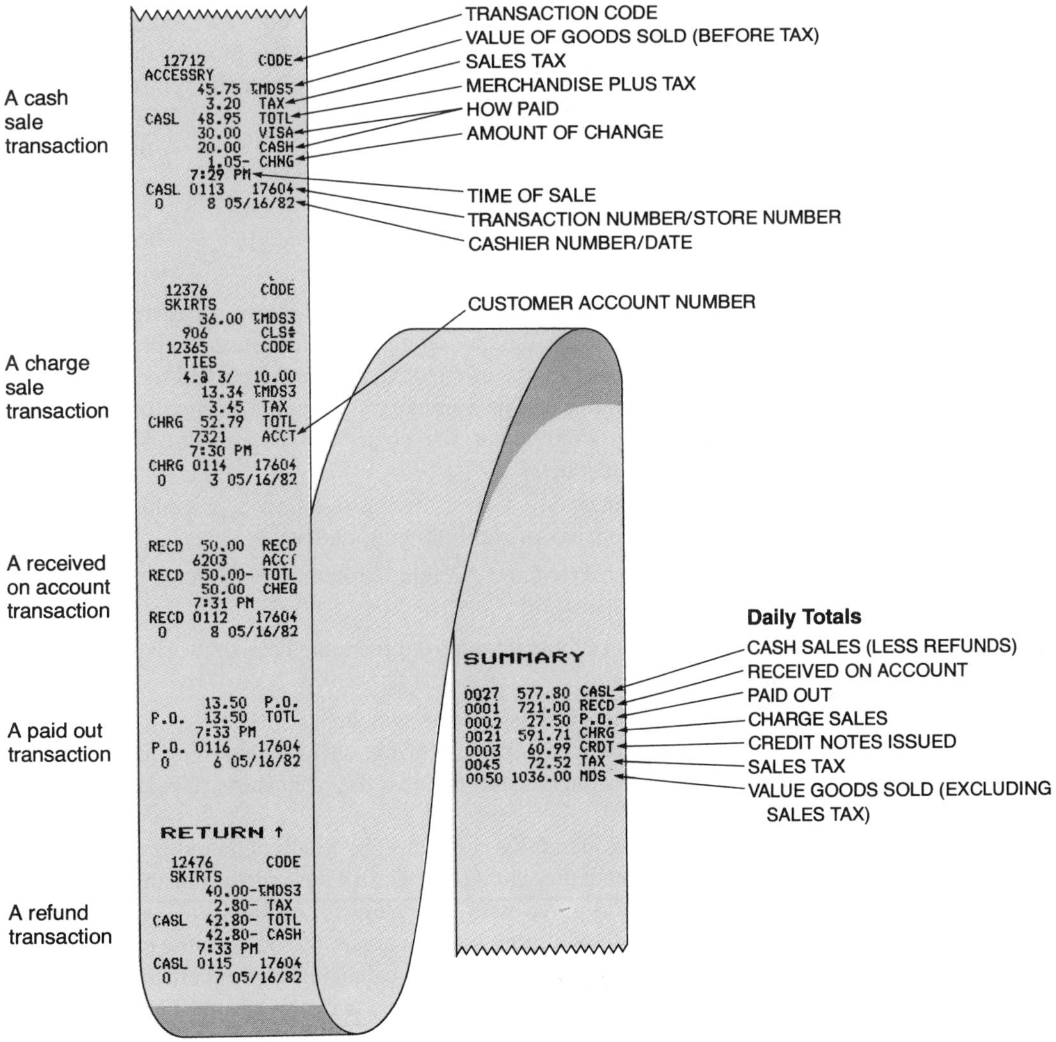

Figure 16.9 Cash register detailed audit tape.

totals are printed out at the end of the day, week, or month as needed. The daily totals are shown in Figure 16.9. Remember that a special key must be inserted in the control lock before the machine will release the totals. The daily totals are used to prove the cash and to build the accounting entry for the day. This end-of-day procedure is explained in the next section.

End-of-Day Procedure

In addition to daily totals on the audit strip, the modern electronic cash register can also print out summary totals for the day on a special form used to prove the cash and to build up the accounting entry. In this text, the form is called the Daily Cash Proof and Accounting Summary. The summary figures are printed out using the document printer device, while under the control of a supervisory person. A completed form is shown in Figure 16.10.

At the end of each business day, the cashier must follow a procedure known as the **daily cash proof**. It consists of the following duties:

1. A copy of the Daily Cash Proof and Accounting Summary form for the day must be obtained from the supervisor.
2. The cash and the vouchers must be removed from the cash drawer and separated from each other.
3. The cash must be proved. This is done in two steps.
   a. Cash is removed equal to the amount of the change fund. This cash is taken out in small bills and coins to start the next day's business. It is kept in a safe place overnight.
   b. The remaining cash is carefully counted. The total is entered on the line for 'Cash in drawer by actual count' in the Cash Proof section of the form. The amount entered should agree with the figure immediately above it for 'Net cash received'. If these two figures do not agree, there is either a cash shortage or a cash overage. The amount must be calculated and recorded on the line that reads Cash Short or on the line that reads Cash Over. In Figure 16.10, a shortage of $10 is recorded.
4. Specific voucher groups are made to agree with their corresponding summary figures. This is done in four categories:
   a. The total of the 'charge sales' slips must agree with the Charge Sales figure on the summary. In the example, the figure is $591.71.
   b. The total of the 'credit sales' must agree with the Credit Notes Issued figure on the summary. In the example, the figure is $60.99.
   c. The total of the 'received on account' slips must agree with the Received on Account figure on the summary. In the example, the figure is $721.00.

DAILY CASH PROOF AND ACCOUNTING SUMMARY DATE *March 12* 19 —	ACCTG SUMMARY LINE	REGISTER TOTALS
CASH PROOF		
Cash sales (less refunds)		577.80
Received on account		721.00
Total cash received		1 29880
Less paid outs		− 27.50
Net cash received		1 271.30
Cash in drawer by actual count	Line 1	1 261.30
Cash short	Line 6	10.–
Cash over	Line 10	
SALES PROOF		
Cash sales (less refunds)		577.80
Charge sales		591.71
Less credit notes issued		− 60.99
Less sales tax	Line 9	− 72.52
Net sales (excluding tax)	Line 8	1 036.00
ACCOUNTS RECEIVABLE SUMMARY		
Received on account		721.00
Credit notes issued		60.99
Accounts receivable credit	Line 7	781.99
Accounts receivable debit - charge sales	Line 2	591.71
PAID OUT SUMMARY		
- *Advertising*	Line 3	13.50
- *Delivery*	Line 4	14.00
-	Line 5	
Total paid out		27.50

ACCOUNTING SUMMARY		DEBIT	CREDIT
Bank	1	1 261 30	
Accounts Receivable	2	591 71	
Expense or Asset - *Advertising Exp.*	3	13 50	
Expense or Asset - *Delivery Exp.*	4	14 –	
Expense or Asset -	5		
Cash Short or Over	6	10 –	
Accounts Receivable	7		781 99
Sales	8		1 036 –
Sales Tax Payable	9		72 52
Cash Short or Over	10		
Balancing Totals		1 890 51	1 890 51

Figure 16.10 The completed daily cash proof and accounting summary form.

d. The total of the 'paid out' vouchers must agree with the Paid Out figure on the summary. In the example, the figure is $27.50.

If any of these totals fail to agree, the audit strip can be used to help locate the errors.

5. The paid out bills must be analyzed and broken down by general ledger account. In Figure 16.10, the paid out total of $27.50 is broken down into $13.50 for advertising and $14.00 for delivery.
6. The accounting summary section must be filled in from data in the four sections above it. Those figures with a line number recorded to their left must be transferred down to the Accounting Summary section. The line number states exactly where to record each item on the accounting summary. When all appropriate figures are transferred to the summary, the accounting entry must be balanced as an accuracy check.
7. The cash, the vouchers, and the daily balance form must be placed in an envelope to be forwarded to the accounting department. The accounting department will check out the contents, see that the money is deposited promptly in the bank, and record the accounting summary in the cash receipts journal as shown in Figure 16.11.

Cash Receipts Journal — Month of March, 19–

Date		Particulars	Other Accounts Cr.			Sales Tax Payable Cr.	Sales Cr.	Acc's Rec'l		Bank Dr.	Amount of Deposit
			Account	P.R.	Amount			Cr.	Dr.		
	12	Cash Summary	Adv. Exp.		13 50	72 52	1 036 –	781 99	591 71	1 261 30	
			Del. Exp.		14 –						
			Cash Short or Over		10 –						

Figure 16.11 The daily accounting summary recorded in the cash receipts journal.

Cash Short or Over

Businesses that deal with the general public for cash are subject to cash shortages and overages due to errors made by their clerks. The way in which a shortage or overage is calculated was discussed in the preceding section.

Some businesses hold their clerks responsible for shortages and overages. That is, the clerks may keep any overages, but must make up any shortages out of their own pockets. In such a business, the shortages or overages are not recorded in the books of account.

Other businesses take a more liberal attitude and accept the shortages and overages. This type of business does record the overages and shortages in the books of account. During the accounting period the overages and shortages are accumulated in a **Cash Short or Over account**. The shortages go into the account as debits since they are losses or decreases in equity. The overages go in as credits since they are gains or increases in equity.

At any particular time, the balance in the account will represent either an expense or income depending on whether it has a debit balance or a credit balance. A debit balance means that the shortages have exceeded the overages and a credit balance means that the overages have exceeded the shortages.

Accounting Terms

sales returns and allowances account
net sales
purchases returns and allowances account
net purchases
cash discount
cash refund
terms of sale
C.O.D.
on account
net 30
net 60
2/10, n/30
1/15, n/60
optical character recognition
change fund
a paid out
detailed audit tape
daily cash proof
cash short or over account

Review Questions

1. What is the simplest way to account for a credit invoice?
2. Under what circumstances does a business maintain a separate account for sales returns and allowances?
3. How is the figure for net sales calculated?

4. How is the figure for net purchases calculated?
5. Under what circumstances would a buyer want a cash refund?
6. Rather than give a cash refund, what alternative might the seller insist on? Explain the seller's purpose.
7. What is the purpose of a cash discount?
8. Explain the meaning of the following terms of sale: C.O.D.; Net 30; 2/10,n/30.
9. What factors help decide the terms granted to a customer?
10. Where are the terms of sale recorded for the customer?
11. How does a business office ensure that it does not miss any cash discounts?
12. Explain how a cash discount is calculated when a return or allowance is involved in the transaction.
13. Not all businesses have a Discounts Allowed account. Explain.
14. Discounts earned are related to what type of transaction?
15. Discounts allowed are related to what type of transaction?
16. Where are discounts shown on the Income Statement?
17. J. Jones pays a bill of $50 with a cheque for $49 because he is entitled to a 2 percent discount. What is the amount of the entry made to his account in the books of the seller?
18. How have cash registers changed in recent years?
19. Give three basic advantages of a cash register.
20. Why are vouchers necessary for certain cash register transactions?
21. Explain the purpose of the detailed audit tape.
22. Explain briefly the end-of-day procedure to be followed by the cash register operator.
23. How does one know if the Cash Short or Over account represents an overage or a shortage?

Exercises

Returns and Allowances

1. Manzer Wholesale Company maintains returns and allowances accounts for both purchases and sales. In general journal form, record the accounting

entries for the following selected transactions. Ignore dates and explanations. The transactions are exempt from sales tax.

Sales Invoice
— No. 372, to Armstrong Co., $141.50, sale of merchandise.
Purchase Invoice
— No. 607, from General Supply, $750, merchandise purchased.
Credit Invoice Issued
— No. 390, to Smith & Associates, $375, defective merchandise returned.
Credit Note Received
— No. 1212, from James Manufacturing Co., $260, allowance given on defective merchandise.

---

2. Northern Building Supplies keeps returns and allowances accounts for both purchases and sales. In general journal form, record the accounting entries for the following selected transactions. Ignore dates and explanations.

Sales Invoice
— No 640, to R. Prentice, $95 plus $4.75 sales tax, total $99.75, for sale of merchandise.
Credit Note Issued
— No 659, to K. Marker, $25 plus $1.25 sales tax, total $26.25 for defective material returned.
Purchase Invoice
— No. 7432, from Ace Insulation Co., $1 025, for insulation.
Credit Note Received
— No 843, from Long Lumber, $350, allowance for inferior grade lumber.

---

3. The data in the Sales account shown below was posted from the three sales journal pages shown beneath. At the time they were posted, the owner was not interested in keeping a separate account for sales returns and allowances. He has now had a change of heart and wants the sales returns and allowances to be kept separately in the future.

1. **Write up the headings in the sales journal for April.**
2. **Show a Sales account and a Sales Returns and Allowances account for the first three months as they would have been if the owner's new policy had been in effect for those months.**

ACCOUNT *Sales* No. 40

DATE		PARTICULARS	PR	DEBIT	CREDIT	Dr Cr	BALANCE
19– Jan.	31		S41		1 308 –	Cr	1 308 –
Feb.	28		S42		1 061 –	Cr	2 369 –
Mar.	31		S43		1 610 –	Cr	3 979 –

Sales Journal *January 19–* *P. 41*

Date		Particulars	Sales Tax Payable CR	Sales CR	No.	Acc's Rec'l DR
Jan.	4	A. Frankland	21 –	420 –	51	441 –
	9	T. Borsch	15 –	300 –	52	315 –
	13	N. Glover	2 85	57 –	53	59 85
	18	P. Swails	12 50	250 –	54	262 50
	21	N. James	4 50	90 –	55	94 50
	29	T. Bruno	8 75	175 –	56	183 75
	30	L. Morris	15 50	310 –	57	325 50
			65 40 (23)	1 308 – (40)		1 373 40 (2)

Sales Journal *February 19–* *P. 42*

Date		Particulars	Sales Tax Payable CR	Sales CR	No.	Acc's Rec'l DR
Feb.	3	B. Carter	16 50	330 –	58	346 50
	7	D. Davidson	14 50	290 –	59	304 50
	15	P. Swails	5 50	110 –	60	115 50
	19	N. Norman	4 75	95 –	61	99 75
	22	R. Allen	23 50	470 –	62	493 50
	24	P. Proctor	10 80	216 –	63	226 80
	28	S. George	2 –	40 –	64	42 –
			53 05 (23)	1 061 – (40)		1 114 05 (2)

Sales Journal *March 19–* *P. 43*

Date		Particulars	Sales Tax Payable CR	Sales CR	No.	Acc's Rec'l DR
Mar.	6	A. Andrews	20 50	410 –	65	430 50
	11	F. Germaine	15 50	310 –	66	325 50
	14	W. Wilson	13 50	270 –	67	283 50
	19	R. Ross	2 50	50 –	68	52 50
	21	M. Kerr	9 –	180 –	69	189 –
	28	C. Fraser	28 –	560 –	70	588 –
	31	N. Topper	3 50	70 –	71	73 50
			80 50 (23)	1 610 – (40)		1 690 50 (2)

4. 1. a. Record the journal entries for both of the following source documents from the point of view of Woods Wholesale. Do not use Returns and Allowances accounts.

b. Record the journal entries again, this time using Returns and Allowances accounts.

2. a. Record the journal entries for both source documents from the point of view of Hanover Hardware. Do not use Returns and Allowances accounts.

b. Record the journal entries again, this time using Returns and Allowances accounts.

WOODS WHOLESALE

NEWCASTLE, NEW BRUNSWICK

SOLD TO: Hanover Hardware
400 Hanover Street
Newcastle, N.B.
E2V 1H4

INVOICE NUMBER 365
DATE July 9, 19--
TERMS Net 30 days

Quantity	Description	Unit Price	Amount
4	3'' Belt Sander	$55.00	$220.00
6	3/8 Reversible Drill	21.00	126.00
			$346.00

WOODS WHOLESALE

NEWCASTLE, NEW BRUNSWICK

CREDIT

SOLD TO: Hanover Hardware
400 Hanover Street
Newcastle, N.B.
E2V 1H4

INVOICE NUMBER 402
DATE July 17, 19--
TERMS Net 30 days

Quantity	Description	Unit Price	Amount
2	3/8 Reversible Drills (returned defective)	$21.00	$42.00

Cash Refunds

5\. 1. **Record the following transaction in general journal form in the books of Copeland's Furniture Mart.**

May 31 Cash Sales Slip, No. 1060, to A. Rosen, sale of goods $55 plus sales tax $2.75, total $57.75; payment received in full.

2\. a. **Record the following transaction in general journal form in the books of Copeland's Furniture Mart, without using Returns and Allowances accounts.**

b. Record the following transaction again, this time using Returns and Allowances accounts.

June 4 Cash Refund Slip, No. 1075, to A. Rosen, return of goods $55 plus sales tax $2.75, total $57.75; cash refunded in full.

Cash Discounts

6. Complete the following schedule by calculating the amount of the payment that is necessary in each case. Where credit notes are involved assume that the discount period is adjusted to start from the date on the credit note.

Date of Invoice	Amount of Invoice	Terms of Sale	Amount of Credit Note	Date of Credit Note	Date Payment is Made	Amount of Payment Required
Mar 12	$ 52.50	2/10,n/30	-	-	Mar 20	
May 18	47.25	Net 30	-	-	May 27	
Sep 4	115.50	3/15,n/60	-	-	Oct 10	
Feb 6	1 050.00	1/20,n/60	$126.00	Feb 18	Mar 6	
Oct 19	588.00	2/10,n/30	42.00	Nov 5	Nov 27	
Aug 27	882.00	2/15,n/60	168.00	Sep 7	Sep 10	

7. Complete the following schedule by calculating the date that payment is required to pick up the discount, and the amount of the payment required.

Date of Invoice	Amount of Invoice	Terms of Sale	Amount of Credit Note	Date of Credit Note	Date Payment is Required	Amount of Payment Required
May 14	$147.00	2/10,n/30	-	-		
Apr 15	315.00	3/20,n/60	May 1	$42.00		
Jun 3	220.05	2/10,n/60	Jun 20	78.75		
Nov 20	59.25	2/15,n/60	Dec 2	36.75		

8. 1. a. In two-column general journal form, record the accounting entry for the invoice shown below in the books of Circle Supply.

900 Park Street — Maple City

Circle Supply

SOLD TO: Watson Construction
1500 Randell Road
Maple City X3Y 7N5

INVOICE NUMBER 715

DATE August 3, 19--

TERMS 2/10,n/30

Quantity	Description	Unit Price	Amount
10 boxes	#10 Woodscrews	$5.50	$55.00
2	Standard Crowbars	4.10	8.20
			63.20
	5% Sales Tax		3.16
			$66.36

b. On August 12 a cheque in the amount of $65.03 is received from Watson Construction. In two-column general journal form, show the accounting entry to be recorded in the books of Circle Supply.

2. Watson Construction charges the merchandise shown on the above invoice to an account called Small Tools and Supplies. Show the journal entries for the above two transactions that will be made in the books of Watson Construction. Use appropriate dates.

---

9. 1. a. In the books of Circle Supply, in two-column general journal form, show the accounting entry to be recorded for the invoice below.

900 Park Street — Maple City

Circle Supply

SOLD TO: Jackson and Jackson
Marmora Road
Maple City X3Y 6T8

INVOICE NUMBER 873

DATE September 3, 19--

TERMS 2/10,n/30

Quantity	Description	Unit Price	Amount
100	General Purpose Connectors	$1.00	$100.00
	5% Sales Tax		5.00
			$105.00

b. Some of the goods are found to be inadequate and are returned for credit. The following credit invoice is issued. Show the accounting entry in general journal form to record this credit invoice in the books of Circle Supply. Circle Supply does not use a Returns and Allowances account.

900 Park Street — **Circle Supply** — Maple City

CREDIT

SOLD TO: Jackson and Jackson
Marmora Road
Maple City X3Y 6T8

DATE September 9, 19-- CREDIT INVOICE NUMBER 891

Quantity	Description	Unit Price	Amount
~~100~~ 10	General Purpose Connectors	$1.00	10.00 ~~$100.00~~
	(Ordered on invoice #873)		
	5% Sales Tax		.50 ~~5.00~~
			~~$105.00~~ 10.50

c. On September 19, a cheque is received in full payment of the sales invoice, less the credit invoice, less the cash discount. Show the accounting entry in general journal form to record the receipt of this cheque.

2. Record the accounting entries to be made for the above transactions in the books of Jackson and Jackson. Use appropriate dates. The goods affect the Supplies account.

Returns, Allowances, and Cash Discounts

10. 1. Give the accounting entries in general journal form for each of the following source documents as they would be made in the books of Circle Supply. Circle Supply uses Returns and Allowances accounts.

2. Give the accounting entries in general journal form for each source document as they would be made in the books of Kitchen Cabinetry. The Supplies account is to be charged for the goods.

900 Park Street Maple City

Circle Supply

SOLD TO: Kitchen Cabinetry
East Side Road
Maple City X3Y 4H2

INVOICE NUMBER 802

DATE Aug. 9, 19--

TERMS 2/10, n/30

Quantity	Description	Unit Price	Amount
1 Ctn	#35 Copper Wire	$65.00	$ 65.00
24	Propane Torch Refills	5.95	142.80
			$207.80
	5% sales tax		10.39
			$218.19

900 Park Street Maple City

Circle Supply

SOLD TO: Kitchen Cabinetry
East Side Road
Maple City X3Y 4H2

DATE Aug. 17, 19--

CREDIT INVOICE NUMBER 851

CREDIT

Quantity	Description	Unit Price	Amount
	Credit to correct price on Propane Torch refills		
24	Propane Torch Refills	5.95	$142.80
	Should be		
24	Propane Torch Refills	5.35	128.40
			$14.40
	5% Sales Tax		.72
			$15.12

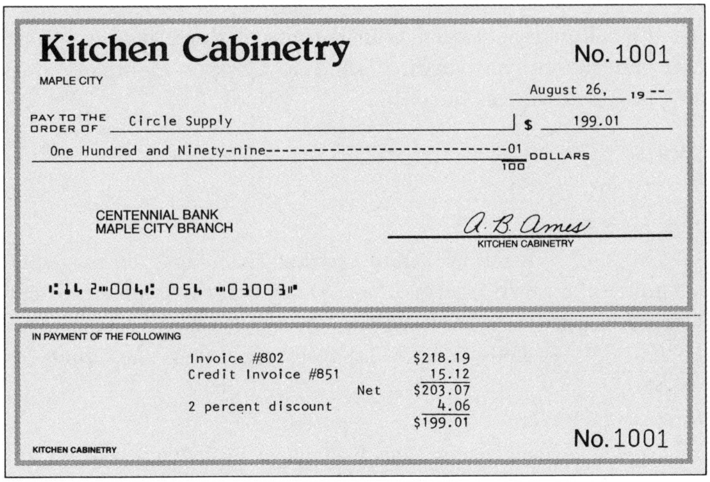

Kitchen Cabinetry No. 1001
MAPLE CITY
August 26, 19--
PAY TO THE ORDER OF Circle Supply $ 199.01
One Hundred and Ninety-nine------------------------------01/100 DOLLARS
CENTENNIAL BANK
MAPLE CITY BRANCH
KITCHEN CABINETRY

IN PAYMENT OF THE FOLLOWING

Invoice #802		$218.19
Credit Invoice #851		15.12
	Net	$203.07
2 percent discount		4.06
		$199.01

KITCHEN CABINETRY No. 1001

Journalizing for Returns, Allowances, Refunds, and for Discounts

11. In the columnar journals provided in the workbook, record the following selected transactions of The Music Store, which sells musical instruments and related merchandise. The Music Store uses returns and allowances accounts. Note: The Music Store does not handle cash refunds as if they were regular cash payments. Rather, the store regards refunds as 'minus' cash sales. Refunds are written up on a cash sales slip with the word REFUND prominently marked, and recorded in the cash receipts journal using the circle method where needed. The money is paid out of the day's cash receipts.

Date	*Source Document*	*No.*	*Terms*	*Amount*	*Tax*	*Total*	*Name*	*Explanation*
May 1	Sales Invoice	373	2/10,n/30	$ 740.00	$37.00	$ 777.00	B. Sloan	Sale of instrument
3	Cash Sales Slip	102		65.00	3.25	68.25	C. Cox	Sale of instrument
7	Purchase Invoice	402	3/10,n/30	1 240.00		1 240.00	Daull Bros	Purchase of instruments
14	Credit Invoice Issued	384		125.00	6.25	131.25	B. Sloan	Defective goods returned
15	Cash Refund Slip	121		65.00	3.25	68.25	C. Cox	Instrument returned
15	Credit Invoice Received	419		105.00		105.00	Daull Bros	Credit for goods returned
20	Cheque Received	375				632.84	B. Sloan	Paying #373, #384
30	Cheque Issued	902				1 100.95	Daull Bros	Paying #402, #419

12. Record the following selected transactions of the Canadian Copper Company in general journal form. Canadian Copper Company does not use Returns and Allowances accounts.

Transactions

October

1 *Purchase Invoice*

— No. 6457, from Dominion Nickel Company, dated September 29, amount, $11 760, terms, Net 30 days, for a shipment of copper.

3 *Cheque Copy*

— No. 750, to Petty Cash, $25, to increase petty cash fund from $25 to $50.

7 *Purchase Invoice*

— No. 354, from Continental Railway, Company, $762.12, in respect to the shipment of copper from Dominion Nickel Company.

8 *Cheque Copy*

— No. 765, to Mallory & Co., $353.99, in payment of their sales invoice No. 6421 for $361.21 less a 2 percent discount.

11 *Cheque Copy*

— No. 784, to Ewing & Barlock, $51.62; cash refund for defective copper bars returned. There was no sales tax on the original transaction.

12 *Cash Receipt*

— Cheque from Kirby Brothers, $116.62, in payment of sales invoice No. 692, dated September 30, having terms of 2/15,n/30.

17 *Cheque Copy*

— No. 801, to Petty Cash, $48.68; replenishing cheque for the following charges: Office Supplies, $17.14; Miscellaneous Expense, $23.22; Delivery Expense, $1.35; Freight-in, $6.97.

25 *Cheque Copy*

— No. 814, to Pearson Bros., $12.14; for the cash purchase of office supplies.

26 *Sales Invoice*

— No. 751, to Toro Fixtures, $643; sale of goods on account; terms of sale, Net 30 days; sales tax 3 percent to be added.

27 *Cheque Copy*

— No. 827, to Commercial Cartage, $412; cash payment for delivery service for the month of September.

30 *Credit Note Received*

— No. 6529, from Dominion Nickel Company, $900; allowance for defective goods on invoice No. 6457.

13. Record the following selected transactions of Wholesale Food Distributors in general journal form. In working out your answers, bear in mind the following:

a. A few of the transactions are dependent on previous ones.

b. Wholesale Food Distributors maintains separate accounts for Purchases Returns and Allowances and for Sales Returns and Allowances.

c. The amounts of certain cheques (receipts and expenditures) have been left for you to decide.

Transactions

November

3 *Sales Invoices*
- — No. 962, Palmer's Grocery, \$496.26; terms, 2/10,n/30; add 5 percent sales tax.
- — No. 963, Grey's Market, \$376.14; terms, 2/10,n/30; add 5 percent sales tax.
- — No. 964, Alec's Groceteria, \$197.26; terms, 2/10,n/30; add 5 percent sales tax.

4 *Cheque Copy*
- — No. 404, to D. K. Knight, \$100, loan to an employee to help him overcome a personal hardship.

5 *Purchase Invoice*
- — No. 213, from Gordon Canners, \$1 260, dated Nov. 2; terms 3/20,n/60, for merchandise purchased.

6 *Bank Debit Note*
- — From City Bank, \$75.10, cheque returned NSF from Doyle's Grocery.

7 *Cheque Copy*
- — No. 412, to Outboard Motor Sales, \$425; instructions from J. D. Doan, the owner, to pay for a new outboard motor delivered to his cottage for his personal use.

8 *Purchase Invoice*
- — No. 5698, from Elmer Canners, \$1 050; for merchandise purchased; terms, Net 60 days, dated Nov. 6.

10 *Credit Note Received*
- — No. 445, from Gordon Canners, \$147, dated Nov. 9; allowance granted on invoice No. 213 for incorrect goods.

10 *Cheque Copy*

— No. 443, to Petty Cash, to replenish petty cash as per the following summary of charges:

Travelling Expenses	$12.92
Delivery Expense	40.89
Building Maintenance	26.14
Miscellaneous Expense	16.19

11 *Cheque Copy*

— No. 447, to Brown Brothers, $475, to pay for C.O.D. delivery of a new office desk.

12 *Cash Receipt*

— Cheque of Grey's Market, paying sales invoice No. 963.

Credit Note Issued

— No. 1007, to Palmer's Grocery, $56.70 including 5 percent sales tax, for defective merchandise returned; discount period adjusted to begin on November 12.

14 *Credit Note Received*

— No. 565, from Burlington Fruit Growers Association, $2 332.80, correcting their invoice No. 412, which was issued incorrectly in the amount of $2 592 instead of $259.20. (**Note:** This is neither a 'return' nor an 'allowance'.)

18 *Cheque Copy*

— No. 474, to G. Simcoe, $47.25; cash refund for defective merchandise that had been returned, $45, sales tax, $2.25.

22 *Cash Receipt*

— Cheque from Palmer's Grocery, paying invoice No. 962 and credit note No. 1007 less discount.

25 *Cheque Copy*

— No. 491, to Gordon Canners, paying sales invoice No. 213 and credit note No. 445 less discount.

26 *Cheque Copy*

— No. 497, to Elmer Canners, paying invoice No. 5698.

30 *Cash Receipt*

— Cheque from Alec's Groceteria, paying sales invoice No. 964.

---

14. Prepare an income statement and a balance sheet from the following partial work sheet.

Work Sheet Master Trading Company Yr. Ended Dec. 31, 19–	Income Statement		Balance Sheet	
	Dr.	Cr.	Dr.	Cr.
Bank			950 20	
Petty Cash			100 -	
Accounts Receivable			37 072 50	
Merchandise Inventory	45 957 06	43 500 -	43 500 -	
Supplies			1 350 -	
Equipment			18 040 -	
Bank Loan				25 000 -
Accounts Payable				26 210 70
Sales Tax Payable				729 16
H. Gander, Capital				41 585 38
H. Gander, Drawings			30 000 -	
Sales		176 350 50		
Sales Returns & Allow's	4 092 -			
Purchases	74 316 20			
Purchases Returns & All's		7 621 90		
Freight-in	592 -			
Advertising	1 074 -			
Bank Charges	516 40			
Car Expenses	4 372 60			
Delivery Expense	5 732 90			
Discounts Allowed	1 372 40			
Discounts Earned		715 25		
General Expense	1 237 37			
Light & Heat Expense	1 576 20			
Rent Expense	12 000 -			
Telephone Expense	789 02			
Wages Expense	37 072 04			
	190 700 19	228 187 65	131 012 70	93 525 24
	37 487 46			37 487 46
	228 187 65	228 187 65	131 012 70	131 012 70

Parts of a Cash Register

15. Identify the parts of the cash register indicated below.

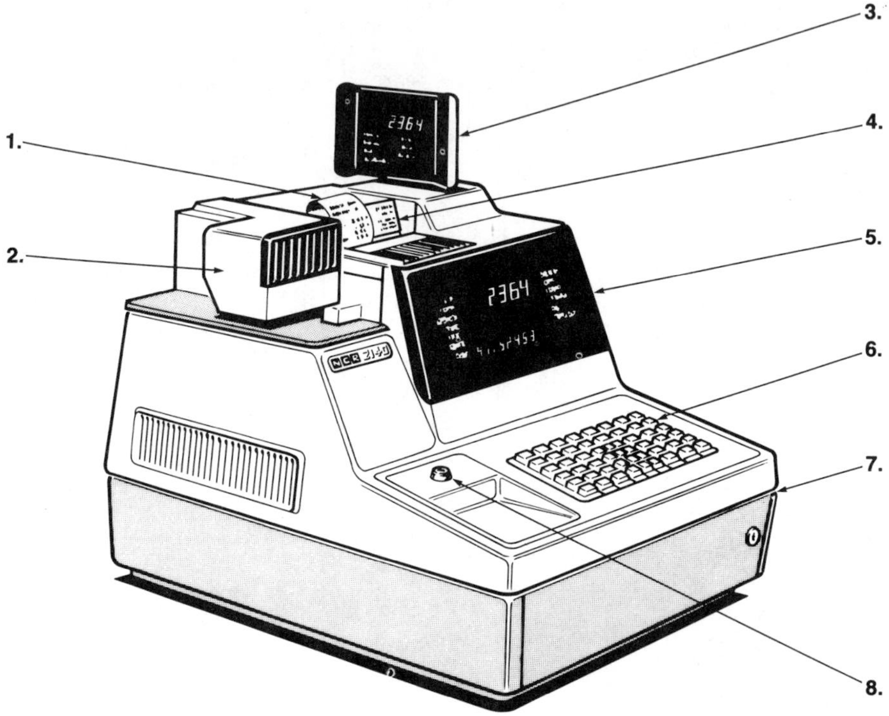

Steps in Cash Register Transactions

16. The eight steps to be followed by the cashier in handling a cash sale are given below in incorrect order. Show the correct order by writing in the proper step number in the space to the right. This exercise also appears in the workbook.

- Money is placed in cash drawer.
- The method and amount of payment are entered into the keyboard.
- 'Cash' key is pressed.
- 'Total' key is pressed.

- A description of the merchandise is entered into the keyboard.
- The cash drawer is closed.
- The cashier's personal number is entered into the keyboard.
- The price of the merchandise is entered into the keyboard.

17. The eight steps to be followed by the cashier in handling a charge sale are given below in incorrect order. Show the correct order by writing in the proper step number in the space to the right. This exercise also appears in the workbook.

- The duplicate sales slip is placed in the slip printer.
- The customer is given a copy of the duplicate sales slip.
- A sales slip in duplicate is prepared.
- The transaction details are entered into the keyboard.
- The 'charge' key is pressed.
- The original of the sales slip is placed in the cash drawer.
- The cashier's personal number is entered into the keyboard.
- The 'total' key is pressed.

Cash Register Controls

18. Prepare a list of all of the control features on a cash register.

Cash Register Detailed Audit Tape

19. Workbook Exercise: Computing audit strip totals.

Cash Register End-of-day Procedure

20. 1. Using the following information, fill in the totals that would be machine-printed by the cash register on the daily balance form. A blank form is supplied in the workbook.

2. Complete the remainder of the form.

3. Show that the vouchers agree with the appropriate summary figures.

Additional Information:

a. *Cash Register Daily Totals*

$1 325.73	CASL
295.00	RECD
40.00	P.O.
925.55	CHRG
87.74	CRDT
141.54	TAX
2 022.00	MDS

b. *Cash on Hand (including $50 Change Fund)*

Currency	$20 × 46
	$10 × 44
	$ 5 × 31
	$ 2 × 30
	$ 1 × 21
Coin	1¢ × 63
	5¢ × 30
	10¢ × 61
	25¢ × 86

c. *Vouchers on Hand*

Sales slip No. 75, Credit note issued for $48.15.
Sales slip No. 76, Charge sale of $124.12.
Sales slip No. 77, Received on account, $75.
Sales slip No. 78, Charge sale of $181.90.
Sales slip No. 79, Charge sale of $218.28.
Sales slip No. 80, Received on account, $125.
Sales slip No. 81, Charge sale of $401.25.
Supplier's bill, $16, for postage.
Sales slip No. 82, Credit note issued for $39.59.
Sales slip No. 83, Received on account, $95.
Supplier's bill, $24, for supplies.

---

21. 1. Using the following information, fill in the totals that would be machine printed by the cash register on the daily balance form. A blank form is supplied in the workbook.

2. Complete the remainder of the form.

3. Show that the vouchers agree with the appropriate summary figures.

Additional Information:

a. *Cash Register Daily Totals*

$1 755.87	CASL
1 470.00	RECD
75.50	P.O.
776.82	CHRG
119.84	CRDT
157.85	TAX
2 255.00	MDS

b. *Cash on Hand (including $50 Change Fund)*

Currency	$20 ×	106
	$10 ×	30
	$ 5 ×	101
	$ 2 ×	65
	$ 1 ×	126
Coin	25¢ ×	92
	10¢ ×	51
	5¢ ×	40
	1¢ ×	127

c. *Vouchers on Hand*

Sales slip No. 102, Received on account, $250.
Sales slip No. 103, Charge sale, $338.12.
Sales slip No. 104, Credit note issued, $44.94.
Supplier's bill, $72 for supplies.
Supplier's bill, $3.50 for miscellaneous.
Sales slip No. 105, Charge sale, $226.84.
Sales slip No. 106, Credit note issued, $74.90.
Sales slip No. 107, Received on account, $500.
Sales slip No. 108, Charge sale, $211.86.
Sales slip No. 109, Received on account, $720.

Journalizing Cash Register Summaries

22. Record the accounting entry for each of the following in the Cash Receipts journal provided in the workbook.

ACCOUNTING SUMMARY		DEBIT	CREDIT
Bank	1	1 777 05	
Accounts Receivable	2	904 30	
Expense or Asset ______	3		
Expense or Asset ______	4		
Expense or Asset ______	5		
Cash Short or Over	6		
Accounts Receivable	7		735 -
Sales	8		1 805 -
Sales Tax Payable	9		126 35
Cash Short and Over	10		15 -
Balancing Totals		2 681 35	2 681 35

ACCOUNTING SUMMARY		DEBIT	CREDIT
Bank	1	3 861 92	
Accounts Receivable	2	1 502 25	
Expense or Asset Misc Expense	3	27 14	
Expense or Asset ______	4		
Expense or Asset ______	5		
Cash Short or Over	6	20 -	
Accounts Receivable	7		1 450 -
Sales	8		3 702 16
Sales Tax Payable	9		259 15
Cash Short and Over	10		
Balancing Totals		5 411 31	5 411 31

Maintaining a Subsidiary Ledger in a Cash Register Environment

23. The following is a summary of the accounts receivable ledger of Select Sales Company on June 1, 19--.

Customer	*Address*	*Sales Slip*	*Amount*	*Balance*
P. J. Carey	88 Kenneth Avenue	141		$ 48.30
M. P. Dewar	94 Belair Drive	151		105.00
D. E. Gale	400 Brewster Street	147		89.25
R. B. Hancock	41 Bisher Avenue	146		31.50
F. Lipton	900 Mandor Drive	99		42.00
G. McDonald	102 Mid-Land Blvd.	96	$21.00	
		157	52.50	73.50
W. Pimm	16 Brent Road	132		63.00
F. Slater	12 Hastings Avenue	104	$15.75	
		125	26.25	
		162	94.50	136.50
				$589.05

Set up the accounts receivable ledger of Select Sales Company as of June 1. If you are using the workbook that accompanies the text, the ledger will be set up for you.

1. **Post to the subsidiary ledger accounts as required for the following transactions. Select Sales Company posts directly from the source documents to the subsidiary ledgers.**

Transactions

June 2 *Partial Cash Register Daily Balance Form*

ACCOUNTING SUMMARY			DEBIT	CREDIT
DEBITS:	Bank	6	641 15	
	Acc's Rec'l (ChargeSales)	*	347 55	
	Other a/c's -	12		
	-	13		
	-	14		
	Cash Short and Over	7	1 00	
CREDITS:	Accounts Receivable	2		195 30
	Sales	18		756 50
	Sales Tax Payable	21		37 90
	Cash Short and Over	8		
BALANCING TOTALS			989 70	989 70

'Charge' Vouchers

Sales slip No. 163	P. J. Carey	$ 47.25
Sales slip No. 164	W. Pimm	65.10
Sales slip No. 165	D. E. Gale	119.70
Sales slip No. 166	M. P. Dewar	115.50
		$347.55

'Received' Vouchers

On sales slip No. 166 from P. J. Carey	Re 141	$ 48.30
On sales slip No. 168 from F. Slater	Re 104, 125	42.00
On sales slip No. 169 from M. P. Dewar	Re 151	105.00
		$195.30

June 2 *Daily List of Mail Receipts*

Cheque from R. B. Hancock Paying sales slip No. 146 $31.50

June 3 *Partial Cash Register Daily Balance Form*

ACCOUNTING SUMMARY				DEBIT	CREDIT
DEBITS:	Bank		6	373 25	
	Acc's Rec'l(ChargeSales)		*	194 25	
	Other a/c's	-	12	10 00	
		-	13		
		-	14		
	Cash Short and Over		7		
CREDITS:	Accounts Receivable		2		94 50
	Sales		18		460 00
	Sales Tax Payable		21		23 00
	Cash Short and Over		8		
BALANCING TOTALS				577 50	577 50

'Charge' Vouchers

Sales slip No. 170	F. Lipton	$ 78.75
Sales slip No. 171	G. McDonald	115.50
		$194.25

'Received' Vouchers
On sales slip No. 172 from F. Slater Re 162 — $94.50

June 4 *Partial Cash Register Daily Balance Form*

ACCOUNTING SUMMARY			DEBIT	CREDIT
DEBITS:	Bank	6	466 35	
	Acc's Rec'l(ChargeSales)	*	135 50	
	Other a/c's -	12		
	-	13		
	-	14		
	Cash Short and Over	7		
CREDITS:	Accounts Receivable	2		63 00
	Sales	18		512 00
	Sales Tax Payable	21		25 60
	Cash Short and Over	8		1 25
BALANCING TOTALS			601 85	601 85

'Charge' Vouchers

Sales slip No. 173	F. Slater	$ 52.50
Sales slip No. 174	W. Pimm	83.00
		$135.50

'Received' Vouchers
On sales slip No 175 from W. Pimm Re 132 — $63.00

June 4 *Daily List of Mail Receipts*

Cheque from F. Lipton	Paying sales slip No. 99	$42.00
Cheque from G. McDonald	Paying sales slip No. 96	21.00
		$63.00

2. Prepare a subsidiary ledger trial balance as of June 4.

Cash Short or Over

24. Assume that the Cash Short or Over account is posted daily as in the account below. Examine the account and answer the following questions.

Cash Short or Over

Date		Particulars	P.R.	Debit	Credit	DR CR	Balance
19– July	3			10 –			
	4			2 –			
	7				5 –		
	10			20 –			
	11				1 –		
	12			5 –			
	14				50		
	17				1 50		
	18			2 –			
	20			1 –			
	24			10 –			
	25				75		
	26			3 –			
	27			10 –			
	28			5 –			
	31			1 –		Dr	60 25

1. **On how many days was there a cash shortage?**
2. **On how many days was there a cash overage?**
3. **Is the net result for the month an overage or a shortage?**
4. **Does this account as it stands represent an expense or an income?**

Using Your Knowledge

25. Wholesale Food Distributors sold merchandise on account to Palmer's Grocery on December 15. The amount of the invoice was $10 000. Terms of the sale were 2/10,n/30. Wholesale Food Distributors received a cheque for $9 800 as payment in full. A few days later Palmer's Grocery returned $2 000 worth of the shipment because it was defective. Wholesale Food Distributors issued a credit memorandum on December 31.

1. **For how much should the credit memo be issued? Explain.**

2. Write the accounting entry for the transaction on the books of each company.

---

26. A cheque for $1 176 was received from a customer within 10 days from the date of sending him a sales invoice for $1 200 with terms of 2/10,n/30. In recording the receipt of the cheque, the accounting clerk entered $1 176 in the Cash column and $1 200 in the Accounts Receivable column of the cash receipts journal. He made no entry in the Discounts Allowed column.

What procedure will bring this error to light?

---

27. Theresa Sprague, the proprietor of Best Wholesale Confectionery, purchased three typewriters for use in her business. One typewriter proved defective and was returned to the supplier, Acme Office Supplies. The accounting clerk debited Accounts Payable/Acme Office Supplies and credited Purchase Returns and Allowances.

1. **Was it wrong for the accounting clerk to credit Purchase Returns and Allowances? Why?**
2. **What effect would this error have on the net income and on the assets if no correction were made?**

---

28. In a large department store, cash registers are used extensively. Give reasons why cash registers are essential in such circumstances.

Cases

Case 1 *Squeeze the Little Man?*

Highway Construction is a large firm that builds major roads and highways. Its contracts frequently involve very large sums of money. Consequently, the size of its accounts receivable is very large. Its accounts payable is also substantial.

Highway Construction obtains large quantities of raw materials, supplies, and services from numerous smaller companies. These are always purchased on credit, and the amounts of money involved are usually large. Individual debts of $100 000 or more are not uncommon. At the time of purchase, Highway Construction always agrees to the supplier's terms of sale. These terms usually request payment within 30 days with no discounts.

In road construction, cash inflows are invariably slower than cash outflows. As a result, Highway Construction is usually in a cash-short position. The company makes no attempt to adhere to the terms of its suppliers. It pays its debts when it can, usually within 90 to 100 days.

A small supplier can seldom afford a 100 day wait for repayment of a large debt. The supplier has its own debts to pay, and a payroll to meet. Therefore, Fred Snell, the chief accountant for Highway Construction, receives many telephone calls urgently requesting immediate payment of accounts.

Fred Snell is experienced at dealing with suppliers. Over the years he has worked out a neat scheme for handling their requests for payment. First, he expresses surprise that the supplier did not know that Highway Construction always takes 90 days to pay its suppliers. Fred then explains that the company only pays within 30 days if a cash discount of at least 2 percent is offered. The supplier is usually desperate for payment and agrees to the 2 percent discount, which at the time seems insignificant.

Fred Snell claims that he makes money for Highway Construction with this scheme, even if he borrows the money at 15 percent interest to make the payment. He has offered to back up this claim with calculations.

Questions

1. Is Fred Snell a sharp businessman? Discuss.
2. Is Fred Snell's policy an ethical one? Discuss.
3. Is Fred correct when he states that he makes money for the company with this scheme? Prove your answer with a calculation.

Career

Peter Lin / General Cashier and Billing Clerk

After Peter Lin finished high school, he immediately enrolled in a Hotel Management program at a community college. This training program included a number of courses in accounting. Peter's first job following graduation was in the credit office at Simpson's, where he received customers' payments and prepared credit invoices for merchandise returned by customers.

Peter left Simpson's to work as a general cashier for the Western Inn in Regina, Saskatchewan. This position involves a variety of duties. Peter cashes cheques for the hotel guests and places their valuables in the vault for safekeeping. He handles all payments from patrons, whether by cash, cheque, or credit card, and makes daily deposits of all cash received from the restaurant, banquet, and lounge sections of the hotel. He also makes sure that each purchase invoice received by the hotel is accurate and that the merchandise has been received. Peter controls four separate cash funds: a current bank account, an in-house bank, a reserve change fund, and the petty cash fund.

Peter supervises four other cashiers. He distributes their payroll cheques and provides each till with a cash float of $200. He collects the detailed audit strips from the cashiers and uses them to prepare the daily cash proof and the accounting summary. He then enters the amounts from the accounting summary in the cash receipts journal. Peter always investigates significant cash shortages or overages, and encourages his staff to keep cash discrepancies at a minimum.

Peter acts as billing clerk as well as general cashier for the Inn. In this capacity, he receives each guest's account from the typist and places it in a file binder. The office manager sends him statements of the charges incurred by each guest. He then posts these amounts to the guests' accounts. Peter reports directly to the controller of the Western Inn, who is the head of the accounting department.

Peter finds the working atmosphere at the Western Inn very attractive. He gets on well with the other employees and enjoys meeting the public. Peter also takes great pleasure in his daily interactions with the Regina community.

Supplementary Exercise
Green Thumb Garden Centre

Introductory Information

The Green Thumb Garden Centre is a business owned and operated by Mr. G. O. Emms. It is a seasonal business which the owner closes down each year from November 1 to March 31. During the season that the business is open, it is operated seven days a week. The most profitable business days are Saturdays and Sundays.

The Green Thumb Garden Centre sells a variety of goods and services. Among these are the following: shrubs, bushes, trees, plants, fertilizers, seeds, bulbs, insecticides, sod, loam, soil, concrete products, and landscaping. All goods and services sold by the business are subject to a 5 percent government sales tax.

Mr. Emms employs a number of workers. Most of these are hired on a part-time basis as they are needed. Once each week, Mr. Emms withdraws from the bank (by means of a cheque made out to Cash) sufficient cash to pay the employees.

Most of the sales of the business are on a cash basis. As a result, the accounting system of the business is geared toward the cash register. In addition to the cash sales, all charge sales and receipts from customers are processed through the cash register. There are relatively few charge customers.

The business accounting system utilizes three special journals as follows:

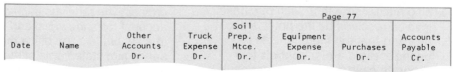

Page 77

Date	Name	Other Accounts Dr.	Truck Expense Dr.	Soil Prep. & Mtce. Dr.	Equipment Expense Dr.	Purchases Dr.	Accounts Payable Cr.

Purchases Journal

Page 47

Date	Name	Other Accounts Dr.	Wages Dr.	G.O.E. Drawings Dr.	Soil Prep. & Mtce. Dr.	Discounts Earned Cr.	Accounts Payable Dr.	Bank Cr.

Cash Payments Journal

Page 65

Date	Name	Other Accounts Cr.	Cash Short & Over Dr.	Discounts Allowed Dr.	Sales Tax Payable Cr.	Sales Cr.	Accounts Receivable Cr.	Bank Dr.

Cash Receipts Journal

At the close of each day's business, a cash register balancing procedure is performed and an accounting summary prepared. A bank deposit is made each day by using a night depository service.

Small expense items are not paid for out of the cash register funds. Mr. Emms maintains a petty cash fund of $100 for this purpose.

The business does not keep perpetual inventory records.

The three ledgers of the Green Thumb Garden Centre as of May 31, 19-- are set up in the workbook. The workbook also contains a cash receipts journal (page 65), a cash payments journal (page 47), and a purchases journal (page 77) for Green Thumb Garden Centre for June 19--.

GREEN THUMB GARDEN CENTRE
GENERAL LEDGER TRIAL BALANCE
MAY 31, 19--

No.	*Account*	*Dr.*	*Cr.*
1.	Petty Cash	$ 100.00	
2.	Bank	3 527.24	
3.	Accounts Receivable	2 469.91	
4.	Inventory — Merchandise and Nursery Stock	10 746.53	
5.	Supplies	595.00	
6.	Land	48 000.00	
7.	Buildings	23 500.00	
8.	Trucks and Tractors	27 500.00	
21.	Bank Loan		$ 20 000.00
22.	Mortgage Payable		22 500.00
23.	Accounts Payable		7 861.87
24.	Sales Tax Payable		160.45
31.	G. O. Emms, Capital		66 175.94
32.	G. O. Emms, Drawings	5 654.60	
41.	Sales		25 042.19
51.	Bank Charges	547.53	
52.	Building Repairs	146.51	
53.	Cash Short and Over	10.04	
54.	Discounts Allowed	95.75	
55.	Discounts Earned		316.70
56.	Equipment Expense	506.86	
57.	Freight-in	256.50	
58.	Light, Heat, and Power	306.75	
59.	Miscellaneous Expense	92.41	
60.	Purchases	10 001.05	
61.	Soil Preparation and Maintenance	2 001.15	
62.	Telephone	519.42	
63.	Truck Expense	1 104.40	
64.	Wages	4 375.50	
		$142 057.15	$142 057.15

GREEN THUMB GARDEN CENTRE
ACCOUNTS RECEIVABLE LEDGER
MAY 31, 19--

Customer	*Address*	*Usual Terms*	*Inv. Date*	*Inv. No.*	*Inv. Amount*
P. Barker	16 Ava Street	Net 30	May 16	398	$ 131.25
J. Bowen	42 Woodlawn Ave.	Net 30	May 14	394	78.75
F. Carson & Sons	165 Pleasant Road	2/10,n/30	May 30	408	541.80
N. Everist	46 Hart Street	Net 30	May 4	375	56.70
O. Harrison	96 Brock Road	Net 30	May 5	377	63.00
P. Pierce	205 Ford Street	Net 30	May 6	379	36.53
A. Renforth	90 Oak Lane	Net 30	May 12	390	178.50
C. Swinton	27 North Cr.	2/10,n/30	May 26	407	1 094.63
Varga Brothers	55 Sharp Drive	2/10,n/30	May 24	402	288.75
					$2 469.91

GREEN THUMB GARDEN CENTRE
ACCOUNTS PAYABLE LEDGER
MAY 31, 19--

Supplier	*Address*	*Terms*	*Inv. No.*	*Inv. Date*	*Amount*	*Account Balance*
Acorn Seed	10 Lynn Road	2/15,n/30	654	May 18	$147.00	
Company			672	May 21	317.10	$ 464.10
Clay Ceramic Co.	74 Pine Street	Net 45	1701	Apr. 24		540.75
Canada Products	100 Willow Ave.	Net 30	B160	May 4	$ 58.80	
			B188	May 12	98.91	
			B249	May 30	35.91	193.62
Kemp Haulage	Summerside	1/10,n/30	747	May 23	$ 52.50	
			754	May 23	52.50	
			760	May 23	52.50	
			772	May 27	52.50	
			795	May 31	78.75	288.75
M & M Chemicals	500 Grand St.	Net 60	1046	Apr. 9		1 932.00
Poplar Finance	200 Crest Rd.	Per Contract				2 560.00
SylvesterConcrete	482-4 Delta Rd.	Net 30	446	May 5		783.51
Triangle Sod	4th Side Road	Net 30	374	May 22		1 099.14
						$7 861.87

1. Journalize the transactions listed below. Post daily to the subsidiary ledgers, directly from the source documents.

Transactions

June 1 *Cash Register Summary*

ACCOUNTING SUMMARY		DEBIT		CREDIT	
DEBITS:	Bank	160	05		
	Acc's Rec'l (Charge Sales)				
	Cash Short and Over	2	00		
CREDITS:	Accounts Receivable				
	Sales			154	33
	Sales Tax Payable			7	72
	Cash Short and Over				
BALANCING TOTALS		162	05	162	05

Purchase Invoice

—From Canada Products, No. B261, $372.75, dated May 31; terms Net 30; for fertilizer for resale.

June 2 *Cash Register Summary*

ACCOUNTING SUMMARY		DEBIT		CREDIT	
DEBITS:	Bank	551	98		
	Acc's Rec'l (Charge Sales)				
	Discounts Allowed	5	78		
	Cash Short and Over				
CREDITS:	Accounts Receivable			288	75
	Sales			256	20
	Sales Tax Payable			12	81
	Cash Short and Over				
BALANCING TOTALS		557	76	577	76

'Received' Voucher

—Voucher No. 416 to Varga Brothers, paying Invoice No. 402 for $288.75 less 2 percent discount; net amount $282.97.

Purchase Invoice

—From Triangle Sod, No. 406, $312.90, dated June 1; terms Net 30; for sod for resale.

Cheque Copies

—No. 661, to Acorn Seed Company, $?, paying Invoice No. 654 less 2 percent discount.

—No. 662, to Kemp Haulage, $?, paying Invoices No. 747, No. 754, No. 760 less 1 percent cash discount.

June 3 *Cash Register Summary*

ACCOUNTING SUMMARY		DEBIT	CREDIT
DEBITS:	Bank	247 20	
	Acc's Rec'l (Charge Sales)		
	Cash Short and Over		
CREDITS:	Accounts Receivable		56 70
	Sales		180 00
	Sales Tax Payable		9 00
	Cash Short and Over		1 50
BALANCING TOTALS		247 20	247 20

'Received' Voucher

—Voucher No. 417 to N. Everist, paying Invoice No. 375 for $56.70.

Cheque Copy

—No. 663, to Petty Cash, $?, to reimburse petty cash fund with respect to the following summary:

Petty Cash Summary June 3, 19--	
Building Repairs	$14.10
Equipment Expense	2.50
Soil Preparation & Maint.	35.50
Truck Expense	17.70
Miscellaneous Expense	26.75

June 4 *Cash Register Summary*

ACCOUNTING SUMMARY		DEBIT		CREDIT	
DEBITS:	Bank	1 00	38		
	Acc's Rec'l (Charge Sales)	330	75		
	Cash Short and Over				
CREDITS:	Accounts Receivable				
	Sales			410	60
	Sales Tax Payable			20	53
	Cash Short and Over				
BALANCING TOTALS		431	13	431	13

'Charge' Voucher

—Voucher No. 418 to Varga Brothers for the sale of merchandise, $315.00 plus 5 percent sales tax; terms, 2/10,n/30; total $330.75.

Purchase Invoices

—From Clay Ceramic Co., No. 1916, $1 003.80, dated June 3; terms, Net 45; flower pots and ornamental garden items (merchandise for resale).

—From M. & M. Chemicals, No. 1193, $784, dated June 3; terms, Net 60; for insecticides etc., for resale.

Cheque Copies

—No. 664, to Sylvester Concrete, $?, paying Invoice No. 446.

—No. 665, to Public Utilities Commission, $14.85, for electricity for the month of May. (**Note:** As soon as this bill was received cheque No. 665 was prepared.)

Bank Statement and Vouchers

—The bank statement and related vouchers and paid cheques arrived from the bank. Included in the vouchers was a debit note for bank charges in the amount of $41.50 for May; this was the first notice for these charges.

At this time, the following bank reconciliation statement was prepared. You will require this statement in order to prepare a reconciliation statement at the end of June.

Green Thumb Garden Centre
Bank Reconciliation Statement
May 31, 19–

Balance per Bk. Statement	3 406 15	Balance per General Ledger	3 527 24
Add: Outstanding Deposit	516 31	Deduct: Bank Interest and Service Charge	41 50
	3 922 46		
Deduct: Outstanding Cheques			
#641 $74.00			
#650 36.50			
#654 29.12			
#655 116.26			
#657 37.40			
#658 42.15			
#659 95.14			
#660 6.15	436 72		
True Balance	3 485 74	True Balance	3 485 74

June 5 *Cash Register Summary*

ACCOUNTING SUMMARY

		DEBIT	CREDIT
DEBITS:	Bank	1 699 90	
	Acc's Rec'l (Charge Sales)		
	Discounts Allowed	21 89	
	Cash Short and Over	1 23	
CREDITS:	Accounts Receivable		1 194 16
	Sales		475 10
	Sales Tax Payable		23 76
	Cash Short and Over		
BALANCING TOTALS		1 693 02	1 693 02

'Received' Vouchers

—Voucher No. 419, to C. Swinton, paying Invoice No. 407 in the amount of $1 094.63 less a 2 percent cash discount; net amount $1 072.74.

—Voucher No. 420, to O. Harrison, paying Invoice No. 377 in the amount of $63.

—Voucher No. 421, to P. Pierce, paying Invoice No. 379 in the amount of $36.53.

Cheque Copies

—No. 666 to Cash, $604.16, wages for the week.

—No. 667, to G. O. Emms, $440, personal drawings of owner.

—No. 668, to Acorn Seed Company, $?, paying Invoice No. 672 less a 2 percent cash discount.

June 6 *Cash Register Summary*

ACCOUNTING SUMMARY		DEBIT	CREDIT
DEBITS:	Bank	847 44	
	Acc's Rec'l (Charge Sales)	852 15	
	Cash Short and Over		
CREDITS:	Accounts Receivable		
	Sales		1 618 66
	Sales Tax Payable		80 93
	Cash Short and Over		
BALANCING TOTALS		1 699 59	1 699 59

'Charge' Vouchers

—Voucher No. 422, to C. Swinton, $516.07 plus 5 percent sales tax, for sale of merchandise; terms, 2/10,n/30; total $541.87.

—Voucher No. 423, to A. Renforth, $295.50 plus 5 percent sales tax, for sale of merchandise; terms, Net 30; total $310.28.

Purchase Invoices

—From Equipment Repair and Supply, 16 Barr St., No. 21, $157.50, dated June 5; terms, Net 30; for repairs to equipment.

—From Canada Products, No. B295, $997.50, dated June 4; terms, Net 30; for fertilizers and chemicals for soil to be charged as follows: Purchases, $871.50; Soil Preparation & Maintenance, $126.

Cheque Copies

—No. 669, to Clay Ceramic Co., $540.75, paying Invoice No. 1701.

—No. 670, to Kemp Haulage, $?, paying Invoice No. 772 less 1 percent cash discount.

—No. 671, to Canada Products, $58.80, paying Invoice No. B160.

June 7 *Cash Register Summary*

ACCOUNTING SUMMARY		DEBIT	CREDIT
DEBITS:	Bank	941 83	
	Acc's Rec'l (Charge Sales)		
	Cash Short and Over	10 00	
CREDITS:	Accounts Receivable		
	Sales		906 50
	Sales Tax Payable		45 33
	Cash Short and Over		
BALANCING TOTALS		951 83	951 83

Cheque Copy

—No. 672, to Public Utilities Commission, $27.50, cash payment of water bill (charge Soil Preparation & Maintenance).

June 8 *Cash Register Summary*

ACCOUNTING SUMMARY		DEBIT	CREDIT
DEBITS:	Bank	611 18	
	Acc's Rec'l (Charge Sales)		
	Discounts Allowed	10 84	
	Cash Short and Over		
CREDITS:	Accounts Receivable		541 80
	Sales		76 40
	Sales Tax Payable		3 82
	Cash Short and Over		
BALANCING TOTALS		622 02	622 02

'Received' Voucher

—Voucher No. 424, to F. Carson & Sons, paying Invoice No. 408 for $541.80 less 2 percent cash discount; net amount $530.96.

Cheque Copies

—No. 673, to M. & M. Chemicals, $1 932, paying Invoice No. 1046.

—No. 674, to Poplar Finance, $175, regular monthly payment on truck.

June 9 *Cash Register Summary*

ACCOUNTING SUMMARY		DEBIT	CREDIT
DEBITS:	Bank	117 60	
	Acc's Rec'l (Charge Sales)	71 40	
	Cash Short and Over		
CREDITS:	Accounts Receivable		
	Sales		180 00
	Sales Tax Payable		9 00
	Cash Short and Over		
BALANCING TOTALS		189 00	189 00

'Charge' Voucher

—Voucher No. 425, to O. Harrison, $68 plus 5 percent sales tax; terms, Net 30; for sale of merchandise; total $71.40.

Purchase Invoices

—From City Gas & Oil Co., 15 Boa Street, No. 1651, $135.68, dated June 8; terms, Net 30; for gasoline and oil used in the trucks and equipment as follows: Trucks, $94.67; Equipment, $41.01.

—From Kemp Haulage, No. 822, $231, dated June 7; terms, 1/10,n/30; topsoil for resale.

June 10 *Cash Register Summary*

ACCOUNTING SUMMARY		DEBIT	CREDIT
DEBITS:	Bank	301 79	
	Acc's Rec'l (Charge Sales)		
	Cash Short and Over		
CREDITS:	Accounts Receivable		78 75
	Sales		211 70
	Sales Tax Payable		10 59
	Cash Short and Over		75
BALANCING TOTALS		301 79	301 79

'Received' Voucher

—Voucher No. 426, to J. Bowen; paying Invoice No. 394.

Cheque Copies

—No. 675, to Northwestern Telephone Company, $25.20, cash payment of telephone bill.

—No. 676, to Kemp Haulage, $?, paying Invoice No. 795 less 1 percent cash discount.

June 11 *Cash Register Summary*

ACCOUNTING SUMMARY		DEBIT		CREDIT	
DEBITS:	Bank	137	66		
	Acc's Rec'l (Charge Sales)	131	25		
	Cash Short and Over				
CREDITS:	Accounts Receivable				
	Sales			256	10
	Sales Tax Payable			12	81
	Cash Short and Over				
BALANCING TOTALS		268	91	268	91

'Charge' Voucher

—Voucher No. 427, to P. Pierce, for the sale of merchandise, $125 plus 5 percent sales tax; terms, Net 30; total $131.25.

Purchase Invoice

—From M. & M. Chemicals, No. 1221, $781.90, dated June 10; terms, Net 60; to be charged to Soil Preparation & Maintenance.

Cheque Copy

—No. 677, to Canada Products, $98.91, paying Invoice No. B188.

June 12 *Cash Register Summary*

ACCOUNTING SUMMARY		DEBIT	CREDIT
DEBITS:	Bank	594 21	
	Acc's Rec'l (Charge Sales)	278 25	
	Cash Short and Over	09	
CREDITS:	Accounts Receivable		178 50
	Sales		661 00
	Sales Tax Payable		33 05
	Cash Short and Over		
BALANCING TOTALS		872 55	872 55

'Received' Voucher

—Voucher No. 428, to A. Renforth, $178.50, paying Invoice No. 390.

'Charge' Voucher

—Voucher No. 429, to F. Carson & Sons, for the sale of merchandise; terms 2/10,n/30; $265 plus 5 percent sales tax; total $278.25.

Cheque Copies

—No. 678, to Cash, $705.19, for the wages for the week.

—No. 679, to G. O. Emms, $350, owner's personal drawings.

—No. 680, to Foster Bros., $44.21, for the cash purchase of miscellaneous items to be charged to Miscellaneous Expense.

June 13 *Cash Register Summary*

ACCOUNTING SUMMARY		DEBIT	CREDIT
DEBITS:	Bank	669 06	
	Acc's Rec'l (Charge Sales)		
	Cash Short and Over	21	
CREDITS:	Accounts Receivable		
	Sales		637 40
	Sales Tax Payable		31 87
	Cash Short and Over		
BALANCING TOTALS		669 27	669 27

Purchase Invoice

—From Acorn Seed Company, No. 756, $82.43, dated June 12; terms, 2/15,n/30; for merchandise for resale.

June 14 *Cash Register Summary*

ACCOUNTING SUMMARY		DEBIT	CREDIT
DEBITS:	Bank	1 112 95	
	Acc's Rec'l (Charge Sales)		
	Discounts Allowed	6 62	
	Cash Short and Over		
CREDITS:	Accounts Receivable		330 75
	Sales		751 26
	Sales Tax Payable		37 56
	Cash Short and Over		
BALANCING TOTALS		1 119 57	1 119 57

'Received' Voucher

—Voucher No. 430, to Varga Brothers, $324.13, paying Invoice No. 418 less 2 percent cash discount.

Purchase Invoice

—From Triangle Sod, No. 452, $787.50, dated June 12; terms, Net 30; for purchase of sod for resale.

Bank Debit Advice

—This debit note from Central Bank stated that $2 000 had been deducted from the business bank account for the purpose of reducing the bank note. Mr. Emms had instructed the bank to make the deduction.

June 15 *Cash Register Summary*

ACCOUNTING SUMMARY		DEBIT		CREDIT	
DEBITS:	Bank	230	21		
	Acc's Rec'l (Charge Sales)				
	Cash Short and Over				
CREDITS:	Accounts Receivable			131	25
	Sales			94	20
	Sales Tax Payable			4	71
	Cash Short and Over				05
BALANCING TOTALS		230	21	230	21

'Received' Voucher
—Voucher No. 431, to P. Barker, $131.25, paying Invoice No. 398.

Cheque Copies
—No. 681, to Government Treasurer, $?, paying the sales tax for the previous month.
—No. 682, to Proud Insurance Company, $278.50, regular monthly mortgage payment.

June 16 *Cash Register Summary*

ACCOUNTING SUMMARY		DEBIT		CREDIT	
DEBITS:	Bank	75	60		
	Acc's Rec'l (Charge Sales)	26	93		
	Cash Short and Over				
CREDITS:	Accounts Receivable				
	Sales			97	65
	Sales Tax Payable			4	88
	Cash Short and Over				
BALANCING TOTALS		102	53	102	53

'Charge' Voucher
—Voucher No. 432, to P. Barker, for sale of merchandise; terms, Net 30; $25.65 plus 5 percent sales tax.

Cheque Copies

—No. 683, to Central Supply, $39.38, for the cash purchase of supplies.

—No. 684, to Mainline Express, $65.85, for the cash payment of express charges, to be charged to Freight-in.

June 17 *Cash Register Summary*

ACCOUNTING SUMMARY		DEBIT	CREDIT
DEBITS:	Bank	758 50	
	Acc's Rec'l (Charge Sales)		
	Discounts Allowed	10 84	
	Cash Short and Over		
CREDITS:	Accounts Receivable		541 87
	Sales		216 50
	Sales Tax Payable		10 82
	Cash Short and Over		15
BALANCING TOTALS		769 34	769 34

'Received' Voucher

—Voucher No. 433, to C. Swinton, $531.03, paying Invoice No. 422 less 2 percent cash discount. Although the payment was received after the discount period it was decided to allow the customer the discount.

Purchase Invoices

—From Equipment Repair and Supply, No. 40, $201.60, dated June 15; terms, Net 30; for truck repairs.

—From Kemp Haulage, No. 856, $211.05, dated June 16; terms, 1/10,n/30; topsoil and fertilizer to improve the condition of the soil on the business's property, to be charged to Soil Preparation & Maintenance.

Cheque Copy

—No. 685, to Kemp Haulage, $?, paying Invoice No. 822 less the cash discount.

June 18 *Cash Register Summary*

ACCOUNTING SUMMARY		DEBIT	CREDIT
DEBITS:	Bank	321 51	
	Acc's Rec'l (Charge Sales)	420 00	
	Cash Short and Over		
CREDITS:	Accounts Receivable		52 50
	Sales		656 20
	Sales Tax Payable		32 81
	Cash Short and Over		
BALANCING TOTALS		741 51	741 51

'Charge' Voucher

—Voucher No. 434, to Varga Brothers, for the sale of merchandise; terms, 2/10,n/30; $400 plus 5 percent sales tax; total $420.

'Credit Note' Voucher

—Voucher No. 435, to P. Pierce, to credit the customer's account for defective merchandise, $50 plus 5 percent sales tax.

Cheque Copy

—No. 686, to The Business House, $15.75, for the cash purchase of items to be charged to Miscellaneous Expense.

June 19 *Cash Register Summary*

ACCOUNTING SUMMARY		DEBIT	CREDIT
DEBITS:	Bank	332 01	
	Acc's Rec'l (Charge Sales)		
	Cash Short and Over		
CREDITS:	Accounts Receivable		
	Sales		316 20
	Sales Tax Payable		15 81
	Cash Short and Over		
BALANCING TOTALS		332 01	332 01

Purchase Invoice

—From Sylvester Concrete, No. 491, $1 236.25, dated June 17; terms, Net 30; patio stones for resale.

Cheque Copies

—No. 687, to Cash, $567.25, wages for the week.

—No. 688, to G. O. Emms, $450, owner's personal drawings.

June 20 *Cash Register Summary*

ACCOUNTING SUMMARY		DEBIT	CREDIT
DEBITS:	Bank	545 03	
	Acc's Rec'l (Charge Sales)		
	Cash Short and Over		
CREDITS:	Accounts Receivable		
	Sales		519 05
	Sales Tax Payable		25 98
	Cash Short and Over		
BALANCING TOTALS		545 03	545 03

Purchase Invoice

—From Triangle Sod, No. 474, $558.08, dated June 19; terms, Net 30; sod for resale.

June 21 *Cash Register Summary*

ACCOUNTING SUMMARY		DEBIT	CREDIT
DEBITS:	Bank	784 71	
	Acc's Rec'l (Charge Sales)		
	Cash Short and Over	9 40	
CREDITS:	Accounts Receivable		
	Sales		756 25
	Sales Tax Payable		37 86
	Cash Short and Over		
BALANCING TOTALS		794 11	794 11

Cheque Copies

—No. 689, to Petty Cash, $?, reimbursement with respect to following summary:

Petty Cash Summary June 21, 19--	
Soil Preparation & Maintenance	$26.15
Sales	35.00
Sales Tax Payable	1.75
Miscellaneous Expense	35.01

—No. 690, to Triangle Sod, $?, paying Invoice No. 374.

June 22 *Cash Register Summary*

ACCOUNTING SUMMARY		DEBIT	CREDIT
DEBITS:	Bank	432 78	
	Acc's Rec'l (Charge Sales)	2 159 50	
	Discounts Allowed	5 57	
	Cash Short and Over		
CREDITS:	Accounts Receivable		278 25
	Sales		2 209 14
	Sales Tax Payable		110 46
	Cash Short and Over		
BALANCING TOTALS		2 597 85	2 597 85

'Charge' Voucher

—Voucher No. 436, to C. Swinton, for the sale of merchandise; terms, 2/10,n/30; $2 056.67 plus 5 percent sales tax; total $2 159.50.

'Received' Voucher

—Voucher No. 437, to F. Carson & Sons, $272.68, paying Invoice No. 429 less 2 percent cash discount.

June 23 *Cash Register Summary*

ACCOUNTING SUMMARY		DEBIT	CREDIT
DEBITS:	Bank	136.77	
	Acc's Rec'l (Charge Sales)		
	Cash Short and Over		
CREDITS:	Accounts Receivable		100.00
	Sales		35.02
	Sales Tax Payable		1.75
	Cash Short and Over		
BALANCING TOTALS		136.77	136.77

'Received' Voucher

—Voucher No. 438, to A. Renforth, $100, on account.

June 24 *Cash Register Summary*

ACCOUNTING SUMMARY		DEBIT	CREDIT
DEBITS:	Bank	107.00	
	Acc's Rec'l (Charge Sales)		
	Cash Short and Over	.10	
CREDITS:	Accounts Receivable		
	Sales		102.00
	Sales Tax Payable		5.10
	Cash Short and Over		
BALANCING TOTALS		107.10	107.10

Purchase Invoices

—From Acorn Seed Company, No. 801, $813.75, dated June 23; terms, 2/15,n/30; merchandise for resale.

—From Clay Ceramic Co., No. 2016, $136.50, dated June 22; terms, Net 45; merchandise for resale.

ACCOUNTING SUMMARY		DEBIT	CREDIT
DEBITS:	Bank	126 47	
	Acc's Rec'l (Charge Sales)	97 23	
	Cash Short and Over		
CREDITS:	Accounts Receivable		
	Sales		213 05
	Sales Tax Payable		10 65
	Cash Short and Over		
BALANCING TOTALS		223 70	223 70

'Charge' Voucher

—Voucher No. 439, to A. Renforth, for sale of merchandise; terms, Net 30; $92.60 plus 5 percent sales tax; total $97.23.

Cheque Copy

—No. 691, to Poplar Finance Co., $182, regular finance payment on tractor.

June 26 *Cash Register Summary*

ACCOUNTING SUMMARY		DEBIT	CREDIT
DEBITS:	Bank	436 13	
	Acc's Rec'l (Charge Sales)		
	Cash Short and Over		
CREDITS:	Accounts Receivable		
	Sales		412 50
	Sales Tax Payable		20 63
	Cash Short and Over		3 00
BALANCING TOTALS		436 13	436 13

Cheque Copies

—No. 692, to Acorn Seed Co., $?, paying Invoice No. 756 less 2 percent cash discount.

—No. 693, to Cash, $505.60, wages for the week.

—No. 694, to G. O. Emms, $400, owner's personal drawings.

June 27 *Cash Register Summary*

ACCOUNTING SUMMARY		DEBIT	CREDIT
DEBITS:	Bank	1 436 29	
	Acc's Rec'l (Charge Sales)		
	Discounts Allowed	8 40	
	Cash Short and Over		
CREDITS:	Accounts Receivable		491 40
	Sales		907 90
	Sales Tax Payable		45 39
	Cash Short and Over		
BALANCING TOTALS		1 444 69	1 444 69

'Received' Vouchers

—Voucher No. 440, to O. Harrison, $71.40; paying Invoice No. 425.

—Voucher No. 441, to Varga Brothers, $411.60; paying Invoice No. 434 less 2 percent discount.

Purchase Invoice

—From Canada Products, No. B340, $330.75, dated June 25; terms, Net 30; for merchandise for resale.

June 28 *Cash Register Summary*

ACCOUNTING SUMMARY		DEBIT	CREDIT
DEBITS:	Bank	730 00	
	Acc's Rec'l (Charge Sales)		
	Cash Short and Over		
CREDITS:	Accounts Receivable		63 00
	Sales		635 21
	Sales Tax Payable		31 76
	Cash Short and Over		03
BALANCING TOTALS		730 00	730 00

'Credit' Voucher

—Voucher No. 442, to C. Swinton, $63.00; credit for merchandise returned.

June 29 *Cash Register Summary*

ACCOUNTING SUMMARY		DEBIT	CREDIT
DEBITS:	Bank	59 01	
	Acc's Rec'l (Charge Sales)	105 00	
	Cash Short and Over		
CREDITS:	Accounts Receivable		
	Sales		156 20
	Sales Tax Payable		7 81
	Cash Short and Over		
BALANCING TOTALS		164 01	164 01

'Charge' Vouchers

—Voucher No. 443, to J. Bowen, for sale of merchandise; terms, Net 30; $30 plus 5 percent sales tax; total $31.50.

—Voucher No. 444, to P. Pierce, for sale of merchandise; terms, Net 30; $70 plus 5 percent sales tax; total $73.50.

Cheque Copies

—No. 695, to Canada Products, $35.91, paying Invoice No. B249.

—No. 696, to First-Rate Repair Service, $233.10, cash payment to be charged to Equipment Expense.

Credit Note Received

—From Triangle Sod, No. 509, $183.75, with respect to inferior goods shipped on Invoice No. 474.

June 30 *Cash Register Summary*

ACCOUNTING SUMMARY		DEBIT	CREDIT
DEBITS:	Bank	88 20	
	Acc's Rec'l (Charge Sales)		
	Cash Short and Over		
CREDITS:	Accounts Receivable		
	Sales		84 00
	Sales Tax Payable		4 20
	Cash Short and Over		
BALANCING TOTALS		88 20	88 20

2. **Balance the journals and post to the general ledger.**

3. **Balance the general ledger, the accounts receivable ledger, and the accounts payable ledger.**

   Note: SAVE THIS SOLUTION. You will need it to prepare a bank reconciliation statement in the next chapter.

17

Accounting Controls

17-1 Internal Control
17-2 Procedures for Control of Cash
17-3 Control of Cash Expenditures
17-4 The Voucher System

Objectives

When you have completed Chapter 17, you should:

1. Understand the concept of internal control.
2. Know the basic features of good internal control.
3. Understand the basic characteristics of a current bank account.
4. Know the specific elements of internal control for cash receipts.
5. Be able to reconcile a bank account.
6. Understand the importance of accounting control over cash payments.
7. Understand a basic system for purchasing.
8. Understand a basic system for receiving.
9. Understand the concept of the voucher system to control expenditures.
10. Know the different records involved in the voucher system.
11. Know how subsidiary ledgers are kept in a voucher register system.

17.1 Internal Control

An accounting system that encourages the employees to be honest and accurate is said to have good **internal control**. No internal control is needed in a small business where the owner does everything alone. But as soon as employees are hired, then accounting controls become important. Where there are numerous employees, a good system of internal control is essential. A business cannot afford to assume that all its employees are honest. Good internal control results in protection against theft and waste, more accurate information, and greater efficiency.

Internal control is a system of accounting designed to protect assets and ensure the reliability and accuracy of accounting records. The most important elements of good internal control are as follows:

1. Where accounting records and documents are prepared, the system should be designed, where possible, so that the work of one person must agree with the work of another person whose work is done independently.
2. The person who records transactions or prepares accounting records should not be able to handle or control assets.
3. All assets should be kept in a safe place. Two authorized persons should be present before access to negotiable assets is allowed. (Negotiable assets are those that can be easily converted into cash.)
4. Powers of approval and authorization should be restricted to a few key employees.
5. Periodically an audit should take place to ensure that the accounting system is followed correctly and to examine the system for weaknesses.
6. Responsibilities should be firmly established. It should be easy to trace the responsibility for errors or missing assets.

Importance of Cash

The word 'cash' can be used in both a narrow and a broad sense. In its narrow sense, cash means dollar bills and coins. In its broad sense, cash also includes cheques, bank balances, and other items such as credit card vouchers or money orders.

Cash in this broad sense is vital to a business. The principal objective of a business is to earn a profit, and this profit must eventually be converted into cash. A business needs cash to pay its bills, to meet its expenses, to reward its owners, and so on.

A quantity of cash is generally kept on hand in the office each day. However, a business keeps most of its cash in the safety of a bank account.

Current Bank Account

We noted in Chapter 2 that a bank offers various types of deposit account to meet the special needs of its customers. The **current bank account** is designed especially for the business person. A business often has several current bank accounts for various purposes, just as an individual might have both a savings and a chequing account.

The special features of a current bank account are as follows:

1. No interest is allowed on the account balance (as compared to the savings account where there is interest).
2. Once a month the bank returns all of the business's cheques that have gone through the bank during the month. These are known as the cancelled cheques.

The bank also includes a credit or debit memo for any deposit or charge that has not originated from the business itself. After these items have been received, the business has a complete record of all its debits and credits at the bank for the month.

3. Once a month the bank supplies the business with a summary of the transactions that have gone through the business's bank account during that month. This summary is known as the bank statement and comes in the same form as a bank statement for a personal chequing account. It is an exact copy of the bank's ledger sheets for the business's account. Today this statement is generally produced by a computer. The monthly bank statement for a business is illustrated in Figure 17.1.
4. The service charge for a current account is approximately 25 cents an entry. However, the bank manager can vary the amount to be charged, and may reduce the charge depending on the number of cheques, the average bank balance, and the size of the bank loan, if any.

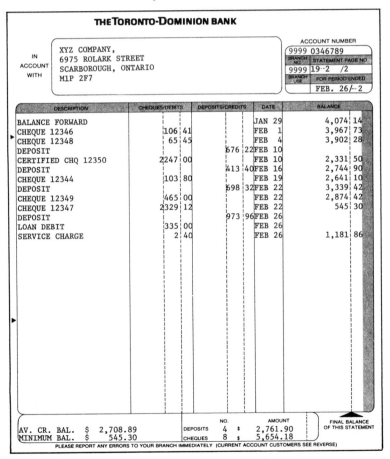

THE TORONTO-DOMINION BANK

IN ACCOUNT WITH
XYZ COMPANY,
6975 ROLARK STREET
SCARBOROUGH, ONTARIO
M1P 2F7

ACCOUNT NUMBER: 9999 0346789
BRANCH NO.: 9999 | STATEMENT PAGE NO.: 19--2 /2
BRANCH USE | FOR PERIOD ENDED: FEB. 26/--2

DESCRIPTION	CHEQUES/DEBITS	DEPOSITS/CREDITS	DATE	BALANCE
BALANCE FORWARD			JAN 29	4,074 14
CHEQUE 12346	106 41		FEB 1	3,967 73
CHEQUE 12348	65 45		FEB 4	3,902 28
DEPOSIT		676 22	FEB 10	
CERTIFIED CHQ 12350	2247 00		FEB 10	2,331 50
DEPOSIT		413 40	FEB 16	2,744 90
CHEQUE 12344	103 80		FEB 19	2,641 10
DEPOSIT		698 32	FEB 22	3,339 42
CHEQUE 12349	465 00		FEB 22	2,874 42
CHEQUE 12347	2329 12		FEB 22	545 30
DEPOSIT		973 96	FEB 26	
LOAN DEBIT	335 00		FEB 26	
SERVICE CHARGE	2 40		FEB 26	1,181 86

		NO.	AMOUNT
AV. CR. BAL. $ 2,708.89	DEPOSITS	4	$ 2,761.90
MINIMUM BAL. $ 545.30	CHEQUES	8	$ 5,654.18

FINAL BALANCE OF THIS STATEMENT

PLEASE REPORT ANY ERRORS TO YOUR BRANCH IMMEDIATELY (CURRENT ACCOUNT CUSTOMERS SEE REVERSE)

Figure 17.1 The monthly bank statement of a business. Courtesy of The Toronto Dominion Bank.

A business would find it almost impossible to operate today without a bank account. Businesses rely on the bank for transfer of funds. A **transfer of funds** takes place every time a cheque or bank credit card voucher is processed. The banks have the equipment to transfer funds almost instantly.

In addition to transfer of funds, the banks offer the time-honoured convenience of keeping money safe for their depositors.

17.2 Procedures for Control of Cash

Internal control regulates all aspects of a business but it is especially needed for cash. Cash is most likely to be stolen outright by employees, or to be embezzled, that is, stolen secretly with the help of falsified accounting records. Cash has no special marks to identify it, and is easily exchanged for other goods or services.

The following are internal control measures specially designed to protect the cash of a business:

1. *Separate duties.* In general, the persons who handle the cash should not be the same ones who keep the records for the cash. For example, the person who opens the mail and prepares the daily list of mail receipts should not be a member of the accounting department. This way, a theft can only take place if two or more employees decide to act in collusion. A mail clerk who acted alone would be easily caught. Suppose, for instance, that the mail clerk managed to cash a customer's cheque for personal use. The customer's account would not get credited with the amount of the payment and there would be a complaint. It would be clear that only the mail clerk had had access to the cheque.

2. *Deposit funds daily.* The total cash receipts for the day should be deposited at the end of that day. In this way the amount of cash in the office is kept to a minimum and theft is not encouraged.

3. *Deposit funds intact.* All the cash receipts of each business day should be deposited intact. The funds should not be used to make payments, or to make short-term loans. This rule is only broken for cash register 'paid outs' which are controlled by the cash register audit strip.

4. *Make all payments by cheque.* Except for petty cash expenditures, all payments should require approval and should only be made by cheque. When payments are made by cheque, and cash receipts are deposited intact, the record prepared by the bank corresponds to the company's own record. It is then possible to compare the externally prepared record against the internally prepared one. This control technique is described later in the chapter.

5. *Mark cheques 'For Deposit Only'.* Mark all cheques 'For Deposit Only' so that each cheque will have to be credited to the business's bank account and none will be cashed in error.

6. *Prepare deposit slips in duplicate.* The deposit slip shows the details of the deposit and is useful if any question arises regarding the deposit. A duplicate of the deposit slip should be stamped by the teller and retained by the business as a receipt for the deposit.

7. *Use cash registers in retail stores.* Cash registers should be used in retail outlets of any size. The cash receipts should be balanced every day. The audit strip and the balanced cash receipts should go different ways for processing, the one to be the source document for the accounting entry, the other to be included with the daily bank deposit.

8. *Reconcile the bank account monthly.* As was indicated in 4, above, the bank's record and the company's record can be compared, or *reconciled*, with each other. If a company has more than one bank account, each one should be reconciled every month.

Bank Reconciliation

Since both the bank and the business keep track of the same funds, you might expect the month-end balance shown by the bank statement to agree with the month-end balance shown by the general ledger Bank account. This is rarely the case. Usually, the two balances are different.

Since the bank statement balance usually differs from the Bank account in the general ledger, how can the accountant be certain that either record is correct? The accountant checks both of these balances by a process known as *reconciling the bank account*. This process is the same as the one you studied in Chapter 2 for a personal chequing account. The accountant thoroughly investigates the two sets of records to find out the precise reasons for any difference.

When the reconciliation is finished, the accountant shows how the records correspond by preparing a **bank reconciliation statement**. An example of a bank reconciliation statement is shown in Figure 17.2.

Steps in Reconciling a Bank Account

The steps in reconciling a bank statement are as follows:

1. Have the following records available: (a) the bank statement and related vouchers received from the bank; (b) the bank reconciliation statement for the previous month end; (c) the general ledger; (d) the cash receipts journal; (e) the cash payments journal; and (f) the general journal.
2. Write the heading Bank Reconciliation Statement on a sheet of paper. Then divide the page down the middle.
3. On one side of the page, enter the balance from the bank statement, which will be the final amount in the Balance column of the bank statement. On the other side of the page, enter the balance from the general ledger, which will be the final balance in the Bank account (after the general ledger is posted and balanced).

Boxwell and Company
Bank Reconciliation Statement
March 31, 19–

Balance per Bank Statement	1 204 90	Balance per General Ledger	1 147 76
		Deduct:	
Add:		Amount of error in	
Late Deposit	300 51	recording cheque #697.	
	1 505 41	Was recorded at $5.60	
		Should have been $6.50	
Deduct:		Difference .90¢	90
Outstanding Cheques			1 146 86
#702 $60.00			
#705 72.40			
#709 51.90		Deduct:	
#710 175.00		Bank Service Charges	
#711 2.75	362 05	deducted on bank statement but not recorded in company books in same month.	3 50
True Balance	1 143 36	True Balance	1 143 36

Figure 17.2 A bank reconciliation statement.

4. Search for the *discrepancy items,* that is, the items causing the difference between the two balances. This is the most difficult and most important part of a reconciliation. It involves comparing in detail the bank's record against the business's record. You are looking for items that are not recorded equally in both records. Techniques for doing this are explained more fully later in this section.
5. Record the discrepancy items on the reconciliation statement, adding or subtracting them as necessary until the two balances are shown to be equal. This step is explained in detail later in this section. You cannot consider the job completed until the point of balance is reached.

Locating the Discrepancy Items

Locating the discrepancy items usually requires a well-organized and skilful search. The following general suggestions will be of some help to you:

1. When comparing the two sets of records, it is never necessary to go back in the books beyond one month. Any differences that occurred before then will be listed on the previous reconciliation statement.
2. The bank's record must be compared in detail against the business's record. When items are found to correspond exactly, they are marked in some way with a coloured pencil. After the comparison is over, the items without coloured marks are the discrepancy items.
3. The most common source of disagreement between the two sets of records is the quantity of uncashed cheques commonly known as the **outstanding cheques**. When a cheque is issued by a business, it is recorded promptly in the books of the business, but it is not recorded in the records of the bank until the time it is cashed. In many cases, this is after some time has passed.
4. A less frequently occurring but fairly common source of disagreement between the two records is the late deposit. A **late deposit** is recorded in the books of the business during a certain month but is not deposited in the bank until the following month. This usually occurs on the last day of the month in businesses that have a one-day delay in the depositing of cash receipts. The late deposit will appear on the bank statement of the following month, usually as the first item in the Deposit column.
5. There are numerous other possible items of disagreement. One of these would be an error made by either a bank employee or a company employee. Another would be a bank service charge that has not yet been recorded in the books of the company.
6. When comparing the records, it is important not to forget the discrepancy items from the previous reconciliation statement. During the current month, most of these items will cease to be items of disagreement. For example, a cheque outstanding on the April 30 reconciliation statement, if cashed during May, will not be an item of disagreement on the May 31 reconciliation statement.

   Some items, however, may not be cleared up in the current month and will have to be carried forward to the new reconciliation. For example, an outstanding cheque appearing on the April reconciliation, if not cashed during the month of May, will continue to be outstanding and must appear also on the May reconciliation.

Recording the Discrepancy Items

The discrepancy items must be recorded on the bank reconciliation statement.

1. All discrepancy items must be included. It is often advisable to group items of a similar nature, such as outstanding cheques.
2. Each item must be recorded on one side of the reconciliation statement only, either on the bank statement side or on the general ledger side. Always choose the side where the item has not appeared as of the reconciliation date. For example, an outstanding cheque, because it represents an item not seen by the bank, would be recorded on the bank statement side. Similarly, an outstanding

bank service charge, because it represents an item not recorded in the company records, would be entered on the general ledger side.

3. Each item represents either an increase or a decrease to the balance. Your common sense should tell you which it is. Just decide what effect the item has on the bank balance and act accordingly. For example, cheques and service charges represent decreases to the bank balance and are therefore treated as deductions on the reconciliation. Similarly, deposits increase the bank balance and are therefore treated as additions on the reconciliation.
4. If all of the discrepancy items are found and entered correctly, the two final totals of the reconciliation statement will balance. If not, then you must repeat the process. The reasons for the difference must be found.

Bringing the Books Up to Date

The general ledger side of the reconciliation lists all of the items by which the Bank account is not currently accurate. These items must be journalized and posted to bring the Bank account up to date.

17.3 Control of Cash Expenditures

In the previous section, you saw how a good system helps to control cash. In this section, you will learn about an effective system for controlling cash expenditures.

The following three cases show what can result when cash expenditures are not controlled. In each of these cases, poor accounting controls result in the payment of bills that were improperly sent to the business.

1. Bruce Ion has a position of authority with Exact Company. He arranges for a major repair to be performed on his home and for the repair bill to be sent to his employer. When the bill arrives on his desk, Bruce approves it for payment. Quite clearly, Bruce Ion has improperly obtained the equivalent of cash from his employer.
2. Fran Boyko has a responsible position with Apex Company. She arranges with a supplier of goods to the company to charge a higher than normal price for them. Fran later approves these inflated bills for payment. She and the supplier split the excess charges.
3. Darren Park is an executive with Supreme Products. He sets up a fictitious company of which he is the sole owner, and through this company sends phony invoices to Supreme Products. Later, he approves the phony bills for payment. The monies paid to the phony company end up in the pocket of Darren Park.

These three cases show that cash can be improperly obtained from a business that has poor accounting controls. Therefore, an effective system is needed to control the expenditure cycle, from the moment the goods are ordered to the time that the cheque is issued for payment. One system of control is known as the voucher system.

17.4 The Voucher System

The **voucher system** is a very popular method of processing expenditure transactions. This system is designed to ensure that all expenditure transactions are right and proper, and that the business papers pertaining to such expenditures are all present and correct.

A voucher system is effective because it controls expenditures through a rigid set of procedures whereby the documents supporting the transactions are 'vouched' (seen to be correct), payment of the obligation is authorized, and the transaction is properly recorded. Every bill received for goods or services, whether it is to be paid right away or some time in the future, must be validated according to these procedures. The business does not issue any cheque unless it is in payment of a previously approved voucher. A **voucher** is any document used in the voucher system as part of the verification process. The features of a voucher system are described on the following pages.

Purchasing Routine

All businesses buy materials, supplies, parts, and services. In some businesses, such as the office of a public accountant, purchasing is a minor, relatively unimportant function. But in other businesses, such as manufacturing companies or large department stores, purchasing is a major function of the business.

Because every item purchased must be paid for eventually, purchasing is really the first step in the expenditure cycle. Figure 17.3 shows a simple purchasing control procedure.

In most businesses, purchases are initiated by key persons such as department heads. The first step in the purchase routine is the preparation of a business document called a purchase requisition.

A **purchase requisition** is a business form requesting the Purchasing Department to order certain goods or services according to given information and instructions. One copy of each purchase requisition is sent to the Purchasing Department. The Purchasing Department is expert in matters related to purchasing. This department keeps available the latest information on sources of supply, new products, latest prices, quality suppliers, means of transportation, and so on.

When the Purchasing Department receives a purchase requisition it proceeds to order the goods. It selects a supplier on the basis of past experience, the instructions of the requisitioner, and the information that it has available. The order is formally placed by means of a **purchase order** which authorizes the supplier to send the goods and to bill the purchaser. The purchase order form specifies all information necessary to the purchase, including quantity, price, part number, description, delivery date, and method of shipment.

Several copies of the purchase order form are prepared. The flowchart in Figure 17.3 indicates the use to which each copy is put.

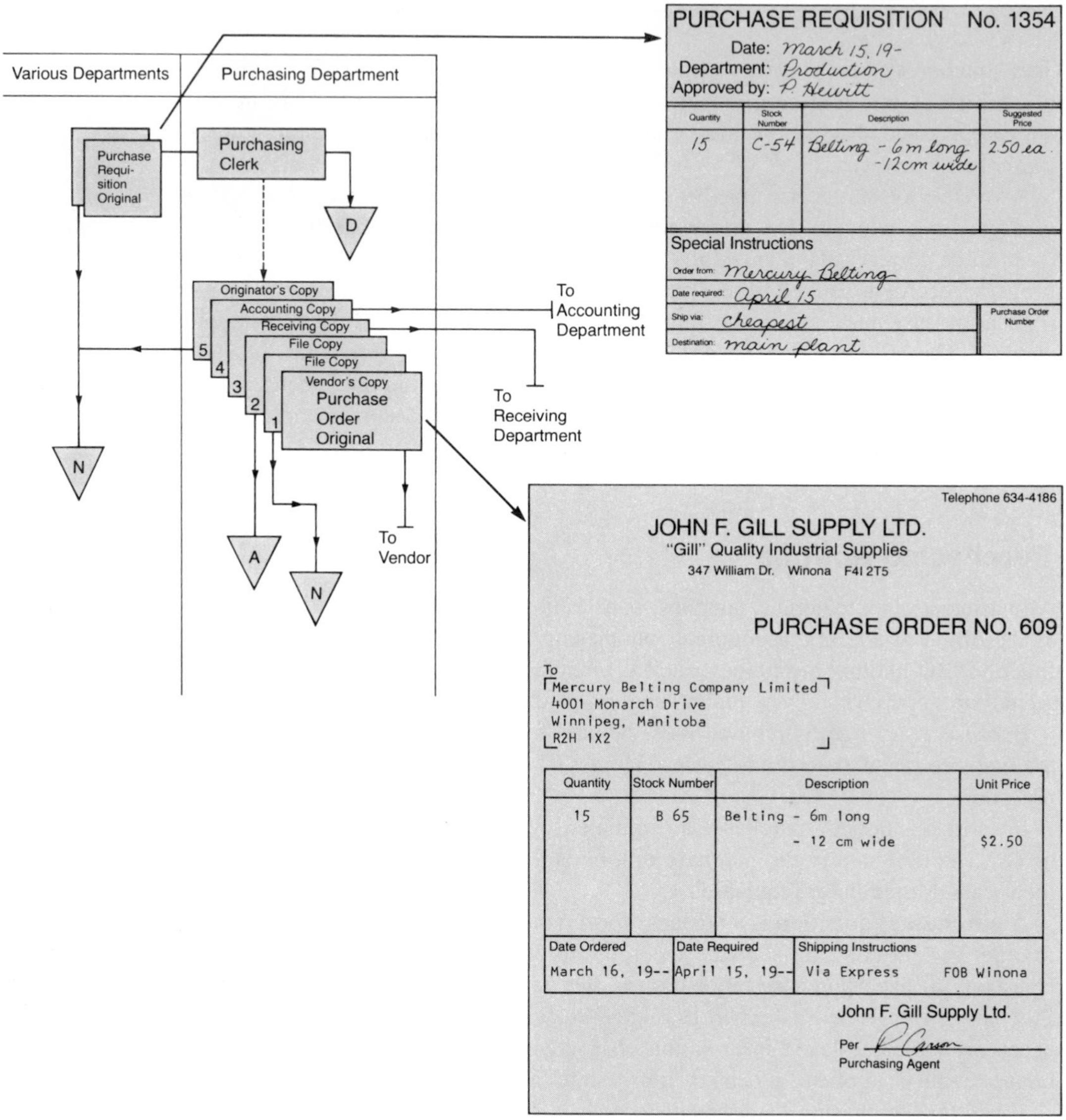

Figure 17.3 A flowchart showing a system for purchasing goods.

Receiving Routine

Figure 17.4 illustrates the receiving routine of a business. One copy of the purchase order is forwarded to the Receiving Department so that the receiver can check the goods when they arrive. The receiver will not accept goods that are clearly in poor condition.

The supplier encloses a **packing slip** with the goods to help the buyer identify

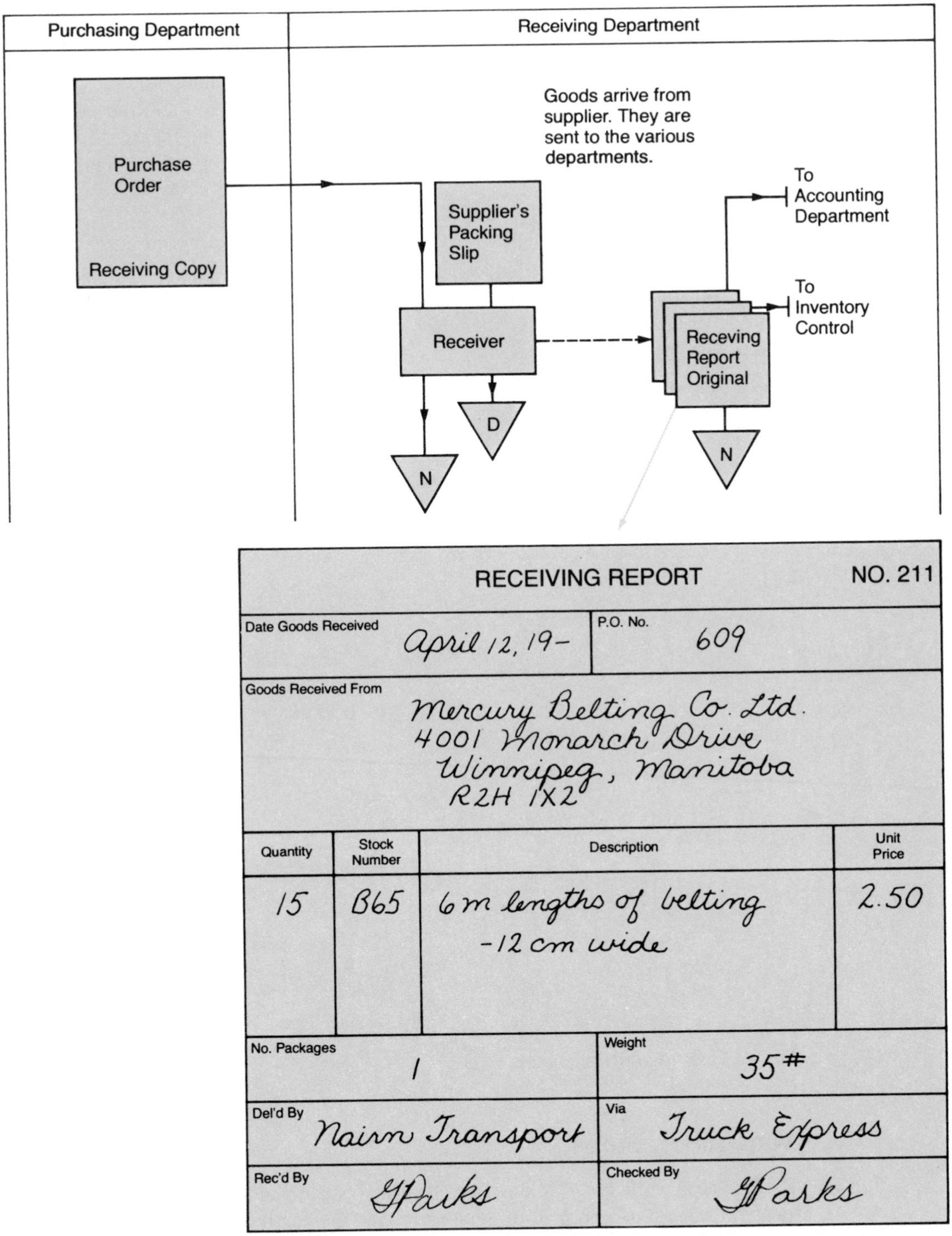
Purchasing Department
Receiving Department
Purchase Order
Receiving Copy
Goods arrive from supplier. They are sent to the various departments.
Supplier's Packing Slip
Receiver
D
N
Receving Report Original
N
To Accounting Department
To Inventory Control
RECEIVING REPORT
NO. 211
Date Goods Received
April 12, 19–
P.O. No.
609
Goods Received From
Mercury Belting Co. Ltd.
4001 Monarch Drive
Winnipeg, Manitoba
R2H 1X2
Quantity
Stock Number
Description
Unit Price
15
B65
6 m lengths of belting
-12 cm wide
2.50
No. Packages
1
Weight
35#
Del'd By
Nairn Transport
Via
Truck Express
Rec'd By
G Parks
Checked By
G Parks

Figure 17.4 A flowchart showing a system for receiving goods.

them. A packing slip is a business paper providing a description of the goods and showing the quantities but not the prices. The packing slip is often merely a carbon copy of the supplier's sales invoice with the prices blocked out.

After checking the goods against the supplier's packing slip and the purchase order, the receiver writes up a **receiving report**. As seen in Figure 17.4, this business form provides all the pertinent details with respect to the goods received.

The Voucher Jacket

An important feature of the voucher system is the **voucher jacket**. This is a file folder containing all the information and documents belonging to a single purchase order. Figure 17.5 illustrates the most common form of voucher jacket, a file folder with printing on it.

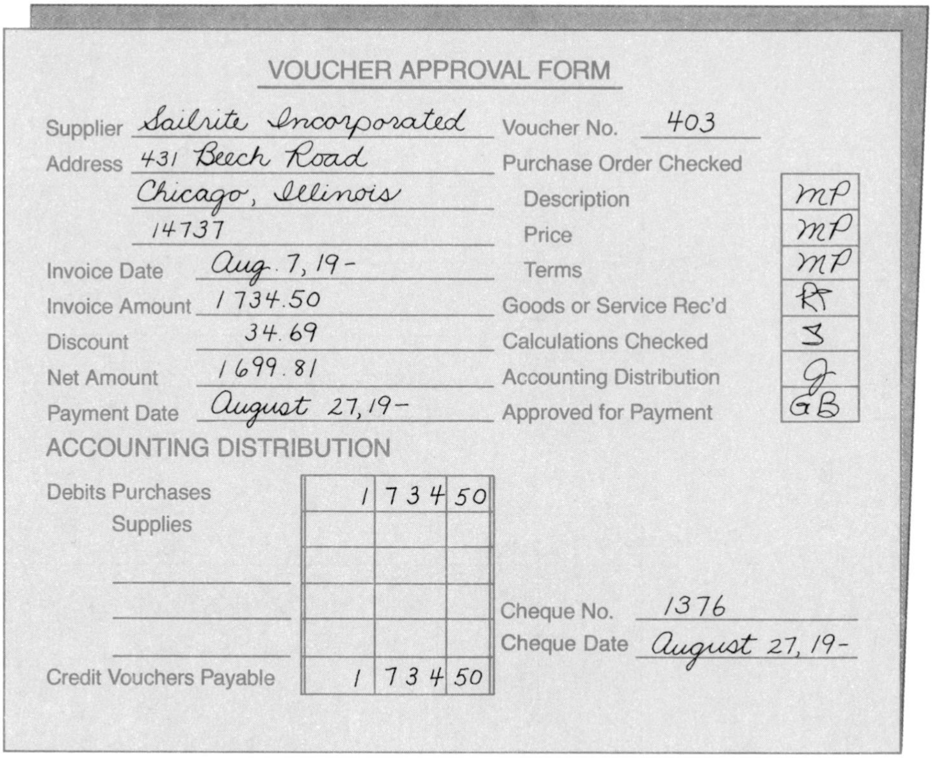

VOUCHER APPROVAL FORM

Supplier	Sailrite Incorporated	Voucher No.	403
Address	431 Beech Road	Purchase Order Checked	
	Chicago, Illinois	Description	mP
	14737	Price	mP
Invoice Date	Aug. 7, 19-	Terms	mP
Invoice Amount	1 734.50	Goods or Service Rec'd	RT
Discount	34.69	Calculations Checked	S
Net Amount	1 699.81	Accounting Distribution	G
Payment Date	August 27, 19-	Approved for Payment	GB

ACCOUNTING DISTRIBUTION

Debits Purchases	1 734	50
Supplies		
Credit Vouchers Payable	1 734	50

Cheque No. 1376

Cheque Date August 27, 19-

Figure 17.5 A voucher jacket.

Verification Steps

The flowchart in Figure 17.6 describes the steps performed in verifying an expenditure, recording it in a book of original entry, and making it ready for payment. This system makes it very difficult to get money out of a business under false pretenses. Collusion among several employees would be needed for fraud. This system is not

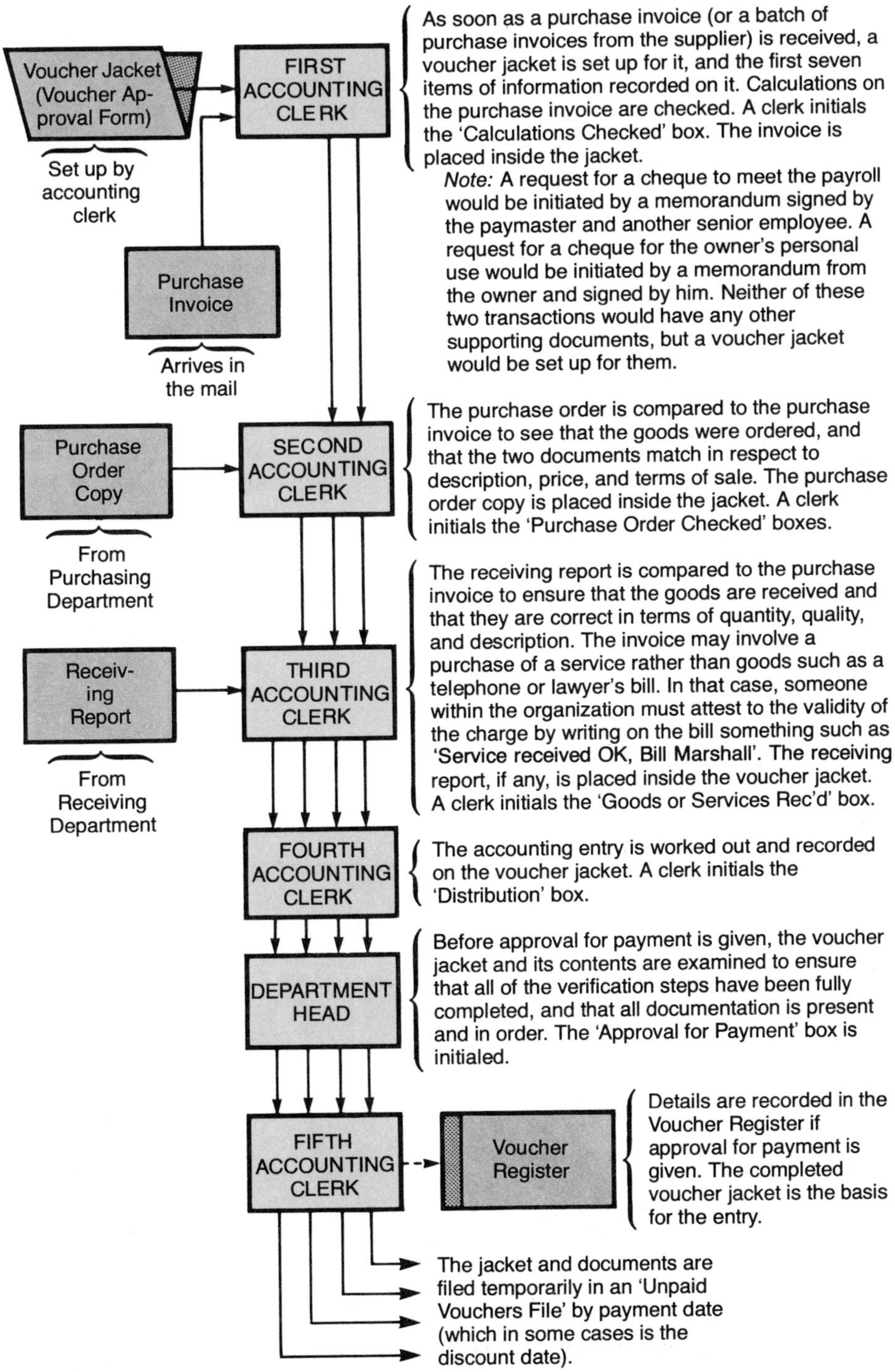
Voucher Jacket (Voucher Approval Form)
Set up by accounting clerk
Purchase Invoice
Arrives in the mail
FIRST ACCOUNTING CLERK
As soon as a purchase invoice (or a batch of purchase invoices from the supplier) is received, a voucher jacket is set up for it, and the first seven items of information recorded on it. Calculations on the purchase invoice are checked. A clerk initials the 'Calculations Checked' box. The invoice is placed inside the jacket.
Note: A request for a cheque to meet the payroll would be initiated by a memorandum signed by the paymaster and another senior employee. A request for a cheque for the owner's personal use would be initiated by a memorandum from the owner and signed by him. Neither of these two transactions would have any other supporting documents, but a voucher jacket would be set up for them.
Purchase Order Copy
From Purchasing Department
SECOND ACCOUNTING CLERK
The purchase order is compared to the purchase invoice to see that the goods were ordered, and that the two documents match in respect to description, price, and terms of sale. The purchase order copy is placed inside the jacket. A clerk initials the 'Purchase Order Checked' boxes.
Receiving Report
From Receiving Department
THIRD ACCOUNTING CLERK
The receiving report is compared to the purchase invoice to ensure that the goods are received and that they are correct in terms of quantity, quality, and description. The invoice may involve a purchase of a service rather than goods such as a telephone or lawyer's bill. In that case, someone within the organization must attest to the validity of the charge by writing on the bill something such as 'Service received OK, Bill Marshall'. The receiving report, if any, is placed inside the voucher jacket. A clerk initials the 'Goods or Services Rec'd' box.
FOURTH ACCOUNTING CLERK
The accounting entry is worked out and recorded on the voucher jacket. A clerk initials the 'Distribution' box.
DEPARTMENT HEAD
Before approval for payment is given, the voucher jacket and its contents are examined to ensure that all of the verification steps have been fully completed, and that all documentation is present and in order. The 'Approval for Payment' box is initialed.
FIFTH ACCOUNTING CLERK
Voucher Register
Details are recorded in the Voucher Register if approval for payment is given. The completed voucher jacket is the basis for the entry.
The jacket and documents are filed temporarily in an 'Unpaid Vouchers File' by payment date (which in some cases is the discount date).

Figure 17.6 A flowchart showing the steps in verifying an invoice and approving it for payment.

used by everyone, but is popular and its verification techniques are common to almost all systems.

Notice that three separate source documents must be matched against each other. The three source documents, along with the voucher jacket, form the basis for the accounting entry. If anything is missing, the documents are given to an accounting clerk for special attention.

The Voucher Register

Figure 17.7 shows a completed page of a voucher register. The **voucher register** is a columnar journal very like the purchases journal with which you are familiar. Recording the vouchers in the voucher register is straightforward. Every voucher jacket is the basis of an accounting entry in this journal. The vouchers are entered in numerical order to make certain that none is missed. There are a number of columns for the debits, but only one for the credit. The credit column is called Vouchers Payable, which is really Accounts Payable by another name. At the end of each month, the register is totalled, balanced, and posted in the usual manner.

This journal contains a special 'Payment' column in which the cheque number and date of payment are recorded at the time each payment is made. These two details are recorded both in the register and on the voucher jacket. A quick look at the Payment column in the register tells you which items have, and which have not, been paid.

VOUCHER REGISTER PAGE 46

DATE	VO. NO.	SUPPLIER	PAYMENT DATE	PAYMENT CHQ.	VOUCHERS PAYABLE CREDIT	PURCHASES DEBIT	SUPPLIES DEBIT	FREIGHT-IN DEBIT	OTHER ACCOUNTS ACCOUNT	PR	DEBIT	CREDIT
19– Feb. 3	361	Pascoe Supply	2/13	902	79 80		79 80					
4	362	Plumbing Market			1 450 –	1 450 –						
8	363	Excel Tools	2/28	905	1 835 –	1 835 –						
8	364	R. Axworthy			300 –				R. Axworthy, Drugs	31	300 –	
10	365	Dick's Paving			250 –				Bldg. Repairs	54	250 –	
12	366	Provincial COOP	2/25	904	740 –	740 –						
12	367	Via Rail			125 –			125 –				
15	368	Payroll	2/15	903	4 926 40				Wages	61	4 926 40	
17	369	Czepak & Sons			276 –	276 –						
17	370	Electro Products			996 –	996 –						
18	371	Metal Products			1 570 –	1 570 –						
24	372	Kelly Trucking			105 –			105 –				
27	373	Lukas's			73 50		73 50					
28	374	Payroll	2/28	906	4 802 60				Wages	61	4 802 60	
					17 529 30	6 867 –	153 30	230 –			10 279 –	
					(21)	(50)	(4)	(51)				

Figure 17.7 A completed page of a voucher register.

The Unpaid Voucher File

After the vouchers are recorded in the voucher register, they are filed in an **Unpaid Vouchers file**, in the order of their date of payment. If there is a discount on the transaction, the date of payment will be the discount date. The vouchers remain in the Unpaid file until the date for payment arrives, at which time they are removed and forwarded to the person in charge of preparing cheques. Cheques are prepared in the usual manner. The tear-off portion of the cheque shows the details regarding the payment for the benefit of the supplier.

Some transactions, such as a cash purchase of supplies, require that payment be made immediately. No change in procedure is made for this type of transaction except that the entire process, from the receipt of the bill or invoice to the issuance of the cheque, occurs on the same day.

The Cheque Register

On the day that a voucher is due for payment, the voucher jacket is removed from the Unpaid Vouchers file, and a cheque is prepared and issued. At that time the cheque number and the date are recorded in the voucher register and on the voucher jacket.

Cheques are recorded in a book of original entry known as the **cheque register**, which is another name for the cash payments journal. Because all expenditures have been recorded previously as vouchers payable, the cheque register is a simple journal. It requires only three columns, as shown in Figure 17.8.

For each cheque, the debit part of the entry is always to Vouchers Payable, and

CHEQUE REGISTER PAGE 76

Date		Particulars	Vou. No.	Vouchers Payable Debit	Discounts Earned Credit	Ch. No.	Bank Credit
19– Mar	3	Plumbing Market	362	1 450 -		907	1 450 -
	5	Bell Phone	375	39 50		908	39 50
	7	Dick's Paving	365	250 -		909	250 -
	7	Metal Products	371	1 570 -	31 40	910	1 538 60
	[illegible]	[illegible] Trucking	[illegible]	[illegible]		[illegible]	[illegible]
	25	Lukas's	373	73 50		920	73 50
	28	Payroll	386	4 851 75		921	4 851 75
	31	Western Bank	387	64 50			64 50
				16 439 90	169 30		16 270 60
				(21)	(41)		(1)

Figure 17.8 A cheque register.

the credits are to Bank and to Discounts Earned, if applicable. At the end of each month, the cheque register is totalled, cross-balanced, and posted in the usual manner.

The Paid Vouchers File

Once the vouchers are paid they are placed in a **Paid Vouchers file**. These paid vouchers are used (1) for reference purposes and (2) as the documented evidence for the transactions.

Accounts Payable Subsidiary Ledger

The voucher system does not use a subsidiary ledger for accounts payable. Also, there are no postings to individual creditors' accounts. The Unpaid Vouchers file takes the place of the subsidiary ledger for accounts payable. Instead of a file of creditors' accounts in the traditional ledger form, the voucher system substitutes a file of voucher jackets in an Unpaid Vouchers file.

The Unpaid Vouchers file is maintained in numerical order, and not in alphabetical order by creditors' names. This is one of the disadvantages of the voucher system. The debt to any one creditor can only be determined by searching through the file and totalling individual items.

The voucher register also acts as a subsidiary accounts payable ledger. The 'open' items in the register are those not marked 'paid' by the entry of a cheque number. These open items are exactly the same as those in the Unpaid Vouchers file. The two records, although different in form, show precisely the same information.

At the end of each month, subsidiary records for accounts payable must be made to agree with the Vouchers Payable control account in the general ledger. In a business that uses the voucher system, the customary manner of doing this is as follows:

1. Take off a listing, with total, of all the open items from the voucher register.
2. Make this listing agree in detail with the unpaid vouchers file.
3. Make the total agree with the general ledger control account. If the totals disagree, the usual search for errors and omissions must be undertaken.

Returns and Allowances with the Voucher System

A business is bound to encounter situations where there are returns and allowances. A good accounting system must be able to handle such situations.

A voucher register handles returns and allowances in the manner shown by the following examples.

Example 1

1. An invoice for $1 300 from PCV Pipe Ltd is approved for payment. It is recorded in the voucher register under voucher No. 614, as shown in Figure 17.9.

VOUCHER REGISTER — PAGE 72

DATE		VO. NO.	SUPPLIER	PAYMENT DATE	PAYMENT CHQ.	VOUCHERS PAYABLE CREDIT	PUR-CHASES DEBIT	SUPPLIES DEBIT	FREIGHT-IN DEBIT	OTHER ACCOUNTS ACCOUNT	PR	DEBIT	CREDIT
Mar	21	614	PCV Pipe Ltd.			1 300 –	1 300 –						

Figure 17.9 An invoice recorded in the voucher register.

2. A credit note for $1 300 from PCV Pipe Ltd is received when goods are found defective and returned. To record this transaction the following steps are necessary.
   a. A voucher jacket is set up for the credit note, in this case No. 702.
   b. Voucher jackets No. 614 and No. 702 are cross-referenced to each other with an explanatory note.
   c. A notation is made in the 'Payment' column of the voucher register, on the line for voucher No. 614, referencing it ahead to voucher No. 702.
   d. The credit note is recorded in the voucher register by an exact reversing entry, using either the circle method or a Returns and Allowances account, as in Figure 17.10.

VOUCHER REGISTER — PAGE 72

DATE		VO. NO.	SUPPLIER	PAYMENT DATE	PAYMENT CHQ.	VOUCHERS PAYABLE CREDIT	PUR-CHASES DEBIT	SUPPLIES DEBIT	FREIGHT-IN DEBIT	OTHER ACCOUNTS ACCOUNT	PR	DEBIT	CREDIT
Mar	21	614	PCV Pipe Ltd	See V	702	1 300 –	1 300 –						
Apr	6	702	PCV Pipe Ltd.			(1 300 –)				Purch Rets & All			1 300 –

Figure 17.10 A credit note for a refund in the voucher register, using a Returns and Allowances account.

Example 2

An invoice for $2 700 from Speciality Products is approved for payment and recorded in the voucher register under voucher No. 714. Several days later, a credit note for $110 is received as an allowance for a minor defect in the merchandise. These two transactions would be recorded as shown below in Figure 17.11.

VOUCHER REGISTER — PAGE 73

DATE	VO. NO.	SUPPLIER	PAYMENT DATE	PAYMENT CHQ.	VOUCHERS PAYABLE CREDIT	PUR-CHASES DEBIT	SUPPLIES DEBIT	FREIGHT-IN DEBIT	OTHER ACCOUNTS ACCOUNT	PR	DEBIT	CREDIT
Apr 10	714	Specialty Products	See V	778	2 700 –	2 700 –						
18	778	Specialty Products			(2 700 –)	(2 700 –)						
					2 590 –	2 700 –			Purch Rets & All			110 –

Figure 17.11 An invoice and a credit note for an allowance recorded in the voucher register.

Notice that, unlike in Example 1, the credit invoice is recorded in the voucher register in two steps as follows:

1. The original invoice is reversed as shown.
2. The accounting entry is set up for the transaction showing the original amount purchased, the amount of the allowance, and the amount payable, as shown.

Accounting Terms

internal control
current bank account
transfer of funds
bank reconciliation statement
outstanding cheque
late deposit
voucher system
voucher
purchase requisition
purchase order
packing slip
receiving report
voucher jacket
voucher register
unpaid vouchers file
cheque register
paid vouchers file

Review Questions

1. Define internal control.
2. Why are accounting controls unnecessary in a very small business?

3. At what stage in the development of a business do accounting controls become necessary?
4. Name six broad principles of internal control.
5. What individual items may be considered as 'cash'.
6. Briefly describe the importance of banking in the business world.
7. Explain why the control of cash is especially important.
8. If a mail clerk made off with a customer's cheque on account, how would the theft be discovered?
9. What is the chief advantage of depositing funds intact and making all payments by cheque?
10. What is the advantage of endorsing a cheque 'for deposit only'?
11. Explain the purpose of a bank reconciliation.
12. What is meant by the term 'discrepancy item'?
13. What is the procedure for locating the discrepancy items?
14. What is an outstanding cheque?
15. What is a 'late' deposit?
16. What is the first step in the 'expenditure cycle'?
17. Where do purchase requisitions originate?
18. Where do purchase orders originate? What is their purpose?
19. What information is on a receiving report?
20. How does the voucher system control expenditures?
21. What documents are matched? Explain.
22. Several persons are involved in the verification process of expenditures. Is this a feature of good internal control? Explain.
23. How can one tell from the voucher register which items are open?

Exercises

Simplified Accounting Control Problems

1. You have just inherited a theatre business and have decided to continue its operation. Describe briefly the system you will adopt to control the revenue from ticket sales. You will not be able to participate directly in this aspect of the business but will have to rely on hired personnel.

2. What controls exist in a gasoline station to prevent an employee from stealing gasoline?

3. Super Sand and Gravel is engaged by Crown Road Builders to deliver loads of stone to the site of a road building project, at a cost of $100 a load. Jim Cox, the

foreman at the site, signs for each load as it is delivered. The signed slips form the basis for the invoice sent by Super Sand and Gravel to Crown Road Builders.

Jim Cox has a friend who is building a new house close to the job site and needs a lot of stone for his large driveway, garage, and parking area. Jim diverts a number of loads from the job site to the home of his friend, and signs for them as if they had been delivered to the road building project.

What weakness in control exists here?

4. Valley Forest is a ski resort with an extensive network of cross-country ski trails. The fee for cross-country skiing is $3 per day, paid at the main chalet. Many people don't bother to pay for the cross-country skiing but merely drive to a remote section of the course and enter and exit freely.

   How can this practice be prevented?

5. A friend of yours works as a waitress in a local restaurant. One evening you are dining at the restaurant while your friend is on duty. You suggest to her that it would be nice if you could have your dinner for free. Your friend replies that she would be sure to be caught.

   What controls exist to prevent hired employees from giving away free food?

Bank Reconciliation Exercises

6. **From the following information prepare a bank reconciliation statement for P. F. Faulkner as of June 30, 19--.**

   a. The balance per the general ledger is $1 291.60.
   b. The balance per the bank statement is $1 118.34.
   c. There is a late deposit of $402.91.
   d. There are four outstanding cheques: No. 75 for $72.00; No. 74 for $35.00; No. 77 for $12.50; and No. 83 for $117.40.
   e. There is a bank service charge shown on the bank statement for $7.25. This was not recorded in the business books.

7. **The Bank account in the general ledger of P. D. French shows a balance of $1 267.91 Dr. at March 31, 19--. On that same date, the bank statement shows a balance of $672.88 Cr. The following items were found to be the items of difference.**

   a. Late deposit of $516.13.
   b. Outstanding cheques of $112.40, $70.23, $16.21, and $19.40.
   c. A cheque of $166.20 which had been cashed by the bank but which had mistakenly not been recorded in the cash payments journal.

d. A cheque of $29.06 which had been cashed by the bank for $29.60 and charged by them as $29.60.
e. Bank service charge of $1.40 recorded on the bank statement on the last day of the month.
f. An NSF cheque for $129 shown on the bank statement on the last day of the month.

1. Prepare a bank reconciliation statement.
2. In general journal form, show the journal entries required in the books of the company.

---

8. Answer the following questions about J. C. Water's bank reconciliation statement as shown below:

J.C. WATERS
BANK RECONCILIATION STATEMENT
MARCH 31, 19--

Balance per bank statement		$2 046.75
Add late deposit, March 31		271.50
		$2 318.25
Less outstanding cheques		
#418	$ 62.80	
#522	103.40	
#523	41.90	208.10
True balance		$2 110.15
Balance per Cash account		$2 186.85
Less bank charges	$ 5.40	
NSF cheque — Walker	71.30	76.70
True balance		$2 110.15

1. Does the $2 046.75 represent the bank balance at the beginning or at the end of the month?
2. Why do you think the March 31 deposit was not included in the bank balance?
3. How does Waters know that there are three cheques outstanding? Why are they subtracted?
4. Is $2 186.85 the cash balance at the beginning or at the end of the month?
5. What is an NSF cheque? Why is it subtracted from the balance per books?
6. A certified cheque for $200 payable to R. Smit is still outstanding. Why is it not part of the outstanding cheques on the bank reconciliation statement?

9. Shown below are all of the records that you will need to reconcile the current bank account of Proctor & Kemp at July 31, 19––.

Note: Normally the bank returns all of the 'paid' cheques to the business along with the bank statement. This cannot be done in a textbook. Instead, on the bank statement in brackets beside each amount in the Cheques column is either an explanation of the charge or the cheque number.

a. Bank reconciliation statement for the previous month end, shown below.

Proctor & Kemp
Bank Reconciliation Statement
June 30, 19–

Balance per Bank Statement		1 406 03	Balance per General Ledger		773 28
Add: Late Deposit		551 00	Deduct: Bank Charge not entered in books of company		
		1 957 03	(1) Service charge	$16.50	
Deduct: Outstanding Cheques			(2) Loan Interest	33.50	50 00
#83	$5.10				
780	71.03				
828	400.00				
846	96.02				
852	123.50				
860	15.00				
871	16.01				
873	17.50				
881	33.60				
886	121.47				
889	60.00				
890	170.00				
891	31.94				
892	27.61				
894	13.82				
898	12.50				
899	18.65	1 233 75			
True Balance		723 28	True Balance		723 28

b. 'Amount of Deposits' column of cash receipts journal for July, page 14.

262.75
312.70
274.19
161.40
700.20
265.92
400.61
396.21
316.40
3 090.38

c. July general journal entry affecting 'Bank', page 9.

Bank	5.10	
Miscellaneous Income		5.10
To cancel outstanding cheque No. 83 issued June 19--		

d. Excerpts from cash payments journal for July, page 18.

Explanation	*Chq. No.*	*Bank Credit*
	900	100.00
	901	171.31
	902	142.19
Loan Interest June		33.50
Service Charge June		16.50
	903	16.41
	904	17.50
	905	10.00
	906	12.40
	907	19.61
	908	31.40
	909	76.39
	910	65.20
	911	500.00
	912	216.75
	914	8.21
	915	2.60
	916	9.40
	917	50.00
	918	50.00
	919	33.19
	920	29.33
	921	65.00
	922	25.00
	923	25.00
	924	419.63
	925	372.60
	926	900.00
		3 419.12

e. Partial general ledger Bank account.

BANK						No. 1	
Date		Particulars	P.R.	Debit	Credit	Balance	DR CR
19--							
June	30					773.28	DR
July	31		CR14	3090.38			
Aug.	31		CP18		3419.12		
Sept.	31		J9	5.10		449.64	DR

f. July bank statement.

Cheques				Deposits	Date	Balance
					June 30	1 406.03
18.65	(899)	31.94	(891)	551.00	July 2	1 906.44
121.47	(886)				3	1 784.97
100.00	(900)	96.02	(846)	262.75	5	1 851.70
12.50	(898)				5	1 839.20
71.03	(780)	27.61	(892)		6	1 740.56
142.19	(902)				6	1 598.37
400.00	(828)			312.70	8	1 511.07
15.00	(860)	13.82	(894)		9	1 482.25
16.01	(871)	171.31	(901)		10	1 294.93
17.50	(904)				10	1 277.43
10.00	(905)			274.19	11	1 541.62
500.00	(911)				12	1 041.62
33.60	(N.S.F. cheque of R.C. Jones)			161.40	15	1 169.42
50.00	(913)				16	1 119.42
170.00	(890)	12.40	(906)		17	937.02
76.39	(909)				19	860.63
31.40	(908)			700.20	22	1 529.43
9.40	(916)	19.61	(907)		23	1 500.42
2.60	(915)				23	1 497.82
				265.92	25	1 763.74
33.19	(919)			400.61	26	2 131.16
17.50	(873)				27	2 113.66
50.00	(917)			396.21	30	2 459.87
25.00	(922)	419.63	(924)		31	2 015.24
165.00	(Promissory Note paid to Arno Bros.)				31	1 850.24
29.00	(Interest on Loan)				31	1 821.24
12.60	(Service Charge)				31	1 808.64

Reconcile the bank account and make the necessary accounting entries in the books of the company.

10. 1. From the following records, reconcile the bank account of Baker and Baker as of April 30, 19--. Record the necessary accounting entries in the books of the business.

a. Previous bank reconciliation statement.

Baker and Baker
Bank Reconciliation Statement
March 31, 19–

Balance per Bank Statement		943 80	Balance per General Ledger	305 08
Add: Late Deposit		216 50		
		1160 30		
Deduct: Outstanding Cheques				
#1207	$23.01			
#1361	14.16			
#1390	17.50			
#1406	36.71			
#1409	19.40			
#1415	141.72			
#1420	13.16			
#1425	51.61			
#1426	36.44			
#1428	18.19			
#1431	76.42			
#1432	19.36			
#1433	14.40			
#1434	85.19			
#1435	19.65			
#1436	116.40			
#1438	78.90			
#1439	25.00			
#1440	50.00	857 22		
		303 08		
Add: Correction of bank error. Cheque #1416 for $110.00 was cashed for $112.00 and charged to account for $112.00.		2 00		
True Balance		305 08	True Balance	305 08

b. Partial cash payments journal for April, page 17.

Date		Chq. No.	Bank CR
19--			
April	1	1441	75.92
	2	1442	80.00
	2	1443	120.00
	4	1444	33.71
	5	1445	10.00
	8	1446	17.50
	9	1447	20.10
	9	1448	10.00
	9	1449	125.00
	10	1450	300.00
	11	1451	14.77
	12	1452	84.33
	15	1453	19.06
	15	1454	69.50
	15	1455	20.00
	16	1456	5.61
	18	1457	3.20
	19	1458	42.75
	20	1459	41.00
	20	1460	18.30
	23	1461	19.00
	23	1462	80.00
	24	1463	100.00
	24	1464	64.70
	25	1465	30.00
	26	1466	10.00
	27	1467	4.50
	27	1468	3.50
	27	1469	12.00
	30	1470	19.00
	30	1471	36.00
	30	1472	7.85
			1497.30

c. ''Amount of Deposit'' column of cash receipts journal for April, page 8.

April	4	216.50
	10	171.41
	15	94.80
	20	156.80
	24	363.85
	27	410.00
	30	94.00
		1507.36

d. April general journal entry affecting Bank, page 9.

Bank	42.75	
Accounts Payable — C. Brown		42.75
To cancel cheque No. 1458 which was issued in error.		

e. Partial general ledger Bank account.

BANK						No. 1	
Date		Particulars	P.R.	Debit	Credit	Balance	DR CR
March	31					305 08	DR
April	30		CR8	1 507 36			
	30		CP 17		1 497 30		
	30		J9	42 75		357 89	DR

f. April bank statement.

Cheques		Deposits	Date	Balance
			Mar 31	943.80
		216.50	Apr 1	1 160.30
116.40 (#1436)	13.16 (#1420)		2	1 030.74
75.92 (#1441)	17.50 (#1390)	216.50	4	
76.42 (#1431)			4	1 077.40
19.40 (#1409)	85.19 (#1434)		5	
10.00 (#1445)			5	962.81
18.19 (#1428)			8	944.62
36.71 (#1406)	50.00 (#1440)	171.41	10	
25.00 (#1439)	120.00 (#1443)		10	
300.00 (#1450)			10	584.32
14.40 (#1433)			11	569.92
78.90 (#1438)	80.00 (#1442)		15	
20.00 (#1455)	20.10 (#1447)		15	370.92
141.72 (#1415)		94.80	16	324.00
51.61 (#1425)	125.00 (#1449)		18	147.39
	(Correct March Error)	2.00	19	149.39
		156.80	20	306.19
36.44 (#1426)	84.33 (#1452)		23	
18.30 (#1460)			23	167.12
100.00 (#1463)		363.85	24	430.97
19.65 (#1435)	16.09 (#1453)		25	395.23
		410.00	27	805.23
DM 5.60 (Service Charge)			27	799.63
INT 36.00 (Interest on Loan)			30	763.63
DM 250.00 (Loan Reduction)			30	513.63
	(Note Collected, R. Smith)	100.00	30	613.63
3.20 (#1457)	4.50 (#1467)		30	605.93

11. From the following records, prepare the bank reconciliation statement for Madison Company as of October 31, 19--. Record the necessary accounting entries in the books of the business.

a. Previous bank reconciliation statement.

Madison Company
Bank Reconciliation Statement
September 30, 19–

Bal. per Bk. Statement	2 1 0 2 69	Bal. per General Ledger	1 6 5 2 95
Deduct: Outstanding		Deduct:	
Cheques		Service Charge $12.50	
#519 $20.00		Loan Interest 36.25	4 8 75
#526 37.50			
#528 105.00			
#529 2.70			
#531 5.19			
#532 74.10			
#533 112.02			
#534 56.94			
#535 85.04	4 9 8 49		
True Balance	1 6 0 4 20	True Balance	1 6 0 4 20

b. Partial cash payments journal.

Page 174

Date		Ch. No.	Bank Cr
19— Oct	1	536	19 05
	1	537	164 02
	2	538	73 74
	3	539	27 60
	3	540	1 95
	4	541	365 12
	5	542	92 06
	8	543	74 09
	8	544	19 65
	10	545	74 02
	11	546	76 75
	12	547	56 21
	12	548	42 96
	15	549	33 21
	17	550	24 02
	19	551	88 61
	22	552	58 36
	22	553	19 05
	23	554	91 50
	24	555	13 30
	24	556	17 50
	26	557	8 61
	29	558	1 047 65
	29	559	319 02
	30	560	1 75
	31	561	2 50
	31	562	19 41
			2 831 71

c. Partial cash receipts journal.

Page 147

Date		Bank Dr	Amount of Deposit
19— Oct	3	16 50	
	3	25 02	
	3	516 95	558 47
	8	104 20	
	8	756 12	
	8	56 12	
	8	96 02	1 012 46
	11	33 40	33 40
	15	17 50	
	15	12 09	29 59
	22	19 06	
	22	502 00	521 06
	24	12 06	
	24	13 50	
	24	91 02	
	24	16 51	133 09
	29	56 93	
	29	83 16	
	29	102 52	
	29	127 06	
	29	31 50	401 17
	31	167 75	
	31	138 44	306 19
		2 995 43	2 995 43
		(1)	

d. October general journal entry affecting Bank.

General Journal — Page 64

Date		Particulars	P.R.	Debit	Credit
19– Oct	4	Bank Charges	54	12 50	
		Bank Interest	56	36 25	
		Bank			48 75
		To record charges picked up			
		from September bank statement.			

e. Bank statement for October.

Cheques				Deposits	Date	Balance
					Sept 30	2 102.69
37.50	(526)				Oct 2	2 065.19
				558.47	3	2 623.66
2.70	(529)	85.04	(535)		4	2 535.92
19.05	(536)				5	2 516.87
74.10	(532)	105.00	(528)		8	2 337.77
73.74	(538)			1 012.46	9	3 276.49
5.19	(531)	27.60	(539)		10	3 243.70
56.94	(534)				11	3 186.76
74.09	(543)	112.02	(533)	33.40	15	3 034.05
96.02	(N.S.F. cheque of J. Marble)				15	2 938.03
164.02	(537)				16	2 774.01
33.21	(549)	19.65	(544)	29.59	17	2 750.74
365.12	(541)				18	2 385.62
76.75	(546)			521.06	22	2 829.93
1.95	(540)	58.36	(552)		23	2 769.62
42.96	(548)				24	2 726.66
				133.09	25	2 859.75
88.61	(551)				26	2 771.14
91.50	(554)				29	2 679.64
13.30	(555)			401.17	30	3 067.51
8.61	(557)	1 047.65	(558)		31	2 011.25
15.20	(Int)	30.20	(Service Charges)		31	1 965.85

f. General ledger account showing October figures.

ACCOUNT Bank — No. 1

DATE		PARTICULARS	PR	DEBIT	CREDIT	Dr Cr	BALANCE
19– Sept	30		—			DR	1 652 95
Oct	4		J64		48 75		
	31		CP174		2 831 71		
	31		CR147	2 995 43		DR	1 767 92

12. Return to your corrected solution for the Green Thumb Garden Centre exercise which followed Chapter 16. This exercise is completed here.

On July 3, the bank statement and related vouchers arrive from the bank. The bank statement appears below. Reconcile the bank account of Green Thumb Garden Centre as of June 30.

THE CENTRAL BANK

In Account With — Green Thumb Garden Centre, Concord Highway

Cheques and Debits				Deposits	Date	Balance
		Balance Brought Forward			May 31	3 406.15
(#650)	36.50	(#660)	6.15	516.31	June 1	3 879.81
(#659)	95.14			160.05	June 2	3 944.72
(#661)	144.06			551.98	June 3	4 352.64
				247.20	June 4	4 599.84
(#662)	155.92	(#663)	96.55	100.38	June 5	4 447.75
(#665)	14.85				June 5	4 432.90
(#657)	37.40			1 669.90	June 8	6 065.40
				847.44	June 8	6 912.84
				941.83	June 8	7 854.67
(#666)	604.16			611.18	June 9	7 861.69
				117.60	June 10	7 979.29
(#667)	440.00	(#668)	310.76	301.79	June 11	7 530.32
(DM)	2 000.00	(Loan Reduction)		137.66	June 12	5 667.98
(#658)	42.15	(#669)	540.75	594.21	June 15	5 679.29
(#681)	160.45			669.06	June 15	6 187.90
				1 112.95	June 15	7 300.85
				230.21	June 16	7 531.06
(#641)	74.00	(#670)	51.97	75.60	June 17	7 480.69
(#671)	58.80	(#677)	98.91	758.50	June 18	8 081.48
(#682)	278.50	(#685)	228.69	321.51	June 19	7 895.80
(#655)	116.26	(#686)	15.75	332.01	June 19	8 095.80
				545.03	June 20	8 640.83
				784.71	June 22	9 425.54
(#673)	1 932.00	(#684)	65.85	432.78	June 23	7 860.47
(#675)	25.20	(#678)	705.19	136.77	June 24	7 266.85
(#679)	350.00	(#687)	567.25	107.00	June 25	6 456.60
(#676)	77.96			126.47	June 26	6 505.11
(#654)	29.12			436.13	June 26	6 912.12
				1 436.29	June 26	8 348.41
				730.00	June 29	9 078.41
(#688)	450.00	(#691)	182.00	59.01	June 30	8 505.42
(#690)	1 099.14				June 30	7 406.28
(DM)	101.10	(Bank Interest)			June 30	7 305.18

Flowcharts on Purchasing Routine and Receiving Routine

13. Study the flowcharts on pages 472 and 473 carefully, and answer the following questions.

1. What is the first step in the purchasing routine?
2. What is the purpose of a purchase requisition?
3. Who prepares a purchase requisition?
4. Where does the original of the purchase requisition go?
5. What is the final destination of the purchase requisition original?
6. What is the function of the purchasing department?
7. What is the chief purpose of the purchase order?
8. Who receives the original of the purchase order?
9. Where do copies No. 3 and No. 4 of the purchase order go?
10. What is the function of the receiving department?
11. What use does the receiving department make of the purchase order copy?
12. What is a packing slip?
13. How many copies of the receiving report are there (including the original)?
14. Where does copy No. 1 go?
15. What does the receiver do with goods that are unsatisfactory?

Questions on Voucher Jacket and Verification Procedure

14. Study the illustration on page 474 and the flowchart on page 475 and answer the following questions.

1. What is a purchase invoice?
2. What is a voucher jacket?
3. What information is put on the voucher jacket by the clerk who sets it up?
4. What use is made of the purchase order copy by the second accounting clerk?
5. What happens to the purchase order copy?
6. What use is made of the receiving report copy by the third accounting clerk?
7. How is an expenditure vouched if there is not a receiving report?
8. How many clerks initial the voucher jacket before the department head receives it?
9. What does the department head do with the jacket and the vouchers before approving it for payment?
10. When is the accounting entry for the transaction recorded in the voucher register?
11. In what order are the accounting entries recorded in the voucher register?
12. What are the source documents for the accounting entry?
13. After the accounting entry is recorded, what happens to the voucher jacket?
14. When is the cheque number written on the voucher jacket?
15. Is the fact that several people are involved in the verification process a factor in the system of internal control?

15. **1. Among your duties as an accounting clerk with Crown Hill Supply is the initial preparation of the voucher jackets from the purchase invoices that arrive in the company's office. For the purchase invoice shown below, set up the initial information on the voucher jacket that appears in the workbook. The next consecutive voucher jacket number is 403.**

2. Assume that you are the accounting clerk responsible for the accounting distribution of vouchers payable. You have just received the following purchase invoice. Complete the accounting distribution section, and initial the voucher jacket in the appropriate box.

BOX 100
CROWN HILL
L4M 4Y8

The Chronicle

CROWN HILL
ONTARIO

PHONE
577-2140

SOLD TO Crown Hill Supply
Crown Hill, Ontario
L4M 4Y8

DATE May 9, 19--

TERMS 2/10,n/30

DESCRIPTION	DLY RATE	AMOUNT
Quarter page ad (copy attached) Run Thursday May 4 to Sunday May 7 Four days	$150	$600

NO. 3874

16. You are employed by Mayfair Manufacturing as an 'expediter' in the payables section. Your job is to work with business papers that for some reason have become a problem. Some of them don't match, while others have errors or omissions on them. You must check out all aspects of problem transactions and resolve difficulties so that the papers can be processed. Most of your company's suppliers can be reached by local telephone.

The three business documents below have come to your desk for resolution. Examine these documents and answer the following questions.

1. **Why do these business papers present a problem? Be specific.**
2. **What details would you check out?**
3. **What solution would you propose?**

lighting fixtures

MAYFAIR MANUFACTURING
1200 HIGH STREET
MONCTON, N.B., E1C 6G9

phone 622-2626

PURCHASE ORDER
NO. 6311

To
Eastbourne Electric
2500 Champlain Street
Moncton, N.B.
E1A 1S9

Quantity	Stock No.	Description	Price
4 doz	724134	Relay switches	$137.50 per doz

Date Ordered	Date Required	Terms
May 30, 19--	June 15, 19--	2%, 15/ n,60
Ship By	**Destination**	**Sales Tax Exempt**
Truck	FOB 1200 High St.	No. 14876

EASTBOURNE ELECTRIC

Phone 701-7010
2500 Champlain Street
Moncton, N.B. E1A 1S9

SOLD TO:	SHIP TO:
Mayfair Manufacturing 1200 High Street Moncton, N.B. E1C 6C9	Same

QUANTITY	STOCK NO.	DESCRIPTION	PRICE	AMOUNT
48	724134	Relay Switches	$137.50	$550.00
		Sales Tax		27.50
		Total		$577.50

DATE	TERMS	P.O. NO.	INV. NO.
June 12, 19--	Net 60	6311	**1764**

RECEIVING REPORT

MAYFAIR MANUFACTURING

No. 906

Date goods received	Purchase order number
June 14, 19–	6311

RECEIVED FROM

Eastbourne Electric
2500 Champlain Street
Moncton, N.B.

Quantity	Stock No.	Description	Price
4 pkgs 10 to a pkg	724 104	relay switches	137.50

No. Packages	Weight	Delivered by	Received by
4	10 #	C.N.	J.X.

Recording in the Voucher Register and Cheque Register

17. At the end of March, Venture Wholesale Supply has the following Vouchers Payable:

a. Vouchers Payable

	1 300

b.

VOUCHERS PAYABLE
MARCH 31, 19--

No.	Supplier	Invoice Amount Gross	Discount	Net	Payment Date
206	Able & Co.	$ 300	—	$300	April 6
207	Doal Bros.	400	—	400	9
210	May Mfg.	150	—	150	15
211	Prior Assoc.	250	5	245	4
213	Ward & Co.	200	—	200	30
		$1 300			

The following purchases were made and cheques issued by Venture Wholesale in the month of April.

PURCHASES

Date	Name	Terms	Amount	Explanation
April				
4	Eastern Co.	Net 30	$380	Merchandise for resale
7	Prov. Hydro	Net 30	70	Power
11	General Supply	2/10,n/30	500	Merchandise $375; supplies $125
12	Via Rail	Net 30	130	Freight-in
14	Payroll	—	700	Wages
18	Eastern Co.	—	380 Cr.	Cancelling invoice of April 4
18	Print Shop	Net 30	50	Advertising
20	Comtech	2/10, n/30	240	Merchandise for resale
21	Data Pro	Net 30	155	Miscellaneous
22	Borge Block	2/10, n/30	1 240	New building under construction
25	C. Abrams	—	300	Drawings
30	Central Bank	—	20	Bank charges
30	Ace Steel	Net 30	425	Merchandise for resale

CHEQUES

Date	Name	Amount	Discount Taken	Explanation
April				
4	Prior Assoc.	$250	$ 5.00	Voucher #211
6	Able & Co.	300	—	Voucher #206
9	Doal Bros	400	—	Voucher #207
14	Payroll	700	—	Voucher #218
15	May Mfg.	150	—	Voucher #210
21	General Supply	500	10.00	Voucher #216
30	Comtech	240	4.80	Voucher #216
30	Central Bank	20	—	Voucher #225
30	Ward & Co.	200	—	Voucher #213

1. **Record these transactions in the voucher register and the cheque register respectively. The next consecutive number for vouchers is 214 and for cheques is 111.**
2. **Total and balance the two registers.**
3. **Post the Vouchers Payable account from each of the two registers.**
4. **Prepare a subsidiary ledger listing of vouchers payable and agree it with the control account.**

---

18. At the end of October, the Unpaid Vouchers file of Boggs Building Supply is as follows. The total of this file is in agreement with the control account in the general ledger.

UNPAID VOUCHERS FILE OCTOBER 31, 19--

			Invoice Amount			
Date	Vo. No.	Supplier	Gross	Discount	Net	Terms
Oct.						
4	220	Ram Industries	$250.00		$250.00	Net 30
4	237	Elgin Supply	316.00	$6.32	309.68	2/30, n/60
10	229	Kohn Hardware	920.00		920.00	Net 30
25	238	High Park Lumber	740.00		740.00	Net 30
28	240	Dashco Doors	165.00		165.00	Net 30
31	242	Noble Transport	320.00		320.00	Net 30
			$2 711.00			

A chart appears below and in your workbook showing the purchase invoices received and the cheques issued in the month of November. Notice that the detail for nine of the cheques is missing.

1. **Study the data and complete the chart below by filling in the missing information.**

TRANSACTIONS

Document	*Number*	*Date*	*Name*	*Amount*	*Terms or Discount Data*	*Explanation*
Purch. Inv.	V 243	Nov 2	Bell Telephone	$ 53.70	Due immediately	Phone bill
Cheque Copy	907	2	Bell Telephone	53.70	—	Paying V 243
Cheque Copy	908					
Cheque Copy	909					
Purch. Inv.	V 244	6	Scholer Insulation	1 250.00	Net 30	Merchandise
Purch. Inv.	V 245	9	Sweet Products	516.00	2/10, n/30	Merchandise
Cheque Copy	910					
Purch. Inv.	V 246	11	Luke's Garage	48.50	Net 30	Gas for delivery
Purch. Inv.	V 247	13	Loo Lighting	856.00	2/10, n/30	Merchandise
Memorandum	V 248	16	P. Waters	500.00	—	Drawings
Cheque Copy	911	16	P. Waters	500.00	—	Paying V 248
Memorandum	V 249	16	Payroll	765.00	—	Wages
Cheque Copy	912	16	Payroll	765.00	—	Paying V 249
Cheque Copy	913					
Purch. Inv.	V 250	20	Economy Electric	497.00	3/10, n.30	Merchandise
Cheque Copy	914					
Purch. Inv.	V 251	23	Local Hydro	75.00	Due immediately	Light and heat
Cheque Copy	915	24	Local Hydro	75.00	—	Paying V 251
Cheque Copy	916					
Purch. Inv.	V 252	27	Hoover Glass	350.00	Net 30	Merchandise
Purch. Inv.	V 253	27	Kline Trucking	185.00	Net 30	Freight-in
Cheque Copy	917					
Cheque Copy	918					
Cheque Copy	919					

Check your completed chart against the following.

Document	No.	Date	Supplier	Amount	Discount Data	Explanations
Chq copy	908	Nov 4	Ram Industries	$250 –	–	Paying V220
Chq copy	909	4	Elgin Supply	309.68	316.00 less 6.32	Paying V237
Chq copy	910	10	Kohn Hardware	920 –	–	Paying V229
Chq copy	913	19	Sweet Products	505.68	516.00 less 10.32	Paying V245
Chq copy	914	23	Loo Lighting	838.88	856.00 less 17.12	Paying V247
Chq copy	916	25	High Park Lumber	740 –	–	Paying V238
Chq copy	917	28	Dashco Doors	165 –	–	Paying V240
Chq copy	918	30	Economy Electric	482.09	497.00 less 14.91	Paying V250
Chq copy	919	31	Noble Transport	320 –	–	Paying V242

2. Record the transactions for November in the voucher register and the cheque register.
3. Total and balance the voucher register and the cheque register.
4. Post the appropriate columns of the voucher register and the cheque register to the Vouchers Payable account provided in the workbook.
5. Prepare a subsidiary ledger listing of vouchers payable. Prepare the listing in order of payment date, as though taken from the Unpaid Vouchers file. Agree the total with the control account.

19. Prepare a list to the best of your ability of the advantages and limitations of the voucher system.

Cases

Case 1 *Conflict of Interest?*

Bill Sloan, a recent accounting graduate, is employed by a national firm of public accountants. Bill is an auditor. He checks the books and records of various companies to ensure that their records are correct, and to help prevent fraud and theft.

While working on an audit of Pacific Manufacturing Company, Bill encounters

Mary Martino, an executive with the company. In the course of the audit, Bill and Mary meet frequently to discuss problem situations. As a result, Bill and Mary become well acquainted. Bill's firm has a strict policy that forbids the dating of members of a client's staff. However, Mary is good-looking and intelligent, and Bill is highly attracted to her. Bill decides to ignore his firm's policy. He feels that it imposes on his personal liberty.

Questions

1. Why does Bill's firm forbid its employees to date members of a client's staff?
2. If you were a senior member of Bill's firm, what would you do when you learned of Bill's actions?

Case 2 *Employee's Wages — How Much?*

The Cycle and Sports Centre is the foremost repair centre for bicycles in the community. There is never a shortage of repair work, and there is always a large backlog of repair work waiting to be done. The Centre depends on this repair work for a substantial portion of its revenue.

One summer, the business hires George Sumac, a university student, to repair bicycles on a part-time basis. George suggests that he and the owners split the repair bills on a 50-50 basis. This will not include any charges for the bicycle parts that the store supplies. The owners, a father and a son, agree to the suggestion.

This arrangement works fine in the first season. George turns out to be an exceptional worker. He repairs bicycles quickly and thoroughly. Customers rarely complain about his work. As George becomes more experienced, however, he begins to turn out a greater volume of repair work. The more work that George turns out, the more he earns in wages. George earns $11 000 in his second year, and $15 000 in his third. The owners, particularly the father, become increasingly concerned. They are not used to paying part-time workers $15 000 in a season.

The owners meet with George to discuss the situation. The father insists that George is overpaid and will have to take a smaller percentage. George argues that he actually works on a piecework basis. He may earn good money, but his work merits it. The more he earns, the more the company earns as well.

The father is unable to accept George's arguments. George refuses to take a cut and gives up his job.

Questions

1. Is the father justified in his claim that the amount paid for part-time work is excessive?
2. Is George right to refuse to take a cut in pay?
3. What will the owners have to do now that George is gone?
4. What factors are the store owners ignoring?
5. Can the store make more money without George's services?

Career

David Steel / Student in Accounts

When David Steel studied accounting in high school, he found his courses interesting and enjoyable. He decided to continue his study of accounting and become a chartered accountant.

David is now a *student in accounts*, working toward a professional degree as a chartered accountant in the Cooperative Educational Program at Waterloo University in Ontario. This program integrates the theory and practice of accounting; four months of each year are spent taking classes and four months are spent gaining practical experience by working for a chartered accountant.

During the four-year program, David will complete nine courses in accounting, two in taxation, one in auditing, two in economics, two in computer science, and four in such business-related areas as law and finance.

At the end of the program, David will graduate with an Honours Bachelor of Arts degree. He then must write the examination for chartered accountants, which actually involves four examinations, each four hours long. Only 53 percent of those who take the exams pass them.

To gain his practical experience, David works with McPherson, Scott and Co., a firm of chartered accountants. McPherson, Scott and Co. have a wide range of clients, including car dealerships, charitable organizations, small manufacturing companies, and trust companies. As a result, David is exposed to the accounting concerns of a variety of businesses.

David's duties this year mostly concern auditing procedures. He examines the internal controls over cash used by his clients. He advises clients when controls are to be strengthened and always recommends that they establish current bank accounts. In addition, he prepares his clients' Bank Reconciliation Statements, using their bank statements, cancelled cheques, and cash journals.

David reviews and analyzes books of accounts to ensure that financial statements are fairly presented. He also helps the chartered accountant to make out tax returns. Finally, David performs general bookkeeping for his clients; this includes recording vouchers in the voucher register and cheques in the cheque register.

The firm of chartered accountants is responsible for supervising the student in accounts for all auditing assignments. The accountants also submit a student evaluation to the university; this is usually reviewed by the student and the accountants together. The student evaluation is made available to prospective employers.

If David succeeds in becoming a chartered accountant, he will have several career choices open to him. He may decide to take a position in industry as an executive officer. Alternatively, he may want to start his own accounting practice or join an accounting firm as a partner. At present, David intends to work for a corporation when he graduates.

David highly recommends the Co-operative Educational Program to all those who wish to advance their business careers. The combination of study and practical application ensures that graduates of the program are well equipped to meet the challenges of today's competitive business world.

18

Payroll Accounting

18-1 Legal Obligations of Employer
18-2 Methods of Paying Employees
18-3 Payroll Deductions
18-4 Recording the Payroll
18-5 Payment to Employees
18-6 Payment of Payroll Liabilities
18-7 Basic Payroll Records

Objectives

When you have completed Chapter 18, you should:

1. Understand the nature of accounting for payroll.
2. Know the three most common methods of paying employees.
3. Be able to calculate common payroll deductions and read government tables of deductions for income tax, unemployment insurance, and Canada Pension Plan.
4. Know how to calculate the employer's contribution for unemployment insurance, Canada Pension Plan, and other employee benefits.
5. Know how to prepare the three basic payroll records: the payroll journal, the payroll cheque, and the employee earnings record.
6. Know the accounting entries to record a complete payroll.
7. Know three different ways to calculate payment to employees.
8. Understand that employer's and employees' contributions out of payroll are to be remitted to the appropriate government department or other organization.
9. Understand how the T4 slip is prepared from the employee earnings record.

The term **payroll** refers to that portion of the accounting process that deals with the salaries and wages paid to employees. The pay period, or period of time covered by the payroll, varies from one business to another. The pay period may be weekly, biweekly (every two weeks), semimonthly (every half month), or monthly.

18.1 Legal Obligations of Employer

The federal government, through legislation such as the Income Tax Act, the Unemployment Insurance Act, and the Canada Pension Plan Act, has set down various regulations for the employer regarding the payroll. In order to fulfil the government requirements, each business must carry out the following procedures:

1. Keep accurate records of all salaries and wages paid to each employee for each pay period.
2. Make appropriate deductions from its employees as set out in the government deduction booklets.
3. Keep full and accurate records of payroll deductions so that they may be audited at the discretion of the government.
4. Remit to the government amounts withheld from employees, along with the employer's own contribution.

18.2 Methods of Paying Employees

There are three basic methods of calculating the pay for employees. Employees are paid either a salary, a wage, or a commission.

Salaries

Salaries are paid to office workers, teachers, supervisors, executives, and civil servants. A **salary** is a fixed sum of money paid to an employee on a regular basis over a given period of time (usually one year). For example, consider the case of Harold Evans, who is employed by Nor-Can Grocers Limited, a food wholesaler. Mr. Evans receives an annual salary of $16 770 and is paid every two weeks (biweekly). His pay for each period is calculated as follows:

$$\underbrace{\$16\,770.00}_{\text{annual salary}} \div \underbrace{26}_{\text{pay periods per year}} = \underbrace{\$645.00}_{\text{per pay period}}$$

Wages

Wages are payment to a worker on an hourly, daily, or weekly basis or by the piece. Payment by the piece means that the workers are paid according to the quantity of goods they produce. Some businesses pay a certain minimum hourly rate plus a piece-work bonus for quantities produced over and above a stated amount per day or per week.

Time Clocks and Timecards

Timecards are often used by workers who are paid by the hour. A **timecard** records the time that the employee starts and finishes work each day.

The timecard permits the Payroll Department to calculate the total hours worked by each employee for each pay period. A mechanical device called the time clock is widely used to accumulate this information. The time clock is illustrated in Figure 18.1.

When the timecard is inserted into a time clock, the mechanism of the clock automatically imprints the time at which the employee is entering or leaving work. Time clocks are usually located near the employee's entrance to the plant, and placed so that they can be viewed by a foreman or supervisor to prevent improper use. The timecard shown in Figure 18.2 is for a one-week period. The times are automatically recorded by the clock in one of six columns: Morning In, Morning Out, Afternoon In, Afternoon Out, Extra In, Extra Out.

Figure 18.1 A time clock. Courtesy of Simplex International Time Equipment Company Ltd.

Completing the Timecard

At the end of each pay period a payroll clerk completes a timecard, such as the one shown in Figure 18.2, for each employee. For each card, the payroll clerk must perform the following procedures:

1. Calculate the number of hours worked each day (both regular and overtime).
   Notes:
   a. For this particular business the regular work week consists of a five-day week of eight hours per day. Any time worked after 5:00 p.m., or on Saturday and Sunday, is to be considered as overtime.
   b. Most business firms have some rules with respect to employees who are late coming to work. We will assume that employees are penalized 15 minutes if they are late by one to 15 minutes, 30 minutes if they are late 16 to 30 minutes, and so on.
2. Total the number of regular hours.
3. Total the number of overtime hours.

Time Card

Week Ended September 14 19 --

Social Ins. No. 603 456 667

Name Burns, Joseph

Day	Morning In	Morning Out	Afternoon In	Afternoon Out	Extra In	Extra Out	Total Hours
M	7:58	12:01	12:59	5:01			8
T	7:56	12:01	12:58	5:02			8
W	8:03	12:00	12:58	5:01			7¾
T	7:58	12:01	12:59	5:01			8
F	7:59	12:01	12:57	5:00	5:57	7:02	8/1
S	7:59	12:02					/4
S							

	Hours	Rate	Earnings
Regular Time	39 ¾	6.80	270.30
Overtime	5	10.20	51.00
Gross Pay			321.30

Figure 18.2 A completed time card.

4. Complete the bottom section of the card. There is space provided to multiply the regular hours by the regular rate, and the overtime hours by the overtime rate. Then, the regular earnings and the overtime earnings are added together to obtain the gross earnings for the employee.

Commission

Commission is paid to salesmen, sales clerks, and sales agents. **Commission** is a stated percentage of the dollar value of sales made by the employee. In most cases, however, a basic salary is paid in addition to the commission to provide the employee with at least a minimum income during difficult periods.

Consider the case of Rod Ferguson, a salesman for Nor-Can Grocers Limited, who receives $195 per week and a commission equal to one-half percent of the net sales made by him. During the last two weeks Mr. Ferguson has sold $29 000 worth of merchandise.

CALCULATION

Basic Salary (2 weeks × $195.00)	=	$390.00
Commission ($\frac{1}{2}$% of $29 000.00)	=	$145.00
Total Earnings for Two Weeks	=	$535.00

18.3 Payroll Deductions

You are probably aware of the factors involved in the preparation of a pay cheque. Employees are hired with the understanding that they will be paid a certain amount per hour, week, or year. However, certain deductions take place before the employee is actually paid.

As we have seen, Harold Evans receives an annual salary of $16 770 payable every two weeks in equal portions of $645. When Evans receives his cheque, however, it is made out in the amount of $500. The difference between $645 and $500 is $145. Harold Evans was not shortchanged. The $145 represents various deductions. The $645, the amount of pay before any deductions are made, is known as the **gross pay**. The $500, the amount of pay after the deductions are made, is known as the **net pay**. The payroll equation, therefore, is as follows:

GROSS PAY − DEDUCTIONS = NET PAY

For Harold Evans:
$645.00 − $145.00 = $500.00

The calculations that are necessary in order to arrive at the net pay for Harold Evans are made on a special columnar paper called a **payroll journal**, payroll summary, or payroll register. Nor-Can Grocers Ltd., the wholesaling firm that employs Evans, uses the payroll journal illustrated in Figure 18.3.

PAYROLL JOURNAL For the 2 Weeks ended May 24 19 —

		Earnings			Deductions										
Employee	Net Claim Code	Regular	Extra	Gross	C.P.P.	U.I. Premium	R.P.P.	Income Tax Taxable Income	Income Tax Ded'n	Health Ins.	Union Dues	Group Life		Total Ded'ns	Net Pay
Harold Evans		645 00	—	645 00											

Figure 18.3 A payroll journal form with gross pay recorded.

Social Insurance Number

The employer is required to withhold a portion of the employee's pay because of government regulations. These deductions include Canada Pension or Quebec Pension contributions, personal income taxes, and unemployment insurance premiums. Naturally, care must be taken to see that employees are credited properly for their contributions. For this purpose, the federal government requires all employees to apply for a Social Insurance Number (SIN) as soon as they start to work.

The Social Insurance Number is a permanent identification number. It is used by government computers to process information relevant to the individual's records. The federal government does not pay out any benefits unless the claimant has a SIN number. Figure 18.4 illustrates the social insurance card, showing the nine-digit number.

Figure 18.4 A social insurance card.

Canada Pension Plan

The first deduction we shall examine is the Canada Pension Plan. Many people are unable, during their productive working years, to accumulate enough savings for the time when they will no longer be able to work. Pension plans are designed to provide an income for those people who retire or who have to stop working because of disabilities. They also provide an income for a wife if she is widowed.

The federal government instituted a pension plan for the Canadian worker which became effective January 1, 1966. This plan is called the Canada Pension Plan (C.P.P.) in English Canada, and the Quebec Pension Plan in Quebec. In English Canada, the plan is administered by the Department of National Health and Welfare of the federal government; in Quebec, it is administered by the provincial government.

Each contributor is guaranteed certain rights under the Plan. Benefits are portable. Once you have contributed to the Plan, you cannot lose the right to the retirement pension based on those years of contribution. If you change jobs in Canada, your pension rights are the same as if you had been in one job all the time. If you leave Canada, you retain your right to the pension you earned before you left.

The Plan covers most types of employment on a compulsory basis. To be covered for a particular year, an employee must be between the ages of 18 and 70 and must earn more than a minimum amount, which is subject to change. In 1982, for example, this amount was $1 600.

Employee Contributions

To avoid the necessity of making individual calculations for each employee, the Department of National Revenue, Taxation Division, publishes a booklet of tables for determining the amount of deduction to be made from each gross pay. Included in this booklet is a set of deduction tables for every possible payroll plan. The most common plans are for pay periods that are weekly, biweekly, semimonthly, or monthly. Each table shows the correct deduction to be made for a wide range of gross earnings. Figure 18.5 shows the two pages for the biweekly deduction for Canada Pension Plan.

To determine the deduction for an employee, look down the 'Remuneration' column until you find the bracket containing the employee's gross pay. You will recall that Harold Evans has a biweekly salary of $645.00. This falls in the bracket of $640.79 to $645.78. The deduction of $10.61 is indicated to the immediate right of the remuneration bracket in the column headed 'C.P.P.' This deduction is then recorded in the payroll journal in the C.P.P. column opposite Evans's name, as shown in Figure 18.6. Note that by using the tables to determine the $10.61 deduction, Harold Evans will reach the maximum annual contribution of $239.40 in the twenty-third pay period, at which time only $5.98 will be deducted. It is the responsibility of the employer to keep track of the total deducted for each employee. Once the maximum is reached, no further deduction for C.P.P. or Q.P.P. is to be made in that calendar year.

CANADA PENSION PLAN CONTRIBUTIONS AND UNEMPLOYMENT INSURANCE PREMIUMS

COTISATIONS AU RÉGIME DE PENSIONS DU CANADA ET PRIMES D'ASSURANCE-CHÔMAGE

BI-WEEKLY PAY PERIOD — *PÉRIODE DE PAIE DE DEUX SEMAINES*

$533.57 – $835.78

Remuneration *Rémunération* From-*de*	To-*à*	C.P.P. *R.P.C.*	U.I. Premium *Prime d'a.-c.*	Remuneration *Rémunération* From-*de*	To-*à*	C.P.P. *R.P.C.*	U.I. Premium *Prime d'a.-c.*	Remuneration *Rémunération* From-*de*	To-*à*	C.P.P. *R.P.C.*	U.I. Premium *Prime d'a.-c.*
$ 533.57 -	534.11	8.64	9.61	$ 573.57 -	574.11	9.36	10.33	$ 613.57 -	614.11	10.08	11.05
534.12 -	534.67	8.65	9.62	574.12 -	574.67	9.37	10.34	614.12 -	614.67	10.09	11.06
534.68 -	535.22	8.66	9.63	574.68 -	575.22	9.38	10.35	614.68 -	615.22	10.10	11.07
535.23 -	535.78	8.67	9.64	575.23 -	575.78	9.39	10.36	615.23 -	615.78	10.11	11.08
535.79 -	536.33	8.68	9.65	575.79 -	576.33	9.40	10.37	615.79 -	616.33	10.12	11.09
536.34 -	536.89	8.69	9.66	576.34 -	576.89	9.41	10.38	616.34 -	616.89	10.13	11.10
536.90 -	537.45	8.70	9.67	576.90 -	577.45	9.42	10.39	616.90 -	617.45	10.14	11.11
537.46 -	538.00	8.71	9.68	577.46 -	578.00	9.43	10.40	617.46 -	618.00	10.15	11.12
538.01 -	538.56	8.72	9.69	578.01 -	578.56	9.44	10.41	618.01 -	618.56	10.16	11.13
538.57 -	539.11	8.73	9.70	578.57 -	579.11	9.45	10.42	618.57 -	619.11	10.17	11.14
539.12 -	539.67	8.74	9.71	579.12 -	579.67	9.46	10.43	619.12 -	619.67	10.18	11.15
539.68 -	540.22	8.75	9.72	579.68 -	580.22	9.47	10.44	619.68 -	620.22	10.19	11.16
540.23 -	540.78	8.76	9.73	580.23 -	580.78	9.48	10.45	620.23 -	620.78	10.20	11.17
540.79 -	541.33	8.77	9.74	580.79 -	581.33	9.49	10.46	620.79 -	621.33	10.21	11.18
541.34 -	541.89	8.78	9.75	581.34 -	581.89	9.50	10.47	621.34 -	621.89	10.22	11.19
541.90 -	542.45	8.79	9.76	581.90 -	582.45	9.51	10.48	621.90 -	622.45	10.23	11.20
542.46 -	543.00	8.80	9.77	582.46 -	583.00	9.52	10.49	622.46 -	623.00	10.24	11.21
543.01 -	543.56	8.81	9.78	583.01 -	583.56	9.53	10.50	623.01 -	623.56	10.25	11.22
543.57 -	544.11	8.82	9.79	583.57 -	584.11	9.54	10.51	623.57 -	624.11	10.26	11.23
544.12 -	544.67	8.83	9.80	584.12 -	584.67	9.55	10.52	624.12 -	624.67	10.27	11.24
544.68 -	545.22	8.84	9.81	584.68 -	585.22	9.56	10.53	624.68 -	625.22	10.28	11.25
545.23 -	545.78	8.85	9.82	585.23 -	585.78	9.57	10.54	625.23 -	625.78	10.29	11.26
545.79 -	546.33	8.86	9.83	585.79 -	586.33	9.58	10.55	625.79 -	626.33	10.30	11.27
546.34 -	546.89	8.87	9.84	586.34 -	586.89	9.59	10.56	626.34 -	626.89	10.31	11.28
546.90 -	547.45	8.88	9.85	586.90 -	587.45	9.60	10.57	626.90 -	627.45	10.32	11.29
547.46 -	548.00	8.89	9.86	587.46 -	588.00	9.61	10.58	627.46 -	628.00	10.33	11.30
548.01 -	548.56	8.90	9.87	588.01 -	588.56	9.62	10.59	628.01 -	628.56	10.34	11.31
548.57 -	549.11	8.91	9.88	588.57 -	589.11	9.63	10.60	628.57 -	629.11	10.35	11.32
549.12 -	549.67	8.92	9.89	589.12 -	589.67	9.64	10.61	629.12 -	629.67	10.36	11.33
549.68 -	550.22	8.93	9.90	589.68 -	590.22	9.65	10.62	629.68 -	630.22	10.37	11.34
550.23 -	550.78	8.94	9.91	590.23 -	590.78	9.66	10.63	630.23 -	630.78	10.38	11.34
550.79 -	551.33	8.95	9.92	590.79 -	591.33	9.67	10.64	630.79 -	635.78	10.43	11.34
551.34 -	551.89	8.96	9.93	591.34 -	591.89	9.68	10.65	635.79 -	640.78	10.52	11.34
551.90 -	552.45	8.97	9.94	591.90 -	592.45	9.69	10.66	640.79 -	645.78	10.61	11.34
552.46 -	553.00	8.98	9.95	592.46 -	593.00	9.70	10.67	645.79 -	650.78	10.70	11.34
553.01 -	553.56	8.99	9.96	593.01 -	593.56	9.71	10.68	650.79 -	655.78	10.79	11.34
553.57 -	554.11	9.00	9.97	593.57 -	594.11	9.72	10.69	655.79 -	660.78	10.88	11.34
554.12 -	554.67	9.01	9.98	594.12 -	594.67	9.73	10.70	660.79 -	665.78	10.97	11.34
554.68 -	555.22	9.02	9.99	594.68 -	595.22	9.74	10.71	665.79 -	670.78	11.06	11.34
555.23 -	555.78	9.03	10.00	595.23 -	595.78	9.75	10.72	670.79 -	675.78	11.15	11.34
555.79 -	556.33	9.04	10.01	595.79 -	596.33	9.76	10.73	675.79 -	680.78	11.24	11.34
556.34 -	556.89	9.05	10.02	596.34 -	596.89	9.77	10.74	680.79 -	685.78	11.33	11.34
556.90 -	557.45	9.06	10.03	596.90 -	597.45	9.78	10.75	685.79 -	690.78	11.42	11.34
557.46 -	558.00	9.07	10.04	597.46 -	598.00	9.79	10.76	690.79 -	695.78	11.51	11.34
558.01 -	558.56	9.08	10.05	598.01 -	598.56	9.80	10.77	695.79 -	700.78	11.60	11.34
558.57 -	559.11	9.09	10.06	598.57 -	599.11	9.81	10.78	700.79 -	705.78	11.69	11.34
559.12 -	559.67	9.10	10.07	599.12 -	599.67	9.82	10.79	705.79 -	710.78	11.78	11.34
559.68 -	560.22	9.11	10.08	599.68 -	600.22	9.83	10.80	710.79 -	715.78	11.87	11.34
560.23 -	560.78	9.12	10.09	600.23 -	600.78	9.84	10.81	715.79 -	720.78	11.96	11.34
560.79 -	561.33	9.13	10.10	600.79 -	601.33	9.85	10.82	720.79 -	725.78	12.05	11.34
561.34 -	561.89	9.14	10.11	601.34 -	601.89	9.86	10.83	725.79 -	730.78	12.14	11.34
561.90 -	562.45	9.15	10.12	601.90 -	602.45	9.87	10.84	730.79 -	735.78	12.23	11.34
562.46 -	563.00	9.16	10.13	602.46 -	603.00	9.88	10.85	735.79 -	740.78	12.32	11.34
563.01 -	563.56	9.17	10.14	603.01 -	603.56	9.89	10.86	740.79 -	745.78	12.41	11.34
563.57 -	564.11	9.18	10.15	603.57 -	604.11	9.90	10.87	745.79 -	750.78	12.50	11.34
564.12 -	564.67	9.19	10.16	604.12 -	604.67	9.91	10.88	750.79 -	755.78	12.59	11.34
564.68 -	565.22	9.20	10.17	604.68 -	605.22	9.92	10.89	755.79 -	760.78	12.68	11.34
565.23 -	565.78	9.21	10.18	605.23 -	605.78	9.93	10.90	760.79 -	765.78	12.77	11.34
565.79 -	566.33	9.22	10.19	605.79 -	606.33	9.94	10.91	765.79 -	770.78	12.86	11.34
566.34 -	566.89	9.23	10.20	606.34 -	606.89	9.95	10.92	770.79 -	775.78	12.95	11.34
566.90 -	567.45	9.24	10.21	606.90 -	607.45	9.96	10.93	775.79 -	780.78	13.04	11.34
567.46 -	568.00	9.25	10.22	607.46 -	608.00	9.97	10.94	780.79 -	785.78	13.13	11.34
568.01 -	568.56	9.26	10.23	608.01 -	608.56	9.98	10.95	785.79 -	790.78	13.22	11.34
568.57 -	569.11	9.27	10.24	608.57 -	609.11	9.99	10.96	790.79 -	795.78	13.31	11.34
569.12 -	569.67	9.28	10.25	609.12 -	609.67	10.00	10.97	795.79 -	800.78	13.40	11.34
569.68 -	570.22	9.29	10.26	609.68 -	610.22	10.01	10.98	800.79 -	805.78	13.49	11.34
570.23 -	570.78	9.30	10.27	610.23 -	610.78	10.02	10.99	805.79 -	810.78	13.58	11.34
570.79 -	571.33	9.31	10.28	610.79 -	611.33	10.03	11.00	810.79 -	815.78	13.67	11.34
571.34 -	571.89	9.32	10.29	611.34 -	611.89	10.04	11.01	815.79 -	820.78	13.76	11.34
571.90 -	572.45	9.33	10.30	611.90 -	612.45	10.05	11.02	820.79 -	825.78	13.85	11.34
572.46 -	573.00	9.34	10.31	612.46 -	613.00	10.06	11.03	825.79 -	830.78	13.94	11.34
573.01 -	573.56	9.35	10.32	613.01 -	613.56	10.07	11.04	830.79 -	835.78	14.03	11.34

See instructions on page 2 * Voir indications à la page 2

Figure 18.5 Pages from the government booklet for Canada Pension Plan contributions and Unemployment Insurance premiums.

CANADA PENSION PLAN CONTRIBUTIONS AND UNEMPLOYMENT INSURANCE PREMIUMS

COTISATIONS AU RÉGIME DE PENSIONS DU CANADA ET PRIMES D'ASSURANCE-CHÔMAGE

BI-WEEKLY PAY PERIOD — *PÉRIODE DE PAIE DE DEUX SEMAINES*

$835.79 – $1,735.78

Remuneration *Rémunération* From-*de*	To-*à*	C.P.P. *R.P.C.*	U.I. Premium *Prime d'a.-c.*
$ 835.79 -	840.78	14.12	11.34
840.79 -	845.78	14.21	11.34
845.79 -	850.78	14.30	11.34
850.79 -	855.78	14.39	11.34
855.79 -	860.78	14.48	11.34
860.79 -	865.78	14.57	11.34
865.79 -	870.78	14.66	11.34
870.79 -	875.78	14.75	11.34
875.79 -	880.78	14.84	11.34
880.79 -	885.78	14.93	11.34
885.79 -	890.78	15.02	11.34
890.79 -	895.78	15.11	11.34
895.79 -	900.78	15.20	11.34
900.79 -	905.78	15.29	11.34
905.79 -	910.78	15.38	11.34
910.79 -	915.78	15.47	11.34
915.79 -	920.78	15.56	11.34
920.79 -	925.78	15.65	11.34
925.79 -	930.78	15.74	11.34
930.79 -	935.78	15.83	11.34
935.79 -	940.78	15.92	11.34
940.79 -	945.78	16.01	11.34
945.79 -	950.78	16.10	11.34
950.79 -	955.78	16.19	11.34
955.79 -	960.78	16.28	11.34
960.79 -	965.78	16.37	11.34
965.79 -	970.78	16.46	11.34
970.79 -	975.78	16.55	11.34
975.79 -	980.78	16.64	11.34
980.79 -	985.78	16.73	11.34
985.79 -	990.78	16.82	11.34
990.79 -	995.78	16.91	11.34
995.79 -	1000.78	17.00	11.34
1000.79 -	1005.78	17.09	11.34
1005.79 -	1010.78	17.18	11.34
1010.79 -	1015.78	17.27	11.34
1015.79 -	1020.78	17.36	11.34
1020.79 -	1025.78	17.45	11.34
1025.79 -	1030.78	17.54	11.34
1030.79 -	1035.78	17.63	11.34
1035.79 -	1040.78	17.72	11.34
1040.79 -	1045.78	17.81	11.34
1045.79 -	1050.78	17.90	11.34
1050.79 -	1055.78	17.99	11.34
1055.79 -	1060.78	18.08	11.34
1060.79 -	1065.78	18.17	11.34
1065.79 -	1070.78	18.26	11.34
1070.79 -	1075.78	18.35	11.34
1075.79 -	1080.78	18.44	11.34
1080.79 -	1085.78	18.53	11.34
1085.79 -	1090.78	18.62	11.34
1090.79 -	1095.78	18.71	11.34
1095.79 -	1100.78	18.80	11.34
1100.79 -	1105.78	18.89	11.34
1105.79 -	1110.78	18.98	11.34
1110.79 -	1115.78	19.07	11.34
1115.79 -	1120.78	19.16	11.34
1120.79 -	1125.78	19.25	11.34
1125.79 -	1130.78	19.34	11.34
1130.79 -	1135.78	19.43	11.34
1135.79 -	1140.78	19.52	11.34
1140.79 -	1145.78	19.61	11.34
1145.79 -	1150.78	19.70	11.34
1150.79 -	1155.78	19.79	11.34
1155.79 -	1160.78	19.88	11.34
1160.79 -	1165.78	19.97	11.34
1165.79 -	1170.78	20.06	11.34
1170.79 -	1175.78	20.15	11.34
1175.79 -	1180.78	20.24	11.34
1180.79 -	1185.78	20.33	11.34
1185.79 -	1190.78	20.42	11.34
1190.79 -	1195.78	20.51	11.34

Remuneration *Rémunération* From-*de*	To-*à*	C.P.P. *R.P.C.*	U.I. Premium *Prime d'a.-c.*
$ 1195.79 -	1200.78	20.60	11.34
1200.79 -	1205.78	20.69	11.34
1205.79 -	1210.78	20.78	11.34
1210.79 -	1215.78	20.87	11.34
1215.79 -	1220.78	20.96	11.34
1220.79 -	1225.78	21.05	11.34
1225.79 -	1230.78	21.14	11.34
1230.79 -	1235.78	21.23	11.34
1235.79 -	1240.78	21.32	11.34
1240.79 -	1245.78	21.41	11.34
1245.79 -	1250.78	21.50	11.34
1250.79 -	1255.78	21.59	11.34
1255.79 -	1260.78	21.68	11.34
1260.79 -	1265.78	21.77	11.34
1265.79 -	1270.78	21.86	11.34
1270.79 -	1275.78	21.95	11.34
1275.79 -	1280.78	22.04	11.34
1280.79 -	1285.78	22.13	11.34
1285.79 -	1290.78	22.22	11.34
1290.79 -	1295.78	22.31	11.34
1295.79 -	1300.78	22.40	11.34
1300.79 -	1305.78	22.49	11.34
1305.79 -	1310.78	22.58	11.34
1310.79 -	1315.78	22.67	11.34
1315.79 -	1320.78	22.76	11.34
1320.79 -	1325.78	22.85	11.34
1325.79 -	1330.78	22.94	11.34
1330.79 -	1335.78	23.03	11.34
1335.79 -	1340.78	23.12	11.34
1340.79 -	1345.78	23.21	11.34
1345.79 -	1350.78	23.30	11.34
1350.79 -	1355.78	23.39	11.34
1355.79 -	1360.78	23.48	11.34
1360.79 -	1365.78	23.57	11.34
1365.79 -	1370.78	23.66	11.34
1370.79 -	1375.78	23.75	11.34
1375.79 -	1380.78	23.84	11.34
1380.79 -	1385.78	23.93	11.34
1385.79 -	1390.78	24.02	11.34
1390.79 -	1395.78	24.11	11.34
1395.79 -	1400.78	24.20	11.34
1400.79 -	1405.78	24.29	11.34
1405.79 -	1410.78	24.38	11.34
1410.79 -	1415.78	24.47	11.34
1415.79 -	1420.78	24.56	11.34
1420.79 -	1425.78	24.65	11.34
1425.79 -	1430.78	24.74	11.34
1430.79 -	1435.78	24.83	11.34
1435.79 -	1440.78	24.92	11.34
1440.79 -	1445.78	25.01	11.34
1445.79 -	1450.78	25.10	11.34
1450.79 -	1455.78	25.19	11.34
1455.79 -	1460.78	25.28	11.34
1460.79 -	1465.78	25.37	11.34
1465.79 -	1470.78	25.46	11.34
1470.79 -	1475.78	25.55	11.34
1475.79 -	1480.78	25.64	11.34
1480.79 -	1485.78	25.73	11.34
1485.79 -	1490.78	25.82	11.34
1490.79 -	1495.78	25.91	11.34
1495.79 -	1500.78	26.00	11.34
1500.79 -	1505.78	26.09	11.34
1505.79 -	1510.78	26.18	11.34
1510.79 -	1515.78	26.27	11.34
1515.79 -	1520.78	26.36	11.34
1520.79 -	1525.78	26.45	11.34
1525.79 -	1530.78	26.54	11.34
1530.79 -	1535.78	26.63	11.34
1535.79 -	1540.78	26.72	11.34
1540.79 -	1545.78	26.81	11.34
1545.79 -	1550.78	26.90	11.34
1550.79 -	1555.78	26.99	11.34

Remuneration *Rémunération* From-*de*	To-*à*	C.P.P. *R.P.C.*	U.I. Premium *Prime d'a.-c.*
$ 1555.79 -	1560.78	27.08	11.34
1560.79 -	1565.78	27.17	11.34
1565.79 -	1570.78	27.26	11.34
1570.79 -	1575.78	27.35	11.34
1575.79 -	1580.78	27.44	11.34
1580.79 -	1585.78	27.53	11.34
1585.79 -	1590.78	27.62	11.34
1590.79 -	1595.78	27.71	11.34
1595.79 -	1600.78	27.80	11.34
1600.79 -	1605.78	27.89	11.34
1605.79 -	1610.78	27.98	11.34
1610.79 -	1615.78	28.07	11.34
1615.79 -	1620.78	28.16	11.34
1620.79 -	1625.78	28.25	11.34
1625.79 -	1630.78	28.34	11.34
1630.79 -	1635.78	28.43	11.34
1635.79 -	1640.78	28.52	11.34
1640.79 -	1645.78	28.61	11.34
1645.79 -	1650.78	28.70	11.34
1650.79 -	1655.78	28.79	11.34
1655.79 -	1660.78	28.88	11.34
1660.79 -	1665.78	28.97	11.34
1665.79 -	1670.78	29.06	11.34
1670.79 -	1675.78	29.15	11.34
1675.79 -	1680.78	29.24	11.34
1680.79 -	1685.78	29.33	11.34
1685.79 -	1690.78	29.42	11.34
1690.79 -	1695.78	29.51	11.34
1695.79 -	1700.78	29.60	11.34
1700.79 -	1705.78	29.69	11.34
1705.79 -	1710.78	29.78	11.34
1710.79 -	1715.78	29.87	11.34
1715.79 -	1720.78	29.96	11.34
1720.79 -	1725.78	30.05	11.34
1725.79 -	1730.78	30.14	11.34
1730.79 -	1735.78	30.23	11.34

"For remuneration in excess of $1735.78:
(a) refer to page 17 under "Employee's Contribution – Calculation Method".
(b) the Unemployment Insurance premium is $11.34."

"Si la rémunération dépasse $1735.78:
a) se reporter à la rubrique «Cotisation de l'employé – Méthode par le calcul», à la page 17;
b) la prime d'assurance-chômage est $11.34."

See instructions on page 2 * Voir indications à la page 2

PAYROLL JOURNAL For the 2 Weeks ended May 24 19 —

Employee	Net Claim Code	Earnings			Deductions									Total Ded'ns	Net Pay
		Regular	Extra	Gross	C.P.P.	U.I. Premium	R.P.P.	Income Tax		Health Ins.	Union Dues	Group Life			
								Taxable Income	Ded'n						
Harold Evans		645 00	—	645 00	10 61										

Figure 18.6 Payroll journal with C.P.P. deduction recorded.

Employer Contributions

The employer is required to contribute an amount equal to that contributed by the employee. We will show how this is handled later in the chapter.

Unemployment Insurance

In Canada, an employed worker pays a portion of earnings into an unemployment insurance fund. These payments are in the form of deductions made by the employer from the employee's pay. If a worker who has made sufficient contributions to the fund becomes unemployed while willing and able to accept employment, that worker receives payments out of the fund to ease financial hardship.

How Much to Deduct?

The amount of premium to be deducted from an employee's pay for unemployment insurance (U.I.) is determined from the Unemployment Insurance Premium tables which are included in the same booklet as the Canada Pension Plan Premium tables (Figure 18.5). To determine the amount of the premium, simply refer to the deduction tables using the gross pay as the insurable earnings.

Recall that Harold Evans is paid on a biweekly basis and his gross pay is $645. His premium of $11.34 is found in the column headed "U.I. Premium" in the biweekly tables. Since both the Canada Pension Plan and the Unemployment Insurance Premium tables are in the same booklet, and since the same remuneration figure is used to determine each premium, both deductions can be obtained and then recorded in the journal with only one referral to the booklet.

Now that we have determined that Harold Evans must contribute $11.34 toward unemployment insurance, this amount is entered in the payroll journal as illustrated in Figure 18.7.

PAYROLL JOURNAL For the 2 Weeks ended May 24 19 —

Employee	Net Claim Code	Earnings: Regular	Earnings: Extra	Earnings: Gross	Deductions: C.P.P.	U.I. Premium	R.P.P.	Income Tax: Taxable Income	Income Tax: Ded'n	Health Ins.	Union Dues	Group Life		Total Ded'ns	Net Pay
Harold Evans		645 00	—	645 00	10 61	11 34									

Figure 18.7 Payroll journal with U.I. deduction recorded.

Employer's Premium

The employer is required to contribute an amount equal to 1.4 times the amount of the employee's unemployment insurance premium. If an employee contributes $11.34, then the employer must contribute an additional $\$11.34 \times 1.4 = \$15.88$. You will be shown how to account for this later in the chapter.

Registered Pension Plans

Employees are often enrolled in private pension plans through their places of employment. In most cases these plans are *registered* plans; that is, they are registered and approved by the government. This allows the employees to deduct for income tax purposes any payments made by them into the fund, up to a given maximum per year. A plan of this kind is known as a **registered pension plan** (R.P.P.) or a registered retirement savings plan (R.R.S.P.).

Usually both the employee and the employer contribute a percentage based on the employee's gross pay. The employees of Nor-Can Groceries Ltd. have an R.P.P., the terms of which require the employees to contribute 5 percent of their gross pay. Deductions are made each pay period.

The entry to record the R.P.P. deduction of $32.25 for Harold Evans is shown in Figure 18.8. The company contributes an equal amount. The accounting for the company share will be discussed later.

PAYROLL JOURNAL For the *2 Weeks* ended *May 24* 19 —

Employee	Net Claim Code	Earnings			Deductions									Total Ded'ns	Net Pay
		Regular	Extra	Gross	C.P.P.	U.I. Premium	R.P.P.	Income Tax		Health Ins.	Union Dues	Group Life			
								Taxable Income	Ded'n						
Harold Evans		645 00	—	645 00	10 61	11 34	32 25								

Figure 18.8 Payroll journal with R.P.P. deduction recorded.

Income Tax

According to Canadian income tax laws, employers are required to make a deduction from the earnings of each employee for personal income tax. The amount to be deducted depends on two factors:

1. The employee's total personal exemption.
2. The amount of taxable income that the employee earns.

Personal Exemption

Every employee is required to fill out a Form TD-1, shown in Figure 18.9. This form is used to calculate the employee's total personal exemption. The total personal exemption is the amount that a person may earn in a year without being taxed. The amount varies with the employee's marital status, and the number and ages of the employee's dependants. This form is completed whenever an employee starts a new job, whenever there is a change in the number or status of the employee's dependants, and also at the beginning of each year.

Figure 18.9 shows Form TD-1 completed for Harold Evans, who is married and has two children. (This form is revised slightly each year. You can obtain a copy of the latest form from the Department of National Revenue.)

Harold Evans has a total personal exemption of $5 856.80 and a net claim code of 8. The *net claim code* is used when referring to the income tax deduction tables. Notice that the family allowance cheques that Mr. Evans receives are deducted when calculating the total personal exemption for Mr. Evans. The annual amount received in family allowance benefits is always deducted from the parent who is declaring the children as dependants on the TD-1 form.

Revenue Canada Taxation — Revenu Canada Impôt

EMPLOYEE'S TAX DEDUCTION RETURN
DÉCLARATION DE L'EMPLOYÉ POUR LA RETENUE DE L'IMPÔT

TD1
Rev. 1980

- **Complete and file one copy of this return with your employer**
  (a) when you commence employment, or
  (b) within **seven** days of any change in your exemptions.
- **This return need not be filed by employees claiming the "Basic Personal Exemption" only.**
- If you do not file this return, as required, income tax will be deducted as though you were a single person without dependants.
- If you believe there are other exemptions that you could claim on your income tax return you may ask your District Taxation Office whether they may be taken into account in arriving at your tax deduction.
- Do not claim a child or other dependant whose net income for the year will exceed $2,990.
- Net income of your spouse or dependants includes any pension or supplement under the Old Age Security Act or any similar Act of a province, benefits under the Canada or Quebec Pension Plan and the Unemployment Insurance Act, 1971.

- **Remettez un exemplaire dûment rempli de la présente déclaration à votre employeur**
  a) au début de votre emploi, ou
  b) dans les **sept** jours suivant tout changement dans vos exemptions.
- **Les employés qui demandent uniquement «l'Exemption personnelle de base» n'ont pas besoin de produire cette déclaration.**
- Faute de produire la présente déclaration, ainsi que vous y êtes tenu, l'impôt sur le revenu sera retenu comme si vous étiez célibataire sans personnes à charge.
- Si vous croyez avoir droit à d'autres exemptions dans votre déclaration d'impôt sur le revenu, demandez à votre bureau de district d'impôt si vous pouvez en tenir compte en calculant votre retenue de l'impôt.
- Vous ne pouvez compter un enfant ou une autre personne à charge dont le revenu net pour l'année dépassera $2,990.
- Le revenu net de votre conjoint ou des personnes à votre charge comprend toute pension ou tout supplément en vertu de la Loi sur la sécurité de la vieillesse ou en vertu de toute loi provinciale semblable, ainsi que les prestations du Régime de pensions du Canada, du Régime de rentes du Québec ou de la Loi de 1971 sur l'assurance-chômage.

FAMILY OR LAST NAME (Print) — *NOM DE FAMILLE (en caractères d'imprimerie)*: EVANS
USUAL FIRST NAME AND INITIALS — *PRÉNOM USUEL ET INITIALES*: HAROLD J.
EMPLOYEE NO. — *NUMÉRO DE L'EMPLOYÉ*: 12650
ADDRESS — *ADRESSE*: 178 NORTH CLARKSON STREET
SOCIAL INSURANCE NUMBER — *NUMÉRO D'ASSURANCE SOCIALE*: 609 779 152
DATE OF BIRTH — *DATE DE NAISSANCE*: Day-Jour 9 | Month-Mois FEB | Year-Année 1949

Complete the "Claim for Exemptions" area on the reverse side and enter your "Net Claim". ▶ $ 5856.80 ◀ Remplissez la section «Exemptions réclamées», au verso, et inscrivez la «Réclamation nette».

Refer to the "Table" below and enter the applicable "Net Claim Code". ▶ 8 ◀ Consultez la «Table» ci-dessous et inscrivez le «Code de réclamation nette» approprié.

Table of Net Claim Codes
Table des codes de réclamation nette

Net Claim for 1980 / *Réclamation nette pour 1980* From – *De* To – *À*	Net Claim Code / *Code de réclamation nette*
$2,890 — $2,940	1
2,941 — 3,430	2
3,431 — 3,760	3
3,761 — 4,030	4
4,031 — 4,470	5
4,471 — 4,800	6
4,801 — 5,300	7
5,301 — 5,890	8
5,891 — 6,380	9
6,381 — 6,870	10
6,871 — 7,300	11
7,301 — 7,740	12
7,741 — 8,040	13
8,041 and up – *et plus*	X
Exemption from Tax Deduction as claimed below / *Exonération de la retenue de l'impôt réclamée ci-dessous*	0

- Your "Net Claim Code" is used by your employer to determine the tax deduction required from your remuneration.
- Votre employeur utilise votre «Code de réclamation nette» pour déterminer l'impôt à retenir sur votre rémunération.

Claim for Exemption from Tax Deduction—*Valid for current calendar year only.*

This area is to be completed by an individual who is receiving remuneration that is subject to tax deduction but who wishes to claim exemption because "Total estimated income from all sources for the year" including taxable benefits and Family Allowance payments, will be less than the "Net Claim" above. No claim may be made here by a person not resident in Canada for the whole year unless your earnings in Canada will be less than your exemptions apportioned to the period of residence in Canada. If you qualify for this exemption, your "Net Claim Code" is "O".

Demande d'exonération de la retenue de l'impôt — *Valable pour l'année civile en cours seulement.*

La présente section doit être remplie par un particulier dont la rémunération est assujettie à la retenue de l'impôt et qui désire en être exonéré parce que le «Total des revenus estimatifs de toutes provenances pour l'année», y compris les avantages imposables et les allocations familiales, sera inférieur à la «Réclamation nette» susmentionnée. Si vous ne résidiez pas au Canada pendant toute l'année, vous ne pouvez demander cette exonération, à moins que vous n'estimiez que vos gains au Canada seront inférieurs à vos exemptions proportionnées à votre période de résidence au Canada. Si vous avez droit à la présente exonération, votre «Code de réclamation nette» est «O».

Income to date this year from all sources—*Revenu de toutes provenances jusqu'ici cette année* ▶ $________
Estimated income for remainder of year from all sources—*Revenu estimatif de toutes provenances d'ici la fin de l'année* ▶ $________
Total estimated income from all sources for the year—***Total des revenus estimatifs de toutes provenances pour l'année*** ▶ $________

Certification
I HEREBY CERTIFY that the information given in this return is true, correct and complete to the best of my knowledge and belief.

Attestation
JE CERTIFIE que les renseignements donnés dans la présente déclaration sont vrais, exacts et complets pour autant que je sache.

Signature Harold Evans   Date January 4 19—

It is a serious offence to make a false return – *Quiconque fait une fausse déclaration commet une infraction grave.*

Warning: An employer should refer a form TD1 containing doubtful statements to the District Taxation Office. Any person who knowingly accepts a form TD1 containing false or deceptive statements commits a serious offence. Employers must retain completed forms TD1 for inspection by officers of the Department of National Revenue, Taxation.

Avertissement: L'employeur doit soumettre toute formule TD1 renfermant des déclarations douteuses au bureau de district d'impôt. Quiconque accepte sciemment une formule TD1 renfermant des déclarations fausses ou trompeuses commet une infraction grave. Les employeurs doivent conserver les formules TD1, une fois qu'elles ont été remplies, aux fins d'inspection par les fonctionnaires du ministère du Revenu national, Impôt.

Form authorized and prescribed by the Minister of National Revenue
Formule autorisée et prescrite par le ministre du Revenu national

Figure 18.9a An employee's TD-1 form, front.

Claim for Exemptions—***Exemptions réclamées***

Basic Personal Exemption—***Exemption personnelle de base*** ▶ $ 2 890

Married or Equivalent Exemption—***Exemption de marié(e) ou l'équivalent***

If applicable, check ☑ and claim **only one** of the 4 items—*S'il y a lieu, cochez ☑ et réclamez **un seul** des 4 articles ci-après.*
If your spouse's net income, while married, will exceed $2,990 in the year, you may not claim this exemption.
Si le revenu net de votre conjoint, pendant le mariage, doit dépasser $2,990 dans l'année, vous ne pouvez pas réclamer cette exemption.

Married and supporting spouse—***Marié(e) et soutien d'un conjoint***

☐ 1. whose net income for the year, while married, will not exceed $460
dont le revenu net pour l'année, pendant le mariage, ne dépassera pas $460 — Claim—*Réclamez* $2,530

☐ 2. whose net income for the year, while married, will exceed $460 but not $2,990
dont le revenu net pour l'année, pendant le mariage, dépassera $460 sans dépasser $2,990 — $2,990

Less: spouse's net income—*Moins le revenu net du conjoint* $ 580

Claim—*Réclamez* $ 2410 ▶ $ 2 410 —

Single, divorced, separated or widow(er)—***Célibataire, divorcé(e), séparé(e) ou veuf(veuve)***

(See information in item A below) *(Voir les indications de l'alinéa A ci-après)*
If the dependant's net income for the year—*Si le revenu net de la personne à charge, pour l'année,*

☐ 3. will not exceed $460, provide details*
*ne doit pas excéder $460, fournissez des précisions** — Claim—*Réclamez* $2,530

☐ 4. will exceed $460, but not $2,990
doit excéder $460, sans excéder $2,990 — $2,990

Less: dependant's *net income—*Moins le revenu net de la personne à charge** $ ______

*Name—*Nom* Claim—*Réclamez* $ ______
Relationship to you—*Lien de parenté avec vous*

Exemption for Wholly Dependent Children—***Exemption pour enfants entièrement à charge***

See information in item B below. Provide details below.
Under age 18 at end of the year—If net income will not exceed $1,910, claim $540. If net income will exceed $1,910 but not $2,990 claim $540 minus one-half the amount in excess of $1,910.
Age 18 or over at end of the year—If net income will not exceed $2,000, claim $990. If net income will exceed $2,000 but not $2,990, claim $990 minus the amount in excess of $2,000.
Voir les indications de l'alinéa B ci-après. Fournissez des précisions.
***Moins de 18 ans à la fin de l'année**—Si le revenu net ne doit pas excéder $1,910, réclamez $540. Si le revenu net doit excéder $1,910 sans excéder $2,990, réclamez $540 moins la moitié du montant en sus de $1,910.*
***Âgé de 18 ans ou plus à la fin de l'année**—Si le revenu net ne doit pas excéder $2,000, réclamez $990. Si le revenu net doit excéder $2,000 sans excéder $2,990, réclamez $990. moins le montant excédant $2,000.*

Name of child (Attach list if space is insufficient)—*Nom de l'enfant (Annexez une liste si l'espace est insuffisant*	Estimated annual net income—*Revenu annuel net estimatif*	Date of birth *Date de naissance* Day *Jour*	Month *Mois*	Year *Année*	If over 21, state school attended or whether infirm—*S'il a plus de 21 ans, indiquez l'école fréquentée ou dites s'il est infirme.*	
DAVID	SON	17	OCT	76		▶ $ 540 —
CATHERINE	DAUGHTER	3	OCT	78		▶ $ 540 —
						▶ $

Exemption for Other Dependants—***Exemption pour autres personnes à charge***

(a) Parents, Grandparents, Brothers or Sisters (including in-laws)—*Père, mère, grands-parents, frères ou soeurs (et ceux du conjoint)*
(b) Aunts or Uncles Resident in Canada (including in-laws)—*Tantes et oncles résidant au Canada (et ceux du conjoint)*
See information in item C below. Provide details and claim estimated cost to you of support of each dependant.
Voir les indications de l'alinéa C ci-après. Fournissez des précisions et réclamez le montant estimatif que vous dépenserez pour l'entretien de chaque personne à charge.

Name and address of dependant *Nom et adresse de la personne à charge* (Attach list if space is insufficient) *(Annexez une liste si l'espace est insuffisant)*	Dependant's – *Personne à charge* Net income in year – *Revenu net dans l'année*	Year of birth *Année de naissance*	Estimated cost to you of support of dependant – *Montant estimatif que vous dépenserez pour l'entretien de la personne à charge*	If over 21, state school attended or whether infirm – *Si elle a plus de 21 ans, indiquez l'école fréquentée ou dites si elle est infirme.*	
					▶ $
					▶ $
					▶ $

Age Exemptions—***Exemptions en raison d'âge***

If you are 65 years of age or over—*Si vous êtes âgé de 65 ans ou plus* — Claim–*Réclamez* $1,810 ▶ $ ______

If your spouse is 65 years of age or over you may claim any unused balance of the exemption amount (maximum $1,810)—*Si votre conjoint a 65 ans ou plus, vous pouvez déduire la fraction inutilisée de l'exemption jusqu'à concurrence de $1,810.* — Unused Balance *Fraction inutilisée* ▶ $ ______

Disability Exemptions—***Exemptions pour invalidité***

For persons totally blind at any time in the year, or confined to a bed or wheelchair for a substantial period each day throughout any 12 month period ending in the year.—*Pour les personnes complètement aveugles à une date quelconque de l'année et pour celles qui doivent garder le lit ou demeurer dans un fauteuil roulant pendant de longues périodes chaque jour au cours de toute période de 12 mois se terminant dans l'année.*

For yourself—*Pour vous-même* — Claim–*Réclamez* $1,810 ▶ $ ______

You may claim any unused balance of the disability exemption (maximum $1,810) to which your spouse, child, grandchild or supported individual (see item A below) is entitled.—*Vous pouvez réclamer toute fraction inutilisée de l'exemption pour invalidité (jusqu'à concurrence de $1,810) à laquelle votre conjoint, enfant, petit-enfant ou personne à votre charge a droit (voir A ci-après).* — Unused Balance *Fraction inutilisée* ▶ $ ______

Student Exemptions—***Exemptions pour les étudiants***

1. Claim $50 for each month in the year you will be a student in full-time attendance at only the following: a university or college or an institution offering job retraining courses.
Réclamez $50 pour chaque mois de l'année où vous fréquenterez à plein temps une université, un collège ou un établissement dispensant des cours de formation professionnelle. ▶ $ ______
2. Claim your tuition fees less the total amount of all scholarships, fellowships or bursaries exceeding $500 which you will receive during the calendar year.—*Réclamez vos frais de scolarité moins le montant global (excédant $500) de toutes les bourses d'études, de perfectionnement (fellowships) ou d'entretien que vous recevrez au cours de l'année civile.* ▶ $ ______

Total—***Total*** ▶ $ 6380 —

Deduct: Taxable Family Allowance Payments (To be received in year for children claimed above.)
Déduire: le montant des versements imposables d'allocations familiales *(À recevoir au cours de l'année pour les enfants nommés ci-dessus.)* ▶ $ 523.20

Net Claim—(Will not be less than $2,890. Enter this amount on reverse side.)
Réclamation nette— *(Ne doit pas être inférieure à $2,890. Inscrire le montant au verso.)* ▶ $ 5856.80

A—Claim exemption for a relative (a) wholly dependent on you or you and one or more other persons and (b) domiciled with you, in a dwelling maintained by you or by you and other persons to whom the dependant is related. (Claim **only** if there is agreement that no other person claims for the same dependant or for the same residence.)

B—Claim exemption for a wholly dependent son, daughter, grandchild, niece or nephew under 21, or any age if in full-time attendance at school, university, or infirm. Claim only for a niece or nephew if (a) you have complete custody and control or (b) the child resides in Canada and the mother is also widowed, separated or divorced and receives no alimony or allowance for child-maintenance, or the father is mentally or physically infirm. Do not claim here for a child claimed in item 3. or 4.

C—Do not claim over the maximum described in the "Wholly Dependent Children" area. If any other person contributes to the support of the dependant, the aggregate claimed by you and the other person must not exceed the allowable maximum. No claim may be made here for a dependant over age 21 who is not mentally or physically infirm (except a brother or sister in full-time attendance at a school or university) or a dependant claimed in item 3. or 4.

A—Réclamez une exemption pour un parent a) qui est entièrement à votre charge ou à votre charge et à la charge d'une ou de plusieurs autres personnes et b) qui vit dans un logement tenu par vous ou par vous et d'autres personnes apparentées à la personne à charge. (Vous n'avez droit à cette exemption **que** s'il a été convenu que personne d'autre n'en présentera pour la même personne ou relativement au même logis).

B—Réclamez une exemption pour un fils, une fille, un petit-fils, une petite-fille, une nièce ou un neveu de moins de 21 ans entièrement à votre charge, ou de tout âge s'il fréquente à plein temps une école ou une université ou s'il est infirme. Vous ne pouvez compter une nièce ou un neveu comme personne à charge que si a) vous en avez la garde et la responsabilité entière ou b) l'enfant demeure au Canada et sa mère est veuve, séparée ou divorcée et ne touche aucune pension alimentaire ou allocation pour l'entretien de l'enfant, ou le père est atteint d'infirmité physique ou mentale. Il ne faut pas faire de demande ici à l'égard d'un enfant compté au nº 3 ou au nº 4.

C—Ne réclamez pas un montant supérieur à celui indiqué à la section «Enfants entièrement à charge». Si quelqu'un d'autre a aidé à subvenir aux besoins de la personne à charge, le montant global compté par vous et cette autre personne ne doit pas dépasser le maximum admissible. Aucune réclamation ne doit être faite ici à l'égard d'une personne à charge âgée de plus de 21 ans qui n'est pas atteinte d'infirmité physique ou mentale (sauf s'il s'agit d'un frère ou d'une soeur qui fréquente à plein temps l'école ou l'université) ou d'une personne à charge comptée au nº 3 ou 4

Figure 18.9b An employee's TD-1 form, back.

Taxable Earnings

Taxable earnings are the gross pay minus the three following items:

1. The employee's contribution to the Canada Pension Plan.
2. The employee's premium for unemployment insurance.
3. The employee's contribution to registered pension plans.

Harold Evans contributed to all three of the above items. His contributions are as follows:

Canada Pension Plan premium	–	$10.61
Unemployment insurance premium	–	$11.34
Registered pension plan premium	–	$32.25
		$54.20

Since gross pay − deductions (C.P.P. + U.I. + R.P.P.) = taxable earnings, then Harold Evans's taxable earnings are $645.00 − $54.20 = $590.80. This figure is recorded in the payroll journal in Figure 18.10.

The general procedure for determining payroll deductions is standard across the country. The amount of individual deductions will vary according to differences in the terms of the plans for different provinces or organizations. For example, the Quebec Pension Plan differs somewhat from the Canada Pension Plan.

PAYROLL JOURNAL For the 2 Weeks ended May 24 19 —

Employee	Net Claim Code	Earnings			Deductions									Total Ded'ns	Net Pay
		Regular	Extra	Gross	C.P.P.	U.I. Premium	R.P.P.	Income Tax		Health Ins.	Union Dues	Group Life			
								Taxable Income	Ded'n						
Harold Evans	8	645 00	—	645 00	10 61	11 34	32 25	590 80							

Figure 18.10 Payroll journal showing taxable income.

Calculating Income Tax Deductions

As with Canada Pension Plan and unemployment insurance, the Department of National Revenue publishes a booklet of tables for personal income taxes. Pages for the biweekly pay period are shown in Figure 18.11. The shaded column along the left-hand side shows biweekly pay brackets. At the top of the thirteen deduction columns are the net claim codes.

To find the correct deduction, locate the appropriate biweekly pay bracket in the shaded area and follow it to the right until you arrive at the correct net claim code column. We have calculated that Harold Evans has a taxable earnings figure of $590.80 and a net claim code of 8. The correct tax deduction for him is $69.85. It is recorded in the journal as illustrated in Figure 18.12.

TABLE 405

BI-WEEKLY TAX DEDUCTIONS
Basis—26 Pay Periods per Year

DÉDUCTIONS D'IMPÔT DE DEUX SEMAINES
Base—26 périodes de paie par année

BI-WEEKLY PAY Use appropriate bracket — PAIE DE DEUX SEMAINES Utilisez le palier approprié	IF THE EMPLOYEE'S "NET CLAIM CODE" ON FORM TD1 IS — SI LE «CODE DE RÉCLAMATION NETTE» DE L'EMPLOYÉ SELON LA FORMULE TD1 EST DE													See note on page 23. Voir remarque p. 23.
	1	2	3	4	5	6	7	8	9	10	11	12	13	
	DEDUCT FROM EACH PAY — DÉDUISEZ SUR CHAQUE PAIE													Column A Colonne A
$ 364.00 - 367.99	41.95	38.75	33.55	29.50	24.05	19.90	17.70	12.95	6.90					
368.00 - 371.99	42.95	39.75	34.55	30.50	25.10	20.85	18.65	13.90	7.85					
372.00 - 375.99	44.05	40.75	35.55	31.50	26.10	21.80	19.60	14.85	8.80					
376.00 - 379.99	45.10	41.75	36.55	32.50	27.10	22.75	20.55	15.80	9.75	3.45				
380.00 - 383.99	46.15	42.75	37.55	33.55	28.10	23.70	21.50	16.75	10.70	4.35				
384.00 - 387.99	47.20	43.85	38.55	34.55	29.10	24.70	22.45	17.70	11.65	5.35				
388.00 - 391.99	48.25	44.90	39.60	35.55	30.10	25.70	23.45	18.65	12.60	6.30				
392.00 - 395.99	49.35	45.95	40.60	36.55	31.10	26.70	24.45	19.60	13.55	7.25				
396.00 - 399.99	50.40	47.00	41.60	37.55	32.10	27.75	25.45	20.55	14.50	8.20				
400.00 - 403.99	51.45	48.10	42.60	38.55	33.10	28.75	26.45	21.50	15.45	9.15				
404.00 - 407.99	52.50	49.15	43.65	39.55	34.15	29.75	27.45	22.45	16.40	10.10	3.75			
408.00 - 411.99	53.60	50.20	44.75	40.55	35.15	30.75	28.45	23.40	17.35	11.05	4.75			
412.00 - 415.99	54.65	51.25	45.80	41.55	36.15	31.75	29.45	24.40	18.30	12.00	5.70			
416.00 - 419.99	55.70	52.35	46.85	42.60	37.15	32.75	30.45	25.45	19.25	12.95	6.65			
420.00 - 423.99	56.75	53.40	47.90	43.65	38.15	33.75	31.45	26.45	20.20	13.90	7.60			
424.00 - 427.99	57.85	54.45	49.00	44.70	39.15	34.75	32.50	27.45	21.15	14.85	8.55			
428.00 - 431.99	58.90	55.50	50.05	45.80	40.15	35.75	33.50	28.45	22.10	15.80	9.50	3.65		
432.00 - 435.99	59.95	56.55	51.10	46.85	41.15	36.80	34.50	29.45	23.05	16.75	10.45	4.60		
436.00 - 439.99	61.00	57.65	52.15	47.90	42.15	37.80	35.50	30.45	24.05	17.70	11.40	5.55		
440.00 - 443.99	62.05	58.70	53.20	48.95	43.25	38.80	36.50	31.45	25.05	18.65	12.35	6.50		
444.00 - 447.99	63.15	59.75	54.30	50.00	44.30	39.80	37.50	32.45	26.05	19.60	13.30	7.45		
448.00 - 451.99	64.20	60.80	55.35	51.10	45.35	40.80	38.50	33.50	27.05	20.55	14.25	8.40	4.10	4.10
452.00 - 455.99	65.25	61.90	56.40	52.15	46.40	41.80	39.50	34.50	28.05	21.50	15.20	9.35	5.10	4.25
456.00 - 459.99	66.30	62.95	57.45	53.20	47.45	42.85	40.50	35.50	29.05	22.45	16.15	10.30	6.05	4.25
460.00 - 463.99	67.40	64.00	58.55	54.25	48.55	43.90	41.55	36.50	30.05	23.40	17.05	11.25	7.00	4.25
464.00 - 473.99	69.25	65.85	60.40	56.15	50.40	45.75	43.35	38.25	31.80	25.15	18.75	12.90	8.65	4.25
474.00 - 483.99	71.90	68.50	63.05	58.80	53.05	48.40	46.00	40.75	34.35	27.65	21.10	15.25	11.05	4.25
484.00 - 493.99	74.55	71.15	65.70	61.45	55.70	51.05	48.65	43.35	36.85	30.15	23.50	17.65	13.40	4.25
494.00 - 503.99	77.20	73.80	68.35	64.10	58.35	53.70	51.30	46.00	39.35	32.70	26.00	20.00	15.80	4.25
504.00 - 513.99	79.85	76.50	71.00	66.75	61.00	56.40	53.95	48.65	41.90	35.20	28.50	22.40	18.15	4.25
514.00 - 523.99	82.50	79.15	73.65	69.40	63.65	59.05	56.60	51.30	44.50	37.70	31.05	24.85	20.55	4.30
524.00 - 533.99	85.25	81.80	76.30	72.05	66.30	61.70	59.25	53.95	47.15	40.25	33.55	27.35	22.90	4.45
534.00 - 543.99	88.15	84.45	78.95	74.70	68.95	64.35	61.90	56.60	49.80	42.75	36.05	29.90	25.40	4.50
544.00 - 553.99	91.10	87.35	81.60	77.35	71.60	67.00	64.55	59.25	52.45	45.40	38.60	32.40	27.90	4.50
554.00 - 563.99	94.05	90.30	84.25	80.00	74.30	69.65	67.25	61.90	55.15	48.05	41.10	34.90	30.45	4.50
564.00 - 573.99	96.95	93.25	87.20	82.65	76.95	72.30	69.90	64.55	57.80	50.75	43.70	37.45	32.95	4.50
574.00 - 583.99	99.90	96.15	90.15	85.40	79.60	74.95	72.55	67.20	60.45	53.40	46.35	39.95	35.45	4.50
584.00 - 593.99	102.85	99.10	93.05	88.35	82.25	77.60	75.20	69.85	63.10	56.05	49.00	42.45	37.95	4.50
594.00 - 603.99	105.75	102.05	96.00	91.30	84.95	80.25	77.85	72.55	65.75	58.70	51.65	45.10	40.50	4.60
604.00 - 613.99	108.70	104.95	98.95	94.20	87.90	82.90	80.50	75.20	68.40	61.35	54.30	47.75	43.05	4.70

TABLE 405

BI-WEEKLY TAX DEDUCTIONS
Basis—26 Pay Periods per Year

DÉDUCTIONS D'IMPÔT DE DEUX SEMAINES
Base—26 périodes de paie par année

BI-WEEKLY PAY Use appropriate bracket — PAIE DE DEUX SEMAINES Utilisez le palier approprié	IF THE EMPLOYEE'S "NET CLAIM CODE" ON FORM TD1 IS — SI LE «CODE DE RÉCLAMATION NETTE» DE L'EMPLOYÉ SELON LA FORMULE TD1 EST DE													See note on page 23. Voir remarque p. 23.
	1	2	3	4	5	6	7	8	9	10	11	12	13	
	DEDUCT FROM EACH PAY — DÉDUISEZ SUR CHAQUE PAIE													Column A Colonne A
$ 614.00 - 623.99	111.65	107.90	101.85	97.15	90.80	85.70	83.15	77.85	71.05	64.00	56.95	50.40	45.70	4.70
624.00 - 633.99	114.55	110.85	104.80	100.10	93.75	88.65	85.95	80.50	73.70	66.65	59.60	53.10	48.35	4.75
634.00 - 643.99	117.35	113.75	107.75	103.00	96.70	91.55	88.90	83.15	76.35	69.30	62.25	55.75	51.00	4.75
644.00 - 653.99	120.20	116.70	110.75	106.00	99.70	94.55	91.90	86.00	79.10	72.05	64.95	58.45	53.70	4.75
654.00 - 663.99	123.05	119.55	113.75	109.05	102.70	97.60	94.90	89.05	81.80	74.75	67.70	61.20	56.45	4.75
664.00 - 673.99	125.85	122.35	116.70	112.05	105.75	100.60	97.95	92.05	84.55	77.50	70.45	63.90	59.20	4.75
674.00 - 683.99	128.70	125.20	119.55	115.10	108.75	103.65	100.95	95.10	87.60	80.25	73.20	66.65	61.90	4.75
684.00 - 693.99	131.70	128.05	122.35	117.95	111.80	106.65	104.00	98.10	90.60	82.95	75.90	69.40	64.65	4.75
694.00 - 703.99	134.80	130.95	125.20	120.80	114.80	109.70	107.00	101.15	93.65	85.85	78.65	72.15	67.40	4.75
704.00 - 713.99	137.90	134.05	128.05	123.60	117.65	112.70	110.05	104.15	96.65	88.85	81.40	74.85	70.15	4.75
714.00 - 723.99	141.00	137.15	130.95	126.45	120.50	115.70	113.05	107.20	99.70	91.90	84.15	77.60	72.85	4.75
724.00 - 733.99	144.10	140.25	134.05	129.30	123.35	118.55	116.05	110.20	102.70	94.90	87.10	80.35	75.60	4.75
734.00 - 743.99	147.20	143.35	137.15	132.35	126.20	121.40	118.85	113.25	105.75	97.95	90.15	83.05	78.35	4.75
744.00 - 753.99	150.30	146.50	140.25	135.45	129.00	124.20	121.70	116.20	108.75	100.95	93.15	85.95	81.10	4.85
754.00 - 763.99	153.40	149.60	143.35	138.55	132.05	127.05	124.55	119.05	111.80	104.00	96.20	89.00	83.80	5.20
764.00 - 773.99	156.50	152.70	146.50	141.65	135.15	129.90	127.40	121.85	114.80	107.00	99.20	92.00	86.75	5.25
774.00 - 783.99	159.65	155.80	149.60	144.75	138.25	133.00	130.25	124.70	117.65	110.05	102.25	95.05	89.80	5.25
784.00 - 793.99	162.75	158.90	152.70	147.85	141.35	136.10	133.35	127.55	120.50	113.05	105.25	98.05	92.80	5.25
794.00 - 803.99	165.85	162.00	155.80	150.95	144.45	139.20	136.45	130.40	123.35	116.05	108.30	101.10	95.85	5.25
804.00 - 813.99	168.95	165.10	158.90	154.05	147.55	142.30	139.55	133.50	126.20	118.85	111.30	104.10	98.85	5.25
814.00 - 823.99	172.05	168.20	162.00	157.15	150.65	145.40	142.65	136.65	129.00	121.70	114.35	107.15	101.90	5.25
824.00 - 833.99	175.15	171.30	165.10	160.25	153.75	148.50	145.75	139.75	132.05	124.55	117.25	110.15	104.90	5.25
834.00 - 843.99	178.35	174.40	168.20	163.40	156.85	151.60	148.85	142.85	135.15	127.40	120.05	113.15	107.95	5.25
844.00 - 853.99	181.75	177.55	171.30	166.50	159.95	154.70	151.95	145.95	138.25	130.25	122.90	116.15	110.95	5.25
854.00 - 863.99	185.10	180.95	174.40	169.60	163.10	157.80	155.10	149.05	141.35	133.35	125.75	119.00	114.00	5.25
864.00 - 873.99	188.50	184.30	177.55	172.70	166.20	160.95	158.20	152.15	144.45	136.45	128.60	121.80	116.90	5.25
874.00 - 883.99	191.85	187.70	180.95	175.80	169.30	164.05	161.30	155.25	147.55	139.55	131.55	124.65	119.75	5.25
884.00 - 893.99	195.25	191.05	184.30	179.05	172.40	167.15	164.40	158.35	150.65	142.65	134.65	127.50	122.60	5.25
894.00 - 903.99	198.60	194.45	187.70	182.45	175.50	170.25	167.50	161.45	153.75	145.75	137.75	130.35	125.40	5.25
904.00 - 913.99	202.00	197.80	191.05	185.80	178.75	173.35	170.60	164.55	156.85	148.85	140.85	133.45	128.25	5.25
914.00 - 923.99	205.35	201.20	194.45	189.20	182.10	176.45	173.70	167.70	159.95	151.95	143.95	136.55	131.20	5.35
924.00 - 933.99	208.75	204.55	197.80	192.55	185.50	179.75	176.80	170.80	163.10	155.10	147.10	139.65	134.30	5.35
934.00 - 943.99	212.10	207.95	201.20	195.95	188.85	183.15	180.15	173.90	166.20	158.20	150.20	142.80	137.40	5.40
944.00 - 953.99	215.50	211.30	204.55	199.30	192.25	186.50	183.55	177.00	169.30	161.30	153.30	145.90	140.50	5.40
954.00 - 963.99	218.85	214.70	207.95	202.70	195.60	189.90	186.90	180.35	172.40	164.40	156.40	149.00	143.60	5.40
964.00 - 983.99	223.90	219.75	213.00	207.75	200.65	194.95	191.95	185.40	177.05	169.05	161.05	153.65	148.25	5.40
984.00 - 1003.99	230.90	226.50	219.75	214.50	207.40	201.70	198.70	192.15	183.80	175.25	167.25	159.85	154.50	5.40
1004.00 - 1023.99	238.45	233.80	226.50	221.25	214.15	208.45	205.45	198.90	190.55	181.85	173.45	166.05	160.70	5.40
1024.00 - 1043.99	246.00	241.35	233.80	228.00	220.90	215.20	212.20	205.65	197.30	188.60	179.90	172.25	166.90	5.40
1044.00 - 1063.99	253.55	248.90	241.35	235.45	227.65	221.95	218.95	212.40	204.05	195.35	186.65	178.60	173.10	5.50

Figure 18.11 Pages from the government booklet for income tax deductions.

PAYROLL JOURNAL For the *2 Weeks* ended *May 24* 19 —

Employee	Net Claim Code	Earnings			Deductions									Total Ded'ns	Net Pay
		Regular	Extra	Gross	C.P.P.	U.I. Premium	R.P.P.	Income Tax		Health Ins.	Union Dues	Group Life			
								Taxable Income	Ded'n						
Harold Evans	8	645.00	—	645.00	10.61	11.34	32.25	590.80	69.85						

Figure 18.12 Payroll journal with income tax deduction recorded.

Health Insurance

Most provinces operate a universal health insurance program. The basic plan generally covers both doctors' fees and hospital expenses. Employers are authorized to deduct from the employee's pay the amount of the premium as set out by the provincial government. The premium for a single person is less than that for a person who is married and has dependent children. The rates to be used for the exercises in this text are shown below.

HEALTH INSURANCE BIWEEKLY RATES

1. Single person	Public ward	$24.00
	Semiprivate	$27.00
2. Family (head and all dependants)	Public ward	$34.00
	Semiprivate	$37.00

In recent years, health insurance plans have developed that provide additional benefits not included in the basic health plans operated by the province. Such programs as Extended Health Care and Dental Health Care are becoming quite common.

Employers often pay a large portion or the entire premium for the health care programs of their employees. For the exercises in this text, assume that the employer pays 75 percent of the cost of health insurance and the employee pays 25 percent.

Harold Evans has no additional health coverage other than the basic programs operated by the province. His employer pays 75 percent of the premium. Mr. Evans has semiprivate coverage.

Harold Evans' portion is calculated as follows:

$$25\% \text{ of } \$27.00 = \$6.75$$

The journal in Figure 18.13 shows the premium for Harold Evans recorded in the payroll journal.

PAYROLL JOURNAL For the 2 Weeks ended May 24 19 —

		Earnings			Deductions										
								Income Tax							
Employee	Net Claim Code	Regular	Extra	Gross	C.P.P.	U.I. Premium	R.P.P.	Taxable Income	Ded'n	Health Ins.	Union Dues	Group Life		Total Ded'ns	Net Pay
Harold Evans	8	645.00	—	645.00	10.61	11.34	32.25	590.80	69.85	6.75					

Figure 18.13 Payroll journal with health insurance deduction recorded.

Union Dues 'Check-off'

The employees of a medium-sized or larger business are often organized into a labour union. Dues to the union are often deducted by the employer and remitted periodically to the union. This obligation of the employer is usually part of the contract negotiated between the employer and the employees.

At Nor-Can Grocers Ltd., the contract contains the following clause:

> The Company will deduct each month from the wages of each employee in the bargaining unit an amount equivalent to the normal monthly Union dues and will remit such sums deducted to the appropriate official of the Union.

The amount that is deducted from the employee's pay depends on the union. The union of Harold Evans requires a deduction of $7.00 each pay period. The journal in Figure 18.14 shows the deduction entered.

PAYROLL JOURNAL For the 2 Weeks ended May 24 19 —

		Earnings			Deductions										
								Income Tax							
Employee	Net Claim Code	Regular	Extra	Gross	C.P.P.	U.I. Premium	R.P.P.	Taxable Income	Ded'n	Health Ins.	Union Dues	Group Life		Total Ded'ns	Net Pay
Harold Evans	8	645.00	—	645.00	10.61	11.34	32.25	590.80	69.85	6.75	7.00				

Figure 18.14 Payroll journal with union dues deduction recorded.

Group Life Insurance

Some firms make it possible for their employees to enrol in some form of group life insurance plan. Premiums for this plan are handled as payroll deductions. Premiums are paid at a specified amount per $1 000 of insurance protection. The amount of insurance that an employee may obtain depends on gross earnings.

Harold Evans has group life insurance and pays a premium of 15 cents per week per $1 000 worth of insurance. He has a total amount of $24 000 of insurance. This means that his premium is 24 × 15¢, which is $3.60 per week, or $7.20 each pay period. The payroll journal in Figure 18.15 shows the premium properly entered.

PAYROLL JOURNAL For the *2 Weeks* ended *May 24* 19 —

Employee	Net Claim Code	Earnings: Regular	Earnings: Extra	Earnings: Gross	Deductions: C.P.P.	U.I. Premium	R.P.P.	Income Tax: Taxable Income	Income Tax: Ded'n	Health Ins.	Union Dues	Group Life		Total Ded'ns	Net Pay
Harold Evans	8	645 00	—	645 00	10 61	11 34	32 25	590 80	69 85	6 75	7 00	7 20			

Figure 18.15 Payroll journal with group life deduction recorded.

Other Deductions

Other deductions may be made from an employee's earnings if authority is granted by the employee. They are handled in a manner similar to those deductions that we have already discussed. Some of these other deductions are charitable donations, credit union contributions, and purchases of bonds or shares of stock.

Calculating Net Pay

At this point, the last deduction to be made from Harold Evans's pay has been entered. There are two steps remaining. First, the deductions are added and the total is entered in the Total Deductions column. The total is then subtracted from the gross pay of $645, giving a net pay of $500. This amount is entered in the Net Pay column of the journal. Figure 18.16 shows the completed calculations for Harold Evans.

PAYROLL JOURNAL For the *2 Weeks* ended *May 24* 19 —

Employee	Net Claim Code	Earnings: Regular	Earnings: Extra	Earnings: Gross	Deductions: C.P.P.	U.I. Premium	R.P.P.	Income Tax: Taxable Income	Income Tax: Ded'n	Health Ins.	Union Dues	Group Life		Total Ded'ns	Net Pay
Harold Evans	8	645 00	—	645 00	10 61	11 34	32 25	590 80	69 85	6 75	7 00	7 20		145 00	500 00

Figure 18.16 Payroll journal showing total deductions and net pay.

Completing the Payroll Journal

The procedure that has been discussed and illustrated for Harold Evans is repeated for each of the employees in the company. One line of the payroll journal is used for each employee. When all the details for all the employees are entered in the journal, the amount columns are totalled as shown in Figure 18.17.

PAYROLL JOURNAL For the 2 weeks ended May 24 19 —

Employee	Net Claim Code	Earnings: Regular	Earnings: Extra	Earnings: Gross	Deductions: C.P.P.	U.I. Premium	R.P.P.	Income Tax: Taxable Income	Income Tax: Ded'n	Health Ins.	Union Dues	Group Life		Total Ded'ns	Net Pay
Harold Evans	8	645 00	—	645 00	10 61	11 34	32 25	590 80	69 85	6 75	7 00	7 20		145 00	500 00
Ronald Baker	7	610 00	—	610 00	10 01	10 98	30 50	558 51	67 25	6 75	7 00	6 60		139 09	470 91
Bob Funston	8	590 00	—	590 00	9 65	10 62	29 50	540 23	56 60	6 75	7 00	6 60		126 72	463 28
Les Williams	1	540 00	—	540 00	8 75	9 72	27 00	494 53	77 20	3 50	7 00	6 00		139 17	400 83
Dennis Murray	8	535 00	—	535 00	8 66	9 63	26 75	489 96	43 35	6 75	7 00	7 20		109 34	425 66
		2920 00		2920 00	47 68	52 29	146 00	2674 03	314 25	30 50	35 00	33 60		659 32	2260 68

Figure 18.17 A completed payroll journal.

Proving the Accuracy of the Journal

The next step is to prove the column totals of the journal. There are three steps to be performed to guarantee accuracy. You should ensure the following:

1. The Regular Earnings column + the Extra Earnings column = the Gross Earnings column.
2. The sum of all the deductions columns = the Total Deductions column.
3. The Gross Earnings column − the Total Deductions column = the Net Pay column.

18.4 Recording the Payroll

Once the payroll journal has been prepared and balanced, the payroll must be recorded in the accounts. To record the payroll for Nor-Can Grocers Ltd., an accounting entry is required for each of the following:

1. The totals from the payroll journal.
2. The employer's liability for Canada Pension Plan.
3. The employer's liability for unemployment insurance.
4. The employer's liability for the registered pension plan.
5. The employer's liability for health insurance.

The Accounting Entries

1. Figure 18.18 shows the totals from the payroll journal recorded in the general journal. The gross pay total is the same as the salaries expense figure. All of the individual deduction columns and the net pay column represent liabilities to be paid in the near future.

GENERAL JOURNAL PAGE 43

DATE		PARTICULARS	P.R.	DEBIT	CREDIT
19– May	24	Salaries Expense		2 920 –	
		Canada Pension Plan Payable			47 68
		Unemployment Ins. Payable			52 29
		Reg'd Pension Plan Payable			146 –
		Employees Tax Deductions Payable			314 25
		Health Insurance Payable			30 50
		Union Dues Payable			35 –
		Group Life Insurance Payable			33 60
		Payroll Payable			2 260 68
		To record payroll totals for May 24, 19–			

Figure 18.18 Totals from the payroll journal recorded in the general journal.

2. Figure 18.19 shows the employer's liability for Canada Pension Plan entered in the general journal. The government booklet on Canada Pension Plan states, 'Every employer is also required to make a contribution on behalf of employees equal to the contributions deducted from them.' Because this employee contributes $47.68 the employer must pay the same amount on his own behalf.

   The accounting entry to record the employer's C.P.P. contribution shows an additional liability of $47.68. Because this comes out of the pocket of the business, it is also an expense of $47.68.

May	24	Canada Pension Plan Expense		47 68	
		Canada Pension Plan Payable			47 68
		Employer's C.P.P. contribution.			

Figure 18.19 General journal entry to record employee's C.P.P. contribution.

3. Figure 18.20 shows the employer's liability for unemployment insurance recorded in the general journal. The government booklet on unemployment

insurance states that the employer's contribution is to be calculated 'at 1.4 times the employees' premium'. Because this employee contributes $52.29, the employer has to pay 1.4 times that amount, or $73.21.

The accounting entry to record the employer's unemployment insurance contribution records the additional liability of $73.21. Because it comes out of the pocket of the business, this contribution is also an expense of $73.21.

May	24	Unemployment Insurance Expense		73 21	
		Unemployment Ins. Payable			73 21
		Employer's U.I. contribution.			

Figure 18.20 General journal entry to record employer's U.I. contribution.

4. Figure 18.21 shows the employer's liability for the registered retirement savings plan recorded in the general journal. The agreement between Nor-Can Grocers Ltd. and its employees states that both the employees and the employer contribute an amount equal to 5 percent of the employee's gross pay toward the registered pension plan. The amount to be contributed by each is $146.00.

May	24	Registered Pension Plan Expense		146 –	
		Reg'd Pension Plan Payable			146 –
		Employer's R.P.P. contribution.			

Figure 18.21 General journal entry for employer's R.P.P. contribution.

5. Figure 18.22 shows the employer's liability for health insurance recorded in the general journal. Nor-Can Grocers Ltd. and its employees have agreed that the employer pays 75 percent and the employees pay 25 percent of the cost of the insurance. Thus, the company pays three times as much as the employees. For this particular pay period, the company must pay 3 × $30.50, or $91.50.

May	24	Health Insurance Expense		91 50	
		Health Insurance Payable			91 50
		Employer's health insurance			
		contribution.			

Figure 18.22 General journal entry for employer's health insurance contribution.

The Effect in the Accounts

Each of the five entries is posted to the appropriate general ledger accounts. The accounts in Figure 18.23 show the effect of the accounting entries for this one payroll.

Canada Pension Plan Payable

19– May	24				47 68	C	47 68
	24				47 68	C	95 36

Registered Pension Plan Payable

19– May	24				146 –	C	146 –
	24				146 –	C	292 –

Health Insurance Payable

19– May	24				30 50	C	30 50
	24				91 50	C	122 –

Group Life Insurance Payable

19– May	24				33 60	C	33 60

Salaries Expense

19– May	24			2 920 –		D	2 920 –

Unemployment Insurance Expense

19– May	24			73 21		D	73 21

Health Insurance Expense

19– May	24			91 50		D	91 50

Unemployment Insce. Payable

19– May	24				52 29	C	52 29
	24				73 21	C	125 50

Employees' Tax Deductions Payable

19– May	24				314 25	C	314 25

Union Dues Payable

19– May	24				35 –	C	35 –

Payroll Payable

19– May	24				2 260 68	C	2 260 68

Canada Pension Plan Expense

19– May	24			47 68		D	47 68

Registered Pension Plan Expense

19– May	24			146 –		D	146 –

Figure 18.23 General ledger accounts with payroll entries recorded.

Observe the following:

1. The amount owed for Canada Pension Plan is the sum of the employee's contribution of $47.68 and the employer's contribution of $47.68, for a total of $95.36.
2. The amount owed for unemployment insurance is the sum of the employee's contribution of $52.29 and the employer's contribution of $73.21, for a total of $125.50.
3. The amount owed for registered pension plan is the sum of the employee's contribution of $146 and the employer's contribution of $146, for a total of $292.
4. The amount owed for health insurance is the sum of the employee's contribution of $30.50 and the employer's contribution of $91.50, for a total of $122.
5. All other payroll liabilities are for the employee's contributions only.

18.5 Payment to Employees

Paying by Cash

When employees receive their pay in cash, each pay envelope must be carefully prepared. In order to have the right number of bills and coins for all of the employees' pay envelopes, it is first necessary to prepare a 'currency requisition' form as shown in Figure 18.24.

This form is taken to the bank together with a cheque drawn on the regular bank account for the total amount of the payroll. The cheque is cashed, and the required number of each of the bills and coins as shown on the form is obtained from the bank. The accounting entry for this cheque is as follows:

Dr. Payroll Payable	$2 260.68	
Cr. Bank		$2 260.68

PAYROLL CURRENCY REQUISITION — PAY PERIOD ENDED May 24 19__

EMPLOYEE	NET PAY	$20	$10	$5	$1	25¢	10¢	5¢	1¢
Harold Evans	500 –	25							
Ronald Baker	470 91	23	1			3	1	1	1
Bob Funston	463 28	23			3	1			3
Leo Williams	400 83	20				3		1	3
Dennis Murray	425 66	21		1		2	1	1	1
NUMBER OF COINS OR BILLS		112	1	1	3	9	2	3	8
DOLLAR VALUE	2 260 68	2 240	10	5	3	2.25	.20	.15	.08

Figure 18.24 A completed payroll currency requisition form.

The employees' pay envelopes are filled with currency and coins as shown by the currency requisition form. Included with each pay envelope is a statement showing the employee's earnings, deductions, and net pay. This statement may be a separate statement or may be printed on the outside of the envelope. The employee's signature is obtained at the time of paying as proof of payment.

Paying by Cheque

Many businesses, especially firms with a large number of employees, prefer to pay by cheque rather than by cash. This eliminates the problem of having large sums of money around. Also, the cancelled cheques serve as evidence that the employees did receive their pay. The cheques for the employees may be drawn on the company's regular bank account or on a special bank account established only to meet the payroll.

Regular Bank Account

A separate cheque, drawn on the regular bank account, is issued to each employee. For each cheque the accounting entry, recorded in the cash payments journal, is as follows:

Dr. Payroll Payable	\$XXX	
Cr. Bank		\$XXX

The sum of all the individual cheques issued in this way will be equal to the total of the Net Pay column of the payroll journal. Since each cheque results in a debit to the Payroll Payable account, the cheques will have the effect of eliminating the balance in this liability account.

Special Payroll Bank Account

To allow the Payroll Department to operate independently and to issue its own payroll cheques, many businesses set up a separate payroll bank account.

Using this method, only one cheque is drawn on the regular bank account for the amount of the total net pay. In the cash payments journal the accounting entry to record this cheque is as follows:

Dr. Payroll Payable	\$XXX	
Cr. Bank		\$XXX

This cheque is cashed and the funds deposited in the special payroll bank account, thereby providing funds for the Payroll Department to meet the payroll obligation. The Payroll Department then issues separate payroll cheques to the employees as necessary. No accounting entries are required for these cheques. When all of the cheques are cashed, the balance in the payroll bank account will be reduced to zero.

18.6 Payment of Payroll Liabilities

To the Federal Government

On or before the fifteenth day of each month, the employer must remit to the Receiver General for Canada all the money deducted from employees during the previous month for Canada Pension Plan, unemployment insurance, and income tax, plus the employer's own contributions for Canada Pension Plan and unemployment insurance. For example, deductions made in August are due by September 15th, deductions made in September are due by October 15th, and so on.

A special two-part form, PD7AR (Tax Deduction—Canada Pension Plan—Unemployment Insurance Remittance Return), is used to make the payment. The upper portion is submitted with the payment while the lower portion is retained for the employer's own records. The payment may be made at any bank or to the appropriate taxation centre.

The correct amount to be sent to the government can be easily worked out. Simply total the balances, as at the end of the previous month, in the accounts for Canada Pension Plan Payable, Unemployment Insurance Payable, and Employees Tax Deductions Payable.

For example, assume that the balances in these three accounts at August 31 are as follows:

Canada Pension Plan Payable	—	$1 455.76 Cr.
Unemployment Insurance Payable	—	210.32 Cr.
Employees Tax Deductions Payable	—	124.32 Cr.
	Total	$1 790.40

One cheque is drawn for the combined amount of $1 790.40 and sent to the government. The accounting entry to record the payment is as follows:

Canada Pension Plan Payable	$1 455.76	
Unemployment Insurance Payable	210.32	
Employees Tax Deductions Payable	124.32	
Bank		$1 790.40

To Other Institutions

Other liabilities resulting from payroll deductions are handled in much the same way. A cheque to the appropriate agency is issued. The accounting entry for the cheque eliminates the liability from the books.

18.7 Basic Payroll Records

You are aware by now of the importance of written documents in the accounting process. There are three important records that are required for payroll: (1) the payroll journal, (2) the payroll cheque or payroll cash statement, and (3) the individual employee's earnings record.

Payroll Journal

The payroll journal was discussed and illustrated in Section 18.3 on payroll deductions. It is prepared for each pay period and is used to accumulate and calculate all of the necessary information about wages and salaries.

Using the Payroll Journal as a Book of Original Entry

The payroll journal can be used in another way. We have been considering the payroll journal as a summary sheet and not as a book of original entry. As a result it has been necessary to journalize the totals of the payroll into the general journal.

Many business firms, regardless of the journal system used, treat the payroll journal as a book of original entry. As a result, the first payroll entry need not be recorded in the general journal but may be posted directly from the payroll journal to the general ledger. It will still be necessary to record in the usual manner entries 2, 3, 4, and 5, as illustrated in Section 18.4 on recording the payroll. This is because the payroll journal shows only the employees' share of Canada Pension, unemployment insurance, registered pension plan, and health insurance. The employer's share of each must be recorded also.

Payroll Cheques or Payroll Cash Statements

In most businesses, the employees are paid by cheque. Attached to each pay cheque is a voucher that shows the employee's gross pay, deductions, and the net pay. A payroll cheque is shown in Figure 18.25.

Businesses that prefer to pay their employees by cash rather than by cheque use a payroll cash statement. It serves the same purpose as the voucher portion of the payroll cheque. It indicates the earnings, the various deductions, and the net pay.

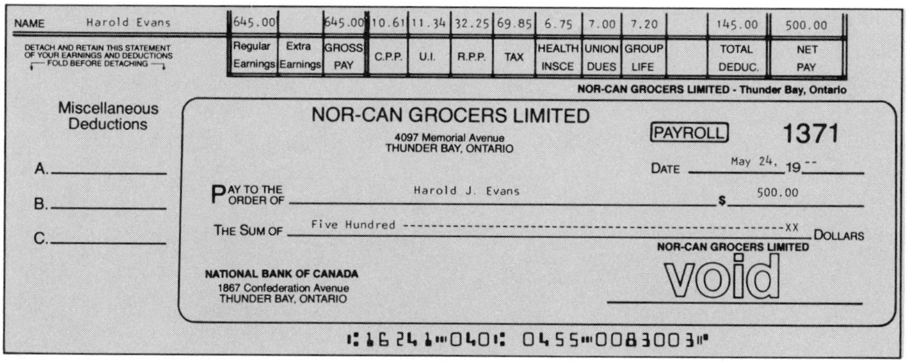

NAME Harold Evans	Regular Earnings	Extra Earnings	GROSS PAY	C.P.P.	U.I.	R.P.P.	TAX	HEALTH INSCE	UNION DUES	GROUP LIFE		TOTAL DEDUC.	NET PAY
DETACH AND RETAIN THIS STATEMENT OF YOUR EARNINGS AND DEDUCTIONS — FOLD BEFORE DETACHING	645.00		645.00	10.61	11.34	32.25	69.85	6.75	7.00	7.20		145.00	500.00

NOR-CAN GROCERS LIMITED - Thunder Bay, Ontario

Miscellaneous Deductions

A. ____________

B. ____________

C. ____________

NOR-CAN GROCERS LIMITED
4097 Memorial Avenue
THUNDER BAY, ONTARIO

PAYROLL 1371

DATE May 24, 19--

PAY TO THE ORDER OF Harold J. Evans $ 500.00

THE SUM OF Five Hundred ------------------------------------XX DOLLARS

NOR-CAN GROCERS LIMITED

void

NATIONAL BANK OF CANADA
1867 Confederation Avenue
THUNDER BAY, ONTARIO

⑆16241⑈040⑆ 0455⑈0083003⑈

Figure 18.25 A payroll cheque for Harold Evans.

Employee's Earnings Record

For each employee, the employer must keep an **employee's earnings record form** on which are accumulated the details of every pay. This form is shown in Figure 18.26.

At the end of the calendar year, the columns of the employee's earnings record are totalled to obtain the information necessary for preparation by the employer of the annual Statement of Remuneration Paid form (T-4 slip). This form is required for income tax purposes. Copies of the T-4 slips are sent to the District Taxation Office and two copies are sent to the employee. The employee attaches one copy to the annual income tax return. The illustration in Figure 18.27 shows a typical T-4 slip.

NAME Evans Harold J. S.I.N. 609-779-152 EXEMPTION CODE 8 BIRTH DATE Feb. 9, 19–

ADDRESS 178 Clarkson St. Thunder Bay MARITAL STATUS DEPENDENTS DEPARTMENT

PHONE 767-5781 DATE STARTED May 10, 19– DATE LEFT

DATE	STANDARD EARNINGS			STANDARD DEDUCTIONS							
May 10	645.00		645.00	10.61	11.34	32.25	69.85	6.75	7.00	7.20	

		1	2	3	4	5	6	7	8	9	10	11	12	13	14	15	16	17
DATE	EMPLOYEE	NET CLAIM CODE	EARNINGS REGULAR	EXTRA	GROSS	DEDUCTIONS C.P.P.	U.I.	R.P.P.	TAX	HEALTH INSCE.	UNION DUES	GROUP LIFE		TOTAL DEDUC'S	NET PAY	CHQ. NO.	C.P.P. TO DATE	INSURED EARNINGS TO DATE
May 24	Harold Evans	8	645.00	–	645.00	10.61	11.34	32.25	69.85	6.75	7.00	7.20		145.00	500.00	1371	10.61	630.00
Jun 7	Harold Evans	8	645.00	–	645.00	10.61	11.34	32.25	69.85	6.75	7.00	7.20		145.00	500.00	1492	21.22	1260.00
Jun 21	Harold Evans	8	645.00	–	645.00	10.61	11.34	32.25	69.85	6.75	7.00	7.20		145.00	500.00	1603	31.83	1890.00

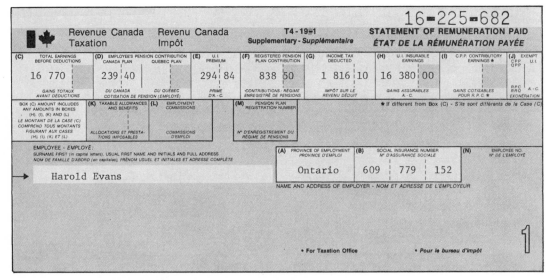

Figure 18.26 An employee's earnings record form.

16-225-682

Revenue Canada Taxation / Revenu Canada Impôt — T4-19–1 Supplementary - *Supplémentaire* — STATEMENT OF REMUNERATION PAID / *ÉTAT DE LA RÉMUNÉRATION PAYÉE*

(C) TOTAL EARNINGS BEFORE DEDUCTIONS / *GAINS TOTAUX AVANT DÉDUCTIONS*	(D) EMPLOYEE'S PENSION CONTRIBUTION CANADA PLAN / *DU CANADA*	QUEBEC PLAN / *DU QUÉBEC*	(E) U.I. PREMIUM / *PRIME D'A.-C.*	(F) REGISTERED PENSION PLAN CONTRIBUTION / *CONTRIBUTIONS: RÉGIME ENREGISTRÉ DE PENSIONS*	(G) INCOME TAX DEDUCTED / *IMPÔT SUR LE REVENU DÉDUIT*	(H) U.I. INSURABLE EARNINGS / *GAINS ASSURABLES A.-C.*	(I) C.P.P. CONTRIBUTORY EARNINGS ★ / *GAINS COTISABLES POUR R.P.C.* ★	(J) EXEMPT CPP QPP / RPC RRQ, U.I. / A.-C. *EXONÉRATION*
16 770	239 40		294 84	838 50	1 816 10	16 380 00		

BOX (C) AMOUNT INCLUDES ANY AMOUNTS IN BOXES (H), (I), (K) AND (L) / *LE MONTANT DE LA CASE (C) COMPREND TOUS MONTANTS FIGURANT AUX CASES (H), (I), (K) ET (L)*

(K) TAXABLE ALLOWANCES AND BENEFITS / *ALLOCATIONS ET PRESTATIONS IMPOSABLES*

(L) EMPLOYMENT COMMISSIONS / *COMMISSIONS D'EMPLOI*

(M) PENSION PLAN REGISTRATION NUMBER / *Nº D'ENREGISTREMENT DU RÉGIME DE PENSIONS*

★ If different from Box (C) - *S'ils sont différents de la Case (C)*

EMPLOYEE - *EMPLOYÉ*:
SURNAME FIRST (in capital letters), USUAL FIRST NAME AND INITIALS AND FULL ADDRESS
NOM DE FAMILLE D'ABORD (en capitales), PRÉNOM USUEL ET INITIALES ET ADRESSE COMPLÈTE

→ Harold Evans

(A) PROVINCE OF EMPLOYMENT / *PROVINCE D'EMPLOI*	(B) SOCIAL INSURANCE NUMBER / *Nº D'ASSURANCE SOCIALE*	(N) EMPLOYEE NO. / *Nº DE L'EMPLOYÉ*
Ontario	609 779 152	

NAME AND ADDRESS OF EMPLOYER - *NOM ET ADRESSE DE L'EMPLOYEUR*

• For Taxation Office • *Pour le bureau d'impôt* 1

Figure 18.27 A T-4 slip for Harold Evans.

Accounting Terms

payroll	**net pay**
salary	**payroll journal**
wages	**registered pension plan**
timecard	**personal exemption**
commission	**taxable earnings**
gross pay	**employee's earnings record form**

Review Questions

1. Give four common payroll periods.
2. For what specific purposes does the government require that employers withhold funds from employees?
3. In general, what kind of records must employers keep regarding the above withholdings?
4. Describe salaries, wages, and commissions.
5. Briefly describe how a timecard works.
6. From the employees' view, are payroll deductions all negative things?
7. What is the purpose of a pension?
8. Why are there registered pension plans, when there is already the Canada Pension Plan?
9. What is the purpose of unemployment insurance?
10. Income taxes are deducted from each pay during the year. How does the government eventually get the right amount from each person?
11. From the employer's view, each of the deductions represents what kind of an account?
12. Give the five accounting entries for payroll that are listed in this book.
13. To which two government funds must the employer contribute?
14. How much must the employer contribute to these two funds?
15. Describe the purpose of a payroll currency requisition form.
16. Theoretically a payroll bank account always ends up with no balance. Explain how this works.
17. When are the amounts that are withheld from the employees' pay turned over to the government?
18. How is the amount of this payment calculated?
19. Name the three basic payroll records.
20. What is the purpose of the employee's earnings record form?

Exercises

Calculating Gross Pay

1. John Alexander earns $24 000 per year. Calculate his gross pay for the following pay periods:

1. Weekly.
2. Biweekly.
3. Semi-monthly.
4. Monthly.

2. Phyllis Marshall earns $30 000 per year. Calculate her gross pay for the following pay periods:

1. Weekly.
2. Biweekly.
3. Semi-monthly.
4. Monthly.

3. In each of the following cases calculate the regular earnings, the overtime earnings, and the gross pay. Assume a regular work week of 40 hours.

	Total Hours	*Regular Rate*	*Overtime Rate*
1.	46	$5.35	time and one half
2.	43	$6.30	double time
3.	$44\frac{1}{2}$	$5.75	straight time
4.	54	$6.05	time and one half
5.	$47\frac{1}{4}$	$5.84	time and one half

4. Greg works in a factory assembling radios. He is paid on a piece-work basis at the rate of $4 for each radio completed. Calculate his gross pay for the week from the following information:

Day	*No. of Units Completed*
Monday	10
Tuesday	9
Wednesday	10
Thursday	12
Friday	11

5. The timecards for two employees are given below.

Time Card							
Week Ended	July 23				19--		
Social Ins. No. 642 393 438							
Name	Frank Windsor						
Day	Morning In	Morning Out	Afternoon In	Afternoon Out	Extra In	Extra Out	Total Hours
M	7·58	12:01	12:58	5.01			
T	8·07	12:00	12·57	5:02			
W	7·56	12:03	12:59	5:00			
T	7:59	12:02	1·01	5:03			
F	7·57	12:02	12:59	5:01			
S							
S							

	Hours	Rate	Earnings
Regular Time		4.85	
Overtime			
Gross Pay			

Time Card							
Week Ended	July 23				19--		
Social Ins. No. 643 461 217							
Name	Ray Peterson						
Day	Morning In	Morning Out	Afternoon In	Afternoon Out	Extra In	Extra Out	Total Hours
M	7·58	12:01	1:00	5:02			
T	7:59	12·00	12·58	5:01	5:59	8:55	
W	7:57	12:01	12·59	5:02			
T	7:56	12·01	12·58	5:03			
F	7·59	12:01	12·59	5:01			
S	7·58	12:01					
S							

	Hours	Rate	Earnings
Regular Time		4.65	
Overtime			
Gross Pay			

1. Determine the total number of hours worked each day and the total number of hours worked during the week. (Move the 'In' times ahead to the nearest quarter hour and the 'Out' times back to the nearest quarter hour.)

2. Calculate the regular and overtime earnings for each. (All hours in excess of 40 hours per week are overtime hours paid at the rate of time and one half the regular rate.)

3. Determine the gross pay for each.

---

6. The Greenfield Real Estate Company pays its salesmen a basic salary of $325 per month plus a 2 percent commission on the sales they make. For each of the salesmen listed below, calculate the commission and the gross earnings.

	Salesmen	*Net Sales*
1.	Bob Rennie	$90 000.00
2.	Mary Hunt	45 500.00
3.	Gerry Anderson	51 300.00
4.	Fay Milroy	39 800.00
5.	Leonard Downes	61 750.00
6.	Peter Chan	42 100.00

Using C.P.P. and U.I. tables

7. 1. The schedule below also appears in the workbook. Complete the schedule by looking up the required deductions for C.P.P. and U.I. and enter them in the appropriate places.

Employee	*Gross Pay*	*C.P.P. Deduction*	*U.I. Deduction*
F. Mazur	$825.60		
C. Koch	645.00		
P. Parsons	548.00		
G. Vittelli	697.43		
Y. Van Del	569.40		

2. You are in charge of the payroll for the above employees.
a. How many deductions will be made during the year for C.P.P.?
b. What will be the amount of the final deduction?

Calculating R.P.P. Deductions

8. Use the following information to calculate the amount of the Registered Pension Plan premium paid by the employees in each case.

	Gross Pay	*R.P.P. Rate*
1.	$ 685.00	3%
2.	1 250.00	7%
3.	785.00	5%
4.	350.00	2%
5.	925.00	6%

Using Income Tax Tables

9. Complete the following schedule in the workbook.

Net Claim Code	Gross Earnings	C.P.P. Deduction	U.I. Deduction	R.P.P. Deduction 6%	Taxable Earnings	Income Tax Deduction	Net Amount After Tax
10	706 29						
8	920 –						
5	534 27						
1	642 90						
2	566 50						
TOTALS							

10. Complete the following schedule in the workbook.

Net Claim Code	Gross Earnings	C.P.P. Deduction	U.I. Deduction	R.P.P. Deduction 5%	Taxable Earnings	Income Tax Deduction	Net Amount After Tax
8	620.15						
3	731.30						
1	531.60						
6	540.20						
4	916.15						
9	718.15						
TOTALS							

Journalizing Payroll Entries

11. The following illustration shows the column totals from the payroll of Hudson Fisheries Limited. The employer matches the employee's contributions to the R.P.P. and pays 75 percent of the health insurance. Prepare the general journal entries to record the payroll.

PAYROLL JOURNAL For the *2 weeks* ended *October 16* 19 —

Employee	Net Claim Code	Earnings: Regular	Earnings: Extra	Earnings: Gross	Deductions: C.P.P.	Deductions: U.I. Premium	Deductions: R.P.P.	Income Tax: Taxable Income	Income Tax: Ded'n	Health Ins.	Union Dues	Group Life		Total Ded'ns	Net Pay
TOTALS		4982.50	1612.95	6595.45	116.35	67.34	329.77	6081.99	1277.22	40.50	84.—	158.50		2073.68	4521.77

12. The following illustration shows the column totals from the payroll of Jackson Associates. The employer matches the employees' contributions to the R.P.P. and the health insurance. Prepare the journal entries to record the payroll.

PAYROLL JOURNAL For the 2 weeks ended March 24 19 —

Employee	Net Claim Code	Earnings: Regular	Earnings: Extra	Earnings: Gross	Deductions: C.P.P.	U.I. Premium	R.P.P.	Income Tax: Taxable Income	Income Tax: Ded'n	Health Ins.	Union Dues	Group Life		Total Ded'ns	Net Pay
TOTALS		1919 25	236 40	2155 65	46 90	31 32	107 78	1969 65	256 05	96 —	32 —	36 —		606 05	1549 60

Full Payroll and Accounting Entries

13. The payroll journal for this exercise appears in the workbook.

1. Complete the payroll journal from the data given below for the two weeks ended August 12, 19--.

a.

Employee	*Hours Worked Week 1*	*Hours Worked Week 2*	*Net Claim Code*	*Hourly Rate**	*Health Insurance Coverage*	*Life Insurance Coverage*
Alex Axelson	40	48	9	$6.75	Family, semi-private	$20 000
Peter Jones	40	40	1	7.20	Single, semi-private	$20 000
Mary Koehler	40	40	3	6.68	Single, semi-private	$40 000
Susan Peterson	46	46	8	6.60	Family, public ward	$40 000
Bob Sauve	40	40	7	8.80	Family, semi-private	$50 000

*Any hours over 40 hours per week are considered to be overtime hours to be paid for at the rate of one and one-half times the regular rate.

b. Each employee is enrolled in the registered pension plan with contributions set at 4 percent of the gross pay. The employer matches the contributions of the employees.

c. The rates for health insurance are those given in the text on page 521.

d. Union dues are $8 every two weeks for every employee.

e. The rate for group life insurance is 20 cents every two weeks for each $1 000 of coverage. The total cost is paid for by the employees.

2. Total the columns of the payroll journal and perform the steps to ensure its accuracy.

3. Journalize the accounting entries to record the payroll journal totals and the contributions required by the employer.

14. The payroll journal for this exercise is set up for you in the workbook.

1. Complete the payroll journal from the data given below for the two weeks ended September 14, 19--.

a.

Employee	*Marital Status*	*Salary for Two Weeks*	*Net Claim Code*
S. Chursa	Married	$560	3
E. Fillion	Married	560	7
D. Hubie	Single	740	2
R. Pitt	Married	650	6
M. Rybar	Married	830	7
G. Sitch	Married	900	4
M. Tabor	Single	950	1

b. Each employee is enrolled in the registered pension plan. Contributions are set at 5 percent of gross pay for both the employee and the employer.

c. The health insurance rates per two-week pay period are as follows:

single person — $18
married person — $24

d. Group life insurance at three times annual salary is compulsory. For this coverage, the employees pay 2 percent of their gross pay.

e. The cost of life insurance is paid entirely by the employee.

f. There is no union in this company.

2. Total and cross-balance the payroll journal.

3. Journalize the accounting entries to record the payroll and the contributions required of the employer.

---

15. 1. From the following information prepare the payroll for the period ended March 15.

a. The payroll journal has the following headings:

Employee
Net Claim Code
Earnings (Regular, Extra, Gross)
Deductions — C.P.P.
— U.I. Premium
— R.P.P.
— Income Tax — Taxable Income
— Deduction
— Health Insurance
— Union Dues
— Group Life Insurancc

b. Each of the employees listed below is employed by E-Z Auto Sales

Limited. They are paid every two weeks. The mechanics are paid on an hourly wage basis as indicated below. Any hours over 40 hours per week are paid at the time-and-one-half rate. They belong to the IAM union local and pay $6.25 in union dues each pay period. The salesmen are paid a basic salary of $280 per week, plus 2 percent commission on all completed sales. Salesmen do not belong to the union.

Employee	*Net Claim Code*	*Hours Worked*	*Hourly Rate*	*Net Sales*	*Health Coverage*	*Group Life Insurance*
Dave Durand	1	80	$6.75		Single, public ward	$20 000
Erika Kuchma	12	80	7.45		Family, semiprivate	$25 000
Glen Nyman	9	86	6.60		Family, public ward	$20 000
Dave Bower	7	86	7.00		Family, public ward	$25 000
Jim Hansen	1			$16 000	Single, semiprivate	—
Terry Sutherland	13			19 600	Family, semiprivate	$25 000
Maria Milani	11			17 500	Family, semiprivate	$10 000

c. The rate of contribution for the R.P.P. is 5 percent of the gross pay. The employer matches the employees' contributions.

d. The employer has agreed to pay 66 percent of the health insurance premiums.

e. Group life insurance is paid entirely by the employees at the rate of 35¢ per $1 000 of insurance each pay.

2. Complete the payroll journal. Where necessary, use the tables and rates provided in this chapter.

3. Prepare all of the accounting entries arising out of the completed payroll. The company uses separate expense accounts for Wages and for Salaries.

Currency Requisition Form

16. Assume that the employees in Exercise 14 are paid on a cash basis. Prepare the payroll currency requisition. Cheque number A39426 is prepared to obtain the necessary funds. Give the accounting entry for the cheque.

17. E-Z Auto Sales Limited in Exercise 15 pays its employees in cash. Prepare a payroll currency requisition.

Recording Remittances for Payroll Deductions

18. The Action Company commences business on January 1, 19--. The company pays its employees every two weeks. The first three payroll summaries are shown below.

	Jan. 14	Jan. 28	Feb. 11
Gross pay	$6 421.05	$6 567.12	$6 308.78
Canada Pension Plan	116.05	121.62	115.00
Unemployment insurance	63.70	64.50	63.05
Registered pension plan	385.26	394.03	378.53
Income tax	963.16	985.07	946.32
Hospitalization	144.47	147.76	141.95
Union dues	95.00	95.00	95.00
Net pay	4 653.41	4 759.14	4 568.93

1. Without explanations, journalize the accounting entries for each of the above payroll summaries. Credit Bank for the net pay figure. Your entries should include the following:

a. The employer's share of C.P.P.
b. The employer's share of U.I.
c. The employer's share of R.P.P. (The employer matches the contributions of the employees.)

2. Post the above entries to T-accounts.

3. On February 15, journalize and post the entries for the remittances for the following deductions of the previous month:

a. Canada Pension Plan, unemployment insurance, and income tax.
b. Hospitalization, paid to the provincial government.
c. Registered pension plan, paid to Federal Insurance Co.
d. Union dues, paid to The Mechanics Union.

Using Your Knowledge

19. Suppose that in Exercise 14 each of the employees is given a 10 percent raise in pay. For the first two employees listed, Chursa and Fillion, calculate the amount of this pay raise for two weeks, and the amount of this pay raise that each takes home. Assume that the only deductions affected by the raise are C.P.P., U.I., R.P.P., and income tax.

20. Mary Watson commenced employment with the Empire Company on January 1 at a salary of $400 for every two weeks. Mary received two $50 pay raises during the year. One took place at the end of 10 weeks, and another at the end of 20 weeks. Mary's employee's earnings record card is partially shown below.

Calculate Mary Watson's yearly totals for the following:

1. Gross pay.
2. Canada Pension Plan.
3. Unemployment insurance.
4. Registered pension plan.
5. Income tax.

Mary Watson

DATE	EMPLOYEE	NET CLAIM CODE	EARNINGS REG	EXTRA	GROSS	DEDUCTIONS C.P.P.	U.I.	R.P.P.	TAX	INSCE.	UNION DUES	GROUP LIFE	RED SHIELD	TOTAL DEDUC'S	NET PAY
Jan 14	Mary Watson	4	400 —		400 —	6 30	5 40	20 —	36 —	18 —		26 50	5 —	117 20	282 80
Jun 3	Mary Watson	4	450 —		450 —	7 20	6 08	22 50	48 65	18 —		26 50	5 —	133 93	316 07
Oct 21	Mary Watson	4	500 —		500 —	8 10	6 75	25 —	61 65	18 —		26 50	5 —	151 —	349 —

21. Matt Cook's T4 slip indicates that his employer has withheld $3 260 in federal income tax from his salary for the year. When Cook prepares his income tax return, he discovers that the total tax he is liable for amounts to $2 820. How can this happen? Explain.

22. Western Electric uses a separate payroll bank account to handle salary and wage payments to employees.
1. Is this a desirable practice? Explain.
2. How would you explain a balance in the bank statement for the payroll account sent to you at the end of the month?
3. Is it possible to have an overdraft in your payroll account? Explain.

Cases

Case 1 *Tampering with T4 Slips*

As a payroll clerk for Triangle Electric, you have discovered that most employees do not attempt to reconcile total income tax withheld as shown on their T-4 slip with the amounts withheld during the year. Accordingly, as payroll clerk, you could understate the amount of tax deduction posted to various employees' earnings records, and overstate the tax posted on your own earnings sheet. Following the end of the year, you could then claim a refund for excess tax shown on your own T-4 slip.

Question

1. Can this be prevented? Explain.

Case 2 *Comparing Wage Increases*

The following salaries and wages are paid by the Magic Tape Company.

Employee		*Salary or Wage*
General Manager:	P. Sanderson	$80 000
Plant Workers:	M. Bailey	8 000
	B. Dorst	9 000
	N. Gehrals	12 000
	V. Ripley	10 000

The owner of this company, P. Epps, grants a 10 percent pay raise to the plant employees to cover a 10 percent rise in the cost of living. Sanderson, the general manager, argues that what applies to the plant employees also applies to him, and he puts in a request for a 10 percent pay increase.

Questions

1. Comment on Sanderson's request, using some simple calculations or figures.
2. Are percentages a fair way to compare earnings?

Case 3 *Wage Increase — How Much Can Be Offered?*

You are the proprietor of Brite Cleaners. The following data is extracted from your most recent income statement.

Revenue:	Cleaning	$134 900
	Storage	5 954
	Tailoring	30 500
		$171 374
Expenses:	Rent	$4 800
	Delivery	2 930
	Wages	104 300
	Supplies used	3 250
	General expense	1 975
	Depreciation	7 560
	Power	4 250
		$129 065
	Net Income	$ 42 309

The employees have requested a 20 percent increase in wages.

Questions

1. Assuming that no other expense is affected, how much would the wage increase cost the company?
2. Can you grant this request and still make a profit?
3. How much would the net income be if the increase were granted.
4. You want to make at least $30 000 per year from the business, and you expect an increase of $5 000 in revenue for the coming year. Calculate the maximum increase that you can grant to your employees, expressed in dollars and as a percentage.

Career

Robert Hunt / Senior Payroll Clerk

Robert Hunt began preparing for a business career by taking a number of accounting courses in high school. After graduation, he continued this preparation by completing one year of business courses at a community college.

Robert left college to work as a bookkeeper for a General Motors dealership. Two years later, he moved to a position as accountant with Suburban Metal Industries, a small manufacturing company. Here, his duties included the control of the general ledger and preparation of the financial statements.

For the past nine years, Robert has been employed by Emerson Electric Company as a senior payroll clerk. In this position, he works with and reports to the General Accountant.

Each week, Robert prepares the payroll for salaried personnel. On each employee's master sheet, he records days worked, vacation pay, rate changes, hospitalization charges, sick leave, changes in personal income tax exemptions, and so on. All this information is then summarized and fed into the computer so that salary cheques can be issued. Another payroll clerk, under Robert's supervision, prepares the payroll in an identical manner for employees who are paid hourly wages.

Robert is responsible for a salaried payroll of 220 employees. In addition, he prepares the confidential payrolls for the executive officers of the company at the head and regional offices. Robert also calculates the commissions earned by the salesmen and agents, and supervises the typing and mailing of the salesmen's commission statements.

Robert distributes all payroll cheques to the respective divisions of Emerson Electric and mails them to out-of-town personnel. Each month, he calculates and remits payroll deductions for C.P.P., U.I.C., Income Tax, Union Dues, Hospitalization, and the Company Pension Plan. At the end of each month, Robert determines the total wages paid during the month and makes the appropriate journal entries.

Robert also maintains a petty cash fund on a weekly basis and supervises the delivery of daily bank deposits. Each month, he prepares and submits sales tax returns to the provincial government. Finally, at the end of each year, he sees that T-4 slips are typed and sent to all employees.

Robert feels that his high school training in accounting gave him an early appreciation of the importance of highly organized work habits and accurate legible record-keeping. These qualities are essential to his position as senior payroll clerk.

19

Adjusting Entries and Classified Statements

19-1 The Work Sheet
19-2 Adjustment for Supplies
19-3 Adjustment for Prepaid Expenses
19-4 Adjustment for Doubtful Accounts of Customers
19-5 Adjustment for Depreciation

Objectives

When you have completed Chapter 19, you should:

1. Understand the reason for adjusting entries.
2. Know how to complete an 8-column work sheet.
3. Be able to work out the adjusting entries for supplies and other prepaid expenses, doubtful debts, and depreciation.
4. Be able to calculate depreciation using the straight-line method and the declining-balance method.
5. Be able to present doubtful debts on the financial statements.
6. Be able to present accumulated depreciation on the financial statements.
7. Know the accounting entries for writing off an account receivable and for recovering an account that was previously written off.
8. Know the purpose of a contra account.

Accounting serves to gather the information for the preparation of the balance sheet, the income statement, and other financial reports. These statements help the managers of a business to make key decisions concerning the welfare of the company.

Financial statements and reports are also used by persons outside the company. A bank that loans funds to a business will require a copy of that firm's financial statements each year. The financial statements allow the bank to evaluate the performance of the business, and, if necessary, to take prompt action to protect its loan. In large public corporations, the law requires that copies of the financial reports be sent to the shareholders annually. This way, the shareholders can follow the financial affairs of companies in which they are part owners. Also, persons who are interested in buying shares of a public company will usually study its financial statements before making a final decision.

Financial statements are used extensively to assist in business decision-making. Therefore, financial statements must be accurate, up to date, and consistent from year to year. The responsibility for these documents rests entirely with the company's accountants. When preparing financial statements, the accountants must ensure that (1) all accounts are brought up to date, (2) all late transactions are taken into account, and (3) all calculations have been made correctly.

Bringing the account data up to date at statement time is known as **making the adjustments**. The accounting entries produced by this process are known as the **adjusting entries**.

An important accounting principle comes into play at this time. The **matching principle** states that all expense items incurred in the earning of revenue must be recorded in the same accounting period as the revenue it helped to earn. Otherwise, the net income figure will not be correct. You will see this principle at work as you study adjustments on the following pages.

The topic of adjustments is discussed both in Chapter 19 and Chapter 20. Only a few adjustments are covered in these chapters. However, these are the most important adjustments and will serve to introduce you to the method for making adjustments of all kinds.

19.1 The Work Sheet

You were shown in Chapter 9 that an accountant uses a work sheet as an aid in organizing the data for the financial statements. An accountant does not begin to write up the financial statements until the work sheet has been completed and balanced.

The first step when preparing the financial statements is to take off a general ledger trial balance at the end of the accounting period on eight-column work sheet paper. In Chapter 9, you worked with six-column paper. Now, two extra columns are needed for the adjustments.

The trial balance figures on the work sheet are taken directly from the general ledger at the end of the accounting period. As a result, they contain the account balances that are not up to date and which require the making of adjustments.

We will begin the study of adjusting entries by preparing the work sheet for Cassidy Cartage, a service business. The general ledger trial balance of Cassidy

Cartage as of June 30, 19-4, the end of an annual accounting period, is shown in the first two columns of the work sheet in Figure 19.1.

Cassidy Cartage — Work Sheet — Year Ended June 30, 19-4.

Accounts	Trial Balance Dr	Trial Balance Cr	Adjustments Dr	Adjustments Cr	Income Statement Dr	Income Statement Cr	Balance Sheet Dr	Balance Sheet Cr
Petty Cash	50 -							
Bank	745 40							
Accounts Receivable	4 027 20							
Allow. for Doubtful Accounts		20 -						
Supplies	516 -							
Prepaid Insurance	1 436 -							
Prepaid Licences	570 -							
Land	17 000 -							
Buildings (Frame)	17 280 -							
Accum. Depr. Buildings		3 283 20						
Furniture and Equipment	5 950 -							
Accum. Depr. Furn. and Equip.		2 142 -						
Automotive Equipment	20 400 -							
Accum. Depr. Auto. Equip.		10 804 -						
Accounts Payable		5 047 20						
Bank Loan		5 000 -						
P. Marshall, Capital		29 116 70						
P. Marshall, Drawings	18 000 -							
Revenue		68 757 -						
Discounts Earned		395 -						
Bank Charges	750 -							
Building Maintenance	757 50							
Light, Heat, and Water	902 40							
Miscellaneous Expense	316 50							
Telephone Expense	416 -							
Truck Expense	11 074 10							
Wages	24 374 -							
	124 565 10	124 565 10						

Figure 19.1 An eight-column work sheet with the balance recorded.

19.2 Adjustment for Supplies

The Supplies account is allowed to become incorrect during the accounting period because it is not convenient to record deductions for supplies as they occur. For this reason, the account balance is incorrect by the cost of all the supplies used up during the period.

To adjust for supplies, it is first necessary to take a physical inventory of the supplies actually on hand on the last day of the accounting period. This involves the preparation of a listing similar to the one shown in Figure 19.2. Each different item must be counted or estimated and the quantity multiplied by the most recent cost price. These listings are then totalled to produce a figure for supplies inventory.

Supplies Inventory
June 30, 19-4

Description	Quantity	Unit Cost	Value
Envelopes, #10, White	4¼ boxes	$ 5.50	$ 23.38
Envelopes, #8, White	4 boxes	4.95	19.80
Envelopes, Manila	1½ boxes	7.50	11.25
Envelopes, C4 Manila	2 boxes	8.75	17.50
Ball Pens, Blue	½ gross	72.00	36.00
Pencils, Black, HB	6 dozen	1.50	9.00
Pencils, Black, F2½	8 dozen	1.50	12.00
Pencils, Red	2 dozen	1.75	3.50
Cellulose Tape, 1 cm	3/4 box	24.00	18.00
Cellulose Tape, 2 cm	1½ boxes	30.00	45.00
Paper Clips, Regular	15 boxes	1.25	18.75
Paper Clips, Small	10 boxes	1.10	11.00
Gummed Labels, Assorted Colours	1¼ gross	75.00	93.75
Elastic Bands, Mixed	5 boxes	1.05	5.25
			$240.00

Figure 19.2 A supplies inventory schedule.

The supplies adjustment accomplishes two things. First, it causes the Supplies account balance to equal the supplies inventory figure. Second, it records the supplies used during the accounting period in an expense account.

The work sheet for Cassidy Cartage shows that the Supplies account balance is $516. The Supplies account can only be adjusted from its present balance of $516 to the inventory figure of $240 with an accounting entry equal to the difference, that is, $276. This figure of $276 represents the supplies used, but unrecorded, during the accounting period.

For Cassidy Cartage the adjusting entry is as follows:

Supplies Expense	276	
Supplies		276

This adjusting entry is recorded on the work sheet in the Adjustments column as shown in Figure 19.3. Observe that this adjustment is coded with the numeral '1' because it happens to be the first adjusting entry on this work sheet.

Notice too that a line for Supplies Expense has been started beneath the trial balance section. This is necessary because the trial balance itself does not include a Supplies Expense account. Whenever an adjustment affects an account that is not included in the trial balance section, that account must be written below the trial balance.

The adjusting entry is not recorded in the journal at this time. As you will see later, all adjusting entries are journalized at one time, along with the closing entries.

Cassidy Cartage	Work Sheet		Year Ended June 30, 19-4					
Accounts	Trial Balance		Adjustments		Income Statement		Balance Sheet	
	Dr	Cr	Dr	Cr	Dr	Cr	Dr	Cr
Petty Cash	50 -							
Bank	745 40							
Accounts Receivable	4027 20							
Allow. for Doubtful Accounts		20 -						
Supplies	516 -			① 276 -			240 -	
Prepaid Insurance	1436 -							
Prepaid Licences	570 -							
Land	17000 -							
Buildings (Frame)	17280 -							
Accum. Depr. Buildings		3283 20						
Furniture and Equipment	5950 -							
Accum. Depr. Furn. & Equip.		2142 -						
Automotive Equipment	20400 -							
Accum. Depr. Auto. Equip.		10804 -						
Accounts Payable		5047 20						
Bank Loan		5000 -						
P. Marshall, Capital		29116 70						
P. Marshall, Drawings	18000 -							
Revenue		68757 -						
Discounts Earned		395 -						
Bank Charges	750 -							
Building Maintenance	757 50							
Light, Heat, and Water	902 40							
Miscellaneous Expense	316 50							
Telephone Expense	416 -							
Truck Expense	11074 10							
Wages	24374 -							
	124565 10	124565 10						
Supplies Expense			① 276 -		276 -			

Figure 19.3 A work sheet showing the adjustment for supplies.

Extending the Work Sheet

When certain that no other adjustment will affect a particular item on the work sheet, the accountant may extend the item. Both the Supplies line and the Supplies Expense line of the work sheet are extended in Figure 19.3. To extend any line of the work sheet, first find the value of the Trial Balance and the Adjustments columns. Then, transfer this value to the proper column of the remaining four.

For Supplies, the value of the first four columns is found to be $240 debit. Since Supplies is a Balance Sheet item (asset), the $240 is transferred to the Balance Sheet Debit column.

For Supplies Expense, the value of the first four columns is found to be $276 debit. Since Supplies Expense is an Income Statement item, the $276 is transferred to the Income Statement Debit column.

19.3 Adjustment for Prepaid Expenses

Expenses that cover a period of time and are paid for in advance are called **prepaid expenses**. They are recorded separately in special prepaid expense accounts. For example, automobile licences are purchased in advance, usually for a period of one year, and are debited to an account called Prepaid Licences. Similarly, insurance coverage is purchased in advance for a period of one to three years, and is debited to an account called Prepaid Insurance.

With the passing of time, prepaid expenses gradually decrease in value and expire. For example, a truck licence that will last one year costs $60 on January 1. This licence gradually diminishes in value as time passes. On June 30, the licence is half expired and has a value of $30. On September 30, the licence is three-quarters expired and has a value of $15.

During the course of an accounting period, however, no attempt is made to keep the prepaid expense accounts accurate. Accuracy is only needed at the end of the accounting period, when the financial statements are written. At that time, the accounts are made accurate by means of adjusting entries on the work sheet.

Prepaid Insurance Adjustment for Cassidy Cartage

Let us make the adjustment for prepaid insurance for Cassidy Cartage. First it is necessary to calculate the value of the unexpired insurance as of the end of the

Prepaid Insurance Schedule
June 30, 19-4

Company	Policy Date	Term	Expiry Date	Number Months Remaining	Unexpired Portion	Prepaid Insurance June 30, 19-4.
Admiral	Aug 1, 19-2	2 yrs	Aug 1, 19-4	1	1/24	$ 20.
International	Mar 1, 19-3	3 yrs	Mar 1, 19-6	20	20/36	240.
Regency	Sep 1, 19-3	1 yr	Sep 1, 19-4	2	2/12	32.
Satellite	Jan 1, 19-4	2 yrs	Jan 1, 19-6	18	18/24	450.
					TOTAL	$ 742.

Figure 19.4 A prepaid insurance schedule.

accounting period. This is done by analyzing the insurance policies and preparing an insurance schedule such as the one shown in Figure 19.4.

The adjustment for insurance must bring the Prepaid Insurance account into agreement with the prepaid insurance calculation. The accounting entry debits Insurance Expense and credits Prepaid Insurance.

The work sheet for Cassidy Cartage shows a balance of $1 436 for Prepaid Insurance. To bring this into agreement with the insurance schedule figure of $742, an adjustment of $694 is needed as follows:

Insurance Expense	$694	
Prepaid Insurance		$694

Cassidy Cartage — Work Sheet — Year Ended June 30, 19-4

Accounts	Trial Balance Dr	Trial Balance Cr	Adjustments Dr	Adjustments Cr	Income Statement Dr	Income Statement Cr	Balance Sheet Dr	Balance Sheet Cr
Petty Cash	50 -							
Bank	745 40							
Accounts Receivable	4 027 20							
Allow. for Doubtful Accs.		20 -						
Supplies	516 -			(1) 276 -			240 -	
Prepaid Insurance	1 436 -			(2) 694 -			742 -	
Prepaid Licences	570 -							
Land	17 000 -							
Buildings (Frame)	17 280 -							
Accum. Depr. Buildings		3 283 20						
Furniture and Equipment	5 950 -							
Accum. Depr. Furn. & Equip.		2 142 -						
Automotive Equipment	20 400 -							
Accum. Depr. Auto. Equip.		10 804 -						
Accounts Payable		5 047 20						
Bank Loan		5 000 -						
P. Marshall, Capital		29 116 70						
P. Marshall, Drawings	18 000 -							
Revenue		68 757 -						
Discounts Earned		395 -						
Bank Charges	150 -							
Building Maintenance	757 50							
Light, Heat, and Water	902 40							
Miscellaneous Expense	316 50							
Telephone Expense	416 -							
Truck Expense	11 074 10							
Wages	24 374 -							
	124 565 10	124 565 10						
Supplies Expense			(1) 276 -		276 -			
Insurance Expense			(2) 694		694 -			

Figure 19.5 A work sheet showing the adjustment for insurance.

The adjusting entry and the items extended on the work sheet are shown in Figure 19.5.

Observe that this adjustment is coded with the numeral '2' and that it requires the opening of an Insurance Expense line.

Prepaid Licences Adjustment for Cassidy Cartage

The adjustment for prepaid licences is similar to that for prepaid insurance. First, it is necessary to calculate the value of the unexpired licences by means of a schedule such as the one shown in Figure 19.6.

PREPAID LICENCES SCHEDULE
JUNE 30, 19–4

Vehicle	*Cost of Licence*	*Term of Licence*	*Unexpired Proportion*		*Prepaid Licences June 30, 19–4*
3-ton van	$250	Jan. 1 to Dec. 31	$\frac{1}{2}$		$125
$\frac{1}{2}$-ton truck	$230	Jan. 1 to Dec. 31	$\frac{1}{2}$		$115
Station wagon	$90	Jan. 1 to Dec. 31	$\frac{1}{2}$		$ 45
				TOTAL	$285

Figure 19.6 A prepaid licence schedule.

The adjustment for licences must bring the Prepaid Licences account into agreement with the Prepaid Licences Schedule. The accounting entry debits Licences Expense and credits Prepaid Licences.

The work sheet for Cassidy Cartage shows a balance of $570 for Prepaid Licences. To bring this into agreement with the schedule figure of $285, an adjustment in the amount of $285 is needed as follows:

Licences Expense	$285	
Prepaid Licences		$285

The adjustment (coded '3') and the items extended are as shown on the work sheet in Figure 19.7.

Cassidy Cartage	Work Sheet				Year Ended June 30, 19-4			
Accounts	Trial Balance		Adjustments		Income Statement		Balance Sheet	
	Dr	Cr	Dr	Cr	Dr	Cr	Dr	Cr
Petty Cash	50 -							
Bank	745 40							
Accounts Receivable	4 027 20							
Allow. for Doubtful Accs.		20 -						
Supplies	516 -			① 276 -			240 -	
Prepaid Insurance	1 436 -			② 694 -			742 -	
Prepaid Licences	570 -			③ 285 -			285 -	
Land	17 000 -							
Buildings (Frame)	17 280 -							
Accum. Deprec. Buildings		3 283 20						
Furniture and Equipment	5 950 -							
Accum. Depr. Furn. and Equip.		2 142 -						
Automotive Equipment	20 400 -							
Accum. Depr. Auto. Equip.		10 804 -						
Accounts Payable		5 047 20						
Bank Loan		5 000 -						
P. Marshall, Capital		29 116 70						
P. Marshall, Drawings	18 000 -							
Revenue		68 757 -						
Discounts Earned		395 -						
Bank Charges	750 -							
Building Maintenance	757 50							
Light, Heat, and Water	902 40							
Miscellaneous Expense	316 50							
Telephone Expense	416 -							
Truck Expense	11 074 10							
Wages	24 374 -							
	124 565 10	124 565 10						
Supplies Expense			① 276 -		276 -			
Insurance Expense			② 694 -		694 -			
Licence Expense			③ 285 -		285 -			

Figure 19.7 A work sheet showing the adjustment for licences.

19.4 Adjustment for Doubtful Accounts of Customers

An element of risk is involved in selling on credit. No matter how carefully the customers' credit ratings are checked, there are always some customers who do not pay. Business people know that this happens, and yet they continue to sell on credit. They reason that the amount gained from the increased sales volume is greater than the loss due to the failure to collect.

A business learns of doubtful accounts as they become increasingly overdue. The longer the account is overdue the less likely it is to be collected.

A business must consider doubtful accounts when preparing its financial statements for the following two reasons:

1. The accounts receivable ledger contains accounts that are doubtful. These must be deducted from the total accounts receivable to show the estimated true value of accounts receivable on the balance sheet.
2. The loss from doubtful accounts must be set up as an expense in the same period as the sales to which they are related. This results in a proper matching of bad debt losses against revenues.

Allowance for Doubtful Accounts

An adjusting entry is made at the end of every accounting period that sets up the estimated value of doubtful accounts as a credit balance in an account called **Allowance for Doubtful Accounts**. The estimated true value of accounts receivable is shown by the Accounts Receivable account and the Allowance for Doubtful Accounts account taken together.

For Cassidy Cartage, the estimated true value of accounts receivable is shown by the following two T-accounts.

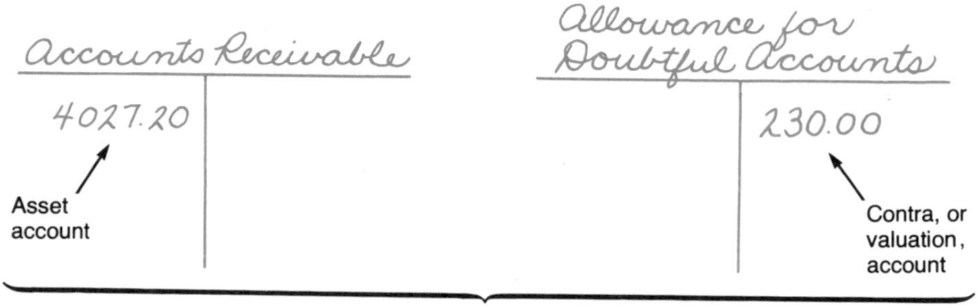

The estimated true value of accounts receivable of $3 797.20 is contained in these two accounts.

The Allowance for Doubtful Accounts account is a **contra account** or a **valuation account**. A contra, or valuation, account is always used together with an asset account to show the true value of the asset account.

Why don't we credit the value of the doubtful accounts directly to the asset account instead of setting it up separately? There is a very good reason for not doing this.

You do not stop trying to collect an account because it is doubtful. Therefore, the doubtful account is not taken out of the subsidiary ledger. Since doubtful accounts remain in the subsidiary ledger, and since the subsidiary ledger must agree with its general ledger controlling account, the doubtful accounts are not credited to the controlling account. Instead, the credit is made to the contra account known as the Allowance for Doubtful Accounts.

Accounts Receivable Aging Schedule

At the end of each accounting period, an **Accounts Receivable Aging Schedule**, such as the one shown in Figure 19.8, is prepared. This schedule is a breakdown of customers' accounts showing how long they have been unpaid. The figure for doubtful accounts comes from this schedule.

Cassidy Cartage Accounts Receivable Aging Schedule June 30, 19-4

Customer	Account Balance	1-30 Days	31-60 Days	61-90 Days	91 Days and Older	Remarks	Allowance for Doubtful Debts
Advance Assocs.	156 50	52 00	29 40	75 10		Will be O.K.	
Barley Brothers	251 20	55 00	94 12	102 08		Will be O.K.	
J. Bowman	35 50	35 50				✓	
M. Carey	165 25	102 10			63 15	63.15 is 7 month old disputed item. Correspondence with customer is proving fruitless.	63 15
Concord Co.	346 56	151 00	94 00	73 25	28 31	Slow but sure. Has been a good customer for over 10 years.	
Devon Bros.	95 62				95 62	Item is 10 months old and customer is in bankruptcy. ✓	95 62
Durnan & Son	114 56	24 00	90 56				
Empire Traders	26 50	26 50					
Young & Young	16 00	16 00					
	4 027 56	2 461 15	841 90	400 07	324 44		230 00

Figure 19.8 An Accounts Receivable Aging Schedule.

Adjustment of the Doubtful Accounts of Cassidy Cartage

Once the figure for doubtful accounts is arrived at by means of the aging schedule, the adjustment for doubtful accounts can be made. There are two aspects of this accounting entry:

Cassidy Cartage	Work Sheet				Year Ended June 30, 19-4			
Accounts	Trial Balance		Adjustments		Income Statement		Balance Sheet	
	Dr	Cr	Dr	Cr	Dr	Cr	Dr	Cr
Petty Cash	50 -							
Bank	745 40							
Accounts Receivable	4027 20							
Allow. for Doubtful Accs.		20 -		(4) 210 -				230 -
Supplies	516 -			(1) 276 -			240 -	
Prepaid Insurance	1436 -			(2) 694 -			742 -	
Prepaid Licences	570 -			(3) 285 -			285 -	
Land	17000 -							
Buildings (Frame)	17280 -							
Accum. Deprec. Buildings		3283 20						
Furniture and Equipment	5950 -							
Accum. Depr. Furn. and Equip.		2142 -						
Automotive Equipment	20400 -							
Accum. Depr. Auto. Equip.		10804 -						
Accounts Payable		5047 20						
Bank Loan		5000 -						
P. Marshall, Capital		29116 70						
P. Marshall, Drawings	18000 -							
Revenue		68757 -						
Discounts Earned		395 -						
Bank Charges	750 -							
Building Maintenance	757 50							
Light, Heat, and Water	902 40							
Miscellaneous Expense	316 50							
Telephone Expense	416 -							
Truck Expense	11074 10							
Wages	24374 -							
	124565 10	124565 10						
Supplies Expense			(1) 276 -		276 -			
Insurance Expense			(2) 694 -		694 -			
Licence Expense			(3) 285 -		285 -			
Bad Debts Expense			(4) 210 -		210 -			

Figure 19.9 A work sheet showing the adjustment for doubtful accounts.

1. *The accounts.* The accounts involved are always the same. The entry is made as follows:

Dr. Bad Debts Expense	XXX	
Cr. Allowance for Doubtful Accounts		XXX

2. *The amount.* The adjustment will be for the amount needed to bring the Allowance for Doubtful Accounts from its existing balance up to the figure shown on the aging schedule.

The trial balance for Cassidy Cartage shows a $20 credit balance in the Allowance for Doubtful Accounts account. The aging schedule shows that the doubtful accounts amount to $230. Therefore, an adjustment in the amount of $210 is needed. The adjusting entry for Cassidy Cartage is as follows:

Bad Debts Expense	210	
Allowance for Doubtful Accounts		210

The adjusting entry (coded '4') and the items extended are shown on the work sheet in Figure 19.9. Observe that, since it is a minus asset, the Allowance for Doubtful Accounts is extended to the credit side of the Balance Sheet column.

Accounts Receivable on the Balance Sheet

The balance sheet for Cassidy Cartage is shown in Figure 19.19 on page 567. In this figure, you will see how the estimated true value of accounts receivable is presented on the balance sheet. The allowance for doubtful accounts figure is deducted from the accounts receivable figure to arrive at the estimated true value of accounts receivable.

Writing Off a Bad Debt

A customer's account becomes known as a **bad debt** when there is no longer any chance that it will be collected. At this point, the account balance is written off, that is, taken out of the books by means of an accounting entry. The entry to write off a bad debt is as follows:

Dr. Allowance for Doubtful Accounts	XXX	
Cr. Accounts Receivable (Customer's name)		XXX

This entry is recorded in the general journal. Remember that the posting to Accounts Receivable must be made twice: once to the general ledger and once to the subsidiary ledger.

Observe that the Allowance account is debited whenever an account is written off. The balance in this account decreases, therefore, with the passing of time. At the end of each accounting period, a balance will remain in the account. If the accounts written off are for less than was previously estimated, the remaining balance will be a credit. If the accounts written off are for more than was previously estimated, the remaining balance will be a debit. This should not present you with a problem at the time of making the adjustment. Just remember to make the adjustment for the amount that will cause the Allowance account to have a balance equal to the figure shown on the aging schedule.

Recovering a Bad Debt

Sometimes a business is lucky enough to collect an account that it has previously written off. Before such a collection can be recorded in the usual manner, the write-off must be reversed.

The following sequence of events illustrates this type of transaction:

1. On March 3 the account of Rex Brooks, in the amount of $75, is written off as uncollectible. The following accounting entry records the write-off:

Allowance for Doubtful Accounts	75	
Accounts Receivable (Rex Brooks)		75

2. On August 5, a cheque is received from Rex Brooks paying his account in full. The following two entries are necessary to record this collection:

a. To reverse the write-off:

Accounts Receivable (Rex Brooks)	75	
Allowance for Doubtful Accounts		75

b. To record the collection:

Bank	75	
Accounts Receivable (Rex Brooks)		75

19.5 Adjustment for Depreciation

With the exception of land, every fixed asset (also known as capital equipment) is used up in the course of time and activity and therefore decreases in value. This decrease in value is known as **depreciation**.

To understand the concept of depreciation, consider the case of a person who purchases a new truck at a cost of $8 000 in order to begin a delivery business. After operating for five years the business is closed down. In the course of its closing, the now-used truck is sold for $500. Clearly, over the five-year period, the truck cost the business $7 500. Just as clearly, the business could not have existed without the truck.

An accurate picture of the profit and loss of the business cannot ignore the $7 500 cost of the truck. Theoretically, the cost must be allocated as an expense of the business at the rate of $1 500 for each of the five years. However, it is impossible to make a precise calculation of depreciation until the end of the life of an asset (that is, until the asset is disposed of). Therefore, depreciation is calculated according to a mathematical formula.

Net Book Value

Contra accounts are used in conjunction with the fixed asset accounts. They record the total amount of depreciation that accumulates during the life of an asset. At the end of every fiscal period, each fixed asset (with the exception of land) is decreased by the amount of the estimated depreciation for the period. However, the reduction in the value of the fixed asset is not credited directly to the asset account but rather to a contra account called the **Accumulated Depreciation** account.

A fixed asset account together with its Accumulated Depreciation account represents the remaining value of the asset, known as the **net book value**. Figure 19.10 illustrates this process.

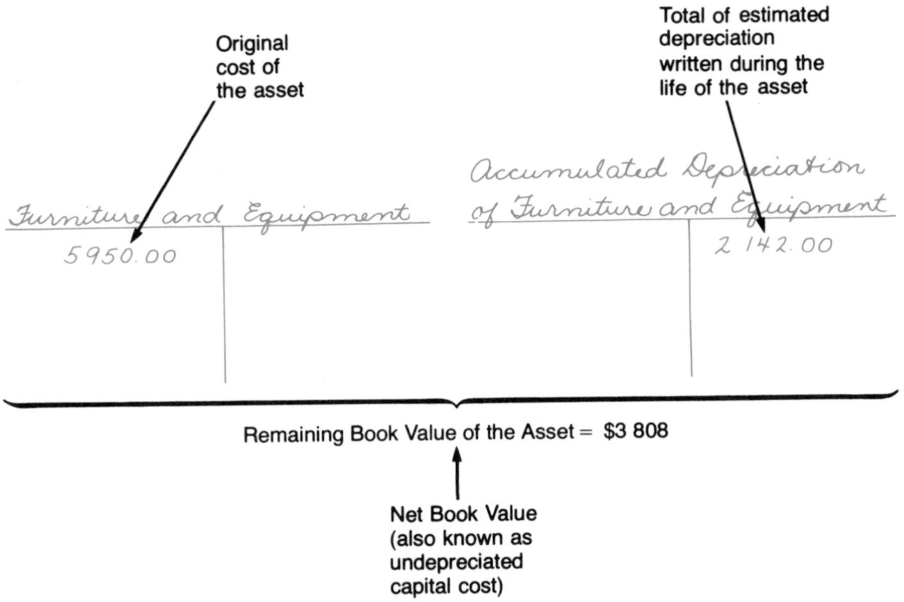

Figure 19.10 Net book value.

Two accounts in respect to a fixed asset are more informative than one account. Two accounts enable the reader to see how much of the asset is used up.

Straight-Line Method of Calculating Depreciation

The simplest method of calculating depreciation is the **straight-line method.** Under this method, the depreciation is computed according to the following formula.

$$\text{Straight-line depreciation for period} = \frac{\text{Original cost of the asset} \quad \text{less} \quad \text{Estimated salvage value}}{\text{Estimated life of the asset}}$$

The following example shows how this calculation works. A business purchases a new truck at a cost of $16 500. It expects the truck to last five years. It estimates that at the end of the five years the truck will be worth $1 500. Applying this data to the formula produces the following calculation:

$$\text{Estimated annual depreciation} = \frac{16\ 500 - 1\ 500}{5} = \frac{15\ 000}{5} = \$3\ 000$$

This gives an estimated annual depreciation figure of $3 000 which does not change from year to year.

Figure 19.11 is a schedule of the straight-line depreciation for the five-year period.

Year	*Depreciation for the year*	*Net Book Value*
Original cost		$16 500
1	$3 000	13 500
2	3 000	10 500
3	3 000	7 500
4	3 000	4 500
5	3 000	1 500

Figure 19.11 A straight-line depreciation schedule.

Observe that the net book value is gradually reduced. At the end of the asset's useful life, the net book value equals the estimated salvage value.

The straight-line method is not restricted to annual depreciation. The asset's useful life can be calculated in months rather than years to produce the estimated depreciation for an accounting period of one month.

Declining-Balance Method of Calculating Depreciation

Depreciation can also be calculated by the **declining-balance method**. Under this method, the estimated annual depreciation is computed by taking a fixed percentage of the remaining cost of the asset. Salvage value is not considered when using this method.

The Canadian government requires that the declining-balance method be used for reporting net income for income tax purposes. The percentages to be used are set forth in government regulation. Figure 19.12 shows some of these percentages.

Class	*Description*	*Percentage*
3	Buildings of Brick, Stone, or Cement	5%
6	Buildings of frame, log, or stucco	10%
8	Furniture and equipment	20%
10	Trucks, tractors, and automotive equipment	30%

Figure 19.12 Government rates of depreciation.

For example, assume that a truck costing $16 500 is depreciated at the rate of 30% per year. Each calculation is based on the remaining cost of the asset. The schedule in Figure 19.13 shows the declining-balance depreciation of the truck over the five years of its life.

Year	*Depreciation Calculation*	*Depreciation for Year*	*Net Book Value*
Original Cost			$16 500.00
1	30% of $16 500.00	$4 950.00	11 550.00
2	30% of $11 550.00	3 465.00	8 085.00
3	30% of $ 8 085.00	2 425.50	5 659.50
4	30% of $ 5 659.50	1 697.85	3 961.65
5	30% of $ 3 961.65	1 188.50	2 773.16

Figure 19.13 A declining-balance depreciation schedule.

The declining-balance method is more difficult than the reducing-balance method. Observe that a new calculation is required each year. Also, the calculation is based on the net book value which changes each year.

To calculate monthly depreciation under the declining-balance method, first calculate the annual depreciation, and then divide this figure by 12.

Calculating the Depreciation for Cassidy Cartage

Cassidy Cartage uses the declining-balance method of recording depreciation. Therefore, the first step in calculating depreciation is to determine the net book values of each of the depreciable assets. These are worked out in Figure 19.14.

Account	*Asset Cost*	*Accumulated Depreciation*	*Net Book Value*
Buildings (Frame)	$17 280.00	$ 1 684.80	$15 595.20
Furniture & Equipment	5 950.00	2 142.00	3 808.00
Automotive Equipment	20 400.00	10 804.00	9 596.00

Figure 19.14 The calculation of net book values for Cassidy Cartage.

The second step is to multiply each of the net book value figures by the appropriate percentage rate to arrive at the depreciation for the year. These calculations are summarized in Figure 19.15.

Asset	*N.B.V.*	*Percentage*	*Depreciation*
Buildings (Frame)	$15 595.20	10%	$1 559.52
Furniture & Equipment	3 808.00	20%	761.60
Automotive Equipment	9 596.00	30%	2 878.80

Figure 19.15 The depreciation calculation for Cassidy Cartage.

An accounting entry for each depreciable asset account is needed to show the effect of the depreciation in the accounts. The basic adjusting entry for depreciation is as follows:

Dr. Depreciation Expense	XXX	
Cr. Accumulated Depreciation		XXX

This entry accomplishes two things:

1. It allocates a share of the cost of the asset against the revenues for the period by recording it as an expense.
2. It updates the accumulated depreciation total by adding the depreciation for the period.

Cassidy Cartage has three depreciable assets, and therefore has three adjusting entries for depreciation. These entries are summarized as follows:

Depreciation of Buildings	$1 559.52	
Accumulated Depreciation of Buildings		$1 559.52
Depreciation of Furniture and Equipment	$761.60	
Accumulated Depreciation of Furniture and Equipment		$761.60
Depreciation of Automotive Equipment	$2 878.80	
Accumulated Depreciation of Automotive Equipment		$2 878.80

On the work sheet, these adjusting entries (coded '5', '6', and '7') and the items extended appear as shown in Figure 19.16. Because the accumulated depreciation accounts are minus asset accounts, they are extended to the credit column of the Balance Sheet columns.

Cassidy Cartage	Work Sheet				Year Ended June 30, 19-4			
Accounts	Trial Balance		Adjustments		Income Statement		Balance Sheet	
	Dr	Cr	Dr	Cr	Dr	Cr	Dr	Cr
Petty Cash	50 -							
Bank	745 40							
Accounts Receivable	4027 20							
Allow. for Doubtful Accs.		20 -		④ 210 -				230 -
Supplies	516 -			① 276 -			240 -	
Prepaid Insurance	1436 -			② 694 -			742 -	
Prepaid Licences	570 -			③ 285 -			285 -	
Land	17000 -							
Buildings (Frame)	17280 -							
Accum. Deprec. Buildings		3283 20		⑤ 1559 52				4842 72
Furniture and Equipment	5950 -							
Accum. Depr. Furn. and Equip.		2142 -		⑥ 761 60				2903 60
Automotive Equipment	20400 -							
Accum. Depr. Auto. Equip.		10804 -		⑦ 2878 80				13682 80
Accounts Payable		5047 20						
Bank Loan		5000 -						
P. Marshall, Capital		29116 70						
P. Marshall, Drawings	18000 -							
Revenue		68757 -						
Discounts Earned		395 -						
Bank Charges	750 -							
Building Maintenance	757 50							
Light, Heat, and Water	902 40							
Miscellaneous Expense	316 50							
Telephone Expense	416 -							
Truck Expense	11074 10							
Wages	24374 -							
	124565 10	124565 10						
Supplies Expense			① 276 -		276 -			
Insurance Expense			② 694 -		694 -			
Licence Expense			③ 285 -		285 -			
Bad Debts Expense			④ 210 -		210 -			
Depreciation of Buildings			⑤ 1559 52		1559 52			
Deprec. of Furn. & Equip.			⑥ 761 60		761 60			
Deprec. of Auto. Equip.			⑦ 2878 80		2878 80			

Figure 19.16 The work sheet showing the adjustment for depreciation.

In Figure 19.19 you will see how the fixed assets and their respective accumulated depreciation figures are presented on the balance sheet. Observe that for each depreciable asset the cost, the accumulated depreciation, and the net book value are shown.

19.6 Completing the Work Sheet and Preparing Financial Statements

After recording the required adjusting entries, it is necessary to complete the work sheet in the following manner:

1. Extend each line that is not already extended. This means that for each such line the value of the Trial Balance columns and the Adjustments columns must be extended to one of the Income Statement columns or to one of the Balance Sheet columns. This must be done carefully and logically. Income and expense items are to be extended to the Income Statement section. Other items are to be extended to the Balance Sheet section.
2. Total, rule, and balance the two Adjustments columns.
3. Total, rule, and balance the last four columns of the work sheet. The technique for doing this is described in Chapter 9.

The completed work sheet for Cassidy Cartage is shown in Figure 19.17.

Financial Statements for Cassidy Cartage

In Chapter 9 you learned that the work sheet is designed to assist the accountant to organize the data needed for the preparation of the financial statements. In this chapter you have seen that certain adjustments are needed on the work sheet so that the data for the statements is correct and up to date.

Remember that the only source of information for the financial statements is the work sheet.

All the information needed to prepare a balance sheet can be found in the Balance Sheet columns of the work sheet. It is unnecessary to look elsewhere. Similarly, all of the information needed for an income statement can be found in the Income Statement columns of the work sheet. It is unnecessary to look elsewhere.

Let us now proceed to the income statement and the balance sheet for Cassidy Cartage. These statements, shown in Figures 19.18 and 19.19, are prepared from the last two sections of the work sheet in Figure 19.7. Be sure to look carefully at the presentation of new items on the statements, in particular items related to bad debts and depreciation.

Cassidy Cartage — Work Sheet — Year Ended June 30, 19-4

Accounts	Trial Balance Dr	Trial Balance Cr	Adjustments Dr	Adjustments Cr	Income Statement Dr	Income Statement Cr	Balance Sheet Dr	Balance Sheet Cr
Petty Cash	50 –						50 –	
Bank	745 40						745 40	
Accounts Receivable	4 027 20						4 027 20	
Allow. for Doubtful Accs.		20 –		(4) 210 –				230 –
Supplies	516 –			(1) 276 –			240 –	
Prepaid Insurance	1 436 –			(2) 694 –			742 –	
Prepaid Licences	570 –			(3) 285 –			285 –	
Land	17 000 –						17 000 –	
Buildings (Frame)	17 280 –						17 280 –	
Accum. Depr. Buildings		3 283 20		(5) 1 559 52				4 842 72
Furniture and Equipment	5 950 –						5 950 –	
Accum. Depr. Furn. & Equip.		2 142 –		(6) 761 60				2 903 60
Automotive Equipment	20 400 –						20 400 –	
Accum. Depr. Auto. Equip.		10 804 –		(7) 2 878 80				13 682 80
Accounts Payable		5 047 20						5 047 20
Bank Loan		5 000 –						5 000 –
P. Marshall, Capital		29 116 70						29 116 70
P. Marshall, Drawings	18 000 –						18 000 –	
Revenue		68 757 –				68 757 –		
Discounts Earned		395 –				395 –		
Bank Charges	750 –				750 –			
Building Maintenance	757 50				757 50			
Light, Heat, and Water	902 40				902 40			
Miscellaneous Expense	316 50				316 50			
Telephone Expense	416 –				416 –			
Truck Expense	11 074 10				11 074 10			
Wages	24 374 –				24 374 –			
	124 565 10	124 565 10						
Supplies Expense			(1) 276 –		276 –			
Insurance Expense			(2) 694 –		694 –			
Licence Expense			(3) 285 –		285 –			
Bad Debts Expense			(4) 210 –		210 –			
Depreciation of Building			(5) 1 559 52		1 559 52			
Deprec. of Furn. & Equip.			(6) 761 60		761 60			
Deprec. of Auto. Equip.			(7) 2 878 80		2 878 80			
			6 664 92	6 664 92	45 255 42	69 152 –	84 719 60	60 823 02
Net Income					23 896 58			23 896 58
					69 152 –	69 152 –	84 719 60	84 719 60

Figure 19.17 The completed work sheet for Cassidy Cartage.

Cassidy Cartage
Income Statement
Year Ended June 30, 19–

Revenue		
Cartage Revenue		68 757 -
Operating Expenses		
Bad Debts Expense	210 -	
Bank Charges	750 -	
Building Maintenance	757 50	
Depreciation of Buildings	1 559 52	
Deprec. of Furn. and Equip.	761 60	
Depreciation of Auto. Equip.	2 878 80	
Insurance Expense	694 -	
Licences Expense	285 -	
Light, Heat, and Water	902 40	
Miscellaneous Expense	316 50	
Supplies Expense	276 -	
Telephone Expense	416 -	
Truck Expense	11 074 10	
Wages	24 374 -	45 255 42
Operating Income		23 501 58
Other Income		
Discounts Earned		395 -
Net Income		23 896 58

Figure 19.18 The income statement for Cassidy Cartage (a service business).

Figure 19.19 The balance sheet for Cassidy Cartage (right).

Cassidy Cartage
Balance Sheet
June 30, 19-

Assets			
Current Assets			
Petty Cash		50 –	
Bank		745 40	
Accounts Receivable	4027 20		
Less Allow. for Doubtful Accs.	230 –	3797 20	4592 60
Prepaid Expenses			
Supplies		240 –	
Prepaid Insurance		742 –	
Prepaid Licences		285 –	1267 –
Fixed Assets			
Land		17000 –	
Buildings	17280 –		
Less Accum. Deprec.	4842 72	12437 28	
Furniture and Equipment	5950 –		
Less Accum. Deprec.	2903 60	3046 40	
Automotive Equipment	20400 –		
Less Accum. Deprec.	13682 80	6717 20	39200 88
Total Assets			45060 48
Liabilities and Equity			
Current Liabilities			
Accounts Payable		5047 20	
Bank Loan		5000 –	10047 20
P. Marshall, Capital			
Balance, July 1, 19-3		29116 70	
Net Income	23896 58		
Drawings	18000 –		
Increase in Capital		5896 58	
Balance, June 30, 19-4			35013 28
Total Liabilities and Equity			45060 48

Accounting Terms

making the adjustments
adjusting entries
matching principle
prepaid expenses
allowance for doubtful accounts
contra account
valuation account
accounts receivable aging schedule
bad debt
depreciation
accumulated depreciation
net book value
straight-line method of depreciation
declining-balance method of depreciation

Review Questions

1. What is the purpose of the work sheet?
2. Give two examples of people outside a business who might read the financial statements of the business.
3. What steps must accountants take to ensure that financial statements are accurate, up to date, and consistent?
4. Explain the meaning of 'adjusting entry'.
5. Where are adjusting entries first recorded?
6. Why is an adjusting entry needed for supplies?
7. Why is it necessary to take an inventory of supplies?
8. What is the accounting entry to adjust the supplies?
9. Why is an adjustment necessary for insurance?
10. Why is it necessary to prepare a prepaid insurance schedule?
11. What is the accounting entry to adjust for insurance?
12. No adjusting entry for licences is necessary for a business that has a December 31 year-end. Explain.
13. Why do business people sell on credit?
14. If no adjustment is made for doubtful accounts, what will be wrong with the financial statements?
15. Explain the purpose of the aging schedule for accounts receivable.
16. How is the estimated true value of accounts receivable calculated?
17. What is a valuation or contra account?
18. Why is the doubtful account figure not credited directly to the Accounts Receivable account?
19. How is the amount of the doubtful accounts adjustment calculated?
20. What is the accounting entry to write off a bad debt?

21. When is a bad debt written off?
22. Depreciation is a matter of allocation, not valuation. Explain.
23. What contra account is associated with the asset account for machinery?
24. How is net book value of an asset calculated?
25. Give the government rates for depreciation as given in the text.
26. Why is the declining-balance method of depreciation more difficult than the straight-line method?

Exercises

1. The general ledger of Salk Company at the end of its annual fiscal period is as follows. These accounts appear in your work book.

1. Using the additional information that is provided, record the year-end adjusting entries in the T-accounts.

2. Prepare an adjusted trial balance.

Account	Debit	Credit
Bank	400	
Accs. Recl.	8 350	
All. Dtfl. Dts.		65
Supplies	1 900	
Prep. Insce.	1 800	
Land	50 000	
Buildings	70 000	
Acc. Depr. Bldg.		6 500
Equipment	96 500	
Accs. Depr. Equ.		24 000
Accs. Payl.		3 200
J. Salk Capital		144 985
J. Salk Drwgs.	30 000	
Revenue		140 700
Bank Charges	200	
Delivery Exp.	1 500	
Light & Heat	1 300	
Misc. Exp.	490	
Telephone Exp.	390	
Wages Exp.	56 620	

Additional Information:

a. Inventory of supplies at the year-end is $850.
b. Unexpired insurance at the year-end is calculated at $625.
c. Doubtful debts at the year-end amount to $245.
d. Depreciation is calculated on a straight-line basis.
e. The building is expected to last 40 years at which time it will be worth $5 000.
f. The equipment is expected to last 15 years after which it will be worth $6 500.

2. The following are the ledger accounts of Sentry Enterprises immediately before making the adjusting entries at the end of an annual fiscal period. These accounts appear in your workbook.

1. Using the additional information that is provided, record the required adjusting entries in the accounts.

2. Prepare an adjusted trial balance. Enclose with a continuous line all of the accounts that would be included in the calculation of net income.

Account	Debit	Credit
Bank	300	
Accs. Recl.	3 500	
Allow. Dt. Dts.		20
Supplies	500	
Prepaid Insce.	400	
Truck	8 000	
Accum. Dep. Truck		5 500
Accs. Payl.		350
Kay Dixon Capl.		3 640
Kay Dixon Drwgs.	10 000	
Revenue		19 000
Advertising	50	
Bank Chgs.	90	
Gas & Oil	1 100	
Light & Heat	3 000	
Misc. Exp.	120	
Rent	1 300	
Telephone	150	
Doubtful Dts. Exp.		
Deprec. Truck		
Insurance Exp.		
Supplies Exp.		

Additional Information:

a. The allowance for doubtful debts should be $170.
b. The supplies on hand amount to $110.
c. The unexpired insurance is valued at $160.
d. Depreciation on the truck is calculated on a straight-line basis. The truck cost $8 000 and is expected to last 6 years, after which it will have a trade-in value of $800.

3. The following partially completed work sheet of Magic Carpet Company also appears in your workbook. Using the additional information provided, complete the work sheet.

Magic Carpet Company	Work Sheet						Yr. Ended Dec. 31, 19–	
	Trial Balance		Adjustments		Income Statement		Balance Sheet	
Accounts	Dr	Cr	Dr	Cr	Dr	Cr	Dr	Cr
Bank	5							
Accounts Recl.	50							
Allowance Dtfl. Dts.		3						
Supplies	4							
Prepaid Insurance	6							
Equipment	40							
Accum. Deprec. Equipment		10						
Accounts Payable		10						
C. Keirsted Capl.		67						
C. Keirsted Drawings	15							
Revenue		105						
Gasoline Expense	12							
Hydro Expense	3							
Miscellaneous Expense	1							
Rent Building	13							
Rent Truck	18							
Telephone Expense	3							
Wages Expense	25							
	195	195						

Additional Information:

a. Depreciation is recorded on a declining balance method at 20 percent.

b. The allowance for doubtful debts at the year-end amounts to $15.

c. Supplies at the year-end are valued at $1.

d. Unexpired insurance at the year-end is calculated at $2.

---

4. Jean De Vries owns a small decorating business called Premium Decorating. A partially completed worksheet for the company, as shown below, is provided in your workbook.

1. **Using the additional information that is provided, complete an 8-column work sheet.**
2. **Prepare a balance sheet for the company.**
3. **Prepare an income statement.**

Premium Decorating	Work Sheet						Year Ended Dec. 31, 19–	
Accounts	Trial Balance		Adjustments		Income Statement		Balance Sheet	
	Dr	Cr	Dr	Cr	Dr	Cr	Dr	Cr
Bank	500 –							
Accounts Rec'l	5 800 –							
Allowance Doubt'l Dts		25 –						
Supplies	2 500 –							
Prepaid Insurance	700 –							
Trucks	13 500 –							
Accummulated Depr. Truck		2 500 –						
Accounts Payable		1 500 –						
J. DeVries Capital		5 665 –						
J. DeVries Drawings	12 500 –							
Revenue		29 250 –						
Bank Charges	200 –							
Gasoline & Oil	1 200 –							
Light & Heat	300 –							
Miscellaneous Expense	90 –							
Rent	1 300 –							
Telephone	350 –							
	38 940 –	38 940 –						

Additional Information:

a. The doubtful debts at the year-end total $350.
b. The unexpired insurance at the year-end amount to $200.
c. The supplies on hand at the year-end are valued at $600.
d. Depreciation on the truck is calculated on a straight-line basis. The truck cost $13 500 and is expected to be usable for 5 years. It will then have a scrap value of $1 500.

Adjustment Calculations and Theory

5. A supplies inventory count is shown below.

INVENTORY ITEM	QUANTITY
Rubber Bands	3 boxes
Envelopes #8	10 boxes
Envelopes #10	4 1/2 boxes
Envelopes, Manila	2 boxes
Typewriting Paper	4M sheets
Letterhead	10M sheets
Copy Paper	4M sheets
Carbon Paper	2 boxes
Paper Clips	12 boxes
Staples	15 boxes
Pencils, Regular	4 doz.
Pencils, Red	2 doz.

1. From this count sheet and the cost price list below, prepare a supplies inventory sheet showing the individual items, the quantities, the cost prices, the extensions, and the final total.

Items	*Cost Prices*
Rubber bands	$.75 per box
Envelopes, #8	$16.90 per box
Envelopes, #10	$17.50 per box
Manila envelopes, C4	$12.40 per box
Typewriting paper	$9.70 per M
Letterhead	$10.50 per M
Copy paper	$3.50 per M
Carbon paper	$2.75 per box
Paper clips	$.50 per box
Staples	$1.85 per box
Pencils, regular	$2.10 per doz.
Pencils, red	$2.40 per doz.

2. If the balance in the Supplies account is $643.10, give the accounting entry to adjust the Supplies.

---

6. A businessman's fiscal year-end is September 30. One of his business expenditures is for truck licences.

1. If he spends $240 on truck licences for the calendar year, calculate the value of prepaid licences at the end of his fiscal year.

4/89.

2. If the balance in the Prepaid Licences account is $300, give the accounting entry to adjust Prepaid Licences.

7. The details of a business's insurance policies are as follows:

Company	*Policy Date*	*Term*	*Premium*
Atlantic	March 15, 19–3	3 years	$ 72.00
Pacific	June 30, 19–4	2 years	120.00
Indian	June 1, 19–4	1 year	84.00
Arctic	September 15, 19–3	3 years	156.00

1. Calculate the value of prepaid insurance as of December 31, 19–4.

2. If the trial balance for Prepaid Insurance is $516, give the accounting entry to adjust prepaid insurance.

8. 1. Calculate the unexpired insurance as of June 30, 19–6 on the following policies. Make your calculations to the nearest half month.

Company	*Policy Date*	*Term*	*Premium*
Gem	June 30, 19–5	3 years	$ 210
Swift	October 1, 19–4	3 years	1 080
Investors	May 1, 19–6	2 years	264
Profitable	January 15, 19–6	1 year	48

2. If the balance in the Prepaid Insurance account is $1 802, give the adjusting entry for insurance.

9. Calculate the depreciation expense in each of the following cases using the declining-balance method and government rates.

Type of Asset	*Asset Account Balance*	*Accumulated Depreciation Account Balance*	*Annual Rate of Depreciation*	*Accounting Period*
Building (Brick)	$ 29 572.50	$13 514.21	5%	Jan. 1 to Dec. 31
Building (Frame)	11 263.00	2 946.50	10%	Jan. 1 to Dec. 31
General Equipment	15 072.13	5 516.20	20%	Jan. 1 to Jan. 31
Automotive Equip.	19 475.43	7 419.21	30%	Jan. 1 to Mar. 31
Building (Frame)	7 500.00	2 946.34	10%	Apr. 1 to Sep. 30
Automobiles	6 500.00	3 050.00	30%	Oct. 1 to Dec. 31
Trucks	15 073.54	8 455.52	30%	Jan. 1 to Mar. 31
Buildings (Brick)	125 900.00	53 542.10	5%	Jan. 1 to Jun. 30
Furniture	4 406.75	2 120.57	20%	July 1 to Dec. 31

10. The following schedule, pertaining to 'adjustment' arithmetic, also appears in your workbook. Complete the schedule by filling in each blank box with the correct figure.

Supplies	*Trial Balance Figure*	*Supplies Closing Inventory Figure*	*Supplies Expense Figure*
1.	$300.00	$100.00	
2.		$175.00	$250.00
3.	$950.00		$740.00
Prepaid Insurance	*Trial Balance Figure*	*Prepaid Insurance Final Calculation*	*Insurance Expense Figure*
1.	$875.00	$325.00	
2.	$925		$315.00
3.		$410.00	$375.00
Allowance for Doubtful Accounts	*Trial Balance Figure*	*Allowance for Doubtful Acc's Figure per Aging Schedule*	*Bad Debts Expense Figure*
1.	$25.00 Cr.	$400.00	
2.	$ 5.00 Dr.	$420.00	
3.	$40.00 Cr.		$565.00
4.	$35.00 Dr.		$530.00
5.		$450.00	$425.00
6.		$480.00	$495.00

11. A company purchases equipment costing $100 000 which it expects to last for 7 years and have a salvage value of $5 500.

1. **For the use of management, prepare a depreciation schedule for the first five years of the assets' life showing depreciation calculated on a straight-line basis.**
2. **Prepare a depreciation schedule for the first five years of the assets' life showing depreciation calculated on a declining-balance basis at the government rate of 20 percent.**

12. A company purchases a truck at a cost of $25 000 which it expects to last 10 years and have a salvage value of $3 500.

1. Prepare two depreciation schedules as follows:

a. A ten-year schedule showing depreciation calculated on a straight-line basis.

b. A ten-year schedule showing depreciation calculated on a declining-balance basis at the government rate of 30 percent.

2. Many accountants claim that, when repairs are also considered, the declining-balance method of calculating depreciation provides a more reliable way to charge the operating expenses of a truck against revenue. Is this argument valid? Explain.

Homework

13. From the following trial balance and additional information, complete the work sheet at December 31, 19–1, the end of a fiscal period of one year.

EDWARD PINKNEY, ARCHITECT
TRIAL BALANCE
DECEMBER 31, 19–1

Bank	$ 10	
Accounts Receivable	400	
Allowance for Doubtful Accounts		$ 5
Supplies	30	
Prepaid Insurance	70	
Equipment	300	
Accumulated Depreciation Equipment		100
Automobile	900	
Accumulated Depreciation Automobiles		270
Accounts Payable		100
E. Pinkney, Capital		350
E. Pinkney, Drawings	2 000	
Fees		4 000
Car Expense	100	
Light and Heat Expense	50	
Miscellaneous Expense	5	
Rent Expense	200	
Telephone Expense	60	
Wages	700	
	$4 825	$4 825

Additional Information:

a. The aging schedule of accounts receivable shows that doubtful accounts amount to $25.

b. The inventory of supplies on hand at the year-end is valued at $10.

c. The prepaid insurance at the year-end is calculated at $30.
d. The depreciation is calculated using the declining-balance method at government rates.

---

14. The following trial balance is for the business of Margaret Akker, a commercial artist, at the end of a fiscal period of one month.

From the trial balance and additional information shown below, complete the work sheet for Margaret Akker.

MARGARET AKKER, COMMERCIAL ARTIST
TRIAL BALANCE
MAY 31, 19–9

Bank	$ 14	
Accounts Receivable	175	
Allowance for Doubtful Accounts	4	
Supplies	45	
Prepaid Insurance	75	
Furniture and Equipment	144	
Accumulated Depreciation of Furniture and Equipment		12
Automobile	220	
Accumulated Depreciation Automobile		36
Accounts Payable		214
Margaret Akker, Capital		378
Margaret Akker, Drawings	35	
Revenue		177
Advertising Expense	5	
Car Expense	30	
Miscellaneous Expense	2	
Rent Expense	25	
Telephone Expense	8	
Wages Expense	35	
	$817	$817

Additional Information:

a. The total of the doubtful accounts is $20.
b. The supplies on hand are valued at $15.
c. The prepaid insurance is valued at $35.
d. Depreciation is calculated on a straight-line basis.
e. It is estimated that furniture and equipment have a life of 12 years with no salvage value.
f. It is estimated that the automobile has a life of 6 years with a salvage value of $4.

---

15. From the trial balance and additional information shown below, complete the work sheet for the year ended September 30, 19–4 for Karen Denby, proprietor of a real estate business.

KAREN DENBY, REAL ESTATE
TRIAL BALANCE
SEPTEMBER 30, 19–4

Petty Cash	$ 100	
Bank	3 800	
Accounts Receivable	10 000	
Allowance for Doubtful Accounts		$ 100
Supplies	500	
Prepaid Insurance	1 000	
Prepaid Licences	400	
Land	50 000	
Building	70 000	
Accumulated Depreciation Building		5 600
Furniture and Equipment	15 000	
Accumulated Depreciation Furniture and Equipment		4 000
Automotive Equipment	17 000	
Accumulated Depreciation Automotive Equipment		6 300
Accounts Payable		400
Bank Loan		100 000
Karen Denby, Capital		40 000
Karen Denby, Drawings	30 000	
Commissions Revenue		96 600
Advertising Expense	4 700	
Bank Charges	8 600	
Car Expenses	8 000	
Light and Heat Expense	2 200	
Miscellaneous Expense	200	
Postage Expense	600	
Commissions Expense	18 000	
Telephone Expense	900	
Wages Expense	12 000	
	$253 000	$253 000

Additional Information:

a. The accounts receivable aging schedule shows a figure of $500 for doubtful accounts.
b. The supplies inventory at September 30 is $200.
c. The prepaid insurance schedule shows a value of $300 for prepaid insurance.
d. The prepaid licences figure in the trial balance represents a licence fee of $200 each for two cars. These fees are for the calendar year.
e. Depreciation is calculated on a straight-line basis.
f. The building is expected to have a useful life of 50 years after which its value will be $5 000.

g. The furniture and equipment are expected to have a useful life of 15 years after which they will have a value of $900.
h. The automobiles are expected to have a useful life of 5 years after which they will have a value of $1 250.

Work Sheet and Statements

16. 1. From the following trial balance and additional information, prepare the work sheet for Janet Gorman, Consultant, for the annual fiscal period ended June 30, 19–0.

JANET GORMAN, CONSULTANT
TRIAL BALANCE
JUNE 30, 19–0

Petty Cash	$ 50.00	
Bank	4 047.50	
Accounts Receivable	7 421.00	
Allowance for Doubtful Accounts		$ 35.00
Supplies	300.00	
Prepaid Insurance	880.00	
Furniture and Equipment	4 596.00	
Accumulated Depreciation Furn. & Equip.		2 242.00
Automobile	8 800.00	
Accumulated Depreciation Automobile		4 488.00
Accounts Payable		521.00
J.P. Gorman, Capital		12 123.50
J.P. Gorman, Drawings	19 500.00	
Revenue		36 072.00
Bank Charges	62.00	
Car Expenses	1 547.50	
Miscellaneous Expense	61.50	
Rent	3 600.00	
Telephone	312.00	
Wages	4 304.00	
	$55 481.50	$55 481.50

Additional Information:

a. The accounts receivable aging analysis showed the doubtful accounts at June 30, 19–0, to be $294.64.
b. The supplies inventory taken at June 30, 19–0, amounted to $80.
c. The prepaid insurance schedule as of June 30, 19–0, showed a total of $200 for unexpired insurance.
d. Depreciation of fixed assets is at government rates.

2. Prepare the balance sheet and the income statement.

17. 1. From the following trial balance and additional information, prepare the work sheet for Dennisson Delivery Service for the half-yearly fiscal period ended June 30, 19–5.

DENNISSON DELIVERY SERVICE
TRIAL BALANCE
JUNE 30, 19–5

Petty Cash	$ 100.00	
Bank	570.00	
Accounts Receivable	12 419.51	
Allowance for Doubtful Accounts	10.00	
Supplies	474.00	
Prepaid Insurance	1 400.00	
Prepaid Licences	1 146.00	
Land	17 000.00	
Buildings (Frame)	21 570.00	
Accumulated Depreciation Buildings		$ 7 046.90
Furniture and Equipment	8 970.00	
Accum. Deprec. Furn. and Equipment		2 946.72
Trucks	48 472.00	
Accumulated Depreciation Trucks		10 407.51
Accounts Payable		3 417.40
Joanne Budd, Capital		58 953.06
Joanne Budd, Drawings	8 900.00	
Revenue		70 721.19
Bank Charges	115.25	
Miscellaneous Expense	219.51	
Telephone	316.25	
Truck Expenses	11 901.32	
Utilities Expense	2 506.00	
Wages	17 402.94	
	$153 492.78	$153 492.78

Additional Information:

a. The accounts receivable aging analysis showed the doubtful accounts at June 30, 19–5, to be $77.12.
b. The supplies inventory taken at June 30, 19–5, amounted to $125.
c. The prepaid licences schedule showed that the value of unexpired licences at June 30, 19–5, amounted to $412.
d. The prepaid insurance schedule as at June 30, 19–5, showed a total of $215 for unexpired insurance.
e. Depreciation of fixed assets is at government rates, declining-balance method. (Remember that the fiscal period is a half-year.)

2. Prepare the income statement and the balance sheet.

18. Tom Franklin is in the plastering business under the name of Tom's Plastering. From the following trial balance and additional information, prepare the work sheet and financial statements for Tom's Plastering for the year ended October 31, 19–1.

TOM'S PLASTERING
TRIAL BALANCE
OCTOBER 31, 19–1

Bank	$ 1 412.10	
Accounts Receivable	5 026.50	
Allowance for Doubtful Debts		$ 37.50
Supplies	416.70	
Small Tools	903.40	
Prepaid Insurance	1 107.80	
Equipment	7 425.00	
Accumulated Depreciation of Equipment		2 673.00
Truck	9 475.00	
Accumulated Depreciation of Truck		2 842.50
Accounts Payable		2 407.35
Tom Franklin, Capital		12 986.60
Tom Franklin, Drawings	25 000.00	
Revenue		56 880.00
Light and Heat Expense	702.40	
Materials Expense	10 043.75	
Miscellaneous Expense	216.70	
Rent Expense	4 800.00	
Telephone Expense	430.00	
Truck Expense	1 840.00	
Wages Expense	9 027.60	
	$77 826.95	$77 826.95

Additional Information:

a. The allowance for doubtful accounts at October 31 is estimated at $312.00.
b. Office supplies on hand at October 31 are valued at $160.
c. Unexpired insurance at October 31 is calculated at $409.50.
d. Depreciation is calculated on the declining-balance method using government rates.

Note: Although you have not been taught the next two items specifically, you should be able to handle them.

e. The small tools at October 31 are valued at $300. The tools represented by the difference from the trial balance figure have been lost, stolen, or broken.
f. Although $10 043.75 has been charged to materials expense, $800 of materials is on hand and unused at October 31.

Cases

Case 1

George Uttz, owner of a large business, has attempted an income tax dodge. George has debited Truck Expense rather than Trucks with the $200 000 cost of several new trucks that he has just purchased.

Questions

1. Has George done anything illegal?
2. What does George stand to gain from his intentional error?
3. If the error is not corrected, what will the immediate tax benefit be if George's tax rate is 40 percent?
4. What other monetary benefit is there besides the saving in income tax?
5. What will the effect be in subsequent years?

Case 2

John Franks, a businessman, seeks your advice in regard to the depreciation method that he should use in his business. To help you explain the two methods, complete the following table in your workbook.

John's only depreciable asset is automotive equipment costing $100 000, expected to last eight years, and to have a salvage value of $5 000.

Year	Net Income Before Depreciation	Declining-Balance at 30%			Straight-Line			Income Tax Gain (or Loss)
		Depreciation for Year	Net Income for Year	Income Tax at 40%	Depreciation For Year	Net Income For Year	Income Tax at 40%	
1	75 000 –							
2	75 000 –							
3	80 000 –							
4	82 000 –							
5	85 000 –							
6	85 000 –							
7	90 000 –							
8	90 000 –							

Questions

1. Under which method is depreciation higher in the earlier years?
2. Which method provides a tax advantage in the early years?
3. What is the net tax advantage or disadvantage after 8 years? (Do not depreciate the asset below the salvage value of $5 000.)
4. Why would a businessman choose the government declining-balance method?
5. Give an advantage or disadvantage of the straight-line method.

Career

Russell Trivett / Management Accountant

After graduating from high school in Grimsby, Ontario, Russell Trivett moved to Toronto and enrolled in the Chartered Accountant's (CA) program. At the same time, he obtained a junior position with Harerson and Clover, a firm of public accountants. Here, Russell's duties included completing customers' tax returns, performing basic accounting functions for small businesses, and preparing financial statements for clients. He also worked with an auditing team that examined accounting procedures for all the firm's clients each year.

Five years later, when Russell received his CA designation, he went to work as an accountant with the Nordberg Company, a manufacturer of mining equipment. In this position, Russell was responsible for keeping track of customers' credit and of the collection of accounts receivable. His duties included aging the accounts receivable, determining the Allowance for Doubtful Accounts, and calculating the year-end inventory of equipment and supplies. Russell reported directly to the general manager.

In search of a more responsible accounting position, Russell next joined EMCO Ltd., a manufacturer of plumbing supplies, as management accountant. At the same time, he enrolled in the Registered Industrial Accountant's (RIA) program, which he completed during evenings and weekends over the next two years.

Russell's responsibilities as management accountant were varied and interesting. He travelled throughout Canada, the United States, and England examining the accounting systems of various branches of the company. He was continually called upon to make major decisions on behalf of head office, such as whether to acquire new companies and whether to participate in various mergers. He established the data processing system for the Canadian branches of EMCO and saw that all corporate policies were carried out. As management accountant, Russell also prepared the yearly work sheet and saw that all accounts were adjusted as required.

Each year, Russell set up schedules of fixed assets to record the year's depreciation expense, using the diminishing balance method. He then used the work sheet to prepare the consolidated financial statements. Russell passed these statements on to his immediate superior, the company controller, for analysis.

Russell eventually began to feel a need for new challenges in his career. Because the top accounting positions at EMCO would remain filled for some time, he decided to look elsewhere for advancement. In the next chapter, we will examine Russell's role as controller for another company.

20

Completing the Accounting Cycle

20-1 Adjusting for Accounts Payable
20-2 Adjusting for Accrued Wages
20-3 Review of Adjustment for Cost of Goods Sold (Periodic Inventory Method)
20-4 Adjusting and Closing the Books of a Proprietorship
20-5 Reversing Entries
20-6 The Accounting Cycle
20-7 Fully Classified Financial Statement

Objectives

When you have completed Chapter 20, you should:

1. Be able to work out the adjusting entries for accounts payable and accrued expenses.
2. Know how to complete an eight-column work sheet for a trading company.
3. Understand the purpose of the closing entries.
4. Be able to record the adjusting and closing entries in the books.
5. Understand the purpose of reversing entries.
6. Be able to work out any required reversing entries.
7. Know the steps in the full accounting cycle.
8. Be able to read fully classified financial statements.

20.1 Adjusting for Accounts Payable

The financial statements cannot be completed until two to three weeks after the end of the accounting period. This period of waiting is necessary to allow time for the late arrival of purchase invoices from suppliers.

Goods and services are often acquired toward the end of an accounting period. The purchase invoices for these goods and services may be delayed until the accounting period is over, that is, until the next accounting period.

The accounting entries for any goods or services should be recorded in the same period as that in which they are used or received. Therefore, for the two or three weeks following the end of the accounting period, each purchase invoice must be examined to see if it pertains to goods or services received prior to the year-end. Those that do must be gathered together and summarized for an adjusting entry.

Assume that an adjustment entry is required for the purchase invoices for Midway Trading Co., shown in Table 20.1.

Table 20.1 Purchase Invoices for Midway Trading Co.

Supplier	*Invoice Date*	*Explanation*	*Amount*
Local Telephone Co.	July 5	Telephone bill for June	$ 15.70
Arrow Garage	July 6	Car repairs in June	35.50
Frank's Supply	July 6	Supplies received in June	45.21
Star Oil Co.	July 10	Gas and oil for cars in June	138.50
Black Lumber Company	July 10	Repairs to building in June	125.00
Public Utilities	July 12	Electricity for June	15.00
Public Utilities	July 14	Water for June	7.81
Jerry's Hardware	July 14	Miscellaneous items in June	20.00

These purchase invoices are summarized in the following accounting entry:

Telephone Expense	$ 15.70	
Car Expense	174.00	
Supplies	45.21	
Building Maintenance	125.00	
Light, Heat, and Water	22.81	
Miscellaneous Expense	20.00	
Accounts Payable		$402.72

The invoices are then absorbed into the normal accounting routine in the new accounting period.

This accounting entry for Accounts Payable is not journalized in the books at this time. It is recorded, however, in the Adjustments section of the work sheet as shown in Figure 20.1.

Midway Trading Company	Work Sheet		Year End	
Accounts	Trial Balance		Adjustments	
	Dr.	Cr.	Dr.	Cr.
Petty Cash	100 -			
Bank	1702 10			
Accounts Receivable	6751 -			
Allowance for Doubtful Accs.		12 50		
Merchandise Inventory	12074 -			
Supplies	370 -		① 45 21	
Prepaid Insurance	794 -			
Land	25000 -			
Buildings (Brick)	42000 -			
Accum. Deprec. Buildings		4095 -		
Furniture and Equip.	3437 20			
Accum. Deprec. Furn & Equip.		1237 40		
Automobiles	17800 -			
Accum. Deprec. Autos.		5340 -		
Accounts Payable		9461 50		① 402 72
Bank Loan		9750 -		
Sales Tax Payable		251 90		
Mary Philip, Capital		68056 70		
Mary Philip, Drawings	12750 -			
Sales		79168 -		
Sales Returns & Allows.	1204 -			
Discounts Earned		516 30		
Bank Charges	1140 50			
Building Maintenance	375 -		① 125 -	
Car Expenses	1846 50		① 174 -	
Discounts Allowed	749 20			
Duty	315 70			
Freight-in	949 -			
Light, Heat, and Water	1417 -		① 22 81	
Miscellaneous Expense	116 40		① 20 -	
Purchases	30616 90			
Purchs. Rets. & Allows.		1520 -		
Telephone Expense	484 -		① 15 70	
Wages	17416 80			
	179409 30	179409 30		

Figure 20.1 A partial work sheet showing the adjustment for accounts payable.

20.2 Adjusting for Accrued Wages

Certain regular expenses, such as wages and interest, are normally accounted for only on the days that payment is made. From one payment date to the next, the liability for such an expense gradually builds up but is not recorded in the books of account. Not until the payment is actually due and paid is the transaction accounted for by means of an accounting entry such as the following:

Wages Expense	$XXX	
Bank		$XXX

Generally, the date of payment for such expenses as wages and interest does not coincide with the date of the end of the fiscal period. For example, consider Figure 20.2.

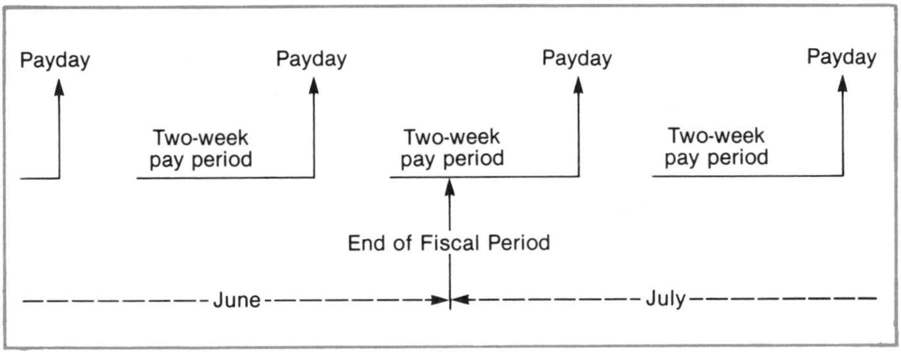

Figure 20.2 A two-week pay period straddling the end of the fiscal period.

The illustration shows that one of the two-week pay periods straddles the year-end. In other words, the date of the end of the fiscal period falls between two paydays.

This situation poses a problem when preparing financial statements. At the end of the accounting period, an unrecorded liability exists which must be taken into consideration when accumulating the information for the statements. In this case, the unrecorded liability is for a portion of two weeks' wages. Items of this nature are known as **accrued expenses** or as **accrued liabilities**. These are expenses or liabilities that have built up during an accounting period, have not been recorded in the accounts, and are not due until sometime in the following accounting period.

Accrued Wages Adjustment for Midway Trading Company

To calculate the accrued wages for Midway Trading Company, wait until the end of the pay period straddling June 30, 19–4, and then compute the portion of the total that pertained to June.

Assume that the total wages for the two weeks amounted to $700.48. Of the ten working days involved, six fell in June and four in July. The accrued wages would then be computed as follows:

Midway Trading Company Work Sheet Year				
Accounts	Trial Balance Dr.	Trial Balance Cr.	Adjustments Dr.	Adjustments Cr.
Petty Cash	100 -			
Bank	1702 10			
Accounts Receivable	6751 -			
Allowance for Doubtful Accs.		12 50		
Merchandise Inventory	12074 -			
Supplies	370 -		① 45 21	
Prepaid Insurance	794 -			
Land	25000 -			
Buildings (Brick)	42000 -			
Accum. Deprec. Buildings		4095 -		
Furniture and Equipment	3437 20			
Accum. Deprec. Furn & Equip.		1237 40		
Automobiles	17800 -			
Accum. Deprec. Autos.		5340 -		
Accounts Payable		9461 50		① 402 72
Bank Loan		9750 -		
Sales Tax Payable		251 90		
Mary Philip, Capital		68056 70		
Mary Philip, Drawings	12750 -			
Sales		79168 -		
Sales Returns & Allows.	1204 -			
Discounts Earned		516 30		
Bank Charges	1140 50			
Building Maintenance	375 -		① 125 -	
Car Expenses	1846 50		① 174 -	
Discounts Allowed	749 20			
Duty	315 70			
Freight-in	949 -			
Light, Heat, and Water	1417 -		① 22 81	
Miscellaneous Expense	116 40		① 20 -	
Purchases	30616 90			
Purchs. Rets. & Allows.		1520 -		
Telephone Expense	484 -		① 15 70	
Wages	17416 80		② 420 29	
	179409 30	179409 30		
Accrued Wages Payable				② 420 29

Figure 20.3 A partial work week showing the adjustment for accrued wages.

$$\frac{\text{In last pay period, number of working days in June}}{\text{In last pay period, total number of working days}} \times \text{Total wages for the last pay period}$$

$$\text{That is,} \quad \frac{6}{10} \times \$700.48 = \$420.29$$

After the accrued wages have been calculated, an adjusting entry must be made on the work sheet. The effect of the adjustment is to increase the wages expense and to set up the accrued liability for wages. The accounting entry debits Wages Expense and credits Accrued Wages Payable.

For Midway Trading Company the adjusting entry is as follows:

Wages Expense	$420.29	
Accrued Wages Payable		$420.29

The adjusting entry on the work sheet is shown in Figure 20.3. Observe that since a Wages Expense account already exists in the Trial Balance section, a new line is not needed for Wages Expense. However, a new line is needed for Accrued Wages Payable because it is a new item. Accrued Wages Payable is a liability and is therefore extended to the credit column of the Balance Sheet section as shown in Figure 20.4.

20.3 Review of Adjustment for Cost of Goods Sold (Periodic Inventory Method)

Trading businesses, which buy and sell merchandise, require an adjustment to determine the cost of the goods that have been sold. This figure is an important one when preparing the income statement. Service businesses, which do not buy and sell merchandise, do not require a cost of goods sold adjustment.

Cassidy Cartage, the business used as an example in the previous chapter, is a service business and therefore does not require a cost of goods sold adjustment. Midway Trading Company, our example for this chapter, is a trading business and does require a cost of goods sold adjustment.

The cost of goods sold adjustment was thoroughly explained in Chapter 13. You should reread Chapter 13 before continuing here.

Cost of Goods Sold Adjustment for Midway Trading Company

Before the cost of goods sold adjustment can be made, it is necessary to take an inventory of the merchandise in stock on the last day of the fiscal period. This job usually requires considerable time and effort and a great deal of systematic organization. In most cases the store or plant must close down until the operation is completed. In an inventory, every item in stock must be counted and listed. The quantity of each item on hand must then be multiplied by its cost price. Finally, the whole listing must be totalled.

Once the inventory figure is available, the cost of goods sold adjustment may be made as follows:

1. On the Merchandise Inventory line, write the opening entry figure (pick up from the Trial Balance Debit column) in the Income Statement Debit column as shown below.

Accounts	Trial Balance Dr.	Trial Balance Cr.	Adjustments Dr.	Adjustments Cr.	Income Statement Dr.	Income Statement Cr.	Balance Sheet Dr.	Balance Sheet Cr.
Merchandise Inventory	12 074 -				12 074 -			

2. On the same line of the work sheet, record the closing inventory figure (in this case $13 750) in the Income Statement *Credit* column and in the Balance Sheet *Debit* column, as shown below.

Accounts	Trial Balance Dr.	Trial Balance Cr.	Adjustments Dr.	Adjustments Cr.	Income Statement Dr.	Income Statement Cr.	Balance Sheet Dr.	Balance Sheet Cr.
Merchandise Inventory	12 074 -				12 074 -	13 750 -	13 750 -	

Observe that the Merchandise Inventory line is in balance at this point.

3. Extend the Purchases line and the Purchases Returns and Allowances line to the Income Statement section of the work sheet as shown below.

Accounts	Trial Balance Dr.	Trial Balance Cr.	Adjustments Dr.	Adjustments Cr.	Income Statement Dr.	Income Statement Cr.	Balance Sheet Dr.	Balance Sheet Cr.
Merchandise Inventory	12 074 -				12 074 -	13 750 -	13 750 -	
Purchases	30 616 90				30 616 90			
Purchases Rets and Alls.		1 520 -				1 520 -		

At this point, the cost of goods sold adjustment is completed. Notice that, in the Balance Sheet columns, the adjustment has provided the correct closing inventory figure for inclusion on the balance sheet. In the Income Statement columns, it has provided the basic ingredients for the cost of goods sold calculation for a trading business.

You can see these entries on the completed work sheet of Midway Trading Company shown in Figure 20.4.

Midway Trading Company	Work Sheet	Year Ended June 30, 19-4						
Accounts	Trial Balance		Adjustments		Income Statement		Balance Sheet	
	Dr.	Cr.	Dr.	Cr.	Dr.	Cr.	Dr.	Cr.
Petty Cash	100 -						100 -	
Bank	1702 10						1702 10	
Accounts Receivable	6751 -						6751 -	
Allowance for Doubtful Accs.		12 50		(3) 465 62				478 12
Merchandise Inventory	12074 -				12074 -	13750 -	13750 -	
Supplies	370 -		(1) 45 21	(4) 269 21			146 -	
Prepaid Insurance	794 -			(5) 468 30			325 70	
Land	25000 -						25000 -	
Buildings (Brick)	42000 -						42000 -	
Accum. Deprec. Buildings		4095 -		(6) 1895 25				5990 25
Furniture and Equipment	3437 20						3437 20	
Accum. Deprec. Furn. & Equip.		1237 40		(7) 439 96				1677 36
Automobiles	17800 -						17800 -	
Accum. Deprec. Autos.		5340 -		(8) 3738 -				9078 -
Accounts Payable		9461 50		(1) 402 72				9864 22
Bank Loan		9750 -						9750 -
Sales Tax Payable		251 90						251 90
Mary Philip, Capital		68056 70						68056 70
Mary Philip, Drawings	12750 -						12750 -	
Sales		79168 -				79168 -		
Sales Returns & Allows.	1204 -				1204 -			
Discounts Earned		516 30				516 30		
Bank Charges	1140 50				1140 50			
Building Maintenance	375 -		(1) 125 -		500 -			
Car Expenses	1846 50		(1) 174 -		2020 50			
Discounts Allowed	749 20				749 20			
Duty	315 70				315 70			
Freight-in	949 -				949 -			
Light, Heat, and Water	1417 -		(1) 22 81		1439 81			
Miscellaneous Expense	116 40		(1) 20 -		136 40			
Purchases	30616 90				30616 90			
Purchs. Returns & Allows.		1520 -				1520 -		
Telephone Expense	484 -		(1) 15 70		499 70			
Wages	17416 80		(2) 420 29		17837 09			
	179409 30	179409 30						
Accrued Wages Payable				(2) 420 29				420 29
Bad Debts Expense			(3) 465 62		465 62			
Supplies Expense			(4) 269 21		269 21			
Insurance Expense			(5) 468 30		468 30			
Depreciation of Bldgs.			(6) 1895 25		1895 25			
Deprec. of Furn. & Equip.			(7) 439 96		439 96			
Deprec. of Automobiles			(8) 3738 -		3738 -			
			8099 35	8099 35	76759 14	94954 30	123762 -	105566 84
Net Income					18195 16			18195 16
					94954 30	94954 30	123762 -	123762 -

Figure 20.4 The completed work sheet of Midway Trading Company, showing the adjustment for cost of goods sold.

Accountant's Working Papers

At the time financial statements are prepared, it is necessary to make numerous inventories, schedules, calculations, and so on pertaining to the work sheet adjustments and the financial statements in general. All papers and calculations related to the preparation of the financial statements are usually collected in one file. These papers are known as the accountant's working papers.

20.4 Adjusting and Closing the Books of a Proprietorship

As you are aware, certain general ledger accounts are allowed to become temporarily incorrect for the sake of convenience during the accounting period. As a result, the information contained in the general ledger cannot be used directly to prepare financial statements. Therefore, the information for the preparation of the financial statements is obtained from the work sheet.

Once the financial statements have been prepared, the accountant must bring the general ledger up to date and prepare the accounts for the next accounting period. This process, known as 'adjusting and closing the books', is usually done before any transactions of the next accounting period are posted.

Objectives of Adjusting and Closing the Books

The process of adjusting and closing the books has three objectives:

1. To adjust those accounts that are not up to date.
2. To close out all Revenue, Expense, and Drawings accounts. This means to cause the accounts to have a nil balance. All of the accounts in the Equity section of the general ledger, except the Capital account, must be closed out to make them ready for the next accounting period. Since these accounts are used to accumulate the revenues, expenses, and drawings during successive accounting periods, they must begin each accounting period with a nil balance.
3. To bring the equity together again in one account — the Capital account. During the accounting period, the owner's total equity is contained in several accounts in the Equity section of the ledger. At the end of each accounting period, the value of the Equity section of the ledger is pulled together into one account — the owner's Capital account. Therefore, the balance in the Capital account usually represents the owner's correct equity only at the very end of an accounting period, or at the very beginning of the next accounting period. Any changes in equity during the period are recorded in the Revenues, Expenses, and Drawings accounts.

Adjusting and Closing Entries for Midway Trading Company

Closing entries were previously discussed in Chapter 10. You must now learn to handle adjusting entries as well. The process of adjusting and of closing the books is outlined below using data from the completed work sheet of Midway Trading Company shown in Figure 20.4.

The adjusting and closing entry process in its final form requires the following five steps. All of the data for these accounting entries is obtained directly from the work sheet, and dated the last day of the fiscal period.

1. Record all and only those adjusting entries that appear in the Adjustments section of the work sheet. For Midway Trading, these are as follows:

June	30	Supplies		45 21	
		Building Maintenance		125 –	
		Car Expenses		174 –	
		Light, Heat, and Water		22 81	
		Miscellaneous Expense		20 –	
		Telephone Expense		15 70	
		Accounts Payable			402 72
		Accounts payable adjustment.			
	30	Wages		420 29	
		Accrued Wages Payable			420 29
		Accrued payroll adjustment.			
	30	Bad Debts Expense		465 62	
		Allowance for Doubtful Accs.			465 62
		Doubtful accounts adjustment.			
	30	Supplies Expense		269 21	
		Supplies			269 21
		Supplies adjustment.			
	30	Insurance Expense		468 30	
		Prepaid Insurance			468 30
		Insurance adjustment.			
	30	Depreciation of Building		1895 25	
		Depreciation of Furn. and Equip.		439 96	
		Depreciation of Automobiles		3738 –	
		Accum. Deprec. Building			1895 25
		Accum. Deprec. Furn. & Equip.			439 96
		Accum. Deprec. Autos.			3738 –
		Depreciation adjustment.			

2. Close out the balances on the credit side of the Income Statement section of the work sheet. Close these to the Income Summary account. The accounting entry is as follows for Midway Trading Co.

June	30	Merchandise Inventory	13 750 -	
		Sales	79 168 -	
		Discounts Earned	516 30	
		Purchases Returns & Allowances	1 520 -	
		Income Summary		94 954 30
		To close out income section credits		
		to Income Summary.		

3. Close out the balances on the debit side of the Income Statement section of the work sheet. Close these to the Income Summary account. For Midway Trading, the accounting entry is as follows:

June	30	Income Summary	76 759 14	
		Merchandise Inventory		12 074 -
		Sales Returns and Allowances		1 204 -
		Bank Charges		1 140 50
		Building Maintenance		500 -
		Car Expenses		2 020 50
		Discounts Allowed		749 20
		Duty		315 70
		Freight-in		949 -
		Light, Heat, and Water		1 439 81
		Miscellaneous Expense		136 40
		Purchases		30 616 90
		Telephone Expense		499 70
		Wages		17 837 09
		Bad Debts Expense		465 62
		Supplies Expense		269 21
		Insurance Expense		468 30
		Depreciation of Buildings		1 895 25
		Deprec. of Furn. and Equip.		439 96
		Deprec. of Automobiles		3 738 -
		To close out income section debts		
		to Income Summary.		

4. Close out the balance in the Income Summary account (the net income or the net loss figure) to the owner's Capital account. For Midway Trading, the accounting entry is as follows:

June	30	Income Summary	18 195 16	
		Mary Philip, Capital		18 195 16
		To close out Income Summary		
		to Capital.		

5. Close out the balance in the owner's Drawings account to the owner's Capital account. The accounting entry is as follows for Midway Trading Co.

June	30	Mary Philip, Capital	12750 –	
		Mary Philip, Drawings		12750 –
		To close out Drawings to		
		Capital.		

After the adjusting and closing entries have been journalized and posted, the following objectives will have been met:

1. All accounts requiring an adjustment will be adjusted.
2. The Capital account will be updated.
3. All other equity accounts will be closed out.

Post-Closing Trial Balance

The closing procedure involves numerous postings and calculations. As a result, there are many possibilities for mechanical errors. One last step is needed, therefore, to be certain that the general ledger is correctly balanced to begin the new accounting period. After posting the adjusting and closing entries, it is common practice to take off a general ledger trial balance, called the 'post-closing trial balance'. This is usually done with an adding machine and paper tape, as illustrated in Figure 20.5. The paper tape is headed and stored for possible future reference.

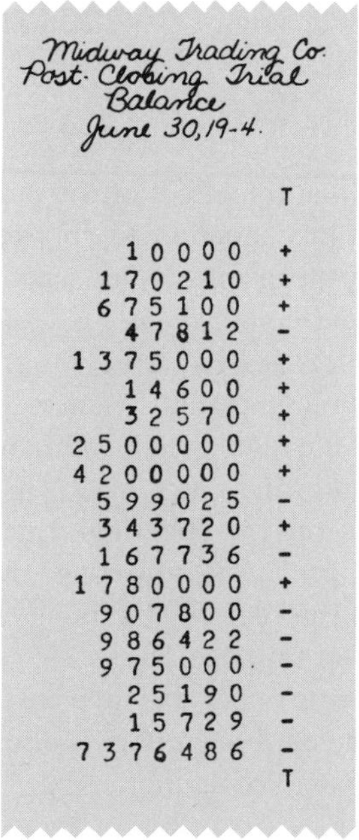

Figure 20.5 A post-closing trial balance prepared on an adding machine.

20.5 Reversing Entries

Reversing Entry for Accounts Payable

Sometimes purchase invoices are received in one accounting period that pertain to goods and services that were received in the previous accounting period. When financial statements are prepared, an adjusting entry is necessary to record these purchase invoices in the proper accounting period.

Once the adjusting entry for accounts payable is made, the purchase invoices are then inserted into the accounting system to be processed by the ordinary accounting routine in the new period. This is necessary because the invoices must be matched with the purchase orders and receiving reports, posted to the subsidiary ledgers, and so on. However, because these purchase invoices are processed through the regular accounting system, they are entered in the books of the business a second time. These particular purchase invoices are recorded in both accounting periods, as shown by the following chart.

END OF ACCOUNTING PERIOD

PERIOD JUST ENDED	PERIOD JUST BEGUN
+ Effect of certain purchase invoices is recorded in the books of the business by means of the accountant's adjusting entry.	+ The same purchase invoices are entered in the books of the business by clerks adhering to the accounting system.

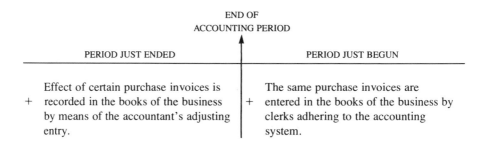

From this chart, you can see that the effect of the purchase invoices is felt in both accounting periods. How can this situation be corrected?

The problem is corrected by means of another accounting entry, called a reversing entry, that is made *early in the new accounting period*. A **reversing entry** is an accounting entry made to cancel out the doubling effect created when an item is recorded in the proper accounting period by an adjusting entry and also in the following period as a result of the regular accounting routine. This reversing entry is exactly the opposite of the adjusting entry made for the invoices in the previous period and completely cancels out the doubling effect.

For Midway Trading Company, the reversing entry for Accounts Payable is shown in Figure 20.6. As you can see, this reversing entry is exactly the opposite of the adjusting entry made earlier on page 585.

The total effect of all the entries for the invoices is described in the following chart. The chart shows that the doubling effect is eliminated in the new accounting period by means of the reversing accounting entry.

July	1	Accounts Payable	402 72	
		Supplies		45 21
		Building Maintenance		125 -
		Car Expense		174 -
		Light, Heat, and Water		22 81
		Miscellaneous Expense		20 -
		Telephone Expense		15 70
		Reversing entry for accounts payable.		

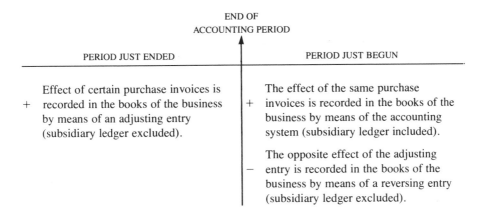

Figure 20.6 A reversing entry for accounts payable.

END OF ACCOUNTING PERIOD

	PERIOD JUST ENDED		PERIOD JUST BEGUN
+	Effect of certain purchase invoices is recorded in the books of the business by means of an adjusting entry (subsidiary ledger excluded).	+	The effect of the same purchase invoices is recorded in the books of the business by means of the accounting system (subsidiary ledger included).
		−	The opposite effect of the adjusting entry is recorded in the books of the business by means of a reversing entry (subsidiary ledger excluded).

Reversing Entry for Accrued Payroll

Reversing entries are necessary for any accounting situation where the following conditions exist:

1. An adjusting entry is made to record an item or items in the accounting period just ended.
2. The same item or items are processed in the new accounting period by means of the regular accounting routine.

Midway Trading Company made an adjusting entry for accrued wages. As a result, six days' wages in the amount of $420.29 were recorded in the accounting period ended June 30. At the same time, the Payroll Department proceeded in its usual manner to calculate the payroll for the ten-day period ended in July which resulted in wages of $700.48 being recorded in the new accounting period. However, this ten-day-wages figure of $700.48 includes the six-day-wages figure of $420.29.

The effect of the above is shown by the following chart.

END OF ACCOUNTING PERIOD

PERIOD JUST ENDED	PERIOD JUST BEGUN
\$420.29 of wages (for 6 days) recorded by adjusting entry.	\$700.48 of wages (for 10 days) recorded through regular accounting routine. This amount includes the \$420.29 shown at left.

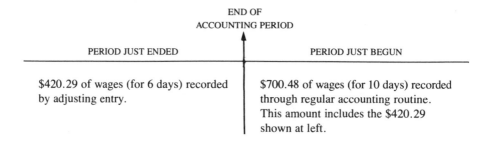

Because the \$700.48 figure includes the \$420.29 figure, the \$420.29 figure is recorded in both accounting periods. This duplication is corrected by means of a reversing entry which cancels out \$420.29 in the new accounting period. The reversing entry is shown below and is exactly the opposite of the adjusting entry made earlier on page 589.

July	1	Accrued Wages Payable	420 29	
		Wages		420 29
		Reversing entry for accrued payroll.		

The total accounting effect is shown by the chart below.

END OF ACCOUNTING PERIOD

PERIOD JUST ENDED	PERIOD JUST BEGUN
\$420.29 of wages (for 6 days) recorded by adjusting entry.	\$700.48 of wages (for 10 days) recorded through regular accounting routine. This amount includes the \$420.29 shown at left.
	\$420.29 of wages (for 6 days) cancelled out by reversing entry.
Net effect: 6 days wages of \$420.29.	Net effect: 4 days wages of \$280.19.

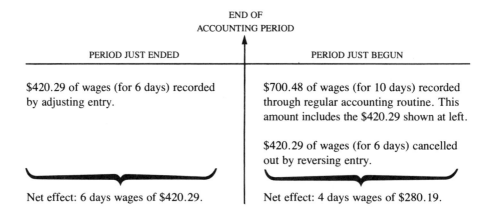

20.6 The Accounting Cycle

The inclusion of the adjusting entries and the reversing entries is the final stage in developing the accounting cycle. Figure 20.7 shows the steps in the accounting cycle in its final form.

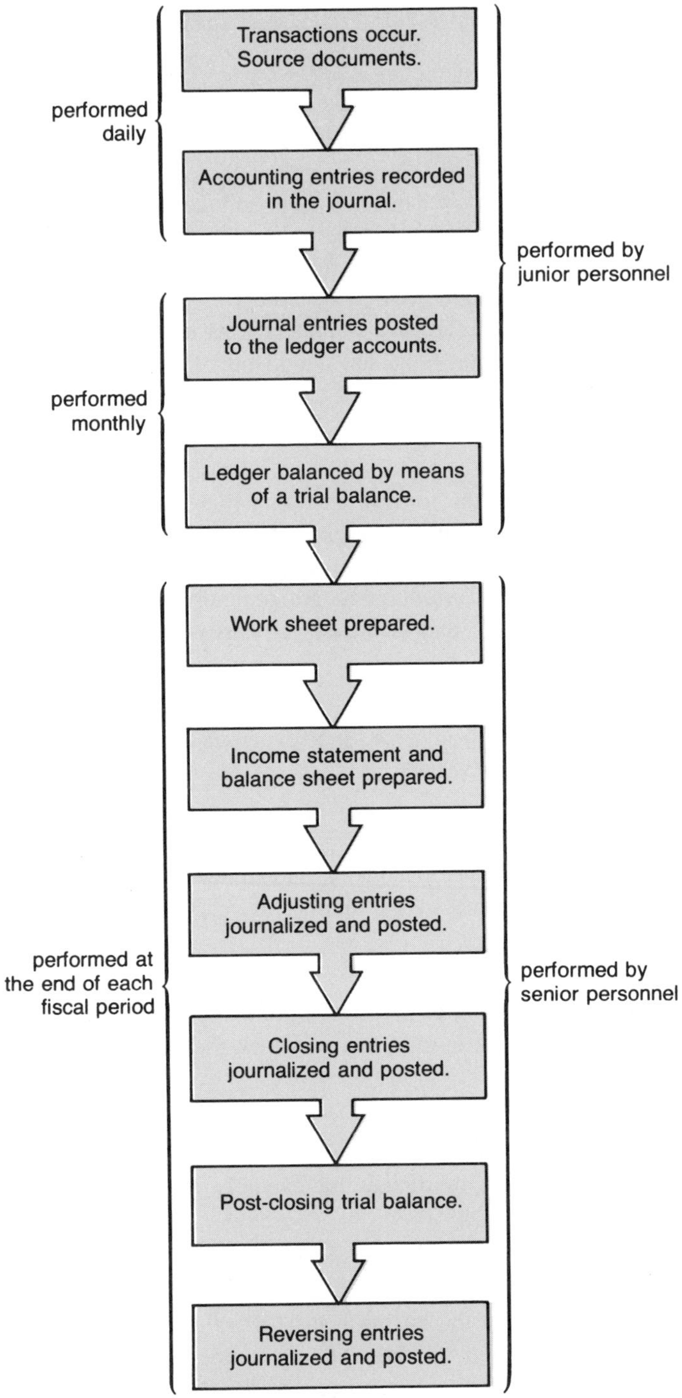

Figure 20.7 The complete accounting cycle.

20.7 Fully Classified Financial Statements

In order to prepare financial statements, one must be familiar with their appearance and organization. There is no single correct form for each of the financial statements. Instead, certain variations exist that are suitable for particular businesses or situations.

Figures 20.8 and 20.9 show the balance sheet and the income statement of Fraser and Associates. These are typical statements for a well-established and profitable trading business. By examining these statements you will see that they are more than just a list of debit and credit items as would appear on a trial balance. The items are grouped and arranged on the financial statements to provide meaningful information in easily readable form. Financial statements of this type are known as **fully classified financial statements**.

Current Assets

These assets are already in the form of cash or will be converted into cash in the ordinary course of business within a period of one year. For example, accounts receivable are ordinarily collected within a period of one year and are therefore classified as current assets. Current assets are generally listed in the order or their liquidity, that is, in the order in which they can easily be converted into cash.

Prepaid Expenses

These expenses are paid for in advance. Such expenses are usually used up or expire within a period of one or two years.

Fixed Assets

These assets, such as buildings, machinery, and equipment, are intended to be used in the operations of the business for a number of years.

Current Liabilities

These liabilities of the business are due within a period of one year. Current liabilities are generally listed in the order in which they must be paid.

Long-term Liabilities

These liabilities of the business are not due for payment within a period of one year. Certain long-term liabilities, mortgages for example, may not be due for several years.

Owner's Equity

This is the owner's share of the business at book value. In other words, owner's equity is the proportion of assets that belong to the owner after providing for payment of all liabilities.

FRASER AND ASSOCIATES
BALANCE SHEET
DECEMBER 31, 19–9

ASSETS

Current Assets			
Petty Cash		$ 100.00	
Bank		1 742.12	
Accounts Receivable	$13 419.05		
Less Allowance for Doubtful Accounts	374.19	13 044.86	
Merchandise Inventory — at cost		15 907.00	
Government Bonds		10 000.00	$ 40 793.98
Prepaid Expenses			
Insurance		$ 416.25	
Supplies		1 530.00	1 946.25
Fixed Assets			
Land		$20 000.00	
Buildings — at cost	$75 742.57		
Less Accumulated Depreciation	12 614.30	63 128.27	
Equipment — at cost	$37 407.56		
Less Accumulated Depreciation	18 316.41	19 091.15	
Automobiles — at cost	$10 407.35		
Less Accumulated Depreciation	5 307.75	5 099.60	107 319.02
			$150 059.25

LIABILITIES

Current Liabilities			
Accounts Payable and Accrued Charges		$12 409.37	
Bank Loan		5 000.00	
Sales Tax Payable		440.72	
Canada Pension Plan Payable		216.40	
Employees' Income Tax Payable		517.42	$ 18 583.91
Long-Term Liability			
Mortgage on Property			42 705.16

PROPRIETORSHIP

Owner's Equity			
D. Fraser, Capital, January 1		$72 017.21	
Add: Net Income for year	$31 742.16		
Less Drawings	14 989.19	16 752.97	
D. Fraser, Capital, December 31			88 770.18
			$150 059.25

Figure 20.8 The classified balance sheet for Fraser and Associates.

FRASER AND ASSOCIATES
INCOME STATEMENT
YEAR ENDED DECEMBER 31, 19–9

Revenue				
Sales			$170 984.76	
Less: Sales Returns and Allowances		$ 3 026.04		
Discount off Sales		1 027.19	4 053.23	
Net Sales				$166 931.53
Cost of Merchandise Sold				
Merchandise Inventory, January 1			$ 18 414.90	
Purchases		$87 314.42		
Less: Purchase Returns & Allowances	$2 016.40			
Discount off Purchases	1 307.51	3 323.91	83 990.51	
Freight-in			2 964.72	
Duty			1 072.12	
Total Cost of Goods Available for Sale			$106 442.25	
Deduct Merchandise Inventory, December 31			15 907.00	
Cost of Merchandise Sold				90 535.25
Gross Trading Income				$ 76 396.28
Selling Expenses				
Advertising and Sales Promotion		$ 2 504.00		
Delivery Expense		1 594.23		
Salesmen's Commissions		10 234.60		
Salesmen's Car Expenses		5 654.30		
Depreciation of Automobiles		2 185.56	$ 22 172.69	
Administrative Expenses				
Bad Debts Expense		$ 304.74		
Bank Charges and Interest		502.10		
Depreciation of Building		7 014.25		
Depreciation of Equipment		4 772.79		
Legal Expense		215.00		
Audit Fee		500.00		
General Expense		95.00		
Insurance Expense		128.00		
Supplies Expense		746.12		
Office Expense		216.40		
Postage Expense		155.03		
Rent Expense		84.00		
Telephone Expense		319.54		
Canada Pension Plan Expense		410.34		
Unemployment Insurance Expense		380.42		
Office Salaries		11 442.83	27 286.56	49 459.25
Operating Income				$ 26 937.03
Other Income				
Interest on Investments				4 805.13
Net Income				$ 31 742.16

Figure 20.9 The classified income statement for Fraser and Associates.

Revenue

Revenue is the gross earnings derived from the regular operations of the business.

Cost of Merchandise Sold

These include all of the elements of cost directly connected with the acquisition of the goods that the business deals in. Included is the actual cost of the merchandise as well as any cost involved in the process of transporting the goods from their place of origin to the premises of the business.

Selling Expenses

These include all expenses of the business that are directly related to the selling and delivery of goods.

Administrative Expenses

These include all expenses of a general nature that are related to the operation of the business. Expenses in this category pertain to such things as the management of the business, the maintenance of the buildings and equipment, and the running of the office.

Other Income and Expenses

These include earnings and expenses that are not derived from the regular operations of the business.

Accounting Terms

accrued expenses
accrued liabilities
reversing entry
fully classified financial statements

Review Questions

1. Explain why an adjusting entry regarding accounts payable is usually necessary.
2. Explain how the 'matching' principle is involved in the accounts payable adjustment.
3. Explain why an adjusting entry regarding accrued payroll is usually necessary.
4. Describe what is involved in taking inventory.
5. What are the accountant's working papers?
6. State the three objectives of adjusting and closing the books.

7. State the five steps in adjusting and closing the books.
8. Why are reversing entries necessary?
9. When are reversing entries recorded?
10. State the ten steps in the full accounting cycle.

Exercises

Calculating Accrued Payroll

1. Based on the following information, calculate the amount of the accrued pay on September 30 and give the accounting entry for it.

a. The fiscal year-end is September 30.
b. The payroll is calculated on a biweekly basis with 10 working days.
c. The first pay in October falls on October 4th.
d. The amount of the first pay in October is $12 000.70.

2. Based on the following information, calculate the amount of the accrued pay on March 31 and give the accounting entry for it.

a. The fiscal year-end is March 31.
b. The payroll is calculated on a weekly basis with 5 working days.
c. The first pay in April falls on April 2nd.
d. The amount of the first pay in April is $20 046.50.

Simplified Work Sheet Adjustments

3. The following partial work sheets appear in the workbook. For each one, record the required adjusting entries and extend the adjusted items to the appropriate columns of the work sheet.

1. At the end of the fiscal period the accrued wages amount to $842.

Work Sheet

Accounts	Trial Balance Dr.	Trial Balance Cr.	Adjustments Dr.	Adjustments Cr.	Income Statement Dr.	Income Statement Cr.	Balance Sheet Dr.	Balance Sheet Cr.
Wages	10 074 11							
	XXXXXXXX	XXXXXXXX						

2. At the end of the fiscal period, the outstanding accounts payable items are as follows:
Telephone, $50; Car Expenses, $210; Miscellaneous Expenses, $35.

Work Sheet

Accounts	Trial Balance Dr.	Trial Balance Cr.	Adjustments Dr.	Adjustments Cr.	Income Statement Dr.	Income Statement Cr.	Balance Sheet Dr.	Balance Sheet Cr.
Bank	500 -							
Accounts Receivable	4 200 -							
Allow. for Doubtful Accts.		110 -						
Supplies	470 -							
Furniture and Equipment	2 850 -							
Accum. Depr. Furn & Equip.		920 -						
Accounts Payable		3 510 -						
J. Smith, Capital		3 395 -						
J. Smith, Drawings	2 700 -							
Sales		9 500 -						
Car Expenses	950 -							
Miscellaneous Expense	175 -							
Rent	1 200 -							
Telephone	315 -							
Wages	4 075 -							
	17 435 -	17 435 -						

3. The closing inventory is $76 365.60.

Work Sheet

Accounts	Trial Balance Dr.	Trial Balance Cr.	Adjustments Dr.	Adjustments Cr.	Income Statement Dr.	Income Statement Cr.	Balance Sheet Dr.	Balance Sheet Cr.
Merchandise Inventory	70 296 50							
Purchases	110 316 40							
Purchases Returns & Allows.		5 764 20						
Freight-in	1 926 70							

Write-off and Recovery of Accounts Receivable

4. At December 31, 19–3, the balance in the Allowance for Doubtful Accounts account was $1 402.63 Cr.

During the 19–4 fiscal period, the following transactions affected the Allowance for Doubtful Accounts account.

March 2	Wrote off the account of T. Kurana in the amount of $185.06.
June 14	Wrote off the account of V. Lengua in the amount of $705.32.
Sept. 16	Wrote off the account of O. Nakashima in the amount of $315.02.
Sept. 26	Recovered the account of J. Goldstein for $216.40 written off two years previously.
Nov. 15	Wrote off the account of J. Pickard in the amount of $216.40.

1. **Give the accounting entry to write-off the account of T. Kurana.**
2. **Give the accounting entries to record the bad debt recovered from J. Goldstein.**
3. **Calculate the balance (before any adjusting entry) of the Allowance for Doubtful Accounts account.**
4. **The allowance for doubtful debts at December 31, 19–4 is estimated at $1 506.12. Give the adjusting entry for doubtful debts.**

---

5. At December 31, 19–6, the balance in the Allowance for Doubtful Accounts accounts was $1 685.09. During the 19–7 fiscal period the following transactions affected the account.

June 4	Wrote off the account of R. Maki in the amount of $505.60
Sept. 9	Recovered the account of P. Simons for $400 which was written off in the previous year.
Dec. 3	Wrote off the account of N. Prentice in the amount of $106.40.

1. **Give the accounting entry to write off the account of R. Maki.**
2. **Give the accounting entries to recover the account of P. Simons.**
3. **Calculate the balance, before any adjusting entry, of the 'allowance' account.**
4. **If the allowance for doubtful debts at December 31, 19–7, is estimated at $1 406.50, give the accounting entry to adjust for doubtful accounts.**

Work Sheets with All Adjustments

6. Prepare a work sheet from the general ledger trial balance of Monarch Marine (after a fiscal period of six months) and the additional information necessary for the adjustments.

MONARCH MARINE
TRIAL BALANCE
SEPTEMBER 30, 19–7

Petty Cash	$ 50.00	
Bank	1 046.57	
Accounts Receivable	10 409.50	
Allowance for Doubtful Accounts		$ 26.17
Merchandise Inventory	39 416.50	
Supplies	497.17	
Prepaid Insurance	395.33	
Land	24 000.00	
Buildings (Brick)	47 000.00	
Accumulated Depreciation Buildings		7 998.37
Equipment	23 469.75	
Accumulated Depreciation Equipment		11 693.24
Delivery Truck	4 200.00	
Accumulated Depreciation Delivery Truck		2 759.40
Accounts Payable		15 609.75
Sales Tax Payable		625.00
Mortgage Payable		3 609.00
B. West, Capital		100 811.73
B. West, Drawings	17 200.00	
Sales Revenue		88 764.20
Bank Charges	62.50	
Building Repairs	752.87	
Delivery Expense	1 459.61	
Discounts Earned		315.12
Freight-in	1 796.14	
Light, Heat, and Water	1 146.19	
Miscellaneous Expense	194.17	
Purchases	42 906.70	
Purchases Returns and Allowances		1 056.92
Telephone	215.90	
Wages	17 050.00	
	$233 268.90	$233 268.90

Additional Information:

a. Purchase invoices received subsequent to the year-end but pertaining to the fiscal period just ended were as follows:

Supplier	*Explanation*	*Amount*
Jack's Hardware	Paint and materials for repairing buildings	$ 19.25
King Oil Company	Gasoline and oil for delivery truck	65.20
Dominion Boats	Boat for resale	565.00
Best Marine Supply	Merchandise for resale	175.00
Dandy Cable	Merchandise for resale	230.45

b. Depreciation is calculated at government rates (half-yearly fiscal period).

c. The accounts receivable aging analysis showed a total for doubtful accounts of $376.45.

d. Inventories taken at September 30, 19–7, were as follows:

Merchandise	$41 759.40
Supplies	255.00

e. The following insurance policies were in force:

Company	*Policy Number*	*Date*	*Term*	*Premium*
Circle	34598	March 31, 19–5	3 years	$72.00
Guarantee	234756	June 30, 19–5	3 years	$40.00
Prairie	190645	September 30, 19–6	3 years	$66.00
Select	23114	September 30, 19–6	3 years	$270.00

f. Wages for the two-week period ended Friday, October 5, 19–7, were $1 214.04. The employees work a five-day week.

Note: Exercise 7 is for students who have studied Chapter 13 on payroll.

---

7. Prepare the work sheet from the following trial balance and additional information for the year ended December 31, 19–5.

GENERAL LIGHTING AND ELECTRIC
TRIAL BALANCE
DECEMBER 31, 19–5

Petty Cash	$ 100.00	
Bank	1 469.25	
Accounts Receivable	119 007.40	
Allowance for Doubtful Accounts	24.50	
Merchandise Inventory	65 759.10	
Supplies	1 059.26	
Prepaid Insurance	470.50	
Furniture and Equipment	4 942.04	
Accumulated Depreciation Furn. & Equip.		$ 2 574.12
Automotive Equipment	6 574.00	
Accumulated Depreciation Autom. Equip.		2 107.15
Bank Loan		25 000.00
Accounts Payable		41 964.75
Sales Tax Payable		940.60
Employees' Income Tax Payable		219.40
R. Brooks, Capital		93 814.11
R. Brooks, Drawings	9 600.00	
Sales Revenue		257 906.40
Sales Returns and Allowances	2 065.70	
Advertising and Sales Promotion	1 075.00	
Bank Charges	34.09	
Bank Interest	1 500.00	
Canada Pension Plan Expense	315.90	
Car Expenses	3 951.40	
Cash Short and Over	29.42	
Discounts Earned		1 095.62
Duty	2 964.15	
Freight-in	1 047.24	
Light, Heat, and Water	312.95	
Miscellaneous Expense	125.94	
Postage	56.05	
Purchases	162 786.97	
Purchases Returns and Allowances		3 746.15
Rent	12 000.00	
Telephone	941.14	
Unemployment Insurance Expense	400.15	
Wages	30 756.15	
	$429 368.30	$429 368.30

Additional Information:

a. The summary of purchase invoices received in 19–6 but which pertain to goods and services received in 19–5 is shown below.

Supplies	$ 49.50
Furniture and Equipment	250.00
Car Expenses	56.55
Freight-in	30.00
Miscellaneous Expense	20.10
Purchases	1 072.16
	$1 478.31

b. The following four accounts are considered to be doubtful:

Customer	*Account Balance*
Morgan & Morgan	$342.19
Perfect Company	255.67
J.A. Swift	12.50
W.A. Wallace	150.00

c. Inventories at December 31, 19–5, are as follows:

Merchandise	$62 056.66
Supplies	742.00

d. Details of insurance policies are as follows:

Company	*Policy Number*	*Date*	*Term*	*Premium*
Northern	90214	Jan. 1, 19–5	3 years	$ 39.00
Alliance	602294	Mar. 31, 19–5	1 year	168.00
Amalgamated	310678	Sept. 30, 19–4	3 years	120.00
Anchor	22230	June 1, 19–4	3 years	90.00
Provincial	123140	Dec. 1, 19–3	3 years	72.00

e. Depreciation is calculated at government rates.

f. Wages for the two weeks ended Friday, January 8, amounted to $1 105.12. The employees work a five-day week and are paid for New Year's Day, a holiday.

Fully Classified Statements

8. The following classification is used in preparing the financial statements of ABC Company:

Current Assets
Prepaid Expenses
Fixed Assets
Current Liabilities
Long-term Liabilities
Owner's Equity
Revenue
Cost of Goods Sold
Selling Expenses
Administrative Expenses
Other Income
Other Expenses

Classify each of the following items into one of the above categories. With a few items a choice is possible.

Accounts Receivable
Accounts Payable
Accumulated Depreciation of Buildings
Advertising
Allowance for Bad Debts
Audit Fee
Bad Debts Expense
Bank
Bank Charges
Bank Loan
Buildings
Canada Pension Plan Expense
Delivery Expense
Depreciation on Automobiles
Depreciation on Building
Discounts Allowed
Discounts Earned
Duty
Employees' Income Tax Payable
F. Franks, Capital
F. Franks, Drawings
Freight-in
General Expense
Insurance Expense
Interest Income
Investment in Bonds
Legal Expense
Merchandise Inventory
Mortgage Payable
Office Expense
Office Salaries
Prepaid Insurance
Postage Expense
Purchases
Rent Expense
Sales
Sales Returns and Allowances
Sales Tax Payable
Salesmen's Commissions
Salesmen's Car Expenses
Supplies
Supplies Expense
Telephone Expense
Unemployment Insurance Expense
Wages

---

9. The following completed work sheet is for Sterling Sales Company.

1. **Journalize the adjusting entries, the closing entries, and the reversing entries.**
2. **Prepare the fully classified financial statements.**

Sterling Sales Company	Work Sheet				Year Ended June 30, 19-2			
Accounts	Trial Balance		Adjustments		Income Statement		Balance Sheet	
	Dr.	Cr.	Dr.	Cr.	Dr.	Cr.	Dr.	Cr.
Petty Cash	50 -						50 -	
Bank	1 292 64						1 292 64	
Accounts Receivable	33 412 94						33 412 94	
Allow. for Doubtful Accs.	5 05			1 407 29				1 402 24
Merchandise Inventory	35 963 15				35 963 15	38 592 -	38 592 -	
Supplies	506 19		65 20	416 39			155 -	
Prepaid Insurance	396 -			150 -			246 -	
Land	35 000 -						35 000 -	
Buildings (Frame)	20 000 -						20 000 -	
Accum. Deprec. Buildings		6 878 -		1 312 20				8 190 20
Furniture and Equipment	4 740 26						4 740 26	
Accum. Deprec. Furn. & Equip.		2 313 04		485 44				2 798 48
Automobiles	16 437 -						16 437 -	
Accum. Depr. Autos.		8 383 -		2 416 20				10 799 20
Bank Loan		25 000 -						25 000 -
Accounts Payable		17 502 12		1 265 09				18 767 21
Sales Tax Payable		607 50						607 50
Mortgage Payable - 13%		39 375 -						39 375 -
O. J. Little, Capital		30 333 01						30 333 01
O. J. Little, Drawings	14 904 15						14 904 15	
Sales		200 205 51				200 205 51		
Sales Returns & Allowances	1 926 50				1 926 50			
Advertising	4 465 17				4 465 17			
Bank Charges & Interest Exp.	1 548 22				1 548 22			
Building Maintenance	1 572 12		50 -		1 622 12			

Delivery Expense	3,416.90		104.32		3,521.22			
Cash Short and Over	26.70				26.70			
Discounts Allowed	2,674.15				2,674.15			
Discounts Earned		742.15				742.15		
Freight-in	1,946.20				1,946.20			
Light, Heat, and Water	1,375.46				1,375.46			
Mortgage Interest Expense	3,839.06		1,279.69		5,118.75			
Postage	392.04				392.04			
Purchases	86,567.50		1,045.57		87,613.07			
Purchases Rets. & Allowances		2,472.19				2,472.19		
Salespersons' Commissions	40,742 -				40,742 -			
Salespersons' Car Expenses	3,974 -				3,974 -			
Telephone	675 -				675 -			
Wages	15,963.12		316.40		16,279.52			
	333,811.52	333,811.52						
Bad Debts Expense			1,407.29		1,407.29			
Supplies Expense			416.39		416.39			
Insurance Expense			150 -		150 -			
Deprec. of Buildings			1,312.20		1,312.20			
Deprec. of Furn. & Equip.			485.44		485.44			
Deprec. of Automobiles			2,416.20		2,416.20			
Accrued Mortgage Int. Pay'l				1,279.69				1,279.69
Accrued Wages Payable				316.40				316.40
			9,048.70	9,048.70	216,050.79	242,011.85	164,829.99	138,868.93
Net Income					25,961.06			25,961.06
					242,011.85	242,011.85	164,829.99	164,829.99

Completing The Accounting Cycle

10. The general ledger trial balance of King Chemical Company, after a fiscal period of one year, is as follows. Additional information is also provided.

KING CHEMICAL COMPANY
GENERAL LEDGER TRIAL BALANCE
DECEMBER 31, 19–3

No. 1	Petty Cash	$ 50.00	
2	Bank	593.74	
3	Accounts Receivable	12 519.50	
4	Allowance for Doubtful Accounts	4.70	
5	Merchandise Inventory	20 416.50	
6	Supplies	575.75	
7	Prepaid Insurance	312.00	
8	Furniture and Equipment	4 010.00	
9	Accum. Deprec. Furn. & Equip.		$ 2 716.50
10	Automobiles	7 800.00	
11	Accum. Deprec. Automobiles		5 124.60
21	Bank Loan		15 000.00
22	Accounts Payable		15 741.62
23	Sales Tax Payable		672.14
24	Employees' Income Tax Payable		602.51
31	F. C. Wallace, Capital		27 441.20
32	F. C. Wallace, Drawings	15 946.15	
41	Sales		140 567.07
51	Bank Charges	141.05	
52	Canada Pension Plan Expense	405.00	
53	Car Expenses	3 509.10	
54	Duty	1 075.92	
55	Freight-in	4 074.75	
56	Light, Heat, and Water	147.16	
57	Miscellaneous Expense	79.52	
58	Postage	112.40	
59	Purchases	73 416.95	
60	Rent	11 760.00	
61	Telephone	565.70	
62	Unemployment Insurance	286.00	
63	Wages	50 063.75	
		$207 865.64	$207 865.64

The general ledger accounts of King Chemical Company are set up for you in the workbook.

Additional Information:

a. The total of the estimated doubtful accounts as shown by the December 31, 19–3, aging analysis is $516.90.

b. Purchase invoices received in January 19–4 pertaining to goods and services received in 19–3 are summarized as follows:

Supplies	$ 75.00
Purchases	967.25
Car Expenses	135.75
Misc. Expense	74.01
	$1 252.01

c. Inventories taken at December 31, 19–3, are as follows:

Merchandise	$18 450.00
Supplies	250.00

d. The prepaid insurance schedule as of December 31, 19–3, showed the value of prepaid insurance to be $116.25.

e. Capital cost allowances are calculated at government rates.

f. The gross wages for the first payroll in January amounted to $1 140. Half of this amount pertained to the 19–3 fiscal year and half to the 19–4 fiscal year. Ignore employer's contributions.

1. **Prepare a work sheet for the company for the year ended December 31, 19–3.**
2. **Prepare a balance sheet and an income statement.**
3. **Journalize the adjusting and closing entries on page 74 of the general journal.**
4. **Post the adjusting and closing entries and calculate the account balances.**
5. **Take off a post-closing trial balance.**
6. **Journalize and post the reversing entries for accounts payable and accrued wages.**
7. **If the first payroll for King Chemical Company in 19–4 is posted immediately, what will be the balance in the Wages Expense account?**
8. **Does this balance correctly reflect the wages expense for the first working week of 19–4?**

---

11. On December 31, 19–4, the end of a fiscal year, the general ledger trial balance of Dominion Furniture is as follows. Additional information is also provided.

DOMINION FURNITURE
TRIAL BALANCE
DECEMBER 31, 19–4

No.	Account	Debit	Credit
No. 1	Petty Cash	$ 50.00	
2	Bank	1 047.21	
3	Accounts Receivable	10 467.04	
4	Allowance for Doubtful Accounts		$ 25.94
5	Merchandise Inventory	12 375.16	
6	Supplies	362.04	
7	Prepaid Insurance	243.00	
8	Land	9 500.00	
9	Buildings — Frame	7 500.00	
10	Accum. Deprec. Buildings		2 579.25
11	Furniture and Equipment	2 150.00	
12	Accum. Deprec. Furn. & Equip.		1 172.00
13	Automobiles	4 875.00	
14	Accum. Deprec. Automobiles		1 462.50
21	Accounts Payable		3 076.21
22	Sales Tax Payable		315.20
23	Employees' Income Tax Payable		84.50
24	Canada Pension Plan Payable		31.10
25	Loan Payable — Due March 31, 19–9		20 000.00
31	J. K. Smit, Capital		8 706.59
32	J. K. Smit, Drawings	12 500.00	
41	Sales		85 904.15
42	Sales Returns and Allowances	2 074.10	
51	Advertising	200.00	
52	Bank Charges	35.00	
53	Building Repairs and Maintenance	746.09	
54	Canada Pension Plan Expense	234.00	
55	Car Expenses	946.80	
56	Cash Short and Over	13.50	
57	Discounts Allowed	1 516.15	
58	Discounts Earned		1 075.21
59	Duty	357.00	
60	Freight-in	907.40	
61	Interest on Loan	900.00	
62	Light, Heat, and Water	112.00	
63	Miscellaneous Expense	56.50	
64	Postage	94.60	
65	Property Taxes	804.90	
66	Purchases	40 915.78	
67	Purchases Returns and Allow.		1 010.44
68	Telephone	212.50	
69	Unemployment Ins. Expense	151.20	
70	Wages and Salaries	14 096.12	
		$125 443.09	$125 443.09

The general ledger accounts of Dominion Furniture are set up for you in the workbook.

Additional Information:

a. The total estimated value of doubtful accounts per the aging analysis is $152.

b. Purchase invoices received in January 19–5 which pertain to goods and services received in 19–4 are summarized below:

Purchases	$1 200.50
Building Repairs and Maintenance	105.00
Car Expenses	41.02
Freight-in	25.00
	$1 371.52

c. Inventories taken at December 31, 19–4, are as follows:

Merchandise	$14 650.00
Supplies	150.00

d. The details of insurance policies as at December 31, 19–4, are as follows:

Company	*Policy Date*	*Term*	*Premium*
Acme	July 1, 19–2	3 years	$ 72.00
Inland	April 1, 19–4	3 years	96.00
Empire	Dec. 31, 19–1	3 years	120.00
Imperial	Sept. 30, 19–4	1 year	36.00

e. Depreciation is calculated at government rates.

f. The gross wages and salaries for the first pay in January 19–5 totalled $305 for 10 working days. Three working days are in 19–4 and seven are in 19–5. Ignore the employer's share.

g. The loan payable of $20 000 bears interest at a rate of 6 percent per annum. Interest payments are made half-yearly on March 31 and September 30. Interest has been paid to September 30 only. (An adjustment is necessary in respect to accrued interest payable.)

1. Prepare a work sheet for Dominion Furniture for the year ended December 31, 19–4.

2. Prepare a balance sheet and an income statement.

3. Journalize the adjusting and closing entries on page 140 of the general journal.

4. Post the adjusting and closing entries and calculate the account balances.

5. Take off a post-closing trial balance.

6. Journalize and post the reversing entries.
7. Post the debit to the Wages and Salaries account of Dominion Furniture for the first pay in 19–5. Calculate the account balance to see if it properly reflects the expense for the new pay period.

Using Your Knowledge

12. At the end of the fiscal year, the accountant for Canadian Auto Supply Company closed the accounts and prepared the balance sheet and the income statement which showed a net income of $22 372.65. He then submitted the two statements to each of the officers of the company.

    When the treasurer received the statements, she compared them with the statements of the preceding year and was surprised to find that the net income had decreased by approximately $4 000. She suspected that something was wrong.

    Upon making an independent check of the books, she found that during the first month of the year, $1 800 had been paid out for insurance, to cover a period of three years. This entire premium had been charged to Insurance Expense for the year. She also found that $2 500 was charged to Office Supplies for the year, but that $2 200 of this was still on hand at the end of the year.
    1. What errors would the treasurer point out to the accountant?
    2. What is the correct net income for the year, assuming that no other errors have been found?
    3. Give the required correcting entries.

13. The accountant for Ruban Enterprises neglected to make any reversing entries for accrued payroll and for accounts payable.

    How will each of these omissions be detected? (Each will be detected differently.)

14. If the following errors are not corrected, state whether the net income will be greater or smaller, and give the amount of the difference.
    1. The $4 200 cost of installing a new machine in a factory was charged to Repair Expense.
    2. A $35.50 credit to Discounts Earned was erroneously credited to Discounts Allowed.
    3. A journal entry in the amount of $1 500 was posted as a $150 debit to Furniture & Fixtures and as a $150 credit to Accounts Payable.

15. The Sutton Hardware Store, owned by C. Wallace, takes inventory only at the end of the calendar year because of the cost and inconvenience involved. The gross profit of the business is stable and averages 40 percent.

The accounts of January 31 had balances as follows:

Inventory January 1 (obtained by actual count of merchandise)	$ 51 920
Sales	103 850
Operating Expenses	29 875
Purchases	45 920

From these facts, estimate the inventory at January 31, and prepare an estimated income statement for January.

16. The comparative statement of income for James O'Halloran shows that his sales have increased 40 percent over the sales of the previous year, but his net income has decreased 15 percent. Give two possible causes.

17. During the taking of physical inventory at December 31, 19--, certain merchandise which cost $2 500 was counted twice. The inventory was therefore overstated by $2 500. What is the effect of this error on the cost of goods sold? On net income for the year? On total assets?

Cases

Case 1 *Why is There a Decrease in Net Income?*

E. C. Percy, owner of Percy Plumbing and Heating, asks you to analyze the operating results of the business for the last two years so that you can tell him the reasons for a decrease in net income.

Your partially completed analysis is shown following the questions, below.

Questions

1. Finish the analysis by completing the Percent columns. (Do not write your answers in the textbook.)
2. Prepare a list of questions and comments for discussion with Mr. Percy. Restrict your comments to significant items only.

Percy Plumbing and Heating
Income Statement
Year Ended March 31, 19-5
(with comparative figures for 19-4)

	19-4 Amount	19-4 Percent of Sales	19-5 Amount	19-5 Percent of Sales
Revenue				
Sales	58 254	100.0	43 534	100.0
Direct Expenses				
Materials Used	29 802		23 978	
Wages	6 380		6 752	
Truck Repairs	776		654	
Truck Licence	80		80	
Gasoline and Oil	650		1 158	
Depreciation of Truck	1 650		1 156	
Insurance	736		918	
Business Licence	370		362	
Depreciation of Equipment	134		108	
Workmen's Compensation	318		384	
Unemployment Insurance	68		90	
Business Tax	14		14	
	40 978		35 654	
Indirect Expenses				
Telephone	870		1 090	
Office Supplies	48		168	
Accounting Fee	160		150	
Postage	60		20	
Interest and Bank Charges	770		526	
Sales Promotion	312		394	
Legal Expenses	362			
Miscellaneous Expenses			122	
	2 582		2 470	
Total Expenses	43 560		38 124	
Net Income	14 694		5 410	

Case 2 *Closing Entries Only Once a Year?*

Janet Porter is the chief accountant for Dolphin Enterprises in Winnipeg, Manitoba. Until recently, management was happy to receive financial statements once a year. However, management recently decided that the income statement should be prepared at the end of each month.

Janet wasn't pleased at having to record the adjusting and closing entries each month. She gave the matter some thought and soon devised a scheme for providing a monthly income statement while still only recording the adjusting and closing entries once a year.

Questions

1. What is Janet's scheme?

Career
Russell Trivett / Controller

Russell Trivett, whom we met in Chapter 19, eventually left EMCO to become the controller for the Robert Hunt Corporation, a manufacturer of doors and windows. As controller, Russell is the chief accounting officer of the company. He oversees the work of more than 60 employees in the cost department, the payroll department, the accounting department, and the computer department.

Russell supervises the preparation of work sheets and the adjustment of all accounts at year-end closing. He prepares the classified financial statements and tax returns for the company. He also interprets and analyzes financial statements and other related data for his immediate superior, the vice president of finance.

Russell plays a key role in the long-term planning and development of the four departments that he oversees. He is in charge of the ongoing development of a computer system to meet the company's expanding needs as efficiently as possible.

As his career has progressed, Russell has found that those who aspire to top positions in accounting must continue to update their accounting knowledge and skills. Russell has also taken several on-the-job courses in management training. As controller, he finds communication and reading skills even more important than mathematical ability. Russell rarely works directly with numbers at this stage in his career. Instead, he spends much of his time presenting planning concepts and financial analyses to his superiors and encouraging his staff to effectively carry out company policies.

Summary Exercise
Universal Lumber Company

Introductory Information

You have taken a position as accountant for the Universal Lumber Company. You are to commence duties on December 15, 19–4, and will work with the present accountant until his departure at the end of the month. During that time, you must become sufficiently acquainted with the company's books, records, and office procedures to take over full responsibility for their preparation.

During the introductory period you learn the following facts and information:

a. The business is three years old.
b. The owner is James Wiseman.
c. The company's fiscal year coincides with the calendar year.
d. The owner demands interim financial statements at the end of each month to show in columnar form the results of operation for the month just completed, as well as the results of operation for the year to date.
e. In the office there is an adding machine and a calculator which are rented by the company from Office Rentals Co. The monthly rentals of $20 and $30 are due on the fifteenth of each month.
f. The company offers a 2 percent discount on all sales if payment is received from the customer within 10 days of the date of the sales invoice.
g. Sales tax at the rate of 10 percent applies on all sales.
h. The company has a National Pacific Railway siding. Most of the material purchased is transported to the company premises by rail.
i. On the fifteenth and on the last day of each month the proprietor draws $725 out of the business.
j. The detailed information in respect to payroll is as follows:
    i. Payday is every other Friday. The first payday in the new year is Friday, January 12.
    ii. All employees are paid on a salary basis.
    iii. The method of payment is by cash. The cash to meet the payroll is obtained by issuing and cashing one cheque for the total amount required.

iv. Each employee is enrolled in the company registered pension plan. Contributions are made at the rate of 5 percent of the gross pay on each pay period. The employer matches the employees' contributions.

v. R.P.P. contributions made by the employees and the employer are accumulated by the company and remitted to the Insurance Company of Canada at the end of each month in which the deductions are made.

vi. Employees' income taxes, employees' and employer's contributions to the Canada Pension Plan, and the employees' and employer's contributions to the Unemployment Insurance Fund are remitted in one cheque to the Receiver General on the fifteenth day of each month following that in which the deductions are made.

vii. The United Appeal Fund contributions of the employees are accumulated by the company and remitted to the local organization at the end of the quarter.

viii. The payroll for January 12 is to be made up from the following minimum information:

Employee	*Weekly Salary*	*Net Claim Code*	*Weekly United Appeal Donation*	*Account to be Charged*
B. Barnes	$265.00	6	$4.00	Wages
T. Crawford	$270.00	3	4.50	Wages
G. Hornbrook	$290.00	7	4.00	Wages
G. Maw	$285.00	12	2.50	Wages
A. Ozolins	$275.00	13	5.25	Wages
F. Sikkema	$280.00	13	2.50	Office Salaries
Accountant (you)	$300.00	1	—	Office Salaries

(Assume for convenience that all employees are at least 18 years of age and under 70 years of age.)

k. The bank reconciliation statement as at December 31, 19–4, is as follows:

UNIVERSAL LUMBER
BANK RECONCILIATION STATEMENT
DECEMBER 31, 19–4

Balance per bank statement			$5555.33
Add outstanding deposit			121.50
			$5676.83
Deduct outstanding cheques			
	635	$ 47.50	
	639	156.20	
	640	300.00	503.70
Balance per general ledger			$5173.13

l. The complete chart of accounts for the business is as follows:

Account Number	*Account Name*
1.	Bank
2.	Petty Cash
3.	Accounts Receivable
4.	Allowance for Bad Debts
5.	Merchandise Inventory
6.	Office Supplies
7.	Prepaid Insurance
8.	Land
9.	Building
10.	Accumulated Depreciation Building
11.	Office Equipment
12.	Accumulated Depreciation Office Equipment
13.	Trucks
14.	Accumulated Depreciation Trucks
20.	Bank Loan
21.	Accounts Payable
22.	Accrued Payroll
23.	Canada Pension Plan Payable
24.	Unemployment Insurance Payable
25.	Registered Pension Plan Payable
26.	Employees' Tax Deductions Payable
27.	United Appeal Payable
28.	Sales Tax Payable
30.	James Wiseman, Capital
31.	James Wiseman, Drawings
32.	Income Summary
40.	Sales
41.	Discount Allowed
50.	Purchases
51.	Freight-in
52.	Bad Debts
53.	Building Maintenance
54.	Depreciation of Building
55.	Depreciation of Office Equipment
56.	Depreciation of Trucks
57.	Insurance Expense
58.	Interest and Bank Charges
59.	Legal Expense
60.	Miscellaneous Expense
61.	Office Expense
62.	Office Supplies Used
63.	Office Salaries
64.	Pension Fund Expense
65.	Power Expense
66.	Property Taxes
67.	Telephone
68.	Truck Expense
69.	Unemployment Insurance Expense
70.	Wages

m. The general ledger trial balance at December 31 is as follows. The complete general ledger is set up for you in the workbook.

	Debit	*Credit*
Bank	$ 5 173.13	
Petty Cash	100.00	
Accounts Receivable	8 642.81	
Allowance for Bad Debts		$ 93.62
Merchandise Inventory	24 812.55	
Office Supplies	650.00	
Prepaid Insurance	352.20	
Land	12 000.00	
Building	17 000.00	
Accumulated Depreciation Building		2 424.63
Office Equipment	1 339.00	
Accumulated Depreciation Office Equipment		653.42
Trucks	11 400.00	
Accumulated Depreciation Trucks		7 489.80
Bank Loan		5 000.00
Accounts Payable		11 416.70
Canada Pension Plan Payable		192.16
Unemployment Insurance Payable		135.12
Employees Tax Deductions Payable		1 226.60
Sales Tax Payable		1 502.17
James Wiseman, Capital		51 335.47
	$81 469.69	$81 469.69

n. The subsidiary ledger trial balances at December 31 are as follows. These accounts are set up for you in the workbook.

Accounts Receivable	
Bayvue Village Estates (Nov. 30)	$2 365.53
Carlton Home Builders (Nov. 30)	1 672.16
Evergreen Gardens (Dec. 27)	1 848.88
Keele Estates (Aug. 23)	120.43
J. Martin (Mar. 16)	10.42
B. Starr (Apr. 1)	83.20
Superior Construction Co. (Dec. 28)	2 542.19
	$8 642.81

Accounts Payable		
Lumber Wholesalers	Terms, N60	$ 5 627.42
Plywood Suppliers	Terms, N60	4 320.60
Wood Moulding Co.	Terms, N60	1 468.68
		$11 416.70

o. The following information is to be used by the accountant to prepare simple financial statements.
   i. *Bad Debts.* The Allowance for Bad Debts is calculated on a specific account basis. The balance in this account at December 31 of $93.62 was to cover J. Martin's account of $10.42 and B. Starr's account of $83.20, both of which were over one year old.
   ii. *Prepaid Insurance.* The annual insurance premium is $2 113.20 payable in advance on each February 28. The Prepaid Insurance account balance of $352.20 at December 31 represents the unused portion (the 2 months of January and February) of the insurance premium calculated as follows: 2/12 × $2 113.20 = $352.20.
   iii. *Fixed Assets.* Fixed assets are depreciated in accordance with the rules and regulations of the federal government. Detailed information in respect to the fixed assets is as follows:

Brick Buildings	
Cost Price	$17 000.00
Rate of Depreciation — 5 percent, reducing balance	
Accumulated Depreciation after 3 years	$2 424.63
Office Equipment	
Cost Price	$1 339.00
Rate of Depreciation — 20 percent, reducing balance	
Accumulated Depreciation after 3 years	$653.42
Trucks	
Cost Price	$11 400.00
Rate of Depreciation — 30 percent, reducing balance	
Accumulated Depreciation after 3 years	$7 489.80

p. Sales tax is remitted on the fifteenth of each month for deductions of the previous month, payable to the Provincial Treasurer.

q. The business uses a synoptic journal and a two-column general journal in its accounting system. The next page number for the synoptic journal is 62, and for the general journal, 31. (**Note:** This exercise may be done using any system of journals preferred. If some other system is used, students are to select their own page numbers.)

1. Read the introductory information and make notes of the business transactions that you will be required to make on your own initiative.

2. Record the accounting entries for the transactions in the journals. You are told directly about most of the transactions but some you must remember to originate yourself, from the notes made according to the introductory information. Post daily to the subsidiary ledgers.

Transactions

January

2 *Sales Invoice*
—No. 1462, to Ontario Carpentry Co., $625 plus sales tax.

3 *Sales Invoice*
—No. 1463, to Evergreen Gardens, $575 plus sales tax.

5 *Cash Receipt*
—From J. Martin, $10.42, on account.
Purchase Invoice
—From Industrial Oil Co. Ltd., $325, for gas and oil used in the trucks; N, 30.

5 *Purchase Invoice*
—From Lumber Wholesalers, $1 214.62, for lumber; N, 60.

5 *Cash Receipt*
—From cash sales, $2 904, including both the amount of the sales and the sales tax for the week.

8 *Cheque Copies*
—No. 641, to Lumber Wholesalers, $2 000, on account.
—No. 642, to Plywood Suppliers, $1 500, on account.

9 *Cash Receipt*
—From Bayvue Village Estates, $2 365.53, on account.

10 *Cash Receipt*
—From Ontario Carpentry Co., $673.75, on account.

12 *Cash Receipt*
—From cash sales, $2 816, including both the amount of the sales and the sales tax for the week.

15 *Purchase Invoice*
—From National Pacific Railway, $156.20 freight on lumber; N,30.

17 *Cheque Copy*
—No. 648, to petty cash, $?, to replenish the petty cash fund for the following petty cash vouchers: Office Expense, $14.12; Truck Expense, $62.40; Building Maintenance, $19.25.

19 *Cash Receipt*
—From cash sales, $2 992, including both the amount of the sales and the sales tax for the week.

20 *Sales Invoice*
—No. 1464, to Bayvue Village Estates, $1 250 plus sales tax.

22 *Cash Receipt*
—From Carlton Home Builders, $1 672.16, on account.

23 *Cheque Copy*
—No. 649, to Wood Moulding Co., $1 468.68, on account.

24 *Cheque Copy*
No. 650, to Local Telephone Co., $37.50, telephone bill for the month.

25 *Cash Receipt*
—From Evergreen Gardens, $2 481.38, on account.

26 *Cash Receipt*
—From cash sales, $2 915, including both the amount of the sales and the sales tax for the week.

29 *Sales Invoice*
—No. 1465, to Carlton Home Builders, $982.49 plus sales tax.
Cash Receipt
—From Superior Construction Co., $2 542.19, on account.

29 *Cheque Copy*
—No. 652, to Yorktown Hydro, $47.89, hydro bill for the month.

30 *Sales Invoices*
—No. 1466, to Ontario Carpentry Co., $3 687.98 plus sales tax.
—No. 1467, to Evergreen Gardens, $4 846.73 plus sales tax.

31 *Sales Invoice*
—No. 1468, to Parker Bros., $400.75 plus sales tax.
Purchase Invoice
—From Lumber Wholesalers, $6 234.65, for lumber received; freight prepaid; N,60.
Cheque Copies
—No. 653, to Lumber Wholesalers, $4 000, on account.
—No. 654, to Municipality of Yorktown, $75, for monthly instalment of property taxes.
Cash Receipt
—From cash sales, $1 870, including both the amount of the sales and the sales tax for the last three days of the month.

3. Balance the journals and post to the general ledger.

4. Balance the general ledger and the subsidiary ledgers as at January 31, 19–5.

5. Prepare the bank reconciliation statement as at January 31, 19–5. The bank statement for January is shown below.

CANADIAN CENTURY BANK

IN ACCOUNT WITH

Universal Lumber Company

DEBITS				CREDITS	DATE	BALANCE
				Balance forward	Dec 31	5 555.33
				121.50	Jan 2	5 676.83
47.50	(635)				5	5 629.33
				10.42	8	5 639.75
156.20	(639)			2 904.00	9	8 387.55
300.00	(640)			2 365.53	10	10 453.08
				673.75	11	11 126.83
2 000.00	(641)	3 224.58	(643)		12	5 902.25
1 500.00	(642)			2 816.00	15	7 218.25
50.00	(644)	95.77	(648)		17	7 072.48
725.00	(645)				19	6 347.48
				2 992.00	22	9 339.48
				1 672.16	23	11 011.64
1 553.88	(646)				24	9 457.76
1 468.68	(649)				25	7 989.08
1 502.17	(647)			2 481.38	26	8 968.29
37.50	(650)	3 224.58	(651)	2 915.00	29	8 621.21
				2 542.19	30	11 163.40
47.89	(652)				31	11 115.51
73.40	Bank Interest				31	11 042.11

6. Using the following information, prepare the work sheet and financial statements, and record the adjusting, closing, and reversing entries as required at the end of the accounting period.

a. The Allowance for Bad Debts at January 31 is to allow for B. Starr's account of $83.20 and Keele Estates' account of $120.43.

b. The lumber inventory at January 31 is valued at $23 773.

c. The office supplies on hand at January 31 are valued at $622.

d. The accrued payroll is to be estimated in the expectation that the gross salaries for the period ending February 9 will be the same as for the period ending January 26.

e. There are no unprocessed accounts payable vouchers pertaining to January.

7. Prepare a post-closing trial balance.

8. Journalize the following transactions for February. Post daily to the subsidiary ledgers.

Transactions

February

2 *Cash Receipt*

—From cash sales, $1 023, including both the amount of the sales and the sales tax for the first two days of the month.

5 *Cash Receipt*

—From Keele Estates, $120.43, on account.

Cheque Copies

—No. 657, to National Pacific Railway Co., $156.20, on account.

—No. 658, to Industrial Oil Co. Ltd., $325 on account.

6 *Cheque Copies*

—No. 659, to Lincoln Motors Limited, $165, repairs to Mr. Wiseman's personal car.

—No. 660, to Large and Small Ltd., $28.91, C.O.D. order of carbon paper.

Cash Receipt

—From Evergreen Gardens, $5 224.77, on account.

9 **Note:** Mr. Maw terminated his employment with the company effective at 5 p.m. S. Sheba was hired to replace him; work to commence on Monday morning February 12. Sheba's salary was set at $265 per week and his TD-1 form showed a net claim code of 1. Sheba made no other commitments.

Cash Receipt

—From Mr. Charles Carlton, owner of Carlton Home Builders, $1 126.94, for balance of his account less the cash discount, plus a cash sale of lumber for $42 with $4.20 additional for sales tax.

Cheque Copies

—No. 662, to John Carmichael, $153.50, painting of buildings.

—No. 663, to Lumber Wholesalers, $5 000, on account.

Sales Invoices

—No. 1469, to Evergreen Gardens, $1 272.68, plus sales tax.

—No. 1470, to Carlton Home Builders, $3 542.01, plus sales tax.

—No. 1471, to Bayvue Village Estates, $1 672.97, plus sales tax.

Cash Receipt

—From cash sales, $2 926, including both the amount of the sales and the sales tax for the week.

12 *Bank Debit Memorandum*

—$120.43, cheque from Keele Estates, deposited on February 5, was returned — 'Not Sufficient Funds'.

Purchase Invoice

—From Wood Moulding Co., $3 742.62, for lumber; N,30.

13 *Purchase Invoice*

—From National Pacific Railway Co., $185.90, for freight charges on lumber; N,30.

Cash Receipt
—From Bayvue Village Estates, $1 375, on account.

15 *Cheque Copies*
—No. 668, to Peter Douglas and Son, $150, cash payment for legal services.
—No. 669, to Plywood Suppliers, $2 820.60, on account.
Cash Receipt
—From James Wiseman, the owner, $3 000, to increase his equity in the business.

16 *Cash Receipt*
—From cash sales, $3 179, including both the amount of the sales and the sales tax for the week.
Cheque Copy
—No. 670, to Tom's Local Garage, $65.42, cash payment of invoice for truck repairs.

19 *Sales Invoice*
—No. 1472, to Ontario Carpentry Co., $2 288.60 plus sales tax.

21 *Cash Receipt*
—From Ontario Carpentry Co., $2 000, on account.
—From cash sales, $2 591.82, for the amount of sales plus the sales tax.

22 *Cheque Copy*
—No. 672, to petty cash fund, $?; to reimburse the petty cash fund for the following petty cash vouchers: Office Expense, $2.10; Truck Expense, $30.72; Office Supplies, $42.60; Miscellaneous Expense, $21.06.

23 *Purchase Invoice*
—From Plywood Suppliers, $2 381.11, for lumber; N,60.
Cash Receipt
—From cash sales, $3 058, including both the amount of the sales and the sales tax for the week.

26 *Purchase Invoices*
—From Industrial Oil Co. Ltd., $258.70, for gas and oil used in the trucks; N,30.
—From National Pacific Railway Co., $200.70 for freight on lumber; N,30.

27 *Cheque Copies*
—No. 673, to Yorktown Hydro, $59.10, cash payment of monthly hydro bill.
—No. 674, to Municipality of Yorktown, $75, for monthly instalment on property tax.
—No. 675, to Local Telephone Co., $37.50, telephone bill for the month.

28 *Cheque Copy*
—No. 676, to Insurance Underwriters, $2 113.20, annual insurance premium.

Sales Invoices
—No. 1473, to Ontario Carpentry, $2 565.53, plus sales tax.
—No. 1474, to Parker Bros., $1 320, plus sales tax.
—No. 1475, to Bayvue Village Estates, $680.70, plus sales tax.
Cash Receipts
—From Parker Bros., $440.83, on account.
—From cash sales, $1 980, including both the amount of the sales and the sales tax for the last three days of the month.

9. Balance the journals and post to the general ledger.

10. Balance the general ledger and the subsidiary ledgers as of February 28, 19–5.

11. Prepare the bank reconciliation statement as at February 28, 19–5. The bank statement for February is shown below.

CANADIAN CENTURY BANK

IN ACCOUNT WITH Universal Lumber Company

DEBITS				CREDITS	DATE	BALANCE
			Balance	forward	Jan 31	11 042.11
				1 870.00	Feb 1	12 912.11
				1 023.00	5	13 935.11
4 000.00	(653)			120.43	6	10 055.54
75.00	(654)	156.20	(657)	5 224.77	7	15 049.11
325.00	(658)				8	14 724.11
725.00	(655)	3 224.58	(661)		9	10 774.53
165.00	(659)	120.43	(N.S.F.)	1 105.33	12	11 594.43
153.50	(662)			2 926.00	12	14 366.93
5 000.00	(663)			1 375.00	14	10 741.93
150.00	(668)			3 000.00	16	13 591.93
786.00	(656)			3 179.00	19	15 984.93
28.91	(660)	65.42	(670)		20	15 890.60
50.00	(664)	96.48	(671)	2 000.00	22	17 744.12
1 253.24	(667)	3 143.32	(672)	2 591.82	22	15 939.38
5 000.00	(D.M. Re Loan Repayment)				23	10 939.38
2 820.60	(669)			3 058.00	26	11 176.78
725.00	(665)	2 463.80	(666)		28	7 987.98
66.30	(Bank Interest)				28	7 921.68

12. Using the following information, prepare the work sheet and financial statements, and record the adjusting, closing, and reversing entries, as required at the end of the accounting period.

a. An analysis of the accounts receivable ledger indicated that B. Starr's account and Keele Estates' account are doubtful.
b. The lumber inventory at February 28 was valued at $20 667.
c. The office supplies on hand at February 28 were valued at $658.
d. Accrued payroll can be estimated on the basis that the gross payroll for the period ending March 9 is the same as for the period ending February 23.
e. The following purchase invoice received in March pertained to goods received in February:

Plywood Suppliers' invoice of March 5, $170.50, for lumber.

13. Prepare a post-closing trial balance.

21

Partnerships

21-1 Formation of a Partnership
21-2 Accounting for Simple Partnerships
21-3 Distribution of Net Income or Net Loss in a Partnership
21-4 Financial Statements of a Partnership
21-5 Adjusting and Closing Entries for a Partnership
21-6 Termination of Partnerships

Objectives

When you have completed Chapter 21, you should:

1. Be able to define 'partnership'.
2. Know the purposes of the partnership form of business organization.
3. Understand how the equity section of a partnership differs from that of a proprietorship.
4. Know the advantages and disadvantages of a partnership.
5. Know the essential features of a partnership agreement.
6. Know of the various provincial partnership acts.
7. Be able to do the accounting for simple partnership formations.
8. Be able to perform the calculations to apportion partnership net income or net loss.
9. Be able to prepare the four financial statements of a partnership.
10. Be able to prepare the adjusting and closing entries for a partnership.
11. Know the four steps in termination of a partnership.

So far you have only studied one type of business organization, the single proprietorship. The text has emphasized basic accounting concepts and skills in as simple a setting as possible. The single proprietorship, however, is not the only type of business organization. Partnerships and corporations are other types of business organization that are very common in the business world. In respect to volume of business, corporations are the most significant by far.

21.1 Formation of a Partnership

A **partnership** exists where two or more persons (called partners) join together in a business and share in its profits or losses. A company's name often indicates if it is a partnership. Names such as H. Gregg & Sons, Peters and Associates, and Black and Morris are typical.

Each province in Canada has its own Partnership Act to govern the operations of partnerships within its provincial boundaries. There is little difference in the partnership acts of the various provinces.

Partnership Accounts

The main difference between accounting for a partnership and for a single proprietorship is in respect to the Capital and Drawings accounts. As you know, a single proprietorship is owned by one person for whom there is a single Capital account and a single Drawings account. Because a partnership is owned by two or more persons, it requires a Capital account and a Drawings account for each of the partners. Partnerships with a number of partners will require a number of Capital and Drawings accounts.

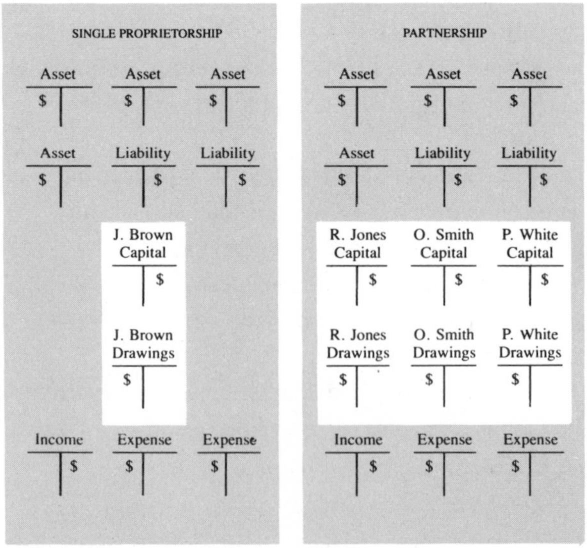

Figure 21.1 A comparison of the accounts for a single proprietorship and for a partnership.

Figure 21.1 offers a simple, graphic comparison of the books of a single proprietorship and those of a partnership with three partners. Observe that the principal difference between the two forms of business organization is reflected in the Capital and Drawings accounts.

Most of the day-to-day accounting for a partnership is the same as for a single proprietorship. The one aspect of partnership accounting that is new to you concerns the Capital accounts.

The Capital accounts represent each partner's individual stake in the business. They must be maintained accurately and in accordance with the wishes of the partners as stated in the partnership contract. The new accounting for the Capital accounts is related to the end-of-accounting-period activity, at which time the partnership net income or net loss is calculated and then distributed to the partners.

Reason for Partnerships

Partnership is a common form of business organization. It is usually chosen for its convenience. Particular circumstances vary, however. To understand why partnerships develop, consider the following simple case histories.

Case 1

Jack Brian has wanted his own business for some time but has lacked the courage to start on his own. He has been afraid of the financial risk and of the heavy responsibility that he would have to bear alone. Then Jack meets Bob James, who agrees to go into business with him. With someone to share the burdens and risks of ownership, Jack finds the courage he needs to change the direction of his career.

Case 2

For several years Bill Salino has been the general manager of a large building firm. Bill knows the business thoroughly and is anxious to go into business for himself. Unfortunately, the nature of the business requires a far greater initial outlay of funds than Bill can raise alone. Bill is frustrated until he meets Bruno Moro who has the necessary funds and who is looking for an opportunity to invest them. The two men agree to enter business as partners. By combining their individual resources, they are able to achieve a goal that neither could reach independently.

Case 3

Over the years, J. R. Hall has built up a profitable and expanding business. Mr. Hall sees a good future in the business for his son. He persuades his son to join him in the partnership of J. R. Hall and Son. The partnership is a convenient way for father and son to share ownership and keep the business in the family.

These simplified case histories demonstrate the following:

1. Partnership allows two or more persons to pool their financial resources and put together funds that could not be raised by any of them separately.
2. Partnership allows two or more persons to bring different resources — money, expertise, personal connections, talent, or experience — together in a business venture.

3. Partnership provides a simple, convenient way for members of a family to cooperate in the operation and continuance of a family business.
4. Partnership allows two or more persons to give each other the emotional support needed to undertake a business venture.

Advantages and Disadvantages of a Partnership

Advantages

1. Compared to the corporation, a partnership is simple to organize. It is usually only necessary to register the firm with the provincial government and to pay a nominal fee in accordance with regulations.
2. A partnership allows for the bringing together of greater financial resources and more varied resources than does the single proprietorship.
3. A partnership is not subject to double taxation as is the corporation. A corporation is itself subject to annual income tax. In addition, the shareholders of the corporation are required to pay personal income tax on any dividends that they receive from the corporation.

Disadvantages

1. A partnership has limited life. The death, insolvency, or incapacity of any of the partners usually ends the partnership automatically by law. The remaining partners must arrange to pay out the departed partner's equity and to register a new partnership in order to carry on the business.
2. There is unlimited liability. Every partner is jointly liable for any or all of the debts of the partnership. This means that an unsatisfied creditor may sue any one partner for total payment of a partnership's debt. If the creditor wins the lawsuit, the sued partner must pay the creditor, even to the extent of selling off personal property and suffering personal hardship. The sued partner in turn has the lawful right to recover from the other partners, but this is usually time-consuming, costly, and inconvenient. In extreme circumstances, the other partners may not be able to pay, in which case the sued partner is the victim of what is essentially unfair treatment.
3. There is mutual agency. This means that all of the partners are bound by the acts of any one of them, provided that the acts are within the normal scope of the firm's activities. If one of the partners happens to make a poor business decision, the others cannot disclaim responsibility except in special circumstances.

Partnership Agreement

The formation of a partnership is not a simple matter. As you have seen, partnerships are formed for various reasons, resulting in a variety of ownership situations.

No one should enter into a partnership without first obtaining legal advice. A lawyer will attend to the registration of the firm, provide professional advice to safeguard the interests of the individual partners, and prepare the partnership agreement. The **partnership agreement** is a legal contract that sets forth the specific terms and conditions of the partnership. The agreement helps the partners to avoid dissatisfaction and poor relationships from the very beginning, and the partnership has a better chance for success and survival.

The following details are included in a partnership agreement:

1. The firm's name and address.
2. The partners' names and addresses.
3. The date of formation of the partnership.
4. The nature of the partnership business.
5. The duties of the individual partners and the amount of time that they are expected to devote to the business.
6. The amount of capital to be contributed by each of the partners.
7. The salaries (if any) to be paid to each of the partners.
8. The rate of interest (if any) to be paid on each of the partners' capital balances.
9. The ratio of sharing income and loss.
10. The procedure to be followed in the case of unforeseen termination of the partnership by the death or bankruptcy of a partner.

Partnership Acts

The Partnership Acts of the various provinces serve as general protective measures for persons who have entered into partnerships. The terms of these acts, however, are not fair in all circumstances. In particular, the condition that 'in the absence of a partnership agreement, profits and losses are to be divided equally' may be unfair in many instances. The possibility of being bound by the terms of a provincial partnership act is a strong reason for ensuring that there is an effective partnership agreement.

21.2 Accounting for Simple Partnership Formations

There is no simple set of rules to be followed in establishing the accounts of a partnership. Circumstances vary greatly and each case must be considered separately. This is one of the reasons why professional opinion should be obtained.

To introduce you to accounting for partnerships, and to add to your understanding of partnerships in general, some additional partnership situations are described below. Bear in mind that these are simplified cases and are not to be thought of as typical. They are meant to show the general accounting treatment of partnerships without any of the legal complexities.

Case 1 *Formation of a new business by investment of cash*

Frank Henderson and Charles Wright had been long-time senior employees of Paper Products Company. The two men were dismissed from their positions when the company was taken over by a large corporation. Both men have worked in the paper products business since leaving high school and have no other skills or experience except in this particular line of work.

For several reasons, the two men decide to establish a paper products business of their own. They agree to form a partnership in which both are equal partners. To establish the business, $50 000 capital is needed to obtain the necessary furniture and equipment. By mortgaging their homes and selling some investments, the two men each raise $25 000 in cash. After obtaining the necessary legal and accounting advice, and depositing the $50 000 cash in a business bank account, the partnership of Henderson, Wright Paper Products is established. The first accounting entry in the new set of company books is the following:

Bank	50 000	
Frank Henderson, Capital		25 000
Charles Wright, Capital		25 000

After the above entries have been posted, the accounts of the business are as follows:

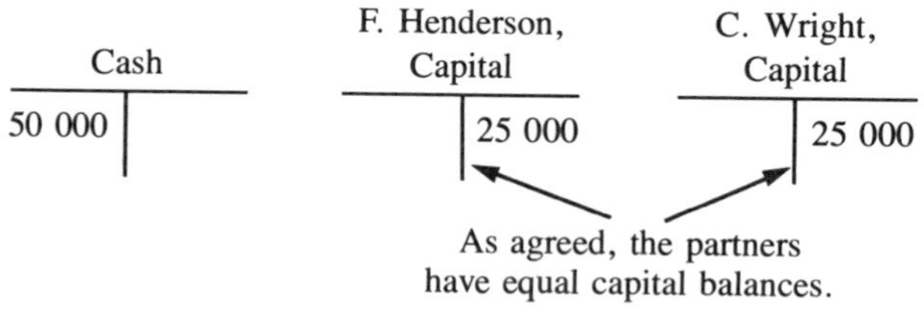

In this situation, the following conditions apply:

1. There is no existing business.
2. An entirely new business is formed.
3. New capital in the form of cash is introduced into the business.
4. No money changes hands privately.

Case 2 *Purchase from the owner of a part interest in an existing business at book value*

Henry Harris is the owner of a well-established and profitable business. He has an equity in the business of $80 000. Because recent expansion has placed a heavy burden on Mr. Harris, he feels the need of assistance at a senior level of responsibility. Jack Soo, a bright young engineer, has agreed to go into business with Mr. Harris and to provide the much needed assistance. The two men form a partnership with the following terms and conditions:

1. Jack Soo is to pay $40 000 to Henry Harris personally for a one-half interest in the business.
2. Net income or net loss of the partnership is to be shared equally.
3. Jack Soo is to gradually assume an equal share of the management responsibility.

After the partnership arrangements have been concluded and the $40 000 has been paid to Mr. Harris, an accounting entry is made in the books of the existing business to establish the partnership. The entry is as follows:

Henry Harris, Capital	40 000	
Jack Soo, Capital		40 000

The books contain the following accounts *before* the above entries are posted:

Cash		Equipment		H. Harris, Capital	
20 000		60 000			80 000

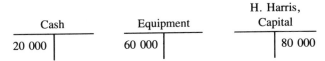

After the above entries are posted, the accounts of the business are as follows:

Cash		Equipment		H. Harris, Capital		J. Soo, Capital	
20 000		60 000		40 000	80 000		40 000

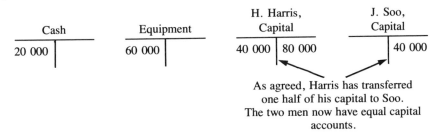

As agreed, Harris has transferred one half of his capital to Soo. The two men now have equal capital accounts.

In this situation, the following conditions apply:

1. There is already an existing business.
2. No new capital is introduced into the business.
3. Any money that changes hands between the partners does so privately, outside of the business.

Case 3 *Introduction into a business of a partner who invests cash and other assets*

T. Wolfe has a small prosperous business which is growing rapidly. Assume that the accounts of her business, in which she has an equity of $75 000, are as follows:

Cash		Equipment		T. Wolfe, Capital	
10 000		65 000			75 000

The business has progressed to the stage where additional facilities and equipment are necessary, but Ms. Wolfe does not have the capital with which to finance the expansion. She has therefore agreed to enter into partnership with R. Hulf on the condition that he contribute $10 000 cash and a building valued at $40 000 to the business. The agreement states that the partners' Capital accounts be kept in a 60:40 ratio and that Wolfe and Hulf share net income or net loss in the ratio of 60:40, respectively. The accounting entry to record the incoming partner's investment is recorded in the existing set of books as follows:

Bank	10 000	
Building	40 000	
R. Hulf, Capital		50 000

After the above accounting entry has been posted, the accounts of the business are as follows:

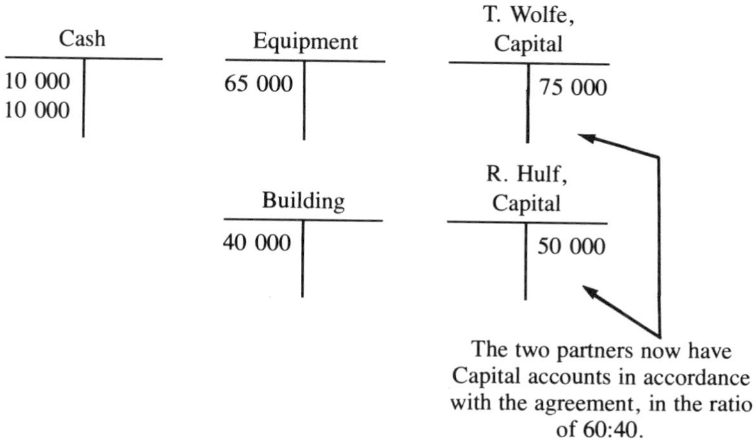

In this situation, the following conditions apply:

1. There is already an existing business.
2. New capital in the form of cash and a building is introduced into the business.
3. No money changes hands privately.

Case 4 *Two existing businesses join together.*

F. Marston and J. Lawson each own a small drugstore. Their stores are located within a few blocks of each other. Their small business operations are threatened by a proposed large shopping centre which will include a large drugstore as one of its units. The new centre is expected to seriously affect the small nearby stores.

Rather than risk financial failure, the two men decide to join together to lease and operate the new drugstore in the shopping centre. In preparation for the move, the two men arrange to have their business assets evaluated by an independent appraiser.

The move to the new store is to take place on July 1, 19––. On that day, the new business is to assume the following assets and accounts payable of the former businesses at the appraised values:

	Marston	*Lawson*
Accounts Receivable	$ 5 000	$ 6 000
Merchandise Inventory	25 000	19 000
Supplies	500	350
Store and Office Equipment	7 500	8 200
Delivery Equipment	4 000	4 800
Total Assets	$42 000	$38 350
Accounts Payable	$12 500	$10 000
Owner's Equity	$29 500	$28 350

The partners agree to the following:

1. Each of them is free to sell or dispose of any other business property as he sees fit.
2. Lawson must bring his equity up to the value of Marston's by contributing cash to the partnership in the amount of $1 150.

The accounting entries to set up the partnership in a new set of books are as follows:

July 1	Accounts Receivable	5 000	
	Merchandise Inventory	25 000	
	Supplies	500	
	Store and Office Equipment	7 500	
	Delivery Equipment	4 000	
	Accounts Payable		12 500
	F. Marston, Capital		29 500
	To record the appraised assets and accounts payable of F. Marston.		
July 1	Bank	1 150	
	Accounts Receivable	6 000	
	Merchandise Inventory	19 000	
	Supplies	350	
	Store and Office Equipment	8 200	
	Delivery Equipment	4 800	
	Accounts Payable		10 000
	J. Lawson, Capital		29 500
	To record the appraised assets and accounts payable and cash contribution of J. Lawson.		

After the above entries have been posted, the accounts of the business are as follows:

Account	Debit	Credit
Cash	1 150	
Accounts Receivable	5 000 6 000	
Mdse. Inventory	25 000 19 000	
Supplies	500 350	
Store & Office Equip.	7 500 8 200	
Delivery Equip.	4 000 4 800	
Accounts Payable		12 500 10 000
J. Lawson, Capital		29 500
F. Marston, Capital		29 500

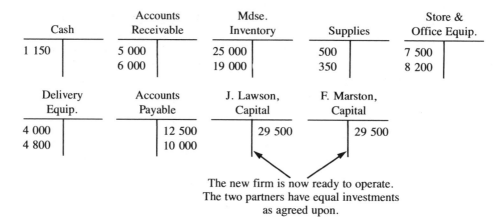

The new firm is now ready to operate. The two partners have equal investments as agreed upon.

In this situation, the following conditions apply:

1. Two existing businesses are joined together.
2. A new business is formed which takes over most of the assets and the accounts payable of the individual proprietorships.
3. No money changes hands privately between the partners.

Note: Cases 1 to 4 describe very simple partnership formations. But partnership formations are seldom simple. Complexities exist in nearly all partnership formations, and professional advice is almost always necessary. The following case shows a more complex but common situation.

Case 5 *Purchase from the owner of a part interest in an existing business at a price greater than its book value*

John De Luca is the sole owner of the only commercial licence to operate a taxi business in the small suburb of Rockton, Ontario. As a result, his taxi business has thrived. Mr. De Luca's investment in the business is $60 000. This includes four cars, a radio and other equipment, and a temporary building. The net income figures for the last three years are $45 000, $48 000, and $50 000, respectively. Profits are expected to continue to grow.

Because Mr. De Luca is nearing retirement age, he is trying to sell a one-half interest in his business. The sale would give him cash for his personal use and would reduce his direct involvement. George Blackburn has expressed interest in the partnership, but the two men have not made a deal.

De Luca tells Blackburn that the business is expected to earn approximately $50 000 annually. As an equal partner, Blackburn would earn $25 000 a year. Therefore, De Luca argues that Blackburn should pay in the range of $200 000 for the partnership.

The book value of a one-half interest in the business is only $30 000. However, Blackburn knows that he cannot expect to buy into the business at book value.

He knows that the price of a business depends more on its earning power than on any other factor.

Eventually the two men agree to a partnership in which Blackburn acquires a full one-half interest in the business by paying De Luca $180 000 privately. Before the new partnership is formed, the accounts of the business are as follows:

Account	Debit	Credit
Cash	2 000	
Autos	28 000	
Equipment	12 000	
Building	18 000	
J. De Luca, Capital		60 000

The following accounting entry admits the new partner to the business:

	Debit	Credit
J. De Luca, Capital	$30 000	
G. Blackburn, Capital		$30 000

After the above entry has been posted, the accounts of the business are as follows:

Account	Debit	Credit
Cash	2 000	
Autos	28 000	
Equipment	12 000	
Building	18 000	
De Luca, Capital	30 000	60 000
Blackburn, Capital		30 000

Equal capital accounts as agreed.

In this situation, the following conditions apply:

1. There is already a new business.
2. No new capital is introduced into the business.
3. Any money which changes hands between the partners does so privately, outside of the business.
4. Part of the business is sold for more than its book value.

Notice that this case is exactly the same as Case 2, except that the price paid is more than the book value of the share. As this case indicates, a business is worth more than its book value when it enjoys above-average profits. These profits may result from good management, superior location, or some other factor.

The sale of a business or the introduction of new partners may occur in a number of ways, and can involve *bonus* payments, or payments for goodwill. **Goodwill** is the value of a business in excess of its book value.

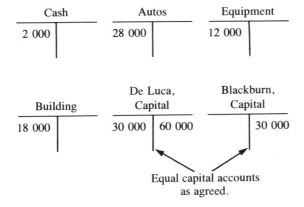

Case 6 *Introduction of a partner who invests cash into the business and agrees to pay a capital bonus to the existing partner*

Jerry Mathews is the proprietor of Ontario Developers, a relatively new company in the business of house building and community development. Although the company is earning above-average profits, it is in a short cash position because of heavy cost outlays in a number of long-term projects. These projects are expected to bring in substantial profits, but not for two or three years.

When exploring sources of additional funds, Mathews meets Barry Richardson. Richardson has money available and is anxious to become a full partner in the business. Richardson agrees to contribute $100 000 in cash to the business for a 50 percent interest in profits and capital.

Mathews's present equity of $50 000 is reflected by the following T-accounts:

Account	Debit	Credit
Cash	1 000	
Equipment	20 000	
Buildings	50 000	
Bank Loan		21 000
J. Mathews, Capital		50 000

The accounting entries to admit Richardson as a partner are as follows:

Bank	$100 000	
B. Richardson, Capital		$100 000
To record the receipt of $100 000 from B. Richardson		
B. Richardson, Capital	$25 000	
J. Mathews, Capital		$25 000
To adjust the partners' capital accounts to a 50:50 ratio; bonus to Mathews		

After these two entries have been posted, the accounts of the business are as follows:

Account	Debit	Credit
Cash	1 000 100 000	
Equipment	20 000	
Buildings	50 000	
Bank Loan		21 000
J. Mathews, Capital		50 000 25 000
B. Richardson, Capital	25 000	100 000

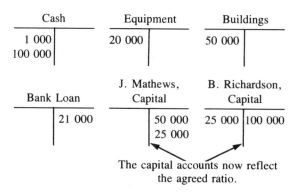

The capital accounts now reflect the agreed ratio.

In this situation, the following conditions apply:

1. There is already an existing business.
2. A new partner introduces new capital into the business.
3. No money changes hands privately.
4. An adjustment is necessary in the partners' capital accounts in order for them to reflect the correct ratio. In this case the adjustment is in favour of the existing partner, who has received what is regarded as a bonus. Under quite different circumstances, the incoming partner could receive a bonus.

21.3 Distribution of Net Income or Net Loss in a Partnership

In a one-owner business, net income, net loss, and drawings are handled in the accounts in a straightforward manner. In a partnership, this process is more complicated. Net income must be properly distributed to the partners' individual equity accounts. This is important for the following reasons:

1. Interest may be paid to the partners based on the balance in their Capital accounts.
2. In the event of a partnership termination, the net assets of the partnership are distributed to the partners in the ratio of their Capital account balances.
3. Income tax law states that the net income of a partnership is deemed to be earned by the individual partners on the last day of the fiscal period. The way in which net income is distributed, therefore, affects the calculation of the partners' individual income taxes.

Factors Affecting the Distribution of Net Income or Net Loss

The following three factors affect the calculation for the distribution of net income or net loss to the partners.

1. *Salaries*. A partner's share of net income (or net loss) often includes some payment for active participation in the running of the business. For example, one partner may participate full-time in the operation of the business and another may not participate at all. Clearly, the one who participates should receive something extra for time and effort. This is generally referred to as salary.

2. *Interest*. A partner's share of net income (or net loss) may include something for the size of his investment in the business. For example, assume that one partner's investment in the business is $100 000 and another's is $20 000. An agreement to pay interest at 8 percent would reward the partners with $8 000

and $1 600, respectively, for the use of their capital. This is generally referred to as interest.

3. *Income- or loss-sharing ratio*. Individual partners expect to receive extra compensation if they bring special talent, connections, or experience to the partnership. For example, a partner may have some special ability or family connections that will bring additional business to the company. This partner will expect compensation as a result.

   Special qualities that are brought to the partnership by the individual partners are taken into account when their **income- or loss-sharing ratio** is decided on. This is the ratio in which the partners share net income or net loss, after first deducting for salaries and interest.

Note: Salaries and interest are prior charges against the net income or net loss when calculating the distribution. In other words, salaries and interest are distributed first. The remaining net income or net loss is then distributed in the income- or loss-sharing ratio.

Statement of Distribution of Net Income

The net income for a partnership is arrived at in the customary manner by means of a work sheet. When the net income is known, the amount that goes to each partner must be calculated. The factors involved in the calculation, discussed in the previous section, are stated in the partnership agreement.

Note: In the absence of a partnership agreement, income and loss are divided equally in accordance with government regulation. Such an equal division does not take into consideration any special contributions of individual partners and may not be fair in all circumstances.

A formal **statement of distribution of net income** must be prepared to show how the net income of the partners is calculated.

Case 1 *Net income greater than salaries plus interest*

Morris and Graves are partners. Their Capital accounts are $50 000 and $20 000, respectively. Their partnership agreement stipulates the following:

1. Graves is allowed a salary of $11 000, and Morris, a salary of $5 000.
2. Interest is allowed on the balances in the Capital accounts at the rate of 10 percent.
3. After allowing for salaries and interest, the balance of the net income is divided equally.

At December 31, 19--, the end of their fiscal year, the partnership net income was $65 312.08. The net income is divided according to the following calculation:

	Morris	Graves	Total
1. Allocate salaries to partners:	5 000 -	11 000 -	16 000 -
2. Allocate interest to partners:	5 000 -	2 000 -	7 000 -
Morris-10% of $50 000 = $5 000			
Graves-10% of $20 000 = $2 000			
Subtotals	10 000 -	13 000 -	23 000 -
3. Determine balance of net income:			
$65 312.08			
less 23 000.00			
$42 312.08 divided equally	21 156 04	21 156 04	42 312 08
Totals to Partners	31 156 04	34 156 04	65 312 08

This calculation is formally presented by means of the statement of distribution of net income as shown in Figure 21.2.

MORRIS AND GRAVES
STATEMENT OF DISTRIBUTION OF NET INCOME
YEAR ENDED DECEMBER 31, 19--

Net Income available for distribution			$65 312.08
	Morris's Share	*Graves's Share*	*Total*
Salary allowed to Graves	$ 5 000.00	$11 000.00	$16 000.00
Interest at 10 percent allowed on Capital account balances	5 000.00	2 000.00	7 000.00
Morris: 10% of $50 000 = $5 000			
Graves: 10% of $20 000 = $2 000			
Balance of net income divided equally	21 156.04	21 156.04	$42 312.08
Totals	$28 656.04	$36 656.04	$65 312.08

Figure 21.2 A statement of the distribution of net income where net income is greater than salaries plus interest.

Case 2 *Net income less than salaries plus interest*

On June 30, 19--, the partnership of Watts, Tate, and Barlow completes a fiscal year with a net income figure of $20 000. The partnership agreement specifies that net income or net loss is to be allocated to the partners according to the following terms:

1. The following salaries are allowed: Watt, $9 000; Tate, $4 500; Barlow, nil.
2. Interest is allowed on Capital account balances at 8 percent. (The partners' Capital account balances are as follows: Watts, $40 000; Tate, $50 000; Barlow, $100 000.)
3. The remaining net income or net loss is to be divided as follows: Watts, 25 percent; Tate, 25 percent; Barlow, 50 percent.

The distribution of net income is calculated as follows for the partnership of Watts, Tate, and Barlow. Notice that in this particular case the total of the salaries and interest is greater than the net income figure. This requires special handling on the statement.

	Watts	Tate	Barlow	Total
1. Allocate salaries to partners:	9 000 -	4 500 -	-	13 500 -
2. Allocate interest to partners:	3 200 -	4 000 -	8 000 -	15 200 -
Watts - 8% of $40 000 = $3 200				
Tate - 8% of $50 000 = $4 000				
Barlow - 8% of $100 000 = $8 000				
Subtotals	12 200 -	8 500 -	8 000 -	28 700 -
3. Deduct: Net Income Deficiency				
$ 28 700.00				
Less 20 000.00				
8 700.00 divided in				
ratio of 1:1:2	2 175 -	2 175 -	4 350 -	8 700 -
Totals to Partners	10 025 -	6 325 -	3 650 -	20 000 -

This calculation is formally presented by means of the statement of distribution of net income as shown in Figure 21.3.

Accounting for the Net Earnings of a Partnership

According to law, a partner participates in a partnership for a share of the earnings of the business, and not for a salary or for interest on an investment. Therefore,

WATTS, TATE, AND BARLOW
STATEMENT OF DISTRIBUTION OF NET INCOME
YEAR ENDED JUNE 30, 19--

Net Income available for distribution				$20 000
	Watts's Share	*Tate's Share*	*Barlow's Share*	*Total*
Salaries allowed to partners	$ 9 000	$4 500	—	$13 500
Interest allowed on Capital accounts at 8 percent	3 200	4 000	8 000	15 200
Watts: 8% of $ 40 000 = $3 200				
Tate: 8% of $ 50 000 = $4 000				
Barlow: 8% of $100 000 = $8 000				
Subtotals	$12 200	$8 500	$8 000	$28 700
Deduct: Net income deficiency in ratio of 1:1:2	2 175	2 175	4 350	8 700
Totals	$10 025	$6 325	$3 650	$20 000

Figure 21.3 A statement of distribution of net income where net income is less than salaries plus interest.

salaries and interest are only seen as mathematical factors in the process of dividing net income. Although salaries and interest are used in the calculations at the end of the fiscal period, they are not entered in the accounts.

The partners usually need to receive money from the business during the year. Any such payments are considered drawings and are debited to the partners' respective Drawings accounts. The partners should know roughly how well the business is doing. Therefore, they base the size of their drawings on the expected net income for the year. In some businesses, drawings are fixed by a formal agreement.

The partners' Drawings accounts and their respective shares of the net income are transferred to their Capital accounts as part of the closing entry process. This process is explained later in the chapter.

21.4 Financial Statements of a Partnership

Financial statements for a partnership include more than the balance sheet and the income statement. A partnership also requires a statement of distribution of net income, which you have just studied, as well as a statement of partners' capital, which will be explained shortly.

Jones, Ross, & Warner — Work Sheet — Year Ended Dec. 31, 19–

Accounts	Trial Balance		Adjustments		Income Statement		Balance Sheet	
	Dr.	Cr.	Dr.	Cr.	Dr.	Cr.	Dr.	Cr.
Petty Cash	100 -						100 -	
Bank	3700 -						3700 -	
Accounts Receivable	37461 -						37461 -	
Allow. for Doubtful Accs.		1956 -		102 -				2058 -
Supplies	1500 -			625 -			875 -	
Prepaid Insurance	900 -			484 -			416 -	
Investment in Property	20000 -						20000 -	
Furniture and Equipment	7000 -						7000 -	
Accum. Depr. Furn. & Equip.		3490 -		702 -				4192 -
Automobiles	12000 -						12000 -	
Accum. Depr. Automobiles		4875 -		2137 50				7012 50
Accounts Payable		5962 -		175 -				6137 -
M. Jones, Capital		19452 12						19452 12
M. Jones, Drawings	18500 -						18500 -	
G. Ross, Capital		15137 09						15137 09
G. Ross, Drawings	14000 -						14000 -	
A. Warner, Capital		25410 79						25410 79
A. Warner, Drawings	22396 -						22396 -	
Sales		82940 -				82940 -		
Advertising	3000 -				3000 -			
Automobile Expense	4600 -				4600 -			
General Expense	350 -		175 -		525 -			
Light, Heat, and Water	600 -				600 -			
Rent	2400 -				2400 -			
Telephone	1290 -				1290 -			
Wages	9426 -		110 -		9536 -			
	159223 -	159223 -						
Bad Debts Expense			102 -		102 -			
Supplies Expense			625 -		625 -			
Insurance Expense			484 -		484 -			
Deprec. Furn. & Equip.			702 -		702 -			
Deprec. Automobiles			2137 50		2137 50			
Accrued Wages Payable				110 -				110 -
			4335 50	4335 50	26001 50	82940 -	136448 -	79509 50
Net Income					56938 50			56938 50
					82940 -	82940 -	136448 -	136448 -

Figure 21.4 The work sheet of Jones, Ross, and Warner.

The financial statements of a partnership are usually constituted as follows:

Statement No. 1 *The Balance Sheet*
Statement No. 2 *The Income Statement*
Statement No. 3 *Statement of Partners' Capital*
Statement No. 4 *Statement of Distribution of Net Income*

When preparing financial statements for a partnership, information found on Statement 4 is needed to complete Statement 3, and information found on Statement 3 is needed to complete Statement 1. Therefore, Statement 4 must be completed before Statement 3, and Statement 3 must be completed before Statement 1. Statement 2 may be prepared at any time because the other statements have no bearing on it.

The study of the preparation of the four statements begins below. The sample statements are based on the simplified work sheet for Jones, Ross, and Warner shown in Figure 21.4.

Statement of Distribution of Net Income (Statement 4)

The net income figure of $56 938.50 to be distributed to the partners is picked up from the work sheet. Additional information necessary to make the calculation is found in the partnership agreement as follows:

1. G. Ross and A. Warner are to receive annual salaries of $5 000 each.
2. Interest is allowed on partners' capital at the rate of 10 percent.
3. After allowing for salaries and interest, the balance of net income or net loss is apportioned in the ratio of 2:1:2 to Jones, Ross, and Warner, respectively.

This information is used to prepare the statement of distribution of net income shown in Figure 21.5.

Statement 4

JONES, ROSS, AND WARNER
STATEMENT OF DISTRIBUTION OF NET INCOME
YEAR ENDED DECEMBER 31, 19--

Net income available for distribution				$56 938.50
	M. Jones	*G. Ross*	*A. Warner*	*Total*
Salaries allowed to partners		$ 5 000.00	$ 5 000.00	$10 000.00
Interest on Capital Accounts	$ 1 945.21	1 513.71	2 541.08	6 000.00
M. Jones $19 452.12 at 10%				
G. Ross $15 137.09 at 10%				
A. Warner $25 410.79 at 10%				
Balance of net income divided in ratio of 2:1:2	16 375.40	8 187.70	16 375.40	40 938.50
Total distribution to partners	$18 320.61	$14 701.41	$23 916.48	$56 938.50

Figure 21.5 The statement of distribution of net income for Jones, Ross, and Warner.

Statement of Partners' Capital (Statement 3)

The **statement of partners' capital** shows the continuity of the partners' Capital accounts for the fiscal period. Except for lack of space, this information would be included in the Equity section of the balance sheet. However, because several partners may have to be accounted for, the information is usually shown on a separate statement.

The statement begins with the Capital account balances as shown on the previous year's statement. It then summarizes the increases and decreases for the current fiscal period, and arrives at the current end-of-period balances.

The information for this statement is usually picked up from the work sheet and from the statement of distribution of net income. The only exception to this occurs when a partner has increased capital investment during the fiscal period so that the balance in the partner's Capital account does not coincide with the figure shown on the prior statement. In this event, it is necessary to analyze the partner's Capital account in order to find the amount of the increase to be shown on the current statement.

For Jones, Ross, and Warner, the statement of partners' capital is shown in Figure 21.6.

Statement 3

JONES, ROSS, AND WARNER
STATEMENT OF PARTNERS' CAPITAL
YEAR ENDED DECEMBER 31, 19--

	M. Jones	*G. Ross*	*A. Warner*	*Total*
Capital Balances January 1	$19 452.12	$15 137.09	$25 410.79	$60 000.00
Add: Share of Net Income for Year (Statement 4)	18 320.61	14 701.41	23 916.48	56 938.50
	$37 772.73	$29 838.50	$49 327.27	$116 938.50
Deduct: Drawings for Year	18 500.00	14 000.00	22 396.00	54 896.00
Capital Balances December 31	$19 272.73	$15 838.50	$26 931.27	$62 042.50

Figure 21.6 The statement of partners' capital for Jones, Ross, and Warner.

Balance Sheet (Statement 1)

The balance sheet of a partnership is the same as for a sole proprietorship, except for the Equity section. The final capital figures are taken from Statement 3. The balance sheet for Jones, Ross, and Warner appears in Figure 21.7.

Statement 1

JONES, ROSS, AND WARNER
BALANCE SHEET
DECEMBER 31, 19--

ASSETS			
Current Assets			
Petty Cash		$ 100.00	
Bank		3 700.00	
Accounts Receivable	$37 461.00		
Less Allowance for Doubtful Accounts	2 058.00	35 403.00	$39.203.00
Prepaid Expenses			
Supplies		$ 875.00	
Insurance		416.00	1 291.00
Investment			
Property — at cost			20 000.00
Fixed Assets			
Furniture and Equipment	$ 7 000.00		
Less Accumulated Depreciation	4 192.00	$ 2 808.00	
Automobiles	$12 000.00		
Less Accumulated Depreciation	7 012.50	4 987.50	7 795.50
			$68 289.50
LIABILITIES			
Current Liabilities			
Accounts Payable		$ 6 137.00	
Accrued Wages		110.00	$ 6 247.00
PARTNERS' EQUITY			
Partners' Capital (Statement 3)			
M. Jones		$19 272.73	
G. Ross		15 838.50	
A. Warner		26 931.27	62 042.50
			$68 289.50

Figure 21.7 The balance sheet for Jones, Ross, and Warner.

Income Statement (Statement 2)

The income statement is prepared in the customary manner. Figure 21.8 shows the income statement for Jones, Ross, and Warner.

Statement 2

JONES, ROSS, AND WARNER
INCOME STATEMENT
YEAR ENDED DECEMBER 31, 19--

Income		
Sales		$82 940.00
Operating Expenses		
Advertising	$3 000.00	
Bad Debts	102.00	
Automotive Expense	4 600.00	
Depreciation of Automobiles	2 137.50	
Depreciation of Furniture and Equipment	702.00	
General Expense	525.00	
Insurance	484.00	
Light, Heat, and Water	600.00	
Rent	2 400.00	
Supplies	625.00	
Telephone	1 290.00	
Wages	9 536.00	26 001.50
Net Income		$56 938.50

Figure 21.8 The income statement for Jones, Ross, and Warner.

21.4 Adjusting and Closing Entries for a Partnership

You have already studied the theory and practice of adjusting and closing entries. However, a slight change in the process is required when adjusting and closing the books of a partnership. A partnership has more than one Capital account and more than one Drawings account.

The adjusting and closing entries process for a partnership is outlined below. Again, Jones, Ross, and Warner are used as the example.

1. The first step in the closing entry process is the same for a partnership as for a

proprietorship. Journalize only those adjustments that appear in the Adjustments column of the work sheet. These are shown below for Jones, Ross, and Warner.

Dec	31	General Expense	175 -	
		Accounts Payable		175 -
	31	Bad Debts Expense	102 -	
		Allow. for Doubtful Accounts		102 -
	31	Supplies Expense	625 -	
		Supplies		625 -
	31	Insurance Expense	484 -	
		Prepaid Insurance		484 -
	31	Deprec. Furniture & Equipment	702 -	
		Accum. Deprec. Furn. & Equip.		702 -
	31	Depreciation Automobiles	2137 50	
		Accum. Deprec. Automobiles		2137 50
	31	Wages Expense	110 -	
		Accrued Wages Payable		110 -
		Adjusting entries for year.		

2. Make an accounting entry that debits each account balance that appears in the credit column of the Income Statement section of the work sheet. Credit the Income Summary account with the column total. The entry for Jones, Ross, and Warner is shown below.

Dec	31	Sales	82940 -	
		Income Summary		82940 -
		To close out Income Section		
		credits to Income Summary		
		account.		

3. Make an accounting entry that credits each account balance that appears in the debit column of the Income Statement section of the work sheet. Debit the Income Summary account with the column total. The entry for Jones, Ross, and Warner is shown below.

				Debit	Credit
Dec	31	Income Summary		26 001 50	
		Advertising			3 000 -
		Automobile Expense			4 600 -
		General Expense			525 -
		Light, Heat, and Water			600 -
		Rent			2 400 -
		Telephone			1 290 -
		Wages			9 536 -
		Bad Debts Expense			102 -
		Supplies Expense			625 -
		Insurance Expense			484 -
		Deprec. Furn. & Equip.			702 -
		Deprec. Automobiles			2 137 50
		To close out Income Section debits			
		to Income Summary account.			

At this point, all of the revenue and expense accounts are closed out, all accounts requiring an adjustment are adjusted, and the Income Summary account has a balance equal to the net income figure.

4. The figures needed to close out the Income Summary account to the partners' Capital accounts can be found on the final line of the statement of distribution of net income. For Jones, Ross, and Warner this entry is as follows:

				Debit	Credit
Dec	31	Income Summary		56 938 50	
		M. Jones, Capital			18 320 16
		G. Ross, Capital			14 701 41
		A. Warner, Capital			23 916 48
		To apportion net income to partners.			

The Income Summary account is now closed out and the partners' Capital accounts have been increased by their respective shares of net income. The Capital accounts for Jones, Ross, and Warner are as follows:

M. Jones, Capital

				Cr 19 452.12
Dec 31			18 320.61	Cr 37 772.73

G. Ross, Capital

Date	PR	Debit	Credit	Balance
				Cr 15 137.09
Dec 31			14 701.41	Cr 29 838.50

A. Warner, Capital

Date	PR	Debit	Credit	Balance
				Cr 25 410.79
Dec 31			23 916.48	Cr 49 327.27

5. The final closing entry closes out each partner's Drawings account to the partner's Capital account. The amounts for this entry are picked up from the work sheet. For Jones, Ross, and Warner, these entries are as follows:

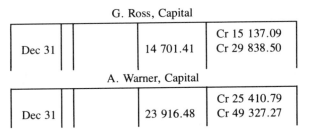

Date		Account	PR	Debit	Credit
Dec	31	M. Jones, Capital		18 500 –	
		G. Ross, Capital		14 000 –	
		A. Warner, Capital		22 396 –	
		M. Jones, Drawings			18 500 –
		G. Ross, Drawings			14 000 –
		A. Warner, Drawings			22 396 –
		To close out Drawings accounts			
		to capital.			

When this five-step closing procedure is complete, the ledger accounts will be adjusted and closed out as necessary. The partners' Capital accounts will then reflect the proper balances as at the fiscal year-end. For the partnership of Ross, Jones, and Warner, the Capital accounts at this stage are as follows:

M. Jones, Capital

Date	PR	Debit	Credit	Balance
				Cr 19 452.12
Dec 31			18 320.61	Cr 37 772.73
Dec 31		18 500.00		Cr 19 272.73

G. Ross, Capital

Date	PR	Debit	Credit	Balance
				Cr 15 137.09
Dec 31			14 701.41	Cr 29 838.50
Dec 31		14 000.00		Cr 15 838.50

A. Warner, Capital

Date	PR	Debit	Credit	Balance
				Cr 25 410.79
Dec 31			23 916.48	Cr 49 327.27
Dec 31		22 396.00		Cr 26 931.27

Clearly, the partners' Capital accounts at this point agree with the statement of partners' capital, and with the Equity section of the balance sheet.

21.5 Termination of Partnerships

A partnership may be terminated for a number of reasons. A partnership may be sold as a going concern, or it may be liquidated, in which case the business ceases to operate. A **liquidation** involves the disposal of the partnership assets for cash, the payment of the partnership debts, the apportionment to the partners of the gain or loss on disposal of the assets, and the payment of the bank balance to the partners.

A partnership is legally terminated upon the death of a partner. The family or estate of the deceased partner is entitled to receive a share in the worth of the business. The remaining partners may wish to continue to operate the business under a new partnership arrangement. In this case, advance provision can be made, often through life insurance, for sufficient funds to pay out the deceased's share. Otherwise, the remaining partners may need to borrow heavily, or even to liquidate the partnership against their wishes.

The accounting for partnership termination is complicated. Termination usually requires the professional services of lawyers and public accountants. The following simplified example will give you a general idea of the process.

Termination of King and Queen Sales

The partnership of King and Queen Sales has two partners, A. King and R. Queen, who have mutually agreed to liquidate the business. Figure 21.9 shows the trial balance of King and Queen Sales at December 31, 19--, after the closing entries are posted.

KING AND QUEEN SALES
POST-CLOSING TRIAL BALANCE
DECEMBER 31, 19--

Bank	$ 5 700.00	
Accounts Receivable	2 300.00	
Allowance for Doubtful Accounts		$ 275.00
Inventory	3 700.00	
Land	12 000.00	
Buildings	33 000.00	
Accumulated Depreciation Buildings		2 925.00
Equipment	12 575.00	
Accumulated Depreciation Equipment		4 075.00
Bank Loan		14 000.00
Accounts Payable		8 000.00
Mortgage Payable		10 000.00
A. King, Capital		20 000.00
R. Queen, Capital		10 000.00
	$69 275.00	$69 275.00

Figure 21.9 The post-closing trial balance of King and Queen Sales.

Conversion of Assets into Cash

The assets must first be converted into cash. On disposal of the assets, gains or losses and any expenses of liquidation are charged to an account called Gain or Loss on Realization.

1. The net accounts receivable are sold to a collection agency at a discount of 25 percent. A cheque for $1 518.75 is received from the collection agency. The following entry records this transaction:

Bank	1 518.75	
Allowance for Doubtful Accounts	275.00	
Gain or Loss on Realization	506.25	
Accounts Receivable		2 300.00
Sale of accounts receivable to Ace Collection Agency at a discount of 25 percent.		

2. The inventory and the equipment are sold at public auction for $2 100.00 and $5 300.00, respectively. The following entries record these transactions:

Bank	2 100.00	
Gain or Loss on Realization	1 600.00	
Inventory		3 700.00
Sale of inventory at public auction.		

Bank	5 300.00	
Accum. Deprec. Equipment	4 075.00	
Gain or Loss on Realization	3 200.00	
Equipment		12 575.00
Sale of equipment at public auction.		

3. The land and buildings with the existing mortgage are sold for $65 000.00 less a 5 percent real estate commission. A cheque for $51 750.00 is received. The following entry records this transaction:

Bank	51 750.00	
Mortgage Payable	10 000.00	
Accum. Deprec. Buildings	2 925.00	
Land		12 000.00
Buildings		33 000.00
Gain or Loss on Realization		19 675.00
Sale of property for $65 000, less 5 percent real estate commission.		

After the above entries are posted, the following accounts remain:

Bank	$66 368.75	
Bank Loan		$14 000.00
Accounts Payable		8 000.00
A. King, Capital		20 000.00
R. Queen, Capital		10 000.00
Gain or Loss on Realization		14 368.75

Payment of Partnership Debts

The partnership debts are normally settled before any allocations to the partners are considered.

1. The bank is directed to deduct from the company bank account an amount that will pay off the bank loan and any accrued interest. A bank debit memo is received debiting the account for $14 097.05 – $14 000.00 principal and $97.05 interest. The accounting entry is as follows:

Bank Loan	$14 000.00	
Gain or Loss on Realization	97.05	
Bank		$14 097.05
Settlement of bank loan and accrued interest.		

2. Cheques are issued in settlement of all accounts payable. The following entry gives effect to these cheques:

Accounts Payable	$8 000.00	
Bank		$8 000.00
Settlement of all outstanding accounts payable.		

After these two entries are posted, the partnership accounts are as follows:

Bank	$44 271.70	
A. King, Capital		$20 000.00
R. Queen, Capital		10 000.00
Gain or Loss on Realization		14 271.70

Apportionment of Gain or Loss on Realization to Partners

The balance in the Gain or Loss on Realization account is apportioned to the partners in the income- and loss-sharing ratio. King and Queen share income and losses in the ratio of 3:2, respectively. Therefore, King receives 3/5 and Queen 2/5 of the balance of $14 271.70, or $8 563.02 and $5 708.68 respectively. The following accounting entry records this apportionment:

Gain or Loss on Realization	$14 271.70	
A. King, Capital		$8 563.02
R. Queen, Capital		5 708.68
Apportionment of gain on realization to partners in the ratio of 3:2 for King and Queen, respectively.		

After this step, the accounts of the partnership are as follows:

Bank	$44 271.70	
A. King, Capital		$28 563.02
R. Queen, Capital		15 708.68

Payment of Cash to Partners

If all of the partners have credit balances in their Capital accounts, the distribution of cash to the partners is made in proportion to their Capital account balances. In this case, the following accounting entry records the payment to the partners:

A. King, Capital	$28 563.02	
R. Queen, Capital	15 708.68	
Bank		$44 271.70
Cheques to partners closing out the partnership.		

Partner with a Deficit Capital Account Balance

Sometimes there is a debit, or deficit, in the partner's Capital account. In this case, the following termination procedure is common. However, this procedure must be written into the partnership agreement to be binding.

1. The partner with the deficit balance makes up the deficit by contributing cash into the business. Otherwise, there would not be enough cash in the bank to pay off the partners with credit balances.
2. If the partner is unable to make up the deficit in cash, then the amount of the deficit is absorbed by the other partners in the income- or loss-sharing ratio that exists between them alone.

   For example, assume that A, B, and C are partners who share income or loss in the ratio of 1:2:3. If A had a deficit balance and couldn't make it up, B and C would absorb it in the ratio of 2:3. If B had the deficit, A and C would absorb it in the ratio of 1:3. And, if C had the deficit, A and B would absorb it in the ratio of 1:2.

Accounting Terms

partnership
partnership agreement
goodwill
income- or loss-sharing ratio
statement of distribution of net income
statement of partners' capital
liquidation

Review Questions

1. What is meant by 'partnership'?
2. From an accounting point of view, where does the main difference between a proprietorship and a partnership lie?
3. Partnerships are formed for a variety of reasons. Describe two situations in which a partnership might be formed.
4. Briefly, and in your own words, note the advantages and disadvantages of the partnership form of business organization.
5. Explain the purpose of the partnership agreement.
6. In your opinion, what are the three most important items contained in a partnership agreement?
7. Explain the reason for a provincial Partnership Act.
8. When forming a partnership, the persons involved should obtain professional assistance. Briefly explain why.
9. In your own words, explain why cash is not always introduced into a new partnership.
10. New accounting theory for partnerships pertains to year-end activity. Why is this so?
11. State the factors that affect the apportionment of net income or net loss.
12. Why would a partner receive interest? Salary?
13. A partnership usually requires two additional financial statements. Name them.
14. In what order would you prepare the four financial statements for a partnership? Explain.
15. The closing entries for a partnership are not exactly the same as for a proprietorship. Explain why this is so.
16. Name the four steps in the termination of a partnership.
17. If a partner has a deficit balance and cannot make it up, how is the deficit dealt with?

Exercises

Simple Partnership Formations

1. Powell and James form a partnership in which Powell contributes $20 000 and James contributes $10 000. The two men agree that their capital interest in the business will be in the ratio of their respective capital contributions.

   Give the accounting entry to establish the partnership.

2. Foster, Harris, and Russell join together to begin a new business. Foster contributes a building valued at $35 000; Harris contributes equipment valued at $25 000; Russell contributes $20 000 cash. The men agree that their capital accounts will reflect their individual contributions.

Give the accounting entry to record the partners' contributions.

3. Fleming is the sole owner of a cleaning business in which he has an equity of $27 000. In order to finance a modernization of the plant, Fleming has agreed to take Monroe into partnership. Monroe has agreed to contribute $27 000 cash into the business for a one-half interest.

Give the accounting entry to record the introduction of Monroe into the business.

4. Krajacich is the sole owner of a men's clothing store. His equity in the business is $22 000. He makes a deal with Gregory to sell him a one-half interest in the business for $15 000 cash. The money is to be paid directly to Baxter. No new funds are introduced into the business.

Give the accounting entry to record Gregory's interest in the business.

5. McLean, Tracey, and Reynolds reach a decision to go into a new business to build recreational trailers. McLean is regarded as a wizard in this field, and his expertise will be his contribution to the partnership. The other men have little to offer in the way of specific skills. Their contribution to the partnership will be $15 000 each in cash. All three men will work full-time in the business. Although Tracey and Reynolds contribute the total cash, the three men agree that all the capital accounts will be equal.

Give the accounting entry to establish the partnership.

More Difficult Partnership Formations

6. I. James, W. Walsh, and P. Norris are sole proprietors working independently as public accountants. They decide to join together in partnership so that each can specialize in a different aspect of accounting and jointly purchase a new office building.

The partnership is to begin on June 1, 19--. At that time, the appraised assets and liabilities of the individual firms are to be transferred to a new set of books for the partnership. It is agreed that capital balances are to be brought up to the level of the partner with the largest equity by the direct contribution of cash to the partnership.

The appraised values of the assets and liabilities on June 1 are as follows:

	I. James	W. Walsh	P. Norris
Assets			
Bank	$ 1 500	$ 1 200	$ 800
Accounts Receivable	4 700	3 800	4 200
Supplies	740	630	315
Office Equipment	1 100	3 000	1 500
Automobiles	5 000	4 200	5 500
Total Assets	$13 040	$12 830	$12 315
Liabilities			
Accounts Payable	$ 1 350	$ 1 700	$ 950
Owner's Equity	$11 690	$11 130	$11 365

Give the accounting entries to set up the new partnership.

---

7. Johnson and Anderson are partners in a prosperous business. They have capital balances of $60 000 and $50 000 respectively, and they share income or loss in the ratio of 3:2.

   Campbell is admitted to the partnership on the condition that she contributes $70 000 cash for a one-third capital interest.

   Record the accounting entries necessary to admit Campbell into the partnership.

---

8. The partnership of Franks, Morris, and Shane has been experiencing financial difficulties. The capital balances of Franks, Morris, and Shane are $75 000, $75 000, and $30 000 respectively. They share income or loss in the ratio of 3:3:2.

   The partners persuade Walker, a management expert, to join the firm. Because of Walker's special skills, the partners agree to give her a one-quarter interest in the firm for only $20 000.

   Record the accounting entries to introduce the new partner into the business.

---

9. C. Fredericks is the sole proprietor of a dry-cleaning business. Her equity is $70 000. M. Masters and T. Fritz agree to become partners in the business. Each agrees to contribute $50 000 in cash for a one-quarter interest.

   Record the journal entry or entries to establish the partnership, continuing the same set of books.

---

10. Adams and Suarez are partners who share profits or losses in the ratio of 1:2. They have capital account balances of $40 000 and $50 000 respectively. Because the business needs additional funds, a third partner, Simms, is admitted. Simms agrees to contribute $54 000 cash for a one-third interest in capital.

    Record the accounting entry or entries to admit Simms to the partnership.

11. A. Hicks is a sole proprietor with an equity of $73 000. To expand his business, Hicks agrees to take in B. McDoal and T. Wilks as partners. McDoal will pay $125 000 and Wilks will pay $135 000 into the partnership. All three partners will have an equal interest in the business.

Record the accounting entries to establish the partnership.

Distribution of Net Income Exercises

12. C. Lemaire, R. Kennedy, B. Henning, and S. Dudley are lawyers in partnership. They have just completed their December 31, 19--, fiscal year with a net income figure of $126 040.28. Their partnership agreement stipulates that Lemaire and Kennedy, the senior partners, are to receive salaries of $12 500 before distributing the remainder of net income equally.

Calculate the net income of each of the partners. Show your calculations.

13. Black and Associates is a loan company with four partners: R. Allen, M. Hamilton, R. Cooper, and T. Cavanaugh. Their respective Capital account balances are $12 000, $24 000, $18 000, and $30 000. Their partnership agreement states that net income or net loss is to be divided in the ratio of their Capital account balances.

Calculate how the partners would divide a net income of $110 040. Show your calculations.

14. For each of the following situations, informally prepare the calculation of distribution of net income or net losses.

	a.		*b.*		*c.*		*d.*			*e.*		*f.*			*g.*		*h.*		
Partners	A	B	A	B	A	B	A	B	C	A	B	A	B	C	A	B	A	B	C
Capital account balances	50 000	50 000	25 000	150 000	100 000	100 000	20 000	20 000	25 000	100 000	10 000	10 000	20 000	80 000	50 000	100 000	20 000	30 000	40 000
Rate of interest on capital	nil		nil		nil		nil			10%		10%			8%		12%		
Salaries	nil		nil		10 000	25 000	nil			nil	15 000	nil	12 000	8 000	40 000	25 000	10 000	12 000	14 000
Income- or loss-sharing ratio	3 : 2		capital accs		1 : 1		4 : 3 : 2			1 : 2		5 : 3 : 1			1 : 1		3 : 2 : 1		
Net income	$60 000		$72 800		$90 000		$135 000			$86 600		$130 000			$60 000		Loss $48 000		

15. A. Barnes, W. Doby, and S. Barnes are partners who share income and loss in the ratio of 4:4:3, respectively. Their partnership agreement further stipulates that S. Barnes receives a salary of $10 000 while the others receive none, and that interest is to be allowed at 9 percent on the Capital account balances held throughout the year. The Capital account balances have been $20 000, $35 000, and $5 500 for A. Barnes, W. Doby, and S. Barnes, respectively.

Prepare a statement of distribution of net income for the year ended April 30, 19--. The net income was $87 199.21.

16. **For the year ended June 30, 19--, Expert Investors had a net income of $19 640.40. Using the additional information shown below, prepare the statement of distribution of net income for Expert Investors.**

Additional Information:

a. The partners are J. Hunter and C. Lamont.
b. The balances in the partners' Capital accounts are: Hunter, $12 000; Lamont, $30 000.
c. Hunter is to receive a salary of $15 000; Lamont, $7 500.
d. Interest is allowed on Capital account balances at the rate of 8 percent.
e. The balance of net income or net loss is divided equally.

17. **For the year ended June 30, 19--, Industrial Suppliers, owned by Farago and George, had a net income of $37 130. Using the additional information below, prepare the statement of distribution of net income.**

Additional Information:

a. The Capital balances are: Farago, $68 000; George, $17 000.
b. No interest is allowed on capital.
c. Farago is to receive a salary of $25 000; George, $20 000.
d. The balance of net income or net loss is divided in the ratio of the partners' capital account balances.

Financial Statements

18. **The work sheet for Frame Brothers appears on page 669, opposite. Additional information is provided below.**

    1. **Prepare the statement of distribution of net income.**
    2. **Prepare the statement of partners' capital.**
    3. **Prepare the balance sheet for Frame Brothers.**

Additional Information:

a. S. Frame receives a salary of $10 000, and G. Frame receives a salary of $8 000.
b. S. Frame and G. Frame divide the remainder of net income in the ratio of 2:1, respectively.

Work Sheet	Frame Brothers				Year Ended Dec. 31, 19–			
Accounts	Trial Balance		Adjustments		Income Statement		Balance Sheet	
	Dr.	Cr.	Dr.	Cr.	Dr.	Cr.	Dr	Cr.
Petty Cash	50 –						50 –	
Bank	312 70						312 70	
Accounts Receivable	9407 16						9407 16	
Allow. for Doubtful Accs.		315 –		(2) 65 –				380 –
Merchandise Inventory	27055 –				27055 –	28575 –	28575 –	
Supplies	740 –			(3) 415 –			325 –	
Prepaid Insurance	316 –			(4) 204 –			112 –	
Furniture and Equipment	19073 –						19073 –	
Accum. Depr. Furn. & Equip.		4907 20		(5) 2833 16				7740 36
Automobiles	26642 90						26642 90	
Accum. Deprec. Automobiles		11373 12		(6) 4580 93				15954 05
Bank Loan		5000 –						5000 –
Accounts Payable		5721 15		(1) 899 27				6620 42
Sales Tax Payable		791 60						791 60
Employees Inc. Tax Pay'l		402 10						402 10
S. Frame, Capital		20000 –						20000 –
S. Frame, Drawings	10583 06						10583 06	
G. Frame, Capital		20000 –						20000 –
G. Frame, Drawings	10566 70						10566 70	
Sales		135702 70				135702 70		
Bank Charges	450 –				450 –			
Canada Pension Plan Exp.	375 –				375 –			
Light, Heat, and Water	970 20				970 20			
Miscellaneous Expense	192 20				192 20			
Purchases	47312 20		(1) 841 60		48153 80			
Rent	12000 –				12000 –			
Telephone	600 –		(1) 57 67		657 67			
Unemployment Insce. Exp.	146 75				146 75			
Wages	37420 –				37420 –			
	204212 87	204212 87						
Bad Debts Expense			(2) 65 –		65 –			
Supplies Expense			(3) 415 –		415 –			
Insurance Expense			(4) 204 –		204 –			
Deprec. Furn. & Equip.			(5) 2833 16		2833 16			
Deprec. Automobiles			(6) 4580 93		4580 71			
			8997 36	8977 36	135518 71	164277 70	105647 52	76888 53
Net Income					28758 99			28758 99
					164277 70	164277 70	105647 52	105647 52

19. The work sheet and additional information for Oakes, Oakes, and Reid appear below:

Work Sheet	Oakes, Oakes and Reid			Year Ended June 30, 19–				
Accounts	Trial Balance		Adjustments		Income Statement		Balance Sheet	
	Dr.	Cr.	Dr.	Cr.	Dr.	Cr.	Dr.	Cr.
Petty Cash	100 -						100 -	
Bank	1498 74						1498 74	
Accounts Receivable	13285 88						13285 88	
Allow. for Doubtful Accs.		24 50		(2) 588 21				612 71
Supplies	412 70			(3) 96 95			315 75	
Prepaid Insurance	804 10			(4) 343 10			461 -	
Investment in Property	70000 -						70000 -	
Furniture and Equipment	5856 -						5856 -	
Accum. Deprec. Furn. & Equip.		1946 90		(5) 781 82				2728 72
Automobiles	16072 84						16072 84	
Accum. Deprec. Autos		7060 21		(6) 2703 79				9764 -
Accounts Payable		1564 97		(1) 145 -				1709 97
Employees Inc. Tax Pay'l		85 -						85 -
Canada Pension Plan Pay'l		30 75						30 75
K. Oakes, Capital		35000 -						35000 -
K. Oakes, Drawings	15200 31						15200 31	
R. Oakes, Capital		35000 -						35000 -
R. Oakes, Drawings	15095 35						15095 35	
B. Reid, Capital		20000 -						20000 -
B. Reid, Drawings	10009 30						10009 30	
Fees Earned		72770 26				72770 26		
Canada Pension Plan Exp.	229 16				229 16			
Car Expenses	3409 07		(1) 90 -		3499 07			
Light, Heat, and Water	1017 15				1017 15			
Miscellaneous Expense	327 63		(1) 55 -		382 63			
Postage	964 46				964 46			
Rent	4800 -				4800 -			
Telephone	633 29				633 29			
Unemployment Insce. Exp.	147 21				147 21			
Wages	13619 40		(7) 500 -		14119 40			
	173482 59	173482 59						
Bad Debts Expense			(2) 588 21		588 21			
Supplies Expense			(3) 96 95		96 95			
Insurance Expense			(4) 343 10		343 10			
Deprec. Furn. & Equip.			(5) 781 82		781 82			
Deprec. Automobiles			(6) 2703 79		2703 79			
Accrued Wages Payable				(7) 500 -				500 -
			5158 87	5158 87	30306 24	72770 26	147895 17	105431 15
Net Income					42464 02			42464 02
					72770 26	72770 26	147895 17	147895 17

Additional Information:

a. Each partner receives an annual salary of $12 000.
b. Interest is allowed on Capital account balances at the rate of 8 percent.
c. K. Oakes, R. Oakes, and B. Reid divide the remainder of net income in the ratio of 3:2:2, respectively.

1. **Prepare the statement of distribution of net income.**
2. **Prepare the statement of partners' capital.**
3. **Prepare the balance sheet.**
4. **Prepare the income statement.**

Adjusting and Closing Entries

20. In a two-column general journal, record the adjusting and closing entries for the Frame Brothers, introduced in Exercise 18. Make sure that your solution to Exercise 18 has been corrected before beginning this exercise.

21. From the work sheet in Exercise 19, prepare the adjusting and closing entries for Oakes, Oakes, and Reid in a two-column general journal. Be sure that your solution to Exercise 19 has been corrected before beginning this exercise.

Partnership Liquidation Exercises

22. Jackson, Johnson, and Koretsky have decided to liquidate their partnership. The post-closing trial balance of the partnership on March 31, 19--, is as follows:

Bank	$ 3 199	
Accounts Receivable	7 061	
Allowance for Doubtful Accounts		$ 350
Merchandise Inventory	12 950	
Supplies	1 720	
Prepaid Insurance	400	
Equipment	15 795	
Accumulated Depreciation of Equipment		4 500
Automobiles	12 500	
Accumulated Depreciation of Automobiles		7 350
Accounts Payable		6 425
E. Jackson, Capital		10 000
C. Johnson, Capital		10 000
F. Koretsky, Capital		15 000
	$53 625	$53 625

From the following information, prepare the accounting entries to liquidate the partnership.

Additional Information:

a. The partners share income and losses as follows: Jackson, 30 percent; Johnson, 30 percent; Koretsky, 40 percent.
b. The accounts receivable are sold to a collection agency for $4 000 cash.
c. The merchandise inventory is sold to another company for $8 000 cash.
d. Insurance is cancelled and a refund cheque for $300 is received from the insurance company.
e. The supplies, equipment, and automobiles are sold at public auction for the following amounts: supplies, $500; equipment, $6 500; and automobiles, $6 200.
f. All of the accounts payable are paid in full.

---

23. The partnership of Gare and Cureo is being liquidated due to the illness of one of the partners. The company books were closed on January 31, 19--. The post-closing trial balance is as follows:

Bank	$ 22.00	
Accounts Receivable	2 950.00	
Allowance for Doubtful Accounts		$ 275.00
Merchandise Inventory	8 942.00	
Supplies	416.00	
Prepaid Insurance	212.00	
Land	20 000.00	
Buildings	17 000.00	
Accumulated Depreciation Buildings		3 680.60
Equipment	6 800.00	
Accumulated Depreciation Equipment		4 609.20
Automobiles	12 710.00	
Accumulated Depreciation Automobiles		8 746.20
Accounts Payable		3 200.00
Bank Loan		2 800.00
Mortgage Payable		25 741.00
C. Gare, Capital		10 000.00
H. Cureo, Capital		10 000.00
	$69 052.00	$69 052.00

Using the following additional information, prepare the accounting entries to liquidate the partnership.

Additional Information:

a. The partners share income and loss equally.
b. $275 of accounts receivable is written off. The balance of accounts receiv-

able is collected quickly by offering a 10 percent cash discount for immediate payment.

c. The merchandise inventory, supplies, and equipment are sold at public auction. The following amounts are realized in cash: inventory, $7 500; supplies, $100; equipment, $2 500.
d. The insurance is cancelled and a refund cheque in the amount of $162 is received from the insurance company.
e. The land and buildings are sold through a real estate agent for $48 000. The agreement calls for the purchaser to take over the existing mortgage on the property and for the seller to pay a real estate commission of 5 percent on the selling price.
f. The owners decide to purchase the two company automobiles at the current market values as determined by an independent car appraiser. C. Gare takes a car with a market value of $2 200; H. Cureo takes a car with a market value of $2 100. The market value of the cars is charged to the partners' respective Capital accounts.
g. The bank loan is settled. Interest of $40 is paid.
h. All of the accounts payable are paid in full.

---

24. The partnership of Rosen, Wolfe, and Stein is being terminated by mutual agreement. The post-closing trial balance at December 31, 19--, the date of termination, is as follows:

Bank	$ 416.20	
Accounts Receivable	5 091.40	
Allowance for Doubtful Accounts		$ 35.00
Merchandise Inventory	10 075.00	
Supplies	216.00	
Prepaid Insurance	437.00	
Land	20 000.00	
Buildings	35 750.00	
Accumulated Depreciation of Buildings		4 024.90
Equipment	9 047.00	
Accumulated Depreciation of Equip.		5 961.75
Automobiles	15 574.35	
Accumulated Depreciation of Autos		5 017.24
Accounts Payable		7 437.16
Bank Loan		10 000.00
Mortgage Payable		27 419.12
A. Rosen, Capital		16 509.14
B. Wolfe, Capital		17 202.64
P. Stein, Capital		3 000.00
	$96 606.95	$96 606.95

Using the following additional information, prepare the accounting entries to liquidate the partnership.

Additional Information:

a. Net accounts receivable are sold to a collection agency at a discount of 50 percent of the gross value.
b. Merchandise inventory is sold to a competitor for $6 000 cash.
c. Supplies are sold for $35.
d. Insurance is cancelled and a refund cheque for $102 is received.
e. Land and buildings are sold for $60 000. The purchaser takes over the existing mortgage. There is no real estate commission.
f. Equipment is obsolete and is disposed of for its scrap value of $1 000.
g. Automobiles are sold for their market value of $4 700.
h. Accounts payable are paid in full.
i. The bank loan is paid off, including $75 of interest owing.
j. Rosen, Wolfe, and Stein divide net income, net loss, and deficits in the ratio of 1:3:4, respectively. P. Stein is personally bankrupt.

Using Your Knowledge

25. Tony Calderone, Jim Kidd, Frank Morris, and Mario Capiletti are experienced construction men who have become acquainted through their work. The men are presently employed by different companies in the house-building industry. Tony is an accountant, Jim is a carpenter, Frank is a heavy-equipment operator and maintenance man, and Mario is a concrete and masonry man.

At a meeting one day the men talk seriously about joining forces to work for themselves. Although they lack some necessary skills, they have a great deal of collective experience and know a great many people in the trades.

The four men discuss their plan with a bank manager. The manager assures them that a substantial line of credit is available, as well as mortgage money for the homes to be built. However, the four men must first invest $50 000 in the business.

Together the men can raise this amount of capital and are eager to proceed with the plan. Jim and Frank believe that they should take on work immediately and work out the details of the business organization later. Tony and Mario are more cautious and insist that the details be worked out in advance.

What course of action should the men follow? Give reasons for your choice.

26. Andrews, Brown, and Collins are all graduate engineers. They form a partnership in which each man is to work full-time in the business. To get the business started, the men contribute cash as follows: Andrews, $25 000; Brown, $20 000; and Collins, $5 000.

The men ask your opinion about their income- or loss-sharing arrangement. State your views in this regard.

---

27. Angela Davidson is a young and talented woman in the photography and graphics field who is anxious to form a business of her own. She believes that many of the people she has worked for would become her clients. Unfortunately, the equipment and special facilities for this line of work are expensive. Davidson needs approximately $40 000, a sum that she does not have.

Jane Edwards is a friend who is willing to put up the required capital for an interest in the business.

If Davidson and Edwards were to form a partnership in which Edwards put up the capital and Davidson did all the work, what profit-sharing arrangement would you suggest for them?

---

28. Fraser and Gregg have formed a partnership in the wholesale auto parts business. Fraser has put up $40 000 and Gregg, $50 000, of the required capital. The two men have agreed that Gregg is to work full time in the business and Fraser is to contribute 25 percent of his time. Neither man brings any particular skills or experience to the business.

These two men have not as yet made a decision regarding the profit-sharing ratio. What suggestions would you make to them?

Cases

Case 1 *How to Keep a Key Employee*

D. R. Johnson is a lawyer with a well-established and highly profitable legal practice. He has built up this practice alone over a period of twenty years. In the past few years, the demands of his business have been exceptionally heavy, forcing him to work many more hours than normal. He has not been able to spend nearly as much time with his family as he would like, and last year he was forced to give up his summer vacation because of an important case.

To help relieve the workload, Mr. Johnson has employed Lorna Fox, a law student, to work with him on a part-time basis. Lorna began working during the summer months, when her classes were not in session, and in the evenings during the school term. The arrangement worked out well for both parties. Lorna proved to be an able and energetic student who soon demonstrated her value. Lorna acquired the experience that she wanted, and Mr. Johnson's workload was reduced considerably.

With Lorna's graduation approaching, Mr. Johnson faces the unpleasant prospect of losing her. Lorna will be a lawyer fully qualified to move into her own office or to take a position with another lawyer. Mr. Johnson has been very happy with Lorna, does not want to see her leave, and, above all, does not want to return to the long, arduous, working days.

Questions

1. What advice would you give to Mr. Johnson? Give reasons for your choice.

Case 2 *A Way Out of the Cash Squeeze?*

Fred Norris is the sole owner of Hilltop Ski Area, which he has developed over the last ten years. The ski area has excellent hills and very reliable snow conditions. Since its beginning, the business has been increasingly profitable. In the most recent fiscal year, its net income figure was $62 000.

Over the years, Fred has used the profits of the business to pay off the large debts that he incurred for the original property and equipment. As a result, the position of the business is regarded as sound, with property presently valued at $1 000 000, and with no large debts. Unfortunately, however, the equipment is either completely worn out or obsolete.

If the ski area is to retain its popularity, Fred must obtain lifts and hill-grooming equipment. The new equipment would cost $600 000 and would last for 15 years. Neither Fred nor the business has that amount of money available. Bank financing is available at an interest rate of $12\frac{1}{2}$ percent, which would cost the business $75 000 a year for the interest alone. Fred believes that the new equipment would attract additional skiers to the area and cause an annual increase in gross revenues of approximately $90 000.

Fred receives an offer from Harry Watson, a man with great confidence in the future of skiing. Harry offers to put up the $600 000 for the new equipment on the condition that he have a one-half interest in all aspects of the business.

Questions

1. What advice would you give to Fred Norris?
2. What is your opinion of Harry's offer? Give reasons for your answer.

Case 3 *How to Avoid Problems of Sudden Termination*

R. Price and G. Nashimo have been partners in a wholesale business for about five years. Although the business is very profitable, the two partners have had to draw heavily on their personal resources in order to get the business started and to see it through an almost immediate period of expansion.

On January 31, 19--, the balance sheet of the partnership is as follows:

PRICE AND NASHIMO
BALANCE SHEET
JANUARY 31, 19--

ASSETS

Current Assets			
Cash		$ 438	
Accounts Receivable	$15 072		
Less Allowance for Doubtful Accounts	2 000	13 072	
Merchandise Inventory		125 000	$138 510
Prepaid Expenses			
Insurance		$ 415	
Supplies		1 432	1 847
Fixed Assets			
Land		$ 35 000	
Buildings	$145 000		
Less Accumulated Depreciation	32 075	112 925	
Furniture and Equipment	$ 72 000		
Less Accumulated Depreciation	48 456	23 544	
Automobiles	$ 12 473		
Less Accumulated Depreciation	5 903	6 570	178 039
			$318 396

LIABILITIES AND OWNERS' EQUITY

Current Liabilities		
Accounts Payable	$112 500	
Bank Loan	50 000	$162 500
Mortgage Payable		65 400
Owners' Equity		
R. Price, Capital	$ 45 248	
G. Nashimo, Capital	45 248	90 496
		$318 396

On February 1, G. Nashimo is killed in an automobile accident. Lawyers for the deceased quickly inform Price that Nashimo's death legally terminates the partnership, and that Nashimo's family is urgently in need of Nashimo's portion of the value of the partnership.

Price is fully aware that he will have to comply with the request of Nashimo's lawyers. He has his own future to think about, however, and hopes to be able to continue to operate the business because it has proven to be successful and profitable.

Questions

1. What problem is Price faced with?
2. What courses of action are open to him?
3. What precautionary measures could he take to avoid a similar situation with a future partnership?

Case 4 *Partnership Agreement Unnecessary?*

Hutton and Inman hastily formed a partnership which was expected to last for only two to three years. They intended to buy and sell metric supplies in order to take advantage of the changeover to the metric system of measurement.

Hutton was an expert on metrication, having lived and worked for a number of years in a country that uses the metric system. Inman knew nothing of the metric system, but expected to study it and become expert in a very short time.

Prior to officially registering the partnership, the two men discussed a tentative income-sharing plan which would compensate each partner according to his contribution of capital, time, and talent. However, because Hutton quickly became very busy, the two men have never gotten together to make an official agreement. The business has carried on without one.

In the process of establishing the business, Inman could raise only $8 000 of the $15 000 that he had promised. Hutton had to come up with his own share of $10 000 plus the $7 000 balance of Inman's share, for a total of $17 000.

The business did well financially thanks to the efforts of Hutton, who did most of the work. Inman never could master the metric system of measurement. He was of little help except to unpack goods that arrived and to package and mail them for shipment. Inman also took a lot of time off for golf in the summer and for curling in the winter.

At the end of the first year of operation, the business had a net income of $38 000. When it came time to discuss the profit split, Inman told Hutton that the Partnership Act specifically stated that the profits had to be divided equally and that there was nothing that either of them could do about it.

Questions

1. Express your views on this situation.

Career
George Ormsby / Auditor

George Ormsby enjoyed the accounting courses he took at his high school in Edmonton, Alberta. Shortly after graduation, he began working for an accounting firm, Thorne Riddell. While employed with this firm, he continued to study accounting evenings and weekends. Eventually he passed his final examinations as a chartered accountant and set up practice on his own.

After a year in his own practice, George joined the firm of McPherson, Scott and Co. as one of six partners. George joined this partnership through a merger, and based his contribution on the yearly gross billing value of his clients. A legal partnership agreement was drawn up outlining the duties of each partner, the division of profits, salaries, and so on.

According to the partnership agreement, a salary account is maintained for each partner. The monthly salaries of the partners are determined in advance each year. At the end of the year, profits are closed out to the Income Summary account and then to the respective capital accounts of the partners.

Each partner in McPherson, Scott and Company is responsible for certain aspects of the business. One partner is in charge of a management committee which carries out policy decisions by signing cheques, approving invoices, arranging contracts, and so on. Another partner is in charge of the preparation of accounts and financial statements for the partnership. Another partner is in charge of personnel, and another partner specializes in tax problems. George performs a variety of special functions for the firm, such as updating and maintaining the manual that outlines the firm's office, accounting, and auditing procedures. He also directs the use of general office forms.

Every two weeks, all the partners attend a lecture and training session for all the firm's employees, including bookkeeping staff and CA students.

These lectures ensure that the whole staff keeps up to date on recent accounting developments.

According to the partnership agreement, George's salary is based on the length of his experience and on his partners' evaluation of his abilities. Profits that are left over at the end of the year are divided among the partners according to the number of extra hours worked by each and the capital investment of each.

As a licenced public accountant, George performs audits for his clients and prepares financial reports for the shareholders of corporations, for lending institutions, and for concerned individuals. George reviews the internal control systems of his clients to ensure that transactions are recorded correctly and that assets are protected from loss or theft. He examines his clients' general books of accounts and participates in the taking of physical inventories to determine the actual value of his clients' assets. He also prepares corporate tax returns for his clients.

One of George's responsibilities is to oversee and advise the students who work for the firm. He warns them that although the field pays well, it can also be very demanding. Good chartered accountants must be willing to meet high professional standards and continually upgrade their skills, particularly in the areas of computer technology, tax regulations, and auditing principles. They must keep informed of new developments in their fields by regularly reading a number of relevant periodicals. Most important, chartered accountants must never shrink from responsibility.

22

Accounting for Corporations

22-1 Characteristics of Corporations
22-2 Advantages and Disadvantages of Corporations
22-3 Accounts of a Corporation
22-4 Dividends
22-5 Different Classes of Shares
22-6 Retained Earnings
22-7 Equity Section — Presentation on the Balance Sheet
22-8 Market Value of Company Shares
22-9 Share Records
22-10 Adjusting and Closing Entries for a Corporation
22-11 Income Tax for Corporations

Objectives

When you have completed Chapter 22, you should:

1. Know the characteristics of a corporation.
2. Know the differences between a public and a private corporation.
3. Know the advantages and disadvantages of the corporate form of business organization.
4. Understand how the equity section of a corporation is different from the equity section of a proprietorship or partnership.
5. Know what organization costs are.
6. Be able to do the accounting for simple share transactions.
7. Be able to explain the meanings of common share, preferred share, par value, and no par value.
8. Know what dividends are.
9. Be able to do the accounting for dividends.

10. Be able to make the calculations for non-cumulative, cumulative, and fully participating dividends.
11. Understand the factors affecting retained earnings.
12. Understand the purpose of appropriations and the accounting for appropriations.
13. Be able to prepare the financial statements for a corporation.
14. Understand the terms *market price* and *issue price* as they pertain to company shares.
15. Know what share records exist and how they work.
16. Be able to record the adjusting and closing entries for a corporation.
17. Be able to do the accounting for the income tax of a corporation.

A **corporation**, also known as a limited company, is an organization that possesses a legal identity independent of the persons who own it. Corporations range in size from small to very large. According to the federal and provincial laws of Canada, the corporation name must include either the word Limited (Ltd.) or the word Incorporated (Inc.). Almost all large business enterprises operate under the corporate form of business organization.

Accounting for corporations can be very complex, particularly for large companies. This chapter does not introduce advanced or specialized accounting theory. Rather, it explains the basic concepts of corporation accounting to give you a general understanding of this prominent form of business organization.

Corporations were originally designed to raise large amounts of capital more easily and to minimize the financial risk involved in costly business ventures. The corporation's structure allows capital to be obtained from a large number of persons. Each individual risks relatively little money for a share in the anticipated profits.

For example, assume that a capital investment of $2 000 000 is required to put a new mine into operation. This capital would be difficult to raise from a few people only. It could be much more easily raised from a large number of persons: 200 000 contributors would only have to pay $10 each. Each contributor would receive a **share certificate** (also known as a stock certificate) indicating the amount of that person's share in the venture. A person who owns shares in a company is a **shareholder** or **stockholder** in the company and receives a portion of the company's profits in proportion to the number of shares owned.

22.1 Characteristics of Corporations

1. A corporation may have different kinds of shares, as will be explained later. However, only the 'common' shares carry the privilege of ownership. The

owners of a corporation are its 'common' shareholders. A small private corporation may have only one shareholder, but a large public corporation usually has many. Each common share in a corporation carries one vote at any shareholders' meeting. A shareholder who owns 50 common shares of a corporation is entitled to 50 votes, whereas one who owns 10 common shares is entitled to 10 votes.

2. An incorporated company is a separate legal entity in the eye of the law. It is regarded as an artificial legal being, separate from those who own it. Its existence continues regardless of anything that may happen to any of its shareholders. It has many of the rights and obligations of a real person. A corporation can buy and sell property in its own name. It can sue or be sued in its own name. It can enter into legal contracts in its own name. And it must pay its own income tax and other taxes.
3. The shareholders have no liability for any actions of the corporation except to the extent of their capital contribution. They have what is known as limited liability. In this respect, the corporate form of business ownership is quite different from the single proprietorship and partnership.
4. For the protection of shareholders and prospective shareholders, corporations are subject to government control. The laws of the federal government in regard to corporations are found in the Canada Business Corporations Act. Each of the provinces has a similar act.

   The federal and provincial acts lay down the numerous rules and regulations that people must strictly follow in forming and operating limited companies. If the scope of a company's operations is national, it will usually choose to operate under the Canada Act. If the scope of a company's operations is confined to a particular province, it will likely choose to operate under the corporations act for that province. One unfortunate aspect of company law is its complexity; parts of it are difficult to read and understand.

   To incorporate a company, a formal request is made to the government by one or more petitioners. Permission, if granted, is given in the form of a document called a **charter** or **letters patent** which contains the following information:

   a. The name of the company.
   b. The purpose of the company.
   c. The address of the head office of the company.
   d. The amount of capital authorized. (**Note:** Authorized capital is the maximum amount of capital that the charter allows the company to raise. If, at a later time, the company wishes to increase the authorized capital, it must apply for permission which may be given in the form of 'Supplementary Letters Patent'.)
   e. The number of shares authorized.
   f. The names, addresses, and occupations of the petitioners for the formation of the company and the number of shares to be taken by each.
   g. The number of directors.

5. Company policy is not decided by the shareholders but by a committee of the shareholders called a **board of directors**. Directors are elected by the shareholders at the annual shareholders meeting. Control of the company is usually in the hands of a few directors who have large holdings of company shares. Directors do not run the day-to-day operations of the company, but they control the affairs of the company by passing bylaws and making policy decisions.
6. The daily operations of the company are controlled by hired company officers or executives. They are the president, vice-president(s), secretary, treasurer, general manager, and so on. The executive positions of a company are established in the bylaws passed by the board of directors.
7. In theory, to control a corporation one must own 50 percent of the shares plus one. In actual fact, because of the wide distribution of shares and the lack of participation by a great many shareholders, a corporation can be effectively controlled with a much smaller percentage holding of shares.

Public and Private Corporations

Business corporations can be either public corporations or private corporations. A **public corporation** obtains its capital by the sale of bonds or shares to the general public. A public corporation has no limit on the number of its shareholders. Most large corporations are of this type.

A **private corporation** must meet certain legal conditions. The number of shareholders cannot exceed fifty, and the corporation's funding must be raised privately instead of publicly by an issue of shares or bonds. Most private corporations are small or medium-sized businesses. They have been incorporated by the owners to allow them to retain control while obtaining the benefit of limited liability to protect their personal assets.

22.2 Advantages and Disadvantages of Corporations

Advantages

1. The liability of the shareholder is limited to the amount of the person's investment in shares of the company.
2. The power of the directors is controlled by government regulations.
3. Large investments of capital can be assembled more easily.
4. The existence of the company continues despite the death, insolvency, or incapacity of any of its shareholders.

5. New capital can be brought into the business by selling additional shares up to the authorized limit.
6. A shareholder is not affected if a company fails or if it is involved in legal entanglements except to the extent of the shares that the person holds in the company.
7. Shares of a public company may be easily acquired or disposed of through a stockbroker.
8. A person can enjoy ownership in a company without having the responsibility of management.

Disadvantages

1. Most individual shareholders have no control over the corporation. The board of directors that controls the corporation is elected by the shareholders at the annual meeting. A shareholder has only one vote per share. Since majority shareholders have the most shares, they also have the most votes. Therefore the majority shareholders are actually the ones who elect the members of the board of directors and decide who will control the corporation.
2. A corporation pays income tax at a high rate. In addition, when the profits of the company are distributed to the shareholders, the shareholders are also required to pay income tax on the money they receive. In effect, this is double taxation.
3. Government controls are quite strict. Corporation law is often difficult to read and to understand.
4. There are fees and legal expenses involved in incorporating a company.
5. Minority shareholders have little influence on the conduct of the business because daily operations are in the hands of hired executives.

22.3 Accounts of a Corporation

The accounts of a corporation differ greatly from those of a proprietorship or partnership in their treatment of the owners' equity. Whereas the accounts of a proprietorship or partnership have Capital and Drawings accounts for each of the owners, the accounts of a corporation have neither.

In very simple corporations, the equities of all the shareholders are recorded collectively in two accounts: (1) the Capital Stock account, and (2) the Retained Earnings account. The general ledger of a corporation appears in simplified form in Figure 22.1. Note that the owners' equity is separated into two parts: (1) capital invested by the shareholders, which is represented by the Capital Stock account, and (2) capital earned by the business, which is represented by the Retained Earnings account.

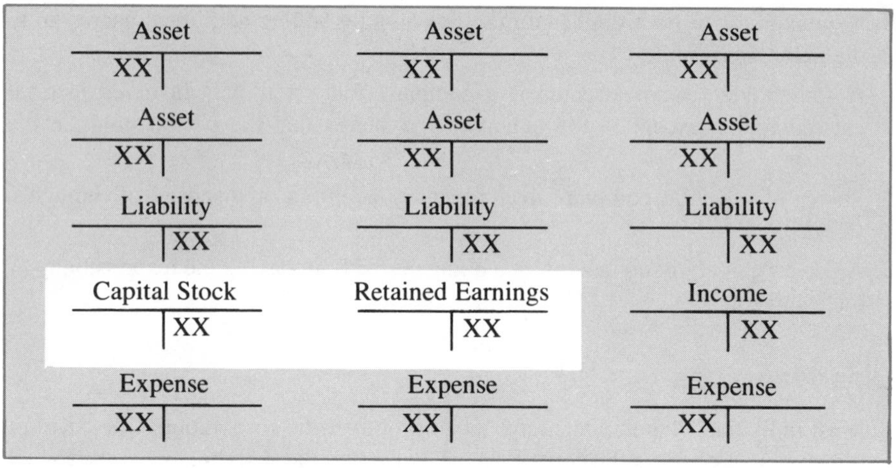

Figure 22.1 The general ledger of a small corporation showing the equities of all the shareholders in two accounts.

Simple Balance Sheet of a Corporation

A simplified balance sheet for a corporation is given in Figure 22.2. The illustration shows how the two components of Shareholders' Equity — Capital Stock and Retained Earnings — are presented.

CROWN INDUSTRIES LIMITED
BALANCE SHEET
JUNE 30, 19--

ASSETS		LIABILITIES	
Current Assets		*Current Liabilities*	
Bank	$10 500	Accounts Payable	$17 800
Accounts Receivable	25 350		
Merchandise Inventory	20 742	SHAREHOLDERS' EQUITY	
	$56 592	*Capital Stock*	
Fixed Assets		Authorized and Issued	
Land	$35 000	10 000 Common Shares	$100 000
Plant and Equipment	75 000	*Retained Earnings*	$ 51 292
	$110 000		$151 292
Organization Costs	$2 500		
TOTAL	$169 092	TOTAL	$169 092

Figure 22.2 The simple balance sheet of a corporation.

Basic Accounting Entries for the Issue of Shares and for Organization Costs

Company Shares

When company shares are sold for cash, the proceeds of the sale are credited to a Capital Stock account. The simplest accounting entry to record the sale of shares is as follows:

Bank	$XXX	
Capital Stock		$XXX
To record the issue of capital stock for cash.		

The Capital Stock account has a credit balance which represents the accumulation of the proceeds from all sales of shares made directly by the company to its shareholders.

Organization Costs

Incorporating a company can be expensive. Initial costs include the fee to obtain the charter from the government, legal fees to company lawyers, and costs for miscellaneous items such as the company seal. Large issues of shares are often sold through an investment dealer, who charges a commission.

Initial costs of incorporation are charged to an account called **Organization Costs.** Accounting theory varies regarding organization costs. Usually, the amount is written off as an expense over a period of years as allowed by government regulation. The item appears on the balance sheet as an added asset.

If organization expenses are paid for in cash, the accounting entry to record them is as follows:

Organization Costs	$XXX	
Bank		$XXX

Often these initial services are not paid for in cash. Instead, shares deemed to be equal in value to the cost of the services are issued in payment. When this happens, the accounting entry is as follows:

Organization Costs	$XXX	
Capital Stock		$XXX

22.4 Dividends

Dividend Policy

Dividends are payments out of retained earnings to the shareholders of a company on a pro rata basis. That is, each share receives an equal dividend. **Retained**

earnings represent a company's net accumulation of earnings available for distribution to shareholders in the form of dividends.

Whether a dividend is distributed or not depends on the directors. They have the ultimate responsibility for deciding on the disposition of retained earnings. Rather than distribute them to shareholders, the directors may decide, for example, to use them for company expansion. The ordinary shareholder has no direct say in this matter. Normally, dividends are not declared unless a company is earning satisfactory profits on a regular basis.

When dividends are declared, they are declared to shareholders of record on a certain date, to be paid at a subsequent time. The date of record, therefore, is important, and is one reason why stock records must be kept current and accurate.

Dividends are usually stated at so much money a share. Once they have been voted by the board of directors, the payment of dividends becomes a legal obligation of the company. If the company fails to make payment, the shareholders can sue in the courts.

The various companies acts protect the interests of shareholders. The acts state that dividends may only be declared if the following two requirements can be met: (1) enough cash must be available to make the payment and (2) the credit balance in the Retained Earnings account must be sufficiently large that the dividend entry will not put the account into a debit position.

Accounting for Dividends

Accounting for dividends is usually done in two steps:

1. When the dividend is declared by the board of directors, the liability is set up in a Dividends Payable account. The Retained Earnings account is reduced by the same amount.
2. The payment of the dividend is recorded at the time payment is made.

Consider this example. Apex Limited is incorporated with 100 000 shares valued at $125 000. Its Retained Earnings account shows a balance of $95 500. On January 10, 19–7, the directors of Apex Limited declare a dividend of 50¢ a share to be paid to shareholders of record on January 31. Payment will be made on February 15.

The following accounting entries record these dividends:

19–7			
Jan. 10	Retained Earnings	$50 000	
	Dividends Payable		$50 000
	To record the declaration of a dividend of 50¢ a share.		
Feb. 15	Dividends Payable	$50 000	
	Bank		$50 000
	Payment of dividend declared Jan. 10.		

22.5 Different Classes of Shares

A corporation may issue more than one class of stock. Each class of capital stock must be kept in a separate account. Figure 22.3 shows a general ledger with more than one capital account. The accounting entries are similar for each class of stock.

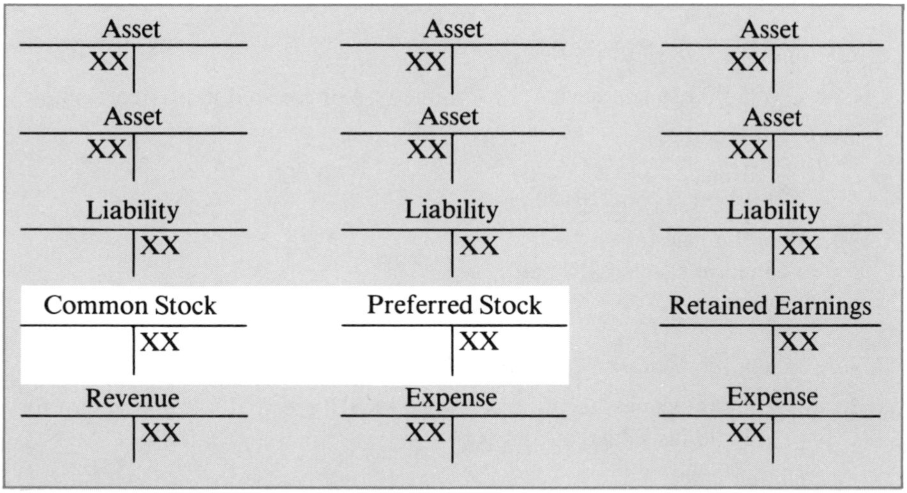

Figure 22.3 The general ledger of a large corporation with separate accounts for each class of capital stock.

Common Shares (Common Stock)

A corporation's basic class of stock is known as **common stock**. The rights of holders of common stock include the following:

1. The right to vote at shareholders' meetings. One vote is granted per share.
2. The right to receive any common dividends that are declared, in proportion to the number of shares held.
3. The right to share in the assets that remain after creditors have been paid if the corporation is liquidated.

Par Value Shares

Before the shares are issued, the directors may decide to set a predetermined value on the shares. This value, known as the **par value**, is printed on the share certificate. The directors usually choose round amounts, such as $10, $25, and $100, as par values to attract buyers.

The shares may be sold for more than par value if the issue is popular and the demand is great. That is, they may be sold at a premium. In most jurisdictions, the law does not permit the sale of par value shares for less than par value, that is, at a discount, except in the case of mining companies.

Some accounting situations that can arise in respect to the issuing of par value shares are explained below.

1. *Sale of par value shares for cash.*

Example: 5 000 shares having a par value of $10 are sold at par for cash.

Accounting entry:

Bank	50 000	
Capital Stock		50 000
To record the sale for cash of 5 000 common shares, $10 par value, at par.		

2. *Sale of par value shares for assets other than cash.*

Example: 5 000 shares having a par value of $10 are sold at par in return for a building valued at $50 000.

Accounting entry:

Buildings	50 000	
Capital Stock		50 000
To record the sale of 5 000 common shares at $10 par for a building located at 751 Cross Place, evaluation of Stone & Associates.		

3. *Sale of par value shares at a premium.*

Example: 1 000 shares with a par value of $100 are sold for cash at a 10 percent premium.

Accounting entry:

Bank	110 000	
Capital Stock		100 000
Premium on Capital Stock		10 000
To record the sale for cash of 1 000 common shares, par value $100, at a premium of 10 percent.		

4. *Sale of par value shares at a discount.*

Example: 2 000 shares having a par value of $25 are sold for $22 each.

Accounting entry:

Bank	44 000	
Discount on Capital Stock	6 000	
Capital Stock		50 000
To record the sale for cash of 2 000 common shares, par value $25, for $22 each.		

5. *Issue of par value shares to pay for organization costs.*

Example: 100 shares having a par value of $10 are issued to pay for the legal fees of incorporation.

Accounting entry:

Organization Costs	1 000	
Capital Stock		1 000
To record the issue of 100 shares, $10 par, to pay legal expenses of incorporation.		

No Par Value Shares

Shares with a par value frequently cannot be sold for the par value figure. To avoid this problem, corporations often sell shares that do not have a par value. This kind of share is known as a **no par value share**.

The advantage of no par value shares is that they can be sold at any price established from time to time by the board of directors. Shares of equal rank, put up for sale at different times, may be sold at different prices according to demand and general market conditions.

The accounting for the issue of no par value shares is simple because no discount or premium situations exist. Consider the following series of share transactions concerning one company's no par value shares.

1. 1 000 no par value common shares are issued for cash at $9 on February 2.

Accounting entry:

Feb. 2	Bank	9 000	
	Capital Stock		9 000
	Sale of 1 000 no par value shares at $9 for cash.		

2. 5 000 no par value common shares are issued for cash at $8.50 on June 15.

Accounting entry:

June 15	Bank	42 500	
	Capital Stock		42 500
	Sale of 5 000 no par value shares at $8.50 for cash.		

3. 500 no par value shares are issued for equipment valued at $5 000 on August 20.

   Accounting entry:

Aug 20	Equipment	5 000	
	Capital Stock		5 000
	Sale of 500 no par value shares for equipment valued at $5 000.		

4. 100 no par value shares are issued on September 1 for legal fees of $1 250 for incorporating the company.

   Accounting entry:

Sept 1	Organization Costs	1 250	
	Capital Stock		1 250
	Issue of 100 shares to pay for legal fees of incorporation.		

5. 5 000 shares are sold through an investment dealer on September 15. Of these, 4 750 are sold to the general public for $59 375 and 250 are kept by the investment dealer to pay for his services valued at $3 125.

   Accounting entry:

Sept 15	Bank	59 375	
	Organization Costs	3 125	
	Capital Stock		62 500
	Issue of 4 750 shares to the general public and 250 to the investment dealer; all at $12.50.		

Preferred Shares (Preferred Stock)

Preferred stock is a stock that carries special privileges, usually in regard to the payment of dividends. If a dividend is declared, the preferred shareholders are paid before the common shareholders. Also, if a corporation is closed down, the preferred shareholders recover their equity before the common shareholders. The dividend attached to preferred shares is generally stated at a certain percentage of the par value of the stock. For example, if a stock were described as 6 percent preferred, par value $100, then the annual dividend would be $6.

Preferred stock is usually issued so that the common shareholders can acquire additional capital from outsiders without relinquishing any control of the company. Preferred stock normally carries no voting rights. Moreover, the preference dividend is restricted to an amount determined beforehand, whereas the amount of a common dividend is limited only by the earning capacity of the company. This means that in a very profitable year a company may pay a much larger dividend to the common stockholders than it is required to pay to the preferred shareholders.

Preferred shareholders do not necessarily receive dividends. If a corporation does not declare a dividend, the preferred shareholder may be in no better position than the common shareholder.

Three Types of Preferred Share

A number of different preferences can be attached to preferred shares. This text deals only with the three common types described in Table 22.1.

Table 22.1 Three common types of preferred share.

Non-cumulative preferred	**Cumulative** preferred	**Fully participating** cumulative preferred
No voting rights.	No voting rights.	No voting rights.
Preferred as to dividends.	Preferred as to dividends.	Preferred as to dividends.
Dividend stated as a percentage of the par value.	Dividend stated as a percentage of the par value.	Dividend stated as a percentage of the par value.
If the preferred dividend is not paid in any year, the preferred stockholders lose their right to receive the dividend.	If the preferred dividend is not paid in any year, the 'arrears' of dividends must be made up in following years before any dividends can be paid to the common stockholders.	If the preferred dividend is not paid in any year the 'arrears' of dividends must be made up in following years before any dividends can be paid to the common stockholders.
		The common stockholders cannot receive proportionately more dividends than the preferred stockholders in any year. This is based on the total capital invested by each group.

Calculating Dividends for the Three Types of Preferred Share

To illustrate how the dividends are calculated under the three different types of preferred share described above, assume the following data for an incorporated company.

Preferred shares: 5 percent; par value, $10; 50 000 shares; total invested, $500 000.
Common shares: no par value; 100 000 shares; total invested, $250 000.

Net incomes earned: Year 1, $30 000; Year 2, $10 000; Year 3, $90 000; Year 4, $150 000.

Dividends paid: Year 1, $30 000; Year 2, nil; Year 3, $60 000; Year 4, $120 000.

The dividend calculations are shown in Table 22.2.

Table 22.2 Dividend calculations for three different types of preferred share.

Year	*Dividend*	*Shares are non-cumulative preferred 5%*		*Shares are cumulative preferred 5%*		*Shares are fully participating cumulative preferred 5%*	
		Preferred	*Common*	*Preferred*	*Common*	*Preferred*	*Common*
1	$ 30 000	$25 000 (note 1)	$ 5 000 (note 2)	$ 25 000	$ 5 000	$ 25 000	$ 5 000
2	nil	—	—	—	—	—	—
3	$ 60 000	$25 000	$ 35 000	$ 50 000 (note 3)	$ 10 000	$ 50 000	$10 000
4	$120 000	$25 000	$ 95 000	$ 25 000	$ 95 000	$ 80 000 (note 4)	$40 000
TOTALS		$75 000	$135 000	$100 000	$110 000	$155 000	$55 000
	$210 000	$210 000		$210 000		$210 000	

Notes: 1. The normal preferred dividend is 5 percent of $500 000 which is $25 000.

2\.

The total dividend	$30 000
Less the preferred dividend	25 000
Equals the balance to common shareholders	$ 5 000

$5 000 divided by 100 000 shares = 5¢ a share

3\.

The preferred dividend in arrears for year 2	$25 000
Plus the preferred dividend for year 3	25 000
Equals the total preferred dividend paid in year 3	50 000

4\.

The normal preferred dividend is 5 percent of $500 000.	$25 000
A proportionately equal dividend to common shareholders is 5 percent of $250 000.	12 500
Total of these two	$37 500

5. For this particular company, whenever a dividend in excess of $37 500 is declared, it is shared by the two groups of shareholders in the ratio of their respective capital contributions, which is 2:1. Therefore, the $120 000 dividend is divided as follows:

   Preferred shareholders: 2/3 of $120 000 = $80 000
   Common shareholders: 1/3 of $120 000 = $40 000

22.6 Retained Earnings

The Retained Earnings account represents a company's accumulation of profits over the years less any dividends paid out. In simple corporations, this account is affected by two types of accounting activity:

1. *Net Income or Net Loss*

   As you will see later, at the end of each fiscal period the net income or the net loss of a company is transferred to the Retained Earnings account. Net income represents a credit to the account and net loss a debit.

   Normally, the Retained Earnings account has a credit balance representing the net accumulation of income from profitable operations. It is possible, however, for the account to have a debit balance — a state of negative retained earnings. This usually follows a severe loss or a series of losses. When the Retained Earnings account has a debit balance, it is known as a **deficit**.

2. *Dividends*

   The shareholders of a company are its owners and expect to receive some of the company profits in the form of dividends. The directors have the power to declare a dividend; that is, to vote a payment to shareholders out of the accumulated net profits in the Retained Earnings account. A dividend payment has the effect of reducing the credit balance in the Retained Earnings account.

Appropriations

Instead of voting for a dividend to shareholders, the directors may decide that it is in the best interests of the company to use cash available from accumulated earnings for some other purpose. The most common other purpose is company expansion. Retained earnings are used in order to save the interest expense on borrowed funds, or to retain company control that might be weakened if new shares were issued. The directors may feel that the company can obtain greater profits as a result of the expansion, and that the shareholders will receive increased dividends in the future.

A substantial credit balance in the Retained Earnings account raises the expectations of the shareholders for dividends. If the directors do not intend to declare dividends, this credit balance can be misleading. Therefore, to avoid misleading the shareholders, the directors normally vote to segregate a portion of the balance in the Retained Earnings account into a special purpose account called an Appropriation account.

An **Appropriation account** is one to which a portion of retained earnings is transferred to restrict its availability for dividends. For example, the directors of Dartco Limited intend to use accumulated company profits to pay for a new building that will cost $250 000. To make their intention clear to the shareholders, the board, on June 5, 19--, votes to appropriate $250 000 to pay for the new building.

The appropriation is entered in the accounts in the following way:

June 5	Retained Earnings	250 000	
	Appropriation for New Building		250 000
	To record resolution of board of directors on June 3, 19--.		

The effect in the accounts is as follows:

RETAINED EARNINGS

Mar 31				Cr 265 000
Jun 5		250 000		Cr. 15 000

APPROPRIATION FOR NEW BUILDING

Jun 5			250 000	Cr 250 000

As the example shows, the appropriation serves to (1) reduce the expectation of receiving dividends by reducing the balance in the Retained Earnings account, and (2) show the purpose for which a particular portion of retained earnings is intended.

In other words, the objective of the appropriation is achieved when cash funds generated from company profits are used to pay for the new building. At that point, the Appropriation account is no longer required and the balance is returned to the Retained Earnings account. This increased balance in the Retained Earnings account is free for dividends as soon as the company builds up sufficient cash, if the directors choose to spend it in that way.

Retained Earnings — Summary

The following diagram shows how income, loss, dividends, and appropriations affect the Retained Earnings account.

RETAINED EARNINGS

Debits: Net Loss Dividends Appropriations made	Credit: Net Income Appropriations returned

Under normal circumstances, the dollar value of credit entries exceeds the dollar value of debit entries, giving the account a credit balance. Payment of a dividend is not allowed if it will create a debit balance in the Retained Earnings account.

The balance in the Retained Earnings account reflects the amount of accumulated earnings retained within the company.

The Retained Earnings account is not closed out to the Common Stock account.

Statement of Retained Earnings

A statement of Retained Earnings is prepared for each set of financial statements. The details are obtained by analyzing the Retained Earnings account. A sample statement is shown in Figure 22.4.

Statement of Retained Earnings

For the year ended December 31, 19-3

	19-3
Balance at Beginning of Year	$ 301 000
Add net income for the year	993 000
	1 294 000
Deduct dividends paid	$ 561 000
Balance at End of Year	$ 733 000

Figure 22.4 The Statement of Retained Earnings for a corporation.

22.7 Equity Section — Presentation on the Balance Sheet

Figure 22.5 gives two samples of the Equity sections of balance sheets as taken from published reports of Canadian companies. The basic components of shareholders'

a.

	19–5	19–4
SHAREHOLDERS' EQUITY		
Share capital		
Authorized		
5 000 000 common shares without nominal or par value		
Issued and outstanding		
2 132 151 shares	**8 450 773**	8 372 435
Retained earnings	**10 865 613**	8 574 373
	19 316 386	16 946 808

b.

	19–8	19–7
SHAREHOLDERS' EQUITY		
CAPITAL STOCK		
Authorized		
4 251 880 class A common shares without par value		
4 000 000 class B common shares without par value		
Issued		
Common shares	**14 564 045**	14 516 670
CONTRIBUTED SURPLUS	**73 720**	73 720
RETAINED EARNINGS	**22 340 595**	18 168 714
	36 978 360	32 759 104

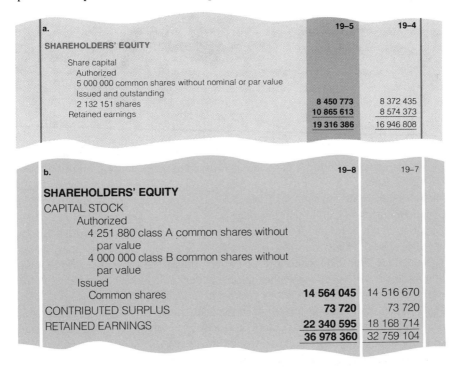

Figure 22.5 The Shareholders' Equity sections of the balance sheets of two public companies: (a) Agra Industries Limited of Saskatoon; (b) Western Canada Broadcasting of Vancouver.

equity, as well as the variation in presentation, are well illustrated by these examples. Observe that in the preparation of these balance sheets the common practice of rounding off large dollar figures to the nearest dollar or thousand dollars has been followed.

Contributed Surplus

In published reports of public companies, an equity item called **contributed surplus** occurs so frequently that it deserves an explanation. Contributed surplus arises primarily from the following:

1. Premium or discount on stock transactions.
2. Gifts of plant or property from outsiders.
3. Donations of stock or assets from shareholders.

When accounting for such transactions, the entries are put into one or more accounts in the Equity section. On financial statements, they are usually combined and shown on the balance sheet as one item called Contributed Surplus.

22.8 Market Value of Company Shares

Shares of a corporation may be bought or sold on the open market. A buyer and a seller simply agree on a price and make the transaction. The share certificate is transferred to the new owner in the manner described in Section 22.9.

Public companies must comply with the requirements of the stock exchange. Shares of these companies are bought and sold ('traded') through the facilities of stockbrokers. The services of stockbrokers can be obtained for a commission. On the basis of instructions from their clients, stockbrokers put through share transactions at the stock exchange building. This procedure is known as trading on the floor of the stock exchange.

The sales data of all transactions on each of the stock exchanges are listed daily in the financial pages of the larger newspapers, as shown in Figure 22.6.

The price of the last trade of any stock is generally regarded as its current 'market price'. The market price of a stock is not a fixed figure, therefore, but may change whenever a new transaction takes place. Prices fluctuate according to buying and selling forces. If investors find a stock attractive they tend to bid the price up. A bad report on a stock will almost certainly cause its market price to drop.

There is no direct relationship between the **issue price** of a stock, as reflected in the accounts, and the **market price** for that stock. The issue price is a one-time price, fixed at the time of issue. The market price fluctuates according to market forces. Generally, if a company is profitable, the market price of its stock will be steady or rising. If it is not profitable, the market price of its stock will fall.

infoPost

Your weekly reference guide

Industrial stocks

Quotations here listed are the official exchange prices for listed stocks.
For unlisted stocks, quotations by unlisted dealers are given.
The Financial Post cannot accept any responsibility for these quotations.

Range 53 Week			Indic. Div. Rate $	Week Ended Mar. 26, 1982						Ind. Yld. %	P/E ratio latest 12 Mos.	latest interim or fiscal period	Earnings per Share		
High $	Low $	Company		High $	Low $	Close or Latest $	Net Chge.	Sales 100s					$	prior or latest fiscal period	$
$7⅞	5	A.G.F. Mgmt. B pfd.	.56	$5⅞	5⅞	5⅞	+⅜	1	T	9.5	6.1	'81 Nov	.97	'80 Nov	.71
$28½	17	Abitibi-Price	1.60	$19¾	17	17½	−2	34	T	9.1	3.1	'81 Dec	5.57	'80 Dec	3.94
$34½	24½	Do. 7.50% A pfd.	3.75	$26	25½	26	+1½	20	T	14.4	...	'80 Dec	x9.21	'79 Dec	x12.59
$48	33	Do. 10% B pfd.	5.00	$36	35¾	36	+1¼	37	T	13.9	...	'80 Dec	x9.21	'79 Dec	x12.59
$16	12	Acklands	.60	L Mar. 12/82		12	.....	nil		5.0	6.3	Aug 9m	.14	'80 Nov	1.98
$14½	12	Do. 6% 2nd cv. pfd.	.96	L Mar. 5/82		12	.....	nil		8.0	...	'80 Nov	x27.22	'79 Nov	x35.44
120	80	Adera Fin. Corp.	p.03	L Mar. 17/82		120	.....	nil		2.5	10.0	'81 Nov	.12	'80 Nov	.12
$14¾	5⅛	Agnico-Eagle Mines	....	$7¼	6⅜	6¾	+⅜	376	T	...	6.6	Jun 6m	.24	'80 Dec	1.30
$10⅜	6½	Agra Industries A	p.10	$8¼	8	8¼	+¼	6	T	1.2	5.3	Jan 6m	.64	'81 Jul	1.69
...	...	Do. B	p.10	none in 1982			.....	nil		...	...	Jan 5m	.64	'81 Jul	1.69
115	26	AHED Corp.	....	L Jan. 29/82		40	.....	nil		...	...	Aug 9m	d.24	'80 Nov	d2.85
$27¾	8	Alberta Energy Co.	p.20	$11¾	10	11¼	+1¼	1141	T	1.8	12.1	'81 Dec	.93	'80 Dec	1.26
$31	22	Alberta Natural Gas	1.32	$23½	22½	23½	+½	23	T	5.6	10.0	Sep 9m	2.04	'80 Dec	2.06
$45¾	21⅞	Alcan Aluminium	1.80	$24	22	22⅞	+¼	3476	T	7.9	7.1	'81 Dec	3.24	'80 Dec	6.70
$23	15	Algoma Central Rlwy.	1.20	$16	15	15⅛	−1⅛	12	T	7.9	5.5	'81 Dec	2.75	'80 Dec	3.14
$49¼	33	Algoma Steel Corp.	1.20	$34¼	33¼	34	+½	25	T	3.5	3.1	'81 Dec	10.85	'80 Dec	8.21
$23	15½	Do. 8% pfd.	t2.00	$16½	16¼	16½	+½	18	T	12.1	...	'81 Dec	x13.08	'80 Dec	x9.42
$14	11	Algonquin Mercantile	.40	L Dec. 11/81		11½	.....	nil		3.5	...	'81 Jun	a7.92	'80 Jun	d.33
$10½	10	Do. pfd.	.40	L Feb. 26/82		10	.....	nil		4.0	...	'81 Jun	a7.92	'80 Jun	d.33
$23½	18	Aluminum Cda pfd.	t2.00	$20½	19½	20½	+1¾	95	M	9.8	...	■'80 Dec	x35.08	'79 Dec	x21.40
400	200	Ambassador Ind.	....	L Nov. 17/81		200	.....	nil		...	...	......	.....	......	.....
$27¼	18	AMCA International	u1.00	$19¼	18¾	19	+¼	1034	T	5.3	9.0	Sep 9m	u1.48	'80 Dec	u1.76
440	05	Amcan Industries	....	25	25	25	+20	70	T	...	...	Jul 9m	d3.17	'80 Oct	d3.14
30	12	AME Limited	p.08	L Mar. 19/82		20	.....	nil		40.0	3.3	'80 Dec	.06	'79 Dec	.08
$16	10	Andres Wines A	.644	$14	13¾	13¾	−¼	37	T	4.7	5.8	Dec 9m	2.29	'81 Mar	1.71
$15½	11	Do. B	.56	$14	14	14	+½	2	T	4.0	5.9	Dec 9m	2.29	'81 Mar	1.71
$22¾	14	AngloCdnTel 4.5% pfd	2.25	$15⅛	15⅛	15⅛	+⅛	1	T	14.9	...	'81 Dec	x17.73	'80 Dec	x17.28
$27	18⅜	Do. $2.90 pfd.	2.90	z$19⅛	19⅛	19⅛	.....	E115	T	15.2	...	'81 Dec	x17.73	'80 Dec	x17.28
$24½	16	Do. $2.65 pfd.	2.65	z$17¾	17¾	17¾	.....	E50	T	14.9	...	'81 Dec	x17.73	'80 Dec	x17.28
$28½	20	Do. $3.15 pfd.	3.15	$22	22	22	+1	3	T	14.3	...	'81 Dec	x17.73	'80 Dec	x17.28
475	110	Anthes Industries	....	125	110	125	+15	56	T	...	4.8	'81 Oct	.26	'80 Oct	.67
$5¼	300	Arbor Capital	p.10	455	425	425	−15	19	T	2.4	9.2	'81 Oct	.46	'80 Oct	.47
30	17	Ardiem Ind. Corp. A	....	24	20	24	+07	120	V	...	...	......	.....	......	.....
$12½	375	Argus Corp.	....	$8½	8¼	8¼	−¼	17	T	...	15.0	Sep 9m	a.36	'80 Dec	a.45
$7¾	375	Do. C pfd.	....	460	450	450	unch.	13	T	...	...	'80 Dec	x3.08	'79 Nov	x4.89
$23¾	16¾	Do. $2.50 A pfd.	2.50	z$16¾	16¾	16¾	.....	E10	T	14.9	...	'80 Dec	x3.08	'79 Nov	x4.89
$23½	16	Do. $2.60 A pfd.	2.60	$17	17	17	+¼	3	T	15.3	...	'80 Dec	x3.08	'79 Nov	x4.89
$25	16¼	Do. $2.70 B pfd.	2.70	$17	16¾	17	+¼	4	T	15.9	...	'80 Dec	x3.08	'79 Nov	x4.89
$19¾	9	Asamera Inc.	.40	$10⅞	10¼	10⅜	+⅜	278	T	3.9	11.7	Dec 9m	u.40	'80 Dec	u1.56
$45⅛	12⅛	Asbestos Corp.	....	$13½	13⅜	13⅜	+¼	8	T	...	4.9	Sep 9m	.96	'80 Dec	.89
$6⅛	305	Astral Bellevue	.12	$6⅛	455	5⅞	+1⅛	2014	T	2.0	21.0	Nov 9m	.13	'81 Feb	.48
$11¼	6½	ATCO Ltd. Class I	.20	$8	6¾	8	+1	126	T	2.5	4.8	Dec 9m	.53	'81 Mar	1.77
$11⅛	6½	Do. Class II	.20	$7½	7	7½	+½	35	T	2.7	4.5	Dec 9m	.53	'81 Mar	1.77
100	70	Aurelian Business	....	76	76	76	−03	5	C	...	...	......	.....	......	.....
03	03	Do. rts.	....	03	03	03	unch.	425	C	...	...	......	.....	......	.....
175	80	Aurora Energy Fund	....	80	80	80	−15	126	C	...	13.3	'80 Dec	.06	'79 Dec	.03
$9	6½	Auto Marine Electric	....	$6½	6½	6½	−⅛	10	V	...	2.4	'80 Nov	2.76	'79 Nov	3.25
$13½	9	Automotive Hardwre A	.60	z$8¾	8¾	8¾	.....	E50	T	6.9	6.0	Sep 9m	1.70	'80 Dec	d.06
...	...	Do. B	y.60	L Apr. 3/80		10⅞	.....	nil		5.5	7.4	Sep 9m	1.70	'80 Dec	d.06
$6	115	Avalanche Ind.	....	145	130	130	−05	100	V	...	...	......	.....	......	.....
$38	19¾	AZL Resources	....	L Feb. 12/82		19¾	.....	nil		...	...	'80 Dec	.11	'79 Dec	1.37
		B													
$11	6¾	Balco Ind.	.16	$8	7⅞	8	+⅛	2	V	2.0	3.1	May 6m	1.17	'80 Nov	1.60
$12⅛	400	Banister Continental	....	$7¼	6½	6½	−⅛	13	T	...	...	Dec 9m	d1.06	'81 Mar	d3.62
$25¼	17	Bank of B. C.	.72	$19	18¼	19	+1	193	T	3.8	6.0	Jan 3m	.86	'81 Oct	4.04
$19½	14¾	Do. $2.28 pf.	2.28	$16	15¾	16	+¼	6	T	14.2	...	■'81 Oct	x22.30	'80 Oct	.....
$31½	20¼	Bank of Montreal	1.96	$22¾	21⅞	22½	+⅝	1921	T	8.7	3.9	Jan 3m	1.10	'81 Oct	6.27
$6	435	Do. wts.	....	$5¼	480	5	+⅛	651	T	...	...	......	.....	......	.....
$34⅜	23¾	Do. $2.85 cv. pf.	2.85	$26⅝	25¼	26¼	+1⅛	123	T	10.9	...	■'81 Oct	x38.15	'80 Oct	.....
$26⅝	18¼	Do. $2.50 pf. A	2.50	$20⅝	19⅝	20⅜	+⅝	332	T	12.3	...	......	.....	......	.....
$31⅜	21⅛	Bank of Nova Scotia	1.84	$23¾	22½	23	+½	2423	T	8.0	4.7	Jan 3m	1.37	'81 Oct	4.83
$19½	7⅝	Banque d'Epargne	1.16	$9½	8½	8½	−¼	11	M	13.6	9.8	'81 Oct	2.12	'80 Oct	2.49
$10	5	Barbecon Inc. A	.20	L Feb. 26/82		5¾	.....	nil		3.5	6.8	Sep 9m	.38	'80 Dec	1.07
$6	5	Do. B	.20	$5	5	5	−1	1	T	4.0	5.9	Sep 9m	.38	'80 Dec	1.07
$11¼	7½	Bathurst Paper pfd.	1.05	L Feb. 26/82		7¾	.....	nil		13.5	...	'80 Dec	x77.64	'79 Dec	x58.52
$9⅝	6	Baton Broadcast A	.30	$7⅝	7½	7½	−⅜	47	T	4.0	9.0	'81 Aug	.63	'80 Aug	.72
$10	6	Do. B	.25	$7⅝	7½	7⅝	−⅛	48	T	3.3	9.8	'81 Aug	.58	'80 Aug	.72
$7	5⅝	Bay Mills	.40	$7	6½	6½	−½	35	T	6.2	3.4	Jan 6m	.58	'81 Jul	1.41
$15⅛	11	BBC Realty Inv.	■p2.14½	$12⅝	11¾	12	−⅜	93	T	17.9	5.6	'81 Dec	2.14	'80 Dec	1.92
$16½	13½	Becker Milk B pfd.	.50	$16	16	16	unch.	1	T	3.1	4.8	Oct 6m	a2.20	'81 Apr	a2.90
250	125	Belding-Corticelli	....	L Mar. 19/82		145	.....	nil		...	...	Mar 3m	d.38	'80 Dec	d.55
$20	16⅞	Bell Canada	1.96	$19⅛	17¾	18¾	+⅝	7147	T	10.5	6.3	■'81 Dec	2.97	'80 Dec	2.00
$57⅛	22	Do. A pfd.	3.20	$22	22	22	−1	1	T	14.5	...	'81 Dec	x15.56	'80 Dec	x9.51
$58	52½	Do. B pfd.	3.34	$55¾	55¾	55¾	+2¼	1	T	6.0	...	'81 Dec	x15.56	'80 Dec	x9.51

Figure 22.6 Part of a financial page showing transactions of the Toronto Stock Exchange.

22.9 Share Records

The Capital Stock account shows the total proceeds from the sale of shares by the company to shareholders. Except in extremely small or private companies, it does not provide any other information about the shareholders. Additional information about the shareholders is required, however, particularly their names and addresses and the number of shares held. This information is kept by the company in a separate book.

The Stock Certificate Book

For all but large public corporations, the detailed information relative to shareholders is kept in a **stock certificate book**. The stock certificate book contains preprinted blank stock certificates and stubs. Each time the company sells a share or shares, details of the transaction are recorded. The company secretary records the name of the buyer (shareholder), the number of shares bought, and the date of issue of the share certificate on the front and back of a blank share certificate and on the attached stub, as shown in Figures 22.7 and 22.8. The share certificate is then detached and exchanged with the purchaser for the price of the shares. The stubs remain in the stock certificate book which acts as the company's permanent record of its shareholders.

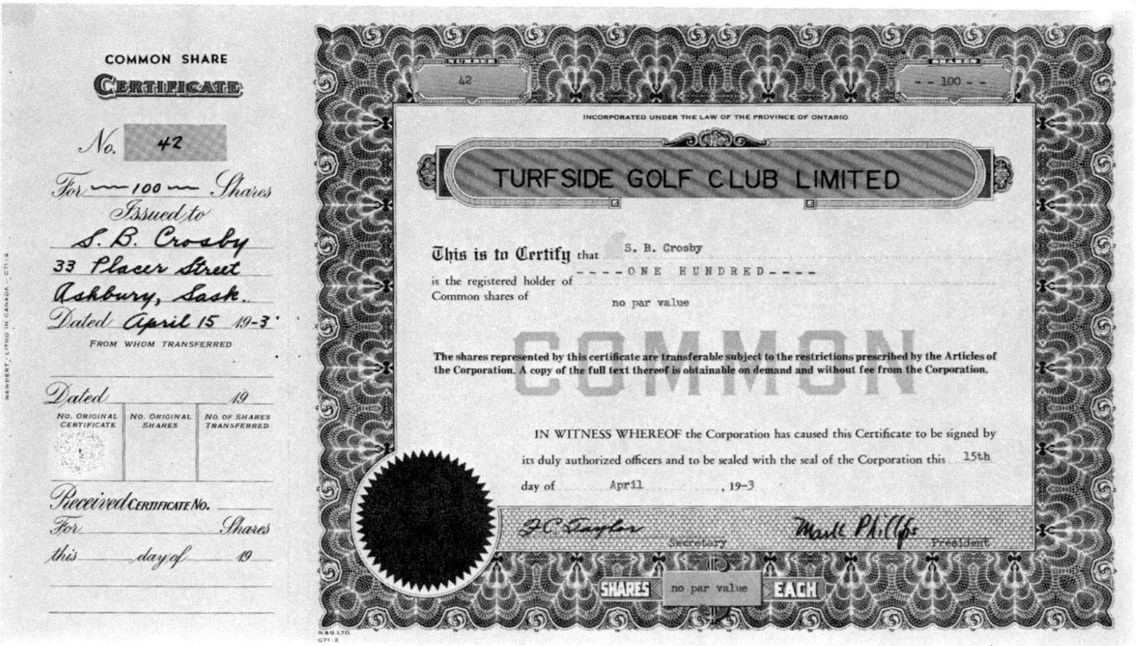
COMMON SHARE
CERTIFICATE
No. 42
For — 100 — Shares
Issued to
S. B. Crosby
33 Placer Street
Ashbury, Sask.
Dated April 15 19-3
FROM WHOM TRANSFERRED
Dated 19
NO. ORIGINAL CERTIFICATE | NO. ORIGINAL SHARES | NO. OF SHARES TRANSFERRED
Received Certificate No.
For Shares
this day of 19

42 — 100 —
INCORPORATED UNDER THE LAW OF THE PROVINCE OF ONTARIO
TURFSIDE GOLF CLUB LIMITED
This is to Certify that S. B. Crosby
is the registered holder of ----ONE HUNDRED----
Common shares of no par value
COMMON
The shares represented by this certificate are transferable subject to the restrictions prescribed by the Articles of the Corporation. A copy of the full text thereof is obtainable on demand and without fee from the Corporation.
IN WITNESS WHEREOF the Corporation has caused this Certificate to be signed by its duly authorized officers and to be sealed with the seal of the Corporation this 15th day of April, 19-3
J.C. Taylor Secretary
Mark Phillips President
SHARES no par value EACH

Figure 22.7 A stock certificate and stub with entries (front).

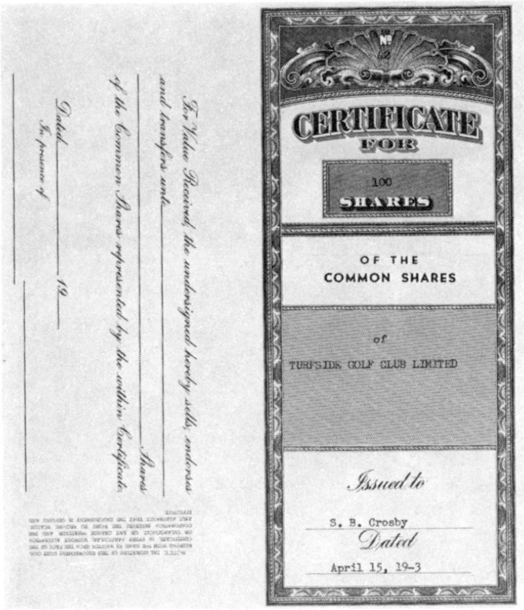

Figure 22.8 A stock certificate and stub with entries (back).

Transferring Shares

An important feature of corporations is the transferability of shares. That is, one person can sell or give shares to another person. When such an exchange takes place, an important procedure must be followed in order both to effect the transfer of stock certificates, and to keep the stock certificate book up to date.

1. The selling shareholder endorses the certificate by completing the reverse side of the share certificate. The selling shareholder indicates the number of shares to be transferred, the name(s) and address(es) of the new shareholder(s), and the date, and then signs the certificate. This is illustrated in Figure 22.9.
2. The endorsed certificate is sent to the secretary of the company.
3. The company secretary, upon receiving the endorsed share certificate, does the following:
   a. Cancels the share certificate and its stub by writing or stamping the word 'cancelled' on each.
   b. Staples the cancelled certificate to its stub in the stock certificate book.
   c. Prepares new certificates, and stubs, as indicated by the endorsement. The new certificate or certificates will be for the same number of shares as the cancelled certificate. More than one new certificate may be necessary for two

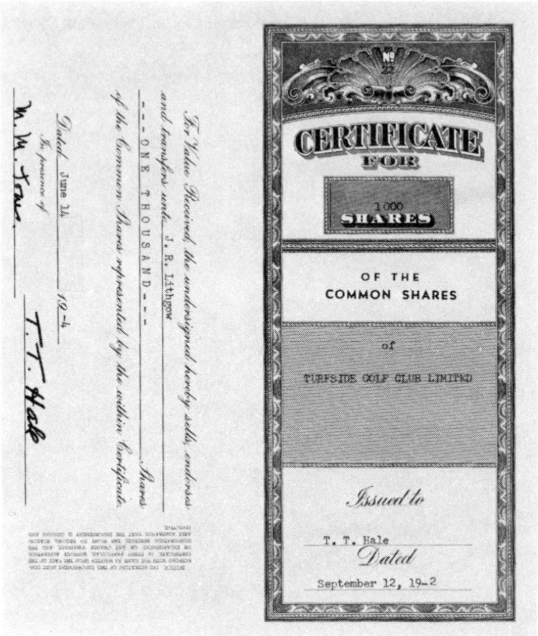

Figure 22.9 An endorsed stock certificate.

reasons. First, if there is more than one buyer, each buyer has to have a record of the number of shares purchased. Second, if the seller has retained a portion of the share value of the old certificate, both seller and buyer need a record of their shares.

4. The company secretary issues the new share certificate(s) to the respective owner(s).

When shares are transferred, money changes hands privately, outside of the corporation. No money is paid by or received by the company, nor is the number of company shares increased or decreased. Therefore, no accounting entries are required in the company accounts.

The stock certificate book is kept as up to date as possible. A corporation requires up-to-the-minute information about its shareholders, so that it can send out notices of meetings, dividend cheques, financial statements, and company reports to the proper persons.

Public corporations, whose shares are traded through a stock exchange, must have their share records maintained by a registrar. Changes in ownership of shares must be effected by a transfer agent. A number of firms are in the business of providing both of these services for corporations.

The Minute Book

The law requires that the actions and decisions of every shareholders' meeting and of every directors' meeting be recorded by the company secretary in a book called the **minute book**. The minute book is an important record of the corporation and an important source of information for its own accounting staff and its outside auditors. It records the company bylaws, dividend declarations, policy decisions, executive appointments, and other company matters.

22.10 Adjusting and Closing Entries for a Corporation

Because there are no individual owners' Capital or Drawings accounts, the process of adjusting and closing the books is changed slightly for a corporation. The following four accounting entries must be journalized and posted:

1. Record all and only those adjusting entries that appear in the Adjustments section of the work sheet.
2. Close out the balances on the credit side of the Income Statement section of the work sheet to the Income Summary account.
3. Close out the balances on the debit side of the Income Statement section of the work sheet to the Income Summary account.
4. Close out the balance in the Income Summary account to the Retained Earnings account.

22.11 Income Tax for Corporations

Corporations, by law, must pay income tax on their earnings at a fairly high rate. Therefore, income tax is an important expense item for a corporation.

The federal law requires a corporation to estimate its income tax in advance and pay it throughout the corporate fiscal year. The procedure for estimating the income tax for any year is set out in government regulations. The corporation must also settle its account for that year within the first three months of its next fiscal year. More specifically, before the last day of each month of each fiscal year, a corporation must remit to the Receiver General an amount equal to one twelfth of its estimated income tax for that year. Then, within three months of the corporation's year-end, the company must remit the balance of any unpaid tax.

To illustrate, assume that Superior Products Limited is incorporated on November 1. Its first fiscal year ends on the following October 31. Assume further that its estimated income tax for the year is $15 000. The required monthly instalment, one twelfth of this amount, is $1 250.

On October 31, the fiscal year-end of the company, twelve instalment payments will have been made. The Income Tax account will have a debit balance of $15 000 as shown in Figure 22.10.

INCOME TAX EXPENSE				
Date	Particulars	Debit	Credit	Balance
Nov 30		1 250		1 250 Dr
Dec 31		1 250		2 500 Dr
Jan 31		1 250		3 750 Dr
Feb 28		1 250		5 000 Dr
Mar 31		1 250		6 250 Dr
Apr 30		1 250		7 500 Dr
May 31		1 250		8 750 Dr
Jun 30		1 250		10 000 Dr
Jul 31		1 250		11 250 Dr
Aug 31		1 250		12 500 Dr
Sep 30		1 250		13 750 Dr
Oct 31		1 250		15 000 Dr

Figure 22.10 A record of monthly income tax payments for Superior Products Limited.

Income Tax Adjustment on the Work Sheet

First, remember that a corporation must itself pay income tax. When preparing the company's work sheet, the Income Tax Expense account is one of the items in the Trial Balance section, as shown in Figure 22.11.

Work Sheet								
	Trial Balance		Adjustments		Income Statement		Balance Sheet	
Accounts	Dr	Cr	Dr	Cr	Dr	Cr	Dr	Cr
Income Tax Expense	15 000 -							

Figure 22.11 A partial work sheet showing income tax expense.

Also remember that the $15 000 figure represents an *estimate* of the company's tax and not the actual tax figure. The actual tax figure still remains to be calculated, based on the company's net income before tax.

Net Income Before Income Tax

Before the company's actual income tax for the year can be calculated, it is necessary to ascertain its *net income before income tax*. The income tax calculation is based on this figure. To find out the company's net income before income tax, perform the following procedures.

1. *Except for the Income Tax line*, complete the work sheet making adjustments as necessary, until you are ready to take column totals.

2. Using an adding machine, total each of the two columns in the Income Statement section and find the difference between them. This figure represents the net income before income tax. (These are not the column totals to be recorded on the work sheet.)

Completing the Work Sheet

Based on the net income before tax figure determined above, and in accordance with government rules and regulations, the actual income tax for the year is calculated. To continue our example, assume that Superior Products Limited has a tax figure of $17 010.

By knowing the income tax expense for the year and the total income tax paid by instalments, it is possible to calculate the balance of income tax either still unpaid or overpaid.

For our example, the following calculation is necessary.

Income tax expense for the year (calculated on tax form)	$17 010
Less income tax paid by instalments	15 000
Equals income tax unpaid and owing	$ 2 010

Once this figure is calculated, an adjusting entry is made on the work sheet. This adjusting entry must correct the Income Tax Expense figure and set up the liability or receivable for the balance. For our example, this adjustment is shown in Figure 22.12.

Work Sheet

Accounts	Trial Balance Dr	Trial Balance Cr	Adjustments Dr	Adjustments Cr	Income Statement Dr	Income Statement Cr	Balance Sheet Dr	Balance Sheet Cr
Income Tax Expense	15000 –		2010 –		17010 –			2010 –
Income Tax Pay'l				2010 –				2010 –

Figure 22.12 A partial work sheet showing the adjusting entry for income tax expense.

The $17 010 figure represents the income tax expense for the year. The $2 010 figure represents the liability for income tax at the company's fiscal year-end.

The work sheet may now be totalled and completed in the usual manner, and the financial statements prepared. The $2 010 liability is included on the balance sheet among the current liabilities. Income tax expense is included on the income statement, usually as the last item before net income for the period. An example of income tax on the income statement is shown in Figure 22.13.

ROBIN HOOD MINES LIMITED

Statement of Income

For the year ended December 31, 19-3

	19-3	19-2
Revenue		
Bullion production	$3 271 000	$1 988 000
Interest	55 000	15 000
	3 326 000	2 003 000
Expense		
Development	285 000	187 000
Mining	367 000	296 000
Milling	198 000	138 000
Fees and charges for the use of underground facilities of parent company	348 000	290 000
Mine management, office and general	161 000	122 000
Head office administration and general	71 000	36 000
Marketing	15 000	9 000
Provision for tax under the Mining Tax Act, Ontario	198 000	131 000
	1 643 000	1 209 000
Operating Income	1 683 000	794 000
Other Expense		
Amortization of deferred development and administrative expenditures	163 000	136 000
Provision for depreciation of buildings, machinery, and equipment	21 000	6 000
	184 000	142 000
Income Before Income Taxes	1 499 000	652 000
Income taxes	506 000	222 000
Net Income for the Year	$ 993 000	$ 430 000

Figure 22.13 The income statement of Robin Hood Mines Limited showing the adjusting entry for income tax expense.

Accounting Terms

corporation
share certificate
shareholder
stockholder
charter
letters patent
board of directors
public corporation
private corporation
organization costs
dividends
retained earnings
common stock
par value
no par value share
preferred stock
non-cumulative dividend
cumulative dividend
fully-participating dividend
deficit
appropriation account
contributed surplus
issue price
market price
stock certificate book
minute book

Review Questions

1. Name one limited company in your community.
2. Give two significant features of the corporate form of business organization.
3. Who owns a corporation?
4. Explain how a corporation acts as an artificial legal being.
5. What is meant by limited liability?
6. Why are corporations subject to greater government control than partnerships or proprietorships?
7. Name the official document that gives approval to the formation of a limited company.
8. Explain the difference between a public and a private corporation.
9. How does a person become a director of a corporation?
10. What does a director do?
11. Name the usual executive officers of a corporation.
12. Give the advantages of a corporation.
13. Give the disadvantages of a corporation.
14. Name the two accounts in which the shareholders' equity of a simple corporation is recorded. Describe how these two accounts separate the equity into two distinct parts.
15. What are organization costs?
16. Explain the difference between a par value and a no par value common share.
17. How is the issue price associated with a no par value share determined?
18. What is a dividend?
19. Is a shareholder assured of receiving dividends? Explain.

20. Give two preferences that are associated with preferred shares.
21. Why might a company choose to issue preferred shares instead of issuing more common shares?
22. What is the name given to negative retained earnings? Explain how negative retained earnings come about.
23. What is the purpose of making an appropriation?
24. What factors affect the retained earnings account?
25. Where does the information for the statement of retained earnings come from?
26. What is contributed surplus?
27. Explain the difference between the book value and the market value of company shares.
28. Explain the purpose of the stock certificate book.
29. Explain the meaning of 'endorsement' as it applies to stock certificates.
30. Shares of public companies change hands daily. How, then, does the company know who is to receive dividends at any given time?
31. How do the closing entries of a corporation differ from those of a proprietorship?
32. What expense does a corporation have that a proprietorship or a partnership does not have?

Exercises

General Information about Corporations

1. Complete each sentence with the most appropriate word or phrase. This question also appears in your workbook.

1. A corporation is also known as a ____________________.
2. As part of the company's name, corporations must always include either the word __________, __________, __________, or __________.
3. The original purposes of a corporation were: a. ____________________ ____________________ b. ____________________.
4. As proof of ownership in a corporation, the owners receive __________ ____________________.
5. A person who has ownership in a corporation is known as a __________ or a __________.
6. Each common share in a corporation carries the right to __________ at the annual general meeting.
7. Private corporations can have no more than ____________________.
8. Private corporations must raise funds ____________________.
9. Shareholders' liability is ____________________.
10. The death, insolvency, or incapacity of any individual shareholder does not affect the ____________________ of a corporation.

11. In a number of respects a corporation has the _________ and _________ of a real person.
12. The laws of the federal government in regard to corporations are found in the _____________________________.
13. To be legally incorporated, a company must receive a _________ or _________ from the government.
14. Shareholders own the company but a corporation is controlled by a _____ ____________________.
15. The daily operations of a corporation are in the hands of _________ __________________.
16. To control a corporation one must theoretically own __________________ ___________________________.
17. Shares of a corporation can be _________ or _________ easily through a ______________.
18. Like a person, a corporation must pay __________________.
19. A corporation does not have a _________ or a _________ for each owner.
20. The equity of all the shareholders is obtained in two basic accounts. These are the ______________ and the ______________.
21. The Capital Stock account of a corporation represents the _____________ ___________________________.
22. The Retained Earnings account of a corporation represents the _________ ___________________________.

Formation of Corporations and Share Transactions

2. J. Franklin Limited is incorporated with an authorized capital of 1 000 shares of common stock having a par value of $10 a share. The petitioners, J. Franklin, R. Franklin, and S. Franklin, each subscribe for 200 shares.
Journalize the following transactions:

Transactions

May

1	Each of the petitioners pays $2 000 cash for his shares.
5	Legal fees for incorporation in the amount of $1 500 are paid.
20	400 shares are sold to T. Wilson for $4 000 cash.

3. E. G. Winters Limited is a company just incorporated with an authorized capital of 100 000 common shares having a par value of $10.
Journalize the following selected transactions of E. G. Winters Limited:

Transactions

February

6	The petitioners pay cash, amounting to $15 000, for their shares.

8 Incorporation expenses of $3 000 are paid by cheque.

15 10 000 shares are sold through an investment dealer to the general public at par. A cheque for the full issue price is received from the dealer.

18 5 000 shares are sold through an investment dealer to the general public at a premium of 2 percent. A cheque for the full price is received from the dealer.

20 A cheque is sent to the investment dealer in the amount of $4 530 representing his commission of 3 percent of the selling price of shares sold.

28 The petitioners are issued shares in consideration of their services in organizing the company. These services are valued at $5 000.

---

4. Plastic Products Limited is a new company which has just received its charter authorizing the issue of 1 000 common shares having no par value. The five petitioners each agree to take 100 shares at a price of $100 per share.

Journalize the following selected transactions.

Transactions

March

3 The petitioners each make payment to the company by cheque for the full price of their shares.

7 Legal and incorporation expenses of $2 000 are paid by cheque.

10 Land valued at $35 000 is acquired in return for 200 shares.

14 300 shares are sold to new shareholders, realizing $51 000 cash.

---

5. Colourful Decor Limited is incorporated with an authorized capital stock of 10 000 shares of no par value.

1. Journalize the following transactions of the company:

Transactions

September

1 2 500 shares are issued in return for cash to each of the three petitioners at a price of $10 a share.

3 Legal fees of incorporation are paid, $2 500.

5 2 500 shares are issued in return for land and a building at an agreed value of $10 000 for the land and $20 000 for the building.

2. Prepare a balance sheet as of September 5, 19–2.

---

6. R. Peters, M. Mowbray, and G. Glen are in the process of changing their partnership over to a limited company. Immediately prior to the changeover, the net assets of the company amounted to $120 000. The partners' Capital account balances were $60 000, $30 000, and $30 000, respectively.

The authorized capital of the limited company is 10 000 shares with a par value of $10.

1. **Calculate the number of shares that each of the partners will receive based on the capital investment ratio.**
2. **Give the accounting entry to convert the partnership into a limited company. With this entry the books of the partnership will become the books of the corporation.**

---

7. **Mountain Mining Company of Canada Limited has three classes of authorized shares:**

   a. No par value common shares.
   b. 8 percent non-cumulative preferred shares having a par value of $10 (known as Class 1 Preferred Stock).
   c. 9 percent cumulative preferred shares having a par value of $10 (known as Class 2 Preferred Stock).

   Journalize the following share transactions of the company:

Transactions

April

2	Sold for cash: 50 common shares for $5 000.
6	Sold for cash: 100 Class 1 preferred shares at par.
9	Sold: 1 200 common shares in exchange for land and buildings valued as follows: Land, $40 000; Buildings, $80 000.
15	Sold for cash: 50 Class 1 preferred shares at a premium of 10 percent.
29	Sold for cash: 100 Class 2 preferred shares at a discount of 5 percent.

---

8. **The trial balance of Ruth Goldberg is shown below.**

RUTH GOLDBERG
TRIAL BALANCE
JUNE 30, 19--

Bank	$ 4 000	Accounts Payable	$ 6 000
Accounts Receivable	10 000	Mortgage Payable	100 000
Land	50 000	R. Goldberg, Capital	33 000
Equipment	75 000		
	$139 000		$139 000

On July 2, Ms. Goldberg receives a charter incorporating her business under the name Goldberg Enterprises Limited. The charter authorizes the issue of 50 000 shares of no par value.

1. **Ms. Goldberg issues 33 000 shares, deemed to have a value of $1, to herself and to members of her immediate family. Record the accounting entry to convert the books from those of a proprietorship to those of a corporation.**
2. **The legal and incorporation expenses of $1 200 are paid by the issue of 1 200 shares to the lawyer. Record the accounting entry for this payment.**

9. Wonder World Limited, an amusement park, is a newly incorporated company authorized to issue 100 000 common shares of no par value and 100 000 8-percent preferred shares having a par value of $100. Five organizing petitioners agree to take 1 000 shares each at a value of $25 a share.

1. Journalize the following transactions:

Transactions

May

6 The five petitioners pay for and receive one-half of the agreed upon shares.

15 Theresa Nyzuk, a lawyer, is given 20 common shares in payment for legal work done in respect to incorporating the company. The work is valued at $500.

21 5 000 preferred shares are sold through an investment dealer at par. Of these, 4 900 are sold to the general public and 100 are kept by the investment dealer in payment for his services valued at $10 000.

26 Legal and other incorporation expenses of $200 are paid for in cash.

29 The petitioners agree to accept the balance of their agreed upon shares as payment for services rendered in incorporating the company.

June

5 Land is purchased for $120 000 cash.

10 Plant and equipment are purchased for $200 000 cash.

15 1 000 preferred shares are sold privately for cash at a premium of 5 percent.

30 2 000 preferred shares are sold privately for cash at a premium of 6 percent.

2. Prepare a simple balance sheet as at June 30.

---

10. Merit Manufacturing Limited is a newly incorporated company with an authorized capital of 100 000 common shares having a par value of $10. The following transactions occurred during its first month.

Transactions

March

3 The three petitioners took 1 000 shares each, valued at $10, as consideration for their efforts in organizing the company.

6 B. Cassidy, a management consultant, was engaged to plan the company layout and organization. He took payment for his services in the form of 600 shares valued at $6 000.

9 50 000 shares were sold to the general public at par. The investment dealer who sold these shares forwarded a cheque to the company for the full amount less a 2 percent commission for her services.

12 Land at a cost of $100 000 was acquired and paid for in cash.

15 Equipment, costing $150 000, was acquired and paid for in cash.

18 Legal and incorporation expenses of $1 500 were paid for in cash.

20 20 000 additional shares were sold to the general public through the same investment dealer at a premium of 5 percent. The full proceeds of the sale, less the dealer's 2 percent commission, were forwarded to the company.

25 25 000 additional shares were sold to the general public through the investment dealer, who was able to sell them at a 10 percent premium. The full proceeds of the sale, less the dealer's 2 percent commission, were forwarded to the company.

31 Equipment costing $600 000 was acquired and paid for in cash.

1. Journalize the above transactions.
2. Prepare a simplified balance sheet for the company as at March 31.

11. W. Murray, M. Walters, and F. Stevens operate a partnership in which they share income and loss and maintain their Capital accounts in the ratio of 3:3:2, respectively. The three men have applied for and received letters patent to incorporate their business under the name of Master Products Limited, effective June 30, 19--. The letters patent authorize capital stock of 16 000 no par value common shares.

After closing the books at June 30, the trial balance of the partnership is as follows:

MURRAY, WALTERS, AND STEVENS
POST-CLOSING TRIAL BALANCE
JUNE 30, 19--

Bank	$ 4 250	
Accounts Receivable	18 450	
Allowance for Doubtful Debts		$ 1 350
Supplies	516	
Prepaid Insurance	1 008	
Land	20 000	
Buildings	35 000	
Accumulated Depreciation of Buildings		4 992
Furniture and Equipment	7 250	
Accumulated Depreciation of Furn. and Equip.		3 538
Automobiles	7 845	
Accumulated Depreciation of Automobiles		4 001
Bank Loan		3 000
Accounts Payable		13 438
W. Murray, Capital		24 000
M. Walters, Capital		24 000
F. Stevens, Capital		16 000
	$94 319	$94 319

The partners have agreed to revalue the land and the buildings and to adjust these accounts to the appraised values immediately prior to incorporation. Any gain or loss on appraisal, and any expenses of appraisal or incorporation, are to be recorded in the partnership accounts as a direct charge or credit to the partners' Capital accounts. It is also agreed that the books of the partnership will continue and become the books of the corporation.

1. **On June 30, journalize the effect of the revaluation of the land and buildings. Land is appraised at $36 000 and buildings at $75 000 (the accumulated depreciation on buildings remaining unchanged).**
2. **Journalize the payments by cheque on June 30 of the following:**
   a. **Appraiser's fee, $1 200.**
   b. **Incorporation and legal fees, $2 640.**
3. **Convert the partnership books into those of the new limited company by closing out the partners' adjusted Capital accounts to a Common Stock account.**
4. **All of the authorized shares are to be distributed to the partners. The distribution is to be made in the ratio of their final Capital account balances as partners.**
   a. **Calculate the number of shares that each partner will receive.**
   b. **Calculate the value per share to be recorded in the company's minute book.**

Dividends

12. **A company is incorporated with fully paid capital stock as follows:**
    a. Common Stock, no par value, 10 000 shares.
    b. Preferred Stock, 8 percent cumulative, par value $25, 50 000 shares.

    1. **Calculate the amount of the preferred dividend for one year.**
    2. **The dividend is declared by the board of directors on January 10. Journalize the accounting entry to record the dividend declaration.**
    3. **The dividend is paid on February 1. Record the accounting entry to pay the dividend.**

13. **Give the accounting entries (without explanation) for each of the transactions shown below for Quality Products Limited. The company has authorized capital stock of 10 000 common shares of no par value, and 25 000 8-percent preferred shares with a par value of $10.**

Transactions

a. Each of the petitioners pays for 1 000 common shares at a value of $5.

b. 10 000 preferred shares are sold to the general public at par. The sale of these shares is handled by an investment dealer who charges $2 000 for his services.
c. Legal and incorporation expenses amounting to $1 000 are paid for in cash.
d. A net income of $126 000 is recorded and closed out of the Income Summary account.
e. The preferred dividend is declared by the board of directors.
f. The preferred dividend is paid.

---

14. The issued capital stock of Marwell Limited is as follows:

a. No par value common shares, 76 700 shares.
b. 6-percent preferred shares, par value $10, 27 500 shares.

1. Calculate the total dividend on the preferred stock.
2. Calculate the total dividend on the common stock if the rate is to be 26 cents per share.
3. Show the journal entries necessary to record the declaration of both of the above dividends. Date of declaration is April 12.
4. Show the journal entries necessary to record the payment of the above dividends. Date of payment is April 30.

---

15. The capital stock of EFG Co. Ltd. has remained as shown below for several years.

a. Common Stock, no par value, 10 000 shares.
b. Preferred Stock, par value $25, 6 percent cumulative, 40 000 shares.

For the last few years the net income of the company has been too small to fully pay the preferred dividends. Dividend payments on the preferred shares have been as follows: 19–2, $50 000; 19–3, $25 000; 19–4, $16 000. 19–5 has been a profitable year, with the company earning a net income of $154 000. It has been proposed that the entire year's profit be paid out in dividends.

If this is done, how much per share will the common shareholders receive? Show your calculations.

---

16. At December 31, 19–7, the end of a fiscal year, Vintage Products Limited has fully paid capital stock as shown below:

a. Common Stock, 500 000 shares of no par value.
b. Preferred Stock, 5 percent cumulative, 100 000 shares, par value of $25 per share.

Dividends on preferred shares are fully paid up to December 31, 19–5. No preferred dividends have been paid since that time.

1. Calculate the total amount of dividends on preferred shares that must be paid before any dividends can be paid on the common shares.
2. On December 31, 19–7, the balance of the Retained Earnings account is

$900 000 Cr. and the balance in the Bank account is $700 000 Dr. Calculate the greatest dividend per share that can be paid on the common shares.

3. **The dividends calculated in both cases above are declared by the directors on January 3, 19–8. Give the accounting entries to record them.**
4. **The dividends above are paid on January 15, 19–8. Give the accounting entries to record the payment.**

---

17. A company has the following capital stock:

a. Common Stock, authorized and fully paid for, 50 000 shares of no par value.
b. Preferred Stock, authorized and fully paid for, 25 000 shares, 8 percent, non-participating, $10 par value.

The company has paid dividends as follows:

Year	*Amount*
1	$70 000
2	nil
3	40 000
4	5 000
5	55 000
6	80 000
7	15 000
8	45 000

1. **Complete the schedule in your workbook showing the dividends to be paid to each class of shares if the preferred shares are non-cumulative.**
2. **Show the dividends to be paid if the preferred shares are cumulative.**

---

18. Fleet Company Limited was incorporated with 10 000 common shares with a par value of $10 and 10 000 10-percent-preferred shares with a par value of $20. All shares were issued and fully paid for.

Over the years, Fleet Company Limited paid the following dividends:

Year	*Amount*
1	$30 000
2	nil
3	15 000
4	25 000
5	36 000
6	39 000
7	42 000
8	36 000
9	45 000
10	12 000
11	50 000
12	42 000

Complete the workbook schedule showing the dividends paid to each class of stockholder under each of the following conditions:

1. **The preferred shares are non-cumulative.**
2. **The preferred shares are cumulative.**
3. **The preferred shares are cumulative and fully participating.**

19. The following is an analysis of the share certificate book of Haskin Associates Limited:

Certificate Number	*Name of Shareholder*	*Number of Shares*	*Date of Issue of Certificates*	*Date of Cancellation of Certificate*	*Comments*
1	E.J. Boynton	50	Mar. 1, 19–1	Apr. 12, 19–5	Replaced by #15
2	A.P. Scully	100	Mar. 1, 19–1	Sep. 9, 19–3	Replaced by #10
3	J. Felton	150	Apr. 30, 19–1		
4	D.T. Tyrone	200	Sep. 6, 19–1	Apr. 6, 19–3	Replaced by #7, #8
5	A. Browser	150	Feb. 19, 19–2		
6	F. Minelli	50	Sep. 20, 19–2		
7	B. Carson	100	Apr. 6, 19–3	Aug. 3, 19–4	Replaced by #12
8	E.J. Boynton	100	Apr. 6, 19–3		
9	A. Browser	1000	July 4, 19–3		
10	J. Felton	100	Sep. 9, 19–3		
11	F. Minelli	500	May 15, 19–4		
12	W. Childs	100	Aug. 3, 19–4		
13	C. Fraser	200	Jan. 19, 19–5		
14	P. Yonge	100	Mar. 16, 19–5		
15	A. Browser	50	Apr. 12, 19–5		

A dividend of $10 a share is declared on October 15, 19–4, to be paid to shareholders of record on December 31, 19–4.

1. **For the purpose of preparing the accounting entry and the dividend cheques, find the names of the shareholders of record on December 31, 19–4, and the total holdings of each.**
2. **Show the journal entry to record the declaration of the dividend.**
3. **Show the journal entry to record the payment of the dividend.**

Retained Earnings

20. The following transactions took place for Black Design Limited:

Transactions

a. Dec. 31, 19–6 Net income of $54 200 closed out.
b. Jan. 10, 19–7 Dividend of $25 000 declared by the board of directors.
c. Jan. 31, 19–7 Dividend of January 10 paid in cash.
d. Dec. 31, 19–7 Net income of $62 700 closed out.
e. Jan. 12, 19–8 Dividend of $30 000 declared by the board of directors.
f. Jan. 31, 19–8 Dividend of January 12 paid in cash.

1. **Journalize these transactions on page 16 of a general journal.**
2. **Post the entries that affect the Retained Earnings account.**
3. **Calculate the ending balance in the Retained Earnings account.**

---

21. The following items were recorded for Meg Limited:

Transactions

a.	Dec. 31, 19–5	Net Income, $76 000 closed out.
b.	Mar. 15, 19–6	Appropriation for New Building, $50 000.
c.	Dec. 31, 19–6	Net Income, $86 000 closed out.
d.	Mar. 15, 19–7	Appropriation for New Building, $50 000.
e.	Dec. 31, 19–7	Net Income, $92 000 closed out.
f.	Jan. 20, 19–8	Declaration of Dividend, $75 000.
g.	Mar. 15, 19–8	Appropriation for New Building, $50 000.
h.	Apr. 20, 19–8	Dividend paid, $75 000.
i.	Aug. 31, 19–8	New building completed and paid for, $150 000.
j.	Dec. 31, 19–8	Net Income, $103 000 closed out.

1. **Show the effect (if any) of these items in the Retained Earnings account that is provided in your workbook.**
2. **Show the accounting entries required for items b., f., h., and i.**
3. **Once the building project is completed, what should be done with the Appropriation account? In your opinion what was the purpose of the account?**

---

22. Shown below is the Retained Earnings account for Morris Switzer Limited. The accountant's comments in analyzing the account are written in the Particulars column. Prepare the statement of retained earnings for the year ended December 31, 19–4.

RETAINED EARNINGS

Date	Particulars	Debit	Credit	Balance
19-3				
Nov 30	Balance Forwarded			CR 102 746.21
Dec 31	Closing of net income		156 212.02	CR 258 958.23
19-4				
Jan 15	Dividend declaration	150 000.00		CR 108 958.23
Jun 30	Appropriation business expansion	100 000.00		CR 8 958.23
Dec 31	Closing of net income		142 012.72	CR 150 970.95

---

23. From the following data, prepare a statement of retained earnings. You must supply any missing data.

Balance at beginning of year	$643 719
Balance at end of year	467 762
Appropriation for new building	70 000
Dividend declared	325 000

Equity Section of Balance Sheet

24. The shareholders' equity of P.R.O. Limited is made up of the following items:

Common Stock
Authorized, 50 000 shares; par value $10; issued and fully paid, 20 000 shares.

Retained Earnings
$7 542.00

Prepare the Shareholders' Equity section of the balance sheet.

25. The shareholders' equity of Alpine Products Limited is comprised of the following:

Common Stock
Authorized, 10 000 shares; no par value; issued and fully paid, 10 000 shares; book value of issued shares, $94 216.

Retained Earnings
$26 412

Appropriation
For land acquisition, $50 000.

Prepare the Equity section of the balance sheet.

26. The shareholders' equity of Kingston Investments Limited consists of the following:

Common Stock
Authorized, 5 000 shares; no par value; issued and fully paid, 5 000 shares; book value of issued shares, $54 260.

Preferred Stock
6 percent cumulative preferred; par value $25; authorized, issued, and fully paid; 20 000 shares.

Contributed Surplus
Premium on preferred stock, $40 000.

Retained Earnings
$157 206

Prepare the Shareholders' Equity section of the balance sheet.

Share Records

27. Workbook Exercise: Filling in data on share certificates.

Work Sheet, Income Tax, End-of-period Accounting

28. Workbook Exercise: Completing a work sheet; preparing financial statements; recording adjusting and closing entries; recording dividend declaration.

29. Workbook Exercise: Completing a work sheet; preparing financial statements; recording adjusting and closing entries.

30. The following information is given for Hall-Parker Toys, Inc:

a. The income tax expense figure in the trial balance section of the work sheet is Dr. $36 000.
b. The tentative totals (excluding the income tax expense figure) of the Income Statement columns of the work sheet are: Dr. $89 076.02; Cr. $170 061.50.
c. The income tax rate is 46 percent.

1. **Calculate the net income before taxes.**
2. **Calculate the income tax expense for the year.**
3. **Calculate the income tax payable or receivable.**

31. The general ledger for the Alice Harper and Associates Limited is provided for you in the workbook. The trial balance from the ledger, prior to completing the work sheet for the year ended December 31, 19–4, is shown opposite. Use the trial balance as well as the additional information to answer the following questions. Additional information is also provided.

Additional Information:

a. The allowance for bad debts should be $350.
b. The supplies inventory is $400.
c. The prepaid insurance is $350.
d. Depreciation is calculated at government rates.
e. The accrued wages are $450.
f. Income tax is at 40 per cent.

1. **Complete the work sheet, using the additional information.**
2. **Journalize the adjusting and closing entries. Ignore dates and explanations.**
3. **Post the adjusting entries to the T-accounts. Ignore dates and cross-references.**
4. **Prepare a post-closing trial balance.**

Work Sheet

Accounts	Trial Balance Dr	Trial Balance Cr
Bank	900 -	
Accounts Receivable	35 400 -	
Allow. for Doubtful Debts		200 -
Supplies	1 475 -	
Prepaid Insurance	1 260 -	
Land	95 690 -	
Buildings	120 000 -	
Accum. Deprec. Buildings		25 450 -
Furniture and Equipment	38 000 -	
Accum. Deprec. Furn. & Equip.		12 500 -
Automotive Equipment	28 000 -	
Accum. Deprec. Auto. Equip.		11 500 -
Bank Loan		20 000 -
Accounts Payable		15 700 -
Employees' Income Tax Payable		
Sales Tax Payable		730 -
Capital Stock - Common		25 000 -
Capital Stock - 8% Preferred		100 000 -
Retained Earnings		12 845 -
Revenue		190 800 -
Advertising	1 850 -	
Bank Charges	2 750 -	
Canada Pension Plan Exp.	750 -	
Income Tax Expense	5 600 -	
Light, Heat, & Water	1 650 -	
Miscellaneous Expense	175 -	
Postage	500 -	
Telephone	1 025 -	
Unemployment Insur. Exp.	300 -	
Wages	29 400 -	
	364 725 -	364 725 -

Challenge Questions

32. A comparative balance sheet and an income statement for Midhurst Company Limited appear below.

MIDHURST COMPANY LIMITED
COMPARATIVE BALANCE SHEET
DECEMBER 31, 19–2 and 19–1

	19–2	19–1
Assets		
Bank	$ 240 000	$ 100 000
Accounts Receivable	280 000	250 000
Inventories	275 000	300 000
Land	90 000	90 000
Buildings	360 000	400 000
Equipment	160 000	200 000
TOTAL ASSETS	$1 405 000	$1 340 000
Liabilities		
Bank Loan	$ 50 000	$ 50 000
Accounts Payable	245 000	210 000
TOTAL LIABILITIES	$ 295 000	$ 260 000
Shareholders' Equity		
Capital Stock	$ 600 000	$ 500 000
Appropriation for New Building	250 000	200 000
Retained Earnings	260 000	380 000
	$1 110 000	$1 080 000
TOTAL LIABILITIES AND EQUITY	$1 405 000	$1 340 000

MIDHURST COMPANY LIMITED
INCOME STATEMENT
YEAR ENDED DECEMBER 31, 19–2

Revenue		$750 000
Expenses		
Cost of Goods Sold	$300 000	
Depreciation	80 000	
Other Expenses	90 000	470 000
Net Income		$280 000

Additional Information:

a. All sales are on account.

b. All purchases of goods and services are on account.

c. There were no additions to fixed assets.

1. **Work out the accounting entries (yearly totals) that caused changes in the balance sheet figures from 19–1 to 19–2.**
2. **Make a list summarizing the changes in Bank.**
3. **Prepare a Statement of Retained Earnings for the year.**

---

33. A simplified comparative balance sheet and an income statement for Snowflake Company Limited are shown below.

SNOWFLAKE COMPANY LIMITED
COMPARATIVE BALANCE SHEET
DECEMBER 31, 19–6 and 19–5

	19–6	19–5
Assets		
Bank	$ 40 000	$ 70 000
Accounts Receivable	67 000	47 000
Inventories	60 000	55 000
Land	80 000	80 000
Buildings	171 000	125 000
Equipment	72 000	90 000
TOTAL ASSETS	$490 000	$467 000
Liabilities		
Bank Loan	$ 20 000	$ 25 000
Accounts Payable	75 000	110 000
TOTAL LIABILITIES	$ 95 000	$135 000
Shareholders' Equity		
Capital Stock	$250 000	$200 000
Appropriation for Expansion	100 000	75 000
Retained Earnings	45 000	57 000
	$395 000	$332 000
TOTAL LIABILITIES AND EQUITY	$490 000	$467 000

SNOWFLAKE COMPANY LIMITED
INCOME STATEMENT
YEAR ENDED DECEMBER 31, 19–6

Sales		$500 000
Costs and Expenses		
Costs of Goods Sold	$220 000	
Depreciation Building	9 000	
Depreciation Equipment	18 000	
Other Expenses	40 000	287 000
Net Income		$213 000

Additional Information:

a. On January 1, 19–6, a major addition to the building was completed at a cost of $85 000 which was paid for in cash.
b. All sales during the year were on account.
c. All purchases of goods and services were on account.
d. Depreciation rates were as follows: Buildings, 5 percent; Equipment, 20 percent.

1. Work out the accounting entries for the year (yearly totals) that caused the changes in the balance sheet figures from year 5 to year 6.
2. Prepare a schedule of changes in Cash for the year.
3. Prepare a schedule of changes in Retained Earnings for the year.

Cases

Case 1 *Raising Additional Capital for Expansion*

Jerry Walker owns a small limited company with his wife and brother. Of a total of 1 000 common shares, Jerry owns 990 and his wife and brother each own 5.

By patiently ploughing the company earnings back into the business and by taking out the minimum in the way of dividends, Jerry has brought the business along successfully. Earnings have been steadily improving but have never been large.

The business has reached a critical point. With a larger plant at a cost of $400 000, it could capitalize on a booming market and be assured of net income (over and above the costs of financing the expansion) in the range of $150 000 annually.

Jerry has no additional capital of his own. The current interest rates are 15 percent or more.

Questions

1. What alternative ways are there for Jerry to finance the expansion?
2. Which method would you recommend? Give reasons for your choice.

Case 2 *Selling Shares on the Instalment Plan*

J. P. Johnson Limited does not require full and immediate payment for its shares. The company has a plan that allows people to *subscribe* for its shares by making a down payment on the purchase price and contracting to pay the balance of the purchase price on an instalment basis.

Question

1. Devise a fair way to handle a situation such as this in the accounts. Consider the extent of the shareholders' liability, the voting privileges of the shareholders, and the presentation on the balance sheet of any new accounts that you may think are necessary. Explain fully.

Case 3 *Control of a Corporation*

An acquaintance of yours, Mr. Farmer, offers to sell you some shares that he owns in a medium-sized and very profitable company. He acquired these shares some time ago as an investment. Mr. Farmer claims that he is selling them because he needs cash to take advantage of another investment opportunity.

Mr. Farmer shows you the following breakdown of the shareholdings of the company:

Mrs. Adams	30 shares	She is a widow who inherited her shares upon the death of her husband. She has shown no interest whatever in the company affairs, and is quite satisfied that it must be an excellent company because she receives a dividend cheque regularly.
R. Baker	40 shares	He acquired his shares from a third person in settlement of a debt. He attends the company meetings regularly and is highly critical of the management. Whenever he suggests a change, however, he is always voted down.
S. Clarke	65 shares	He is the secretary-treasurer of the company, a position that he has held for 15 years. He is also one of the three company directors.
M. Dunn	100 shares	He is the general manager, president, and a director of the company which he started 15 years ago.
C. Everett	10 shares	He had his shares given to him. He does not know anything about the company and is not interested. He would be willing to sell his shares for a fair price.
Mr. Farmer	150 shares	
Mrs. Greig	35 shares	Mrs. Greig is a wealthy lady who travels a great deal. She has had no known direct involvement in any affairs of the company. It is not known how she acquired her shares.
H. Harris	70 shares	He has been the vice-president for the last ten years, is the brother-in-law of the president, and is also a director.

Mr. Farmer believes that the company could earn substantially higher profits with new management. By acquiring his shares, you would become the shareholder with the largest individual holdings. You would stand a good chance of gaining control of the company by getting the support or acquiring the shares of the four small shareholders. He points out that the three men who run the company own only 235 shares out of a total of 500.

Mr. Farmer is asking $50 000 for his shares. This is a fair price. You have the management skills, the technical expertise, and the experience to handle the company.

Question

1. Decide on a course of action and give reasons for your decision.

Case 4 *Control Without a Majority of Shares*

The Jones family owns 24 percent of the common stock of a large corporation. It is common knowledge that this family has control of the company.

Question

1. How can the Jones family control the company without having the theoretical 50 percent of the shares plus one?

Case 5 *Controlling a Stock Promoter*

Jake Takem, a young and aggressive entrepreneur, saw a chance to make some quick and easy money if he could come up with $50 000. Unfortunately Jake was broke, but he had heard that corporations raise money by selling shares to the public. He decided to explore this possibility. He surmised that if he were to set up a company with 100 000 shares, he could keep control by putting 50 001 shares in his own name, and he could sell the remaining 49 999 to the general public at $1 each. Without putting up a cent of his own he then would have close to the $50 000 he needed. Jake was quite pleased with the whole scheme.

To put his plan into action, Jake first paid a visit to a lawyer and explained his plan. The lawyer informed Jake of the following:

a. He would have to comply in all respects to the numerous requirements of the Companies Act.
b. He would have to seek permission from the government to set up his company by applying for Letters Patent and paying a fee.
c. Most important, he would have to prepare a *prospectus* for which there are page upon page of legislative requirements.

Hearing all of this annoyed Jake. He left the lawyer's office in an angry mood exclaiming about the unfairness of government regulations and about oppression of the little man.

Question

1. Is Jake right? Does government regulation work for or against the little man? Explain.

Case 6 *Should Dividends be Declared?*

The board of directors of Grover Contracting Company Limited is meeting on January 10, 19–4, to decide on the payment of dividends to shareholders. The following data have been collected for the meeting to help the directors in their discussion:

Net income, year ended December 31, 19–3	$150 000
Cash on hand, January 10, 19–4	95 000
Retained earnings, January 10, 19–4	156 750
Total current assets, January 10, 19–4	99 000
Total current liabilities, January 10, 19–4	104 000

Capital Stock:

Common: 50 000 shares, no par value, issued and fully paid. (The last common dividend was $2 a share for the 19–2 year.)

Preferred, 6 percent cumulative: 150 000 shares, issued and fully paid, par value $1 500 000. (Preferred dividends are fully paid up to and including the 19–2 year. There were no preferred dividends in 19–3.)

Questions

1. Based on the above information, what decision should the directors make? Give your opinion and show your calculations.
2. If you believe that a dividend should be paid, give the accounting entries to record the declaration of the dividend and the payment of the dividend.

Case 7 *Buying the Shares of a Company?*

John Church, the owner of a corporation, has decided to get out of the catering business. A number of legal hassles with the income tax department and with other corporations have been putting a lot of strain on him. John has put the 10 000 company shares up for sale at the very fair price of $20 a share, for a total of $200 000.

Cynthia Pollock wants to purchase the business and has offered $200 000 for it. But this offer is not for the shares of the company, only for its assets and liabilities.

Questions

1. Why is it to Cynthia's advantage to buy the assets and the liabilities rather than the share certificates, which carry with them the ownership of the assets and liabilities?
2. Why is it to John's advantage to sell the shares?

Career

Rita Iacello / Vice President of Finance

Because Rita Iacello did not anticipate a career in accounting, she did not take any accounting courses in high school. She regretted this when, after graduating, she became an inventory clerk for a large food-processing corporation. To supplement her on-the-job accounting training with a broader knowledge of accounting principles, Rita enrolled in the Registered Industrial Accountant's (RIA) program.

From inventory clerk, Rita was promoted to cost accounting manager and then to general accounting manager. Over the course of her career, Rita has also held the positions of assistant controller, controller, and director of finance. These positions have involved a wide variety of accounting responsibilities, including cost accounting, pricing, controlling the budget, supervising accounts payable, preparing the payroll, and controlling the general ledger. She has also monitored the company's internal control system and effectively coordinated accounting procedures throughout the corporation.

Rita is now vice president and corporate controller. She is responsible for every accounting operation and financial decision that occurs in the company. She directs the preparation and analysis of the Income Statement, the Balance Sheet, and the Statement of Retained Earnings. She coordinates the preparation of all budgets and financial forecasts. She designs and administers the company's cash management program and makes sure that the company's assets are effectively managed. She also acts as the company liaison with external auditors.

Rita monitors and updates all of the company's accounting systems and internal control measures. Recently, she has been in charge of developing a computerized system to meet the company's accounting needs. She highly recommends computer education to anyone entering today's ever-changing business world.

As Vice President in Charge of Finance, Rita must coordinate the financial features of all three corporate divisions which process chocolate, soft drinks, and general food, respectively. To keep herself informed of trends in these areas, Rita spends much of her free time reading trade journals and research reports. She believes that those who enter top managerial positions must be prepared to devote as much time and energy to their careers as is necessary.

23

Analyzing Financial Statements

23-1 Comparative Financial Statements
23-2 Common-size Financial Statements
23-3 Trend Analysis
23-4 Key Ratios and Relationships

Objectives

When you have completed Chapter 23, you should:

1. Know who analyzes financial statements and for what reasons.
2. Be able to prepare and read comparative financial statements.
3. Be able to prepare and read common-size financial statements.
4. Be able to prepare and read trend analyses.
5. Be able to calculate and interpret the following key ratios and relationships: current ratio; quick ratio; collection period; return on owner's investment; inventory turnover; net income percentage; earnings per share; debt/equity ratios; price-earnings ratio.

The financial statements of a company show the financial position of a business simply and clearly. Nonetheless, financial statements by themselves do not always satisfy the needs of the readers. Owners, managers, bankers, other creditors, prospective purchasers, and shareholders all require specialized information that is not directly provided by standard financial statements. This information can be obtained, however, when certain techniques of analysis are applied to the financial statements.

For example, bankers who are asked to loan money to a business normally request financial statements covering several years of operation. The bankers then analyze these statements to find out the borrower's ability to repay bank loans. In particular, bankers are interested in the trend of the company's net income, the company's potential for growth, and the worth and saleability of the company's assets should they have be sold to pay off a loan.

Prospective investors in a company are interested in the trend of the company's earnings, its potential for growth, and the market price of the company's shares if it is a corporation.

The management team of a company examines the financial statements more thoroughly than any other group. Management compares the statements with those of previous years, makes a number of specific calculations about such items as inventory or accounts receivable, and works out trends and projections for the future. Management performs this detailed analysis to eliminate areas of weakness, promote areas of strength, and institute sound planning, efficiency, and control.

In a few cases, management pays little attention to the day-to-day operations of the business. Managers of this sort are only aware of the condition of their businesses after the accounting period is over and the financial statements have been prepared by outside accountants. Managers who do not keep in close touch with the financial affairs of their businesses run a greater risk of failure than those who are well informed.

All wise executives study financial statements carefully and analyze them thoroughly. In particular, they look for unfavourable trends and areas of weakness that require correction. In unsuccessful businesses, the areas of weakness are soon painfully apparent.

Business people use several methods to obtain meaningful information from financial statements. A number of these are discussed in the following pages.

23.1 Comparative Financial Statements

A simple and effective analysis of a business can be made by comparing data from year to year. This comparison is usually made on **comparative financial statements** that present the figures for successive years side by side, along with the amount of change. Figures 23.1 and 23.2 show the comparative financial statements of Astra Supply Co. Ltd.

ASTRA SUPPLY CO. LTD.
COMPARATIVE BALANCE SHEET
DECEMBER 31, 19–2 and 19–1

	19–2	*19–1*	*Change*
ASSETS			
Current Assets			
Bank	$ 1 000	$ 4 000	—$ 3 000
Accounts Receivable	39 000	17 500	21 500
Merchandise Inventory	48 000	35 000	13 000
Prepaid Expenses	2 050	2 100	— 50
Total Current Assets	$ 90 050	$ 58 600	$31 450
Plant and Equipment			
Land	$ 70 000	$ 70 000	
Buildings	216 500	227 900	—$11 400
Office Equipment	7 200	7 500	— 300
Automotive Equipment	21 370	30 100	— 8 730
Total Plant and Equipment	$315 070	$335 500	—$20 430
Total Assets	$405 120	$394 100	$11 020
LIABILITIES			
Current Liabilities			
Bank Loan	$ 40 000	$ 50 000	—$10 000
Accounts Payable	10 100	9 050	1 050
Accrued Liabilities	3 000	2 700	300
Total Current Liabilities	$ 53 100	$ 61 750	—$ 8 650
Shareholders' Equity			
Common Stock, Par Value $25; 12 000 shares	$300 000	$300 000	
Retained Earnings	52 020	32 350	$19 670
Total Shareholders' Equity	$352 020	$332 350	$19 670
Total Liabilities and Equity	$405 120	$394 100	$11 020

Figure 23.1 A comparative balance sheet.

ASTRA SUPPLY CO. LTD.
COMPARATIVE INCOME STATEMENT
YEARS ENDED DECEMBER 31, 19–2 and 19–1

	19–2	*19–1*	*Change*
Revenue			
Net Sales	$330 400	$308 580	$21 820
Cost of Goods Sold			
Merchandise Inventory, January 1	$ 35 000	$ 32 700	$ 2 300
Net Purchases	181 432	150 022	31 410
Goods Available for Sale	$216 432	$182 722	$33 710
Less Merchandise Inventory, Dec. 31	48 000	35 000	13 000
Cost of Goods Sold	$168 432	$147 722	$20 710
Gross Profit	$161 968	$160 858	$ 1 110
Operating Expenses			
Advertising	$ 5 500	$ 5 750	—$ 250
Car Expenses	8 010	7 450	560
Depreciation of Buildings	11 395	11 395	
Depreciation of Office Equipment	1 800	1 800	
Depreciation of Automotive Equipment	10 700	10 700	
Insurance	1 050	1 350	— 300
Interest and Bank Charges	6 400	6 000	400
Miscellaneous Expense	310	300	10
Power	1 340	1 210	130
Supplies	400	475	— 75
Telephone	475	462	13
Wages	36 600	30 560	6 040
Total Operating Expenses	$ 83 980	$ 77 452	$ 6 528
Net Income Before Income Tax	$ 77 988	$ 83 406	—$ 5 418
Income Tax	30 800	33 033	— 2 233
Net Income	$ 47 188	$ 50 373	—$ 3 185

Figure 23.2 A comparative income statement.

When examining comparative financial statements, management looks for items that show extraordinary, or unusual, change. These items are then studied in greater depth to find out the reasons for the change. Of course, management will encourage factors that cause favourable change, and perhaps apply them in other areas. Management will try to eliminate factors that cause unfavourable change.

On the comparative financial statements of Astra Supply Co. Ltd., a number of items show extraordinary change. These items are subjected to further investigation. Figures 23.1 and 23.2 show the following changes:

1. Accounts receivable have more than doubled. Although sales have increased, they have not increased nearly enough to have caused a doubling of accounts receivable. Because this large increase is negative, management will be forced to take corrective action. Management will ask questions such as the following: Has there been an ill-advised change in credit-granting policy? Does the accounts receivable figure include any large uncollectible accounts? Does the collection policy of the company need to be strengthened?
2. Sales have increased by $21 820. On the surface, this appears positive. However, management breaks this increase down into two possible components. Management must separate the amount of increase that results from an increase in items sold from the amount that results from an inflationary rise in prices. If the sales increase of Astra Supply Co. Ltd. is merely the result of inflation, then it is not really a positive change.
3. Both Purchases and closing Merchandise Inventory have increased significantly. The dramatic increase in these two items points to a potentially unhealthy situation. If the increases are the result of large-scale buying at special low prices, then the changes are favourable. However, if the increases have been caused by overbuying, buying at excessive prices, keeping more inventory on hand than is necessary, or keeping an inventory that includes unsaleable goods, then the changes are unfavourable and require quick remedial action.
4. While sales have increased by $21 820, gross profit has only increased by $1 100. Undoubtedly this situation is related to the increased Purchases and closing Inventory, but it could indicate that prices are too low and should be reviewed.
5. Wages have increased by $6 040. If this results from a necessary rate increase granted to employees, then it must be taken in stride. However, if it results from employees working below their potential and working more hours at overtime rates, then corrective action is necessary.
6. Insurance has decreased by $300. This is good if it results from a definite premium savings. The increase is not good if it results from the lapse of some policies through negligence.

23.2 Common-size Financial Statements

Financial statements can be prepared in a form that presents data differently. **Common-size statements** show individual items as percentages of a selected figure, known as the base figure. As an example, examine the condensed common-size comparative income statement shown in Figure 23.3.

COMMON-SIZE INCOME STATEMENT

	19–4	*19–4*	*19–5*	*19–5*
Sales	$145 000	100.0%	$157 000	100.0%
Cost of Goods Sold	80 000	55.2	88 000	56.1
Gross Profit	$ 65 000	44.8%	$ 69 000	43.9%
Operating Expenses	30 000	20.7	32 000	20.4
Net Income	$ 35 000	24.1%	$ 37 000	23.5%

Figure 23.3 A common-size income statement.

To help you to understand the value of common-size statements, observe the following:

1. On an income statement, the sales figure for each year is selected as the base figure and is given the value of 100.0 percent.

2. In each year, the other financial figures are converted to percentages of the sales figure. To make this simple calculation, use the sales figure as the denominator of a fraction and multiply by 100. For the Cost of Goods Sold figure in 19–4, the calculation is as follows:

$$\frac{80\ 000}{145\ 000} \times 100 = 55.2\%$$

3. The percentage analysis reveals information not seen by a straight comparison of dollar figures. For example, Figure 23.3 provides the following data:
   a. The costs of the goods sold is rising faster than the selling price of the goods sold, resulting in a decreased percentage gross profit.
   b. Although operating expenses have increased by $2 000, they are being controlled. This is seen by comparing 20.4 percent for this year to the 20.7 percent of the previous year.
   c. The bottom line shows an increase in net income. This may appear favourable at first sight, but appears less so when the percentage figures are examined.

On a common-size balance sheet, the total assets figure (which equals the total liabilities and equity figure) is selected as the base figure and given the value of 100 percent. Other figures on the statement are then calculated as percentages of this base figure.

A condensed common-size balance sheet is shown in Figure 23.4.

COMMON-SIZE BALANCE SHEET YEARS ENDED DECEMBER, 19–5 and 19–6				
	19–6	*19–6*	*19–5*	*19–5*
ASSETS				
Current Assets				
Cash	$ 2 000	1.9%	$ 1 000	.8%
Accounts Receivable	12 000	11.8	15 000	12.8
Merchandise Inventory	7 000	6.9	10 000	8.6
Total Current Assets	$ 21 000	20.6%	$ 26 000	22.2%
Plant and Equipment				
Land	$ 27 000	26.5%	$ 27 000	23.1%
Building	39 000	38.2	39 000	33.3
Equipment	15 000	14.7	25 000	21.4
Total Plant and Equipment	$ 81 000	79.4%	$ 91 000	77.8%
Total Assets	$102 000	100.0%	$117 000	100.0%
LIABILITIES AND EQUITY				
Current Liabilities				
Accounts Payable	$ 16 000	15.7%	$ 21 000	18.0%
Shareholders' Equity				
Common Stock	$ 50 000	49.0%	$ 50 000	42.7%
Retained Earnings	36 000	35.3	46 000	39.3
Total Shareholders' Equity	$ 86 000	84.3%	$ 96 000	82.0%
Total Liabilities and Equity	$102 000	100.0%	$102 000	100.0%

Figure 23.4 A common-size balance sheet.

23.3 Trend Analysis

Analyzing by percentages is very useful in determining trends. A **trend analysis** presents financial data in percentages, for a number of periods, so that tendencies can be seen that are not evident when looking at the dollar figures alone. In a trend analysis, the figures for the first period are selected as the base figures and given the value of 100 percent. The figures for subsequent periods are then expressed as percentages of the base figures. Figures 23.5 and 23.6 show how this is done. Two steps are involved:

1. Important data are accumulated in dollars for a selected number of periods as shown in Figure 23.5.

WESTWIND COMPANY LIMITED
COMPARATIVE INCOME STATEMENT SELECTED DATA
19–1 to 19–5

	Year 1	*Year 2*	*Year 3*	*Year 4*	*Year 5*
Sales	$65 000	$67 700	$70 900	$74 750	$78 000
Cost of Goods Sold	32 100	33 000	34 000	35 000	35 600
Gross Profit	$32 900	$34 700	$36 900	$39 750	$42 400
Operating Expenses	20 700	22 350	23 200	25 250	28 000
Net Income	$12 200	$12 350	$13 700	$14 500	$14 400

Figure 23.5 A schedule of income statement data for a five-year period.

2. The dollar amounts are converted to percentages using the year 1 figures as the base year. The resultant trend analysis is shown in Figure 23.6.

WESTWIND COMPANY LIMITED
COMPARATIVE INCOME STATEMENT SELECTED DATA
IN PERCENTAGES FROM 19–1 to 19–5

	Year 1	*Year 2*	*Year 3*	*Year 4*	*Year 5*
Sales	100	104	109	115	120
Cost of Goods Sold	100	103	106	109	111
Gross Profit	100	105	112	121	129
Operating Expenses	100	108	112	122	135
Net Income	100	101	112	119	118

Figure 23.6 A trend analysis of income statement data for a five-year period.

This trend analysis clearly shows the following tendencies:

1. Sales have experienced a steady and satisfactory rate of increase.
2. Cost of goods sold has risen steadily, but the rise has not been as steep as for sales. This indicates that the cost of merchandise has been well controlled.
3. The excess of sales over cost of goods sold has resulted in an exceptional climb in the rate of gross profit.
4. Operating expenses have risen more steeply than any other item, particularly in year 5.
5. Net income has not kept pace with gross profit. In year 5, net income actually declined.

From this trend analysis, we can conclude that Westwind Company Limited has experienced a steady rate of growth, and has been able to improve its rate of gross profit over the 5-year period. An important factor has been its ability to control the cost of goods sold. However, it has not shown the same ability to control its operating expenses. As a result, net income, although showing a healthy increase over the 5-year period, has fallen off in year 5.

23.4 Key Ratios and Relationships

Several meaningful ratios and numbers may be worked out to provide insights into specific aspects of financial data. A number of these are discussed below.

Current Ratio

Calculation:

$$\text{current ratio} = \frac{\text{total current assets}}{\text{total current liabilities}}$$

For Astra Supply Co. Ltd., this calculation is derived from items on the balance sheet in Figure 23.1, as follows:

$$\text{current ratio} = \frac{90\ 050}{53\ 100} = 1.7$$

Interpretation:

The **working capital** of a business is the difference between the total current assets and the total current liabilities (for Astra, \$90 050 less \$53 100 = \$36 950). The **current ratio** measures a business's ability to pay its debts in the normal course of business operations. This is important because a business that is unable to pay its debts for any length of time will have to close down.

The general standards for interpreting current ratios are as follows:

Current Ratio	*Interpretation*
2	good
1.5	fair
1	precarious*
less than 1	dangerous

*Except in regard to specialized companies such as public utilities.

Quick Ratio

The **quick ratio** is also known as the **acid-test ratio**.

Calculation:

$$\text{quick ratio} = \frac{\text{current assets (excluding inventory)}}{\text{current liabilities}}$$

For Astra Supply Co. Ltd., the calculation is as follows:

$$\text{quick ratio} = \frac{90\ 050 \text{ less } 48\ 000}{53\ 100} = \frac{42\ 050}{53\ 100} = .79$$

Interpretation:

The calculation of the quick ratio includes only current assets, those that can be converted into cash within a short period. Therefore, the quick ratio measures a business's ability to pay its debts within a short period, say two months. A ratio of below 1 is considered to be unhealthy.

Collection Period

Calculation:

$$\text{collection period} = \frac{\text{accounts receivable}}{\text{charge sales for year}} \times 365$$

For Astra Supply Co. Ltd., the calculation is as follows:

$$\text{collection period} = \frac{39\ 000}{330\ 400} \times 365 = 43.1$$

Interpretation:

The **collection period** figure gives an indication of the number of days it takes the business to collect an account receivable. The meaning of the figure depends on the business's usual terms of sale and its discount policy. A general rule of thumb is that the figure should be less than $1\frac{1}{2}$ times the usual credit period. If a discount is offered, the figure should be much lower.

For Astra Supply Co. Ltd., the figure of 43.1 is acceptable if the credit period is normally 30 days.

Inventory Turnover

Calculation:

$$\text{inventory turnover} = \frac{\text{cost of goods sold}}{\text{average merchandise inventory}}$$

For Astra Supply Co. Ltd., the calculation is as follows:

$$\text{inventory turnover} = \frac{168\ 432}{\frac{48\ 000 + 35\ 000}{2}} = 4.1$$

Interpretation:

The **inventory turnover** figure represents the number of times the business has been able to sell its usual inventory. To be most useful, the figure must be compared with those of previous years, or even better, with those of other companies in the same line of business. A relatively high figure is considered to be a sign of good performance.

The figure of 4.1 for Astra is low, as one might expect for a company which has experienced inventory-related problems. A healthy figure for a supply company would be in the neighbourhood of 8 to 10.

Net Income Percentage

Calculation:

$$\text{net income percentage} = \frac{\text{net income}}{\text{net sales}} \times 100$$

For Astra Supply Co. Ltd., the calculation is as follows:

$$\text{net income percentage} = \frac{47\ 188}{330\ 400} \times 100 = 14.28\%$$

Interpretation:

The net income figure of a business is the ultimate measure of its success. The net income figure in dollars can be misleading. **Net income percentage** expresses net income as a percentage of total sales. As shown by the following schedule, an increase in net income and a decrease in net income percentage is possible.

	Year 1	*Year 2*
Sales	$500 000	$525 000
Net Income	$ 50 000	$ 50 500
Net Income %	10.0%	9.6%

By themselves, the dollar figures incorrectly suggest that the business's profit performance is perfectly satisfactory.

Return on Owner's Invested Capital

Calculation:

$$\text{return on owner's investment} = \frac{\text{net income}}{\text{owner's average equity}} \times 100$$

Assume the following data for Astra Supply Company: beginning capital, $210 000; ending capital, $220 000; net income, $37 500.

For Astra Supply Company, the calculation is as follows:

$$\text{return on owner's investment} = \frac{37\ 500}{\frac{210\ 000 + 220\ 000}{2}} = 17.4\%$$

Interpretation:

The **return on owner's investment** measures how well the business is doing relative to the owner's investment in it. The owner can then compare this figure with other investment possibilities.

When interest rates are high, for example, the owner might be able to get as high a return on invested capital by lending it out for interest. The owner could then have the same income without the responsibility and pressures of running a business. However, the capital can't be taken out of the business until a buyer for the business has been found. In other words, the capital invested in a business is not always available to the owner for reinvestment.

Earnings Per Share

Calculation:

$$\text{earnings per share} = \frac{\text{net income (after income tax)}}{\text{number of common shares outstanding}}$$

For Astra Supply Co. Ltd., the calculation is as follows:

$$\text{earnings per share} = \frac{47\ 188}{12\ 000} = \$3.93$$

Interpretation:

The **earnings per share** figure is used to measure the performance of a corporation and its executive officers. The figure is used by shareholders and by prospective investors. The earnings per share figure may be used in two ways:

1. It can be used in a comparative analysis over a number of periods to determine trends and stability.
2. It can be compared against the same figure for other companies to determine the relative merits of each for investment purposes.

Earnings per share figures are usually published in the financial statements of public corporations.

Debt/Equity Ratios

Calculation:

$$\text{debt ratio} = \frac{\text{total liabilities}}{\text{total assets}}$$

$$\text{equity ratio} = \frac{\text{total equity}}{\text{total assets}}$$

For Astra Supply Co. Ltd., the calculations are as follows:

$$\text{debt ratio} = \frac{53\ 100}{405\ 120} = .13 \text{ or } 13\%$$

$$\text{equity ratio} = \frac{352\ 020}{405\ 120} = .87 \text{ or } 87\%$$

Interpretation:

The **debt ratio** and the **equity ratio** are complementary; that is, in percentage terms, they add up to 100. The two ratios show the proportion of the total assets acquired by borrowed money relative to the proportion of total assets acquired by invested capital.

Prospective lenders are especially interested in these two figures. They like to see a high proportion of owners' money in a business. Owners with a high stake in the business are highly committed to its success.

Prospective lenders would undoubtedly view the ratios for Astra Supply Co. Ltd. quite favourably. Were the two figures reversed, so that the owners had only a 13 percent investment in the business, creditor confidence would be low. Any request for money would probably be declined.

Price-Earnings Ratio

Calculation:

$$\text{price-earnings ratio} = \frac{\text{current market price per share}}{\text{earnings per share}}$$

Assuming a market price of $47 a share for the stock of Astra Supply Co. Ltd., the calculation is as follows:

$$\text{price-earnings ratio} = \frac{47}{3.93} = 12$$

Interpretation:

The **price-earnings ratio** measures the confidence that outside investors (represented by the stock market quotation) have in the stock of a company. The price-earnings ratio is used to help evaluate alternative investment opportunities, and is of little value by itself.

Suppose, for example, that two companies that manufacture the same item have price-earnings ratios of 14 and 19, respectively. This is like saying that if the two companies were equal in all other respects, then one company's stock would sell for $14 and the other's would sell for $19. Quite clearly, the $14 stock would be the better buy. (**Note**: Stock ratio figures should not, however, be confused with real stock prices.)

Accounting Terms

comparative financial statements
common-size statements
trend analysis
current ratio
working capital
quick ratio
acid-test ratio
collection period
inventory turnover
net income percentage
return on owner's investment
earnings per share
debt ratio
equity ratio
price-earnings ratio

Review Questions

1. Name three groups that require special financial data.
2. What two aspects of a business are of particular interest to bankers?
3. Which group will examine and analyze financial statements most thoroughly?
4. Explain how simple comparative financial statements work.
5. What does the analyst look for in simple comparative financial statements?
6. What does management do about items that are positive? Negative?
7. Explain how common-size financial statements work.
8. What is the base figure for a common-size income statement?
9. What is the base figure for a common-size balance sheet?
10. Explain how a trend analysis works.
11. What does the current ratio measure?
12. What does the quick ratio measure?
13. Explain the meaning of the collection period calculation.
14. What type of business has a low inventory turnover? A high inventory turnover?
15. Which of the key figures is the ultimate measure of the success of a business?
16. Why is the return on invested capital of particular importance today?
17. Who are the principal users of the earnings per share figure?
18. Give two reasons why a low debt ratio would be considered favourable.
19. What does the price-earnings ratio measure?
20. Who uses the price-earnings ratio?

Exercises

Simple Comparative Financial Statement Calculations

1. The comparative balance sheet of Acton Company for the years ended December 31, 19–4 and 19–5 appears below. Complete the Net Change column of the statement, showing decreases preceded by a minus sign. This question appears in your workbook.

ACTON COMPANY
COMPARATIVE BALANCE SHEET
DECEMBER 31, 19–4 and 19–5

	19–4	*19–5*	*Net Change*
ASSETS			
Current Assets			
Bank	$ 9 800	$ 4 500	$
Accounts Receivable	31 700	27 400	
Merchandise Inventory	29 050	30 250	
Prepaid Expenses	3 050	3 100	
Total Current Assets	$ 73 600	$ 65 250	$
Plant and Equipment			
Land	$ 57 000	$ 57 000	$
Buildings	107 500	127 500	
Equipment	65 900	74 900	
Total Plant and Equipment	$230 400	$259 400	$
Total Assets	$304 000	$324 650	$
LIABILITIES AND EQUITY			
Current Liabilities			
Accounts Payable	$ 10 450	$ 11 350	$
Bank Loan	20 000	25 000	
Total Current Liabilities	$ 30 450	$ 36 350	$
Owner's Equity			
C. Price, Capital	$273 550	$288 300	$
Total Liabilities and Equity	$304 000	$324 650	$

2. The comparative income statement for Arcade Enterprises for the years ended December 31, 19–6 and 19–7 appears below. Complete the Net Change column of the statement, showing decreases preceded by a minus sign. This question appears in your workbook.

ARCADE ENTERPRISES
COMPARATIVE INCOME STATEMENT
YEARS ENDED DECEMBER 31, 19–6 AND 19–7

	19–6	*19–7*	*Net Change*
Revenue			
Net Sales	$221 450	$230 602	$
Cost of Goods Sold			
Opening Inventory	$ 48 290	$ 50 290	$
Net Purchases	107 050	105 035	
Goods Available for Sale	$155 341	$155 325	$
Less Closing Inventory	50 290	47 250	
Cost of Goods Sold	$105 051	$108 075	$
Gross Profit	$116 399	$122 527	$
Operating Expenses			
Advertising	$ 2 575	$ 3 040	$
Bad Debts	940	850	
Bank Charges	1 100	1 250	
Car Expenses	4 875	5 902	
Depreciation of Automobiles	11 360	9 400	
Depreciation of Equipment	11 637	10 300	
Insurance	1 596	1 695	
Light, Heat, and Power	1 272	1 530	
Miscellaneous Expense	390	425	
Rent	12 050	14 000	
Supplies Used	912	1 200	
Telephone	516	602	
Wages	20 072	24 312	
Total Expenses	$ 69 295	$ 74 506	$
Net Income	$ 47 104	$ 48 021	$

3. The results of operations for C. Simpson for the years 19–1 and 19–2 are shown opposite. This exercise appears in your workbook.

C. SIMPSON
COMPARATIVE INCOME STATEMENT
YEARS ENDED DECEMBER 31, 19–1 AND 19–2

	19–1	*19–2*	*Net Change*
Revenue			
Sales	$361 800	$345 884	$
Cost of Merchandise Sold			
Opening Inventory	$ 25 072	$ 31 719	$
Purchases	137 916	146 209	
Freight-in	3 812	4 702	
	$166 800	$182 630	$
Deduct: Closing Inventory	31 719	35 080	
Cost of Goods Sold	$135 081	$147 550	$
Gross Trading Income	$226 719	$198 294	$
Selling Expenses			
Advertising	$ 1 076	$ 1 102	$
Delivery Expense	5 192	4 865	
Salesmen's Salaries	26 437	25 096	
Car Expenses	9 711	9 542	
Depreciation of Automobiles	7 215	5 767	
Total Selling Expenses	$ 49 631	$ 46 372	$
Administrative Expenses			
Bad Debts	$ 574	$ 2 472	$
Depreciation of Building	2 075	1 904	
Depreciation of Equipment	1 974	1 812	
Legal and Audit	500	550	
Insurance	400	416	
Office Expenses	372	1 450	
Rent	10 000	12 000	
Telephone	317	450	
Canada Pension Plan Expense	356	375	
Unemployment Insurance Expense	412	475	
Wages	12 902	15 074	
Total Administrative Expenses	$ 29 882	$ 36 978	$
Total Expenses	$ 79 513	$ 83 350	$
Net Income	$147 206	$114 944	$

1. To this comparative statement add a third column to show the changes from 19–1 to 19–2. Show decreases preceded by a minus sign.
2. In your opinion, what are the two principal factors causing the decrease in net income?

Simple Common-Size Financial Statement Calculations

4. Complete the following simplified statement by calculating the percentages to one decimal place. This exercise appears in your workbook.

SPRUCE COMPANY
BALANCE SHEET
DECEMBER 31, 19–8

	Amount in thousands	*Percentage*
ASSETS		
Bank	$ 240	.
Accounts Receivable	60	.
Merchandise Inventory	180	.
Land	860	.
Buildings	1 800	.
Equipment	1 500	.
	$4 640	100.0
LIABILITIES AND EQUITY		
Bank Loan	$ 400	.
Accounts Payable	300	.
Mortgage Payable	1 600	.
Owner's Equity	2 340	.
	$4 640	100.0

5. Complete the following simplified income statement by calculating the percentages correct to one decimal place. This exercise appears in your workbook.

MORRIS AND ASSOCIATES
INCOME STATEMENT
YEAR ENDED DECEMBER 31, 19–8

	Amount in thousands	*Percentage*
Revenue		
Net Sales	$1 050	100.0
Cost of Goods Sold		
Merchandise Inventory, January 1	$ 300	.
Net Purchases	400	.
Merchandise Available for Sale	$ 700	.
Less Merchandise Inventory, December 31	325	.
Cost of Goods Sold	$ 375	.
Gross Profit	$ 675	.
Operating Expenses		
Advertising	$ 10	.
Car Expenses	50	.
Depreciation of Equipment	20	.
Depreciation of Automobile	30	.
Light, Heat, and Power	90	.
Wages	200	.
Total Operating Expenses	$ 400	.
Net Income	$ 275	.

6. The operating figures for the James Company are shown below. Convert each amount into a percentage of the sales figure. Make the calculations to one decimal place. Record these percentages in a column immediately to the right of the money figures.

This exercise appears in your workbook.

	Amount in thousands	*Percentage*
Revenue		
Sales	$48 075	.
Operating Expenses		
Bad Debts	$ 315	.
Supplies Expense	157	.
Licences	250	.
Insurance	975	.
Depreciation of Building	1 020	.
Depreciation of Furniture and Fixtures	1 675	.
Depreciation of Automobiles	3 072	.
Bank Charges	215	.
Building Maintenance	1 574	.
Light, Heat, and Water	2 746	.
Miscellaneous Expense	105	.
Telephone Expense	747	.
Truck Expense	2 769	.
Wages	10 437	.
	$26 057	.
Operating Income	$22 018	.
Other Income		
Discounts Earned	$ 746	.
Net Income	$22 764	.

7. **The partially completed comparative income statement for Lunar Company is shown below. This exercise appears in your workbook.**

LUNAR COMPANY
COMPARATIVE INCOME STATEMENT
YEARS ENDED DECEMBER 31, 19–8 AND 19–9

	19–8 Amount	Percent	*19–9* Amount	Percent
Revenue				
Net Sales	$2 000	.	$2 400	.
Cost of Goods Sold				
Opening Inventory	$ 80	.	$ 50	.
Net Purchases	900	.	1 200	.
Goods Available for Sale	$ 980	.	$1 250	.
Less Closing Inventory	50	.	72	.
Cost of Goods Sold	$ 930	.	$1 178	.
Gross Profit	$1 070	.	$1 222	.
Operating Expenses				
Advertising	$ 30	.	$ 36	.
Car Expenses	70	.	96	.
Depreciation of Car	240	.	240	.
Light and Heat	100	.	84	.
Wages	400	.	384	.
Total Expenses	$ 840		$ 840	
Net Income	$ 230	.	$ 382	.

1. **Complete the percent columns of the statement.**
2. **State the four most significant aspects of this statement, as indicated by the change in percentage.**

Trend Analysis

8. The current assets and the current liabilities of Goodenough Company for a 5-year period are shown below. This exercise appears in your workbook.

GOODENOUGH COMPANY

	Year 1	*Year 2*	*Year 3*	*Year 4*	*Year 5*
a. Current Assets	$50 702	$51 716	$53 237	$55 265	$57 800
b. Current Liabilities	$30 406	$31 014	$31 622	$32 534	$33 447
a. minus b. Working Capital					

1. **Complete the above schedule by calculating the working capital for the five-year period.**
2. **Prepare a percentage trend analysis from the above schedule in the space indicated below.**

GOODENOUGH COMPANY
WORKING CAPITAL TREND ANALYSIS

	Year 1	*Year 2*	*Year 3*	*Year 4*	*Year 5*
Current Assets					
Current Liabilities					
Working Capital					

9. The income statement for Gorry and Associates is given below.
1. **Prepare a percentage trend analysis.**
2. **Comment on each line of the analysis in terms of performance and meaning.**

GORRY AND ASSOCIATES
INCOME STATEMENT DATA
19–1 to 19–5

	Year 1	*Year 2*	*Year 3*	*Year 4*	*Year 5*
Sales	$120 000	$121 200	$124 800	$125 950	$128 500
Cost of Goods Sold	65 000	66 300	67 600	68 250	70 200
Gross Profit	$ 55 000	$ 54 900	$ 57 200	$ 57 700	$ 58 300
Operating Expenses	30 000	30 600	31 500	32 700	33 600
Net Income	$ 25 000	$ 24 300	$ 25 700	$ 25 000	$ 24 700

Simple Key Ratios

10. The balance sheet and income statement for Saturn Sales Company are shown below.

SATURN SALES COMPANY
BALANCE SHEET
DECEMBER 31, 19–5

ASSETS			
Current Assets			
Bank		$ 3 400	
Accounts Receivable		33 070	
Merchandise Inventory		27 400	$ 63 870
Prepaid Expenses			
Supplies			1 500
Plant and Equipment			
Land		$ 50 000	
Buildings		125 000	
Equipment		69 000	244 000
Total Assets			$309 370
LIABILITIES AND EQUITY			
Current Liabilities			
Bank Loan		$ 35 000	
Accounts Payable		17 970	$ 52 970
Long-Term Liability			
Mortgage Payable			65 700
Owner's Equity			
P. Shawn, Capital, January 1		$194 895	
Net Income	$40 805		
Withdrawals	35 000		
Increase in Capital		5 805	
P. Shawn, Capital, December 31			200 700
Total Liabilities and Equity			$309 370

SATURN SALES COMPANY
INCOME STATEMENT
YEAR ENDED DECEMBER 31, 19–5

Revenue			
Sales			$335 286
Cost of Goods Sold			
Merchandise Inventory, January 1	$ 26 500		
Purchases	226 500		
Merchandise Available for Sale	$253 000		
Less: Merchandise Inventory December 31	27 400		225 600
Gross Profit			$109 686
Operating Expenses			
Bank Charges		$ 3 200	
Depreciation of Building		6 250	
Depreciation of Equipment		6 900	
Power		1 800	
Miscellaneous Expense		350	
Telephone		425	
Car Expense		2 940	
Wages		57 016	78 881
Net Income			$ 30 805

Calculate the following:

1. **Current ratio.**
2. **Quick ratio.**
3. **Collection period.**
4. **Inventory turnover.**
5. **Net income percentage.**
6. **Rate of return on owner's investment.**
7. **Debt ratio.**
8. **Equity ratio.**

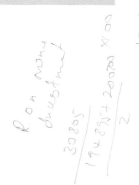

11. The balance sheet and income statement of Venus Sales Company are shown below.

VENUS SALES COMPANY
BALANCE SHEET
DECEMBER 31, 19–7

ASSETS		
Current Assets		
Bank	$ 2 200	
Accounts Receivable	35 450	
Merchandise Inventory	38 800	$ 76 450
Prepaid Expenses		
Insurance	$ 700	
Supplies	1 000	1 750
Plant and Equipment		
Land	$ 75 000	
Building	195 000	
Equipment	70 000	340 000
Total Assets		$418 200
LIABILITIES AND EQUITY		
Current Liabilities		
Bank Loan	$ 25 000	
Accounts Payable	10 800	$ 35 800
Long-Term Liability		145 900
Shareholders' Equity		
Capital Stock, no par value, common shares		
Authorized, 20 000 shares		
Issued and fully paid, 20 000 shares	$150 000	
Retained Earnings	86 000	236 500
Total Liabilities and Equity		$418 200

VENUS SALES COMPANY
INCOME STATEMENT
YEAR ENDED DECEMBER 31, 19–7

Revenue		
Sales		$438 317
Cost of Goods Sold		
Merchandise Inventory, January 1	$ 38 800	
Purchases	285 050	
Merchandise Available for Sale	$323 850	
Less: Merchandise Inventory, December 31	41 600	282 250
Gross Profit		$156 067
Operating Expenses		
Bank Charges	$ 3 000	
Car Expenses	2 850	
Depreciation of Building	9 750	
Depreciation of Equipment	14 000	
Power	2 400	
Miscellaneous Expense	375	
Telephone	480	
Wages	66 012	$ 98 867
Net Income		$ 57 200

Calculate the following:

1. **Current ratio.**
2. **Quick ratio.**
3. **Collection period.**
4. **Inventory turnover.**
5. **Net income percentage.**
6. **Earnings per share.**
7. **Debt ratio.**
8. **Equity ratio.**
9. **Price-earnings ratio, if the market price of the stock is $43.**

Using Your Knowledge

12. The condensed financial statements of Magnus Company for the years 19–5 and 19–6 are shown below. This exercise also appears in your workbook.

MAGNUS COMPANY
COMPARATIVE BALANCE SHEET
DECEMBER 31, 19–5 AND 19–6

	19–5	*19–6*	*Net Change*
ASSETS			
Bank	$ 13 000	$ 960	$
Accounts Receivable	29 500	35 200	
Merchandise Inventory	37 450	38 950	
Prepaid Expenses	3 700	2 600	
Land	64 500	64 500	
Buildings	90 000	166 500	
Equipment	75 000	146 400	
Automobiles	30 000	21 000	
	$343 150	$476 110	$
LIABILITIES AND EQUITY			
Bank Loan	$ 40 000	$200 000	$
Accounts Payable	26 500	18 700	
Mortgage Payable	125 300	112 770	
Owner's Equity	151 350	144 640	
	$343 150	$476 110	$

MAGNUS COMPANY
COMPARATIVE INCOME STATEMENT
YEARS ENDED DECEMBER 31, 19–5 AND 19–6

	19–5 Amount	19–5 Percent	19–6 Amount	19–6 Percent
Sales	$289 500	.	$309 120	.
Costs of Goods Sold	142 750	.	155 700	.
Gross Profit	$146 750	.	$153 420	.
Operating Expenses				
Advertising	$ 1 500	.	$ 1 500	.
Car Expenses	4 000	.	4 050	.
Depreciation of Building	4 250	.	8 500	.
Depreciation of Equipment	18 000	.	29 280	.
Depreciation of Automobiles	9 000	.	9 000	.
Power	3 500	.	3 950	.
Interest and Bank Charges	16 530	.	36 530	.
Supplies Used	1 000	.	1 100	.
Wages	36 700	.	38 900	.
Total Operating Expenses	$94 480	.	$132 810	.
Net Income	$52 270	.	$ 20 610	.

1. Complete the Net Change column of the comparative balance sheet.

2. Complete the Percent column of the comparative income statement.

3. Answer the following questions related to the income statement:

a. By how many dollars have sales increased?

b. By how many dollars has net income decreased?

c. Do the percentages indicate that the profit decline is caused by the cost of goods sold or the operating expenses?

d. State the three operating expenses that show the greatest increases.

4. State the three balance sheet items that show the greatest increases.

5. From the above data write a brief explanation describing the factors that caused the profit decline. Explain also, with reasons, whether you believe this condition is permanent.

---

13. The following is the partially completed common-size comparative income statement for two companies in the same line of business. You are preparing this analysis with a view to making an investment in one of the two companies. This exercise appears in your workbook.

COMMON-SIZE COMPARATIVE INCOME STATEMENT
YEAR ENDED DECEMBER 31, 19–3

	Dollars		Percentage of Sales	
	Co. A	Co. B	Co. A	Co. B
Sales	$200 000	$150 000	.	.
Cost of Goods Sold				
Opening Inventory	$ 50 000	$ 25 000	.	.
Purchases	123 000	81 200	.	.
Goods Available for Sale	$173 000	$106 200	.	.
Less Closing Inventory	57 000	24 000	.	.
Cost of Goods Sold	$116 000	$ 82 200	.	.
Gross Profit	$ 84 000	$ 67 800	.	.
Operating Expenses				
Advertising	$ 5 000	$ 4 000	.	.
Bank Interest	900	10 000	.	.
Depreciation Building	10 000	—	.	.
Depreciation Equipment	4 500	3 000	.	.
General Expense	1 900	1 500	.	.
Insurance	500	400	.	.
Postage	750	350	.	.
Property Tax	2 000	—	.	.
Rent	—	18 000	.	.
Telephone	450	300	.	.
Wages	13 740	9 500	.	.
Total Expenses	$ 39 740	$ 47 050	.	.
Net Income	$ 44 260	$ 20 750	.	.

1. Complete the common-size income statement.

2. Answer the following questions:

a. Which company has the larger net income?
b. Which company has the larger percentage net income?
c. Which company has the larger investment in inventory?
d. Which company has the larger gross income percentage?
e. Which company does not own its own building?
f. What are the three clues to question 'e'?
g. If the owners' equities are $80 000 for Company A, and $30 000 for Company B, calculate the respective returns on owners' investment.
h. Which company gives the greater return on owners' investment?
i. Which company has the greater interest-bearing debt?
j. How much is Company B disadvantaged by not owning its own building?

k. Listed below are factors that favour Company A or Company B. For each one, indicate the company favoured.

i. Greater net income.
ii. Higher gross income percentage.
iii. Greater return on owners' investment.
iv. More established, owns own building.
v. Lower inventory.
vi. Lower expense.
vii. Greater potential to reduce expenses.
viii. Greater share of market (sales).
ix. Fewer interest-bearing debts.

---

14. Certain financial data pertaining to Anson Company are given below. This exercise appears in your workbook.

ITEM 1

STATEMENT OF OWNER'S EQUITY
YEAR ENDED DECEMBER 31, 19–8

Beginning Balance	$542 000
Add: Net Income from Operations	83 000
Profit on Sale of Land	200 000
	$825 000
Deduct: Drawings for Year	50 000
Ending Balance	$775 000

ITEM 2

ANSON COMPANY
INCOME STATEMENT
YEAR ENDED DECEMBER 31, 19–8

Revenue		$700 000
Cost of Goods Sold		475 000
Gross Profit		$225 000
Operating Expenses		
Depreciation of Building	$ 4 000	
Depreciation of Equipment	18 000	
Other Expenses	120 000	142 000
Net Income		$ 83 000

ITEM 3

ANSON COMPANY
COMPARATIVE BALANCE SHEET
YEARS ENDED DECEMBER 31, 19–7 AND 19–8

	19–7	*19–8*	*Net Change*
ASSETS			
Current Assets			
Bank	$ 4 000	$509 000	$
Merchandise Inventory	50 000	50 000	
	$ 54 000	$559 000	$
Fixed Assets			
Land	$380 000	$ 80 000	$
Buildings	80 000	76 000	
Equipment	90 000	72 000	
	$550 000	$228 000	$
Total Assets	$604 000	$787 000	$
LIABILITIES AND EQUITY			
Current Liabilities			
Bank Loan	$ 20 000	—	$
Accounts Payable	42 000	$ 12 000	
	$ 62 000	$ 12 000	$
Owner's Equity			
R. Anson, Capital	$542 000	$775 000	$
Total Liabilities and Equity	$604 000	$787 000	$

1. Complete the Net Change column of the balance sheet.

2. Answer the following questions:

a. What caused the decrease in Buildings?
b. What caused the decrease in Equipment?
c. What caused the decrease in Land?
d. Does Anson Company sell on credit? Explain.
e. How much did the company make on the sale of the land?
f. For how much was the land sold?

g. The bank balance increased by $505 000. Prepare a schedule that shows the increases to bank and the decreases to bank that resulted in the net increase of $505 000.

Increases	1.		
	2.		
		Total Increases	________
Decreases	1.		
	2.		
	3.		
		Total Decreases	________
		Net Increase	________

---

15. The following data applies to Calvino Company.

a. The collection period is 36.5.
b. The current ratio is 1.3.
c. The inventory turnover is 12.0.
d. The net income percentage is 12.5.
e. The debt ratio is 15.

Use this data to fill in the missing information on the following partially completed financial statements.

INCOME STATEMENT
YEAR ENDED DECEMBER 31, 19–8

Revenue		
Sales		$170 000
Cost of Goods Sold		
Opening Inventory		
Purchases		$128 500
Goods Available for Sale		
Closing Inventory		
Cost of Goods Sold		$129 000
Gross Profit		$
Operating Expenses		$
Net Income		$

BALANCE SHEET
DECEMBER 31, 19–8

ASSETS	
Current Assets	
Bank	$ 3 700
Accounts Receivable	
Merchandise Inventory	10 500
Total Current Assets	$
Plant and Equipment	
Land	$ 35 000
Buildings and Equipment	
Total Plant and Equipment	$
Total Assets	$
LIABILITIES AND OWNER'S EQUITY	
Current Liabilities	
Bank Loan	$ 15 000
Accounts Payable	
Total Current Liabilities	$
Owner's Equity	
Beginning Capital	$134 750
Add: Net Income	
Deduct: Drawings	$
Ending Capital	$
Total Liabilities and Owner's Equity	$

Cases

Case 1 *To Lend or Not to Lend?*

In the city of Kempenfelt, population 150 000, Paul Ego owns the most popular store for stereo and electronic equipment. Paul's store is extremely modest, but the ideal location connects two heavily populated areas of the city with the downtown core. Paul also offers excellent quality, prices, and service.

Paul Ego's financial position is shown by the following comparative financial statements.

COMPARATIVE BALANCE SHEET

ASSETS	19–5	19–6	19–7	19–8
Cash	$ 1 520	$ 907	$ 4 340	$ 3 090
Accounts Receivable	18 910	19 500	22 750	24 800
Merchandise Inventory	11 100	11 700	12 800	17 500
Prepaid Expenses	521	546	506	526
Store Equipment	5 975	4 975	4 175	3 575
Total Assets	$38 026	$37 628	$44 571	$49 491
LIABILITIES AND EQUITY				
Bank Loan	$10 000	$10 000	$15 000	$15 000
Accounts Payable	12 397	13 099	12 342	15 537
Capital Stock	10 000	10 000	10 000	10 000
Retained Earnings	5 629	4 529	7 229	8 954
Total Liabilities and Equity	$38 026	$37 628	$44 571	$49 491

COMPARATIVE INCOME STATEMENT

	19–6	*19–7*	*19–8*
Sales	$ 90 000	$105 000	$115 000
Cost of Goods Sold	44 600	50 000	55 775
Gross Profit	$ 45 400	$ 55 000	$ 59 225
Operating Expenses			
Depreciation	$ 1 000	$ 800	$ 600
Other Expenses	20 000	24 000	26 900
Total Expenses	$ 21 000	$ 24 800	$ 27 500
Net Income	$ 24 400	$ 30 200	$ 31 725
Drawings	$ 25 500	$ 27 500	$ 30 000

Questions

1. Complete the schedule of key ratios and numbers that appears in your workbook.
2. Construct a general statement about this business, giving your opinion of its profitability, efficiency, weaknesses, and so on.

Paul Ego has learned recently that a national chain of electronic and stereo specialists is opening a branch store within a year in a large new downtown mall. To meet this competition, Paul will have to restructure his store, and provide greater room, variety, and convenience in more modern surroundings.

Paul wants to acquire the empty property next door and build a modern store with plenty of parking. This new store would cost $180 000 ($55 000 for the land, $125 000 for the building). A mortgage on the property at 15 percent in the amount of $140 000 is available. Paul has no savings of his own but expects to be able to borrow the $40 000 down payment from the bank at 15 percent.

To prepare for this bank loan, Paul has had a public accountant prepare a set of estimated financial statements for 19–9. These statements appear below.

ESTIMATED FINANCIAL STATEMENTS, 19–9

1. BALANCE SHEET

ASSETS	
Cash	$ 2 483
Accounts Receivable	22 800
Merchandise Inventory	20 000
Prepaid Expenses	546
Land	55 000
Building	118 750
Store Equipment	19 675
Total Assets	$239 254
LIABILITIES AND EQUITY	
Bank Loan	$ 65 000
Accounts Payable	22 500
Mortgage Payable	139 000
Capital Stock	10 000
Retained Earnings	2 754
Total Liabilities & Equity	$239 254

2. INCOME STATEMENT

Sales	$160 000
Cost of Goods Sold	72 500
Gross Profit	$ 87 500
Operating Expenses	
Deprec. Equipment	$ 3 900
Deprec. Building	6 250
Mortgage Interest	21 000
Bank Interest	9 750
Other Expenses	27 800
Total Expenses	$ 68 700
Net Income	$ 18 800

3. CASH FLOW STATEMENT

Beginning Bank Balance		$ 3 090
Funds Received From:		
Bank Loan	$ 50 000	
Collections from Customers	162 000	$212 000
		$215 090
Funds Paid For:		
Downpayment New Building	$ 40 000	
Owner's Drawings	25 000	
Paid to Suppliers	95 857	
Mortgage Interest	21 000	
Mortgage Principal	1 000	
Bank Interest	9 750	
New Equipment	20 000	212 607
Ending Bank Balance		$ 2 483

Questions

3. Using the estimated data above, work out the eight ratios and comment on them in the schedule provided in your workbook.

4. Answer the following questions related to the projected figures:
   a. What factors caused the decrease in net income?
   b. Is the sales figure realistic?
   c. Are the expenses figures realistic?
   d. Are the statements thoughtfully prepared?
   e. Has anything been omitted?

5. Assume that you are the bank manager asked to lend Paul Ego $40 000 for expansion. Write a statement giving your impression of the request and stating what additional information you need. Finally, decide whether or not you would grant the loan, and state your reasons.

Case 2 *Which Company to Invest In?*

As an investor in the stock market, you are trying to decide which of two companies to invest in. You have obtained the following financial data for analysis of the two companies.

a. Condensed balance sheets as of June 30, 19–3.

	Co. A	*Co. B*
ASSETS		
Cash	$ 5 000	$ 800
Accounts Receivable	25 000	27 000
Merchandise Inventory	21 300	18 000
Land	150 000	80 000
Buildings	250 000	175 000
Equipment	100 000	90 000
Total Assets	$551 300	$390 800
LIABILITIES AND EQUITY		
Bank Loan	$ 30 000	$100 000
Accounts Payable	7 500	15 000
Long-Term Liabilities	150 000	80 000
Capital Stock	240 000	100 000
Retained Earnings	123 800	95 800
Total Liabilities and Equity	$551 300	$390 800

b. Comparative income statements for the years ended June 30, 19–1, 19–2, and 19–3.

COMPANY A	19–1	19–2	19–3
Sales	$330 000	$338 000	$344 000
Cost of Goods Sold			
Opening Inventory	$ 20 500	$ 21 300	$ 22 500
Purchases	198 800	204 200	205 500
Goods Available for Sale	$219 300	$225 500	$228 000
Less Closing Inventory	21 300	22 500	23 000
Cost of Goods Sold	$198 000	$203 000	$205 000
Gross Profit	$132 000	$135 000	$139 000
Operating Expenses	$ 72 000	$ 73 000	$ 74 000
Net Income	$ 60 000	$ 62 000	$ 65 000
COMPANY B			
Sales	$151 000	$185 000	$231 000
Cost of Goods Sold			
Opening Inventory	$ 17 000	$ 16 000	$ 17 500
Purchases	65 000	86 500	119 500
Goods Available for Sale	$ 82 000	$102 500	$137 000
Less Closing Inventory	16 000	17 500	18 000
Cost of Goods Sold	$ 66 000	$ 85 000	$119 000
Gross Profit	$ 85 000	$100 000	$112 000
Operating Expenses	$ 60 000	$ 70 000	$ 75 000
Net Income	$ 25 000	$ 30 000	$ 37 000

c. Additional Information:

i. Current stock market prices: Company A — $26; Company B — $78.
ii. Number of shares outstanding: Company A — 30 000; Company B — 10 000.

Questions

1. Complete the following schedule in your workbook by filling in all the blank areas.

Key Ratios and Numbers	*Company A*			*Company B*			*Company Favoured*
	Yr. 1	*Yr. 2*	*Yr. 3*	*Yr. 1*	*Yr. 2*	*Yr. 3*	
Current ratio							
Quick ratio							
Collection period (terms are 30 days)							
Inventory turnover							
Gross profit %							
Net income %							
Earnings per share							
Debt ratio							
Price-earnings ratio							

Trend Percentages	*Company A*			*Company B*			*Company Favoured*
	Yr. 1	*Yr. 2*	*Yr. 3*	*Yr. 1*	*Yr. 2*	*Yr. 3*	
Sales							
Cost of Goods Sold							
Gross Profit							
Operating Expenses							
Net Income							

2. What additional information would you like to help you make your decision?
3. If you have $7 800 to invest, which of the two companies would you select? Write a paragraph giving the reasons for your choice.

Case 3 *Which Company to Invest In?*

An investment analyst has compiled the following information in respect to three public companies:

	X Ltd.	Y Ltd.	Z Ltd.
Number of common shares	50 000	400 000	120 000
Number of preferred shares	nil	nil	nil
Total shareholders' equity	$650 000	$4 600 000	$1 800 000
Net income for last five years			
19–6	250 000	1 400 000	480 000
19–5	200 000	1 500 000	475 000
19–4	175 000	1 800 000	510 000
19–3	125 000	2 400 000	435 000
19–2	75 000	2 500 000	450 000

The current market values of the stocks are as follows:

X Ltd.	Y Ltd.	Z Ltd.
$90	$35	$60

In all three companies, the total earnings are regularly paid out in dividends.

Questions

1. In the columns provided in your workbook calculate the following:
   a. The net book values per share.
   b. The earnings per share for the 19–6 year.
   c. The average earnings per share for the last five years.
2. What factors influence the market price of the companies' shares?
3. Explain the difference in the market price of the shares of the three companies.
4. If you were required to select one of the three companies to invest in, which company would you select? Assume that you have $100 000 to invest. Explain your choice.

Case 4 *Analyzing Corporate Data*

The following analysis of Mannheim Limited has been made by an investment company.

Year	*Number of Common Shares*	*Amount of Dividends Paid on Common Shares*	*Amount of Net Income*	*Market Value Per Share*
19–1	50 000	$62 500	$215 000	$48
19–2	57 000	62 700	275 000	55
19–3	67 000	63 650	375 000	57

Questions

1. Calculate the rate of dividend for each year.
2. Calculate the rate of earnings per share for each year.
3. In your opinion, why is the market value of the stock increasing at a time when the rate of dividends is decreasing?

Case 5 *Is the Manager Competent?*

Bill Mallon had owned and operated a retail business for several years. Last year he retired and hired Joan O'Brien as the new manager at an annual salary of $15 000. Joan promised to expand the business and to increase profits. Mr. Mallon left on a world cruise for a year, and Joan was given a free hand to run the business.

Upon his return, Mr. Mallon is eager to see how the business has done under Joan O'Brien. He anxiously compares the most recent statement, reflecting Joan's work, with the statement of the previous year, when he was manager. At first glance,

Mr. Mallon is disappointed with the results. He must now decide whether to retain Joan as manager or seek someone else.

Income statements for the two most recent years appear below, as well as additional data. Analyze this information and answer the questions that follow.

MALLON ENTERPRISES
INCOME STATEMENT

	19–1 (Mallon)	*19–2 (O'Brien)*
Sales	$315 000	$375 000
Cost of Goods Sold		
Opening Inventory	$100 000	$110 000
Purchases	200 000	170 000
Goods Available for Sale	$300 000	$280 000
Less Closing Inventory	110 000	55 000
Cost of Goods Sold	$190 000	$225 000
Gross Profit	$125 000	$150 000
Operating Expenses		
Advertising	$ 2 000	$ 7 000
Bad Debts	300	2 500
Bank Interest	10 000	5 000
Car Expense	3 000	3 100
Depreciation of Car	1 500	1 500
Delivery Expense	9 000	8 000
Depreciation of Delivery Truck	3 600	—
Light and Heat	1 700	2 000
Miscellaneous Expense	300	350
Rent	13 000	16 500
Telephone	400	500
Wages and Salaries	24 500	40 000
Loss on Sale of Truck		2 000
Total Expenses	$ 69 300	$ 88 450
Net Income	$ 55 700	$ 61 550

Additional Information:

The following policy changes were made by Joan O'Brien:

a. More money was spent on advertising in an attempt to increase sales.
b. Credit was granted more freely in an attempt to increase sales.

c. The size of the inventory was reduced, but not the number or variety of products.
d. The delivery equipment was sold and an outside trucker was hired to make deliveries.
e. Neither the plant nor the facilities were expanded.

Questions

1. Did the increase in advertising and the more liberal credit policy have the desired effect?
2. Calculate the net gain from the above policy.
3. Indicate a direct monetary gain caused by the reduction of inventory.
4. Was there a financial saving from the change in the method of delivery? If so, how much was the saving?
5. Which expense increases could Joan not prevent?
6. Why did Wages and Salaries increase so much?
7. Which expense(s) are non-recurring?
8. In your opinion, did Joan O'Brien manage the business competently? Explain fully with figures to back up your opinion.

Career
Kim Brady / Senior Accounting Clerk

Kim Brady enrolled in the Certified General Accountancy (CGA) program while still at high school in Vancouver, B.C. She graduated from high school with an average of 80 percent and won several academic awards.

Kim's first employer was Barry Demers, a Registered Industrial Accountant (RIA). Kim kept the clients' books and performed all accounting work up to the taking of the trial balance for the general ledger.

Kim next worked for Emerson Electric as a junior cost clerk. In this position, she coded invoices for the computer, calculated the cost of goods sold, prepared reports on the distribution of labour in the company, and determined the costs of production. She reported directly to the supervisor of the cost department.

Emerson Electric was very satisfied with Kim's work, and she was soon promoted to senior cost clerk. In this capacity, she learned how to analyze and interpret financial statements. She compared budgeted costs to actual costs and analyzed profits in detail to determine future trends.

At present, Kim works for Sterling Drugs, a leading manufacturer of drugs and household items. As senior accounting clerk of a company that employs over 300 personnel, Kim holds a highly responsible position. She analyzes all the figures on the Income Statement, the Balance Sheet, and the Manufacturing Statement and presents her findings to management. She examines current ratios and quick ratios, and conducts an analysis of profits. She also investigates any figures that vary from those of the previous month.

Kim is also involved in the analysis of financial statements. She compares budgeted expenses to actual costs and reviews accounts to see if they are out of line. She prepares monthly journal entries and makes the adjustments for accrual and deferral. She also prepares schedules of fixed assets, manufacturing costs, and inventory costs. Her training on the job has enabled her to use computer terminals and to keypunch journals and maintenance budget data into the computers.

Kim has now completed four of the five levels required for her CGA designation. She looks forward to completing the program and becoming a full-fledged accountant. In future, she hopes to become increasingly involved with the analysis of financial statements and the planning of company budgets.

Kim's work involves considerable contact with the computer. She has taken a number of on-the-job training courses to learn how to use computer terminals and how to keypunch information onto cards for computer processing. Kim is careful to ensure that all pertinent journal entries and budget data are stored in the computer for future use in planning and analysis.

24

Accounting and the Computer

24-1 Basic Concepts of Data Processing
24-2 Components of a Computer System
24-3 Computer Applications in Accounting
24-4 Developing a Computerized System
24-5 Computer Applications in Accounting at Save-More
24-6 Internal Control
24-7 Computer Use in Accounting
24-8 Computerized Accounting in the Future

Objectives

When you have completed Chapter 24, you should:

1. Understand what data processing is, how it works, and how a computer system deals with data processing.
2. Have a general understanding of how a computer operates.
3. Understand how computerized systems handle the following accounting routines: accounts receivable; accounts payable; inventory; billing; payroll; budget; cost accounting; financial statements; and financial decisions.
4. Know the benefits of computerized accounting routines.
5. Know the steps necessary to develop a computerized accounting system.
6. Know how to ensure that the computer system operates efficiently.
7. Know what procedures are used to protect the system from abuses.
8. Know the computer operations of a business.

As you have seen, accounting provides the method for processing the data, or information, that managers of a business need to know. First, various business papers, such as invoices, receipts, and cheques, are sorted into groups of similar transactions; some concern money paid out, others involve money received, and so on. Next, each separate transaction is recorded in the appropriate journal. Then the daily entries are posted to the ledger. Finally, and most importantly, conclusions are drawn from this information.

Why is this last step so vital? In order to be successful, a business must try to increase profits and lower expenses. To achieve this, a business needs to have certain information. How much profit has the business produced? How much debt is owed? How much inventory is in stock? To answer these and other questions, the accountant must organize and interpret the vast amounts of financial data available. With this information, the accountant can make informed business decisions.

As our world becomes more and more complex, the world of business also continues to grow. As business expands, the amount of paperwork grows and the amount of data increases. Over the years, the business world has searched for faster, cheaper, and more efficient ways to deal with increasingly vast quantities of data. The computer is the fastest and most sophisticated tool invented so far to process information.

Today's world has been called the age of the computer. Certainly, computers are used in most areas of our lives. They can be found in business, government, medicine, the arts, education, communications, and the home. Can you list ten specific uses of the computer in our society?

In this chapter, we will look at how the computer has affected the accounting work done by business. However, let's first examine the general topic of data processing.

24.1 Basic Concepts of Data Processing

What is Data Processing?

Most people associate data processing with a statement from the bank or a billing from a credit card company. But such financial information is just one form of data.

The word **data** is the plural of **datum**, meaning fact. Thus data are facts that describe persons, places, things, or events. Data can be made up of letters, numbers, words, symbols, or charts.

We all process facts about the world around us every day. We do not need a computer to tell us when to use an umbrella or how to time a roast-beef dinner. In a very general sense, our brains act as data processors. Information is received by them, stored, and acted upon.

Data processing is the handling of facts to achieve a desired result. Data processing takes place every time a shipping clerk prepares an invoice for payment, a bank teller sorts cheques, or a typist prepares a customer's monthly statement of account.

Data Processing Cycle

The computer is one method of processing data, and mental calculation is another. However, no matter what method you use to process data, certain basic steps must be followed. The following steps form the data processing cycle:

1. **Recording** is the copying of data from a source document onto a form that can be easily handled for processing.

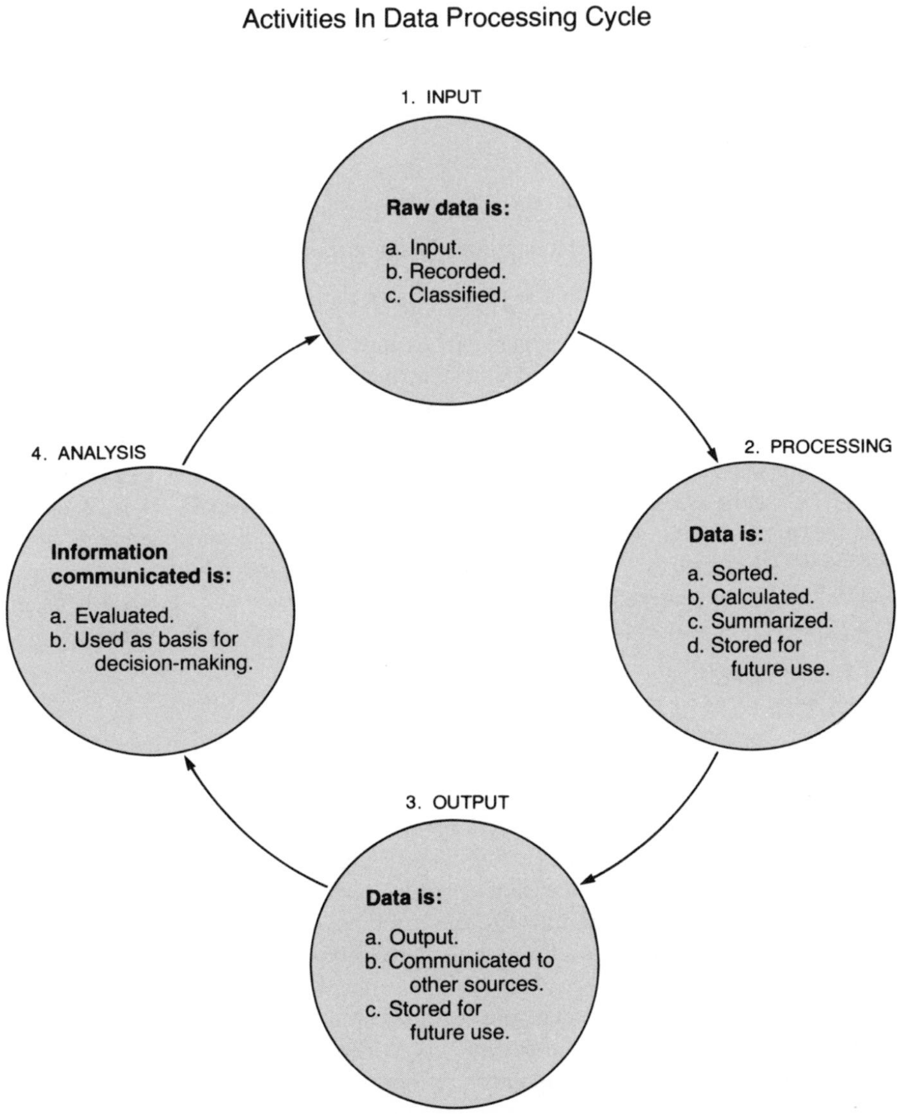
Activities In Data Processing Cycle
1. INPUT
Raw data is:
a. Input.
b. Recorded.
c. Classified.
2. PROCESSING
Data is:
a. Sorted.
b. Calculated.
c. Summarized.
d. Stored for future use.
3. OUTPUT
Data is:
a. Output.
b. Communicated to other sources.
c. Stored for future use.
4. ANALYSIS
Information communicated is:
a. Evaluated.
b. Used as basis for decision-making.

Figure 24.1 The flow of data and information within any business takes place in a definite cycle.

2. **Classifying** is the arranging and grouping of data according to a common characteristic.
3. **Sorting** is the process of placing data in order according to a common characteristic or classification.
4. **Calculating** (or computing) is the process of performing the mathematical operations of adding, subtracting, multiplying, or dividing.
5. **Summarizing** is the organizing and printing of data so that the main points are emphasized and the data is presented in a useable form.
6. **Communicating** is the process of reporting the summarized data to those people who need the information.
7. **Storing** is the filing of data for future use.

These seven steps can be combined into three very basic functions: input, processing, and output.

1. **Input** involves the recording and classification of data for processing.
2. **Processing** refers to how the computer manipulates the data.
3. **Output** is the final result of the processing of data.

The combined activities of input, processing, and output comprise the data processing cycle. Figure 24.1 shows these activities.

A definite flow of data and information takes place within any business. Data are organized and processed to produce useful information. That information is then used to support a decision. The decision causes action to take place. The results of this action can be assessed and measured, producing additional data. These data can then be processed to produce new information which, in turn, supports new decisions. Therefore, the flow of data and information through a business is cyclical and recurs in the same sequence. Remember that, no matter what method is used, data processing always takes place to convert data into useful information.

Electronic Data Processing — the Computer

There are three methods of processing data: manually (by hand), mechanically (by machine), and electronically (by computer).

So far, this course has taught you to process accounting data manually. All businesses used to keep records in this way (Figure 24.2). The manual method involves the use of pens, pencils, paper, ledgers, work sheets, and other devices.

Mechanical data processing refers to the machines most businesses use to help them process data. Adding machines, calculators, typewriters, and cash registers are the most common office machines.

Today, many businesses use electronic equipment to process data. In recent years, the electronic computer has developed quickly to meet business needs. In **electronic data processing** (EDP), the computer can perform all the necessary operations automatically and with minimal human involvement.

The **computer** is an electronic device made from electronic components. It functions to input, process, and output data, and uses the flow of electricity for

Until the late 19th century, pen and paper were the accountant's only equipment.

The adding machine and the accounting machine first allowed accountants to perform some tasks mechanically.

The computer has now almost replaced the traditional pen and paper in the accounting office.

Figure 24.2 The equipment used in accounting has changed radically in the twentieth century.

these operations. An electrical current can go around the world seven times in one second. Therefore, a computer can process data at very high speeds, sometimes performing more than 1 000 000 operations per second. Because the computer is not bored by repetition, it can perform repetitive operations very efficiently. Moreover, the computer does not make as many errors as humans do.

Because it can process and store data, the computer has been compared to the human brain. However, a computer cannot think for itself. It can only act on the instruction it receives from humans.

The Development of the Computer

The earliest computers were not designed for use in business. Rather, they performed calculations for the scientist and the engineer. The first general-purpose computer, the Mark I, was developed in 1944. The first computer for business, UNIVAC I, was produced in 1951. The early computer models, such as the one shown in Figure 24.3, were extremely large. This is because these computers used vacuum tubes. (Old television sets and radios, made in the 1950s or earlier, also used these tubes.) The vacuum tube was essentially an electronic switch. By 1959, the vacuum tube had been replaced by a tiny electronic device called a transistor. The introduction of the transistor enabled computers to become smaller and more efficient.

In the mid 1960s, the computer became even smaller due to the development of the **integrated circuit**. The vacuum tube and the transistor form only parts of an electrical circuit. Circuits also contain resistors, capacitors, wires, and other components to control the behaviour of the electrical current. In earlier computers, these components were wired together one by one. However, integrated circuits are produced as single units. They contain dozens of components joined together in a

Figure 24.3 The Mark 1, the first general-purpose computer. Courtesy of IBM.

single process. Integrated circuits are produced on **silicon chips**, thin layers of silicon so tiny that a thimble could hold nearly 50 000 of them. Computers with integrated circuits were much smaller and could operate much faster than their predecessors.

In the 1970s, the use of computers grew tremendously. This was largely due to the development of a large-scale integration (LSI) of computer circuits. By 1975,

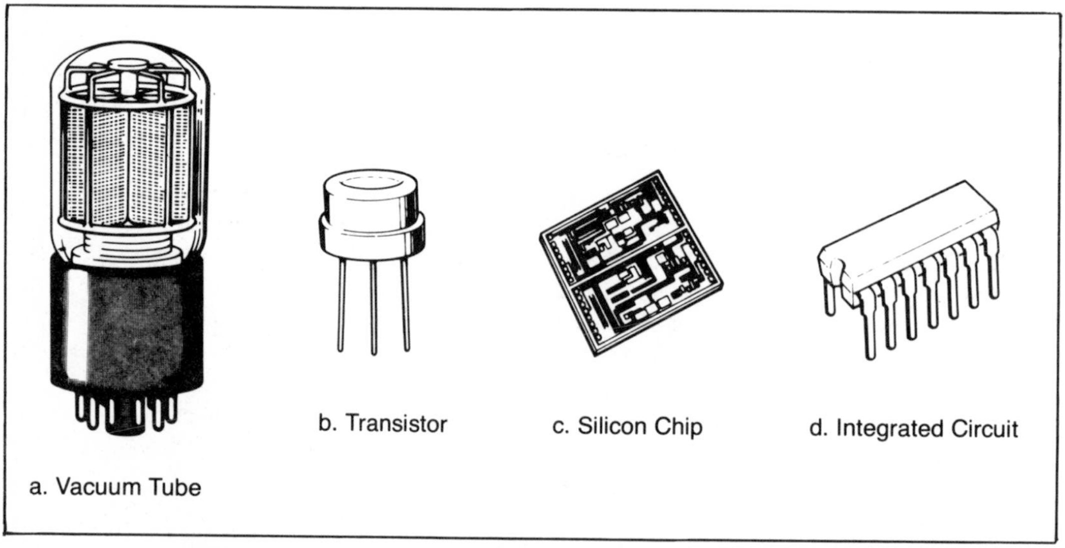

Figure 24.4 Computer technology has developed from the use of the unwieldy vacuum tube (a) to the smaller transistor (b) to the tiny silicon chip (c) and, finally, to the large-scale use of the integrated circuit (d). (Not drawn to scale.)

chips carried between 10 000 and 20 000 transistors. Today, chips can carry over 20 000 transistors. As a result, microprocessors have developed entire computers on one tiny integrated chip.

Figure 24.4 illustrates the vacuum tube, the transistor, the silicon chip, and the integrated circuit.

Types of Computer

Computers today are smaller and more reliable than earlier models. They also consume less power and process far more information. Computers can be classified by size and speed.

1. *Super-computers.* The super-computer is the biggest and fastest machine available today. Super-computers can quickly perform billions or even trillions of calculations. Because they are extremely expensive to operate, super-computers are only used when maximum speed and power are so vital that their cost is unimportant.
2. *Large computers.* Large computers are much less expensive to operate than super-computers, and are used by large organizations such as corporations and universities. Figure 24.5 shows a typical business computer-room setup.

Figure 24.5 A computer room.

3. *Mini-computers.* Mini-computers handle many tasks at a more reasonable cost than large computers. They are used in such varied operations as banking, inventory control, airline reservations, and car rentals. Mini-computers have become almost as powerful as the large computers. However, they work much more slowly. Because they cost much less to operate, mini-computers are used by small companies that do not need the capacity or speed of large computers.
4. *Micro-computers.* Micro-computers are even smaller than mini-computers. They offer considerable computer power, low cost, and flexibility. Therefore, they are ideal for operations that handle limited amounts of data. As shown in Figure 24.6, the micro-computer is increasingly used in small businesses, in education, and in the home.

Computer design is changing all the time. At present, the trend is toward reduced size, reduced cost, and increased computer speed and storage capacity. Smaller and less expensive machines will appear in the very near future, as the computer continues to increase its influence on our lives.

Advantages and Limitations of Computers

The following major advantages result from the use of the computer to process data.

1. The computer processes data more quickly than any other form of data processing.
2. The computer is more versatile than any other machine for data processing.
3. The computer processes data continuously with minimal human intervention, once it has received data and instructions.
4. The computer can store data and instructions for long periods of time and produce them quickly on demand.
5. The computer is more accurate than any other system.

The computer provides the accountant with very fast access to information. As a result, the accountant can make quicker, better-informed decisions. The computer also improves the speed and quality of customer service.

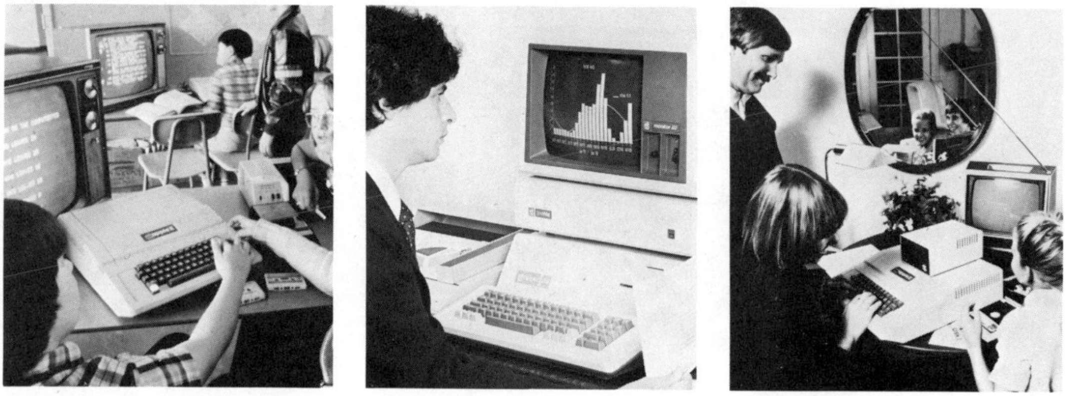

Figure 24.6 Micro-computers are being used in the classroom, the office, and the home. Courtesy of Apple Canada Inc.

In a manual accounting system, you have learned that the possibility of errors increases when tasks are boring and repetitive. The computer does not get bored. By taking over repetitious tasks, the computer provides greater accuracy and frees employees for more meaningful and creative work.

Most companies accumulate a great many documents with information on accounts, sales, inventory, customers, production, and employees. As business files grow larger, specific items of data become harder to find. Besides reducing paperwork, the computer can store large amounts of data using far less space than paper files. The computer can also find specific data very quickly.

However, the computer does have limitations. It cannot initiate operations; it can only respond to the data and the instructions it receives. Moreover, computer processing is expensive. Besides the high cost of equipment itself, qualified personnel must be hired to operate it. Nonetheless, despite these limitations, the computer is usually more cost effective than a manual system.

24.2 Components of a Computer System

Although computers differ in size, speed, and degree of complexity, they are all data-processing systems. All computers perform four basic operations: input, processing, storage, and output.

Each of these operations is performed by a physical component. The four components are interconnected with one another to form a computer system. The physical components of a computer system, known as the computer's **hardware**, are illustrated in Figure 24.7.

In order to operate, a computer must also be given a set of logical instructions to follow. A set of instructions is called a **program**. Computer programs are referred to as **software**.

In this section, we will look at the four operations of a computer system, beginning with input.

Figure 24.7 The computer and all its peripheral equipment, such as terminals and printers, are referred to as hardware. Courtesy of IBM.

Input

Computers cannot read data in the same way that we can. Before data can be fed into a computer, they must be converted into a form that the computer can understand.

There are various ways to feed data into a computer. The form that data take for computer entry is called an **input medium**. Input media include punched cards, punched tape, magnetic tape, magnetic disks, documents with data printed in magnetic ink or a special style of optical character, and terminals. First the data are coded or recorded on these input media. Then the data are fed into the computer using an input device.

Punched Cards

Under this input system, data are taken from source documents and transferred onto cards. Holes are punched in appropriate places using a predetermined coding system. Figure 24.8 shows one of these **punched cards**. The holes represent digits, letters, and special characters.

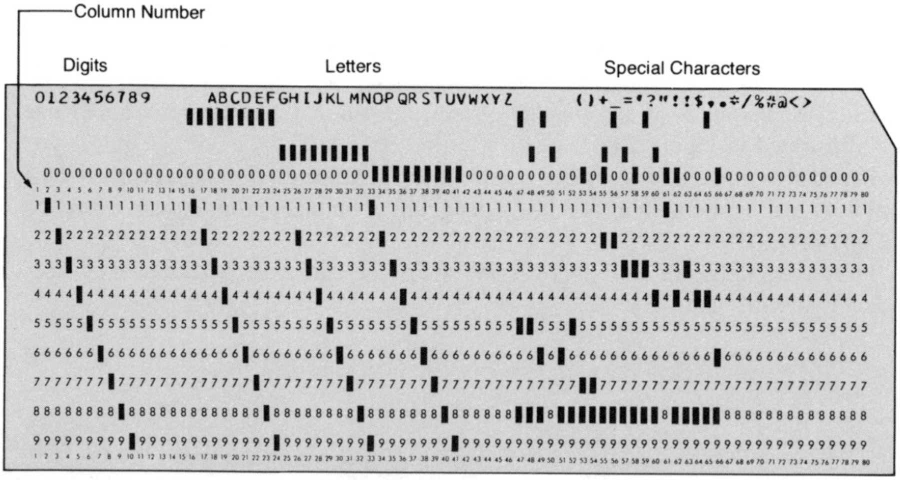

Figure 24.8 Punched cards sometimes accompany the customer's bill. The card is returned with the payment.

Punched Paper Tape

Punched paper tape can be compared to a continuous series of punched cards. See Figure 24.9.

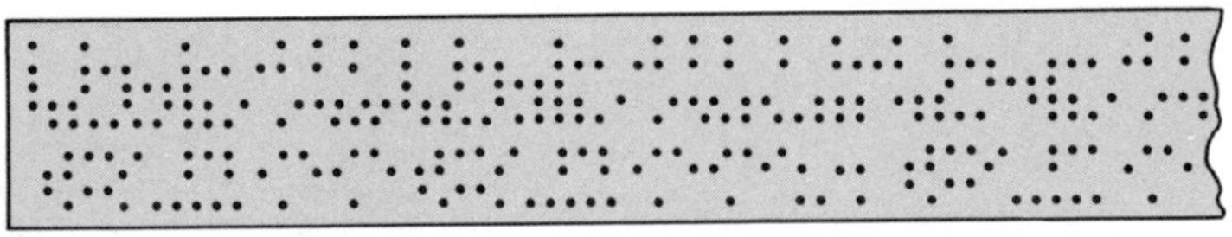

Figure 24.9 A punched tape.

Magnetic Tape

Magnetic tape uses the principle of a common tape-recorder. Data are recorded as 'magnetized' spots on the tape, which is usually reel-to-reel or cassette.

Magnetic Disk

A **magnetic disk** looks like a 45 rpm phonograph record. (Figure 14.10) This disk, often called a **diskette** or **floppy disk**, is a thin circular metal plate that has been coded on both sides with a recording material. Far more data can be recorded on disk than on tape. Also, the data can be retrieved 300 to 400 times faster.

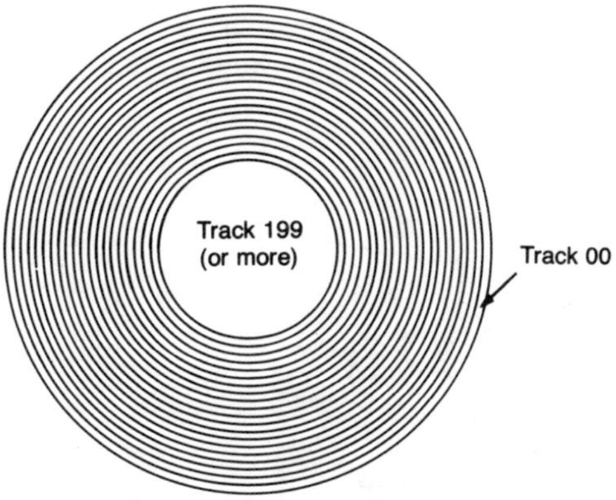

Figure 24.10 A magnetic disk. Data are stored on a series of concentric circles called tracks.

Character Recognition

Character recognition involves printing a special type of coding on a source document. The coding is then read by a special device. Have you ever noticed the special coding on a bank cheque, seen in Figure 24.11? The bank uses character recognition to process the cheque.

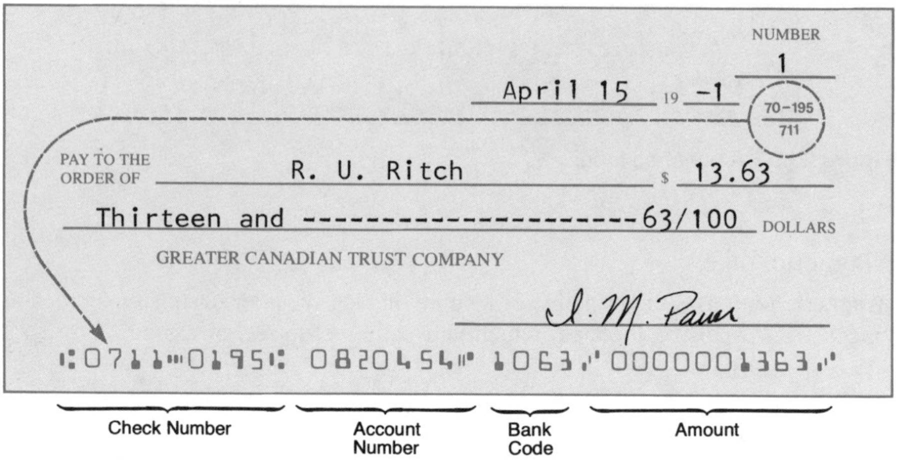

Figure 24.11 A bank cheque uses a special type of coding for processing by the computer.

Terminals

The **terminal** is a form of electronic typewriter. As a person types, the typewriter converts each key-stroke into an electronic impulse that is fed into the computer.

Figure 24.12 A CRT display terminal (left) is a soft copy terminal. It provides temporary output only on the screen. A printer (right) is a hard copy terminal. It provides a written copy of the output. Courtesy of Apple Canada Inc.

Figure 24.12 shows the two types of terminal. A **hard copy terminal** issues a printed record of the data that are entered into the computer. With a **soft copy terminal,** the characters appear as a light pattern on a television screen. A soft copy terminal is often called a CRT (Cathode Ray Tube). The CRT is faster and less expensive than a hard copy terminal because it does not produce a printed record.

Table 24.1 summarizes the six ways to input data into a computer.

Table 24-1 Input Media and Devices

Medium	*Device*	*Purpose*	*Typical Speed Ranges*	*Use*	*Advantages or Disadvantages*
Punched cards	Card reader	Input of source data on 80- and 96-column punched cards	100–2 000 cards per minute	Low-volume applications in small or medium computer systems	Low cost but low speed, bulky media, not correctable, not reusable.
Paper tape	Paper tape reader	Low-speed input of low-volume files	100–2 000 characters per minute	Low-volume applications for small systems	Simple and inexpensive but bulky and fragile, not correctable, not reusable
Magnetic tape	Magnetic tape reader	High-speed input of large-volume sequential files	50 000–1 000 000 characters per second	High-volume processing (inventory, payroll)	Inexpensive with fast transfer rate, correctable, sequential, direct, reusable
Magnetic disk	Magnetic disk unit	High-speed input of data	50 000–1 000 000 characters per second	High-volume processing	Large capacity, fast, correctable, but expensive, reusable
Special paper or print	Character readers	Input reading from source documents	700–3 000 characters per second	Applications requiring high-volume data input from source documents	Direct input, but limitations with input format
Cathode ray tube	CRT display terminals	Keyboard entry of input data and inquiries	Limited to speed capabilities of operator	Low-volume or inquiry applications	Convenient and low cost — use limited to sitting at terminal

Processing

After data have been fed into the computer, they must then be processed. Remember that processing refers to the manipulation of data by the computer.

Every computer system contains a **central processing unit** (**CPU**), whose main purpose is to process data. The CPU acts as the brain of the entire computer system. It takes data from the input device and processes the data according to the instructions of the program. It then sends the results to an output device for recording.

The CPU is composed of three units: the primary storage (memory) unit, the arithmetic-logic unit, and the control unit. Figure 24.13 illustrates three components of a CPU. The units may be contained in one cabinet or in separate cabinets connected by cable.

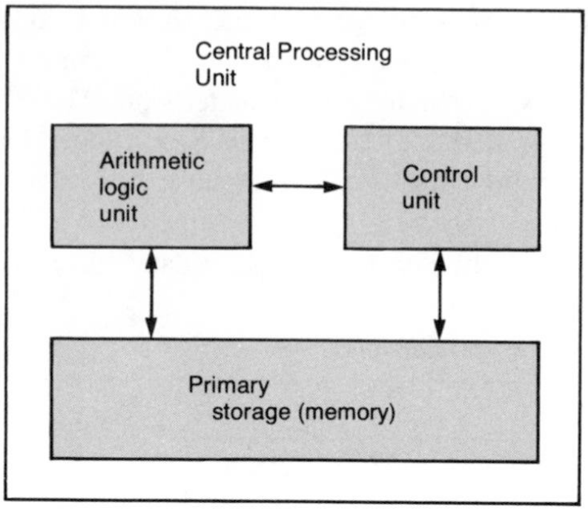

Figure 24.13 The components of a CPU .

Primary Storage (Memory) Unit

The word 'storage' means the same for a computer as the word 'memory'. The storage unit of the CPU is referred to as **primary storage**. Storage devices outside the CPU are called **auxiliary storage**.

All data must be stored in the computer before they can be processed. The computer stores three things:

1. Data from input devices.
2. Sets of instructions (programs) that tell the machine what to do.
3. The final results of the processing.

Computer storage operates somewhat like a huge electronic filing cabinet. Computer 'files' are completely indexed and available to the computer on demand. The primary storage unit of the CPU contains many storage areas called cells. Each cell can store a fixed amount of data. Each cell also has a unique location and address somewhat like a postal box in a post office.

Arithmetic-Logic Unit (ALU)

The **arithmetic-logic unit** actually processes the data by performing a variety of arithmetic and logic operations such as comparing relative values. For these operations, data are taken from storage and placed in temporary storage areas called registers. The arithmetic processing takes place in these registers. When an arithmetic operation is finished, the result is transferred from its register to storage. The registers are then free for the next operation.

Control Unit

The **control unit** of the CPU directs and coordinates all units of the computer. The control unit does not input, output, process, or store data. Rather, it initiates these activities and controls their sequence.

The control section's operations are controlled by a program stored in the computer's main memory. This program is a series of instructions outlining the exact sequence of steps the computer must follow to process a given set of data.

The control unit controls the following:

1. Input devices.
2. Storage and the retrieval of data from the storage unit.
3. Output devices.
4. The order in which instructions are to be carried out.

Auxiliary Storage

Primary storage is used for the temporary storage of data. If data are to be kept, they are stored in auxiliary or secondary storage units outside the computer. Auxiliary storage consists of data held outside the primary storage or memory of the computer for later use. When needed, the data can be transferred to the primary storage, processed, and then returned to auxiliary storage.

Access time is the average time required to locate and retrieve a piece of data from storage. The use of auxiliary storage means the data must be located in the auxiliary storage and then transferred to the primary storage.

For auxiliary storage, access time depends on what type of storage device is used. A sequential-access storage device requires more access time than a direct-access storage device. In **sequential-access storage**, stored data are retrieved in the order in which they were stored. In other words, before item 325 can be located, the first 324 items must be read. In **direct-access storage**, data can be retrieved without a search through the preceding items in storage. Thus item 325 can be located virtually immediately.

The major sequential-access storage media are punched cards, punched paper tape, and magnetic tape. The major direct-access storage media include magnetic disks, diskettes (floppy disks), and magnetic drums. You read about the first two devices when you studied input media. The magnetic drum operates much like the magnetic disk. The drum, shown in Figure 24.14, is a heavy metal cylinder with a thick outer layer of magnetic oxide.

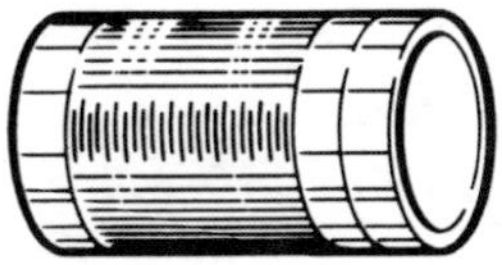

Figure 24.14 A magnetic drum is a heavy metal cylinder coated with a thin layer of magnetic oxide.

Output

After the computer has processed the information, it must be presented in a meaningful form. The presentation of the data is known as the output. Output is the final link in the data-processing cycle.

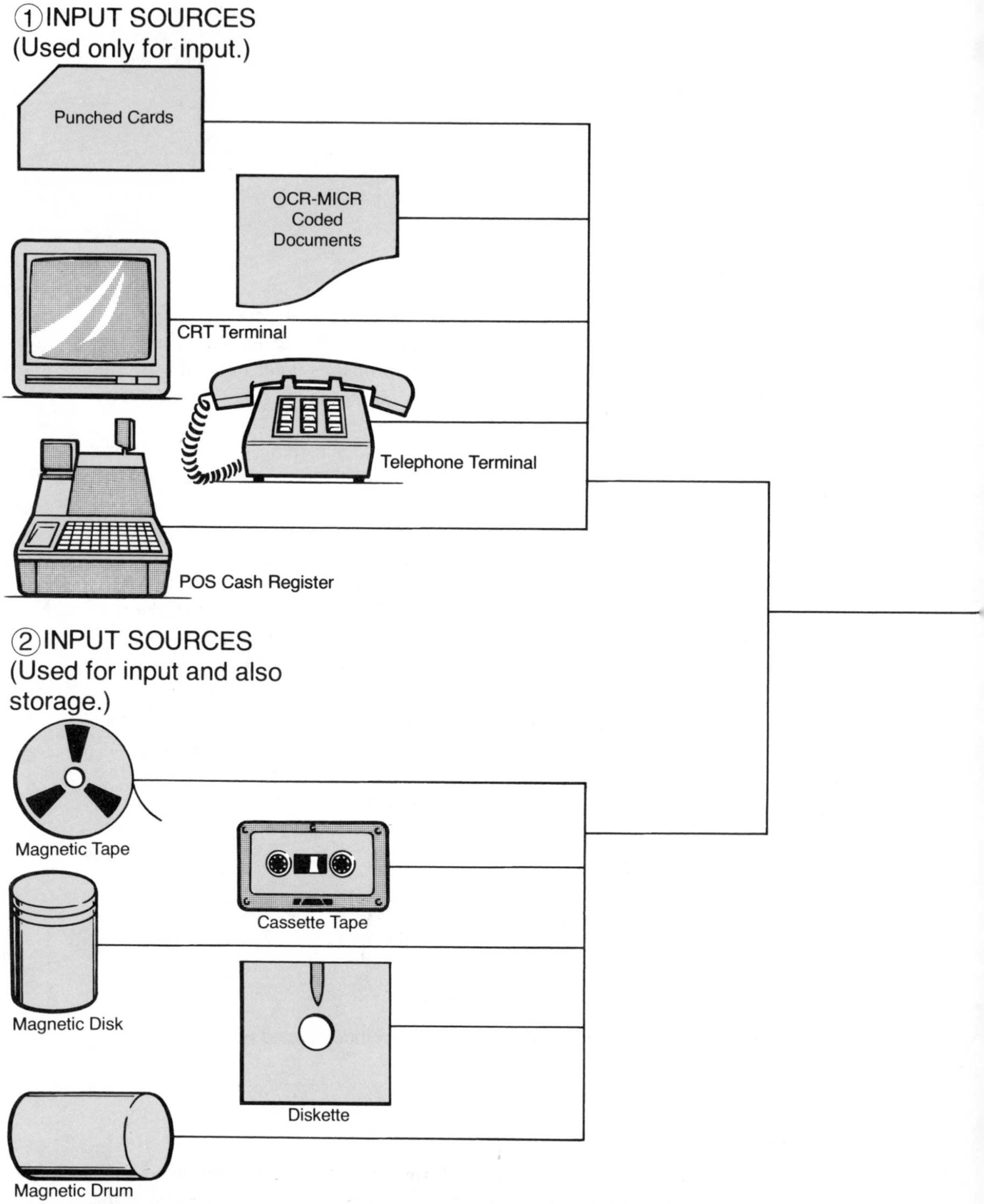

Figure 24.15 A flowchart showing the common devices for input, output, and storage that are used along with the CPU to carry out computer programs.

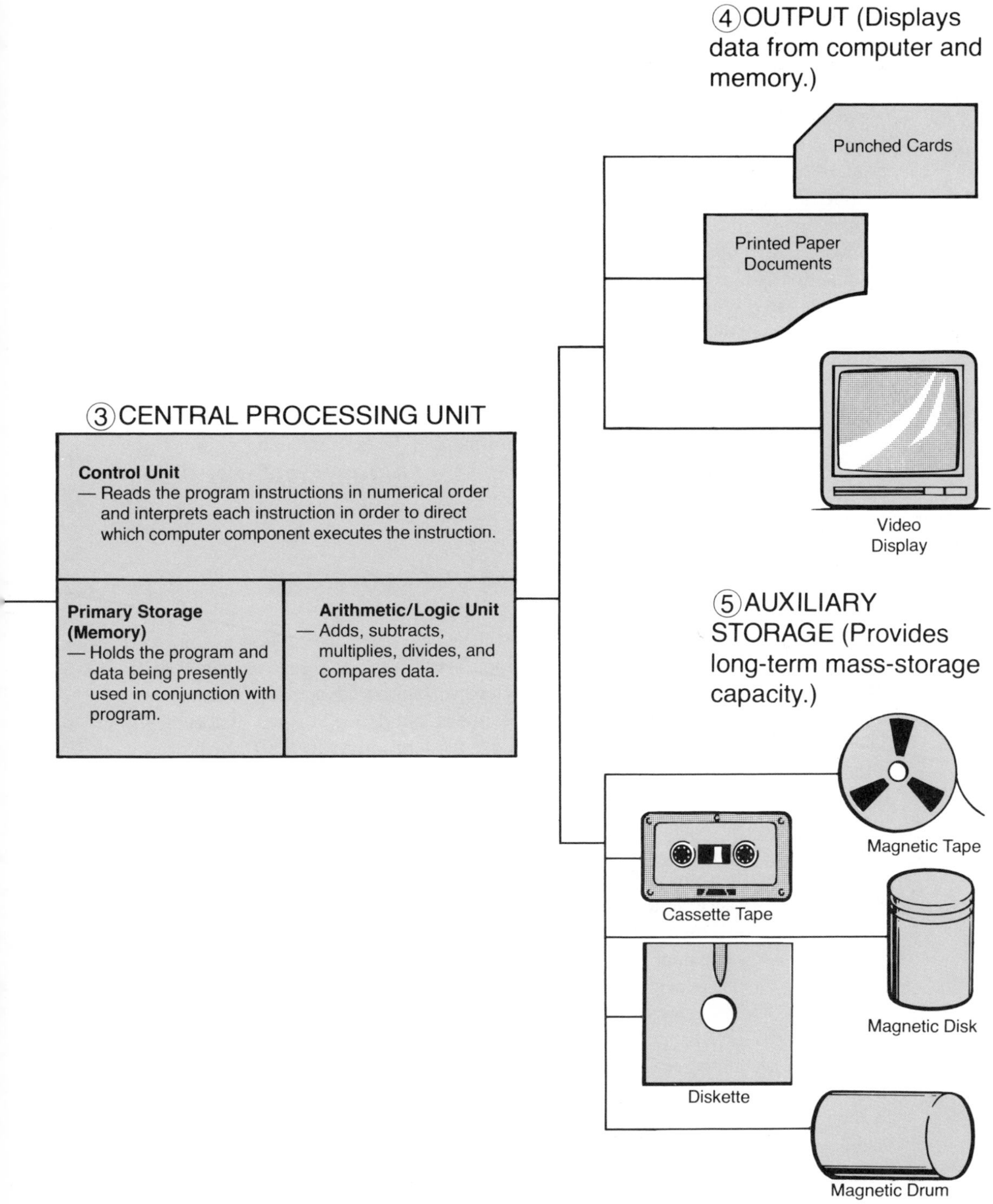
③ CENTRAL PROCESSING UNIT
Control Unit
— Reads the program instructions in numerical order and interprets each instruction in order to direct which computer component executes the instruction.
Primary Storage (Memory)
— Holds the program and data being presently used in conjunction with program.
Arithmetic/Logic Unit
— Adds, subtracts, multiplies, divides, and compares data.
④ OUTPUT (Displays data from computer and memory.)
Punched Cards
Printed Paper Documents
Video Display
⑤ AUXILIARY STORAGE (Provides long-term mass-storage capacity.)
Magnetic Tape
Cassette Tape
Magnetic Disk
Diskette
Magnetic Drum

There are two kinds of computer output. Output intended for immediate use must be presented in a form that people can read. An example is a printed copy. Output that is to be stored for future use must be presented in a form that can be read again by the computer.

An output device is connected to the CPU. Most output devices produce some form of print, whether on paper, cards, film, or screen. These devices, called printers, are classified as either hard-copy devices or soft-copy devices. **Hard-copy output** devices produce a physical record of the information. Hard-copy output includes punched cards, paper tape, or a printed report. **Soft-copy output** devices produce only a temporary copy of the output information. An example of soft-copy output is a display on the screen of a computer terminal.

Output for machine use is usually stored on magnetic tape and various direct-access storage devices. Output for use by people is usually provided by printers, terminals, and microfilm.

In this section, you were introduced to the components and operation of a computer system. Figure 24.15 summarizes this information. In the remaining sections of this chapter, you will learn how the computer is changing the nature of accounting in the modern business world.

24.3 Computer Applications in Accounting

Now that you know something about computers, you are ready to look at some of the accounting work that computers perform. However, let's first review a few points about electronic data processing. The two biggest advantages of using the computer to process data are its tremendous speed and its high degree of accuracy. The computer also has an enormous capacity to store information. It can process information according to very involved instructions. Then it can make that information available in a variety of desired forms.

What significance do these factors have for the field of accounting? When processed by computer, information is more complete and more immediately available than when processed by hand or by machine. The computer can collect vast quantities of accounting data and transform the data into meaningful reports. In addition, the computer performs a great deal of the routine accounting work. Therefore, the accountant has more time to interpret accounting reports and use them to make management decisions.

When the computer was first introduced to business in the early 1950s, it was used to process large batches of paperwork. Later, the computer was used to handle fundamental accounting operations; it routinely processed large amounts of accounting data, such as payroll, inventory, accounts receivable, accounts payable, and posting to ledger accounts. Today, the computer can be used for nearly every phase of accounting operations. Moreover, it performs these procedures more quickly and accurately than the numerous clerks needed to perform them manually.

Recently, computers have begun to play a role in decision-making. More and more, they are helping businesses to use information efficiently. Computers are now able to predict and evaluate the outcomes of business policies, and even to make policy recommendations. Today the computer plays an integral part in every phase of business operation.

There are seven primary accounting tasks that computers can perform:

1. Sales.
2. Purchases.
3. Inventory.
4. Accounts receivable and accounts payable.
5. Payroll.
6. Budget.
7. All other accounting routines.

We will look at each of these accounting functions in Section 24.5.

24.4 Developing a Computerized System

Save-More is a chain of discount department stores with over 200 branches located across Canada. This company is in the process of switching to computerized accounting. Save-More plans to use the computer for a variety of functions. All branches are to be connected to the main computer which is located at the head office. The links between the branches and Head Office will be provided by telephone lines. The telephone company rents this service to firms such as Save-More so that they can transmit information from one place to another. Figures 24.16 and 24.17 illustrate this network.

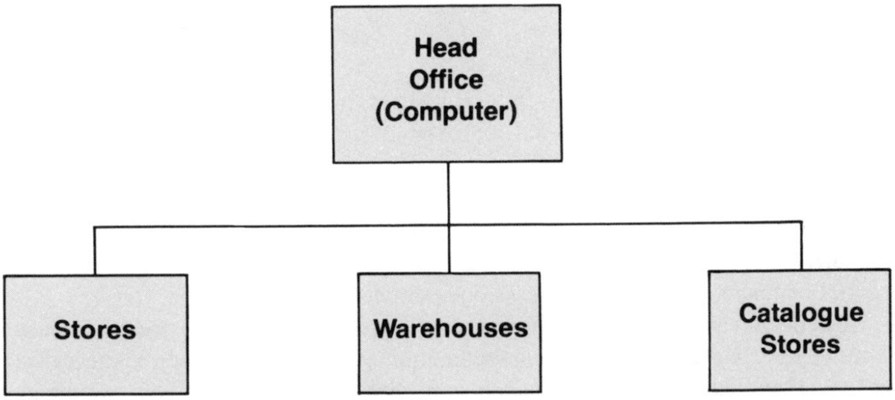

Figure 24.16 All Save-More operations throughout Canada are connected by computer terminals or computerized cash registers to the main computer at the head office. This is known as distributed processing.

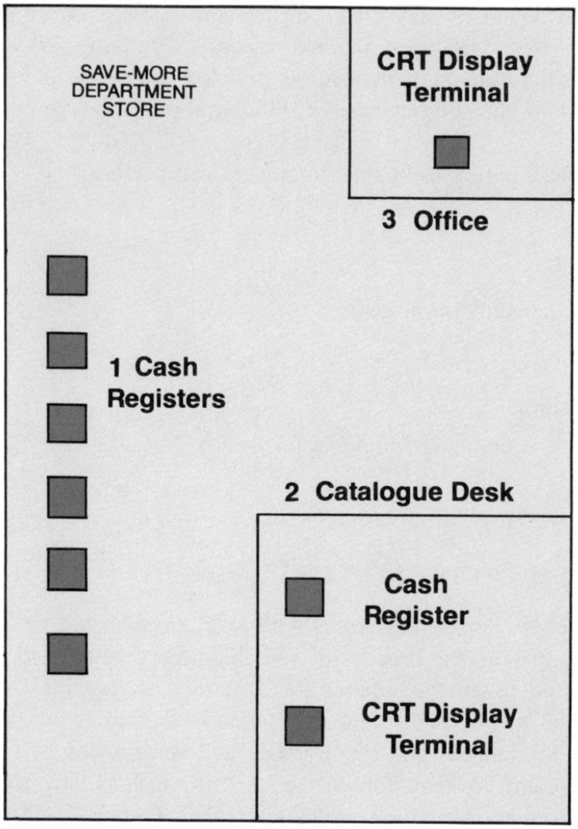

1 All the cash registers are computerized.

2 The cash register is computerized. The terminal is to check stock in warehouses and process orders.

3 The terminal allows office personnel to monitor the cash registers and communicate with Head Office.

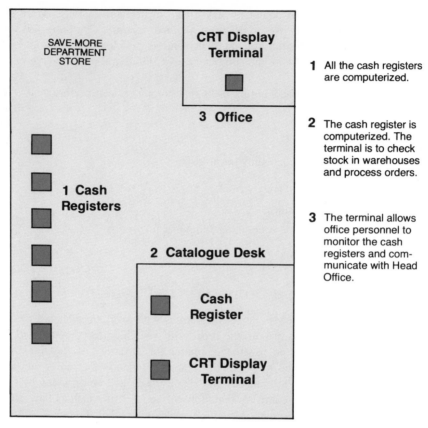

Figure 24.17 Each store has three departments that are connected to the head-office computer. Each catalogue store has the same setup as the catalogue department in the department store.

Systems Development

When Save-More management decided to computerize its operation, it found that more was involved than just buying a computer and installing it. Save-More found that systems development was necessary. A **system** is a group of parts that function together as a unit. Save-More needs a group of parts, from cash registers to a central computer, that can operate as one complete whole.

Systems development involves four steps. First, the company's computer needs must be clearly analyzed. Then, computer equipment must be chosen to meet those needs. Third, computer programs must be obtained to operate the equipment. Finally, methods must be designed to ensure that the computer is operating at maximum efficiency.

To analyze the company's computer needs, representatives of the computer manufacturer work alongside Save-More management. Senior accounting staff play a substantial role in determining the computer's place in accounting operations. Today, accounting personnel must have at least a basic knowledge of computer operations so they can discuss the company's use of the computer intelligently.

The company's computer needs are met through the careful selection of computer hardware. Save-More requires a very large central computer that can handle enormous amounts of data processing. The computer has to be able to handle computerized cash registers in over 200 stores, terminals in warehouses, and terminals for the phone-order departments, and still meet the needs of personnel at Head Office. The system must also have extra capacity for future expansion. If necessary, Save-More will rent out the extra capacity until needed.

After the computer equipment is purchased, computer programs (software) are needed to operate that equipment. There are three sources of software. First, the manufacturer of the computer equipment may work closely with Save-More computer personnel to provide the necessary programs. Second, company programmers may be employed in the Save-More computer department to create new programs. Third, Save-More may hire an independent software company that specializes in writing computer programs.

Each of these three sources can be used alone or in combination with the others. Save-More is likely to buy its software initially. Over the years, its own programmers can then continually modify the software based on the changing needs of the company.

The testing of computer efficiency is the responsibility of Save-More. Initially, the entire system is tested with every possible variety of sample transaction. However, ongoing testing is also necessary to ensure that the computer system is operating correctly to meet the company's computer needs.

System Assistance Process

A computer system is very complex and very expensive. It cannot be used effectively unless operated correctly. In order to guarantee the correct operation of the system, the computer manufacturer offers **system assistance**; that is, training programs for Save-More employees. Trained Save-More personnel then take over the training of new employees.

At Save-More, store personnel will be trained to operate computerized cash registers. Management in the stores must learn special procedures concerning adjustments. For example, when a mistake over $25 is made by a cashier, the supervisor or head cashier will have to insert a special key into the machine and key a certain code. Many personnel in Head Office and in the warehouses must be trained to use computer terminals. The computer department will undergo intensive training on the features of Save-More's particular system. And, finally, Save-More management personnel will have to learn how to use the system effectively.

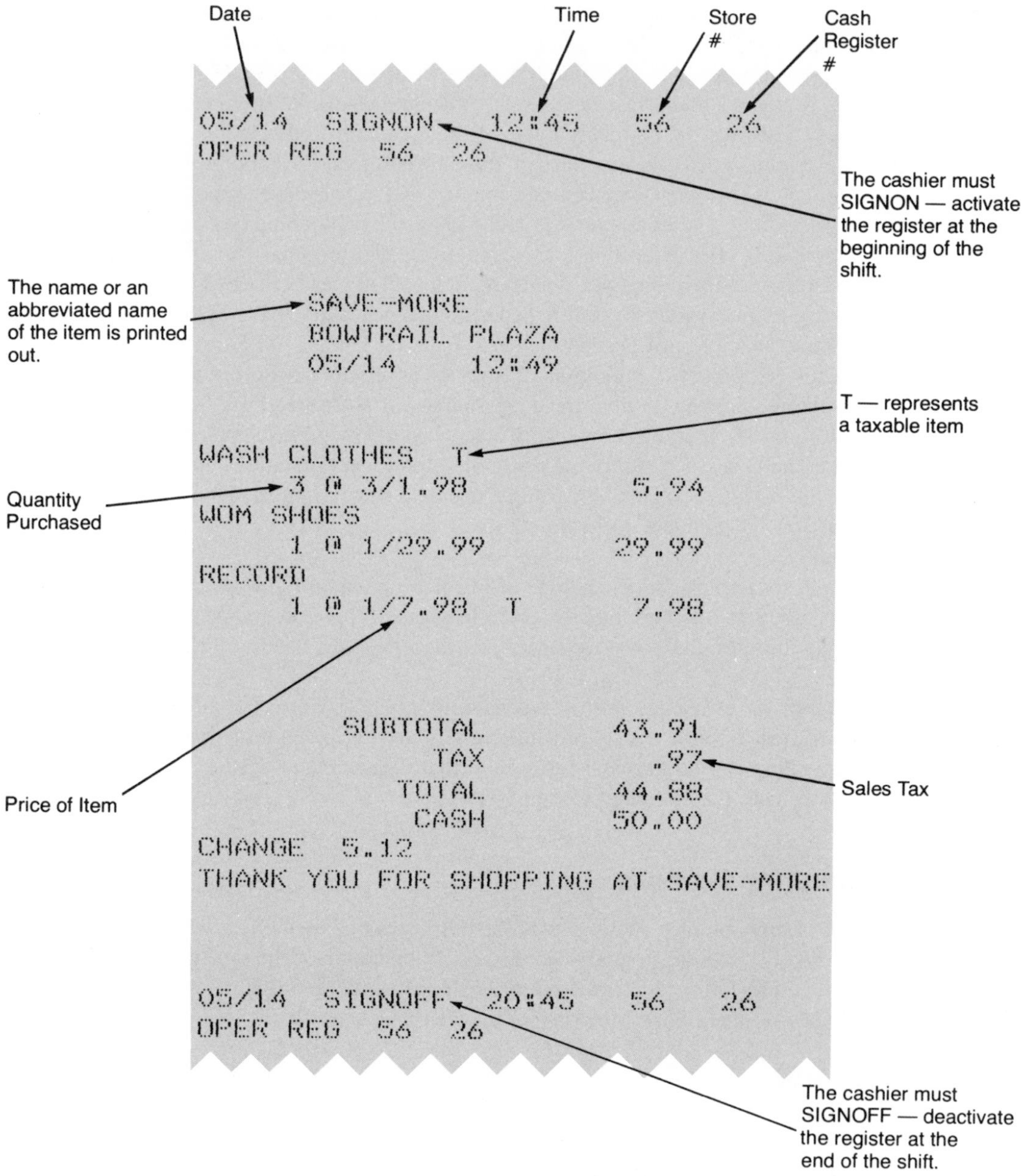

Figure 24.18 A computerized bill from Save-More.

24.5 Computer Applications at Save-More Stores

In this section, we will take a look at the major accounting work that the newly installed computer performs for the chain of Save-More stores. The Save-More computer system has applications in terms of sales, purchasing, inventory, accounts receivable, accounts payable, payroll, budget, and a few other accounting routines.

Sales

The Save-More chain of stores uses four different methods for sales. Sales are made through the stores, through the warehouses, through catalogue stores, and through telephone orders. Data from all four methods of sale are directly fed to the Save-More computer. The computer system keeps a running total of sales from all sources and a running total of inventory. Sales that require further action, such as delivery or billing of accounts receivable, are passed on by the computer to the correct department.

Sales by Stores

Each store has computerized cash registers that are connected to the main computer. As you read in Chapter 16, electronic cash registers, often called point of sale (POS) terminals, are far more efficient than mechanical cash registers. The electronic cash register updates the sales record, the customer account, and the inventory record while each transaction is taking place.

The cashier records sales by one of two methods. By the first method, the cashier punches in the code number of the item, the amount purchased, and the price. By the second method, which just applies to certain items, the cashier punches only the code number of the item and the amount purchased; the computer has already stored the price and prints it out when the code is received. Save-More uses the second approach to save money on price tags for small items with large numbers of sales.

For both methods, after all the customer's purchases have been punched in, the computer calculates any tax payable and prints out the final price. Figure 24.18 shows a sample bill.

Save-More also operates two experimental stores near its head office. The experimental stores make use of the character recognition form of input that we discussed in Section 24.2. Have you ever noticed the series of parallel lines or bars on the labels of packaged products in food stores? Figure 24.19 shows this

0 61143 13180

Figure 24.19 The UPC is a universal code that identifies the item to the store's computer. The cashier runs the code over the scanner.

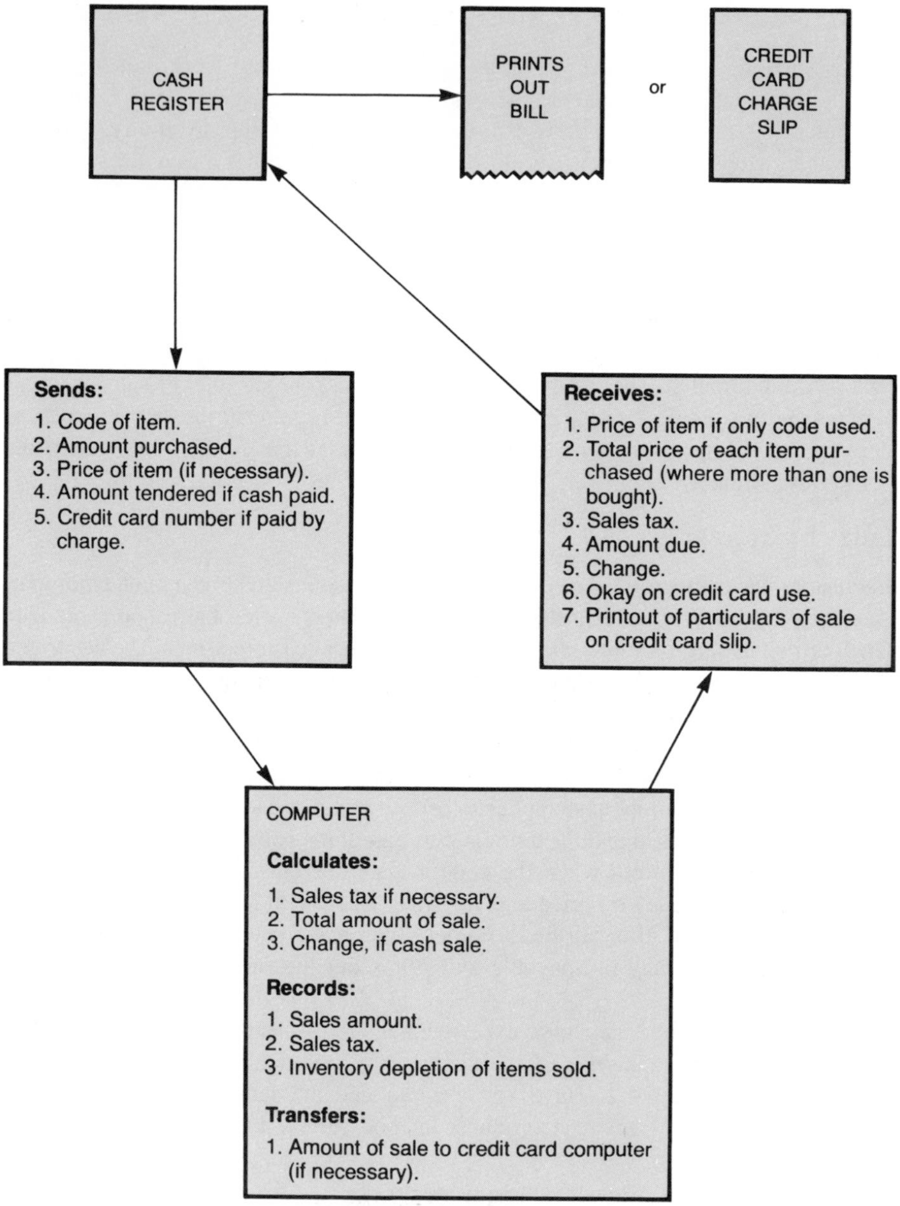

Figure 24.20 How sales information travels through a computer system.

code, called a Universal Product Code (UPC). In its two experimental stores, Save-More has installed UPC readers at the checkout counters. A UPC scanner reads the code with a laser beam. The scanner can ring up sales more quickly and accurately than a cashier can. The prices of all items are stored in the computer. When the computer receives the UPC that identifies the item, it sends back the price to be printed on the cash register tape. Thus, the cashier does not have to key in any prices.

The use of computerized cash registers allows the Save-More computer to keep up-to-date information on the operations of all its stores. The central computer notes that a particular store has registered a sale, notes it in the sales records, and subtracts the item from that store's inventory record. As a result, an up-to-the-minute record of total sales and inventory is kept for each store. Management in Head Office can obtain daily printouts of each store's sales and inventory records by simply accessing the computer. Figure 24.20 shows how sales information travels through the computer system.

The POS cash register is useful for credit-card purchases. Save-More accepts all major credit cards like Visa and MasterCard. The cash register has a space where the blank credit-card slip is inserted. The cashier keys in the account number and then lets the cash register take over. The Save-More computer checks the validity and credit limit on the card with the credit-card company's computer. If there is something wrong, it flashes a code to the cashier indicating what action is to be taken, and refuses to process the blank credit-card slip. Otherwise, the credit-card slip is printed up by the register.

Warehouse Sales Invoices

Save-More does a limited amount of special selling to other businesses from some of its warehouses. For example, it may sell 50 beds to a motel owner. These sales are written up as sales invoices by a salesman. The invoices are then entered by terminal to the computer at the end of the business day. All the information from these sales on account is entered into a type of computerized sales journal and into the necessary account receivable, as shown in Figure 24.21.

Telephone Orders

The warehouses also have office staff that are employed as telephone order clerks. All telephone orders are received by a clerk sitting at a computer terminal. The clerk uses the terminal to check whether or not the requested item is available in stock. The terminal is linked to the computer which has a complete inventory record of the stock in every warehouse. When possible, merchandise is shipped from the warehouse closest to the customer. Should the item be out of stock there, the clerk can use the terminal to check the other Save-More warehouses. Therefore, the customer knows immediately whether the item is available.

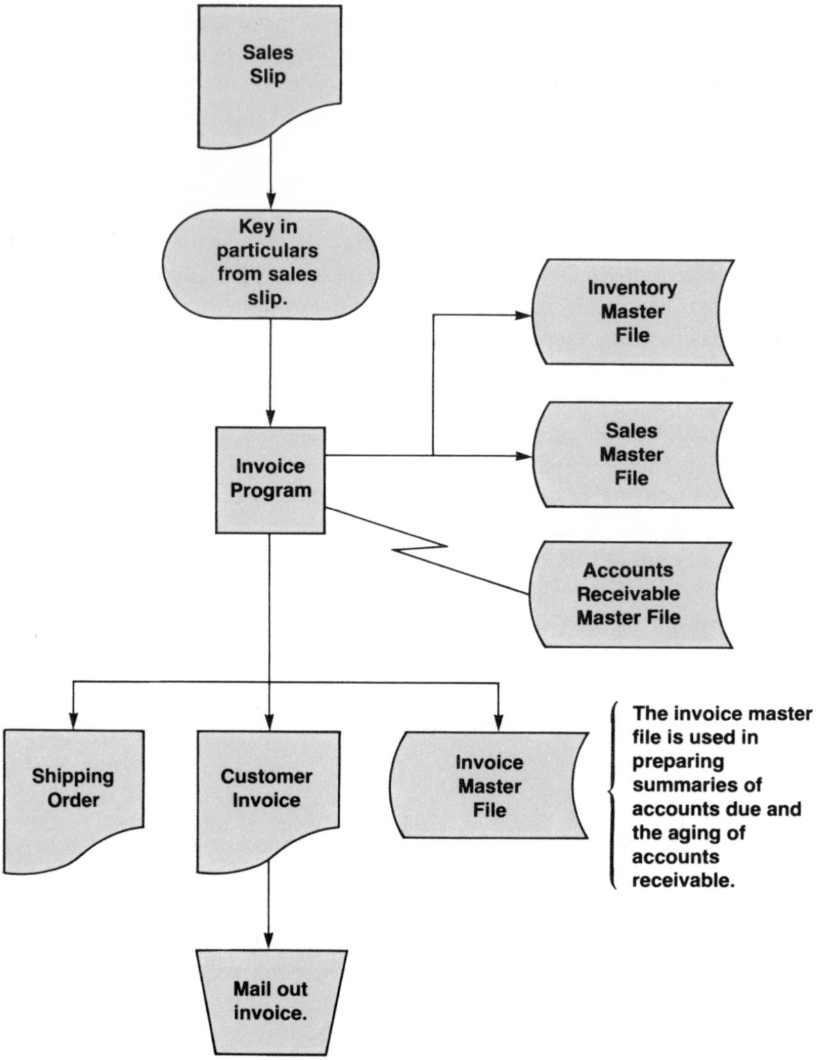

Figure 24.21 Processing a warehouse sale.

If the stock is available, the clerk takes down the order and gets the customer's name, address, phone number, and credit card number if the order is charged. The clerk then sends this information through the terminal to the main computer. The computer records the sale and either bills the credit-card account or sets up an account receivable for the customer.

The computer then sends a shipping order to the shipping department in the warehouse. If the purchase is not charged, the shipping order instructs the delivery person to collect the payment. Figure 24.22 shows how a telephone order is processed.

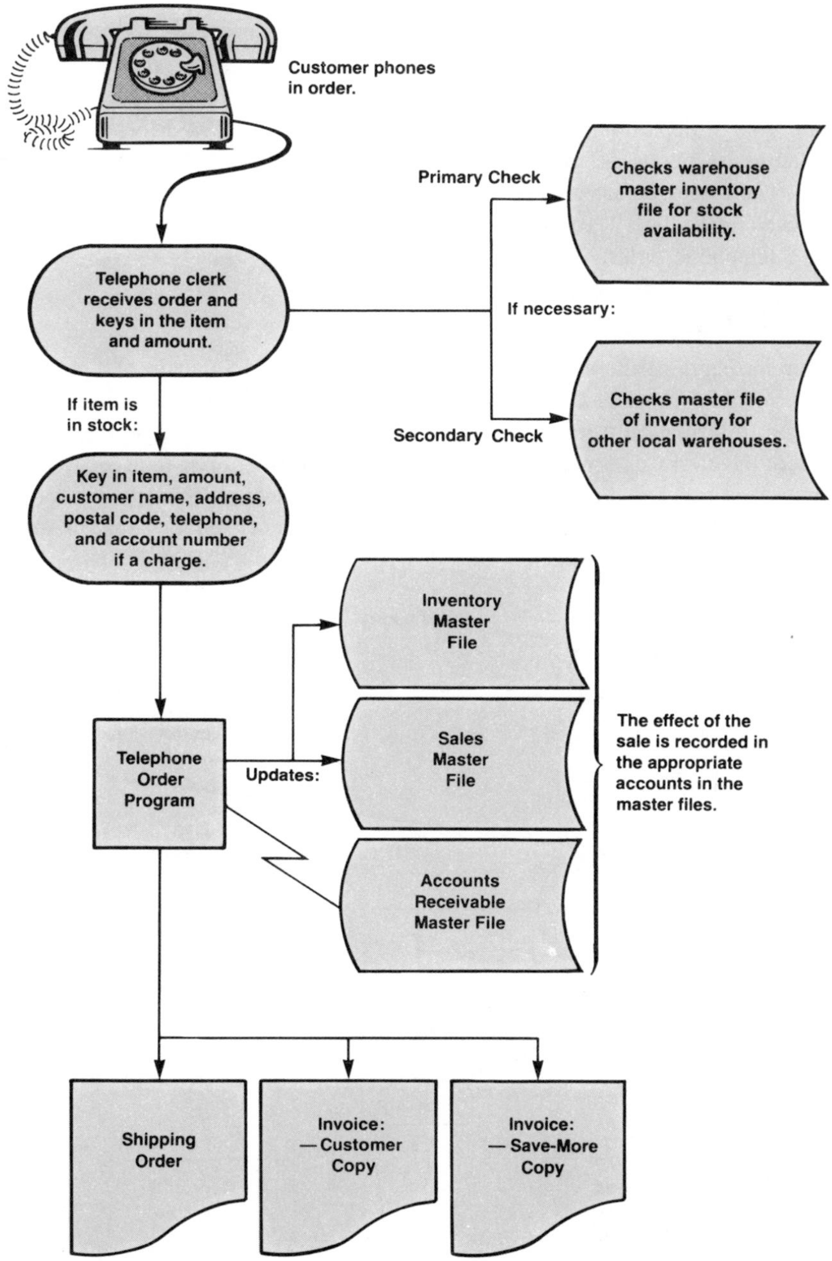

Figure 24.22 Processing a telephone order.

Catalogue Stores

Save-More has catalogue departments in many of its stores as well as small catalogue stores in some of Canada's smaller towns where it would not pay to operate a large department store. A customer can use the Save-More catalogue to order items by phone or can come to the catalogue store and make the order in person. The catalogue store has a CRT display terminal so that stock availability can be checked immediately. The actual processing of the order follows the same pattern as for a telephone order.

Purchasing

The purchasing department of Save-More is run by Arnold Soladam. All purchasing is performed through Head Office using the computer system. As a purchase order is created, information from the form is entered through a terminal to the computer by one of the clerks in Arnold's department. This information is then recorded on a computerized purchases-pending master file. The records on this file are sorted in numerical sequence. The file contains such information as vendor name, item, unit cost, date ordered, date expected, and description.

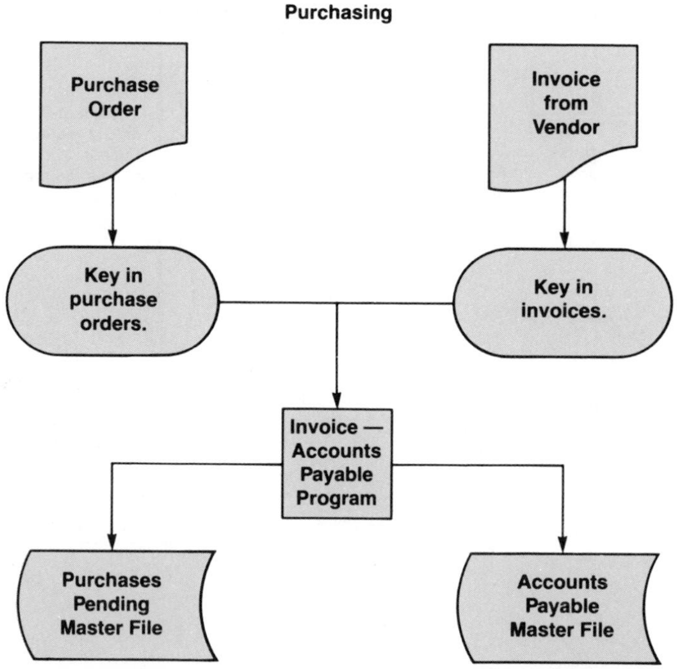

Figure 24.23 The program should create master files of the purchases and the accounts payable. These files will then be used to process the payments when data on the receipt of the purchases are received.

Shipments are sent directly to the warehouses or sometimes the stores. The supervisor of the receiving department can find information on any incoming shipment by using the terminal in the shipping department to check the purchases pending file. A receiving clerk can also use this terminal to record the receipt of the shipment and indicate damage, shortage, and so on.

The centralized storage of data on all purchases helps the members of Arnold's department to do their jobs effectively. The computer provides information on virtually every aspect of the purchasing process, such as whether merchandise purchased from a certain supplier tends to arrive on time. Perhaps the most important use of the computer in purchasing is the efficient handling of accounts payable, a process illustrated in Figure 24.23.

Inventory

Perpetual inventory is much easier to keep with a computerized inventory system. As we have seen, the Save-More computer keeps a complete inventory record of all

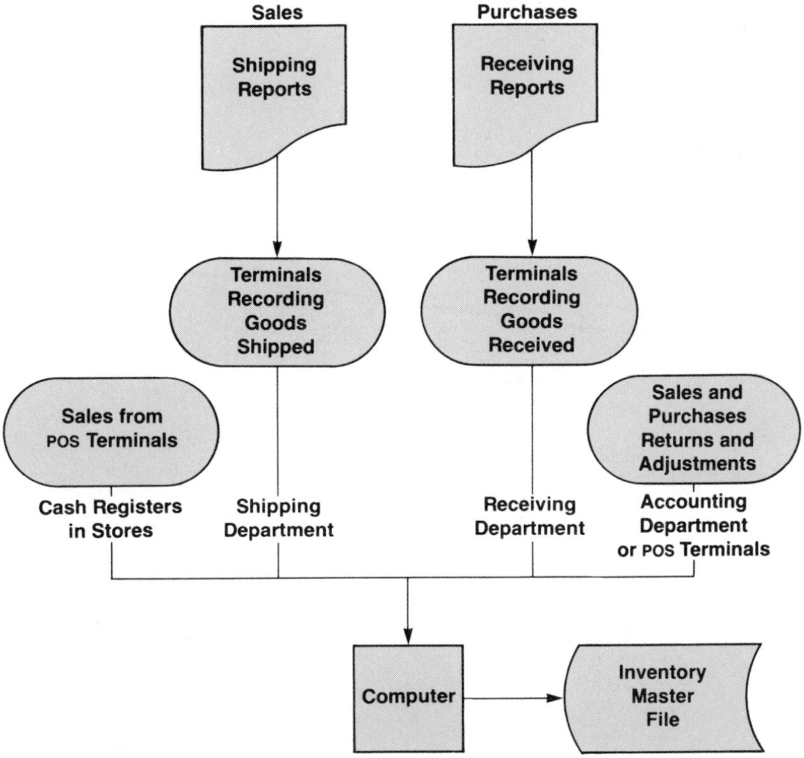

Figure 24.24 A variety of transactions affect inventory, from a sale or return of merchandise by a customer in a Save-More store to the receiving or shipping of goods at warehouses.

stock in Save-More stores and warehouses. Nonetheless, with all perpetual inventory systems, a physical inventory must be taken occasionally. The computer reviews the results of the physical inventory and reports any discrepancies between its records and what is actually in stock. The accounting department can then study the shortages.

The computer is also programmed to automatically monitor stock levels in stores and warehouses. A minimum and a maximum amount are assigned to each item in every store and warehouse. When the quantity of an item falls below its minimum amount, the computer instructs the purchasing department to replenish the stock. The computer also reports the exact quantity needed to bring the stock up to its maximum amount.

Figure 24.24 shows the types of accounting transaction that affect the Save-More inventory. The first is sales. As we have seen, each time a sale is entered into the computer, the inventory record of that item records the amount sold and adjusts the inventory total downward. The second is purchases. When the receiving clerk

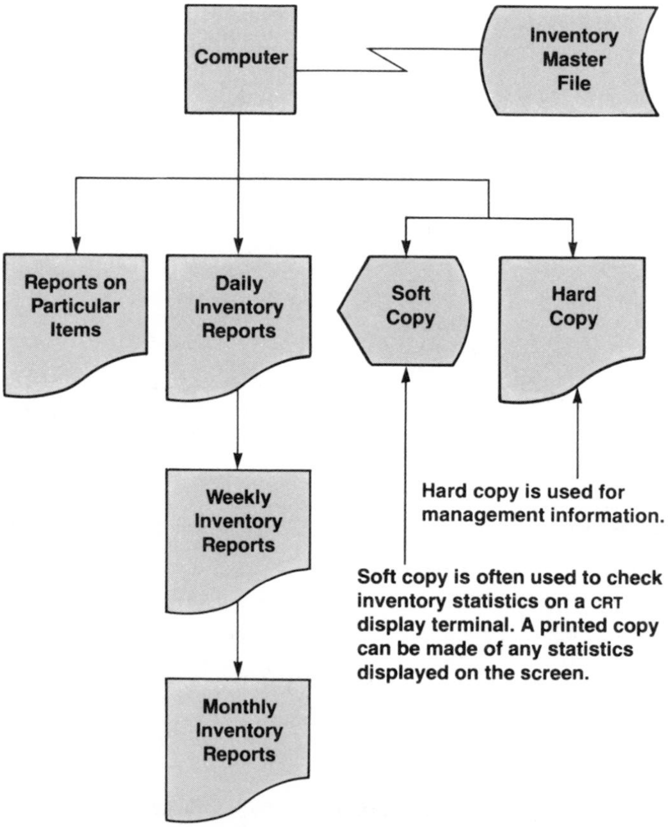

Figure 24.25 Inventory reporting. As adjustments are made to inventory, the computer can provide information on the updated records. Management can check everything from the stock of a particular item in a particular store to the total value of the inventory owned by Save-More.

records the receipt of goods in the purchases pending file, the information is simultaneously recorded in the inventory records as well. The computer then adjusts the inventory record upward. The third type of transaction concerns adjustments for purchases or sales returns and allowances. These are entered into the computer which then makes the necessary adjustments to the records. The last type of transaction concerns deliveries. The shipping clerk in the warehouse uses the terminal to record all deliveries that are sent in response to telephone orders and so on.

Figure 24.25 shows how Save-More's computer provides perpetual inventory information. The computer allows Save-More management to effectively control millions of dollars in inventory. The accounting department has a complete, centralized perpetual inventory system at its fingertips. Moreover, the benefits of such a system are felt throughout the company. For example, Head Office can instantly verify whether a shipment has been received and the vendor should be paid. Or management can more easily decide such issues as whether too much money is tied up in inventory.

Accounts Receivable

Earlier in the text, you learned how accounts receivable operates in manual accounting. Remember that an accounts receivable system has several objectives:

1. To maintain a correct set of customer records.
2. To collect and process payments.
3. To bill customers at certain intervals.
4. To produce statistics on overdue accounts for the credit department.
5. To produce statistics concerning customers and their buying habits.
6. To handle customer enquiries to the file.

In the accounts receivable department of Save-More, several employees work under the supervision of Yvonne Tremblay. This department is responsible for all procedures related to the accounts receivable subsidiary ledger and the billing of clients.

The primary duties of Yvonne's department are as follows:

1. To handle accounts receivable activities related to sales on account.
2. To handle the billing and receipt of payment of accounts receivable.
3. To make adjustments to accounts receivable when necessary.
4. To provide financial information for analysis of accounts receivable.

The computer is programmed to perform all these functions. Yvonne and her workers provide support for the computer programs by entering data, providing specific instructions and requests, and manually checking the computer's operation.

Sales on Account

The computer is programmed to perform the company's journalizing and posting. Clerks in store, catalogue, and warehouse locations across Canada enter the sales data into the computer through terminals. As seen in Figure 24.26, Yvonne and her workers are primarily concerned with monitoring this operation.

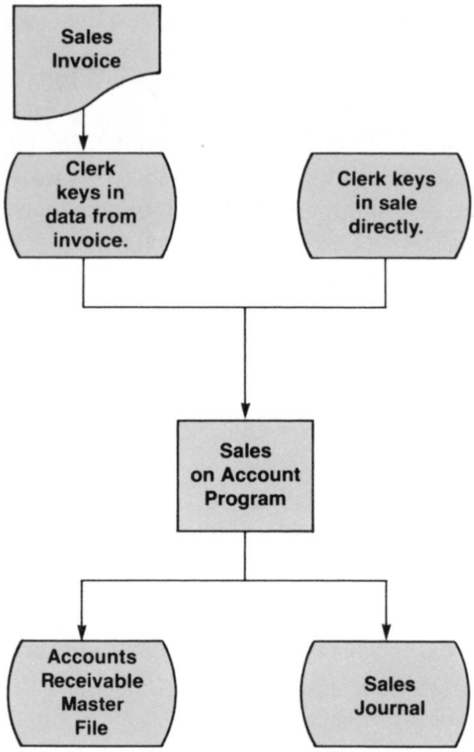

Figure 24.26 The accounts receivable department monitors a system in which sales data are fed directly to the computer for journalizing and posting.

Billing and Receipt of Payment

Most billing is now done directly by the computer. The same program that records the sale can also issue the bill. For example, when a phone order is received for which a delivery person collects payment, the computer automatically sets up a temporary account to show that money is owed by that customer. Because this account receivable is set up without the involvement of Yvonne's department, Yvonne and her staff must monitor the computer to learn the details of each transaction.

Input preparation is another major duty of the accounts receivable department. A copy of every invoice is sent to Yvonne's department. Each invoice is checked off manually against a computer printout of the invoices issued. This is done as a safeguard on the system.

Each bill sent to a customer has a portion that is sent back with the customer's payment. This stub contains information that must be prepared for input into the computer. Yvonne's department uses this information, and information found on other documents, to enter all payment data into the computer. The documents used by Yvonne's department are illustrated in Figures 24.27, 24.28, and 24.29.

15458-5694

SAVE-MORE
5219 CANADA WAY
BURNABY, B.C. V5E 3N4

DATE					SHIP
M	D	Y	CUSTOMER	JAMIE MCKILLOP	
			ACCOUNT	859 264	
11	21	82	ADDRESS	1583 KAMLOOPS STREET	34
				VANCOUVER, B.C. V5K 3W1	

QUANT	CAT #	DESCRIPTION	PRICE	AMOUNT
1	8H-1289-4	KLEENER VACUUM		
3	8H-2356	VACUUM CLEANER BAGS		

SHIPPING COPY 1

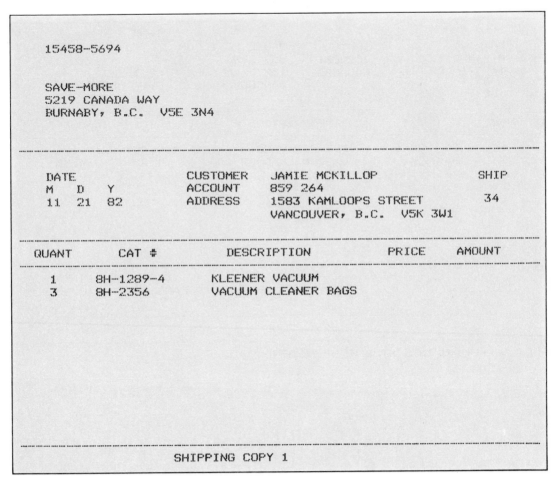

Figure 24.27 The computer outputs a shipping order of the purchase to be delivered.

```
15458-5694

SAVE-MORE
5219 CANADA WAY
BURNABY, B.C.   V5E 3N4
-------------------------------------------------------------------------------
DATE
M   D   Y          CUSTOMER   JAMIE MCKILLOP                  SHIP
11  21  82         ACCOUNT    859 264
                   ADDRESS    1583 KAMLOOPS STREET             34
                              VANCOUVER, B.C.   V5K 3W1
-------------------------------------------------------------------------------
QUANT    CAT #          DESCRIPTION              PRICE      AMOUNT
-------------------------------------------------------------------------------
  1    8H-1289-4     KLEENER VACUUM              199.95      199.95
  3    8H-2356       VACUUM CLEANER BAGS           1.45        4.35





                                              SUBTOTAL      204.30
                                              TAX            14.30
                                           PLEASE PAY       218.60
-------------------------------------------------------------------------------
                       CUSTOMER  2
-------------------------------------------------------------------------------
PLEASE RETURN THIS STUB WITH PAYMENT

15458-5694                                  DATE  11/21/82

               SAVE-MORE
               5219 CANADA WAY
               BURNABY, B.C.      V5E 3N4

ACCT   859 264                              AMOUNT DUE:  218.60
```

Figure 24.28 Notice that the bottom of the bill is to be returned with the payment.

Assume that you work in Yvonne's department. To key the information through a terminal into the computer, you would perform the following steps.

1. At the beginning of the day, you first key in a code that gives your terminal

15458-5694

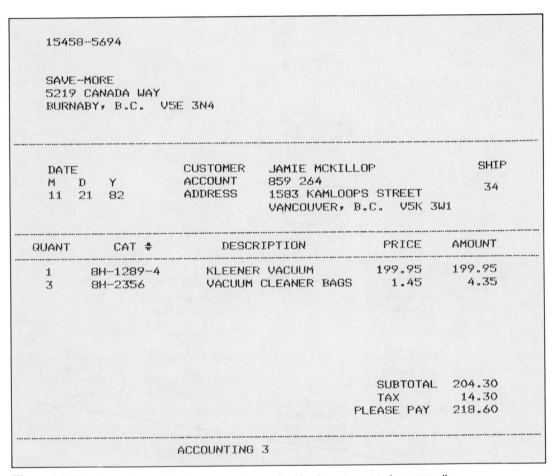

SAVE-MORE
5219 CANADA WAY
BURNABY, B.C. V5E 3N4

DATE					SHIP
M	D	Y	CUSTOMER	JAMIE MCKILLOP	34
11	21	82	ACCOUNT	859 264	
			ADDRESS	1583 KAMLOOPS STREET	
				VANCOUVER, B.C. V5K 3W1	

QUANT	CAT #	DESCRIPTION	PRICE	AMOUNT
1	8H-1289-4	KLEENER VACUUM	199.95	199.95
3	8H-2356	VACUUM CLEANER BAGS	1.45	4.35
			SUBTOTAL	204.30
			TAX	14.30
			PLEASE PAY	218.60

ACCOUNTING 3

Figure 24.29 A copy is sent to the accounts receivable department to be manually checked against the computer printout.

access to the computer. The code informs the computer that you are entering data on payments received from customers and tells the computer what program to use when processing this data. Each accounting routine has a different code to turn on a preset format.

2. Next you fill in the spaces on the screen with the information from each payment stub that is returned. This should take perhaps 10 to 15 seconds for each stub. The computer then posts this information almost simultaneously.
3. At the end of the day, you must reconcile the total amount of accounts receivable entries with the amount of money to be deposited in the bank. This verifies that all payments received were recorded and deposited. Figure 24.30 shows the route used to record these payments.

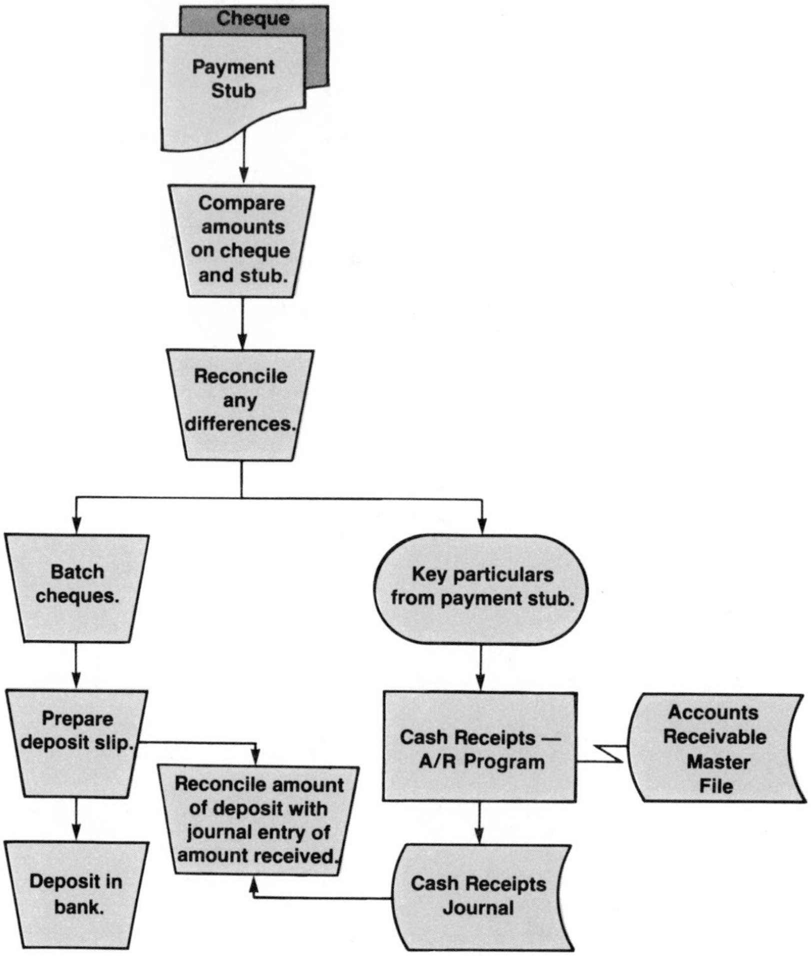

Figure 24.30 The computer posts and journalizes the data that have been entered. The deposit of cheques is prepared manually. This amount is then checked manually against the amount the computer has recorded as received.

Adjustments to Accounts Receivable

As stated earlier, all billing is done automatically by the computer. Once a month the computer produces a bill for each customer indicating the purchases for the month, any amounts past due, and the total amount due. Save-More's computer is programmed to add 2 percent interest per month automatically to any overdue account and to generate past-due notices.

This billing system has a number of advantages. Through their terminals, customer service personnel can immediately obtain up-to-date information on customers' accounts. Customer enquiries can therefore be answered quickly and accurately. Customer complaints concerning discrepancies in the accounts can be cleared up easily and efficiently.

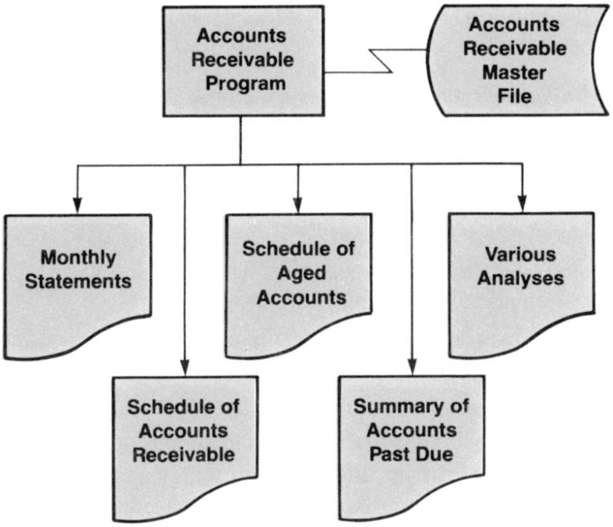

Figure 24.31 Using a set program, an operator can instruct the computer to produce whatever information is required.

Providing Financial Information

The introduction of the computer has meant that much of the routine work such as posting has been replaced by a variety of computer-related tasks. These include the input of data, the supervision of computer activities, the relaying of output information to other departments and the providing of information on accounts receivable.

The computer can produce financial information on accounts receivable very quickly. As you have discovered, the manual preparation of a Schedule of Accounts Receivable is extremely time-consuming. The computer, however, can print out the entire schedule at a speed of approximately one account every two seconds. Figure 24.31 shows the types of financial information that are automatically produced by the computer for Yvonne and her co-workers.

Accounts Payable

As you know, the accounts payable department of a business pays the bills that are received from vendors, suppliers, or manufacturers. The accounts payable department of Save-More, run by Hanif Khan, uses the computer for routine tasks much as Yvonne's department does. However, the specific tasks performed by the computer are different. The three main duties of Hanif's department are to record accounts payable, to prepare cheques, and to provide information for the use of management.

All accounts payable are listed on a master accounts payable file. When a new account is required, a clerk in Hanif's department enters the pertinent information into the file, via a terminal. Information from bills is also entered into the computer by clerks in Hanif's department. The computer then posts this information to the proper record in the accounts payable pending file.

To handle a purchase by Save-More of merchandise on account, Hanif's department follows these steps:

1. The invoice for the merchandise is received by the accounts payable department.
2. The invoice is entered into the accounts payable pending file.
3. The purchases pending file is checked by the computer to see if there is a receiving report. Under the old manual system, a clerk would have had to match up the purchase order slip, the receiving report, and the invoice. Under the computer system, all three pieces of information are stored in the computer and are matched automatically, as seen in Figure 24.32.
4. In accordance with its program, the computer checks each day to see which accounts are due for payment and which should be paid to take advantage of discounts.
5. The computer provides a list of the accounts to be paid. Once this is approved by members of Hanif's department, the computer will generate the required cheques and place the necessary accounting entries in the accounts payable master file. Figure 24.33 illustrates the paying of accounts by computer.

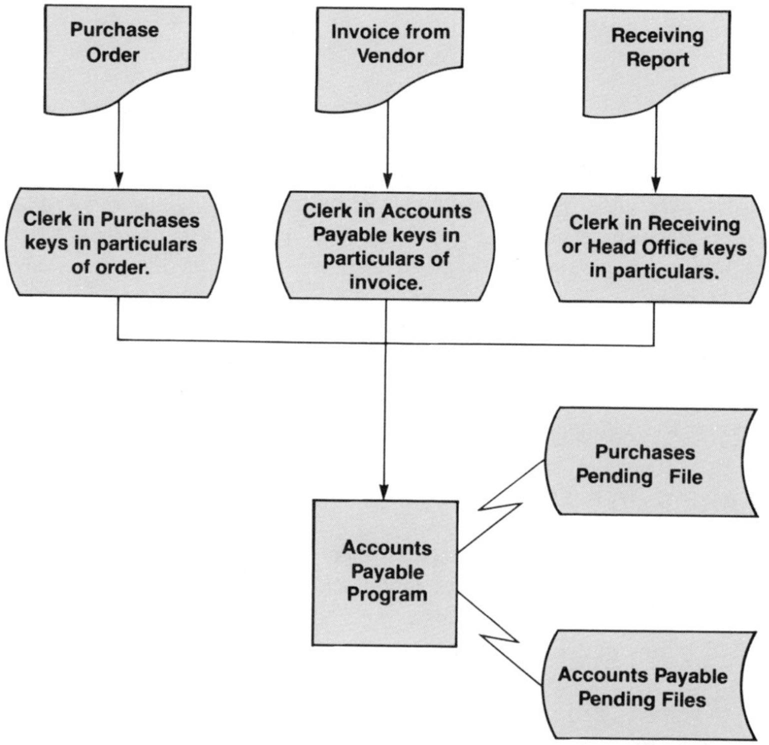

Figure 24.32 The purchases pending file contains the purchase requisition information and the receiving report. The accounts payable pending file contains the invoices from vendors.

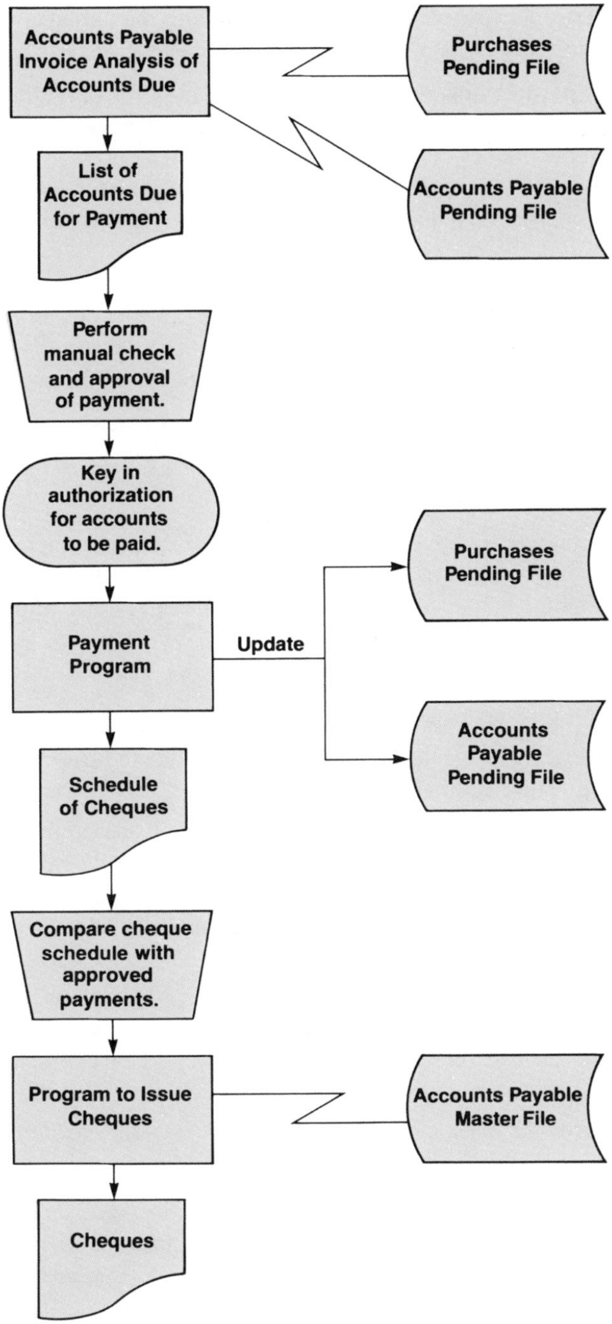

Figure 24.33 The program will produce a list of the accounts that are close to the payment date. Once the authorization is given, it will print the cheques and update the necessary accounts payable files.

6. The computer produces a final printout, specifying the amounts of all cheques issued. This printout is then verified against the authorized list.

The accounts payable department is also responsible for providing information for use by Save-More management. This information allows management to know how and at what rate money is spent, as well as how much is owed at any particular moment. The computer can provide this information quickly and efficiently. It can produce a Schedule of Accounts Payable, for example, in the time that it takes to print the material on the page.

Finally, Hanif works with senior members of his department to check routine procedures run by the computer. This check ensures that such benefits as discounts are taken advantage of where possible, that the routine payments are made before interest is charged, and that aging of accounts payable is performed.

Payroll

All payroll information on Save-More employees is kept on a payroll master file. Each employee has a separate record on this file. The record contains basic employee information, including name, address, identification number, rate of pay, number of exemptions, and other required payroll data.

The payroll is completed according to the following steps:

1. The payroll program is fed into the computer.
2. The employee records on the payroll master file are fed into the computer or linked for use via an auxiliary storage unit.
3. The employee identification number and hours worked are fed into the computer, along with any adjustments such as paid sick days or unpaid absences. This input is not necessary for salaried employees. Their pay will be calculated automatically by the computer unless an adjustment is necessary for sick-day deductions.
4. The computer calculates each employee's gross pay, deductions, and net pay for the week and year-to-date. This information is stored with the payroll information already on the payroll files. This record forms a sort of computerized payroll journal.
5. The computer prints out a cheque and deduction stub for each employee.

Under its old manual payroll system, Save-More kept a bookkeeper at each one of its two hundred stores and warehouses. The bookkeeper made up the payroll and drew the cheques on a local bank account. The payroll information was then sent to Head Office and recopied into one total payroll record for the company.

Figure 24.34 compares a manual payroll system to a computerized system. Notice that the computerized system means that one payroll is done instead of two hundred. The computer can also prepare all necessary payroll reports, such as those needed to record income tax, unemployment insurance, and Canada Pension Plan deductions. Figure 24.35 shows the complete computerized payroll system.

Save-More system under manual payroll system.

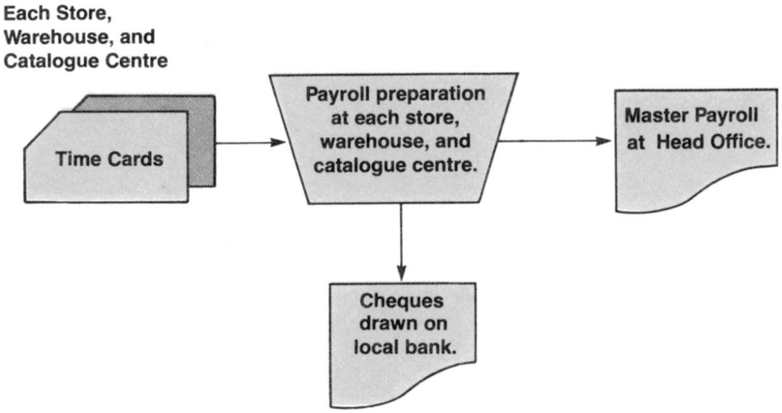

Two payroll journals are kept, one locally and one at Head Office for all the operations.

Save-More system under computerized payroll system.

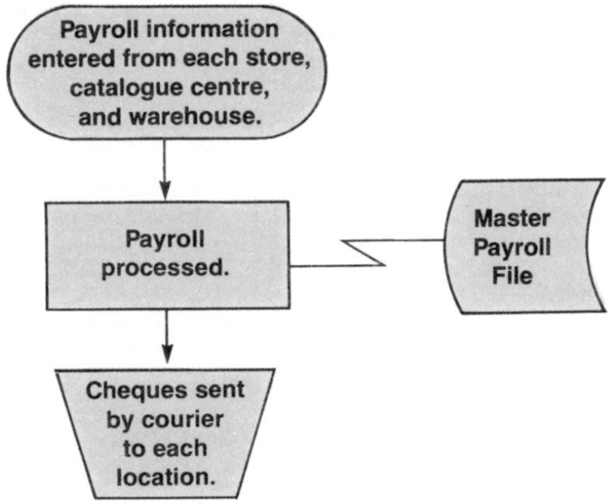

All payroll is done centrally in one session at Head Office and the cheques are sent by courier.

Figure 24.34 A comparison of payroll systems.

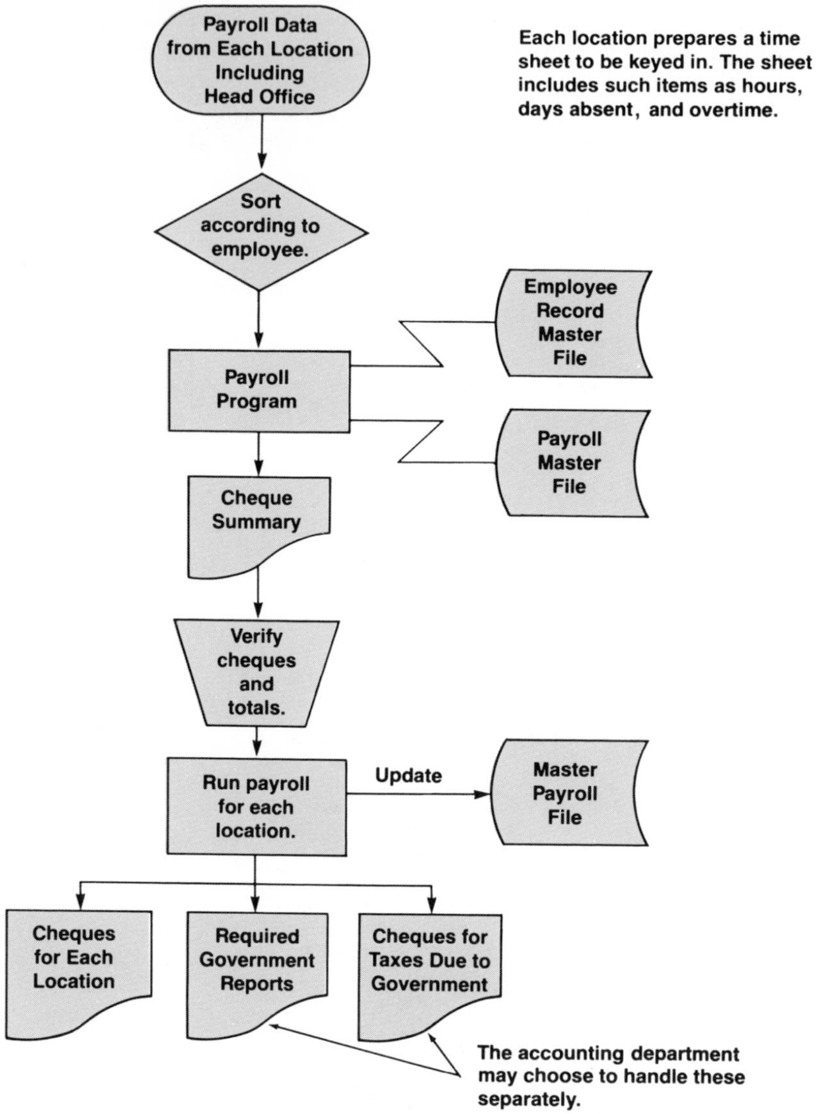

Figure 24.35 A computerized payroll system.

Budget

The computer's major advantage for budgeting is its ability to produce interim budget reports quickly and easily. At Save-More, the computer produces a budget report for each department at Head Office, each store, and each warehouse. The report shows the expenditures for the month and the year-to-date, allowing various levels of management to control expenses. For example, if a report shows that the salaries expense of one store is much higher than the salaries expenses of other stores with the same amount of sales, management can order an investigation. Figure 24.36 illustrates a budget report.

BUDGET SUMMARY 03/31/-2 9:45
DEPARTMENT: ADVERTISING 124
ITEM: ADVERTISING EXPENSES

NUMBER	DESCRIPTION	BUDGET	PAID	REMAINING $	SPENT%
124-1150	OUTDOOR PLANT	12 000	2 250	9 750+	18.75%
124-1151	NEWSPAPER	95 000	18 690	76 310+	19.67%
124-1152	TELEVISION	70 000	13 800	56 200+	19.71%
124-1153	RADIO	30 000	3 500	26 500+	11.67%

TOTAL ADVERTISING BUDGET	207 000
TOTAL SPENT TO DATE	38 240
AMOUNT REMAINING	130 520
SPENT %	18.47%

Figure 24.36 Perhaps one of the greatest decision-making uses of the computer is the ability to access budget information quickly. For example, the budget for radio advertising could be broken down by the week, by the day of the week, by city, by region, etc. The information on any of these breakdowns is available from the computer in a matter of seconds.

Other Accounting Routines

The computer can also handle all other accounting routines. However, the more complicated accounting routines will require some paperwork. For example, a Save-More executive who is touring stores throughout the country pays for the trip with an expense account. Before the tour begins, the computer issues a cheque to the executive as advance money. At the end of the trip, the executive submits a written report of expenses, along with receipts. The computer then uses this information to reconcile the expense account with the money that was advanced.

The computer can then take this information one step further and prepare a monthly budget report indicating how much is being spent on expense accounts. If travel is proving too expensive, management might decide to use a less expensive method of communication, like the telephone.

Today, the accounting personnel at Save-More use the computer for every accounting routine. The computer can even perform such complex operations as calculating depreciation expenses. Save-More has found that the computer has allowed it to expand its business operations with a minimum of confusion and expense.

24.6 Internal Control

Save-More's enormous dependence on the computer for accounting operations has made certain precautions necessary. All companies with computerized systems must institute some means of **internal control**.

When Save-More purchased the computer system, it was tested thoroughly for use in every possible type of transaction. Moreover, the system came equipped with several built-in controls. For example, the Save-More computer will not print payroll cheques of more than $5 000 without special authorization. This prevents anyone in the payroll department from leaving town with a cheque for a large amount of money.

Save-More management insists on constant monitoring of the accounting programs that are run by the computer. The monitors look for one of three things:

1. A program error, sometimes called a **bug**. This is most often caused by an unusual accounting transaction. The bug is a fault in the program that does not allow it to process something correctly. For example, a bug in a payroll program would occur if the program did not deduct C.P.P. payments; the program would have a bug in it because it could not correctly calculate payroll.

   When faced with a bug, the programmer must rewrite the program to correct the error. Sample data are run with programs to try to detect errors before they become a problem. This procedure is commonly referred to as 'debugging'.
2. An error by a computer operator, such as the input of incorrect data.
3. An alteration to the accounting program or an unauthorized computer routine.

The accountants and the senior computer programmers should test the accounting programs regularly. The accounting processes performed by the computer should be frequently checked.

Unfortunately, a computer does not leave a paper trail. In fact, an embezzler can easily destroy the evidence of a crime by wiping out part of the computer's memory. To help ensure that accounting procedures are free of error and that any tampering is detected, Save-More insists that all senior accounting personnel understand enough about computer programming to work directly with computer personnel.

Last year, Save-More sent Susan Rochester of the accounting department to Calgary on a week-long seminar on **data security** in computers. The seminars examined various tricks used to defraud companies through their computers. The following is a short summary of Susan's report on the seminar.

Data Security — Submitted by Susan Rochester

It is important that procedures be set up immediately to protect the security of data in our computers. Measures need to be designed in order to prevent the following situations:

1. Unauthorized people acquiring knowledge about the financial position of the company or data concerning company personnel.
2. Important data being accessed and later destroyed in error.

3. Important data being accessed and deliberately altered by unauthorized personnel.

As you know, important data are already given **security codes**. A person wishing to obtain important information has to know the proper access code before the computer gives up the data. I believe that we should consider having the computer automatically produce a new security code each day for very important data. Company personnel who have the right of access to the data would be given this new number daily.

Besides using senior accounting personnel to monitor the system, Save-More has instituted one other major internal control measure. A **duplicate file** is kept of all information in the computer. This means that if, say, the investment file were accidentally erased, there would be a duplicate copy.

The duplicate copies of all files are stored on magnetic tape reels which are kept in a special bank vault on the first floor of the Save-More Head Office building. Two different members of the computer department plus the bank manager are needed to open this special vault; each has a third of the combination. Keeping duplicate files means extra work for the computer and the computer operators. However, this work is worthwhile as it provides insurance against the loss or damage of the original records.

Save-More is only one example of a computerized company. Each company has different needs and uses different procedures to meet those needs with a computer system.

24.7 Computer Use in Accounting

As we have seen, the computer offers many different benefits to a company. The following is a list of the basic accounting and financial applications of the computer in the business world.

Accounting Applications

1. *Sales.* The computer processes all sales, sends necessary data to the accounts receivable and shipping departments, and analyzes the sales performances of salespersons for management purposes.
2. *Billing.* The computer processes information on shipping orders and sends out invoices.
3. *Inventory Control.* The computer processes all receiving and shipping of goods, and reports all changes in inventory to the appropriate source.
4. *Accounts Payable.* The computer processes all purchases and issues cheques.
5. *Accounts Receivable.* The computer processes all sales on account, issues billings, and issues monthly customer statements.

6. *Payroll*. The computer processes data on employee earnings, calculates and records the payroll, and issues cheques.
7. *Accounting*. The computer uses data from all available sources to produce ledgers, journals, trial balances, balance sheets, and any other accounting reports that are needed.

Financial Applications

1. *Financial Analysis*. The computer uses data to control the company's financial position. It analyzes that position, analyzes economic factors, such as interest rates and inflation rates, and plans budgets.
2. *Credit*. The computer provides information for decisions on the granting of credit to customers. It also analyzes bad debts and provides information on the bad debts ratio.
3. *Investment*. The computer keeps up-to-the-minute records of cash deposits, withdrawals, and transfers. It also provides analysis for the investment of excess funds and short-term notes, stocks, and bonds.

24.8 Computerized Accounting in the Future

In this chapter, we have introduced you to the increasing role of computers in accounting. We have discussed both the advantages of using computers and possible problems associated with their use.

The computer is an invaluable tool for recording information and providing data for financial decisions. A computerized system is far faster than any manual method of accounting; in a few millionths of a second, a computer can perform tasks that require hours of manual labour. Accountants must accept that all accounting will eventually be done by computer.

The computer continues to offer untapped potential for further use in accounting. As a result, a basic knowledge of computers is essential to any person entering today's business world. Many accountants are learning computer programming, especially audit accountants who are increasingly called upon to audit computerized rather than written records.

Computers have already had a large impact on accounting procedures. And, just as telephones and typewriters revolutionized business practices early in the century, computer technology promises to utterly transform the accounting department of the future in ways that cannot even be guessed. The time is coming when an accountant who cannot work with the computer will be as rare as a secretary who has never learned to type.

Accounting Terms

data
data processing
recording
classifying
sorting
calculating
summarizing
communicating
storing
input
processing
output
electronic data processing (EDP)
computer
integrated circuit
silicon chip
hardware
software
program
input medium
punched cards
magnetic tape
magnetic disk
diskette
floppy disk
character recognition
terminal
hard copy terminal
soft copy terminal
central processing unit (CPU)
primary storage
auxiliary storage
arithmetic-logic unit
control unit
access time
sequential-access storage
direct-access storage
hard copy output
soft copy output
system
systems development
system assistance
internal control
computer bug
data security
security code
duplicate file

Review Questions

1. We live in an age of computers. List ten specific uses of the computer in our society in order to prove this statement.
2. What are data? Where do data come from?
3. a. Define data processing.
b. Explain why data processing is so important in business.
4. Name the seven steps in the data-processing cycle and briefly explain each.
5. The seven parts of the data processing cycle can be summarized in three basic procedures. Explain each of these procedures. In your answer, also explain which of the seven steps are included in which procedure.
6. What is the difference between manual, mechanical, and electronic data processing?

7. What is a computer?
8. Why has the use of computers grown tremendously since the 1950s? In your answer, briefly describe the major improvements that took place as more efficient computers were developed.
9. Briefly explain each of the four types of available computer.
10. a. What are the major advantages of using a computer system to process data?
    b. What are the major limitations of computers?
11. Explain the difference between computer hardware and software.
12. a. List the six basic ways to enter data into a computer.
    b. Briefly describe each of these methods of data input.
13. a. List the major components of the Central Processing Unit (CPU).
    b. Briefly explain each of these components.
14. How do primary and auxiliary storage differ?
15. a. What is the difference between sequential-access storage and direct-access storage?
    b. Which type of storage is better? Give reasons for your answer.
16. Briefly describe the two different types of output device.
17. What are the major advantages in using a computer to handle accounting data?
18. Briefly explain the four necessary steps in systems development.
19. Systems assistance requires computer manufacturers to train company personnel. List each category of employee at Save-More that would require training and explain what training the employees in each would receive.
20. What are the Save-More cash registers called? How do they operate?
21. List the advantages of the Save-More cash registers over ordinary electric cash registers.
22. Explain the steps in processing a telephone order.
23. Explain how the computer has helped to improve Save-More's purchasing department.
24. How can the computer help in the reordering of stock?
25. What are the four types of transaction that affect the computer inventory records?
26. Give specific examples to show how computerized inventory records have helped in management decisions.
27. List the main objectives of an accounts receivable system.
28. Explain the advantages of computerized accounting for handling accounts receivable that are overdue.
29. Why would a billing process generated by a computer be interconnected with the computerized accounts receivable records?
30. How can computerized accounts receivable records help a company to make financial decisions?
31. Explain the advantages of computerized accounting for handling accounts payable. Give specific examples.
32. Explain how the computer can help businesses to take advantage of discounts offered by vendors.
33. Briefly describe the steps involved in using the computer to do payroll.

34. What are the major advantages in using a computerized payroll system instead of a manual system?
35. What advantages does a computerized budget system have over a manual method?
36. Why are internal controls in a computer system necessary?
37. List three specific things that a person monitoring a computer system for internal control might try to detect.
38. What are three security problems that could result if a dishonest employee tried to use the computer to defraud the company? Indicate some specific action that the firm could take in order to avoid these problems.
39. What are the seven basic accounting applications of the computer? Briefly describe each.
40. Briefly describe the three basic financial applications of the computer.

Exercises

Data Processing

1. Assume that your school has a central computer system with a terminal and other related equipment. List all the school functions that this computer system operates.

2. a. List all the types of financial document that your family handles (e.g., the telephone bill).
b. Sort this list under the following headings: household expense, living expense, and recreation expense.

3. Sort the following data into three categories: paid weekly, paid monthly, or paid yearly.

telephone bill	property taxes	salaries expense
hydro bill	insurance	heating bill
leased truck	mortgage payment	magazine subscription

4. Sort the following data into two categories: money in or money out.

cheque from debtor	refund from tax department
cheque paying an account payable	rent expense
credit memorandum	cheque to vendor
money order from an account receivable	bank draft sent to supplier

5. List the data that the school's computer would need to create your student record. (Think back to any information sheets you filled out for registration at the beginning of the year.)

6. a. List the data that the computer would need to calculate each of your final marks and your final average.
b. List all the steps that the computer would perform to process this information.

The Computer

7. You learned that there are four basic types of computer. Listed below are a number of businesses. Suggest which of the four types of computer each business would use. Give reasons to support your decisions.

national weather service	department store
steel manufacturer	lawyer
medical clinic (40 doctors)	insurance company
hardware store	Revenue Canada

8. Visit several local computer stores. Make sure each store sells a different type of micro-computer. Talk to the salespeople and obtain literature on the products. Prepare a report comparing the different types of micro-computer available.

9. Obtain literature on software offered by micro-computer companies and independent software companies. Make a list of all the possible accounting programs available.

10. Arrange to visit a local company that has a computer department. Write a report on the company's hardware and software applications.

What Is Needed?

11. List the places in your school where computer terminals might be placed for use. Assume the terminals are linked to a central computer.

12. Save-More is thinking of converting all its stores to cash registers that use optical scanners to read the UPC. These scanners are already used in two Save-More stores. Prepare a report listing the accounting advantages of this conversion.

13. List the reasons a perpetual inventory kept by computer might be incorrect.

14. You are the manager of the accounts receivable department. Prepare a list of all the expenditures for which you would like to receive a monthly budget report.

15. Save-More is interested in introducing the Save-More Credit Card. Suggest the steps necessary in setting up the computer to handle such a credit card.

Assisting the Programmer

16. Maria Padopoulos has been hired to write a payroll program for your company. This program will perform all calculations, record all necessary accounting entries, and issue cheques. However, Maria has a very limited knowledge of accounting. To assist her in planning the program, you have been asked to write down the step-by-step routine used to complete the company payroll.

All employees, including management, punch a time clock and are paid by the hour. Those who work over 40 hours are paid double time. Deductions are made for U.I., C.P.P., income tax, and medical and dental insurance. At present, you use a one-write system consisting of the employee earning record, the payroll journal, and the cheque.

List each step necessary to complete the payroll for your company. Make sure that you do not leave out any details. The first few steps in the process are given as examples.

Step 1. Gather time cards from time clock rack.
Step 2. Sort consecutively by employee number.

17. Sven Nielsen of the Save-More computer department has been ordered to write a computer program to process cash refunds in stores. At present, this accounting activity is still performed manually. A form is filled out in the Returns Department and the customer takes it to any cashier for the money. The refund slips are processed at the end of the day as cash refunds from that particular cash register. Each slip lists the quantity, description, and price of goods that are returned.

Save-More intends to install a cash register with a CRT computer terminal link in each refund department. The refund will be handled by computer. To prepare for this changeover, Sven has asked you to write down the refund process.

List Save-More's refund procedure step by step in as much detail as possible.

Cases

Case 1 *Planning for Expansion*

Kwick Convenience Stores has 25 retail outlets in the greater Vancouver area. The stores sell fresh fruits, vegetables, and gourmet items such as nuts, cheeses, and baked goods. An average store has gross sales of $16 000 per week. There is a rapid turnover on many items, especially fruits, vegetables, and cheeses.

Each morning, buyers for Kwick Convenience buy fresh goods at a large food warehouse. The warehouse is a centralized complex of wholesalers dealing in all types of foodstuff. Kwick's buyers pride themselves on buying the freshest and finest quality products. The goods are then shipped to stores via company trucks.

In the afternoon, the manager of each store does a periodic physical inventory. The manager then prepares a list of what items need to be reordered. The inventory clerk and the preparation of the list take about an hour of the manager's time.

A clerk from the main office phones each store every night and takes the order. A clerk must be kept full-time on this job. Once the order has been taken, a master list of required goods is prepared for the buyers. The buyers use this list to buy goods at the warehouse the next day. All this is done manually using preprinted forms listing the inventory stock of each store.

Each morning, the assistant manager of Head Office studies the inventory lists from each store. Stores that are overstocked on certain items have the overstock moved to stores that are understocked on those items. This is again done by company truck. This system is somewhat lacking because it often takes days to move highly perishable goods.

Kwick Convenience intends to open ten new stores in the next two years. This will make the inventory control system even more awkward.

Questions

1. Identify areas in which employee time is being used unproductively.
2. Explain how a computer system could ensure that time was used more efficiently in these areas.
3. Explain how a computer system could be used for inventory control.

Case 2 *Purchasing A Computer System*

Moretone Pianos is owned by Sylvia Buntic of Regina, Saskatchewan. The company has gross sales of about $750 000 per year. An accounting staff of two clerks and a supervisor handle the accounts for about 600 customers and 50 suppliers. They also prepare the payroll for 53 employees, and perform any other relevant tasks. The one-write system is used wherever possible.

Sylvia has read that a small computer can improve the efficiency of her accounting department. She decides to buy one although neither she nor her accounting staff know anything computers. She calls a computer company and arranges to discuss her accounting needs with a representative. After several discussions, the representative tells Sylvia that a minimum system for her needs would require the following investments:

Computer	$ 95 000
Support equipment	25 000
Programs	6 000
Renovations for a special computer room	12 000
	$138 000

A one day computer-training session for the accounting personnel is included in this price.

Questions

1. Would you purchase the system? Give reasons for your decision.
2. What guarantees would you seek from the computer supplier? What concrete action could you take to make sure the guarantees are carried out?

Case 3 *Dealing With A Computer System*

Sylvia decides to buy the system discussed in the previous case. There are problems right from the start of operations. Duplicate payments are sent to suppliers. Some invoices are not sent. Overtime rates are not calculated properly and employees receive overtime pay for regular hours.

The system is supposed to supply Sylvia with additional information to help her make better management decisions in such areas as the costing of contracts. However, because Sylvia's accounting personnel are continually trying to input and output information and make corrections, they never get around to processing the information she needs.

Questions

1. Identify and explain the major causes of the problems with Sylvia's computer system.
2. Suggest solutions to the problems.

Case 4 *Inventory Case Study*

Paul Nastomi owns fourteen stores located at various streets and shopping malls in Toronto, Ontario. The stores are called Echo Electronics and sell stereo equipment, radios, televisions, videotape machines, and all types of electrical part. The chain of stores is extremely successful and gross sales are approaching $20 million a year. This success has been largely due to Paul's insistence on personal control, knowledgeable staff, excellent service, low prices (profit is made on volume), and a large inventory of merchandise for customer selection. A head office is located on the second floor of the main store, and a warehouse is adjacent to the main store.

The head office consists of two departments. The first department purchases merchandise for the company. Paul personally directs this department and then coordinates sales with the store managers. The second department is an accounting department consisting of five people under the supervision of an employee who is a Certified General Accountant. A Chartered Accountant occasionally provides Paul with financial advice and, once a year, audits the books.

The accounting procedure is as follows:

a. All accounting records are kept using the five-journal, three-ledger system.
b. All sales are recorded in triplicate. One copy is given to the customer and two copies are sent to head office.
c. At the end of each day, the store manager deposits the cash receipts and credit card invoices in the bank. A daily sales and cash receipts summary is sent to the head office. The duplicate sales copies are sent to the head office once a week.
d. All purchased merchandise is first sent to the warehouse and then sent to the various stores. Copies of receiving and shipping reports are sent to accounting.
e. The accounting department handles all accounting data from the stores, warehouse, and other sources such as creditors. The clerks handle all routine matters involving the business. The Certified Accountant supervises their work and handles all non-routine accounting transactions.

Paul has three business problems. The first is related to inventory control. At present, each store manager orders stock from the warehouse when a particular item is low in the store. Then, when the item is low in the warehouse, new stock is ordered for the warehouse. Paul has been finding problems with this system. One store might be overstocked on an item while another must order from the warehouse. Paul feels that he has far too much money invested in inventory. He used to have the store manager phone all other stores before ordering something from the warehouse. However, this was found to be too time-consuming.

Paul's second problem is the number of personnel required to staff the accounting department. As business has increased, Paul has found it necessary to hire more personnel. Presently he is considering hiring at least one and perhaps two more people for the accounting department.

Paul's third problem is related to his personnel problem. He intends to open four new stores in the next year in some new shopping centres that are being built in outlying suburban areas. To handle the increased workload, he will have to hire even more personnel and move to a larger building with more office space.

Question

1. Prepare a report on how a computer could help Paul.

Case 5 *A Matter of Ethics*

You work for a very large company that does hundreds of millions of dollars worth of business. The company is completely computerized, and all accounting information is stored in the computer. You work in the accounts receivable department.

When a payment is received, you record the receipt through a computer terminal and credit the amount to the customer's account. You work with a person named Robert.

Robert has a cousin who buys goods from your firm amounting to about $10 000 a year. Robert covers his cousin's purchases by informing the computer that there has been a sales return or an allowance on the goods bought by his cousin. In this way he saves his cousin about 15 percent of the total cost.

Robert argues that a loss of a few thousand dollars will never be found in a computer handling hundreds of millions. He states that he is safe because there are no slips of paper to give him away. You know about Robert's activities.

Questions

1. What, if anything, should you do? Defend your action.
2. How would you ensure that people like Robert cannot enter false information into the computer?

Career
Alan Rettig / Computer Accountant

After Alan Rettig graduated from high school, he attended the University of Windsor to obtain a Bachelor of Commerce degree. His first job was managing the garden centre at a neighbourhood Woolco department store. He was in charge of purchasing all the merchandise for that department and reported directly to the General Manager.

Alan left Woolco to work for International Carriers Ltd., a public transportation company employing 500 people. He joined this firm as a billing clerk, preparing the freight bills. Next, he worked as a payroll clerk, where he was responsible for all the drivers' time cards. In this position, Alan first encountered computers; he prepared payroll data for entry into the firm's computer system.

Alan currently works for International Carriers Ltd. as a computer accountant and programmer. Because his educational background did not include courses in electronic data processing and computer programming, Alan had to learn about computers through on-the-job training. In his position as both accountant and programmer, Alan is responsible for three phases of the accounting system: payroll, billing, and accounts receivable.

In the payroll system, the rates of pay and deductions are based on the employee's classification, such as driver, dock worker, or mechanic. For each employee, the number of regular and overtime hours worked is keypunched on cards and fed into the computer. This input is sorted by means of employee number, terminal (city), and department. The computer reports the

total amount of the cheques issued so that Alan can transfer the proper amount of money to the payroll account.

The company's billing system also uses punched cards. When freight is moved, a sales invoice is typed. Information from these invoices is keypunched onto cards and fed through the computer. These records are then sorted by customer number. Periodically, a journal is printed, showing each invoice typed for that period. Alan audits each invoice. If correct, the information is printed on a statement and mailed to the customer as a bill.

The company's system for accounts receivable does not use punched cards to record payments. Information from cheques that are received are keyed onto the screen of a terminal. The amount of each cheque is then applied against the invoice that it pays. According to Alan, the advantage of this system is that it supplies up-to-date information concerning the status of a particular customer's account.

In his position as computer programmer, Alan makes sure that all information received from the payroll and billing departments has been placed on punched cards. He also takes all the printouts from the computer, examines them for accuracy, and forwards them to various departments as reports. For these audits, Alan reports directly to the data-processing manager.

Alan firmly believes that the future of accounting lies with the computer. Because of his interest in computer programming, Alan attends many company-sponsored training programs at IBM to further his knowledge and skills in this important field.

Glossary

A

Access Time The average time required by the computer to locate and retrieve a piece of data from storage.

Account A specially ruled page used to record financial changes. There is one account for each different item affecting the financial position. All of the accounts together form the ledger.

Account balance The value of an account showing the dollar amount and an indication as to whether it is a debit or a credit value.

Account form of balance sheet A balance sheet on which the information is presented in a side-by-side, or horizontal, format. *Contrast* Report form of balance sheet.

Accounting controls A set of accounting procedures designed to ensure the accuracy and reliability of the information contained in accounting records.

Accounting cycle The total set of accounting procedures that must be carried out during each fiscal period.

Accounting entry All the changes in the accounts caused by one business transaction, expressed in terms of debits and credits. For each accounting entry, the total of the debit amounts will equal the total of the credit amounts.

Accounting period The period of time over which the earnings of a business are measured. *Same as* Fiscal period.

Accounts payable The money that a business owes to its ordinary creditors. This money is a liability of the business.

Accounts payable ledger A book or file containing all the accounts of ordinary creditors representing amounts owed to them by the business.

Accounts receivable The money that is owed to a business by its customers. This money is considered an asset of the business.

Accounts receivable aging schedule A detailed breakdown of customers' accounts showing how long they have been unpaid.

Accounts receivable ledger A book or file containing all the accounts of debtors (customers) representing amounts owed by them to the business.

Account title The name of the item for which an account is prepared, entered at the top of the account page.

Accrued expense An expense incurred during an accounting period for which payment is not due until a later accounting period. This results from the purchase of services which at the time of accounting have only been partly performed, are not yet billable, and have not been paid for.

Accrued liability A developing but not yet enforceable claim by another person for payment in regard to services that have only been partly performed.

Accrued revenue Revenue that has been earned in an accounting period but for which no claim can be enforced in that accounting period against the customer. It arises from the sale of services which at the time of accounting have been only partly performed, are not yet billable, and have not been paid for.

Accumulated depreciation The total credit representing the expired cost of fixed assets since the assets were placed in use by a business.

Acid-test ratio The ratio of current assets, excluding inventory, to current liabilities. *Same as* Quick ratio.

Adjusting entry An entry made before closing the books for the period to apportion amounts of revenue or expense to the proper accounting periods or operating divisions. For example, the apportioning of wages between accounting periods when the current period ends between two paydays.

Administrative expenses Expenses of a general nature related to the operation of a business, such as building maintenance, heating, and so on.

Aging The analysis of accounts or notes receivable by classifying the amounts according to the length of time for which they have been due.

Allowance for doubtful accounts An account that records the estimated value of accounts receivable that may be uncollectible.

Appropriation account An account to which some retained earnings are transferred to restrict their availability for dividends.

Arithmetic-logic unit The unit inside the computer's CPU that actually processes the data by performing a variety of arithmetic and logic operations.

Asset Anything owned that has a dollar value. *Contrast* Liability.

Auxiliary storage Any data storage device that exists outside the central processing unit of the computer. *Contrast* Primary storage.

B

Bad debt An account or note receivable that is uncollectible.

Balance column account The most commonly used type of account, in which there are three money columns, one for the debit amounts, one for the credit amounts, and one for the amount of the balance. *Same as* Three column account.

Balance sheet A statement showing the financial position (the assets, liabilities, and capital) of an individual, company, or other organization on a certain date.

Bank advice A notice sent by the bank to a depositor announcing that the bank has initiated an increase or a decrease in the depositor's bank account. *Same as* Bank memo.

Bank memo A notice sent by the bank to a depositor announcing that the bank has initiated an increase or a decrease in the depositor's bank account. *Same as* Bank advice.

Bank reconciliation A routine procedure to find out the reasons for a discrepancy between the balance on deposit as shown by the bank and the balance on deposit as shown by the depositor.

Bank reconciliation statement A statement accounting for the differences between a bank account as reflected in the books of the bank and the same account as reflected in the books of the depositor.

Bank statement A copy of the bank's ledger sheet, sent by the bank at regular intervals along with the cancelled cheques to customers who have current accounts or chequing accounts.

Board of directors The committee of persons elected by the shareholders of a corporation to supervise its affairs.

Book of original entry Any journal; that is, the book that contains the first, or original, record of each transaction. *Same as* Journal.

Books of account The journal and the ledger. The journal provides a daily record of transactions as they occur. The ledger provides detailed information on each account.

Business transaction A financial event that changes the values in certain accounts and that therefore affects the financial position of the business.

C

Calculating Performing the mathematical operations of adding, subtracting, multiplying, or dividing.

Canada Pension Plan A national pension plan sponsored by the Canadian government.

Capital The difference between the total assets and total liabilities of a business. *Same as* Net worth, Owner's equity.

Cash discount A reduction that may be taken in the amount of a bill provided that the full amount is paid within the discount period shown on the bill.

Cash payments journal A special columnar journal in which are recorded the accounting entries for all transactions that directly cause a decrease in the bank balance.

Cash receipts Cheques or cash received by the business, usually from customers paying their bills or from cash sales. Cash receipts are generally deposited in the bank on a daily basis.

Cash receipts journal A special columnar journal in which are recorded the accounting entries for all transactions that directly cause an increase in the bank balance.

Cash receipts list A business paper, prepared daily, that lists the monies received by a business from customers on account and other sources.

Cash refund The return of money to the buyer by the seller in respect to deficient goods that were paid for.

Cash short or over account An account in which are entered, throughout the accounting period, the cash shortages and overages that result when the amount of money at the end of the day does not agree with the transaction records.

Central processing unit (CPU) The unit of a computer that takes data from the input device, processes it according to the instructions of the program, and sends the results to an output device for recording.

Change fund A small quantity of money, usually about fifty dollars, kept in the drawer of a cash register to make change for customers.

Character recognition The process in which data are recorded through a special type of coded printing on a source document, and are then read by a special device. *See* Optical character recognition.

Charge To record an amount on the left-hand side of an account. *Same as* Debit.

Charter The document by which a corporation is created under the provisions of the Canada Business Corporations Act, or the corresponding act of a province. *Same as* Letters patent.

Chart of accounts A list of the accounts of a business and their numbers, arranged according to their order in the ledger.

Cheque A written order by a depositor to the bank authorizing the bank to pay out a sum of money to a given person or organization.

Cheque copy A copy of a cheque, used as the source document for a payment made by cheque.

Cheque register In a voucher system, a simple columnar journal in which is recorded each cheque issued in payment of a purchase invoice.

Chequing savings account A bank account that allows the use of cheques and also offers some interest on savings.

Classified financial statement A financial statement in which data are grouped according to major categories.

Classifying The arranging and grouping of data according to a common characteristic.

Closing entry An entry made at the end of an accounting period for the purpose of transferring the balances in nominal accounts (revenue, income, expense, or loss) to the capital (or retained earnings).

C.O.D. (Cash on delivery) A term of sale whereby goods must be paid for at the time they are delivered.

Collection period The ratio of accounts receivable to charge sales for the year, multiplied by 365. It indicates the average number of days it takes the business to collect an account receivable.

Commission An amount paid periodically to a salesperson or an agent calculated as a percentage of the amount of goods or services sold by that person.

Common-size statements Financial statements that show individual items as percentages of a selected figure, known as the base figure.

Common stock The class of capital stock representing the residual equity in the company's assets and earnings. *Contrast* Preferred stock.

Communicating Reporting the summarized data to those people who need the information.

Comparative financial statements Financial statements that present the figures for successive years side by side, along with the amount of change.

Computer An electronic machine which, by means of stored instructions and information, performs rapid, often complex calculations or compiles, correlates, and selects data.

Computer bug An error in a computer program.

Computer internal control The measures taken by a company to monitor its computer system for program errors, operator errors, program alterations, and unauthorized routines, and to protect itself against computer-related loss, damage, and theft.

Contra account An account that must be considered along with a given asset account to show the true value of the asset account. *Same as* Valuation account.

Contributed surplus For a corporation, an equity item arising primarily from premiums or discounts on stock transactions, gifts of plant or property from outsiders, and donations of stock or assets from shareholders.

Control account A general ledger account, the balance of which represents the sum of the balances in the accounts contained in a subsidiary ledger.

Control unit The unit inside the computer's CPU that directs and coordinates all functions of the computer.

Corporation A legal entity as determined by statute, separate and distinct from its owners, with a capital divided into shares which, when issued, are held by shareholders. The liability of the shareholders is limited to the amount of the capital for which they have subscribed. *Same as* Limited company.

Correcting journal entry An accounting entry to rectify the effect of an error.

Cost of goods sold The total cost of goods sold during an accounting period.

Credit To record an amount on the right-hand side of an account. *Contrast* Debit.

Credit invoice A business form issued by a vendor to reverse a charge that has been made on a regular sales invoice. The reason for the reversal is explained in detail on the invoice. *Same as* Credit note.

Credit note A business form issued by a vendor to reverse a charge that has been made on a regular sales invoice. The reason for the reversal is explained in detail on the note. *Same as* Credit invoice.

Creditor Anyone who is owed money by the business. *Contrast* Debtor.

Cross balancing The procedure whereby the total of all the debits in a journal is checked against the total of all the credits in the journal to make sure that the two totals agree.

Cross-referencing Part of the posting sequence in which the journal page number for a given entry is recorded in the appropriate account, and the account number, in turn, is recorded on the journal page.

Cumulative dividend A dividend paid at a fixed annual rate on preferred stock, which, if not paid in one year, is carried forward as an additional priority of the preferred shareholder in future income distributions. *Contrast* Non-cumulative dividend.

Current asset Unrestricted cash, an asset that will be converted into cash within one year, or an asset that will be used up within one year.

Current bank account A type of deposit account offered by the bank specifically to meet the needs of businesses.

Current liability A short-term debt, payment of which is expected to occur within one year.

Current ratio The ratio of current assets to current liabilities.

Customer's statement of account A record of customer's account for a one-month period, showing purchases made during the period, payments received during the period, and the unpaid balance remaining. Statements of account are usually sent out each month by a business to its customers.

D

Daily cash proof The procedure by which, at the end of the business day, the amount of money in the cash register is checked in detail against the vouchers and audit tape that record the day's transactions.

Daily interest chequing account A bank account that offers some interest, calculated on a daily basis, on fluctuating savings, and that also permits the use of cheques.

Daily interest savings account A bank account that offers fairly high interest, calculated on a daily basis, on fluctuating savings. Cheques cannot be used with this account.

Data (datum) Facts; units of information.

Data processing The manipulating of facts to achieve a desired result.

Data security The measures taken by a company to protect itself against computer-related fraud. *See* Security code.

Debit To record an amount on the left-hand side of an account. *Contrast* Credit.

Debt ratio The ratio of the total liabilities of a business to the total assets. This measures the proportion of total assets acquired through borrowed money. The debt ratio is complementary to the equity ratio. *See* Equity ratio.

Debtor Anyone who owes money to the business. *Contrast* Creditor.

Declining-balance method of depreciation A method of calculating the annual depreciation of an asset as a fixed percentage of the remaining value of the asset. Under this method, the asset's annual depreciation becomes progressively smaller. The percentages to be used are determined by government regulation.

Deficit In a corporation, the financial condition that results when there is a debit balance in the Retained Earnings account.

Delivery expense Transportation charges on outgoing merchandise. *Contrast* Freight-in.

Depreciation The decrease in value of a fixed asset over time. For accounting purposes, this decrease is calculated according to a mathematical formula.

Detailed audit tape In a cash register, a paper tape that provides a continuous record of all transactions that occur during the day.

Direct-access storage A method of data storage that allows data to be retrieved virtually immediately, without a search through the data that precede them in storage. *Contrast* Sequential-access storage.

Discounts allowed An expense incurred by a business when it offers a cash discount to customers.

Discounts earned Income acquired by a business when it takes advantage of cash discounts offered by its suppliers.

Discrepancy item An item arising out of a transaction that has not been recorded equally in both the bank statement and the records of the depositor. *See* Bank reconciliation.

Diskette A thin circular metal plate, coated on each side with a recording material, on which data are recorded for computer input or for storage. *Same as* Floppy disk, Magnetic disk.

Dividend An amount of earnings declared by the board of directors for distribution to the shareholders of a corporation in proportion to their holdings, having regard for the respective rights of various classes of stock.

Double entry system of accounting The system of accounting in general use in which every transaction is recorded both as a debit in one or more accounts and as a credit in one or more accounts. Under this system, the total of the debit entries equals the total of the credit entries.

Doubtful account An account receivable that may not be collectible.

Drawings A decrease in owner's equity resulting from a personal withdrawal of funds or other assets by the owner.

Duplicate file A file containing a copy of all information stored in the computer, kept as a precaution against loss or damage of the original.

E

Earnings per share The net income (after income tax) of a company divided by the number of common shares outstanding. This figure measures the performance of a corporation and its executives.

Electronic data processing (EDP) The use of electronic equipment to record and manipulate information.

Employee's earnings record form A form used to provide a cumulative record of all the payroll data during a calendar year for a particular employee. One is prepared for each employee.

Equity ratio The ratio of the total equity to the total assets of a business. This measures the proportion of total assets acquired by invested capital. The equity ratio is complementary to the debt ratio. *See* Debt ratio.

Expense A decrease in equity as a direct result of business activity. *Contrast* Income, Revenue.

F

Financial position The status of a business, as represented by the assets, liabilities, and owner's equity.

Fiscal period The period of time over which earnings are measured. *Same as* Accounting period.

Five-journal system An accounting system in which five journals are kept in process at the same time, each one recording transactions of a particular type.

Fixed asset A long-term asset held for its usefulness in producing goods or services.

Floppy disk A thin circular metal plate, coated on each side with a recording material, on which data are recorded for computer input or for storage. *Same as* Diskette, Magnetic disk.

Flowchart A pictorial, step-by-step representation of a system or procedure.

Forwarding The process of continuing an account or journal on a new page by carrying forward all relevant information from the completed page.

Freight-in Transportation charges on incoming merchandise. *Contrast* Delivery expense.

Fully classified financial statement A financial statement on which the items are grouped and arranged to provide meaningful information in easily readable form.

Fully participating dividend A cumulative dividend paid at a fixed annual rate on preferred stock, which carries an additional provision; namely, that the common stockholders cannot receive proportionately more dividends than the preferred stockholders in any year. *See also* Cumulative dividend.

Fundamental accounting equation The equation that states that total assets minus total liabilities are equal to owner's equity. A − L = OE.

G

General journal voucher A slip of paper on which one general journal entry is recorded. A file of these vouchers functions in the same way as a general journal in book form.

General ledger A book or file containing all the accounts of the business other than those in the subsidiary ledgers. The general ledger accounts represent the complete financial position of the business.

Goodwill An intangible asset of a business that has a value in excess of the sum of its net assets.

Gross pay Earnings before deductions.

Gross profit In a trading business, the excess of net sales over the cost of goods sold.

H

Hard copy output A physical record of the information received from the computer, such as a printed copy. *Contrast* Soft copy output.

Hard copy terminal A computer terminal that issues a printed record of data that are entered into the computer. *Contrast* Soft copy terminal.

Hardware The physical components of a computer system.

I

Impress method The method of handling petty cash in which the removal of monies is only recorded in the accounts at the time when the fund is replenished.

In balance A state in which the total value of all the accounts (or columns in a journal) with debit balances is equal to the total value of all the accounts (or columns in a journal) with credit balances. *Contrast* Out of balance.

Income An increase in equity as a direct result of business activity. *Same as* Revenue. *Contrast* Expense.

Income- or loss-sharing ratio The ratio in which partners share net income or net loss, after first deducting for salaries and interest.

Income statement A financial statement that summarizes the items of revenue and expense, and shows the net income or net loss of a business, for a given fiscal year.

Input The recording and classification of data for processing by a computer.

Input medium The form that data take for computer entry, such as punched cards, magnetic disk, and so on.

Insolvency The inability of an individual or organization to pay debts as they become due.

Integrated circuit An electronic circuit produced as a single unit on a silicon chip.

Internal control The plan of organization and all the coordinated methods used to protect assets, ensure accurate, reliable accounting data, encourage efficiency, and adhere to company policies.

Inventory turnover For a trading business, the cost of goods sold figure divided by the average merchandise inventory. This represents the number of times the business has been able to sell its inventory in a year.

Issue price of stock The price received for stock at the time it is issued by the corporation. *Contrast* Market price of stock.

J

Journal A specially ruled book in which accounting entries are recorded in the order in which they occur. A transaction is recorded in the journal before it is recorded in the ledger. *Same as* Book of original entry.

Journal entry An accounting entry in the journal.

Journalizing The process of recording entries in the journal.

L

Late deposit A deposit that is made on the last day (usually) of the period covered by the bank statement but which does not appear on the bank statement until the following period.

Ledger A group or file of accounts that can be stored as pages in a book, as cards in a tray, or as tape on a reel. *See* Account.

Ledger sheet In banking, a simple business form, showing a customer's deposits, cheques, and other deductions, as well as a running balance of the customer's account.

Letters patent The document by which a corporation is created under the provisions of the Canada Business Corporations Act, or the corresponding act of a province. *Same as* Charter.

Liability A debt of an individual, business, or other organization. *Contrast* Asset.

Limited company A legal entity as determined by statute, separate and distinct from its owners, with a capital divided into shares which, when issued, are held by shareholders. The liability of the shareholders is limited to the amount of the capital for which they have subscribed. *Same as* Corporation.

Liquidation The winding up of the affairs of an organization. The accounts of its debtors and creditors are settled, and any remaining assets are distributed among its owners.

Liquidity The ease with which an asset can be converted into cash.

Long-term liability A liability which, in the ordinary course of business, will not be liquidated within one year.

M

Magnetic disk A thin circular metal plate, coated on each side with a recording material, on which data are recorded for computer input or for storage. *Same as* Diskette, Floppy disk.

Magnetic tape A tape on which data are recorded as magnetized spots. The tape may be reel-to-reel or cassette.

Making the adjustments The process of updating the account data at statement time.

Market price of stock The price of the most recent trade of the stock, which fluctuates according to buying and selling forces. *Contrast* Issue price of stock.

Matching principle An accounting principle whereby each expense item incurred in the earning of revenue must be recorded in the same period as the revenue it helped to earn.

Merchandise Goods that are bought for the purpose of being sold at a profit.

Merchandise inventory The goods handled by a merchandising business. *Same as* Stock-in-trade.

Merchandising business A business that buys goods to resell them at a profit. *Same as* Trading business.

Minute book For a corporation, the book in which are recorded the actions and decisions of every shareholders' meeting and of every directors' meeting.

N

Net book value The value of a fixed asset that remains after the accumulated depreciation of the asset has been deducted.

Net income The difference between total revenues and total expenses if the revenues are greater than the expenses. *Contrast* Net loss.

Net income percentage The ratio of the net income of a business to net sales, expressed as a percentage.

Net loss The difference between total revenues and total expenses if the expenses are greater than the revenues. *Contrast* Net income.

Net pay Earnings after deductions.

Net purchases The figure obtained by subtracting the balance of the Purchases Returns and Allowances account from the balance of the Purchases account.

Net sales The figure obtained by subtracting the balance of the Sales Returns and Allowances account from the balance of the Sales account.

Net 60 A term of sale whereby the full amount of the invoice is due 60 days after the date of the invoice.

Net 30 A term of sale whereby the full amount of the invoice is due 30 days after the date of the invoice.

Net worth The difference between the total assets and total liabilities of a business. *Same as* Capital, Owner's equity.

No par value share A share of capital stock which has no nominal or face value.

Nominal account An account that accumulates data for only one fiscal period at a time. Revenue, expense, and drawings accounts are nominal. *Same as* Temporary accounts.

Non-cumulative dividend A dividend paid at a fixed annual rate on preferred stock, which, if not paid in any year, will never be paid for that year. *Contrast* Cumulative dividend.

NSF cheque A cheque that was not cashed when presented to the issuer's bank because there were not sufficient funds in the issuer's bank account to cover the amount of the cheque.

O

On account A term of sale whereby the full amount of the invoice is due at the time the invoice is received, but a brief time, usually 25 days, is given to make payment. *For other uses, see* Payment on account, Purchase on account, Receipt on account, Sale on account.

1/15, n/60 A term of sale whereby, if the bill is paid within 15 days of the invoice date, a cash discount of 1 percent may be taken. Otherwise, the full amount of the invoice is due 60 days after the invoice date.

One-write system An accounting technique that uses collated business forms and carbon paper to prepare more than one business paper at the same time.

Opening an account The process of setting up a new account in the ledger.

Opening entry The first accounting entry in the general journal, the entry that records the beginning financial position of a business, thereby opening the books of account.

Opening the books The whole process of beginning a set of books of account for a business, individual, or organization.

Optical character recognition A particular form of character recognition in which data are recorded by specially-coded printing and read by a special device. An example of optical character recognition is the use of an electronic cash register to record the data contained in the Universal Product Codes of store merchandise. *See* Character recognition, Universal Product Code.

Organization costs The initial costs of incorporating a company.

Out of balance A state in which the total value of all the accounts (or columns in a journal) with debit balances does not equal the total value of all the accounts (or columns in a journal) with credit balances. *Contrast* In balance.

Output The final result of the processing of data.

Outstanding cheque A cheque that is issued and recorded, but not cashed, during the period covered by a bank statement, and that therefore does not appear on the bank statement. *See* Discrepancy item.

Owner's equity The difference between the total assets and total liabilities of a business. *Same as* Capital, Net worth.

P

Packing slip A business paper providing a description of the goods and the quantities shipped, but not the prices. It is enclosed with the goods by the supplier to help the purchaser to identify them.

Paid out A small expenditure that is paid out of funds in a cash register.

Paid vouchers file A file containing vouchers that have been paid. Paid vouchers are used for reference purposes and as documented evidence for the transactions they record.

Partnership The relationship that exists between persons carrying on a business in common for shared profits. Does not apply to the members of a corporation.

Partnership agreement A legal contract that sets forth the specific terms and conditions of a partnership.

Par value The nominal or face value of a share.

Payment on account Money paid to a creditor to reduce the balance owed to that creditor.

Payroll The total process of calculating and preparing the employees' earnings.

Payroll journal A sheet of columnar paper on which are recorded the calculations to determine each employee's net pay.

Pencil footings Tiny pencil-figure totals used in accounts and journals. *Same as* Pin totals.

Periodic inventory method A method of accounting for merchandise inventory in which the record of items in stock is updated only at the end of an accounting period. *Contrast* Perpetual inventory method.

Perpetual inventory method A method of accounting for merchandise inventory in which the record of items in stock is kept up to date on a daily basis. *Contrast* Periodic inventory method.

Personal chequing account A bank account that pays no interest on savings and is designed for those who write a lot of personal cheques.

Personal exemption The amount of annual income that a person may earn that is exempt from tax; that is, tax-free. The amount varies with the person's marital status and number of dependents.

Petty cash fund A small quantity of cash, usually no more than $200, that is kept in the office for small expenditures.

Petty cash voucher A form that is filled out when money is removed from the petty cash fund and no bill for the expenditure is available.

Physical inventory The procedure by which the unsold goods of a merchandising business are counted and valued at the end of a fiscal period.

Pin totals Tiny pencil-figure totals used in accounts and journals. *Same as* Pencil footings.

Post-closing trial balance The trial balance that is taken after the closing entries have been posted.

Posting The process of transferring the accounting entries from the journal to the ledger.

Preferred stock A class of capital stock with special rights or restrictions compared with other classes of stock of the same company. The preference generally involves the distribution of dividends at a stipulated rate. Such stock usually carries no voting rights to elect the company's directors. *Contrast* Common stock.

Premium savings account A bank account that offers fairly high interest on savings at intervals of at least one month. Cheques cannot be used with this account.

Prepaid expense An expense, other than for inventory or capital, with benefits that extend into the future and that is paid for in advance.

Price-earnings ratio The ratio of the current market price per share of stock to the earnings per share. This measures the confidence that outside investors have in the stock of a company.

Primary storage The storage unit inside the computer's CPU. *Contrast* Auxiliary storage.

Private corporation A corporation that must raise funding privately and that cannot have more than fifty shareholders. *Contrast* Public corporation.

Processing The manipulation of data by the computer.

Program A set of logical instructions outlining the exact sequence of steps the computer must follow to process a given set of data. *See* Software.

Public corporation A corporation that obtains its funds from the sale of bonds or shares to the general public. *Contrast* Private corporation.

Punched cards Cards on which data are recorded for computer input or storage via holes punched according to a predetermined coding system.

Punched paper tape A paper tape on which data are recorded for computer input or storage as holes according to a predetermined code.

Purchase invoice The name given to a supplier's sales invoice in the office of the purchaser. *See* Sales invoice.

Purchase on account A purchase that is not paid for at the time it is made; also called a purchase on credit.

Purchase order A business form initiated by the Purchasing Department authorizing the supplier to ship certain goods or to perform certain services as detailed on the form, and to send a bill for these goods or services.

Purchase requisition A business form requesting the Purchasing Department to order certain goods or services according to information and instructions recorded on the form. Only key personnel, such as department heads, are usually authorized to issue purchase requisitions.

Purchaser In any business transaction, the party that buys. *Contrast* Vendor.

Purchases account The account used by a merchandising business to record the cost of merchandise purchased for resale. 'Purchases' is short for 'Purchases of Merchandise for Resale'.

Purchases allowance From the buyer's position, an agreement with the seller of deficient goods that the goods will not be returned, but that the price will be decreased by means of a credit note.

Purchases journal A special columnar journal in which are recorded the accounting entries for all transactions involving the buying of goods or services on account.

Purchases return From the buyer's position, the return of deficient goods to the seller in exchange for a credit note or replacement.

Purchases returns and allowances account The account in which is accumulated the amount of returns and allowances on merchandise purchased.

Q

Quick ratio The ratio of current assets, excluding inventory, to current liabilities. *Same as* Acid-test ratio.

R

Receipt on account Money received from a debtor to reduce the balance owed by that debtor.

Receiving report A business form initiated by the Receiving Department that contains detailed information about goods received from suppliers.

Recording The copying of data from a source document into a form that can be easily handled for processing.

Registered pension plan A private pension plan, registered and approved by the government, for which contributions, up to a given maximum, are tax-free.

Replenishing petty cash The procedure whereby the petty cash fund is renewed when it reaches a lower limit.

Report form of balance sheet A balance sheet on which the information is presented in a one-above-the-other, or vertical, format. *Contrast* Account form of balance sheet.

Retained earnings The accumulated balance of income less losses of a corporation, after the dividends and other appropriate charges or credits have been taken into account.

Return on owner's investment The ratio of the net income of a business to the owner's average equity, expressed as a percentage.

Revenue The gross proceeds from the sale of goods and services (generally after deducting returns, allowances, and discounts).

Reversing entry An entry made at the beginning of an accounting period to bring forward any accrued amounts set up at the end of the preceding period.

S

Salary A fixed amount paid regularly to an employee for services, regardless of the number of hours worked. Salary is usually set at a certain amount per week, per month, or per year, and is paid weekly, half-monthly, or monthly.

Sale on account A sale for which no money is received at the time it is made; also known as a sale for credit.

Sales allowance From the seller's position, an agreement with the buyer of deficient goods that the goods will not be returned, but that the price will be decreased by means of a credit note.

Sales invoice A business form, prepared whenever goods or services are sold on account, showing a description of goods or services, the price, and other information.

Sales journal A special columnar journal in which are recorded the accounting entries for all sales of merchandise on account.

Sales return From the seller's position, the return of deficient goods by the buyer in exchange for a credit note or replacement.

Sales returns and allowances account The account in which is recorded the amount of returns and allowances on merchandise sold.

Sales tax A percentage tax based on and added to the price of goods sold to a customer.

Security code A code, known only to a few authorized personnel, that must be entered into the computer before access can be gained to important information. The security code is a data security measure, designed to protect the company against computer-related fraud.

Selling expenses Expenses of a business directly related to the selling and delivery of goods.

Sequential-access storage A method of data storage that only permits data to be retrieved in the order in which they were stored, requiring a search through all the data that precede the desired data in storage. *Contrast* Direct-access storage.

Service business A business that sells a service, not a product.

Share One of the equal parts into which each class of the capital stock of a corporation is divided.

Share certificate A certificate given to each shareholder in a corporation, showing the amount of that person's share in the ownership of the company.

Shareholder The legal owner of shares of a corporation. *Same as* Stockholder.

Shareholders' equity The interest of the shareholders in the net assets of a limited company.

Shipping order A business form originated by the Order Department (a division of the Sales Department) on which is recorded detailed information in respect to goods or services shipped to customers.

Silicon chip A minute layer of silicon, capable of carrying over 20 000 transistors.

Soft copy output A temporary copy of the information received from the computer, such as an image on the screen of a computer terminal. *Contrast* Hard copy output.

Soft copy terminal A computer terminal that shows data, as they are entered into the computer, as images on a television screen. A soft copy terminal does not produce a printed record. *Contrast* Hard copy terminal.

Software The programs, or sets of instructions, that direct a computer's operation.

Sorting Placing data in order according to a common characteristic or classification.

Source document A business paper, such as an invoice, that is the original record of a transaction and that provides the information needed when accounting for the transaction.

Statement of distribution of net income A statement that shows how the net income of a business is divided among its partners.

Statement of partners' capital A statement that shows the continuity of partners' Capital accounts for a fiscal period.

Stock certificate book For all but large public corporations, the book that contains the stock certificate stubs, on which is written detailed information concerning shareholders.

Stockholder The legal owner of shares of a corporation. *Same as* Shareholder.

Stock-in-trade The goods handled by a merchandising business. *Same as* Merchandise inventory.

Storing Filing data for future use.

Straight-line method of depreciation A method of calculating the depreciation of an asset whereby the depreciation is apportioned equally to each year of the asset's life. *Contrast* Declining-balance method of depreciation.

Subsidiary ledger A separate ledger that contains a number of accounts of a similar type, such as the accounts receivable ledger or the accounts payable ledger. The accounts in a subsidiary ledger make up the detailed information in respect to one particular control account in the general ledger.

Summarizing Organizing and printing data so that the main points are emphasized and the data are presented in a useable form.

Synoptic journal A multi-columned journal with a number of selected special columns and two general columns. The special columns are used to record the more frequently occurring items; the two general columns are used to record the less frequently occurring items. Each of the special columns is reserved for a specific type of entry as indicated in the column heading. At posting time, the totals of the special columns are posted to the general journal, and not the individual items contained in the columns.

System A group of parts that function together as a unit. In computer terminology, all the components needed to computerize a given operation.

System assistance A training program in computer operation, offered by the computer manufacturer to the employees of its customer.

Systems development The process by

which an organization's computer needs are analyzed, computer equipment is chosen, computer programs are obtained, and monitoring methods are designed.

T

Taking off a trial balance The process of comparing the total value of the debit accounts in a ledger with the total value of the credit accounts in a ledger.

Taxable earnings These equal the employee's gross pay after the premiums for Canada Pension Plan, unemployment insurance, and any registered pension plan have been deducted.

Temporary account An account that accumulates data for only one fiscal period at a time. Revenue, expense, and drawings accounts are temporary. *Same as* Nominal account.

Terminal A form of electronic typewriter that feeds data into the computer by converting key-strokes into electronic impulses. *See* Hard copy terminal, Soft copy terminal.

Terms of sale The conditions agreed to at the time of sale, between the buyer and the seller, in respect to the length of time allowed for payment and whether a cash discount can be taken.

Three-column account The most commonly used type of account, in which there are three money columns, one for the debit amounts, one for the credit amounts, and one for the amount of the balance. *Same as* Balance column account.

Timecard A card that records the times that an employee starts and finishes work each day. A timecard is usually for a one- or two-week period.

Trading business A business that buys goods in order to sell them at a higher price for profit. *Same as* Merchandising business.

Transfer of funds The movement of funds into or out of a bank account.

Transposition error A mistake caused by the interchanging of digits when transferring figures from one place to another. The trial balance difference that results from such an error is always exactly divisible by 9.

Trend analysis A document that presents financial data in percentages, for a number of periods, so that tendencies can be seen that are not evident when looking at the dollar figures alone.

Trial balance A special listing of all the accounts balances in a ledger, the purpose of which is to see if the dollar value of the accounts with debit balances is equal to the dollar value of the accounts with credit balances. *See* Taking off a trial balance.

Two-column general journal A simple journal with two money columns, one for the debit amounts and one for the credit amounts.

2/10, n/30 A term of sale whereby, if the bill is paid within 10 days of the invoice date, a cash discount of 2 percent may be taken. Otherwise, the full amount of the invoice is due 30 days after the invoice date.

U

Unemployment insurance A national insurance plan against unemployment, sponsored by the Canadian government.

Unpaid vouchers file The file that contains the vouchers of a business prior to their date of payment. The vouchers are filed in the order of their date of payment.

V

Valuation account An account that must be considered along with a given asset account to show the true value of the asset account. *Same as* Contra account.

Vendor In any sales transaction, the party that sells. *Contrast* Purchaser.

Voucher A business document that establishes the validity of accounting records.

Voucher jacket A file folder, containing all the information and documents belonging to a single purchase order.

Voucher register A columnar journal in which all vouchers are recorded in numerical sequence.

Voucher system A rigid set of procedures by which the documents supporting all expenditure transactions must be verified before any payments are authorized.

W

Wages An amount paid periodically to an employee based on the number of hours worked or the quantity of goods produced. Wages are usually paid on a weekly basis.

Work sheet An informal business form prepared in pencil on columnar bookkeeping paper, used to organize and plan the information for the financial statements.

Working capital The difference between the current assets and the current liabilities of a business.

Write off To transfer to income all or a portion of the balance in an asset or liability account.

Index

A

Abbreviations, on financial statements, 38
Access time, 785
Accountant's working papers, 592
Account balances, 75–76
  calculating, 75
  interpreting, 75–76
Account form of balance sheet, 33–37, 167, 168
Accounting
  careers in, *see* Careers in accounting.
  objectives of, 2
  professional accountancy, 4, 7–8
  study of, 3–4, 6, 7–8
  usefulness to business, 2
Accounting controls, 241
Accounting cycle, 120–21, 176, 198
  steps in the complete accounting cycle, 599
Accounting entry, defined, 76
Accounting equation, fundamental, 33
Accounting office, 4–6
Accounting organizations, 7–8
Accounting period, 134–35, 188
Accounting standards, 101
Accounting terms, 19, 40, 57, 80, 102, 121, 145, 176, 199, 221, 252, 290, 332, 362, 413, 480, 533, 568, 603, 663, 707, 742, 817
Accounts, 66
  chart of, 139–40, 141
  of a corporation, 685–87
  numbering the, 112–14
  opening, 114
Accounts payable, 35
  accounting procedure for, 244–45
  adjusting entries for, 585–86
  balance sheet presentation for, 240
  computerized system for, 808–810, 815
  reversing entry for, 596–97
  summary of accounting entries for, 245
Accounts payable subsidiary ledger, 238, 478
Accounts receivable, 35
  adjusting entries for doubtful accounts, 554–58
  analyzed on comparative financial statements, 733
  balance sheet presentation for, 240
  collection period, 738
  computerized system for, 801–807, 815
  flowcharting of procedure for, 241–44
  subsidiary ledger for, 238
  summary of accounting entries for, 244
Accounts receivable aging schedule, 555
Account title, 114
Accrued expenses, 587
Accrued liabilities, 587
Accrued wages, adjusting for, 587-89
  reversing entries for, 597–98
Accumulated depreciation, 559
Acid-test ratio, 738
Adding machine method of taking off a trial balance, 78–79
Adjusting entries, 546–68
  for accounts payable, 585–86
  for accrued wages, 587-89
  adjusting and closing the books of a proprietorship, 592–95
  for a corporation, 703
  cost of goods sold, 589–91
  depreciation, 558–63
  doubtful accounts, 554–58
  financial statements, 565–67
  for a partnership, 656–59
  prepaid expenses, 550–53
  supplies, 547–50
  work sheet, 546–47, 550, 563–65
Administrative expenses, 603
Allowance for doubtful accounts, 554–55
Analyzing financial statements, 729–42
  common-size statements 734–35
  comparative statements, 730–33
  key ratios and relationships, 737–42
  trend analysis, 736
  use of computers in, 816
Analyzing transactions, 56–57, 70–74
Appropriation account, 695–96
Arithmetic-logic unit, 784
Assets, 32
  accounts receivable as, 35
  claims against, 37–38
  in fundamental accounting equation, 33
Audit tape, detailed, 408–410
Automated accounting system:
  numbering of accounts in, 114
  for producing customers' statements, 249–50
Auxiliary storage, 784

B

Bad debts, 557
  recovering, 558
  writing off, 557–58

Balance column account, 112
  compared with T-account, 112
Balance sheet, 31–40
  account form, 33–37, 167, 168
  for a business, 35–37
  classified, 168, 169, 171, 601
  common-size, 734–35
  comparative, 731
  of a corporation, 686, 697–98
  equity section of, 172, 173, 174, 697–98
  features of, 36–37
  of an individual, 33–35
  of a partnership, 655
  presentation for merchandise inventory, 273
  report form, 167, 168
  updating, 56
  with subsidiary ledger system, 240
Balancing, 246–47
  the columnar journal, 320
  general ledger, 247
  subsidiary ledger, 247
Bank accounts, business, 19, 97, 464–66
Bank accounts, personal, 10–19
  types of, 11
Bank advice, 218–19, 220
Banking, for business, 19, 97
Bank memo, 218–19, 220
Bank reconciliation, 14–18, 467–70
  locating the discrepancy items, 468–69
  recording the discrepancy items, 469–70
Bank statements, 13, 14
Billing, computerized, 802–805, 807, 815
Bills, 100, 101
Board of directors, 684
Bookkeeping cycle, 120–21, 176, 198
Bookkeeping period, 134–35, 188
Books of account, 111. *See also* Journal; Ledger.
Budgeting, use of computer for, 812–13
Business
  banking and, 19, 97
  complexity of, 3–4
  usefulness of accounting to, 2
Business papers, *see* Source documents.

C

Calculating, 774
Canada Business Corporations Act, 683
Canada Pension Plan, 511–14, 528
  employee contributions, 511–13
  employer contributions, 514, 525
Capital, 32
  See also Owners' equity.
  changes in, 56
  return on invested capital, 740
  using the computer for information on investments, 816
Capital accounts, 135, 137
  and closing entries, 191, 195, 197, 592
  for partners, 636, 637, 640–47, 654, 658–59, 663
Capital stock account, 685, 686, 687, 700
Careers in accounting, 4, 29–30, 47–48, 110, 129, 161, 187, 209, 271, 306, 349, 381–82, 439, 503–504, 544, 583, 622, 679–80, 728, 770, 826–27
Cases, 27–28, 45–46, 64, 90, 108–109, 128, 159–60, 184–86, 206–208, 229–30, 269–70, 302–305, 347–48, 379–80, 437–38, 501–502, 542–43, 582, 619–21, 675–78, 724–27, 761–69, 822–25
  simplified cases in partnership, 637, 639–47
Cash
  See also Petty cash fund.
  control of cash expenditures, 470
  meaning of term, 97
  "narrow" and "broad" sense of word, 464
  payment of payroll by, 528–29, 531
  payment on termination of partnership, 663
  procedures for control of, 466–70
Cash disbursements journal, 358–59
Cash discounts, 394–99
  accounting for, 395–97
  defined, 394
  on the income statement, 398, 399
  terms of sale, 394–95
Cash payments journal, 358–59
Cash receipts journal, 356–57
Cash receipts list, 217–18, 220
Cash refunds, 392–93
  "no cash refunds" policy, 393–94
Cash registers, 399–413
  features, 401
  point-of-sale terminals, 399, 792
  stand-alone electronic cash registers, 399, 400
  using, 401–413
Cash sale, recording, 402
Cash sales slip, 211–12, 220
Cash short or over, 412–13
Catalogue stores, and use of computerized order system, 798
Central processing unit (CPU), 783–85
Certified General Accountants (CGAS), 7
Change fund (float), 402
Character recognition, 401, 781–82, 783, 792
Charge, *see* Debit.
Charge sale, 394
  recording, 403
Charge sales slip, *see* Sales invoice.
Charter, 683
Chartered Accountants (CAS), 7–8
Chart of accounts, 139–40, 141
Cheque copy, 216–17, 220, 245

Cheque register, 477–78
Cheques, 11, 97
  NSF, 353
  outstanding, 15
  payroll, 529, 531
Claims against the assets, 37–38
Classified financial statements, 168–73
Classifying, 774
Closing entries, 188–97
  adjusting and closing the books of a proprietorship, 592–95
  for a corporation, 703
  making, 192–97
  for a merchandising business, 282–84
  objectives of, 190–92
  for a partnership, 656–59
C.O.D. (cash on delivery), 394
Collection period, 738
Columnar journal, *see* Synoptic journal.
Columnar paper, use of, 38
Commission, 509
Common shares, 682, 683, 689
Common-size statements, 734–35
Communicating, 774
Company Law, 683, 688
Comparative financial statements, 730–33
Computer bug, 814
Computer-based accounting systems
  for accounts payable, 808–810, 815
  for accounts receivable, 801–807, 815
  billing, 802–805, 807, 815
  for budgeting, 812–13
  computerized accounting in the future, 816
  and internal control, 814–15
  for inventory control, 288–90, 799–801, 815
  numbering of accounts in, 114
  for payroll, 810–12, 816
  for production of customer's statement of account, 250–51
  for purchasing, 798–99, 800
  for sales, 792–98, 800, 815
  summary of accounting and financial applications of computers, 815–16
  systems development, 789–91
Computers
  See also Computer-based accounting systems; Flowcharting.
  accounting applications of, 788–89, 792–816
  advantages and limitations of, 778–79
  and banking, 11–12, 18–19
  components of a computer system, 779–88
  development of, 775–77
  financial applications, 816
  future role in accounting of, 816
  operations of, 774–75, 779
  systems development, 789–91
  types of, 777–78
Contra accounts, 554–55, 559
Contributed surplus, 698
Control accounts, 239
Control unit, 784–85
Corporations, 3, 681–707
  accounts of, 685–87, 697–98
  adjusting and closing entries for, 703
  advantages of 684–85
  characteristics of, 682–84
  costs of incorporating, 687
  defined, 682
  disadvantages of, 685
  dividends of, 687–88
  income tax for, 703–706
  private, 684
  public, 684
  regulations concerning, 683
  retained earnings for, 694–97
  share records of, 700–703
  shares of, 689–94, 698–99, *see also* Shares.
Correcting errors in the books, 118–19
Correcting journal entry, 118–19
Cost of goods sold, 274, 603
  analyzed on common-size statement, 734
  calculating, 275–76
  review of adjustment for, 589–91
Credit, 69
  buying and selling on, 96
  in the expanded ledger, 140–41
  rules of debit and credit, 69–74
  and use of computers, 816
Credit balance, 75, 76
Credit invoices (credit memos), 311–314, 389
  purpose of, 314
Creditors, 35
Cross balancing, 320, 361
Cross-referencing, 116–17
  in the five-journal system, 361–62
  in the synoptic journal, 323
Current assets, 169
CRT (Cathode Ray Tube), 782–83
Cumulative dividend, 693, 694
Current assets, 169, 600
Current bank account, 464–66
Current liabilities, 169, 600
Current ratio, 737–38
Customer's statement of account, *see* Statement of account.

D

Daily cash proof, 410, 412
Data, defined, 772
Data processing
  cycle, 773–74
  definition of, 772
  electronic, 774–75, 783–85, 788, *see also* Computer-based accounting systems.

Data security, 814–15
Date, recording in journal, 92–93
Debit, 69
in the expanded ledger, 140–41
Debit and credit, rules of, 69–74
Debit balances, 75, 76
Debtors, 35
Debt ratio, 741
Debts, settlement on termination of partnership, 662
"Debugging," 814
Declining-balance method of calculating depreciation, 560–63
Deficit, 695
Delivery expense, 278
Depreciation adjustment for, 558–63
accumulated depreciation account, 559
declining-balance method, 560–63
net book value, 559
straight-line method, 560
Detailed audit tape, 408–410
Direct-access storage, 785
Discounts, *see* Cash discounts.
Discounts allowed, 398
Discounts earned, 398
Discrepancy items, in personal bank records, 15, 468, 469–70
Dishonoured cheques, 353
Diskettes (floppy disks), 781, 783
Distributed processing, 789
Distribution of net income or net loss in a partnership, 647–51
statement of distribution of net income, 648–50, 653
Dividends, 687–88
accounting for, 688
calculating dividends for the three types of preferred share, 693–94
Double-entry system of accounting, 76
Double taxation, 638, 685
Doubtful accounts, adjustment for, 554–58
Drawings accounts, 137, 138–39
closing entries for, 190–92, 195, 197
for partners, 636, 651, 659
Dual purpose sales slip, 213–14
Duplicate file, 815

E

Earnings per share, 740
Electronic cash registers, *see* Cash registers.
Electronic data processing (EDP), 18–19, 774–75, 783–85, 788. *See also* Computer-based accounting systems; Computers.
Employee's payroll deductions, *see* Payroll: deductions.
Employee's earnings record, 532
Employer's legal obligations *re* payroll, 506
contributions for CPP and UIC, 525–26
payroll deductions 509–524, (*see* Payroll: deductions *for details*)
payroll records, 524–28, 530–32
remittance of payroll liabilities, 530
End-of-day procedure on cash register, 410–12
"Entry," different meanings of term, 113
Equation analysis sheet, 50
updating, 51–56
Equity, *see* Owners' equity.
Equity ratio, 741
Equity section
of balance sheet, 172, 173, 174
of ledger, 131, 135–39, 190, 191
Errors
correcting, 118–19
in subsidiary ledger balance, locating, 248
transposition, 145
in trial balance, detecting, 142–45
Expense accounts, 137–38
closing entries for, 190–92, 193, 197
Expenses, 131
accrued, 587
administrative, 603
prepaid, 550–53, 600
selling, 603

F

Fees form, 99
Financial position, 32
changes in, 49–57
use of computer to analyze, 816
Financial statements, 565–67
analyzing, 729–42 (*see* Analyzing financial statements *for details*)
balance sheet, *see* Balance sheet
classified, 168–73
common-size, 734–35
comparative, 730–33
fully classified, 600–603
income statement, *see* Income statement
of a partnership, 648–50, 651–56
typewritten, 175
work sheet and, 168
Fiscal period, 134–35, 188
Five-journal system, 353–62
cash payments journal, 358–59
cash receipts journal, 356–57
posting in, 361–62
purchases journal, 360–61
sales journal, 357, 358
Fixed assets, 169, 600
Floppy disks, 781, 783

Flowcharting, 240–41
of procedure for accounts receivable, 241–44
of procedure for balancing the general ledger, 143
of a simple perpetual inventory system, 286–87
of two-journal system, 330
Forwarding procedure, 119–20
in the synoptic journal, 320–21
Freight-in, 278, 280–82
Fully classified financial statements, 600–603
Fully-participating dividend, 693, 694
Fundamental accounting equation, 33

G

Gain or loss on realization, apportionment to partners, 662
General journal, 92–96
vouchers, 331
General ledger, 239
balancing, 247
posting to, 246, 315
Goodwill, 645
Gross pay, 509
Gross profit, 134
Group life insurance, payroll deductions for, 522–23

H

Hard-copy output, 788
Hard-copy terminals, 782
Hardware, 779
Health insurance, provincial
employer's contributions for, 526, 528
payroll deductions for, 521-22, 528

I

Impress method of handling petty cash, 308–11
"In balance," 77
Income, *see* Revenue.
net, *see* Net income.
Income- or loss-sharing ratio, 648, 662, 663
Income statement, 131–34
cash discounts on, 399
classified, 602
common-size, 734
comparative, 732
for a merchandising business, 276
for a partnership, 656
returns and allowances on, 391–92;
showing income tax expense on, 706
Income tax, 134
corporate, 703–706
Income tax, payroll deduction for, 516–21
calculating income tax deduction, 519–21
personal exemption, 516
taxable earnings, 519
Information system, accounting department in, 97, 98
Input, 774
Input media, 780–83
Insurance, analyzed on comparative financial statements, 733
Integrated circuits, 775–77
Interest, to partners, 647–48, 651
Internal control, 463–66
with computerized systems, 814–15
Inventory, *see* Merchandise inventory.
Inventory control, *see* Periodic inventory method; Perpetual inventory method.
Inventory turnover, 739
Investment, *see* Capital; Owners' equity.
Issue price of shares, 698

J

Journal, 92, 111
two-column general, 92–96
Journal entries, steps in recording, 93–94
Journalizing, 92, 93–94
business practices and, 96–97
with the five-journal system, 356–61
in the synoptic journal, 314–19, 328

L

Large computers, 777
Large-scale integration (LSI), 776, 777
Late deposits, 15, 469
Late discounts, 397–98
Ledger, 66, 91–92, 111
balancing, 77–80
equity section of, 131, 135–39, 190, 191
expanded, 131, 135–39, 189
forms of, 66–67
general, 239, 246, 247
growth of, 236–37
simple, 65–80
subsidiary, *see* Subsidiary ledger.
Ledger accounts, 66–68
important features of, 68
Ledger sheets, 12–13
Letters patent, 683
Liabilities, 32
accrued, 587
current, 169, 600
in fundamental accounting equation, 33
long-term, 600
Limited liability, 3, 683
Liquidation, of partnership, 660

Liquidity, 36
Long-term liabilities, 600
Loss, net, 131, 166–67

M

Magnetic disks, 781, 783
Magnetic drums, 785
Magnetic tape, 781, 783
Manufacturing business, 3
Market price of shares, 698
Matching principle, 546
Memory (of computer), 784
Merchandise, 273
Merchandise inventory, 273–76
- account, 277, 280–82
- analyzed on comparative financial statements, 733
- balance sheet presentation for, 273
- computerized inventory control system, 288–90, 799–801, 815
- inventory pattern, 274–75
- periodic inventory method, *see* Periodic inventory method.
- perpetual inventory method, *see* Perpetual inventory method.
- relationship to net income, 274
- turnover of, 739

Merchandising business, 3
- new accounts for, 277–78

Micro-computers, 778
Mini-computers, 778
Minute book, 702–703
Mutual agency, 638

N

Neatness, importance in accounting, 39, 118
Net book value, 559
Net claim code, for personal income tax, 516
Net income, 131, 166–67
- before income tax, for a corporation, 704–705
- relationship of merchandise inventory to, 274
- statement of distribution of, for a partnership, 648–50, 653

Net income percentage, 739
Net loss, 131, 166–67
Net pay, 509
- calculating, 523

Net purchases, 391
Net sales, 390
"Net 60," 394
"Net 30," 394
Net worth, 32
"No cash refunds" policy, 393–94
Nominal accounts, closing entries for, 190–97. *See also* Drawings accounts; Expense accounts; Revenue accounts.
Non-cumulative dividend, 693, 694
Non-routine entries
- to subsidiary ledgers, 246
- to synoptic journal, 328

No par value shares, 691–92
NSF cheques, 353
Numbering the accounts, 112–14

O

"On account," 96
"1/15, n/60," 394
Opening an account, 114
Opening entry, 95, 96
Opening the books, 95
Optical character recognition, 401, 781–82, 783, 792
Organization costs, 687
"Other income and expenses," 603
"Out of balance," 77
Output, 774, 785, 788
Outstanding cheques, 15, 469
Owners' equity, 32, 600
- in corporation accounts, 685, 686
- equity ratio, 741
- in fundamental accounting equation, 33
- return on, 740
- revenue and expense related to, 131

Ownership, forms of, 3

P

Packing slip, 472, 474
Paid out, recording, 406
Paid vouchers file, 478
Partnership accounts, 636–37
Partnership Acts, 639
Partnership agreement, 638–39
Partnerships, 3, 635–63
- accounting for net earnings of, 650–51
- adjusting and closing entries for, 656–59
- advantages and disadvantages of, 638
- cases, 637, 639–47
- distribution of net income or net loss in, 647–51, 653
- financial statements of, 648–50, 651–56
- formation of, 636–39
- termination of 660–63

Par value shares, 689–91

Payroll
computerized system for, 810–12, 816
deductions, 509–524 (*see* Payroll deductions)
legal obligations of employer regarding, 506 (*see also* Employer's legal obligations *re* payroll)
methods of payment, 506–508
payments to employees, 528–29, 531
payment of payroll liabilities, 530
recording, 524–28, 530–32
Payroll deductions, 509–524
calculating net pay, 523
Canada Pension Plan or Quebec Pension Plan, 511–13, 528
completing the payroll journal, 524
group life insurance, 522–23
health insurance, 521–22, 528
income tax, 516–21
registered pension plans, 515–16, 528
Social Insurance Number, 510
unemployment insurance, 514–15, 528
union dues 'check-off', 522
Payroll journal, 509–510
completing, 524
using as a book of original entry, 531
Pencil footings, 75, 320
Periodic inventory method, 273, 276–80
cost of goods sold adjustment, 589–91
limitations of, 279–80
Perpetual inventory method, 273, 284–90
adjusting perpetual inventory, 288
computerized inventory control system, 288–90, 799–801, 815
flowchart of a perpetual inventory system, 286–87
Personal chequing accounts, 11
Personal exemption from income tax, 516
Personal income tax, payroll deductions for, 516–21
Petty cash fund, 308–311
Petty cash voucher, 309
Physical inventory, 278–79
Pin totals, 75, 320
Point-of-sale terminals, 399, 792
Post-closing trial balance, 197, 595
Posting, 114
in the five-journal system, 361–62
to the general ledger, 246, 315, 323
steps in, 114–16
from the synoptic journal, 322–27
Posting reference, 92, 114, 116, 117
in the five-journal system, 361–62
in the synoptic journal, 326–27
Preferred shares, 692–94
three types of, 693
Prepaid expenses, 600
adjustment for, 550–53
Prepaid insurance adjustment, 550–52
Prepaid licenses adjustment, 552–53
Price-earnings ratio, 741–42
Primary storage (memory), 784
Private corporations, 684
Processing, 774
See also Data Processing; Electronic data processing.
by computer, 783–85
distributed, 789
Producing business, 3
Profit
analyzed on comparative financial statements, 733
as goal of business, 1
gross, 134
Profitability, 134
Program, 779
Proprietorship, 3
adjusting and closing the books of, 592–95
Public corporations, 684
Punched cards, 780, 783
Punched paper tape, 780, 781, 783
Purchase invoices, 100, 214–16, 220, 245
adjusting entries for, 585
reversing entries for, 596–97
Purchase orders, 471, 472
Purchaser, 212
Purchase requisition, 471
Purchases, analyzed on comparative financial statements, 733
Purchases account, 277–78, 280–82
Purchases journal, 360–61
Purchases returns and allowances account, 390–91. *See also* Returns and allowances.
Purchasing
routine, 471, 472
use of computer in, 798–99, 800

Q

Quebec Pension Plan, 511
Quck ratio, 738

R

Ratios and relationships, in financial analysis, 737–42
Receipt on account, recording, 403
Receiving reports, 474
Receiving routine, 472–74
Recording, in data processing, 773

Recording transactions, 49–56
Recordkeeping, basic practices in, 38–39
Records, business, 2. *See also* Source documents.
Records, personal, 13–14
 reconciliation with bank records, 14–18
Records of shares, *see* Share records.
Registered Industrial Accountants (RIAS), 7
Registered pension plans
 employer's contributions to, 526, 528
 payroll deductions for, 515–16, 528
Registered retirement savings plans (RRSPS), *see* Registered pension plans.
Replenishing petty cash, 309–311
Report form of balance sheet, 167, 168
Retained earnings, 685, 686, 687–88, 694–97
 statement of, 696–97
Return for credit or refund, recording, 406
Return on owner's investment, 740
Returns and allowances, 312–14, 389–92
 adjustments for, in computerized system, 801
 on the income statement, 391–92
 purchases returns and allowances account, 390–91
 sales returns and allowances account, 389–90
 with the voucher system, 478–80
Revenue, 131, 603
Revenue accounts, 135, 137
 closing entries for, 190–92, 193, 197
Reversing entries, 596–98
 for accounts payable, 596–97
 for accrued payroll, 597–98
Ruled lines, use of, 39

S

Salaries, 506
 of partners, 647, 648, 651
Sales
 accounting applications of computers in, 792–98, 800, 815
 analyzed on comparative financial statement, 733
 terms of sale, 394–95
Sales account, 278
Sales invoice, 212–13, 220
 correction or cancellation of, 311, 312–14
 entry of warehouse sales invoices into computerized system, 794, 796
Sales journal, 357, 358
Sales returns and allowances, 389–90
 adjustments for, in computerized system, 801
Sales tax, 350–52
 accounting for, 351–52
 remitting, 352
Savings accounts, 11
Security code, 815
Selling expenses, 603
Sequential-access storage, 785
Service business, 3
 income statement for, 132
Share certificate, 682
Shareholders, 682, 684
 records of, 700
Shareholders' equity, 685, 686
 presentation on balance sheet, 697–98
Share records, 700–703
 minute book, 702–703
 stock certificate book, 700–702
Shares
 accounting entry to record sale of, 687
 classes of 689–94
 earnings per share, 740
 market value of, 698–99
 price-earnings ratio for, 741–42
 records of, *see* Share records
 transferring, 701–702
Silicon chips, 776, 777
Social Insurance Number, 510
Soft-copy output, 788
Soft-copy terminals, 782-83
Software, 779
Sorting, 774
Source documents, 97–101, 210–21
 number of copies of, 221
Statement of account, 248–51
 automated accounting system, 249–50
 computer-produced system, 250–51
 and the customer, 251
 manual system, 248
Statement of distribution of net income, 648–50, 653
Statement of partners' capital, 654
Stock, *see* Shares.
Stock certificate book, 700–702
Stock exchange, 698, 699
Stockholders, *see* Shareholders.
Stock-in-trade, 273
Storing, 774
Straight-line method of calculating depreciation, 560
Subsidiary ledgers, 235–52
 balancing, 247
 locating errors in, 248
 non-routine entries to, 246
Summarizing, 774
Summary exercises, 231–34, 383–88, 623–34
Super-computers, 777
Supplementary exercise ("Green Thumb Garden Centre"), 440–62

Supplies adjustment, 547–50
Synoptic journal, 314–28, 329
- cross balancing, 320
- forwarding in, 320–21
- journalizing in, 314–19, 328
- posting, 322–27

System, 790
System assistance, 791
Systems development, 789–91

T

T-account, 68
- calculating the balance of, 75
- compared with balance column account, 112

Taxable earnings, 519
Telephone orders, and use of computerized system, 796–97
Temporary accounts, closing entries for, 190–97
Terminals, 782–83
Termination of partnerships, 660–63
- partner with deficit capital account balance, 663

Terms of sale, 394–95
Three-ledger system, *see* Subsidiary ledgers.
Timecards, 507–509
Trading business, income statement for, 133
Transactions
- analyzing, 56–57, 70–74
- evidence of, 101, 211
- recording, 49–56, 97

Transfer of funds, 466
Transposition error, 145
Trend analysis, 736–37
Trial balance, 77–80
- detecting errors in, 142–45
- importance of, 79–80
- post-closing, 197
- procedure unchanged in expanded ledger, 141–42
- taking off, 77–79

Turnover of inventory, 739
Two-column general journal, 92–96
Two-journal system, 329, 330
"2/10, n/30," 394

U

Unemployment insurance
- employer's contribution, 515, 526–26
- payroll deductions for, 514–15, 528

Union dues, payroll deductions for, 522
Universal Product Code (UPC), 792
Unlimited liability, 638
Unpaid vouchers file, 477, 478

V

Valuation account, 554
Vendor, definition of term, 212
Voucher, 471
Voucher jacket, 474
Voucher register, 476, 478
Voucher system, 471–80
- accounts payable subsidiary ledger, 478
- cheque register, 477–78
- paid vouchers file, 478
- purchasing routine, 471, 472
- receiving routine, 472–74
- returns and allowances with, 478–80
- unpaid vouchers file, 477, 478
- verification steps, 474–76

W

Wages
- analyzed on comparative financial statements, 733

Work habits, developing good, 57
Working capital, 737
Work sheet, 163, 170, 546–47
- completing, 563–65
- extending, 550
- and financial statements, 168
- for a merchandising business, 280–82
- preparation of, 163–67
- as source of data for closing entries, 192